UNDERSTANDING
HEALTH

Understanding Health

Senior Consultant

William M. Kane

Executive Director,
American College of Preventive Medicine,
Washington, D.C.

Consultants

Peggy Blake

Health Education Consultant
MA, Educational Administration and Supervision
University of North Carolina, Chapel Hill

Robert Frye

Health Education Consultant
MPH Health Education, University of
North Carolina, Chapel Hill

Eloise Miller

Health Curriculum Coordinator
Anoka-Hennepin Public Schools, District 11
Minnesota

Michael Whittington

Department Head, Health Education
Lakewood High School,
Lakewood, California

RANDOM HOUSE SCHOOL DIVISION
NEW YORK

The Second Edition

Project Editor: Charles Roebuck

Manufacturing Supervisor: Lenore Zani

Cover Design: Thomas Vroman Associates, Inc.

Cover Photograph: Ray Hoover

Apple: Steuben Glass

Developed for Random House by Visual Education
Corporation, Princeton, New Jersey

Editor: Linda Perrin

Associate Editor: Susan Tischler

Copy Editor: Susan Garver

Text Design: Pencils Portfolio

Picture Researcher: Judith Burns

Writer Researchers: John Drexel, Marc Epstein,
                   Jodine Mayberry

Library of Congress Catalogue Card Number: 86-42835

Understanding Health.

   "Developed for Random House by Visual Education Corporation,
Princeton, New Jersey"—T.p. verso.
   Includes index.
   1. Health—Juvenile literature. I. Kane, William, 1947-
II. Random House (Firm)   III. Visual Education Corporation.
[DNLM: 1. Health Education. QT 210 U55]
RA777.U64   1987   613   86-42835

ISBN 0-676-39683-6

Manufactured in the United States of America

Preface

Understanding Health has two principal aims. The first is to help you to recognize the value of attaining and maintaining good health. If you know the benefits and rewards of good health, you are more likely to find the motivation to achieve it. The second aim is to give you the knowledge you need in order to get healthy and stay healthy. Good health is not a matter of good luck. You need to know what you can do to promote your own health and to prevent disease. Outlined below are some of the features that enable this second edition of *Understanding Health* to accomplish its aims.

Comprehensive Content

An introductory chapter explains the basic principles of good health. It also introduces you to the two main themes of this book: that your health is largely a matter of your own responsibility and that decisions you make now could help prevent the onset of a number of diseases as you get older. In addition, Chapter 1 describes the government's guidelines for improving the health of the American people. Its publication, *Promoting Health/Preventing Disease,* lists a series of health-related goals for the nation, and focuses public attention on programs that promote health. *Understanding Health* presents information that will help you in achieving those goals that are important to you.

Each chapter then concentrates on a specific topic, paying particular attention to issues that are of major concern today. In the chapters on mental health, for example, you'll read about dealing with stress, coping with competition, and handling depression. There is also a discussion of the eating disorders anorexia and bulimia.

Chapters on physical fitness and nutrition provide sensible guidelines on exercise and diet. You'll learn how you can establish a fitness program to suit your needs, and you'll learn why you need to eat a variety of foods. A discussion of overweight and underweight explains how you can achieve a long-term weight change.

A section on the life cycle takes you from conception and birth through adolescence and marriage to death, explaining the physical, mental, and emotional changes that occur as you mature. You'll read about the changing nature of marriage and about the trend toward marrying at a later age. You'll also find out about new ideas for caring for the elderly.

The abuse of drugs, alcohol, and tobacco is a matter of grave national concern. *Understanding Health* explores the role of drugs in American society. It explains how use can lead to abuse and what is being done to help people who have drug-related problems. Most importantly, it helps you make decisions about the role drugs will play in your life.

Because most Americans today die from chronic, rather than infectious, diseases, *Understanding Health* pays particular attention to cardiovascular diseases and cancer. You will learn how these chronic diseases develop, what factors contribute to them, and what you can do to try to prevent them.

Accidents, not disease, are the leading cause of death among young people. *Understanding Health* explains why drinking and driving is a lethal combination and suggests what you can do to help prevent accidents on streets and highways.

Environmental pollution is another cause of national concern. You'll learn of the efforts that are being made to clean up the environment, and you'll find out what you can do to help protect the land, air, and water from further damage.

Finally, you'll discover what's happening to the American health care system. A major overhaul of our hospitals and other medical facilities is underway. You need to understand the significance of the changes so that you can make informed decisions about your medical care in the years to come.

Learning Activities

One of the primary concerns of *Understanding Health* is to stimulate thought and discussion. It places great emphasis on helping you understand what you read. At the beginning of each chapter you will find a series of questions to help you focus on the main themes of the chapter. The sections listed below also appear in each chapter and will help you review what you have read, discuss important issues, and conduct your own investigations.

- *Check Your Understanding.* This series of questions appears at the end of each section. The questions will help you review and better understand what you have just read.
- *Do you Remember?* This is a vocabulary exercise designed to help you master words and terms that may be new to you. Key words and terms are highlighted in the text by the use of italic type. The most important and most commonly used terms are defined in the glossary at the end of the book.

- *Think and Discuss.* A series of discussion questions appears at the end of each chapter. These questions encourage you to examine your own attitudes and values about issues that are important to maintaining good health.
- *Follow-Up.* Each chapter also has a series of suggestions for individual activities. Some activities ask you to locate and evaluate information from newspapers, magazines, and other sources. Others encourage you to investigate and report on health services. Many of the activities are designed to help you discover the relationship between what you read in this textbook and what goes on in your own life and community.

Special Features

Two different kinds of features appear at intervals throughout the text. The *How to...* features offer useful advice and information in a list format. The *Talking Point* features expand upon the main text with discussions of important and timely topics. This second edition of *Understanding Health* includes a number of new features in both categories (for example, How to Cope with Competition, The Aerobics Boom, and Look-alike and Designer Drugs.

A Practical Approach

Understanding Health is a book designed not just to be read, but to be used. It provides practical guidelines for establishing a healthy life style. Your good health is not just a matter of luck. It is the outcome of intelligent, informed decisions made by the person who knows you best—yourself.

Contents

UNDERSTANDING
HEALTH

CHAPTER 1

What Is Health?

After reading this chapter, you should be able to answer these questions:

1. Is is true that if you're not sick, you're healthy?
2. What is the major health hazard in the United States today?
3. What areas of health care are receiving the most attention?
4. What can you do to promote your own health?
5. What is preventive medicine? What is the difference between preventive medicine and traditional medicine?

The average American born in the 1980s can expect to live for 75 years or more. Most of us take this fact for granted. Yet just a few decades ago it was very unusual for people to live that long. Americans born in 1900, for instance, had an average life span of just over 49 years. Every decade since then, however, advances in medicine and science, combined with improved health practices, have added nearly four years to our life expectancy. Today, in the words of the Surgeon General of the United States, "the health of the American people has never been better."

Not only are we Americans healthier than ever before, but we are also far more health-conscious. Books on nutrition and exercise climb the best-seller lists. Running, bicycling, and aerobics are very popular. We spend our money on sports clothes and fitness equipment. We are openly expressing our concern about such public health issues as hazardous wastes, radiation, and unnecessary food additives.

Yet despite advances in medicine, science, hygiene, and health-consciousness, many Americans—rich and poor, young and old, rural and urban—are not as healthy as they might be. Those who smoke or who are overweight, for example, could be healthier. So could those who get little exercise or who drink excessively.

Health is not just a matter of physical well-being. Emotional and mental health are equally important. And in this respect, too, many Americans are not as healthy as they might be.

This textbook shows what you can do to promote your own physical, mental, and emotional health. The emphasis throughout is on prevention. Many diseases can be prevented. And many of the factors that contribute to today's big killers—cardiovascular disease and cancer—can be controlled. Thus, the habits you form now and the life style you choose will have a direct bearing on your overall health in the years to come.

In this first chapter we'll discuss just what is meant by health. You'll learn what the major health hazards are, and you'll discover how attitudes toward health care are changing.

SECTION **1**   **Our Potential for Health**

Many people think that health is simply the absence of disease. If you're not sick, you're healthy. Right? Wrong.

We can easily see how this is so if we compare two people with typical nine-to-five jobs. Both are 35 years old. One smokes several packs of cigarettes a day, has three or more drinks every evening, is overweight, and is often anxious. The other does not smoke, drinks alcohol rarely, exercises regularly, and is relaxed and confident. Both people may pass all laboratory tests and be declared free of disease. But are they equally healthy? No.

Because many Americans confuse well-being with the absence of disease, they settle for less than the best possible health. We know a great deal about how to promote health and avoid disease. We know about the hazards of smoking, the risks of drugs, the value of good diet and exercise. But this knowledge does not automatically assure us good health. Good health comes only from *acting* on such knowledge. Not all of us do.

Matters of Definition

The World Health Organization has defined health as "a state of complete physical, mental, and social well-being, not merely the absence of disease or infirmity." Some people have criticized this definition for being too idealistic. However, it does set forth a goal toward which public health leaders and individuals can aim.

The fact that the definition includes goals for mental and social well-being is extremely important. Boredom, anxiety, loneliness, or general unhappiness can affect the way we function. These emotional states can actually lower the body's physical resistance to disease. They can also lead people to drink excessively, use drugs excessively, or overeat. Such behavior will, of course, damage physical health.

The link between physical, mental, and social well-being has, then, been clearly established. By recognizing this link and by paying attention to the various factors that contribute to well-being, we can gain more control over our own health.

Factors Beyond Our Control

Certain factors that have a bearing on our health are beyond our control, however. We cannot, for instance, choose the genes that we inherit from our parents. Those genes determine our body shape, our physical constitution, and our inborn resistance to disease. They also influence our emotional make-up and our susceptibility to certain diseases.

Also beyond our control is the environment in which we grow up. We can't choose the type of family into which we are born. It may be rich or poor, well educated or poorly educated, black or white, argumentative or peaceful. All of these factors have an influence on our health. So do the neighborhood we live in and the people with whom we come into contact during our formative years.

For each one of us, then, certain aspects of our health are already determined. However, many important factors are well within our control. Let's consider the three parts of the World Health Organization's definition of health in turn.

Figure 1.1 People who exercise regularly find that it does more than provide a sense of physical well-being. It contributes to a feeling of mental well-being as well.

Physical Well-being

We can keep our bodies healthy by exercising regularly. The human body is designed for movement and it needs exercise in order to function properly. Different kinds of exercise enable us to build up strength, suppleness, and stamina—the three main elements of physical fitness.

Exercise improves the efficiency of the lungs and cardiovascular system. It may also serve as an effective defense against heart disease. The heart is a muscle. It will perform less efficiently if it is not kept in good shape. This is true of all our muscles and joints. If used properly, they will remain in good condition. If neglected, they will deteriorate—even in young people.

In other ways, too, we can influence our own physical health, for better or worse, through the choices we make or the habits we form. For example, smoking cigarettes damages the lungs and causes cancer. We can choose between risking our health or not smoking. Similarly, too much exposure to the sun can damage the skin and even cause skin cancer. It takes just a simple decision to spend a bit less time in the sun or to wear protective clothing.

Physical well-being is also influenced by our eating habits. Overeating leads to overweight. And overweight can contribute to a variety of disorders, including high blood pressure and heart disease. Eating too little can also lead to health problems. We need a well-balanced diet in order to function properly. Teenagers, with their rapidly growing bodies, need to pay particular attention to what they eat.

Mental Well-being

Mental health, like physical health, is more than just the absence of illness. People in good mental health feel comfortable with themselves and with others. They are able to love and be loved. They can work well and play well. And they can cope successfully with the normal problems and stresses of life.

Beyond this, people in good mental health are energetic and enthusiastic about life. They are relaxed, confident, and usually optimistic. They do not avoid life's problems. Rather, they see that coping with problems provides an opportunity for personal development. They welcome new experiences and are not afraid to ask for help when they need it.

Social Well-being

You probably don't realize it, but your involvement in the society in which you live

Figure 1.2 People in good mental health feel comfortable with themselves and with others.

Figure 1.3 This hospital volunteer is not only maintaining her own social health, but is contributing to the well-being of others as well.

Figure 1.4 Bicycling is healthy in more ways than one—it is good exercise, good for the environment, and good fun.

plays a part in your overall health. Until recently, health specialists paid little attention to the social aspect of well-being. Now, however, more and more health experts are recognizing that our social relationships are relevant to our health.

At one level, social health is concerned with the people with whom we come into contact. Our relationships with our parents, friends, neighbors, and acquaintances all have a bearing on our health. Conflicts with parents or friends are stressful, and stress can have adverse effects on our bodies and our minds. People who enjoy close, supportive relationships and who get along well with their families are likely to be healthier than those who don't.

At a higher level, social health is concerned with our roles within society as a whole. For a society to function well, its members need to recognize certain basic needs. Each one of us can contribute to the well-being of our own society in a variety of ways.

You could, for example, volunteer your time or money to help others or to work for important causes. Or you could aim for a life style that minimizes waste of natural resources, conserves energy, and reduces environmental pollution. For instance, you might choose to walk or ride a bicycle rather than drive a car. This would not only help society, but it would also be good for your physical and mental health.

Taking responsibility for your personal health also contributes to social health. If you look after yourself, you are less likely to become a burden to others because of illness. Ideally, people with high levels of social health give more to the world than they take from it.

CHECK YOUR UNDERSTANDING

1. How has the World Health Organization defined health?
2. Describe some of the health-determining factors that are beyond our control.
3. List three practices that can affect our physical well-being. What happens to muscles and joints that are not used?
4. Describe the characteristics of mentally healthy people.
5. Explain the different levels of social well-being. How does taking care of your own health contribute to social well-being?

SECTION 2 Promoting Health/Preventing Disease

Americans spend more money on health care than any other people in the world. We have some of the world's most sophisticated medical technology and many well-trained doctors. Yet millions of Americans suffer disabilities and die prematurely of causes that are partially or totally preventable.

What are these causes of disability and premature death? According to a report issued by the Department of Health and Human Services, *the major health hazard in our society is our life style*. The most harmful components of that life style are:

- use of tobacco
- excessive use of alcohol
- lack of exercise
- improper diet
- non-use of car safety belts

Together, these *risk factors*, which are preventable, contribute heavily to cancer, coronary heart disease, stroke, and unintended injuries— all leading causes of death and disability.

Individual Health Habits

The very large role that personal behavior plays in determining health was shown in a study of some California residents. Over a period of five and one-half years, researchers studied the health habits of nearly 7,000 people in Alameda County, California. The results of the study clearly show that individual health habits influence not only the amount of illness a person experiences, but also how long he or she lives. The specific habits associated with good health and longer survival are:

1. not smoking cigarettes
2. drinking alcohol in moderation (no more than two drinks a day), if at all
3. eating breakfast
4. not eating between meals
5. maintaining normal weight
6. sleeping seven or eight hours each day
7. exercising at least moderately

While there may be no surprises in this list, their impact on well-being is remarkable. The study found, for instance, that a 45-year-old man following six or seven of these habits lived an average of 11 years longer than did men of the same age who followed three habits or less. For women, the life expectancy difference was 7 years. In addition, men in their mid-fifties who followed six or seven habits were in about the same physical condition as men 20 years younger who followed only three or less.

The study also showed that personal health habits had a far greater impact on health than did income level, gender, or age. Detailed information about the impact of these personal habits on health will be found throughout this textbook.

Today's Diseases

In this century a number of diseases have been brought under control. Smallpox, polio, tuberculosis, and diphtheria once caused widespread death and disability. Now, thanks to vaccines, immunization programs, and other preventive measures, they are no longer significant threats. Indeed, smallpox has been completely wiped out. Not a single case of it exists anywhere in the world.

However, as one group of diseases comes under control, a new problem appears. Today, the leading causes of death in the United States are chronic diseases—diseases that last a long time and that generally worsen slowly. Heart disease and cancer, the two major killers today, are chronic diseases. These diseases are "new" in the sense that years ago many people died from other diseases before a chronic disease had time to develop. Chronic diseases also tended to go undiagnosed in the past because doctors did not have the knowledge or diagnostic equipment that they have today.

The medical profession continues to find ways to treat chronic diseases, but because these diseases are not caused by a single, simple infection, they have no single, simple cure. The

Figure 1.5 There are more than 35 million ex-smokers in the United States today.

best that the medical profession can do is treat them once they develop.

The chronic diseases *can* be prevented, however. By taking certain preventive measures, individuals can greatly reduce their chances of suffering a chronic disease.

Objectives for the Nation

The United States government has attempted to reorganize the health care system and focus the attention of the American people on programs that promote health and prevent disease. In 1980 it published *Promoting Health/Preventing Disease*. This list of health objectives for the nation sets a series of goals that are to be attained by 1990.

You know from personal experience that if you want to reach goals, you have to be realistic when setting them. Let's say you decide you want to get in shape by walking 4 miles three times a week. Because you haven't exercised for a while, you begin by getting a physical. Then you set realistic goals when you begin your program—½ mile the first few times, 1 mile the next few times—building up to 4 miles in three or four weeks. If you don't set such goals, you'll probably try to do too much at first, get tired, and give up.

In setting its health objectives, the government tried to be realistic. It couldn't expect *every* American to give up smoking, cut down on salt, or change other harmful habits by the year 1990. But it could expect a certain number to have changed their life style in significant ways by then.

Promoting Health/Preventing Disease focuses on 15 priority areas. Each area is concerned with a particular health problem.

The 15 areas on which the government chose to focus its efforts are the following:

1. smoking
2. alcohol and drugs
3. nutrition
4. physical fitness and exercise
5. control of stress and violent behavior
6. high blood pressure
7. family planning
8. pregnancy and infant health
9. immunization
10. sexually transmitted diseases
11. toxic substances
12. occupational safety and health
13. accident prevention and injury control
14. fluoridation and dental health
15. control of infectious diseases

For each area, *Promoting Health/Preventing Disease* explains the nature and extent of the problem. It then suggests specific disease-preventing and health-promoting measures and states the objectives to be attained by 1990. In the case of alcohol and drugs, for example, one of its suggestions is to introduce nationwide educational programs that will result in a reduction of the number of automobile accidents that involve the use of alcohol. It provides a specific goal: to bring the number of deaths involving drunk drivers down to 9.5 per 100,000 people. In 1975 there were 11.5 deaths involving drunk drivers per 100,000 people.

The government emphasizes the need for action by Americans in all walks of life. In particular, it calls upon industry and labor, schools, churches, and consumer groups to play an active role in promoting health. Health professionals can do only so much. They need the voluntary cooperation of community organizations if they are to carry out their functions.

Consider the nation's immunization programs, for example. Health professionals have the capability and equipment to immunize all Americans against a variety of life-threatening diseases. Yet every year, Americans die from these diseases because they never received the immunizations. Health professionals can't visit every home to provide the immunizations. They have to rely on individuals coming to them. Schools and employers can help. They can inform people of the value of immunizations and encourage individuals to take advantage of them. In some cases, the services can be provided at school or at work.

Action at the individual level, then, remains an important key to a healthy nation. There is much that each one of us can do to promote our own health and that of the society we live in. In this book, you'll learn to help yourself and, by so doing, to help the nation attain the government's health objectives by 1990.

CHECK YOUR UNDERSTANDING

1. What is the major health hazard in our society?
2. Compare the kinds of diseases Americans once faced with the kinds of diseases that are now most common.
3. What is the purpose of *Promoting Health/Preventing Disease?*
4. List the areas for which the government has drawn up health objectives.
5. Why does the government emphasize the need for Americans to take responsibility for the quality of their health?

SECTION **3** **The Wellness Approach**

Good health, as we have seen, is not just the absence of illness. Nor is it just feeling so-so or okay. Rather, it is a sense of total well-being—physical, emotional, mental, and social.

To achieve this feeling of wellness, you need to play a conscious and active role in promoting your health. You need to recognize that your health is affected by a number of factors. These factors include your heredity, eating habits, home and working environment, physical condition, and relationships with others. Detailed information about how these factors affect your health is given throughout this book.

Changing Habits

Adopting good health habits is far easier than changing bad ones. It's much easier, for example, to refuse to start smoking than to give up

a two-pack-a-day habit. As a teenager, you are beginning to form your own life style. The decisions you make now and the habits you form will affect your health for years to come.

But what about the millions of Americans whose life style already threatens their health? What chance do they have of changing the habits that harm them? Much depends on the individual and on the kind of support she or he receives. Given the right encouragement and the right environment, people can change deeply ingrained habits.

This is demonstrated by the nation's experience with smoking. The Surgeon General's first Report on Smoking and Health came out in 1964. For the first time, Americans began to realize just how harmful cigarette smoking was. It is now estimated that more than 35 million Americans have successfully quit smoking.

Campaigns to prevent heart disease have also succeeded in making people change their

Figure 1.6 One way of managing stress is to find some time every day to relax and be by yourself.

habits. So have programs to control high blood pressure and to teach diabetics to take better care of themselves.

Public education has, then, achieved some success in making people change their habits. But there is still a long way to go. Millions of Americans, including over 6 million teenagers, continue to smoke. Over 15 million Americans have drinking problems. Obesity is widespread. And, despite the seeming mania for aerobics, jogging, and other forms of physical activity, millions of Americans get little or no exercise.

Good health is not hard to achieve, but it is easy to damage. By taking positive health action, you can enjoy a state of wellness for decades. Neglect and abuse of the human body simply doesn't make sense.

Preventive Medicine

Traditionally, Americans went to doctors only when they were sick, and, until recently, many doctors only diagnosed and treated illness. Most

Figure 1.7 To achieve a feeling of wellness, you need to think carefully about what is important to you. Then you need to develop a life style that matches your values.

physicians had little to do with prevention. Their job was to cure people when they were sick. That tradition is changing as more and more people become concerned with maintaining, not just regaining, their health.

Americans have long been dissatisfied with their health care system. They say that it is too complex and too expensive. They also think that it places too much emphasis on cure and not enough on prevention. Some health professionals have responded to the criticisms by becoming involved in *preventive medicine*. Physicians who practice preventive medicine are concerned about stopping a disease before it starts. They identify the individual risk factors of patients and help patients take action to reduce their chances of becoming sick or disabled.

Individual Responsibility

Physicians can do only so much. You as an individual have the primary responsibility for your own health care. In order to take charge of your own health, you must examine your life style. What are your habits? How often do you exercise? How much stress do you experience? How do you deal with stress? Do you use tobacco, drink, or take drugs? Is your weight under control? Do you buckle your car safety belt? How do you get along with friends and family? What do you want to achieve in life? By examining the various elements in your life and by identifying your particular health risks, you can decide which ones need most attention.

The most important benefit of wellness is, of course, that you feel terrific. You feel capable of achieving things that are important to you. Taking an active approach to wellness will also save you money. You reduce the likelihood of illness or accidents, so you are less likely to run up medical bills.

Medical care is very expensive in the United States. Americans spend billions of dollars in health care every year, and more than 90 percent of the money goes for treatment. A very small percentage is devoted to research, prevention, and health education. The percentages are changing, however. Concerned groups and individuals have already brought about a number of reforms that will help focus this country's attention on disease prevention and health promotion.

In the meantime, the sad truth is that Americans spend more money on alcohol and tobacco—which are known to cause disease—than they do on disease prevention and medical research. Obviously, much needs to be done to

Figure 1.8 The decision to smoke or not to smoke is up to each individual. Unfortunately, Americans spend more money on alcohol and tobacco than on disease prevention and medical research.

persuade people to take more responsibility for their health.

It's Up to You

Each of us chooses our own general life style. We decide the work we do, what we eat, and whether we use tobacco or drink alcohol or use drugs. We also control the amount of exercise we get, the physical risks we run, and when we see a physician. In cooperation with other people, we can also have some influence over the quality of our neighborhoods and over the amount of pollution to which we are exposed.

It's up to you to be responsible for your own life style. This simple commitment is the first step toward long and healthy life. No one else can make this commitment for you. No one else can sleep, exercise, buckle up, or eat balanced meals on your behalf. Indeed, you are the only one who is in a position to take responsibility for your own health. Only you can know all the forces—physical, mental, social, economic, cultural—that influence your health. You are the only one who can shape your behavior in ways that affect your health.

In order to maintain health, you need to understand how the body functions and what risk factors apply to you. You also need to understand the link between emotional, mental, and physical health. This book discusses these and other aspects of health. It will enable you to make informed decisions about your own health.

Good health is something you can choose to strive for. But it is not the result of a one-time decision. It grows from a series of decisions lasting your whole life. Each decision has a bearing on whether or not you will enjoy a feeling of wellness. It's up to you.

CHECK YOUR UNDERSTANDING

1. List five factors that affect the state of your health.
2. In what specific areas has public education had some success in helping people change their health habits?
3. What is preventive medicine?
4. What kinds of knowledge must you gain in order to take care of your own health?

CHAPTER SUMMARY

- The World Health Organization has defined health as a "state of complete physical, mental and social well-being, not merely the absence of disease or infirmity."
- Certain factors that influence our health are beyond our control. These include our genetic inheritance and the environment in which we grow up.
- We can maintain physical health by exercising regularly, avoiding unnecessary hazards, and eating a well-balanced diet.
- A person in good mental health is energetic, confident, relaxed, and able to cope with the problems and stresses of life.
- Our social health is influenced by our relationships with other people and by our roles within society as a whole.

- *Promoting Health/Preventing Disease* is a list of health objectives for the nation. It aims to control and prevent the most common causes of death and disability.
- Most infectious diseases have been brought under control in the United States today. The big killers are chronic diseases and unintended injuries.
- To achieve a feeling of wellness, a person has to play a conscious and active role in promoting health.
- The aim of preventive medicine is to stop a disease before it starts.
- Americans spend more money on alcohol and tobacco than they do on medical research, disease prevention, and health education.
- Good health grows from a series of informed decisions that will affect an individual for life.

It has long been said that a healthy body and a healthy mind go hand in hand. Doctors know that poor mental health contributes to poor physical health, and vice versa. Part 1 of this book explores the relationship between health and the mind. It emphasizes that good mental health is not just a matter of luck. Just as people can actively promote physical fitness, they can also take certain measures to attain mental fitness.

Chapter 2 looks into the nature of emotions. It explains why people must satisfy some basic emotional needs in order to achieve optimal health. Chapter 3 turns to mental health and mental disorders. Many mental disorders occur when people fail to understand their emotions or when they lose the ability to control or express their feelings. The chapter focuses on some strategies that people can develop for promoting mental health.

In a fast-paced society such as ours, we are continually exposed to many types of stress. Stress can be a stimulating challenge, but many people find it difficult to cope with. Chapter 4 looks at stress, at its effects on health, and at ways of reducing its negative effects.

CHAPTER 2

Emotional Development

After reading this chapter, you should be able to answer these questions:

1. What five stages do you go through when you experience an emotion?
2. How does your body react to fear?
3. What are some signs that your self-esteem is strong?
4. What is a defense mechanism? What are some examples of defense mechanisms?
5. What is meant by emotional maturity?

When Larry put pencil to paper in art class, he felt a surge of pleasure. He could even feel his heart beat faster. Then and there, he knew drawing was going to be very important to him. Sheila, on the other hand, felt bored and impatient in art class. She yawned a lot and hitched around in her seat. Drawing just wasn't for her. Next semester she would try to find an activity that felt better.

For Larry and Sheila, the same activity had aroused very different feelings. These feelings, or emotions, had in turn affected them physically. Just as important, their emotions had affected their decisions about future activities.

Our behavior is determined in great part by our emotions. As for Larry and Sheila, emotions provide important cues about what is good or bad, right or wrong, for each of us. The emotion itself can rarely be called good or bad. Rather, it is the way we deal with it that matters. Boredom, for instance, might seem like a negative emotion. But in Sheila's case, it was her signal to change activities.

Why one person feels one emotion and someone else another in the same situation is a complicated matter. Our emotional patterns are determined by many influences. There is evidence that our emotional make-up starts to develop before we are born, determined in part by the genes we inherit. A person's emotional development also depends heavily on his or her culture and surroundings.

Along with the emotional differences between individuals, there are also similarities. We all have the same basic repertoire of feelings and the same emotional needs. We experience the same kinds of conflicts and use the same coping mechanisms to help us deal with emotional problems.

Learning the nature of your emotions and how they develop is an important step toward understanding and shaping your own emotional pattern. In this chapter we shall look at those aspects of emotions. We shall also look at ways to cope with the sometimes confusing emotional responses we have to ourselves and to the world around us.

SECTION **1**   # The Nature of Emotions

What are emotions? Many people would answer this question by giving examples. Emotions are such things as anger, love, fear, hope, and joy. Put simply, emotions are feelings. These feelings are experienced both physically and mentally. Physical changes, such as clammy hands or queasy feelings in your stomach, are one part of experiencing an emotion. The other part takes place in your mind. Although you may not be aware of it, your mental evaluation of a situation is the basis for your feelings about it. That is, what you think about a situation causes your feelings about it.

Stages of Emotional Response

When you experience and express an emotion, you go through five stages. The first stage is *perception,* which is becoming aware of something through your senses. Usually, you perceive an event by seeing or hearing it. Sometimes, though, this stage occurs in the imagination, as when you become anxious about a possible future event. *Appraisal,* the second stage, is judging how beneficial or harmful the event is. At this stage you think about whether the event is favorable or unfavorable for you. Once you have made this appraisal, the third and fourth stages occur— the *emotion* itself and the *physical changes* that go with it. The final stage is *action,* which is what you do in response to the situation.

Michael experienced these five stages as French class began. When he saw his teacher opening his grade book, he knew it was a sure sign of a surprise oral quiz. The first stage he experienced was perception—seeing what was happening. Michael's appraisal (stage two) was "Boy, am I in trouble!" The emotion he felt, fear (stage three), affected him physically (stage four). His heart started beating faster, and he could even see his hands shaking slightly. Recognizing how frightened he felt prompted him to take action (stage five). He picked up his notes and started flipping through them before the quiz began.

Gil experienced a similar emotional reaction on the opening night of the school play. Just before he stepped into the spotlight, he felt butterflies in his stomach. What if he forgot his lines? What if the audience didn't like him? He reminded himself that even famous actors and actresses experience stage fright. He also realized that the fear was exhilarating; it would help him give a better performance.

Values

Your emotions are closely related to your *values.* These are your beliefs about what is good and bad, important and unimportant, moral and immoral. Thus, if you value friendship, making friends and spending time with them will be activities that bring you pleasure and satisfaction. If you value a sport such as tennis, you will feel good while you play it and devote time to getting better at it. People who value owning things will try to earn money to buy them.

Values also relate to your feelings about large issues such as fairness and morality. When something happens that goes against your beliefs about right conduct, you will feel emotions such as anger or sorrow. If the wrong

Figure 2.1 Gil's stage fright went through five stages. (1) *Perception:* "There are many people in the audience." (2) *Appraisal:* "They may not like my performance." (3) *Emotion:* Fear. (4) *Bodily changes:* Butterflies in the stomach. (5) *Action:* Repeating his lines to himself.

is righted, you will feel relief and satisfaction. The strong feelings that are part of your value system play a major role in your decisions about how you want to live your life.

Emotions and the Body

Everybody has experienced the bodily sensations that come with emotions. We've all had, at one time or another, sweaty palms, a racing heart, a red face, tensed muscles, or clenched teeth.

What causes these physical reactions to happen during emotional experiences? The answer can be found in the body's *autonomic nervous system.* This system helps the body to respond when action is called for. It also helps the body calm down and restore itself when needed. This is all done without conscious effort on your part. That is why you may blush when you are embarrassed, even though you try very hard not to.

There are two parts in the autonomic nervous system. The *sympathetic system* goes into action when you face an emergency or a threat. The situation could be extreme cold, lack of food, an upcoming examination, a disagreement, a date, or team tryouts.

The sympathetic system speeds up your heart to increase the flow of oxygen and nutrients to the body. It increases the rate of breathing so that more oxygen is taken into the body. It increases the size of the blood vessels leading to the muscles that are needed. It also decreases the size of the blood vessels leading to the digestive and other systems not necessary for these tense situations.

The *parasympathetic system,* on the other hand, tends to conserve energy or build the body back up after it has faced a threat. It reduces the heart rate and the breathing rate. It increases the size of the blood vessels running to the digestive system and reduces the size of those running to the muscles.

The actions of the autonomic nervous system help us to deal with stressful situations. Sometimes, though, the physical changes that accompany our emotions have a negative side. There are often times when a person cannot act immediately. You may have felt angry or frus-

Figure 2.2 Our emotions are closely related to our values. If you value friendship, spending time with friends will bring you pleasure.

trated over something but were unable to express those emotions. Your body prepared you for action, but you kept your feelings bottled up inside. If the body is continually preparing for an emergency but never releasing emotional tensions, health problems may result. Backaches, migraine headaches, asthma, high blood pressure, and stomach ulcers are all thought to be related to this kind of stress. Physical exer-

cise provides one way of relieving this common type of stress.

There is also a positive side to the physical effects of emotions. Pleasant emotions such as love and joy produce feelings of relaxation, comfort, and well-being. Frequently, the positive and negative effects of emotions are mixed together. Emotions also give intensity, variety, and purpose to life. Aroused emotions motivate people to reach their goals—to win a race, write a song, or achieve success in their work.

CHECK YOUR UNDERSTANDING

1. Describe the five stages you go through when you experience and express an emotion.
2. What are values? Give an example of how values can determine a person's behavior.
3. How does a situation that makes you feel threatened affect your body? What is the name of the body system that controls those changes?
4. What can happen if a person does not get a chance to release emotional tensions?
5. What kinds of feelings do positive emotions produce?

SECTION **2**   **Emotional Needs**

We all have certain basic physical needs that must be met in order for us to survive. We need air to breathe, water to drink, food to eat. But do we also have basic emotional needs? According to psychologist Abraham Maslow, we definitely do. Maslow distinguished two categories of human needs, *basic needs* and *growth needs*.

The basic needs include the obvious physical needs for food and water. But they also include certain emotional needs, such as the needs for affection, security, and self-esteem. If these basic needs are not met, a person will feel a

lack and try to make up for it. Some of these basic needs, such as the need for food, take priority over others.

The growth needs are all psychological needs. They include the needs for justice, goodness, and beauty. The growth needs do not have any set order of importance. Their relative importance depends on the individual. One person, for example, may feel a much stronger need for beauty than another. And while the growth needs usually take a back seat to the basic needs, there are always exceptions. A poor artist may choose to buy paint instead of food. A dedicated soldier may volunteer to risk his life on the battlefield instead of maintaining his safety.

In general, though, people who lack a basic need do not feel free to consider the growth needs. And if the growth needs go unfulfilled, a person may develop emotional problems. Of all the emotional needs, the need for love and the need for self-esteem are perhaps the most important. These, then, are the needs we shall look at more closely.

The Need for Love

Psychologists have performed studies to find out about our basic emotional needs and how they develop. Harry Harlow carried out a series of studies with monkeys that had been taken from their parents at birth.

In one set of studies, Harlow wanted to test whether the young monkeys would become attached to parent-substitutes because these substitutes gave them food. In the cages, he set up two kinds of parent-substitutes for each monkey: a wood-and-wire model and a soft terry-cloth doll. In some cages, the wood-and-wire model held a bottle of food; in other cages, the terry-cloth doll held the bottle. Harlow found that the monkeys ran to the terry-cloth doll when they were frightened, whether or not the terry-cloth parent-substitute held a bottle. He realized that touch is a very important element in establishing relationships.

In another set of studies, Harlow wanted to see how monkeys who had neither parents nor substitutes would act as they grew up. The monkeys that had been isolated showed differing degrees of apathy or fear. They were indifferent to other monkeys and preferred to crouch alone

Figure 2.3 Harry Harlow showed that a lack of love or attention could cause emotional problems in young monkeys. When monkeys raised with terry-cloth substitute parents were placed alone in a cage with a strange object, they were frightened. But when the terry-cloth substitute was also in the cage, the young monkeys were simply curious.

off to the side. As adults, they did not seem to know how to mate, how to play, or how to defend themselves. The monkeys with cloth parent-substitutes were less disturbed than those with no parents at all. But they were not well adjusted to normal monkey life. Those who were allowed to play with other baby monkeys grew up somewhat normally. Contact with other monkeys turned out to be a fairly good substitute for attention from a parent. To grow up completely normally, however, the monkeys needed contact with both a parent and other baby monkeys.

Children who, like Harlow's monkeys, are deprived of their parents at an early age may have emotional problems. Severe problems can develop when a child forms no attachment to an adult or when a relationship is broken off when the child is very young. Lack of continuing close relationships is a problem for some children in orphanages and other institutions. Sometimes such children do not get the warmth, attention, and sense of security they need. These children may then have problems relating to other people.

The need to give and receive love continues throughout our lives. It is important for both emotional and physical health. People who enjoy close, satisfying relationships with others seem to be less prone to disease and to live longer than people who do not.

Satisfying the need for love, then, means building close relationships with others. It means showing your family and friends that you care about them. Giving and accepting affection help you to like yourself and to fulfill the needs of the people who are close to you.

Figure 2.4 Self-esteem is the belief that you are competent and worthy of living.

The Need for Self-Esteem

Self-esteem—which means having a favorable opinion of yourself—is another basic emotional need. One psychologist has defined it as a "conviction that one is competent to live and worthy of living." Without self-esteem, a person is likely to act in self-destructive ways.

Darla, for instance, always seems to end up with a boyfriend who treats her badly. When she does go out with someone who treats her well, she finds herself thinking, "How terrific can *he* be if he thinks *I'm* special?" She then loses interest in him and stops seeing him. Darla doesn't realize it, but she lacks the self-esteem that makes people feel worthy of love. So she chooses boyfriends who treat her in the way she unconsciously thinks she should be treated.

People who think well of themselves act very differently. They like themselves and find it natural for other people to like them too. They also do things that are good for themselves. When Jonah, who has a positive attitude toward himself, started seeing Barbi, all went well. But then Barbi began to break dates at the last minute. She also became very critical of Jonah and wanted him to change all sorts of things about himself. Rather than going along with Barbi and trying to change himself, Jonah felt annoyed. He decided that he was a worthwhile person just as he was and that he would find someone who could appreciate him.

High self-esteem, or a positive estimate of one's worth, is characterized by self-confidence, independence, assertiveness, self-respect, pride, self-acceptance, and expressiveness. Low self-esteem, or a negative estimate of one's worth, is demonstrated by submissiveness, passivity, helplessness, timidity, self-doubting, self-punishing, and feelings of inferiority, powerlessness, and unworthiness.

Psychologists cite four sources of self-esteem:

- *Power* is a sense that comes from having the ability to influence the circumstances of your life in important ways.
- *Connectedness* is the feeling of satisfaction that arises from the acceptance, attention, and affection of others.
- *Standards* are role models or reference points that provide you with examples that help you establish meaningful values and goals.
- *Uniqueness* is the special sense of self that comes from acknowledging qualities that make you special and different.

High self-esteem does not depend on success in all four sources. For example, someone may have high self-esteem because he or she feels specially talented, without feeling accepted by others, identifying with a role model, or being particularly powerful.

CHECK YOUR UNDERSTANDING

1. Give examples of basic needs and growth needs.
2. What do Harry Harlow's experiments with monkeys tell us about the need for close relationships with others?
3. How can lack of love affect a person's physical well-being?
4. What is self-esteem? How can a lack of self-esteem affect a person's behavior?
5. What are four sources of self-esteem?

SECTION **3** # The Development of Emotions

Just as you are physically different from anybody else, so your emotional make-up is unique too. Nobody else feels or acts exactly as you do. The source of your uniqueness is the complicated interplay between the traits you inherit, the environment in which you grow up, and the experiences you have. All of these factors contribute to your emotional development.

Genetic Factors

Genetic factors are those characteristics that are present from birth. You inherit genes from your parents. The genes determine such physical characteristics as the color of your eyes and hair and how tall you will become. There is also evidence that at least part of your emotional make-up is inherited.

From the moment of birth, all babies are capable of expressing four basic emotions—pleasure, displeasure, excitement, and depression. The facial expressions used to show these emotions are the same in everyone, regardless of race or culture. Even people born blind and deaf smile to express happiness. Apparently, the genetic programming that controls such emotional signals is similar in everyone.

But at the same time, there are distinct differences in the way individual babies express themselves. Some are active while others are passive. Some cry a lot; others cry little. Some demand constant cuddling; others seem con-

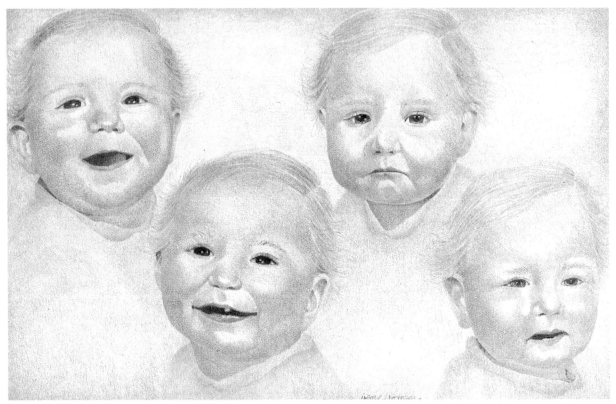

Figure 2.5 From the moment of birth, babies are able to express four basic emotions—pleasure, displeasure, excitement, and depression.

tent to be left alone. Such differences seem to indicate that human beings inherit some tendency toward certain emotional states.

The physical characteristics that children inherit can also play a role in emotional development. Studies have shown that children who are large and well coordinated are more likely to be chosen as leaders by other children. They are also more likely to score higher in IQ tests and tend to have greater self-esteem. On the other hand, children who are awkward and whose physical abilities are poorly developed might be left out of things while growing up. Those children may experience more stress and unhappiness as a result.

Environmental Factors

Your emotional development is greatly influenced by the environment in which you grow up. The term *environment* refers to all the people and things that surround you. It includes your parents, friends, relatives, your home, the area in which you live, your school—even movies and television. All of these environmental factors have an effect on you.

One of the ways that children are influenced by other people is through *modeling,* or imitation. Children watch the way adults and other children act in certain situations and are likely to do the same thing if placed in a similar situation. Usually, they imitate the people who are most significant in their lives—parents, teachers, friends, and maybe TV and sports stars.

Modeling may be one of the most important influences on emotional development. Psychologists who stress its importance encourage parents and teachers to provide good models for children and to shield them from bad models, such as violent characters in television shows, movies, and books.

Another way the environment influences emotional development is through *conditioning,* which is learning to do things that earn *reinforcements,* or rewards. Receiving rewards for certain actions makes people more likely to repeat those actions. They are less likely to repeat behavior for which they are not rewarded. Sometimes, though, punishment becomes a reward. Most children, for example, would consider being reprimanded by a teacher a punishment. But a child who needs attention may find that disrupting the class is the best way to get that attention. Even though the response is in the form of a reprimand, it is still attention and it becomes a reward.

In general, though, positive consequences for actions are considered rewards. Thus, chil-dren learn to follow household rules by being praised for their efforts. Teenagers dress like the other members of their group because they receive approval from their friends. The rewards people get for certain behaviors make them continue those behaviors.

The type of behavior rewarded is that which the people giving the reward consider to be "right." There are different kinds of rewards—attention, praise, special privileges, gifts. All help to encourage an individual to behave according to the values of the people giving them.

Sometimes this can lead to conflict. The different people in an individual's environment may have different values. As a result, a person may risk being punished by one group in order to get approval from another. For example, you may decide to dress and act in ways that

Figure 2.6 Environmental influences on young children include their families, their homes, and even their toys.

please your friends. But when you do that, you feel uncomfortable because your parents do not approve. Conflicts such as this are common, especially during the teenage years, when young people are developing their own systems of values.

Stages of Emotional Development

The first person to suggest that emotional development occurs in stages was Sigmund Freud, the founder of psychoanalysis. According to Freud, children go through five major stages of development. At different stages, children take pleasure in different parts of the body. By the end of each stage, children learn to channel their behavior in ways that are acceptable to society. Freud believed that this adapting determines how a child's personality develops.

Freud proposed that the first stage of emotional development is the *oral stage*, when the focus of pleasure is the baby's mouth. The source of pleasure is the mother's breast. When babies are weaned from the breast, they feel frustrated by not getting what they want, and they express their feelings.

The second year of life, Freud thought, is taken up by the *anal stage*. Children at this stage gain pleasure from the process of eliminating solid wastes. Soon, though, this freedom is curbed by toilet training.

Freud saw a major conflict coming between the ages of three and five. During this *phallic stage*, as he called it, children take pleasure in their genitals and become very aware of the differences between males and females. They also try to gain the affections of the parent of the opposite sex. Without realizing it, they become rivals with the parent of the same sex. Eventually, this conflict is resolved to the point where boys identify with their fathers and girls identify with their mothers.

Freud thought that children next enter a *latency stage*, when sexual desires are pushed into the background. Children become concerned with exploring the world and learning new skills. According to Freud, when puberty occurs, sexual feelings return, and the *genital stage* begins. In this stage of emotional development, the person focuses on sexual intercourse, deriving as much satisfaction from giving pleasure as from receiving it.

Today, many psychologists disagree with certain aspects of Freud's theories. Still, his work has had a lasting effect on the study of human development. His belief that the experiences of early childhood affect adult personality and behavior remains one of the cornerstones of modern psychology.

Swiss psychologist Jean Piaget was influenced strongly by Freud's theories. Piaget focused on how young children need to interact with their parents and others in order to grow. He kept detailed diaries about the development

Figure 2.7 According to Freud, children try to gain the affection of the parent of the opposite sex during the phallic stage of development. For a while, they become rivals with the parent of the same sex.

of his own children. He found consistent patterns that he divided into stages of thinking abilities. He thought that children first learn that there are external objects and that actions have consequences (*sensorimotor stage*). Then they begin to imagine objects and use words to communicate with others (*preoperational stage*). Next they develop the ability to solve problems with physical objects (*concrete operational stage*). In the final stage, according to Piaget, children can deal with abstract concepts (*formal operational stage*).

Another psychologist, Erik Erikson, was also influenced by Freud's theories. He concentrated on how people grow and develop in regular stages. He identified eight stages because he thought that emotional development continues after adolescence. The names he gave the stages come from the basic conflict that the child must resolve at each stage in order to grow.

During the first stage that Erikson described, infants gain awareness of their bodies and learn to trust the people who care for them (*basic trust vs. mistrust*). As toddlers, the children's sense of individuality emerges. They learn to see themselves as people who still depend on their parents but who are separate from them (*autonomy vs. shame and doubt*). At the next stage, children begin to use their imaginations, explore their surroundings, and play by themselves. Pride in their accomplishments gives them greater self-esteem (*initiative vs. guilt*).

During the next stage, children's surroundings expand to include their neighborhoods and schools. As they meet the demands of schoolwork and new relationships, children in middle childhood learn to be realistic and solve practical problems (*industry vs. inferiority*).

Adolescence brings a renewed quest for identity and direction, which can cause conflicts and confusion for young people (*ego identity vs. role confusion*). In general, these uncertainties are a necessary part of maturing. A gradual acceptance of new responsibilities eases the transition to adulthood, the stage at which people face the demands of jobs and close relationships (*intimacy vs. isolation*).

However, emotional development does not end in adolescence, according to Erikson. Adults continue to become more understanding and accepting of themselves and others. For many adults, the middle years bring productive work and a chance to guide the next generation (*generativity vs. stagnation*). The final stage of development comes with old age. People who have coped with earlier conflicts successfully will have the conviction that life has meaning and that death need not be feared (*integrity vs. despair*).

A common theme in these three different theories of emotional development is that young children need to interact with their parents and others in order to adapt to society. Freud, Piaget, and Erikson all thought that humans grow and develop in regular stages. But each focused on different elements of the development process.

CHECK YOUR UNDERSTANDING

1. What four emotions can all babies express?
2. Define modeling and conditioning.
3. Briefly explain Sigmund Freud's five stages of emotional development.
4. What was a basic difference between Freud's theories of emotional development and those of Erikson?

SECTION **4** **Dealing with Emotions**

Jennifer feels so anxious and uneasy that she is having trouble paying attention to her schoolwork. She is no longer enjoying the interests and friendships that used to make her happy. Yet she has no idea why she has been feeling so upset. What causes such troublesome feelings?

Reynaldo explodes when he gets angry at his mother or his teachers. Later he feels miserable and blames himself for losing control. How can he learn to deal with his feelings?

Our emotions can trouble us in many ways. One problem is that they often seem to have no reasonable cause. You may find yourself feeling depressed or angry for no apparent reason. Physical changes during adolescence are one cause of unpredictable emotional reactions. The maturing process alters the body's chemical balance and this can cause moodiness.

Sometimes we don't understand our emotions because the reason for them is buried in our *unconscious mind*. The *unconscious* was Sigmund Freud's term for the part of the mind of which a person is not aware. Without our realizing it, unconscious forces shape our personalities and influence our actions. For example, Nancy took an instant dislike to her new neighbor, but she did not know why she felt as she did. If she could have examined her unconscious mind, she would have discovered the reason. The neighbor reminded her of a babysitter she once feared and disliked. Nancy had made the unconscious judgment that all people who look like the baby-sitter are to be feared and disliked. This unconscious judgment surfaced in the feelings she had toward her new neighbor.

In addition to mysterious emotions, people often experience conflicting emotions. They have two or more feelings about the same event. For example, Jason felt excited about going away to college. He looked forward to the freedom and independence. Yet, at the same time he felt afraid. He had never lived away from home before and knew he would miss his family and friends. Conflicts such as this are common and normal because no one has a totally consistent set of values.

Defense Mechanisms

Emotional conflicts can sometimes be so upsetting that people need to find relief from the anxiety they cause. The human mind has a number of ways of coping with anxiety and providing temporary relief. These methods of coping are called *defense mechanisms*. They are automatic, unconscious reactions that help people to reduce or avoid painful feelings. Some use of defense mechanisms is essential to emotional health. Too much dependence on them, though, can be a sign that someone is having difficulties coping with the problems of everyday living. Some of the common defense mechanisms are the following:

1. *Repression* is "forgetting on purpose." A person pushes a shameful or unpleasant thought or experience out of the conscious mind. She or he believes that it never existed. Repression is usually an unconscious process. People don't realize they are doing it. Nevertheless, the feelings remain, influencing behavior. Repression is the most fundamental of the defense mechanisms.

2. *Displacement* is venting feelings on someone or something other than the person or situation that caused them. A child who is angry at her mother for denying her another cookie may yell at her cat instead.

3. *Sublimation* is transforming unacceptable impulses into acceptable ones. A boy who feels particularly aggressive toward others can play on the football team, where aggressive behavior is acceptable.

4. *Escape* is running away from problems through daydreaming, fantasy, books, movies, even excessive sleep. Children who have unhappy home lives have been known to build up elaborate fantasy worlds.

5. *Regression* is going back to behavior more appropriate to an earlier stage of life. An eight-year-old boy who has grabbed something away from his brother may use baby talk as a way of avoiding responsibility for his actions.

6. *Identification* is choosing another person as an ideal and then trying to be like that person. A teenage boy might identify with a famous rock star. He might dress like the star and wear the same hairstyle in order to share in the star's success.

7. *Rationalization* is providing a substitute reason for an act. It is an attempt to justify an action rather than admit to one's failures or mistakes. Common rationalizations include "I would have done better if I'd had more time"; "The game was rigged"; "The teacher doesn't like me."

8. *Projection* is shifting one's own undesirable attitudes or feelings to somebody else. The aim is to protect one's self-esteem. A college student who cheats on a test, but who doesn't want to admit it to himself or herself, may accuse others of cheating.

Talking Point

Identity Formation

Teenagers are often preoccupied by the need to establish a sense of personal identity. On the one hand, each one of us wants to develop an identity that reflects our personal needs, goals, and desires. On the other hand, a person's identity has to fit in somehow with society's rules and expectations. In order to answer the questions "Who am I?" and "What do I want to become?" you need to confront and resolve many questions about your role in society. These are some of the questions you need to ask yourself:

- What do I believe?
- What do I value?
- What kinds of friends do I make? What kind do I want?
- How do I handle my emotions?
- How do I interact with other people?
- What do I want in life?
- Do I want to get married or remain single?
- Do I want to have children? How many?
- What kind of career do I want?

As you become more independent, you are challenged to "be yourself" and to share being yourself with others. You must take into account your needs, desires, and attributes when you make choices about friendships, roles, first sexual encounters, and other decisions.

Trying to establish a sense of who and what you are can sometimes be confusing. The confusion may occur when you find it too hard to make a decision. You might, for example, find yourself torn between family and friends. You value the time you spend with your family, but you want to spend more of your leisure hours with your friends. Only you can decide how to divide your time, but it's not always an easy decision. You might also find that the process

of figuring out what is important to you causes you to change your mind a lot. One week popularity seems more important than anything else. The next week, you decide that good grades matter most. The next week, friends and schoolwork take a back seat to your efforts to raise funds for environmental protection.

Some teenagers who are confused about their own identity turn to a ready-made identity instead. They choose heroes or cliques, and try to be just like the people they have chosen. For a while they might be very critical of people who are different from the group they have chosen to identify with. This unwillingness to accept differences may be a natural defense mechanism for people who are confused.

Erikson views the formation of identity as a time of uncertainty. He characterizes it as a time when

> "Deep down you are not quite sure . . . that you really know who you are, that you know what you want to be, that you know what you look like to others, and that you will know how to make the right decisions without once and for all committing yourself to the wrong friend, sexual partner, leader, or career."

There are no easy ways of dealing with the confusion that accompanies identity formation. Nobody else can make decisions for you, or answer the questions you have in your mind. You're not alone, though. Identity formation is a process that everybody goes through. To some extent, it's a process that continues throughout life.

Adapted from *Adolescence and Depression*, U.S. Department of Health and Human Services, Public Health Service, Alcohol, Drug Abuse, and Mental Health Administration, © 1985.

9. *Denial* is refusing to accept some aspect of reality. A heavy smoker may deny scientific reports on the dangers of smoking.

Emotional Control and Expression

Your internal defense mechanisms are not the only forces that keep your emotions under control. The society you live in also affects the way you express your emotions. Each society places value on the expression of certain emotions and the control of others.

American society, for example, has traditionally encouraged men to be strong, aggressive, and independent and to keep their emotions under control. Women, on the other hand, have been expected to be sensitive, dependent, and highly emotional.

Today the traditional sex roles are changing. Men and women have more freedom to do and be whatever feels comfortable to them. Many of the ingrained ideas about emotional expression are changing. It seems likely, then, that both men and women will be able to express a wider range of emotions without fear of rejection.

The Role of the Individual

Not all the forces that shape your emotional landscape are out of your hands. You can take an active part in helping to determine your emotional life and your emotional well-being. You can accomplish this by doing as much as you can to make your life consistent with your values and goals.

One of the first steps in doing this is to decide what your values and goals are. Once you gain this kind of self-knowledge, you can place yourself in situations that provide you with positive emotions.

The experiences of Mark Weston illustrate this process. Because of his size and coordination, Mark played football. It was something that was always expected of him, and he came to expect it of himself. It took a long time for him to realize that hitting people made him uncomfortable. The body contact of football simply didn't fit in with his values and attitudes.

Figure 2.8 American society has traditionally taught boys to be aggressive and competitive.

Figure 2.9 Thinking about your goals and values is the first step toward reaching emotional maturity.

But Mark enjoyed sports and considered physical activity vital to his sense of well-being. So he found one that involved competition without body contact. He joined the track and field team and became a shot putter, something he thoroughly enjoyed. By adjusting his activities to his values, Mark created a positive emotional setting for himself.

Of course, there are many aspects of life that you cannot control. In such cases, you need different methods of coping in order to achieve emotional well-being. Cassie, for example, found out that her parents were getting a divorce, and she became extremely upset. She reached the point where she could not face her problems alone, so she went to the school counselor. He helped her realize that part of her pain was caused by her belief that she was to blame.

Once Cassie understood that she was not at fault in the breakdown of her parents' marriage, she felt a great sense of relief. She still had painful feelings to cope with, but these were appropriate feelings. If you are in a similar situation, talking to a trusted adviser, teacher, or other adult can help you cope. Such talks will not change the situation, but they can help you by allowing you to ventilate your feelings.

Emotional Maturity

What Mark and Cassie learned will help them reach emotional maturity. Emotional maturity is not a matter of being happy or contented all the time. Everyone faces conflicts and disappointments. In fact, according to some psychologists, conflicts such as those described above challenge people to develop emotional maturity.

There are several aspects to emotional maturity. They include the abilities to accept yourself and to form relationships with others. The emotionally mature person can also work effectively and enjoy leisure time. She or he can also cope with life's challenges in the most appropriate way. People who are emotionally mature have the ability to make the best of life and of themselves.

CHECK YOUR UNDERSTANDING

1. What is the unconscious mind?
2. Describe five common defense mechanisms. What does an overdependence on such mechanisms suggest?
3. How does a person's society affect his or her expressions of emotion?
4. Describe one way you can help to determine your own emotional life.
5. List five aspects of emotional maturity.

CHAPTER SUMMARY

- The five stages of experiencing and expressing an emotion are perception, appraisal, the emotion, the accompanying physical changes, and action.
- The autonomic nervous system produces the physical changes that accompany an emotion. It prepares the body to meet an emergency and helps to calm it down afterward.
- In addition to having certain basic physical needs, people also have emotional needs. Abraham Maslow divided emotional needs into two categories, basic needs and growth needs. The two most important emotional needs are the need for love and the need for self-esteem.
- Emotional development is influenced by genetic factors and environmental factors (family, friends, home, school).
- Freud, Piaget, and Erikson all developed psychological theories about emotional development that emphasized the importance of children interacting with others and adapting to society as they grow.
- Our defense mechanisms help us to cope with emotional conflicts. Some of the common defense mechanisms are repression, displacement, sublimation, escape, regression, projection, and denial.
- Because of changes in our society, it seems likely that men and women will be able to express a wider range of emotions than they have in the past.
- In order to control your emotional well-being, you must first decide what your values and goals are.
- People who are emotionally mature accept themselves and can form relationships with others. They can also work effectively and enjoy their leisure time.

DO YOU REMEMBER?

Give brief definitions of these terms:

perception	autonomic nervous system	basic needs	modeling
appraisal	sympathetic system	growth needs	conditioning
values	parasympathetic system	self-esteem	defense mechanism

THINK AND DISCUSS

1. How many different influences can you think of that affect the development of a person's value system?
2. Is it possible to be friends with someone whose values are very different from your own? Why or why not?
3. What ways besides exercise can you think of to relieve the stress caused by unexpressed emotions?
4. What kinds of emotions do you think motivate people such as athletes to achieve their goals?
5. In what ways might too strong a belief in the genetic determination of emotions be harmful?
6. How would you help a child develop self-esteem?
7. How are leisure activities an important part of emotional well-being?
8. Which of the defense mechanisms do you think are most frequently used? Why?
9. How would a childhood with no disappointments or problems affect a person?
10. What do you think are the most common emotional conflicts teenagers have to face?
11. What seem to be the topics of most popular songs? Why?

FOLLOW-UP

1. Look up some studies on identical twins separated at birth and reunited in adulthood. Write a report on what these cases suggest about the inherited aspects of emotions.
2. Interview four people about their leisure-time activities and the emotional benefits they think they gain from these activities. Discuss the results with your class.
3. Contact a local hotline volunteer and find out what teenage problems the hotline deals with most frequently. Also find out the ways the hotline suggests for coping with these problems. Report your findings to the class.
4. Visit your local library or bookstore and draw up a list of popular self-help books. What trend do you see in their titles? Post the list in your classroom.
5. Make a poster illustrating the workings of the autonomic nervous system during stress. Display the poster in your classroom.
6. Draw up a list of local hotlines and other agencies that offer counseling services. Post the list in your classroom.

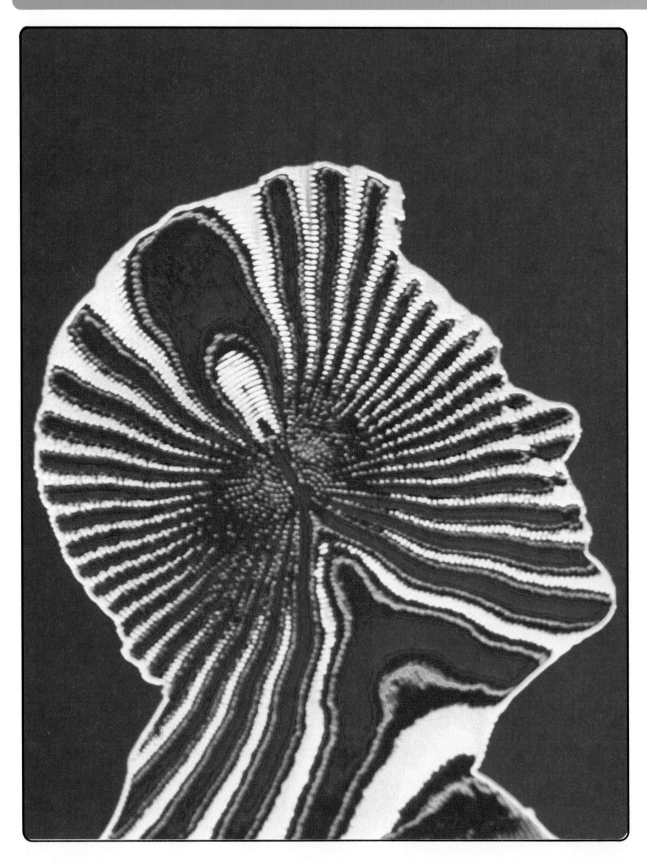

CHAPTER 3

Mental Health and Mental Disorders

After reading this chapter, you should be able to answer these questions:

1. Why do we have trouble defining mental illness?

2. What are the most common mental health problems in the United States today?

3. What is meant by a personality disorder?

4. How can you tell if someone is having a serious emotional problem?

5. What can you do to help someone who is troubled?

It looked bad for a while. Kim stopped showing up for the usual handball game after class. In fact, nobody saw him any more outside of class. In school he had always been lively and joking. Now he was distant and dreamy. Normally talkative, he now spoke little. He was preoccupied and seemed always to be tired. His marks, normally above average, began to go down.

Kim's teachers and classmates were worried about him. Finally, one of the teachers went to talk with Kim's parents. The teacher discovered that there was no cause for concern. Kim was carving a wooden model of the old fishing boat his family had once owned in Korea. It was to be a birthday present for his grandfather, and he had only one week left to finish it. He worked on it every spare moment and late into the night.

Were Kim's teachers and friends wrong to worry about him? No, they were not. The changes they had noticed in Kim could very well have been the symptoms of a serious emotional problem. Such a problem, neglected, could lead to a crippling mental disorder.

As you can see from this story, it is not always easy to recognize a mental health problem. There is a fine line between good mental health and poor mental health. It is not always obvious when the line has been crossed.

Poor mental health affects hundreds of thousands of people. Most people go through periods when they feel depressed and unable to cope with their problems and responsibilities. Usually, though, they find a way of dealing with such feelings. But some people develop serious mental disorders for which they need professional help.

In this chapter we will discuss some of the characteristics of mental health and explain some of the things you can do to promote your own mental health. Then we will examine some of the more common mental disorders and the various ways of dealing with them. Finally, you will learn how to help people with problems and how to get professional help when it is needed.

SECTION **1** # Promoting Mental Health

Mental health is more than the absence of mental illness. There are degrees of mental health, just as there are degrees of physical health.

Here's an illustration of what we mean by degrees of mental health. Roberto is an average student but a gifted artist. Ever since he was old enough to hold a crayon, he has been drawing. And he draws very well. Even though he is very talented, however, he never lives up to his promise. Somehow, whenever he is entered in a drawing competition, Roberto is late getting his work in. Or it is not the right size. Or it is done sloppily. His art teacher knows he could do better. But Roberto just won't—or can't—apply himself.

One characteristic of mental health is a person's desire to achieve goals that he or she knows can be attained. In Roberto's case, something is holding him back. We can't say that Roberto is mentally ill; he isn't. He has good relations with his family and good friends in school. His academic record is fair. He is not destructive of himself nor of anyone else. Yet, he is not all he could be either.

Kelly, on the other hand, is an average student and an outstanding soccer player. She is one of the smallest girls in her class. Yet, despite her size, she is able to play against much bigger girls. She has quick reflexes and great speed. She works hard at developing her playing skills. At practice she is almost always the last one off the field. She enjoys playing and does it with enthusiasm.

People like Kelly, who enjoy what they do, seem to get more out of life. Perhaps the most obvious sign of a good state of mental health is a certain zest for what one is doing. Without this zest, you may do reasonably well, be moderately popular, feel relatively secure, and yet find that it is all a little flat. When you have a high degree of mental health, you are better able to reach your maximum potential. You are at your best in your work, your play, and with your friends. In short, you are enjoying yourself more.

How to Improve Your Mental Health

Enjoying oneself is not the goal of mental health. It is a by-product of mental health. Gaining mental health does not mean complete freedom from everyday problems. This is not realistic, nor possible. What mental health involves is the ability to cope with problems while keeping a good psychological balance.

How can you go about improving your mental health? There is no single easy answer. Still, there are some things you can do to promote your mental health. A number of important ones are listed below.

1. Set realistic goals for yourself, then achieve them.
2. Practice being alone without outside distractions. Learn to be comfortable with yourself.
3. Identify your good qualities. Be proud of them and of yourself.
4. Make the most of your physical appearance.

Figure 3.1 Liking yourself and treating yourself well
are important to your mental health.

5. Be yourself. Express yourself openly and honestly.

6. Recognize and face your fears, guilts, and hostilities. Accept these as part of being human.

7. Try to see the value in both good and bad emotional experiences.

8. Practice sharing your feelings with others.

9. Build friendships by giving and accepting affection.

10. Join in family, club, or other group activities. Share goals and values.

11. Maintain your physical health.

12. Accept responsibility for what and who you are and for what you do.

13. Develop worthwhile skills.

14. Take advantage of opportunities for new experiences. Learn to enjoy good experiences.

15. Learn from both successes and failures. Make full use of all your experiences.

16. When someone upsets or annoys you, try to put yourself in that person's place.

17. Allow yourself to be pleased with what you are and excited about what you are becoming.

18. Ask for help when you feel you could use it. Understand that accepting help may be good for the person who helps you as well.

19. Recognize that nobody's perfect, including yourself.

Helping Others

You can often help yourself by helping other people. You can help by your behavior. Be warm and honest with others. Accept them for what they are. Listen to other people, weighing carefully what they say. If they seem under stress, try to help them define the problem. Work with them to figure out possible solutions to what is troubling them. Help those close to you to face the consequences of their decisions. Do not, however, be quick to judge another's actions. Finally, you can help others to find positive ways of expressing their emotions. You may find that in acting as a good friend or family member, you yourself have grown.

CHECK YOUR UNDERSTANDING

1. What is one obvious sign of good mental health?
2. What are the benefits of mental health?
3. List 10 ways to promote your mental health that you consider especially helpful.
4. List seven ways you can help others with their emotional problems.

SECTION **2**   **What Is Mental Illness?**

A man living in a small town in the Ozark Mountains of Missouri has a vision. He believes God has spoken to him. He begins preaching to his neighbors. Soon the whole town is in a state of religious fervor. People say he has a "calling." His reputation as a prophet and a healer spreads. One day he ventures down into the city of St. Louis and attempts to hold a prayer meeting on a main street. He is arrested. When he tells the police that he talks with God, they take him to a mental hospital.

A high school junior moves to a new town with her family. She doesn't like the new school. She has trouble sleeping and feels tired all the time. She finds it hard to make new friends and feels unable to keep up with her schoolwork. It is hard for her to concentrate. She sees a doctor who tells her she is in perfect health.

She tells her family about her depression. She says she thinks she is mentally ill and needs to see a psychotherapist. Her family ridicules the idea. All she needs to do, they say, is cheer up. The schoolgirl wonders if she could solve her problem by running away or jumping off a bridge.

Defining Mental Illness

Who is right in the illustrations above? The "prophet" or the police? The schoolgirl or her parents? It is not always easy to identify a serious mental disorder. What seems abnormal to some is considered normal by others. Many people in our society—and in other societies—feel that having visions is an important part of religion. Others feel that hearing voices or having visions is a sign of mental disturbance. Had the "prophet" stayed at home in the Ozarks, he might have been considered perfectly normal. In St. Louis, however, he was thought to be mentally ill. This was because his behavior

Figure 3.2 There are no hard-and-fast rules for defining mental illness. What seems abnormal to some may be considered normal by others.

was so different from what the people in St. Louis considered normal.

But just being different doesn't mean that you are disturbed. Sometimes, not going along with the crowd can be the most healthful thing to do. When your friends plan to go riding with someone who has been drinking, for example, your refusal to go along may be the only sensible act in the group.

In the case of the high school student, she herself decided that she was disturbed because she was depressed. But occasional depression is not necessarily a sign of mental disturbance. Everyone feels low from time to time.

The problem is that there are no hard and fast rules for defining mental illness. Even the experts disagree. However, various definitions have been devised, and we shall look at some of the more common ones.

Normal and Abnormal

Some people say that whatever most people in a society do is normal. Therefore, behavior that is different from that of the majority is abnormal. In our society, for instance, taking 10 showers a day would be considered abnormal behavior. This is true because few people take 10 showers a day.

But does abnormal behavior indicate mental illness? Sometimes it does. However, this definition has serious limitations. Most people, for instance, are not particularly creative. Does that mean that highly creative people such as Shakespeare or Einstein were abnormal? Does it mean they were mentally ill? Obviously not. Defining mental illness in terms of normal and abnormal behavior is not always, then, a useful standard.

Legal Insanity

The terms *sane* and *insane* are not used much by workers in the mental health care field. They are mainly legal terms that even lawyers are wary of using. People used to be considered legally insane if they were unable to understand the difference between right and wrong or if they were unable to control their actions. Such definitions have never been easy to apply. The notions of "right" and "wrong" are sometimes hard to pin down. It is even harder to determine whether a person really does understand that what he or she did was wrong. It is equally difficult to determine whether a person could have acted differently in a specific situation. In criminal cases, some defendants enter a plea of innocent on the grounds of temporary insanity. Should they be excused because sanity returned after the criminal acts were committed? The legal approach to defining mental illness has been difficult to use.

Adjustment to Society

Some psychiatrists say that a normal person is one who can get along—physically, emotionally, socially—in the world. Such people are able to earn their living; feed, clothe, and house themselves; and make friends. The abnormal or mentally ill people are the ones who cannot do these things. They cannot adjust to their society. They may not be able to hold a job. They may be unable to cope with the demands of daily life. They may have so much trouble with personal relationships that they avoid people.

This approach to defining mental illness is the one most often used by workers in the mental health care field. It is valuable in that it stresses ability to function rather than a standard of behavior. There are problems with this approach, however. If a society has gone wrong, it may be a sign of health *not* to be able to adjust to it. Thus, people who find it impossible to function in a cruel or repressive society—Nazi Germany, for example—may be the most healthy ones in it.

The Need for Caution

As we have seen, there are various ways of defining mental illness, none of them entirely satisfactory. However, the fact that it is difficult to define mental disorders does not mean that they do not exist. What it does mean is that we should be very cautious about judging a person to be mentally ill.

If a person behaves in a way that we don't understand, he or she is not necessarily mentally disturbed. We may all behave a little strangely under stress. In addition, mild disturbances are quite common. It is only when a person's problems become so severe that he or she cannot cope with everyday life that it becomes an illness.

The Scope of the Problem

Mental disturbances are a huge public health problem. It has been estimated that 1 of every 10 Americans now needs some form of treatment for mental health problems. In large urban areas, 1 out of 5 people suffers from serious emotional problems. Moreover, mental illness affects teenagers as often as adults. An estimated 10 million people under the age of 18 have mental disorders. At least 1.4 million in this age group suffer from problems serious enough to need professional care.

Many social problems have underlying psychological problems as the cause. These include such widespread and destructive problems as delinquency, divorce, alcoholism, drug abuse, crime, even accidents. The economic cost of mental illness to the nation is conservatively estimated at $40 billion a year.

More important than these figures, though, is the personal cost of mental illness. People suffering from mental illness miss out on the very things that make life worth living: happiness, love, achievement, creativity, motivation, and personal relationships.

CHECK YOUR UNDERSTANDING

1. Why is it difficult to define mental illness?
2. Explain the limitations of defining mental illness in terms of normal or abnormal behavior.
3. Describe the adjustment-to-society approach to defining mental illness.
4. What is the estimate of how many Americans have mental health problems that need treatment?

SECTION **3**   # Types of Mental Illness

Mental illness is much more common than most people realize. Because of the problems of definition, however, it is difficult to say exactly how many people suffer from mental illness. It is also difficult to say how many types of mental illnesses there are.

A study done by the National Institute of Mental Health projected that almost one out of every five adult Americans—29 ' million people—suffers from mental health problems. The most common problems, the study found, were related to anxiety (8 percent of the population). People who have mental problems stemming from drug and alcohol abuse were next (6 to 7 percent). Depression was the third most common problem (5 to 6 percent). Schizophrenia, an often severe and incapacitating mental disorder, was found in 1 percent of the population. Antisocial personality problems were also found in 1 percent of the population.

Psychologists have classified the major kinds of mental illnesses into categories. They call these categories *disorders*. Psychologists sometimes also use two other terms to describe how severe a mental illness is. A *neurosis* is a mild disorder that causes distress but does not interfere with a person's everyday activities. Most anxiety disorders are considered neuroses. A *psychosis* is a severe mental disorder that prevents a person from functioning. Schizophrenia is an example of psychosis. Depression ranges in severity and can be either a neurosis or a psychosis.

Depression

Depression is the name for a large range of similar problems. A depression is a disorder that affects a person's mood. Depression has been called the common cold of mental disorders. This is because it is so widespread. It has been estimated that during any given year 1 out of every 20 people may suffer some form of significant depression.

Depression ranges in intensity from occasional feelings of the blues to feelings of extreme sadness and hopelessness. Most of us at one time or another are depressed. We get a bad grade on an exam, break up with our steady date, lose a tight ball game, move to a different city. Naturally, we feel "down" for a while. But then we get back into the swing of things. There are new challenges to be met. We change our mood and we get going again. In such cases, depression is not much different from a mild cold. We feel bad for a while. Eventually, the feeling goes away, possibly without our having done anything special to get rid of it.

Severe depression is a different matter. Among the signs of serious depression are sadness, feelings of hopelessness, loss of appetite, inability to sleep (or, sometimes, excessive sleep), and loss of self-esteem. The most common sign of depression, however, is loss of the ability to feel pleasure. Depressed people no longer enjoy the things they used to enjoy.

Some people have a *manic-depressive illness*. These people experience periods when their moods alternate between extreme sadness and extreme joy. This can be a very serious illness, and is usually treated with medication.

The causes of severe depression are not well understood. It does seem, however, that both

Figure 3.3 Among the signs of serious depression are sadness, feelings of hopelessness, and loss of self-esteem.

Talking Point

Anorexia and Bulimia

Two emotional disorders that have increased in incidence in recent years are anorexia and bulimia. Both disorders involve an obsession about body weight. The largest percentage of sufferers are young women. Both conditions can be life-threatening.

People suffering from anorexia diet to the point of emaciation. Their self-image becomes totally distorted. Even when they are down to 65 or 70 pounds, they still see themselves as fat.

Most anorexics come from middle-class backgrounds. One theory about their condition is that it is a result of profound insecurity. These young women are afraid that they won't be able to live up to their parents' expectations. By dieting, they "cheat" the process of maturing. Their bodies don't gain the curves associated with womanhood. Excessive dieting also causes menstruation to cease. Anorexics effectively manipulate their bodies so that they can cling on to childhood.

Like anexoria, bulimia seems to affect most frequently young women from middle-class backgrounds. These women alternate between a binge and a purge cycle. First, they eat enormous quantities of food at one sitting. Then, to prevent the possibility of weight gain, they make themselves vomit or take large quantities of laxatives.

Bulimics are usually high achievers who, for some reason, lack self-esteem. They may go through the binging and purging cycles for years. They hide their condition by buying their food at many different stores and by withdrawing from family and friends.

Anorexia and bulivia need to be treated professionally. Patients need medical attention for their physical condition and psychiatric help to find the underlying cause of the disturbance.

psychological and biological factors are involved. Usually, depression is related to a stressful event—loss of a job, the death of a loved one, physical illness, and so on. But this is not always the case. Sometimes there seems to be no single event that causes depression.

In recent years scientists have found that people's moods vary with their brain chemistry. Nerve impulses in the brain are transmitted by certain chemical substances. Sometimes the amounts of chemical substances are too low in certain key parts of the brain. When this happens, people feel depressed. So depression can have a biological base.

Anxiety Disorders

Like depression, anxiety disorders affect a person's moods. Most people feel anxious at times. For example, you may feel anxious about meeting new people. But as you enter into a new situation, your anxiety is likely to go away. Your anxiety was a natural reaction to a situation you thought might be difficult. Anxiety disorders are different. They are based on vague or imagined fears rather than on realistic fears.

Some people are very afraid of objects or situations they know are not really dangerous. These fears are called *phobias*. A common phobia is claustrophobia, the fear of small, enclosed spaces. When someone suffers from a phobia, she or he tries to avoid the object or situation at all costs. Other people's anxieties result in obsessive and compulsive behavior. They persist in acting in certain ways, even though they know their actions are absurd. Other people suffer from another type of anxiety disorder called panic attacks. These are sudden, intense feelings of fear. Symptoms include shortness of breath, rapid heartbeat, dizziness, numbness, sweating, and trembling. Most panic attacks last several minutes, but some can continue for hours.

Schizophrenia

So far we have been discussing mood disorders. Other disorders affect a person's thoughts rather than moods. *Schizophrenia* is one of the thought

Figure 3.4 Although neurotic people may become anxious about vague or imagined dangers, they can still function satisfactorily in most areas of daily life.

disorders. It is also the most common type of psychosis. The word *schizophrenia* means "split mind."

Schizophrenia is a disease that affects about 1 percent of the population. Schizophrenic people are severely disturbed. Often they have *delusions*—false beliefs that cannot be corrected by logical argument. Sometimes they have *hallucinations*—experiences during which they see or hear things that are not there.

The schizophrenic person also suffers from extreme mood changes. In addition, she or he may respond inappropriately to a situation—for instance, by laughing at the news of someone's death. Schizophrenics frequently suffer from *paranoia* too. Paranoid people may feel that everyone is plotting against them. Or they may feel that they are the greatest leaders in the world.

There is some proof for thinking that schizophenia has a physiological basis. Much promising work has been done on genetic, or inherited, factors as a cause of schizophrenia. Other evidence points to an imbalance in the chemical make-up of the brain. Also important are sociological factors. Schizophrenia has been shown to occur more frequently in the lowest social classes of urban populations. Another factor is severe stress. Although much work has been done, the cause of the illness is still not known. Keep in mind that there are many kinds of schizophrenia. Remember, too, that this is not the same as multiple personality disorder—a popular subject of books and movies.

Substance-Abuse Disorders

Some disorders affect both moods and thoughts. Disorders related to the abuse of drugs and alcohol—substance-abuse disorders—are in this category. According to one recent estimate, nearly one in five teenagers experiences serious alcohol-related emotional problems.

Drug and alcohol abuse are related to various mental disturbances and can cause or be caused by a variety of psychological problems. After using drugs or alcohol for a period of time, people can develop a *tolerance* to the substance. Their bodies need larger amounts of the substance for it to have an effect on them. As people use these substances more and more frequently, they run the risk of growing dependent upon them. They first become *psychologically dependent*. This means that they depend upon the drug for their sense of well-being. People can also become *physically dependent*. When someone is physically dependent on a substance, his or her body has come to treat the substance as something it needs, like water or oxygen. If the person does not use the substance, there is physical pain, called *withdrawal*.

Both the physical and emotional components of substance-abuse disorders are difficult to treat. Experts are not sure about the causes of these disorders. They think that heredity, environmental factors, personality, and chemical imbalances are all involved.

Personality Disorders

Personality disorders are different from the problems we have been discussing. They are not really disorders of specific moods or thoughts; they affect all of a person's thoughts and actions. Personality disorders are distinguished by the intensity and pattern of antisocial characteristics displayed by the person suffering from them.

Personality disorders are shown by extreme difficulties in personal relationships. For example, someone with an antisocial personality disorder is unable to live by ordinary social and moral rules. He or she might be intelligent, lively, attractive to others, and from a "good" home. However, people with this disorder are also irresponsible, dishonest, and unable to establish any deep relationship of love or trust. They feel no anxiety or guilt when they do something wrong, and punishment has no effect on them.

Personality disorders have no single cause, and the causes are often undiscoverable. Psychologists have theories that these disorders are inherited, caused by brain damage, or learned from unfortunate experiences during childhood.

Psychosomatic Reactions

Psychological stress often produces physical symptoms. If the mental stress is prolonged, it can result in a physical ailment. Often the person is not aware that the origin of the physical problem is *psychosomatic*—involving mind and body. Severe psychological stress may be a component in such physical problems as backaches, migraine headaches, asthma, hypertension, and ulcers. This subject will be treated in more detail in the next chapter.

Suicide

People suffering from severe depression or from other mood or thought disorders need help to deal with the problems. The majority do obtain that help from family, friends, or professionals. A small minority, however, choose another way out: they attempt or commit suicide.

How to...
Recognize the Signals of a Potential Suicide

A suicide attempt is a dramatic plea for help. A person is showing that he or she feels hopeless. And often suicide is not an act done on the spur of the moment. It is one that a person thinks about and plans.

Yet far too often no one recognizes the potential suicide's despair. When that happens, a person who really wanted to live dies. You should know how to identify the warning signs of suicide. Here are some things to be aware of:

1. Watch out for extremes of mood. Suicidal people may be hopelessly depressed and withdrawn from life. Or they may be so agitated that they can't eat or sleep.
2. Watch out for sudden changes in mood. Severe depression, followed by elation, followed by depression again are warning signals. They may mean that someone is struggling with the desire to live and the even stronger desire to die.
3. Be concerned when people start giving away the things they love. They may be telling you that they no longer have any reason to live.
4. Be alert for a crisis that may bring about a suicide attempt. Events such as the loss of a job, the death of a parent, or the breakup of a relationship may be overwhelming to suicidal people. They may feel that there is no way to cope with life as it is.
5. Listen for a suicide "plan." Suicidal people often talk about their death wish long before they try to kill themselves.
6. Take *every* suicide attempt seriously. People who threaten to take their lives are crying for help. They want someone to save them from an unbearable situation.
7. Be wary of people who quickly bounce back from a suicide attempt and act as if nothing had happened. They may try to kill themselves again within a short time unless they receive help.

Remember, most suicides really wanted to live. Suicide is preventable—if you know how to help.

Adapted from *Suicides: Do They Want to Die?* (New York: St. Vincent's Hospital and Medical Center of New York, n.d.).

Every year about 30,000 suicides are reported in the United States. However, the actual number of suicides committed each year may be as high as 100,000. Some suicides are covered up by families and friends to avoid shame or guilt. In addition, some people make their suicides look like accidents to spare their families pain.

Of the 30,000 reported suicides, about 5,000 involve teenagers and young adults. It is thought that for each completed suicide in this age group, there are 100 to 110 attempts. In recent years, the number of teenage suicides has increased sharply, so much so that suicide is now the third most common cause of death, after accidents and homocides, for people aged 15 to 24. Although four times more males than females in this age group commit suicide, many more females than males attempt suicide.

Many young people go through periods of deep depression. They are at a stage in their lives when they have to make important decisions. They also have to come to terms with the physical and emotional changes in their lives. To feel depressed about such matters is natural, but it is usually a temporary feeling.

Some young people attempt suicide not because they really want to end their lives. Rather, they may want to draw attention to their unhappiness to punish someone who has made them unhappy. They are confused, angry, and hurt. Their thinking patterns become distorted, and they fail to see the possible outcome of their actions.

You may be able to prevent a suicide by listening to friends carefully and acting promptly. Read the box on page 43 to learn how to recognize the signals of a potential suicide. If you're with someone who feels suicidal, get help. Call a responsible adult or the police. Do not leave the person alone. Every suicide attempt or threat should be treated seriously.

Many communities now have suicide prevention centers and suicide hotlines. These are places operated by vounteers trained to talk to callers who need special help in coping with personal crises.

CHECK YOUR UNDERSTANDING

1. What are some of the signs of a severe depression?
2. Explain the difference between anxiety and fear.
3. What is schizophrenia?
4. Why is substance abuse considered to be a mental health problem?
5. List some of the ways you can help prevent a suicide.

SECTION **4**   # Types of Treatment

It is true that we do not fully understand the causes of most mental illnesses. Nevertheless, mental illnesses can, in many cases, be successfully treated. There are two basic methods of treatment: psychotherapy and drug therapy. The two are frequently used together.

Psychotherapy

Psychotherapy is used to help people understand and overcome the causes of their mental disorders. Psychotherapists work with their clients to get at the problems that are bothering them. The therapists talk to and listen to their clients. They use their skills and insights to help people change their approaches to life. With a new outlooks on themselves and on life, the clients can function more effectively.

There are two main types of psychotherapy: insight therapy and behavior therapy. Insight therapy involves helping clients understand why they behave as they do. Many insight therapists place considerable emphasis on the client's experiences in early life. This approach is based on the belief that a person's childhood experiences may have led to mental or emotional disorders in later life. Behavior therapy, on the other hand, emphasizes life in the present. Clients concentrate on altering undesirable behavior patterns. Many psychotherapists use both kinds of therapy.

There are several kinds of workers in the psychotherapy field. They are distinguished one from the other by the amount and type of their training. *Psychiatrists* are medical doctors (M.D.'s). In addition, they have three more years of training in the medical specialty of psychiatry. *Psychologists* do not have the medical training of psychiatrists. They usually have a Ph.D. in psychology. Although they have great skill and success in therapy, they cannot treat physiological illnesses or prescribe medicines as psychiatrists can. *Social workers* generally work on a broader scale of problems, including income and housing, as well as doing counseling. They usually have a master's degree in social work.

There are many other people with training in guidance and counseling who work in mental health. Most forms of psychotherapy can be carried out by people without medical training. Warmth, compassion, understanding, and intelligence are what are needed for helping disturbed people. Therapists with these qualities, plus the ability to understand human behavior, can be successful no matter what their training.

Figure 3.5 Behavior therapy can often help people overcome phobias, such as this woman's fear of snakes.

Group Therapy

There are therapies that treat people in groups rather than individually. Group therapy techniques do not allow patients to experience the intimacy of individual therapy. However, they do have some advantages. They allow more people to be treated at lower fees. This is important because the cost of private therapy can be very high. The chief advantage of group therapy, though, is that it concentrates on improving people's relations with other people. Certain problems that do not respond to individual therapy seem to respond to group therapy. Possibly, the emotional support of the group helps more than the expertise of a single therapist. This seems especially true if the members all have a similar problem, such as drug dependence or alcoholism.

Self-help groups are not strictly therapy groups as they are not led by a professional. Usually, they are groups formed by people who share common problems. There are groups for alcoholics, widowed people, single parents, cancer patients, and many others. They can be extremely effective in helping their members cope with their specific problem.

Family Therapy

Recently, therapists have come more and more to treat families or couples as a unit. If one spouse comes in for counseling, the therapist invites the other partner to join too. If a child is having emotional problems, she or he may be treated with the parents.

Family therapy is an exciting and valuable addition to psychotherapy. It enables family members to communicate with each other. They learn to see others' problems as well as their own.

For instance, many families or couples unconsciously assign roles to each member. There may be a "strong" one, a "weak" one, a "scapegoat," a "caretaker." Sometimes the assigned role becomes too confining or burdensome for the person. He or she may show signs of disturbance. Family therapy assumes that all members of the family are contributing to the problem. The therapy tries to bring out in the

Figure 3.6 Many people have found that group therapy can help to solve their mental health problems. The emotional support of a group is especially effective when all members have a common problem, such as drug dependence or alcoholism.

open all the expectations and communication patterns of the family. It does this in order to readjust inappropriate roles. It also encourages mutual support and understanding.

Drug Therapy

The 1950s saw a revolution in the treatment of mental illness. It was discovered that certain drugs could relieve many symptoms of serious mental disorders. This discovery has made it possible for many people suffering from severe mental disorders to be treated on an outpatient basis.

Three main types of medications are used in therapy for mental disorders: antipsychotic drugs, antidepressants, and antianxiety drugs. Antipsychotic drugs, or major tranquilizers, are used to treat serious disorders such as schizo-

phrenia. Schizophrenic patients who take these antipsychotic drugs become less withdrawn, less confused, have fewer hallucinations, and become less hostile.

Another class of drugs, antidepressants, make some depressed people happier. One of these drugs, lithium, is used to control the extreme mood swings of manic-depressive patients. The drugs in this class can have severe side effects, so they must be given under close medical supervision.

The antianxiety drugs are used to reduce excitability and cause drowsiness. The most commonly used drugs in this group are Valium, Librium, and Miltown. Thse drugs help people cope with difficult periods in their lives. They are also prescribed to relieve various neurotic problems, psychosomatic problems, and symptoms of alcohol withdrawal. If the drugs are taken properly, there are few side effects. However, prolonged use may lead to dependence, and heavy doses taken along with alcohol can result in death. Nevertheless, the drugs do allow people who otherwise would be hospitalized to lead productive lives. They are commonly used with one or more of the other types of therapy.

CHECK YOUR UNDERSTANDING

1. Explain what the different types of psychotherapy have in common.
2. Describe the advantages of group therapy.
3. What is the value of family therapy?
4. What are the advantages of drug therapy for mental disorders? The disadvantages?

SECTION **5** # When and How to Get Help

How can you tell when someone—including yourself—needs treatment for a mental disorder? How do you handle your own problems? How do you help someone else? Where do you turn for professional help? We will discuss some of the answers to these questions below.

Coping with Everyday Living

We all face problems in our daily lives. We are sometimes frightened, embarrassed, threatened, frustrated. We are made to feel anger, guilt, inadequacy. Usually, we overcome such feelings. Occasionally, though, we face situations that are beyond our ability to cope. At such times, we may experience symptoms of psychological disturbance.

Sometimes such symptoms can be avoided by the use of certain strategies. For one thing, you can try to avoid unreasonable problems. If, for instance, you find you always argue with another student in your school, you can make plans to see as little of the student as possible. Find different friends. Go to different places.

You can also try to develop skills for coping with problem situations. The more practice you get in trying different strategies—and the more successful you are—the better adjusted you become. Here are some examples:

1. John wanted to become a paramedic. However, when he looked at the required chemistry course, he knew it was not for him. Rethinking goals and switching to another subject is reasonable coping behavior. On the other hand, switching courses because of a minor setback—a bad grade on one exam—is not good coping.

2. Choosing your own interests is vitally important for your growth. Ben decided to quit the football team and to take up swimming, even though his father wanted him to play football. Such a change may be good for developing Ben's reliance on his own feelings. However, if Ben had quit the football team because he was angry with his father and wanted to hurt him, it would not have been helpful.

3. The best way to get rid of extreme acrophobia (fear of heights) is not suddenly to walk to the edge of a roof and look over. Instead, people should accustom themselves to high places gradually. They should go step by step. The same applies to many other fears and phobias.

4. Suppose you feel you just cannot speak in public. Try to speak to a group whose members not only understand your fear but share it. The desire of all the members to overcome the fear will give support to each one.

5. Everyone runs out of energy now and then. If you find yourself overwhelmed by the pressure and pace of your life, take it easy for a while. Withdraw from some activities. Get away by yourself until you feel like reengaging with the world.

Most importantly, avoid developing behavior patterns that are destructive to yourself or to others. Kicking a younger brother who angers you may vent the anger. But it also causes you to feel stupid and guilty. A better solution may be to express your anger in words. This allows the other person to take a part in resolving the conflict.

Signs of Mental Disorders

How can you tell when a person's coping strategies are not sufficient? How can you distinguish between the normal disturbances everyone has and a disorder that needs help? What are the warning signs of mental disorder?

In addition to the symptoms described already, the following are other signs:

1. a prolonged and intense anxiety (This is a feeling that something bad is going to happen when there is no real reason for such a feeling.)

2. a severe and persistent depression (Here the person feels low, unhappy, uncaring. A depressed person often has little energy or motivation, withdraws from most activities, and finds it hard to do anything.)

3. a sudden change in mood or behavior that is uncharacteristic (A generally passive person may become very aggressive, change her or his patterns of dress, speech, or actions, and appear strange and reckless.)

4. one or more physical complaints (The person may begin to complain of headaches, nausea, pains, sleeplessness, shortness of breath, or the like. Yet there is no medical cause for the complaints.)

5. performance falling far short of earlier promise (Here the person's actions in work, play, or relationships suddenly fall much below what he or she is capable of doing.)

How You Can Help

You can listen. Maybe because so few of us listen much, we underestimate its value. If someone you know has a problem, it may help

Figure 3.7 The best way to help a friend in mental distress is to listen, to be supportive, and to suggest outside help if necessary.

a great deal just to let her or him talk about it. Do not be critical. Show that you feel the problem along with the person. Learn to indicate your sympathy. Use responses such as "I can tell you're worried" or "I've been down myself. It can be a terrible feeling."

Usually, it is better to let the person think up ways of coping than for you to rush in with advice. It is always good, though, to encourage and reassure the disturbed person. That is primarily what you are there for. You want to create a calming and supportive situation in which the person is better able to deal with the problem.

Sometimes such talks will not be enough. Despite your efforts, you find that the person is not feeling better. The problem remains unresolved. Then it is time to get outside help. It is better to get such help too early rather than too late. Many tragic outcomes of mental problems could have been avoided if people who knew about the problems had sought help sooner.

You should first encourage the disturbed person to seek outside help for himself or herself. A good contact might be a school counselor, a member of the clergy, or a family physician. In any case, you should recommend someone the disturbed person knows and trusts. If the disturbed person will not seek outside help, you, as a friend, or a family member may make the first contact. Then plan with the outside party how to get help to the person.

Dealing with Emergencies

Sometimes there is no time for talk. A crisis arises. The disturbed person poses a danger to herself or himself or to others. In such cases, those nearby must get professional help even against the express wishes of the disturbed person. One source of help is a hospital emergency room. If the person is too violent to be taken there, call the police. In most communities the police are trained to cope with such emergencies both humanely and effectively.

Many communities have a crisis hotline. People in trouble can telephone at any time, day or night. They will receive immediate counseling, sympathy, and comfort. Hotlines

Figure 3.8 People who call this suicide hotline can receive immediate counseling, sympathy, and comfort at a time of emotional crisis.

have been set up in many communities to handle such specific problems as alcoholism, rape, battered women, runaway children, and suicide. Also, they can provide just a shoulder to cry on if that is all the person needs.

Community Mental Health Centers

In earlier days the mentally ill were sent to mental hospitals called asylums. These institutions were often built in isolated rural areas. The removal of the patients from their familiar surroundings sometimes made their problems worse and made it harder for them to readjust to society later. Patients released from mental hospitals often needed help in coping with the outside world. If the hospital was a long way away from the patient's home, such help was hard to get. Eventually, it was seen that if the patient was to return successfully to his or her community, the community would have to help.

Congress passed a law in 1963 to provide community mental health services for people in need of such help. Hospitals began releasing patients who would otherwise have been kept in for long-term treatment. Today, it is estimated that 2 million people who, earlier, would have been in hospitals now are being treated in their communities or are not receiving any treatment at all.

Two-thirds of the mentally ill now live with their families and receive professional help from hospitals or clinics on an outpatient basis. While some benefit enormously from the support provided by family members, others cause family members to suffer great hardship. Mental health workers think that the families of mentally ill people need professional assistance to help them deal with a mentally ill family member. Some families do receive counseling, but for many the help is simply not available.

Not every mentally ill person has a family to turn to. The growing number of homeless mentally ill people has prompted mental health workers to question the practice of releasing these patients from hospitals. Lacking any kind of support system, many of them are unable to find jobs or gain acceptance in a community. The plight of the homeless has been receiving widespread publicity. Mental health professionals hope that this publicity will lead to reforms in our mental health care system.

CHECK YOUR UNDERSTANDING

1. Describe four strategies that can help you cope with everyday problems.
2. List five signs of mental disorders.
3. What kind of atmosphere should you create when trying to help someone deal with a problem? What should you do if you see that the problem persists?
4. List three sources of aid in a crisis situation.

CHAPTER SUMMARY

- Good mental health is more than just the absence of mental illness. There are degrees of mental health.
- There are many things you can do to promote your mental health. These include setting yourself realistic goals, accepting yourself for what you are, and sharing your feelings with other people.
- There are no hard and fast rules for defining mental illness. In general, when a psychological problem is severe enough to prevent someone from coping with everyday life, it is then considered an illness.
- It is estimated that 1 out of every 10 Americans needs some form of treatment for mental health problems.
- The most common mental disorders are said to be anxiety-related. These include phobias, obsessive-compulsive behavior, and attacks of panic. The second most common disorders are related to substance abuse.
- More than 5 percent of the people in the United States suffer significant depression. Depression

can range in intensity from occasional feelings of the blues to feelings of extreme sadness and hopelessness.
- A common form of psychosis is schizophrenia, in which people exhibit severely disturbed thinking, moods, and behavior. Personality disorders are shown by extreme difficulties in personal and social relationships.
- Most people who feel suicidal are suffering from major depressions that need treatment. Researchers are looking into the cause and prevention of suicide.
- Medications can be used to relieve the symptoms of many serious mental disorders. There are three types of medications used in therapy for mental disorders: antipsychotic drugs, antidepressants, and antianxiety drugs.
- Psychotherapy helps people understand and overcome the causes of their mental disorders. Among the forms of psychotherapy are individual therapy, behavior therapy, group therapy, and family therapy.
- Among the warning signs of mental disorder are

- prolonged anxiety, severe depression, sudden mood changes, physical complaints, and below-normal performance levels.
- You may be able to help a disturbed person simply by listening to him or her. If that doesn't help, you should obtain outside help.
- Among the many sources of help for mentally disturbed people are a school counselor, member of the clergy, family physician, crisis hotline, hospital emergency room, and community mental health center.

DO YOU REMEMBER?

Give brief definitions of these terms:

neurosis	manic-depressive illness	delusion	psychosomatic
psychosis	phobia	hallucination	psychiatrist
depression	schizophrenia	paranoia	psychologist

THINK AND DISCUSS

1. What are some of the problems caused by trying to be perfect and expecting perfection in others?
2. What might be the dangers of becoming involved with an unqualified "therapist" who is really a quack?
3. Think of a famous person you consider to be in good mental health and one you think is in poor mental health. On what do you base your opinions?
4. Why do you think making the most of your physical appearance can be beneficial to your mental health?
5. How can helping others help you learn about yourself?
6. Why do you think depression is so common among teenagers?
7. What would you do if a friend told you he or she felt like committing suicide?
8. Many people react with scorn to the idea of therapy. What reasons can you think of for this reaction?
9. Why do you think some people develop eating disorders? What can they do to help themselves?

FOLLOW-UP

1. Find out more about behavior therapy. Write a report that describes the kind of work being done with this therapy.
2. Most phobias have complex Greek names. Make a chart that lists the names of phobias on one side and their definitions on the other. Display the chart in your classroom.
3. Learn more about the differences between psychologists and psychiatrists. Write a report that explains these differences.
4. Find out about the facilities in your community for helping people with mental health problems. Post the information in your classroom.
5. Contact a local hotline to find out some of the common reasons people give for wanting to commit suicide, as well as the techniques volunteers use to prevent suicides. Discuss your findings with your class.
6. Ask your librarian or teacher to recommend a book about a person who has recovered from mental illness. Prepare a short synopsis for the class.

4

Living with Stress

After reading this chapter, you should be able to answer these questions:

1. What is stress?
2. How can stress be good for you?
3. Does the body respond to stress? How?
4. What are some diseases that people under stress are likely to develop?
5. Can you learn to cope with stress?

Six months after a woman's husband dies, she develops cancer. A man wins $15,000 at the race track. While collecting the money, he collapses and dies of a heart attack. A high school senior has to give a speech to the student body. The morning of the speech she wakes up with a headache after a sleepless night. Another student can't keep still right before he's about to play an important football game. During exam week more than the usual number of students come down with the flu.

All of these people may be victims of stress. They have had to face a stressful situation—or one that seemed stressful to them. Stressful situations are ones that present a challenge to a person's ability to adapt to them. A student facing an exam, a football game, or a first date is undergoing a challenge. In one way or another, the student feels pressure and the need to adjust to it. The student feels stress.

People react to stressful situations in different ways. Some high-strung, or very nervous, people react strongly to stress. They routinely come down with illnesses or suffer accidents in stressful situations. Others are able to adapt to similar situations without undue difficulty. Still others have learned to control their reactions to stress and to lessen the effects of stress on their physical and emotional health.

Yet stress is also a normal part of life. It can, in fact, be crucial to people's well-being. Without the challenge of stressful situations, human beings might never feel the need to develop their potential.

This chapter discusses the paradox that stress can both help you and cause you harm. It also deals with the causes of stress and how people respond to it. It explains the body's stress mechanism and discusses the relationship between stress and disease. Finally, it explores how you can learn to cope with the stresses of life.

SECTION **1** # What Is Stress?

The word *stress* can be confusing because it is used in different ways. For example, we might talk about the stresses of city living. By that we mean such factors as noise and traffic that cause us to feel strain and tension. Or we might say that a person is suffering from stress. In this case, the word is used to mean the strain or tension itself.

For clarity, in this chapter we will follow the practice of stress researchers. They use the word *stressor* when they refer to situations or things that cause stress. Examples of stressors in a city might be rushing crowds, wailing sirens, traffic jams, and the like. The illness of a parent or a separation from one's family can also be stressors.

Researchers use the word *stress* to refer to the individual's reaction to stressors. Thus, in this chapter we will use the word *stress* when we are talking about the body's internal responses to a stressful situation—to a stressor.

Negative Effects of Stress

You are probably aware of the negative effects of stress. You feel bad; perhaps you get headaches and upset stomachs. Such unpleasant physical reactions can keep you from coping with the stressor. Reggie, for example, got a migraine headache two days before his final exam. As a result, he was not able to study as much as he should have. Likewise, Tina was so anxious about her upcoming relay race in a dual track meet that she couldn't sleep. She showed up tired and nervous and, as she feared, did not do well.

Both Reggie and Tina suffered from the negative effects of stress. Their physical reactions to the stressor prevented them from doing what was necessary to adapt to it.

Positive Effects of Stress

Stress can have positive effects too, though. If you've ever watched any major sporting event, you may begin to understand. Picture Chris Evert Lloyd before a Wimbledon championship or Kareem Abdul-Jabbar before an important basketball game. Both of them are under stress to do their best. They will have to "get up" for the stressor—the match or game. Stress can, then, help people to meet a challenge. Think of a challenge in your life such as getting up the nerve to talk to someone you've been wanting to meet for over a month. That anxious feeling could be just the push you need to make the first move.

Stress is often useful in pushing you to do your best. The trick is to develop the ability to use stress positively rather than to be defeated by it. By understanding what stress is you can minimize its harmful effects.

Causes of Stress

To be alive is to experience stress. The stressors in modern life seem endless. They include everything, both inside and outside your body, that challenges you to adapt either physically or emotionally. Some stressors clearly affect you physically. These include heat, cold, glare, pollution, and sudden or continued noise. Other stressors affect you psychologically. These include events or situations that bring out such emotions as fear, anxiety, depression, anger, joy, and love. A math class can make you anxious. A birthday party can make you happy. And you can become depressed from being lonely.

Stressors, then, are not necessarily bad. Many of the good things in life are stressors.

Figure 4.1 Stress can be a good thing, as when it helps an athlete meet the challenge of a competition.

Thus, an argument with a parent is a stressor, but so is going out on a date. Feeling left out is a stressor, but so is being popular. Not having enough money is a stressor, but so is sudden wealth. A busy schedule that leaves little time for relaxation is a stressor, but so are idleness and boredom. Hard physical work and strenuous exercise are both stressors. Driving in heavy traffic is a stressor, and so is watching a horror movie. All illnesses are stressors.

The important point is that stress comes in many forms. Whether the stressor is basically positive or negative, a challenge must be met.

Life Changes

The most significant stressors, either good or bad, are major changes in the pattern of a person's life. Much research has been done to as-

sess the impact of such life changes. Different researchers have developed scales for measuring the stress that a person goes through. The best-known one was developed in the early 1970s by Dr. Thomas H. Holmes and Dr. Richard H. Rahe.

Holmes and Rahe first made a check list of 43 typical life events (see Table 4.1). They then asked hundreds of people from all age groups and all walks of life to rate these events. The ratings were based on a scale of 1 to 100. Marriage was arbitrarily placed at 50 to give the people in the study a point of reference. The people were asked to assign numbers which indicated the amount of adaptation they felt each event demanded.

In their responses, the people agreed that the event with the highest stress was the death of a spouse. It got a rating of 100 Life Change Units (LCUs). Being fired rated 47, and changing

Figure 4.2 Even a trip abroad can be a stressful event. Vacations rank forty-first on Holmes and Rahe's check list.

TABLE 4.1   **Life Change Scale**

Rank	Life Event	Value
1	Death of spouse	100
2	Divorce	73
3	Marital separation	65
4	Jail term	63
5	Death of close family member	63
6	Personal injury or illness	53
7	Marriage	50
8	Fired at work	47
9	Marital reconciliation	45
10	Retirement	45
11	Change in health of family member	44
12	Pregnancy	40
13	Sex difficulties	39
14	Gain of new family member	39
15	Business readjustment	39
16	Change in financial state	38
17	Death of close friend	37
18	Change to different line of work	36
19	Change in number of arguments with spouse	35
20	Mortgage over $10,000	31
21	Foreclosure of mortgage or loan	30
22	Change in responsibilities at work	29
23	Son or daughter leaving home	29
24	Trouble with in-laws	29
25	Outstanding personal achievement	28
26	Wife begin or stop work	26
27	Begin or end school	26
28	Change in living conditions	25
29	Revision of personal habits	24
30	Trouble with boss	23
31	Change in work hours or conditions	20
32	Change in residence	20
33	Change in schools	20
34	Change in recreation	19
35	Change in church activities	19
36	Change in social activities	18
37	Mortgage or loan less than $10,000	17
38	Change in sleeping habits	16
39	Change in number of family get-togethers	15
40	Change in eating habits	15
41	Vacation	13
42	Christmas	12
43	Minor violations of the law	11

Source: T. H. Holmes and R. H. Rahe, "The Social Readjustment Rating Scale," *Journal of Psychosomatic Research,* 1967.

schools rated 20. Notice that both positive events and negative events are listed. The death of a grandmother can be a serious life change. So can the birth of a new baby brother or sister.

Holmes and Rahe then took their scale to thousands of United States Navy officers and men serving aboard ships. These men were asked to take this scale and calculate their own life change units. The researchers found that the higher a person's LCU scores, the more likely he was to have become ill. Men with LCU scores below 150 remained in good health. Of those with scores between 150 and 300, about half became ill. And, of those with scores over 300, some 70 percent became sick. Since that time, investigators have applied the Holmes-Rahe scale to various groups of people. They, too, have found that high scores are often linked to disease. (Stress and disease are discussed in detail in Section 3.)

The specific number value of an LCU may not be the same for everyone. Nevertheless, it is evident that such life changes do have an impact, for better or worse, on overall well-being.

Environmental Stressors

Until recently, people paid little attention to the stressors in such environments as homes, workplaces, and recreational facilities. They simply assumed that human beings could adapt to almost any environment. Now, however, increasing attention is being paid to such environmental stressors as noise, glare, air pollution, and insufficient light. In some workplaces, pollution is checked regularly. In others, soundproofing is installed to dampen noise.

If you examine a large department store, you will see that much is done to create a pleasant environment. Store owners and managers try hard to minimize stress from noise and glare in order to make their customers feel comfortable. Often the floors are carpeted to reduce noise, and the lights are subdued. Frequently, soft music is played in the background. Large shopping malls usually have plants and trees to give a pleasant feeling to the area. Often fountains are included to soothe the shopper with the sound of rushing water and to mask other noises.

Store owners provide pleasant surroundings because they know that people respond negatively to environmental stress. In a place that is crowded, noisy, and hectic, the only desire people have is to get away as soon as possible. This does not help business. So merchants go to great expense to give their stores as inviting and as relaxed an atmosphere as they can.

CHECK YOUR UNDERSTANDING

1. What is the difference between a stressor and stress?
2. How can a feeling of stress have a positive effect?
3. According to the Holmes-Rahe scale, what are the 10 most stressful life changes?
4. What frequently happens to people who are under a great deal of stress?

SECTION 2   How We Respond to Stress

Some people will say a glass is half empty. Others will say it is half full. Similarly, different people react differently to the same stressor. In one person a stressor arouses great anxiety and distress. In another, the same stressor appears as no more than a simple challenge.

For example, Janet and Peter both have an economics exam on Friday. Janet has a solid B grade average. She has turned in her homework regularly and has kept up with her classwork. Peter, on the other hand, dislikes economics. He has trouble with his homework and barely passes the tests. Naturally, Janet and Peter have different feelings about the exam on Friday. She feels confident about passing and, in fact, hopes to do well enough to raise her average. He has been worried all week and fears that this test will cause him to fail the course.

Circumstances also have a lot to do with the way people react to stressors. Willie Joe, for example, broke his ankle in football practice the day before the season started. He was upset at missing the season. But since he was only a junior, he knew he would have a chance to play the next year. How different his situation was from that of Gavin, a senior, who had to miss the season because he came down with hepatitis. Gavin was hoping for a good year and an athletic scholarship. It was his only chance of affording a college education. Willie Joe viewed his situation as a tough break while Gavin viewed his situation as a tragedy.

This is one criticism of the Holmes-Rahe scale for rating life changes. It is hard to assign a value to a life change without knowing the circumstances of the person undergoing the change. Losing a job may not mean much to someone with a large fortune. But to a person with financial problems, the loss of a job may seem like the end of the world. The impact of any stressor on a person varies with many factors. Some of these factors are the person's age, social status, income, cultural background, stage in life, and previous experiences.

People's responses to stressors are also affected by how much control they have—or think they have—over the situation. The impact of a stressor on someone who feels unable to do anything about it can be overwhelming. On the other hand, if a person feels he or she can do something, the stressor may be viewed as a welcome challenge.

Personality Differences

The amount of stress in a person's life also depends to a large degree on the individual's personality. Researchers have described two basic kinds of personalities, which they call Type A and Type B. Type A people are hard-driving, hurried, and tend to have a short fuse. They are often praised for their dedication and their obvious desire to succeed. Type B people, on the other hand, are outwardly composed and relaxed. They tend to speak more softly and be less aggressive than Type A people.

Type A people are more likely to feel stress than those who are Type B. Recent research indicates that Type A people are also more apt to have heart disease and other stress-related diseases. When Type A people change their impatient behavior by learning to relax, they reduce their risk of developing heart disease.

Signs of Stress

You go to a party where you know almost no one. Your throat suddenly feels dry and you develop a nervous cough. Your best friend, in the same situation, tends to giggle a lot, even when there's nothing to giggle about. Later on,

Figure 4.3 Type A people tend to be hard-driving, impatient, and always in a hurry. They experience more stress than the more relaxed Type B personalities.

when you and your friend feel at home with the group, you find that the cough and the giggle disappear. Or maybe you were not aware of them at all.

There are many signs of stress. The signs vary from person to person and from time to time in the same person. A cough, a giggle, a nagging pain in the back—all these can be symptoms of stress. Some people get physically sick with nausea and diarrhea, while others have nightmares. Still others drink alcohol or use drugs. Some people get angry and loud when they are under stress, while others withdraw and get very quiet.

There is a tendency, however, for any one person to respond to stress with the same symptom. The first step in coping with stress is to become aware of how your own body responds. That will enable you to recognize when you are under stress.

The Stress Mechanism

Whenever the brain perceives a stressor, it activates the body. In the brain is an organ called the *hypothalamus*. The hypothalamus is a control center. It tells the body that a stressor is present by activating two systems. The *autonomic nervous system* releases adrenaline into the bloodstream. The *endocrine system* releases hormones that travel through the bloodstream to the adrenal, thyroid, and other glands. When the two systems are activated, the heart rate increases and blood pressure rises. In addition, blood leaves the stomach area and goes to the arms, legs, and brain. There is no need to digest food if the brain says it is time to run or fight. Scientists call this arousal of the body under stress the *fight-or-flight mechanism*. It prepares the body for action.

This initial response to stress is called the *alarm stage* of the stress mechanism. The next stage is the *resistance stage*. In this stage the body tries to resist the stressor. The length of this stage depends on the nature of the stressor and its intensity and on the body's ability to adapt to it. Once people get used to a stressor, they do not experience as much emotional stress.

Figure 4.4 The physical and emotional symptoms of stress vary from person to person.

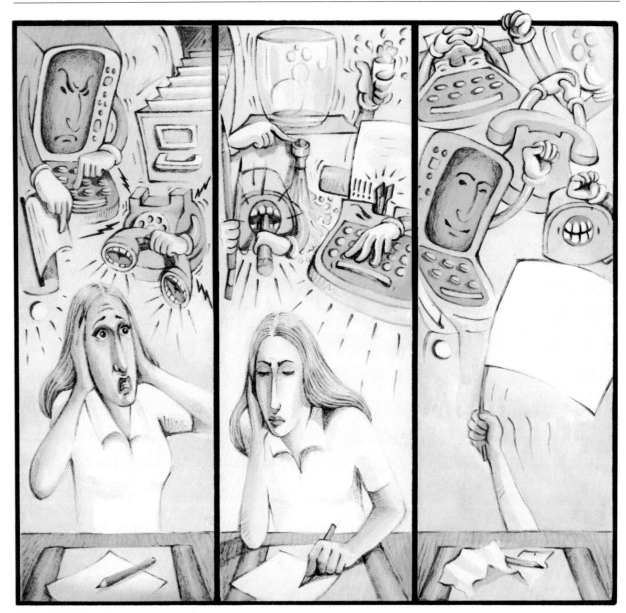

Figure 4.5 The three stages of the stress mechanism—alarm, resistance, and exhaustion.

Eventually, however, if a severe stressor continues too long, the third stage of the stress mechanism occurs. This is called the *exhaustion stage*. Quite simply, the body's ability to resist the stressor is used up. It can no longer resist the stressor. In the most extreme cases, the person who reaches the exhaustion stage dies.

While death as a result of prolonged stress is rare, other physical damage is not. Even when people get used to a stressor, their bodies may continue to react. For example, when Rita graduated from high school and went to work in a large office, she found herself exposed to a great deal of noise. Typewriters clattered all day long. Telephones rang constantly. Machines hummed and rattled endlessly. As a new employee, Rita was extremely conscious of the noise and felt acute stress. Her pulse and blood pressure rose. She had many second thoughts about the job. Moreover, she developed headaches and indigestion frequently.

After a while, however, Rita became used to the office. She adapted to noise—at least emotionally—and became less aware of it. But even though she adapted emotionally to the stressor, her body continued to react. In time, her health was affected. She developed an ulcer, which is a stress-related disease.

Living with stress is not always simple. You may not be doing as well as you think you are.

CHECK YOUR UNDERSTANDING

1. List six factors that affect a person's reaction to a stressor.
2. Describe Type A and Type B personalities.
3. What are some of the physical signs of stress?
4. Describe the three stages of the body's stress mechanism.

SECTION **3** **Stress and Disease**

Excessive stress is linked to a wide range of diseases, both physical and mental. People who are under great stress are more likely to have ulcers, heart attacks, or infections, or to die suddenly. In addition, they are more apt to have accidents or athletic injuries.

Mental illnesses linked to stress include schizophrenia and depression. People under stress are more likely to be hospitalized with these diseases and to attempt suicide.

Numerous studies have established the link between stress and diseases. Researchers have found, for example, that people are far more likely to become ill during the year following a divorce. They have also found that the death rate among widows and widowers is very high during the first year of widowhood. In fact, 10 times as many widows and widowers die during that year as do other people in the same age group.

In addition, the stressful Type A personality pattern is believed by some to be a major cause of heart disease. In one study, more than 3,500 men were observed over a 10-year period. It was found that those with Type A behavior were almost three times more likely than those with Type B behavior to develop heart disease. Not all scientists accept the idea that personality in itself contributes to heart disease, however. They point out that other risk factors, such as cigarette smoking and high blood pressure, are more common among Type A personalities. Thus, the personality itself may not cause heart disease. Rather, it may be the risk factors associated with the personality that do.

Individual Responses to Stress

Why should one person under stress develop an ulcer and another asthma? Why should one student get the flu or a cold during exam week, while others get headaches or feel tired? And why are most students not sick at all?

Part of the reason seems to be that certain people inherit certain weaknesses. One person might have inherited defective genes that make her or him more likely to have an ulcer. Another might have a genetic defect in the nervous and cardiovascular systems. In times of stress, the blood flow to that person's head may change and cause headaches. Yet another person may have a defective respiratory system. Stress may cause that person to have colds.

Anybody who is ill is under some stress, of course, since disease itself is a stressor. And the way people react emotionally to a disease can affect the course of the disease. Some people, for example, feel angry or afraid when they suspect that they have cancer or heart disease. Their anger or fear makes them put off seeing a doctor. By so doing, they reduce their chances of being treated successfully.

Psychosomatic Illness

You may often hear someone say about an illness: "Oh, it's only psychosomatic." *Psychosomatic* refers to bodily (somatic) illnesses brought on by a person's psychological stress. Some people think that a psychosomatic illness is not real, that "It's all in the mind." Nothing could be further from the truth. Psychological factors *can* affect physical health. By the same token, physical factors can affect a person's psychological state. The following two examples illustrate the interplay between psychological and physical stress and a person's mental and physical well-being.

Evelyn loves science and does well in it. So well, in fact, that she won a statewide competition in physics. Just after that, she noticed that her best friends at school became very cool toward her. She began to worry about being liked. She felt lonely, and even doing well in her schoolwork didn't make her feel any better. She developed what seemed to be a perpetual case of the sniffles and a nagging cough that wouldn't go away.

Evelyn was suffering from psychological stress. Just when she thought she would be most happy, she was most miserable. Her psychological stress led directly to a weakened physical state and a nagging, unpleasant ailment.

Jeff, on the other hand, is in good physical health and has no problems with his friends. He is on the first-string basketball team, and the city championship is coming up. At this time, his mother injures her back in a fall. His father, a salesman, is on the road. This means Jeff has an extra work load at home. He has to do all the laundry and shopping and prepare meals for himself and his little sister. He has to do all of this after coming home from a hard practice. Then he has to do his schoolwork after he has finished that.

He feels pressured. Even though he understands that his mother needs him, he still gets irritated. One night he yelled at his sister and walked out of the house slamming the door. He knows things will ease up when his mother recovers, but that doesn't help his mood. He finds himself impatient with everyone, and even his teammates are beginning to resent it.

Jeff is experiencing several outside stressors: the upcoming game, his extra work load, and his regular schoolwork. These have created physical stress for him. He is tired all the time,

Figure 4.6 Anxiety about a difficult exam can cause such psychosomatic problems as headaches, colds, or general fatigue.

and his short temper is a result. Thus, we see that physical stress can lead to a change in psychological state. Jeff is normally a vigorous, secure young man. Now he is a tired, grumpy one.

The point to remember is that there is no split between the mind and the body. The ancient Romans used to say "mens sana in corpore sano." This means "a sound mind in a sound body." They understood that if either one was ill or under stress, the other would be affected also.

CHECK YOUR UNDERSTANDING

1. List some of the diseases people under stress are likely to develop.
2. Why do some researchers reject the theory that personality in itself can lead to heart disease?
3. Why do different people develop different physical ailments under stress?
4. What are psychosomatic illnesses?

SECTION **4** **Coping with Stress**

Fortunately, there are many ways of coping with stress. You can learn to minimize its impact on you. You can learn to cope with it.

Stress Can Be Helpful

One important discovery researchers have made is that a certain amount of fear and worry about a stressful situation can be helpful. Indeed, it may even be necessary for coping successfully with the situation.

As an example, investigators cite a study of people going into surgery. The people reacted to the situation in three different ways. Some were moderately fearful, asking questions about the operation and showing tension from time to time. They showed they were concerned about the dangers of the situation. Others were highly fearful. They tried to postpone the operation and slept poorly. The third group gave little evidence of feeling fear. They were cheerful and optimistic and gave no indication that they felt they would come to harm.

Interestingly, the ones who made the best emotional adjustment after the operation were the first group—the moderate worriers. It seems that their "constructive worrying" had prepared them for what was to come. The highly fearful ones remained in that state, showing great anxiety after the operation.

They were very reluctant to help in the recovery procedures. And the outwardly calm ones were most likely to be resentful and angry. They had not come to terms with the fact that the operation would have unpleasant effects. When they found themselves uncomfortable, they became emotionally upset. This study indicates that a little worry and apprehension before a stressful situation can help people cope with it. It helps them to build inner defenses and prepare for what is to happen.

You may have noticed something similar when one of your classmates was preparing to give a report to the class. You saw how he or she practiced, worrying about what it would be like to stand in front of the whole class. This worrying and anticipation probably helped the student. A student who did not worry might have an unpleasant surprise. She or he may be caught off guard and suddenly freeze up.

Avoiding Unnecessary Stressors

One way of dealing with stress is to avoid unnecessary stressors. You can do this by avoiding potentially stressful situations or circumstances. For example, overwork is a stressor. It makes you feel anxious and tired. If you let school assignments pile up, you will suddenly find you have too much to do. You will feel

How to...
Cope with Competition

As a teenager, you're probably more aware than ever before that life is very competitive. You compete with others in sporting events. You compete for leadership positions in school. You compete with others for the attention of people you admire.

As an adult, you'll find that competition does not stop. Whether in the workplace, on local committees, in politics, or on the tennis court—people are always trying to challenge each other.

Coping with competition is not always easy. It puts a lot of pressure on you. If you set your heart on winning and then lose, you have to deal with that awful feeling of disappointment. With the right attitude, you can learn to enjoy the excitement and stimulation of healthy competition. Here are some guidelines that will help you prepare for, and even look forward to, your next competition.

- Look at competition as an opportunity to fulfill personal goals or as an occasion for excitement and enjoyment.
- Recognize that it's okay to lose. You grow and learn from losing. Being a perfectionist can hurt you.
- Keep competition fun. People who can relax and enjoy competition are better able to concentrate on their performance. You are bound to suceed at some activities and fail at others. If winning is important, the sensible response is to try harder next time.
- Everybody benefits from competition. But not all of us belong in the same types of activities. Explore activities you like.
- Be prepared for any competition you enter. Know the rules. Learn to concentrate and to follow instructions. Consider the experience and level of development of the people you are competing against.
- Acknowledge losing without shame or embarrassment. It's not necessary to rationalize when you lose. You can feel bad about losing and still like and respect the person who beat you. The prospect of winning is only one of the reasons to participate in an activity. Nobody wins all the time.
- When you are on the winning side, be gracious. A winner doesn't need to brag or hurt the feelings of the losing side. A warm glow of satisfaction is the best reward.
- Learn to recognize and accept your strengths and weaknesses. Everyone is unique. You can learn from observing others, but don't use comparison to put yourself down. Choose goals that are challenging but reasonable. Reassess your goals as competitive situations arise.

pressured and too rushed to do your best work. You can avoid this stressor by scheduling your time better.

In your relationships with other people you will often experience stress. You can avoid this by limiting the time you spend with people you know will make you anxious. You can also modify your own behavior, so that you don't bring about a stressful situation.

Another way to avoid unnecessary stress is to prepare for situations that tend to make you anxious. If you have something difficult to say to someone, try going over it with a friend. Kate did this when she decided to spend less time with the boy she had been dating. She didn't want to hurt his feelings and she wanted to make sure he understood the reasons for her decision. So she talked the situation over with her girlfriend. Talking about it helped her to figure out just what her reasons were. It also helped her to decide how she was going to explain her decision to the boy.

Controlling Stress Responses

You can deliberately develop skills to help you cope with stress. Sometimes something as simple as getting away from a situation for a few hours or for a weekend can help. You can also try to alter the way you interpret a stressful situation. For instance, if a teacher is abrupt with you, you might feel anxious. You probably think he or she is angry with you. But think about it; there might be another explanation. Perhaps the teacher has had a bad night's sleep, or is feeling sick, or is troubled by things that have nothing to do with you. Or say a friend passes you in the hall and ignores you. Your immediate reaction might be to feel hurt and assume that the friend is upset with you. But it's also possible that the friend is preoccupied and simply didn't see you. Once you begin to think of alternative explanations for stressful events, you may be able to reduce your own stress.

Open, honest communication can also relieve stress. Many of the interpretations we make are incorrect. If we check out our assumptions with another person, we learn the truth and, in the process, feel relief from stress.

Drugs

Some doctors prescribe drugs such as mild tranquilizers for people under stress. The drugs are useful for easing the severe effects of stress. However, they do have drawbacks. They can cause adverse reactions. They can prevent people from facing up to a stressful situation. And there is always the possibility of developing a dependency on them. Drugs should be seen as a short-term measure only. They are useful for crises, but they are not appropriate as a day-to-day method of coping with normal stress.

Exercise

Physical exercise is most useful in controlling stress. It stimulates the fight-or-flight behavior and probably burns off stress hormones. Many people find that jogging, walking, and other forms of continuous, rhythmic exercise help to release tension. Exercise also helps them to stay in good physical health, of course.

Relaxation

Many techniques of relaxation have been developed for dealing with stress. Some are fairly simple; others are elaborate and require extensive training.

One method is known as *progressive relaxation*. To practice this, first lie down in a comfortable place, and then alternately tense and relax each major muscle group in turn. Start with the hands and arms then move on to the head, eyes, mouth, neck, shoulders, back, chest, abdomen, buttocks, thighs, calves, and feet.

To relax by *meditation*, set aside a block of time (about 15 to 30 minutes) once or twice a day. Take a comfortable sitting position in a quiet place where there are few distractions. Concentrate on a calming mental picture or think of a word or phrase and repeat it over and over to yourself. Breathe slowly and easily. Feel yourself relax. Studies have shown that meditation reduces the psychological feelings of stress. It can also reduce pulse rate, blood pressure, muscle tension, and other physical aspects of stress.

Figure 4.7 A few hours of quiet relaxation are sometimes all that are needed to cope with a stressful situation.

Figure 4.8 For centuries, people have used the martial arts to achieve physical and mental relaxation. This woman is practicing tai chi.

Yoga is a popular system of exercise, body control, and relaxation. Yoga can vary from simple stretching exercises to elaborate forms of body-mind control. People experienced in the advanced forms of yoga can do incredible things such as alter their heart rate and body temperature. This comes with discipline and training.

You may be surprised to find that the martial arts of the Far East are other systems of relaxation. *Karate, kung fu, judo,* and *tai chi* all appear to focus on combat. Yet they require a great deal of control of a person's perceptions and reactions. They involve learning an "inner order" that is itself a form of relaxation.

Hypnosis, although not a form of relaxation, has been used to help people relax. The hypnotist asks the person to go limp, feel the weight of the body pressing downward, and erase all tension from the muscles.

Stress and Life Style

Perhaps the most basic way of controlling stress in your life lies in reordering your life style. Some people seem to be in tune with their surroundings and their relationships with people. They are at ease with their environments. These people probably experience less stress than those who are in constant conflict with their environments. Being in tune does not mean being passive. It does not mean you should ignore problems. Instead, it means recognizing your limits and trying to keep an inner calm. Someone who can remain calm can generally cope with a situation that is difficult. Again, this does not mean ignoring your feelings. If you are angry about something, it is important to deal with the thing that is making you angry.

Danny, for instance, was frequently angry. When he lost his temper at the school outing, no one was surprised. "Happens all the time," his classmates said and thought no more of it. But Danny thought about it that night. He had no idea what made him fly off the handle so often. He would have liked to talk to his parents about it, but he didn't want to bother them. Ever since his baby sister had become seriously ill, they had been very busy with her. Danny sat and watched TV for a while. Then he switched it off, said good-night to his parents, and went to bed—angry.

Danny knew he had a problem. He was afraid it would get worse if he didn't talk about it. So finally he had a long discussion with his parents. The discussion helped all three realize that Danny needed more attention from his parents. They set about finding ways of spending more time together. Danny became more a part of the family, and all three shared in the care of the infant. When Danny goes to bed now, he isn't angry.

Danny was lucky to have someone help him face the real cause of his anger. If you find that you are responding negatively to a whole range of events and stressors, you should think of looking for the underlying stressor that causes that response.

A stress-controlled life style is likely to be balanced between work and play, rest and exercise, and a host of other human activities. It is also likely to be flexible, allowing for changing needs and new experiences. As already mentioned, you will not avoid stress completely. And, as you understand now, you probably wouldn't want to. But the emphasis should be on control.

It has been said that no first-rate performer fails to have stage fright before going on. Performers use this tension to help them prepare for the show and to give an edge to their performance. In the same way, if you can control your stress and make it work for you, you can also give an edge to your performance.

CHECK YOUR UNDERSTANDING

1. How can "constructive worrying" before a stressful situation help people cope with it?
2. Describe two ways to avoid unnecessary stressors.
3. Explain three things you can do to help yourself cope with stress.
4. Briefly describe three techniques of relaxation.
5. What are the characteristics of a stress-controlled life style?

CHAPTER SUMMARY

- An event or situation that causes stress is called a stressor. The body's physical and emotional reaction to a stressor is called stress.
- Stress can have positive as well as negative effects. It can help you to perform better.
- Anything that challenges us to adapt, either physically or emotionally, is a stressor. The most significant stressors are major changes in the pattern of a person's life.
- Different people react differently to the same stressor. Among the factors that influence a person's reaction to a stressor are age, social status, income, stage in life, personality, and previous experience.
- Signs of stress may include coughing, giggling, back pains, nausea, diarrhea, nightmares, anger, and withdrawal.
- When a person encounters a stressor, the brain activates two systems—the autonomic nervous

system and the endocrine system. The effect is to increase heart rate and blood pressure and to cause other changes that prepare the person for fight or flight.

- The three stages of the stress mechanism are the alarm stage, the resistance stage, and the exhaustion stage.
- Excessive stress is linked to a wide range of diseases, physical and mental.
- Among the techniques for coping with stress are "constructive worrying," avoiding unnecessary stressors, preparing for stressful situations, and seeking alternative interpretations of events. Drugs, exercise, and relaxation can also help people deal with stress.
- A stress-controlled life style is likely to be balanced between work and play, rest and exercise, and a host of other activities.

THINK AND DISCUSS

1. What kinds of jobs do you think involve the most stress? The least stress? Why?

2. What do you think would happen to a child brought up in an environment with almost no stressors?

3. What time of day seems to be the most stressful? The least stressful? Why?

4. What special stressors do you think famous people have to deal with?

5. What aspects of school do you think are most stressful? Why?

6. In what kinds of activities do you think feelings of stress would help a person? Hinder a person? Why?

7. Would you want a life totally without stress? Why or why not?

8. In what kinds of situations would you want to have a Type A person around? A Type B person? Why?

9. Why do you think some employers try to control the stressors in their workers' environments?

10. Do you think people living 100 years ago dealt with more or fewer stressors? Explain.

FOLLOW-UP

1. Put together a Holmes-Rahe-type life change scale that lists stressful situations most likely to affect teenagers. Compare your scale with those of your classmates.

2. Find out more about yoga or another relaxation technique. Write a report on your findings.

3. Make a list of the changes you would make to the physical environment in your school in order to reduce stress. Read the list to your class.

4. Read some accounts by noted actors and actresses about their experiences with stage fright and how they dealt with it. Write a report on what you read.

5. Find information on psychologists who use exercises such as running to treat patients with stress-related depression. Write a report on your findings.

6. Interview four people to find out what aspects of their jobs they consider most stressful, and why. Report your findings to your class.

Personal Health Care

To a great extent, your health is in your hands. You can improve your chances for good health by exercising regularly, eating sensibly, and following a basic health care routine.

Part 2 covers some aspects of personal care that make big differences to the way you look and feel. Feeling healthy depends largely on being physically fit. Chapter 5 examines the components of physical fitness and explains the benefits of various types of exercise.

Chapter 6 presents the basics of nutrition. It explains why you need a variety of foods to stay healthy and how poor eating habits can increase your chances of becoming sick. It also discusses the problems associated with being overweight and explores ways of losing weight and keeping weight under control.

Certain parts of the body need special attention. Chapter 7 focuses on the care of the teeth, eyes, skin, hair, and feet. The emphasis is on preventive care. The habits you develop now will affect the way you look and feel for years to come.

CHAPTER 5

Physical Fitness

After reading this chapter, you should be able to answer these questions:

1. Why do you need exercise?
2. What is physical fitness?
3. How can you decide what level of fitness is right for you?
4. What is aerobic exercise? What makes it different from other kinds of exercise?

If you've ever done any baby-sitting, you may have an idea of how demanding young children can be. Linda Schreiber knows, for she is the mother of quadruplets. One dismal, rainy day, the quads had just about worn her out. She was so tired and edgy that she didn't know whether to scream or cry. Instead, her husband suggested she go outside and run. She did, rain and all.

Since that afternoon, Linda Schreiber has run nearly every day. She runs for the pleasure it gives her. It has made her thinner, stronger, and calmer. Linda Schreiber has the ability and determination of a special kind of athlete. She has become a marathon runner, and something of a celebrity as the author of *Marathon Mom*.

Although running marathon races takes both dedication and ability, Linda Schreiber is not all that unusual. Millions of Americans jog for exercise. Many others try different forms of exercise to keep fit. Sales of recreational equipment from bicycles and running shoes to canoes and hiking boots are booming. More than 50,000 companies in the United States sponsor fitness programs for their employees. Americans, in other words, have turned to exercise in a big way. They are getting into shape not just because they want to look better but also because it makes them feel less tense and more energetic.

Back in 1961, fewer than one in four Americans exercised regularly. Some 25 years later, the figure had more than doubled. In a recent

Gallup poll, 59 percent of the respondents said they exercised regularly. Polltaker George Gallup has said that the fitness boom is the biggest change in behavior he has ever witnessed.

The shift to regular exercise has important health benefits. In fact, it may be the most important shift toward good health in American life in this century.

SECTION **1** # Why We Need Exercise

Until fairly recently in human history, people had to be fit in order to survive. They needed physical skills to find and grow food, build homes, and escape from danger. But they did not need to make a conscious effort to exercise. The kind of work they did kept them fit. They bent to plant seeds. They stretched to load hay. They walked behind plows. They hauled water in heavy buckets. Physical exercise was a routine part of everyday life. For some people, such as farmers and construction workers, it still is. But many Americans no longer do physical work.

Think of the jobs done by the adults you know. Does the work involve many different kinds of movement and exercise? Or is their work done mostly while sitting at a desk or standing in one place on an assembly line? Many modern jobs just don't provide exercise. Yet our bodies, like those of our ancestors, are designed for movement. They need exercise.

True, our survival no longer depends on physical fitness. Even severely handicapped people can lead productive lives. Nevertheless, some level of physical activity is essential for everyone. And we can achieve fitness only if we work actively toward it. The tragedy is that too many people simply accept physical deterioration—and early aging. There are better alternatives.

Inactivity and Health Problems

For years health researchers had noticed that inactive people had more health problems than active people. Some of their studies compared the cardiovascular systems of people who did active work (such as carpentry or delivering mail) with those of people who sat in one place

Figure 5.1 Like these factory workers, many people get little exercise on the job.

most of the day. In every study the active people suffered less heart disease. And in every age group their death rates were lower than the death rates of inactive people.

Physical fitness is one of the health areas selected for special attention by the federal government. In its publication *Promoting Health/Preventing Disease*, it emphasizes the physical and emotional benefits to be gained from regular exercise, but it also says that most Americans do not get enough physical activity. In fact, the government suggests that the number of Americans who exercise regularly is much smaller than that reported by the opinion polls.

Promoting Health/Preventing Disease lists some of the health problems connected with inadequate physical activity:

- obesity
- heart disease
- high blood pressure

- injuries to muscles, ligaments, tendons
- injuries and pain in bones and joints
- respiratory diseases
- stress
- depression and anxiety

The connection between this gloomy list and lack of exercise is simple. The body is like a finely tuned, complicated machine. If it is cared for, the different parts keep working well. If it is neglected, those parts get creaky and rusty. They break or injure more easily.

Have you ever broken an arm or a leg? If so, you know what happened when the cast came off. Your muscles had begun to *atrophy*. That is, the muscles had begun to waste away from lack of use. Bones and joints, too, had gotten weaker because of disuse. That's what happens to people who do not exercise. Parts of their bodies begin to grow weak. Because their muscles and bones are weak, such individuals are more prone to injury than fit people. Their bodies also tend to age faster.

Many people who don't exercise are also overweight. That's because the human body has a system for storing fat. In times when food was scarce, the fat storage mechanism helped people to survive. But in these days of overeating and underexercising, the same mechanism threatens our health and survival.

Released Tension

Exercise may provide people with the means of expressing or releasing tension when they are under stress. Primitive human beings survived, in part, through their "fight or flight" reactions. When danger threatened, the body reacted by releasing *adrenaline* into the bloodstream. This hormone sharpened and quickened physical reactions. It helped people fight the danger or flee from it.

In modern life, we all face stressful situations from time to time, even though we do not have to confront the dangers that threatened our ancestors. And our bodies react in the same way. You have probably felt the reaction of adrenaline yourself. When you are startled or frightened or excited, you feel a quick surge

through your body. Your heart beats faster. This response gives you extra energy in emergencies.

Often, though, your body releases adrenaline when there really isn't any action you can take. It happens when you panic because you are facing a test you aren't prepared for. It happens when you are late for an appointment and then get caught in a traffic jam. As the adrenaline surges through your body, you tense up, ready for action. The result is *stress*. Your muscles are poised for action, but you can't act. You feel jumpy, irritable, tense.

People under stress are often required to sit still and appear relaxed and calm. But unresolved stress is hard on the body. It makes your heart beat faster and causes high blood pressure. Stress is also thought to contribute to a variety of *degenerative*, or wearing out and aging, processes. The digestive and cardiovascular systems are particularly affected.

Exercise, then, enables people to release tension and achieve relaxation. Obviously you can't get up and run laps around the classroom every time you feel tense. But you can exercise regularly in ways that will help reduce the stress on your body.

Figure 5.2 For people under stress, regular exercise is an effective way to release tension.

Figure 5.3 Physical activity is especially important for young people, whose growing bodies need exercise in order to develop properly.

Fitness for Young People

Exercise is necessary for fitness at any age, but it is especially important for young people. In the development years from birth to age 20, the body is constantly changing and growing. It needs exercise to ensure that the muscles, bones, heart, lungs, and other organs develop properly.

Children who don't get any exercise may develop permanent physical handicaps. The handicap may not show up until middle age. Middle-aged men and women who did not exercise when they were children may suffer from a variety of disorders, such as those mentioned earlier. Medical treatment can sometimes bring relief when those disorders strike. But it is sad to realize that many people suffer years of pain and discomfort simply because they did not get adequate exercise during their childhood.

CHECK YOUR UNDERSTANDING

1. Why do people today need to make a conscious effort to exercise?
2. List eight health problems associated with inadequate physical activity.
   when they are not used?
4. Explain how exercise can reduce stress.
5. Why is exercise particularly important for young people?

SECTION **2**   # The Elements of Fitness

Lizzie is a cheerleader who walks with the grace of a dancer. She does bending and stretching exercises to look good. Yet when Lizzie climbs three flights of stairs to get to science class, she huffs and puffs. José has built a fine-looking set of muscles by doing pull-ups and working with weights. Yet he's clumsy at basketball because his body is stiff and rigid. He can't pivot and twist easily. Claire can bicycle 25 kilometers (15 miles) without tiring. Yet she hurt her back moving some stage props.

Each of these young people would seem at first glance to be physically fit. Each of them exercises regularly. Yet something is missing in their fitness programs.

The three main elements of physical fitness are strength, suppleness, and stamina. All three elements must be present for anyone to be completely fit.

Strength

Strength is the basic muscular force needed for movement. Everyone needs strength for ordinary activities. You use strength to push a lawn mower, to carry grocery bags, to lift things.

Figure 5.4 Weight training is the quickest and most direct way to improve strength.

The quickest and most direct means of improving strength is through weight training, a form of *isotonic* exercise. Isotonic exercises develop strength by repeated movements with the use of weights. *Calisthenics,* such as push-ups, pull-ups, and sit-ups, are also isotonic exercises that involve weight training. The weight is your own body.

Isometric exercises, on the other hand, involve little movement. In isometric exercises you push or pull against an unmoving object. You use muscle tension to build strength. Pushing against a tension bar is an isometric exercise. If you clasp your hands in front of you and pull, you are doing an isometric exercise. Such exercises add strength to individual muscles but do not tune up the entire body.

Most fitness experts strongly recommend isotonic exercises because they do more for your whole body than isometric exercises. Athletes generally do isotonic exercises for general conditioning.

Suppleness

If you've seen Mikhail Baryshnikov dance on television or in a movie, you've seen a superbly trained body that combines strength with suppleness. He can lift a ballerina into the air. Yet his body can bend, twist, and stretch with ease. Or picture Dr. J on the basketball court. He twists and bobs and pivots with speed and grace.

Figure 5.5 By stretching and bending before a race, this runner is keeping her muscles supple and reducing her risk of injury.

Figure 5.6 The three main components of fitness: (*top left*) strength, for lifting and carrying; (*bottom left*) suppleness, for reaching and bending; (*right*) stamina, for building long-term reserves of energy.

Suppleness, or flexibility, is the quality of muscles, bones, tendons, and ligaments that permits your joints a full range of movement. You may be supple in some joints but not in others. You may even find that the joints on one side of your body are suppler than the same joints on the other side. Many people, for instance, have a greater range of movement in one shoulder than the other.

You can improve suppleness by doing bending and stretching exercises. By keeping supple, you reduce the risk of injury. When a person who is out of shape does an unusual activity—for example, playing in a Sunday volleyball game or moving furniture—he or she may strain or pull a muscle.

As people get older, they tend to lose flexibility. Their joints get stiff. Some loss of flexibility is inevitable with aging, but regular exercise will slow this aging process.

Stamina

Stamina, or endurance, is the quality that enables you to use energy to keep up movements over a long period of time.

You build stamina by doing regular, sustained exercises of the whole body. In stamina workouts, you use the large muscles and put the major joints through a wide range of motion. Excellent whole-body exercises include running, bicycling, swimming, and cross-country skiing. You can also build stamina with weight training if you use light weights and repeat the exercise many times.

Stamina builds reserves of strength. Once you begin to work out regularly to build stamina, instead of feeling tired from a workout, you will feel energetic. By spending energy, you actually build up energy reserves.

Trained and Untrained

People who lead sedentary lives offer a marked contrast to those who exercise frequently and intensely enough to build up strength, suppleness, and stamina. Compared with the untrained person, the trained individual is leaner and stronger, moves faster, and recovers more quickly after exercise. Fitness training also strengthens the cardiovascular system, so trained people are less likely than untrained people to get heart and blood vessel diseases.

There is also evidence that fitness training postpones the aging process. People who are unfit may have middle-aged bodies by the time they are 21. On the other hand, there are vigorous "youngsters" in their sixties and beyond.

Your own old age is a long way off, of course. But now is the time to start building up the strength, suppleness, and stamina that will make it more enjoyable for you.

CHECK YOUR UNDERSTANDING

1. What are the three elements of physical fitness?
2. Describe the differences between isotonic and isometric exercises. Which type do experts recommend? Why?
3. What is suppleness? What kinds of exercises improve suppleness?
4. Describe the characteristics of a stamina workout.
5. List some of the benefits of fitness training.

SECTION **3**　# How Fit Is Fit Enough?

For Olympic athletes, being fit means grueling hours of training. If your dream is an Olympic medal, your physical fitness goal will be very different from that of a person who just wants to feel fit without devoting too much time to it.

Not everyone has the ability to be a great athlete. Yet virtually anyone can make her or his body fitter by exercising regularly. Each person has to decide how fit she or he wants to be. When making your own decision, take into account your personal goals, abilities, and life style. How much time are you willing to devote to exercise? What do you want to achieve from your fitness program? Should fitness take precedence over other aspects of your life?

Only you can decide how fit is fit enough for you. However, health scientists and doctors have defined certain standards that will help you make this decision.

Reducing the Risk of Injury

People should, for example, be *fit enough to enjoy active living with minimal risk of injury.* They should be strong and supple enough to be able to work and play without risk of muscle or joint injury. They should not hurt muscles or joints doing ordinary things such as pushing a lawn mower, lifting a baby, swimming a few laps, or playing a game of tennis.

You might wonder why it isn't enough to do the things you like and develop the muscles for just those activities. Why bother with other

	ACTIVITY	COMMENT
	Bowling	Not taxing enough to promote endurance.
	Paddleball, Squash, Handball, Racquetball	Not sufficiently continuous unless played competitively. (Competitive environment in a hot room is dangerous to anyone not in excellent physical condition.)
	Table Tennis, Badminton, Volleyball, Doubles Tennis	Can have endurance benefits only if played vigorously and continuously.
	Singles Tennis	Can provide benefit if played by skilled player who keeps moving for 30 minutes or more.
	Calisthenics and Ballet Exercises	Many of these will promote endurance if continuous, rhythmic, and repetitive.
	Skating	Dynamic and aerobic if done continuously.
	Walking	Good, dynamic, aerobic exercise at 5.5 kilometers (3.3 miles) per hour or more.
	Cycling	Good, dynamic, aerobic exercise at 12.5 kilometers (7.5 miles) per hour or more.
	Running	Dynamic, aerobic, endurance-building exercise at 8 kilometers (5 miles) per hour or more.
	Swimming	Excellent isotonic, aerobic exercise when done steadily and continuously.
	Aerobic Dancing	Excellent conditioning exercise, easily adaptable to varying capacity levels.
	Cross-Country Skiing	Superior activity for fitness training. Improves cardiovascular fitness, body tone, muscle strength, and flexibility.

Figure 5.7 Relative merits of various exercises for stamina training.

Talking Point
The Aerobics Boom

Mention aerobics, and many people think immediately of dance and calisthenic exercises. You have probably seen aerobic exercise records in record stores or read advertisements for aerobic exercise classes in your local newspaper. Nationwide, there are about 10,000 exercise centers, most of which offer aerobics sessions. Film stars and television personalities have even made videocassettes in which they teach aerobic exercises. Today, aerobics is probably one of the most popular ways of working out. But aerobics means more than just dance and calisthenic exercises.

The word *aerobics* was coined in 1967 by Kenneth H. Cooper, a physician who helped develop fitness exercises for Air Force pilots and NASA astronauts. In a book titled *Aerobics*, he described exercises that can strengthen the heart, lungs, and circulatory system. *Aerobics* literally means "with oxygen." When you do aerobic exercises, your heartbeat and pulse rate increase to bring more oxygen into your bloodstream. This extra oxygen allows your body to work harder.

You have probably practiced some aerobic exercises without even knowing it. Jogging, swimming, and cycling are all aerobic because they increase the flow of oxygen in the bloodstream. Brisk walking, ice-skating, and cross-country skiing are also aerobic.

Physicians and medical researchers have found that these exercises strengthen the heart and reduce the possibility of cardiovascular disease. As the heart becomes better conditioned, everyday physical tasks become easier to do. This is because a strong heart does not have to work as hard as a less-healthy heart does to pump the same amount of blood. Regular aerobic exercise also helps reduce blood pressure, lower the amount of cholesterol in the bloodstream, and increase lung capacity and efficiency. Not surprisingly, this type of exercise can also help you control your weight.

In addition to the physical benefits, aerobic exercise has emotional benefits. People who exercise aerobically often say that they feel less anxious than they did before they began exercising. This is probably because vigorous exercise produces natural substances in the bloodstream, called *endorphins*. Scientists believe that endorphins relieve depression and stress. Studies have also shown that smokers who do aerobic exercises are highly motivated to quit smoking.

The aerobics boom seems to have attracted people who had not previously been motivated to get much exercise. You don't have to join a class or pay money to get aerobic exercise. For example, if you need a few groceries, you can walk to the local supermarket instead of driving, or you can ride a bicycle to school or work instead of taking the bus. You'll soon notice a difference in how you feel.

---

exercises? Why work on strength if you just want to lose weight and look good?

The reason is that your body adapts to the demands made upon it. That's all it does. If you don't push it further, it goes no further. Yet you need reserves of strength, flexibility, and stamina for the times you demand more of your body. If you are unfit and then do something you are not used to doing, such as carrying suitcases or going canoeing, your muscles may ache. You may feel stiff and sore. You may even injure muscles or joints with unexpected activity.

When young people strain muscles or pull tendons, their bodies usually snap back quickly. But older people begin to lose this ability. If a person does nothing more strenuous than rake the leaves or carry out the garbage, the body adapts to these limits. Even slight exertion beyond the normal could produce injury or fatigue. Therefore, extra training beyond the routine daily demands is needed. The body needs reserves for the times when unusual demands are made upon it.

Calisthenic exercises are useful for developing strength and suppleness. Bending and stretching exercises and other controlled no-strain movements are excellent for keeping bones, joints, and muscles in shape. Once you have reached minimal levels of fitness, you might add exercises such as push-ups and pull-ups to your program.

Protection Against Heart Attack

Another standard of fitness that is often cited is *fit enough to protect against heart attack.* There is, of course, no absolute protection against heart attack. But stamina training (to be described in detail later) does appear to reduce the risks.

Here's what happens. Suppose you decide to train for stamina by swimming. As you swim, your heart begins to beat faster and harder. It pumps more blood through your body with each beat. After you have trained for a while, your heart will pump fewer times. Yet each pump will send more blood to your muscles. You won't feel as tired, even after swimming for an hour, because you have improved your stamina. At the same time you will have strengthened your heart and artery system.

The normal pulse rate of a resting adult is about 70 beats per minute. It can be 80 to 90 beats in untrained individuals. By comparison, the resting pulse rate of a person who has built up stamina can be 55 to 60 beats a minute, or even less.

When you are fit, your heart doesn't have to pump as often because each pump delivers more blood. Therefore, a fit person's heart beats several thousand times less every day than an unfit person's heart. This appears to reduce the wear and tear on the heart valves and blood vessels.

There are other benefits. Your whole breathing system works better if you train. Your lungs take in more oxygen, and your blood does a better job of delivering oxygen to the body. Stamina training also helps to keep weight down by burning calories. And it helps to reduce tension and stress.

As mentioned earlier, you have to decide for yourself how fit you want to be. You have learned the importance of strength, suppleness, and stamina. You are aware both of the benefits to be gained from training and of the dangers of neglecting your body. It's now up to you to act upon that knowledge.

CHECK YOUR UNDERSTANDING

1. List two standards of physical fitness.
2. Why does your body need reserves of strength, flexibility, and stamina?
3. What kinds of movements can keep your bones, joints, and muscles in shape?
4. Describe the changes your heart undergoes in stamina training. How does this reduce wear and tear on your heart?

SECTION **4** # Planning for Fitness

Not long ago two boys were in a ski shop. They waited while the owner chatted with a tall, slim, older man who looked about 55 and leaned on a cane. When the older man left, the owner asked the boys if they had noticed him.

The gentleman, the owner said, was 70 years old. Yet he hoped to get his damaged leg back into shape before ski season was over. The reason for the cane? Someone had crashed into him while he was riding his 10-speed bike.

How to...
Develop a Daily Fitness Program

Today is the best day to start your own daily exercise program. After all, the sooner you start, the sooner you will discover the rewards of increased suppleness, strength, and stamina. You don't need special equipment or clothing. Exercise is free. All you have to invest is some time and effort. So look below for an easy-to-follow program of daily exercise, one that will help you become fit at a comfortable pace. Start it today, and find yourself starting to look better and feel better—for free.

To increase your suppleness:

Do 10 to 15 minutes of stretching exercises. Do not bounce! The idea is to hold the stretched position for several seconds. Aim at working up to the ability to hold each stretch for 30 to 60 seconds.

To increase your strength:

1. Do several sit-ups, keeping your knees bent to protect your back. Breathe normally, and do not strain to do more than you are capable of.

2. Now do several push-ups in any way that feels comfortable. You can keep your lower body on the floor if that works best for you. Again, breathe normally and do not strain yourself.

To increase your stamina:

1. Start the aerobic part of your exercise program with a daily walk. Gradually work up to a point where you can walk briskly for one hour without stopping. Do not allow yourself to get out of breath or to be unable to talk during this activity.
2. Once you are able to walk briskly for one hour, you can substitute a different aerobic activity for that time. Running, bicycling, swimming, and jumping rope all fit into that category.
3. Always start any aerobic activity by warming up for 5 to 10 minutes at a slower rate. At the end of the activity, cool down in the same manner. DO NOT end your exercising with a burst of increased activity.

Not everyone can achieve the kind of fitness that will keep him or her skiing or cycling at 70. Yet anyone at any age can train his or her body into better physical condition. Fitness is a lifetime enterprise, with lifetime rewards. And more Americans are taking up the fitness idea every year.

If you want to be fit, you will have to work at it regularly. A once-a-week basketball or touch football game won't keep your body in peak form. In fact, feverish exercise once in a while can do even more harm than good.

What Exercise Is Best?

There are hundreds of ways to exercise. How do you find the ones that will work best for you? Remember that you need to build and maintain strength, suppleness, and stamina. No one form of exercise will achieve this. The trick is to find a combination that gives you a balanced fitness program.

For instance, you can make the central part of your fitness program swimming, which is good for building strength and stamina. To it you would add a few exercises to promote flexibility. If you like mountain climbing, you may need to add some exercises to build stamina for climbs. You might also need to add some limbering-up exercises to keep your body supple. If you like tennis, you might work to build flexibility—to become a better player and avoid injuries. You might also run or swim to build endurance for playing that second or third set.

A good exercise program, then, should combine calisthenic movement (stretching, bending, twisting) with stamina training. As you train for stamina, you will also build strength. Calisthenics should fully stretch the muscles and joints as gently as possible. Remember that short, quick bursts aren't as helpful as slow, gentle moves. Some people exercise to music because it helps avoid jerky movements.

Athletes routinely warm up for sports with calisthenics. You've seen football players touching their toes and doing body twists before games. These exercises limber up the body for peak performance. They also keep joints and muscles flexible, thereby helping to prevent injury.

As you begin to get older, such limbering-up exercises will become more important. With age, the body loses some of its suppleness. Muscles and joints become less resilient, less able to snap back. Exercising won't stop the aging process, but it will slow down the effects of aging on your body. It will also leave your body feeling more vigorous and energetic.

Stamina Training

Many experts consider stamina training the most important form of exercise for adults. You have read how stamina training helps the heart and breathing systems and how it relieves stress and tension. Since exercise burns calories, stamina training has another benefit too. Most people who regularly swim, jog, bicycle, or do other stamina-building exercises lose extra pounds and stay in good shape.

The principle behind stamina training is *aerobics*. You read about the growing popularity of aerobic exercises on page 79. Aerobic exercises increase stamina by strengthening the

Figure 5.8 Swimming is an aerobic exercise that improves both strength and stamina.

heart, lungs, and circulation. These systems play a vital role in bringing oxygen to the rest of the body and carrying waste gases out of individual cells. Some types of aerobic exercises are vigorous walking, running, jogging, jumping rope, swimming, bicycling, and certain kinds of dancing.

Exercise in which the demand for oxygen exceeds the supply is termed *anaerobic*. Anaerobic means "without oxygen." An example of an anaerobic exercise is sprinting 400 meters (440 yards) at full speed. The sprinter goes so fast that her or his body can get only part of the oxygen it needs during the sprint.

Oxygen is necessary for body cells to extract energy from food. When the body can't deliver enough oxygen for the demands being made on it, some additional energy is available anaerobically—that is, without oxygen. In this process, sugar, or glucose, in the body breaks down to provide the needed energy. However, the process causes the body to feel extreme fatigue.

Studies have shown that controlled aerobic exercise done long enough and hard enough gives better results than anaerobic spurts. The "with oxygen" exercises are more comfortable and less hazardous. They are also less likely to cause fatigue.

How Long and How Often?

To benefit from aerobic, or stamina, exercises, you need to do them for at least eight minutes. Less exercise than that produces little or no improvement. In the beginning, you may not be able to work out that long, but you can build up to it.

Once you reach an 8-minute workout, your body will begin to develop stamina, and you will be able to work out for longer periods. Between 15 and 30 minutes of aerobic exercise are generally thought to be sufficient for normal individuals interested in general fitness. Progress will be greater if you train for up to an hour. Training for more than an hour gives less additional benefit, although athletes who want to reach peak fitness levels may work out for several hours a day.

How frequently should you do your aerobic workouts? Research has shown that the benefits of aerobic workouts last about two days. Therefore, experts suggest that you work out at least every other day. Every day is best, but three times a week is the minimum for solid improvement. One researcher found that people in a three-day-a-week exercise program made twice the progress in six months that people in a two-day-a-week program made.

Recreational Sports

Recreational sports such as basketball, baseball, hockey, soccer, or volleyball may seem to be the best way to get exercise. They are fun, and you can do them with friends. Yet as a way to maintain fitness, such sports are not as useful as other things you could do. Competitive sports involve quick spurts of activity rather than continuous, rhythmic movement. They are also likely to lead to overexertion.

Of course, most people participate in sports because they enjoy them. And competitive sports do provide an opportunity for some exercise. But as part of a physical fitness program, they need to be combined with calisthenics and stamina training.

Overdoing It

It's easy to get so enthusiastic about getting fit that you do too much too soon. Your body needs to build its strength, suppleness, and stamina over a period of time. If you do too much, you may injure yourself or become so tired that you can't do any more exercise for several days.

If you begin exercise training gradually and make steady, slow progress, you will reduce the chance of overexertion. But mistakes are possible, and you should watch for these warning signs of overexertion:

- pulse rate higher than 120 beats per minute two minutes after you have stopped exercising
- feeling quite tired more than 10 minutes after a workout (You should feel relaxed and pleasantly tired, not exhausted.)

Figure 5.9 A pulse count is the best practical way to determine your heart rate. As soon as possible after a period of exercise, take your pulse. Count the number of pulse beats that occur in a 10-second period, and multiply this number by six to get the per-minute rate.

- continuing fatigue and difficulty in sleeping
- fatigue a day after the workout
- chest pains (Anytime this happens, you should consult a doctor.)

If you notice any of these signs, you should reduce your level of activity and change your exercise program.

Sports medicine specialists urge people to exercise—*in moderation.* In addition to the problems of overexertion, certain injuries can occur from too much exercise. People who jog to excess, for example, may suffer knee injuries or inflammations of the bones and joints.

In addition, a number of medical conditions can be aggravated by physical exertion. If you have any doubts about your ability to exercise, have your doctor approve your fitness program before you start. The doctor will be familiar with your physical condition and past medical history and will know whether strenuous exercise could harm you. Medical clearance is particularly important for people who have been inactive or who are over 35.

Fitness Fads

You've seen them—the ads that promise that you will look wonderful and feel fit for just a few minutes' effort a day. Don't believe them. Fitness fads that promise shortcuts to a well-tuned body rarely work, and some may actually be harmful.

There are the food-for-fitness fads, for instance—special diets that promise miracles. Yet they rarely result in permanent weight loss or body improvement. In fact, food fads may harm your body by depriving it of needed nutrients.

Programs that promise to reduce fat from certain parts of your body, such as your waist or thighs, are useless too. You'll never be able to lose fat in just one place. Your fat is distributed according to your body type. Exercise will help tone muscles in certain areas, but not necessarily in the place you would choose.

Some fitness gadgets and devices can be useful, but they are certainly not essential. Weights and springs, for example, are fine for building strength, but they have little use in developing stamina. Exercise bicycles and treadmills provide stamina training. Perhaps they may motivate you to exercise. But you don't need them. You can get just as much useful exercise by running in place.

A Plan for You

Only you can choose a fitness program that will work for you. There is virtually an infinite variety of exercise options that you can adjust to your needs and goals. Your program need not be complex or elaborate, but it should always include some form of controlled, continuous, rhythmic exercise that will raise your heart rate.

As a typical example, suppose a young woman of 18 begins to run regularly. To maintain suppleness and avoid stiffness, she spends at least five minutes before and after running doing stretching and bending exercises.

During four workouts in her first week, she experiments by varying the rate at which she runs. One run is very slow, one slow, one moderate, and one fast. She takes her pulse rate after each one. She jots down the rate at which she ran and the pulse rate after each run.

She finds that her most comfortable speed is about 3 kilometers (1.8 miles) in about 18 minutes. In the first 3 minutes of such a run, her pulse rate rises to 23 to 24 beats for 10 seconds.

It stays at about that level for the rest of the run. This would be a good pulse rate for a beginner.

Over a three-month period she very slowly increases the rate at which she runs, as well as the distance. By the end of four months she can run 6 kilometers (3.7 miles) in 30 minutes. By that time she has improved her level of fitness. She feels more energetic, stronger, and has lost weight.

Once she has reached a good level of fitness, she no longer needs to run as often. Three days a week for 30 minutes will maintain the fitness level she has achieved. If she wants to train to a higher level, she can run either farther or faster, or both.

To supplement the running, she should also do about 15 minutes a day of stretching and bending exercises. These, too, should be continued after she reaches the desired fitness level.

You can translate this plan into some other activity. Instead of running, the main activity could be rowing, swimming, or cycling. The main activity should have controlled, continuous movement. Many people like to vary the main activity from day to day or season to season. Some combine swimming and bicycling, for example, or cross-country skiing and running.

Lifelong Benefits

We have already seen how regular exercise seems to slow down some of the effects of aging. We have seen that it reduces wear and tear on the heart from stress and tension.

Exercise is no cure-all, of course. Even superbly trained athletes slow down with age. Baseball players are typically considered "old" at 35. Football players are "old" at 30, and competitive swimmers at 25.

From about 25 on, most people should try to do less "occasional" exercise that has short, violent bursts of movement. Instead, they should concentrate on rhythmic and continuous exercises.

It does take time and determination. But the benefits of regular exercise will pay off more

Figure 5.10 Regular exercise seems to slow down some of the effects of aging. Many older people continue to enjoy a variety of physical activities.

and more every year that you keep your body in good physical shape. You will be able to pack more work and more play into your days than someone who is out of shape and unfit. With a lifelong commitment to exercise, you will look better, feel better, and perhaps even live longer.

CHECK YOUR UNDERSTANDING

1. What are the characteristics of a balanced fitness program?
2. Compare aerobic with anaerobic exercises.
3. How many minutes of stamina exercise are necessary for improvement? How frequently should such workouts occur?
4. What are two of the drawbacks of competitive sports?
5. List the warning signs of overexertion.
6. What characteristics should the main activity in an exercise program have?

CHAPTER SUMMARY

- The human body is designed for movement and needs exercise.
- Inactive people are more likely than active people to be overweight, to have high blood pressure, and to have other health problems.
- Exercise enables people to release tension and achieve relaxation.
- The three main elements of fitness are strength, suppleness, and stamina. All three elements must be present for someone to be completely fit.
- One should be strong and supple enough to be able to work and play without risk of muscle or joint injury.
- One should be fit enough to protect against heart attack. Stamina training appears to reduce the risks.
- A good exercise program should combine calis-

thenic movement (stretching, bending, twisting) with stamina training.
- Aerobic exercise is exercise in which the body's oxygen needs are met. In anaerobic exercise the demand for oxygen exceeds the supply. Controlled aerobic exercise gives better results than anaerobic spurts.
- Most competitive sports are not as useful for maintaining fitness as calisthenics and stamina training.
- To avoid overexertion and injury, one should begin exercise training gradually and make slow, steady progress.
- A fitness program can bring lifelong benefits. People who exercise regularly look better, feel better, and may even live longer.

DO YOU REMEMBER?

Give brief definitions of these terms:

atrophy	strength	calisthenics	aerobic exercise
adrenaline	isotonic exercise	suppleness	anaerobic exercise
degenerative	isometric exercise	stamina	

THINK AND DISCUSS

1. What causes can you think of for the physical fitness boom in this country?
2. How do current fashion trends reflect the American interest in fitness? In what ways might these trends affect people who do not exercise?
3. Some companies provide their employees with exercise facilities. Why do you think they do this?
4. Athletes in sports such as swimming and gymnastics usually retire by the age of 20, while athletes such as marathon runners and weight lifters may not peak until they are in their thirties. What reasons can you give for this difference?
5. Many people who start a physical fitness program soon give up, saying that it's "boring," "lonely," or "too hard." What measures do you recommend to help such people stick to a program?
6. What are some of the positive and negative ways in which television has affected sports and our attitudes toward sports?
7. One simple way for people to get more exercise is to walk up and down stairs instead of taking elevators. What other changes in daily habits can you think of to help people increase the amount of exercise they get?

FOLLOW-UP

1. Write a description of your own exercise program. Now that you've read this chapter, what changes would you make in this program?
2. Visit a local sporting goods store and catalog the number of different sports for which they carry equipment. Interview the manager about the ways in which customers and their needs have changed over the years.
3. Make a map of your community that locates all the different public and private sports facilities available to residents. Post the map in your classroom.
4. Choose an Olympic or professional athlete you admire and find out what his or her training schedule is like. Write a report on your findings.
5. Look through some recent newspapers and magazines for advertisements of physical fitness devices. Cut out the ads and paste them on a large piece of poster board. Circle the claims you consider suspicious and discuss them with your class.

CHAPTER 6

Nutrition and Weight Control

After reading this chapter, you should be able to answer these questions:

1. Why do you need a variety of foods?
2. What kinds of foods provide you with energy?
3. How can you be sure of getting a balanced diet?
4. Why do some people eat too much? Why do other people eat too little?
5. How can you maintain the weight that is right for you?

When the bell sounded, Nicole and Jessie grabbed their lunches and found some seats in the cafeteria. As they unpacked their lunches, Nicole was startled by the amount of food Jessie pulled out of her bag. Besides a thick tuna fish sandwich, Jessie had a container of salad, an orange, a banana, and a yogurt.

Nicole looked down at her own lunch. It was half the size of Jessie's—just a bologna sandwich, a bag of potato chips, and a can of vanilla pudding. Yet Jessie was slim, and Nicole was—well, "pleasingly plump" was how her mother described her.

"How do you do it?" Nicole asked. "How do you eat so much and not gain weight?"

Jessie explained. Not only was her lunch less fattening than Nicole's, but it also provided her with more of the materials her body needed to work properly. Whereas Nicole would be tired and hungry after school, Jessie would still feel fresh and satisfied; that would make it easy for her to run, which also helped to keep her weight down.

Jessie and her family, like many Americans, had recently become interested in *nutrition*, the science of food. By reading some popular books on the subject, they had learned that eating does a lot more than fill a person's stomach. It also feeds all the cells in the body and provides the material for new cells. And it provides the fuel the body needs to work efficiently.

They had also learned that poor eating habits can contribute to a wide variety of problems, ranging from obesity to cancer, heart disease, and diabetes. By changing their diet, Jessie's family had lessened their chances of developing these problems. They also found that eating to enhance their health actually enhanced their enjoyment of food.

In this chapter you will learn some of the things Jessie's family learned. You will also learn how to deal with weight problems by changing your habits rather than by trying to stick to a difficult diet. If you learn to eat properly now, you will be taking an important step toward feeling good—and looking good—throughout your life.

SECTION 1 The Basics of Nutrition

Australia's koala feeds only on the eucalyptus tree. It is obviously a nutritious and satisfying diet for this mammal. Humans could barely function on such a monotonous diet. We must have a variety of foods because no one food contains all the nutrients our bodies need. *Nutrients* provide energy, build and maintain cells, and regulate the body's natural functions. Without the proper nutrients, the body becomes weak and prone to disease.

The nutrients we need are carbohydrates, fats, proteins, vitamins, and minerals. In addition, water and fiber, although not nutrients, are essential in our diet.

Carbohydrates

What does a gallon of gasoline have in common with a loaf of bread? Both are made up primarily of carbon, and both are forms of fuel. While gasoline provides the energy for cars, bread and other *carbohydrates* provide energy for the human body. There are two kinds of carbohydrates: *simple carbohydrates*, consisting of sugars, and *complex carbohydrates*, consisting of starches. In general, Americans eat too many simple carbohydrates and too few complex carbohydrates.

Almost any food that tastes sweet contains simple carbohydrates, or sugars. Fruits, some vegetables, milk, and milk products all contain these simple carbohydrates. Sugar is also an ingredient in many processed foods, such as candies, cakes, pies, and preserves. The sugar that is added to these products generally comes from sugar cane or sugar beets.

Complex carbohydrates, or starches, are found in potatoes, pasta, peas, beans, and rice, corn, and other grains. Both simple and complex carbohydrates provide energy. However, complex carbohydrate foods are better for you because they are generally rich in other nutrients as well, and they should be the body's major source of energy.

Figure 6.1 Every physical movement, from a tennis stroke to a heartbeat, requires energy. We get nearly all of this energy from carbohydrates and fats

In the body, the liver converts carbohydrates into a sugar called *glucose*. Glucose is the only substance that the body can burn as energy. Glucose that is not used up is stored in your liver and muscles. These tissues can hold only a certain amount of glucose, however, and what cannot be stored in your liver or muscles is converted into fat and stored in the fatty tissues of your body. Besides providing energy, carbohydrates are needed to process fats. If you eat too few carbohydrates, fat waste products build up in your blood.

Americans, as we have said, tend to eat too much sugar. In particular, we eat too many foods that have been sweetened with sugar, such as pies and candy. These foods are not recommended by nutritionists because they tend to be high in sugar and calories, but they contain few other nutrients. Foods high in calories are linked to obesity.

Certain sugary foods are also linked to tooth decay. The most damage is done by foods that stick to the teeth, such as caramel or taffy, especially if they are eaten between meals and before bedtime. Mouth bacteria feed on the sugar and increase the build-up of plaque on the teeth. These bacteria also act on the sugar to produce acids that attack tooth enamel.

Nutritionists recommend that we get less of our energy from simple carbohydrates and more from complex carbohydrates. They say that 50 to 65 percent of the foods we eat should consist of complex carbohydrates. Such foods are high in fiber, vitamins, and minerals, as well as complex carbohydrates. Properly prepared, they are nutritious, filling, and not fattening.

Unfortunately, however, foods containing complex carbohydrates have gained a bad reputation over the years. People often think that they are high in calories. The first foods that many Americans cut back on when they want to lose weight are bread, pasta, and potatoes. These foods are *not* high in calories; the fats we put on them, such as butter, oil, or sour cream, make them fattening. People who want to lose weight should cut down on fats and sugars, not starches. Diets low in complex carbohydrates make people feel weak and tired. It is far better to cut out the butter on the baked potato than the baked potato itself.

Fats

Fats serve a number of vital purposes in the body. Like carbohydrates, they are a source of energy, though not as efficient a source. Fats dissolve and store certain vitamins, help form hormones, and help make blood clot. In addition, fatty tissue helps cushion your body's bones and vital organs from being damaged by falls and shocks. Because fats move slowly through the digestive tract, they help you feel satisfied when you have eaten.

Fats are contained in meats and dairy foods, in fish, and in certain vegetables and nuts. There are two main kinds of fats: saturated and unsaturated. *Saturated fats* are solid at room temperature. The fats in meats, in certain dairy products, and in two plants oils, coconut and palm oil, are saturated. *Unsaturated fats* are liquid at room temperature. Examples of unsaturated fats are olive oil, peanut oil, and corn oil.

Saturated fats are believed to increase the amount of cholesterol in the body. *Cholesterol* is a fatlike substance that is carried in the bloodstream. Most of your body's cholesterol is produced in your body by your liver. It is not taken directly from food, but is manufactured from digested fats.

Cholesterol plays both good and bad roles in the human body. It is necessary to form various hormones. It also enables the body to digest fats and to produce vitamin D. However, cholesterol may form painful stones in the gall bladder. It may also form deposits on the inner walls of the arteries, a serious condition called *atherosclerosis* (see Chapter 17). Scientists know, too, that there is a relationship between the level of cholesterol in the blood and the risk of heart disease.

Saturated fats may serve as the starting material for the body's production of more cholesterol. Unsaturated fats, in contrast, do not have adverse effects on blood cholesterol. In fact, because the body does not use them as the raw material for cholesterol, such fats may help lower blood cholesterol.

Eating enough fat is not a problem in the United States, except, possibly, in the poorest areas. Most Americans eat too much fat, especially saturated fat. Fat contains more calories

Figure 6.2 A diet high in fat can contribute to obesity. Serious health problems such as heart disease and cancer are linked to obesity.

per gram than carbohydrates or protein, and it is our most "fattening" nutrient. Not only is a high-fat diet linked to obesity, but it may also contribute to heart disease and cancer. The daily diet of most Americans consists of nearly 45 percent fats. Between 20 and 30 percent would be healthier, and no more than 10 percent of your diet should consist of saturated fats. You can cut down on fats by eating less red meat and by trimming fat from meat before you cook it. You can also cut down on the amount of butter, oils, and fried foods that you eat.

Proteins

Every cell in your body is made of protein. Each day your body must make thousands of new cells to replace those that wear out. If you are still growing, you must make cells to meet that demand as well.

The raw material for these new cells comes from the proteins in the plants and animals that you eat. First, your body breaks these proteins down into smaller segments called *amino acids*. These tiny particles are then combined in various ways to make up body tissues.

It takes 23 different amino acids to make up human protein. Your body can manufacture only 15, and the other 8, called *essential amino acids*, must come to you ready-made in the food you eat. Meat, eggs, milk, and other foods from animals have all 8 of the essential amino acids and are therefore said to contain *complete protein*. Grains and vegetables do not have all 8 amino acids. They contain *incomplete protein*, and need to be combined with other foods to form complete protein. Such combinations include cereal with milk, rice with beans, and macaroni with cheese.

Most Americans eat twice as much protein as they need to meet their daily requirement. They also get too much of their protein from foods high in fat, such as meats and dairy products. Nutritionists advise us to eat less total protein and to get more of our protein from plant foods. Many of the complex carbohydrate foods described earlier, such as potatoes, pasta, rice, corn, and beans, are excellent sources of protein.

Eating *less* protein than you need can have serious effects as well. Even slight protein shortages can affect the body's functions. Over time, tiredness and irritability can occur. The body may form fewer antibodies, catch diseases more easily, and get well more slowly than it should.

Figure 6.3 Animal products, such as meat, fish, milk, and eggs, supply us with complete protein.

TABLE 6.1	**Major Vitamins**	
Vitamin	**Sources**	**Effects of Deficiency**
A	Liver, eggs, fortified milk and other dairy products, carrots, fruits, vegetables	Night blindness, eye infections, increased susceptibility to respiratory infections, cracking and drying of skin, hemorrhage
B$_1$ (Thiamine)	Whole-grain or enriched cereals, liver, nuts, beans, pork, wheat germ	Beriberi, muscular weakness, loss of appetite, faulty digestion
B$_2$ (Riboflavin)	Liver, green vegetables, milk, eggs, cheese, fish, lean meat, whole-grain or enriched cereals	Cracking of the mouth corners, sore skin, bloodshot eyes, sensitivity to light
Niacin	Yeast, liver, kidneys, lean meat, wheat germ, eggs, nuts, fish	Pellagra, diarrhea, skin rash, mental disorders, depression, death
B$_6$ (Pyridoxine)	Yeast, wheat bran and germ, liver, kidneys, meat, whole grains, fish, fruits, vegetables	Scaliness around eyes, nose, and mouth; mental depression; confusion; convulsions
B$_{12}$	Meat, liver, kidneys, eggs, milk, cheese	Anemia, irritability, drowsiness, depression
Folic acid	Fruits, vegetables, grains, nuts, orange juice, dairy products	Anemia, diarrhea
C	Citrus fruits, tomatoes, cabbage, broccoli, potatoes, green peppers, strawberries	Scurvy, anemia, unhealthy skin and gums, retarded healing, hemorrhage
D	Fish-liver oils, butter, eggs, milk, liver, fortified milk	Poor development of bones and teeth, rickets (softening of bones)
E	Plant oils, vegetables, wheat germ, butter, lettuce, watercress, grains, nuts, seeds, margarine	Changes in make-up of blood
K	Leafy vegetables, eggs, liver, tomatoes, meat	Poor blood clotting (hemorrhage)

Vitamins

Vitamins, along with minerals, are often called "micronutrients·" They are required only in tiny amounts. They are needed to trigger certain chemical reactions in the body. For example, calcium cannot become part of the bone structure without the presence of vitamin D. The major vitamins and their food sources are listed in Table 6.1. The table also shows the possible effects of a diet that is deficient in one or more of the vitamins.

Americans frequently add vitamins to their normal diet. They spend between $300 million and $500 million a year on vitamin supplements. Most of them are unnecessary. People would be wiser to spend their money on nu-

trients in the form of food. Of course, if you have a vitamin deficiency, your doctor may prescribe vitamins.

Some vitamins may not harm you if you have too many of them. The B group of vitamins and vitamin C cannot remain in the body in excessive amounts. What the body does not need, it excretes.

Too much of vitamins A, D, E, and K can harm you, however. These vitamins cannot be excreted. Instead, they are stored in fatty tissues. If too many of them build up, the body's normal functions may be disrupted. Too much vitamin D, for example, can cause harmful calcium deposits to form in your body. Because of this hazard, the Food and Drug Administration (FDA) has limited the amount of vitamin D that can be added to foods.

Minerals

At least 20 *minerals* are needed by your body in small amounts every day to help it form tissues and vital chemical substances. These minerals also help regulate your body's fluid levels. Some of the necessary minerals and their sources are listed in Table 6.2. If you eat a balanced diet, with a wide variety of vegetables, fish, and meat products, and if you drink enough water each day, you will probably not need to take mineral supplements.

Iron is one of the most important minerals because it helps red blood cells carry oxygen. Women of childbearing age need twice as much iron as men of the same age because they regularly lose large amounts through menstruation. Iron is the one nutrient that some people need to supplement. No one should take iron supplements, however, before consulting a doctor.

Although *salt* (sodium chloride) is a necessary mineral, most Americans eat far more salt than they need. Excess salt has been linked to congestive heart failure, kidney disorders, and toxemia (blood poisoning) during pregnancy. Too much salt is also linked to increased blood pressure in people who have a tendency for high blood pressure.

The average American consumes the equivalent of 2 to 4 teaspoons of salt per day. Most people need only about a quarter of a teaspoon of salt daily. Salt is hard to avoid, even if you deliberately stop using table salt, because most processed foods contain salt. In addition, we tend to acquire a "salt habit," because we become accustomed to eating food that is highly salted. Many doctors and nutritionists suggest a low-salt diet for children to prevent them from forming this habit, and many baby food manufacturers have removed salt entirely from their products. Most doctors recommend that you add no salt to your food.

A well-balanced diet usually includes enough *calcium,* an important mineral that keeps bones and teeth hard and performs other vital functions. However, some people do not get enough calcium. Calcium deficiency is more common in women than in men. A depletion of calcium in the bones can cause osteoporosis, a condition in which bones do not develop properly and become brittle and susceptible to breaking. It

is important that you get enough calcium when you are young in order to prevent osteoporosis from developing in your later years. Your doctor should be able to tell you whether or not you need calcium supplements.

Water

Water, in itself, has no nutritional value. However, it is perhaps the most important component in the diet. Your body can go without food for long periods. Without water, it can survive no longer than four days.

TABLE 6.2 **Minerals**

Mineral	Sources
Calcium	Dairy products, leafy vegetables, apricots
Chloride	Table salt, dried apricots, beans, beets, brown sugar, raisins, spinach, yeast
Cobalt	Vitamin B_{12}
Copper	Kidneys, liver, beans, Brazil nuts, whole-meal flour, lentils, parsley
Fluoride	Fish, meat, cheese, tea, drinking water in some areas
Iodine	Iodized salt, seafood
Iron	Liver, meat, shellfish, lentils, peanuts, parsley, dried fruits, eggs
Magnesium	Available in most foods
Manganese	Wheat germ, nuts, bran, leafy vegetables, cereal grains, meat
Phosphorus	Peas, beans, milk, liver, meat, cottage cheese, broccoli, whole grains
Potassium	Available in most foods
Sodium	Table salts, dried apricots, beans, beets, brown sugar, raisins, spinach, yeast
Sulfur	Nuts, dried fruits, barley, oatmeal, beans, cheese, eggs, lentils, brown sugar
Zinc	Shellfish, meat, milk, eggs

Figure 6.4 Raw vegetables, often eaten in salads, are a good source of water and fiber.

Water plays many roles. It brings nutrients to all body cells and carries their wastes to the kidneys. It is needed for the many chemical reactions that occur during digestion. Water also controls body temperature. It conducts heat efficiently and cools the body by evaporation through the skin (perspiration). Water in the body tissues also cushions vital organs and lubricates the joints and central nervous system. Water, in fact, makes up about 60 percent of a person's weight.

You should take in about 2 quarts of water every day. Most people get only about half of that amount by drinking water and other liquids. The rest comes from food. Surprisingly, many foods are mainly water. Most fruits, for instance, are almost 90 percent water. A "dry" food such as bread is actually about 35 percent water.

The weather, your physical activity, and your diet all affect the amount of water you need each day. A salty meal or snack, high-protein foods, and alcohol all tend to raise the sodium content of your body fluids. More water is then needed to dilute the fluids to their normal state.

Fiber

Fiber is a necessary nonnutrient in the human diet. It is also known as roughage or bulk. Fiber is present in whole grains, fruits, vegetables, and meat.

Fiber is a necessary aid to digestion. In the colon, which is part of the large intestine, fiber and large amounts of water unite with other waste products. This combination forms large, soft stools that are easily eliminated. Enough fiber in the diet results in large and frequent bowel movements. They relieve pressure in the colon. This helps to prevent *diverticulosis,* a

Talking Point

Fiber

"An apple a day keeps the doctor away."

This old saying may be truer than you think, although you could just as well substitute a carrot or a bowl of bran cereal for the apple. All these foods are high in fiber, and fiber helps keep your body healthy in a variety of ways.

Fiber is found in the plants that we eat. It contains no nutrients, so the body absorbs nothing from it as it passes through the digestive system. Fiber does, however, perform a very useful role. As it passes through the digestive system, it speeds the elimination of food wastes and helps prevent or relieve disorders of the digestive tract such as constipation, irregularity, spastic colon, and diverticulosis.

Studies suggest that a diet high in fiber might also protect people against cancer of the colon because the fiber cleanses the colon of cancer-causing agents. Nutritionists, therefore, consider fiber to be a very important part of a healthful diet.

Different foods contain different kinds of fiber. Bran cereals and whole-grain breads contain cellulose and hemicellulose, which act in the body as a laxative. These types of fiber absorb water and help form large, soft stools that are eliminated frequently.

The kinds of fiber found in fruits and vegetables—pectins and gums—help reduce the amount of fat carried in the bloodstream. A diet that combines these kinds of fiber with foods low in fat can substantially reduce the amounts of cholesterol and triglycerides in the blood. Excessive amounts of these substances in the blood contribute to cardiovascular disease.

Fiber can also play a role in controlling diabetes. Diabetics who are placed on a high-fiber, low-fat diet can greatly reduce their dependence on insulin. The fiber in the diet slows the release of sugar into the bloodstream, which reduces the need for sudden, large doses of insulin.

Fiber helps the body in another way too. It can help you control your weight. Because fiber makes you feel full, it helps you stop feeling hungry between meals. As a result, you'll be less tempted to reach for a snack a couple of hours after a meal.

disorder in which the intestinal wall weakens and bulges out. Fiber also helps the body produce such nutrients as vitamin K. Some studies suggest that adequate fiber intake also lowers the risk of colon cancer and possibly other cancers as well.

Calories

A *calorie* is a measure of the energy found in food. The amount of energy your body needs for each process or action also is measured in calories. For example, an apple contains about

100 calories. Those 100 calories give you enough energy to walk 20 minutes.

Carbohydrates and proteins each contain 4 calories per gram. Fat contains 9 calories per gram. Therefore, a teaspoon of butter contains more than twice as many calories as a teaspoon of sugar. There are no calories in vitamins, minerals, and water. Though fiber contains calories, humans cannot digest fiber and therefore cannot gain its calories.

Not everyone needs the same number of calories to keep in good health. Many factors affect how much energy your body needs. A nutritionist prescribing a balanced diet would need to know your age, height, sex, weight, and level of physical activity. We will discuss calories and body weight later in this chapter.

CHECK YOUR UNDERSTANDING

1. Give examples of the two kinds of carbohydrates. In what ways does your body use them?
2. List five functions of fats in the human body. What is the difference between saturated and unsaturated fats?
3. Where does your body get the raw material to make new cells?
4. Why does the human body need vitamins and minerals?
5. What two nonnutrients are necessary in the human diet? What does each one do?

SECTION **2** **A Balanced Diet**

When Linda woke up, she knew it was time to see a doctor. Once again, after a full night's sleep, she could hardly drag herself out of bed. And if today was anything like yesterday, she would be so tired after school she would have to take a nap. What could be the matter with her?

At the doctor's office, Linda found out what was wrong. She had *anemia*. Her blood was not carrying the oxygen her body cells needed to function properly. The doctor explained to Linda that her anemia was caused by a lack of iron in her diet. Linda couldn't understand this. After all, she ate a lot. She wasn't skinny, was she?

The pamphlet the doctor gave Linda provided the answer. Linda was getting enough calories, but not enough of all the nutrients her body needed. She needed to add foods such as lentils, spinach, and dried fruits to her diet, so her blood would have the iron it needed to attract oxygen. In other words, she needed a balanced diet, one that would enable her body to keep its own delicate chemical balance.

The Food Groups

Achieving a balanced diet is not difficult once you know about the five food groups. You need daily servings from four of the five groups. The numbers of servings given below are those recommended by the Food and Nutrition Board of the National Research Council. The board makes no recommendations for the fifth group, which includes sugars, fats, and oils. In fact, most Americans eat too much from this last group, which includes junk food.

Meat Group Included in this category are meats, poultry, fish, eggs, as well as beans, peas, and nuts. They are all excellent sources of protein. These foods also supply B vitamins and iron. You should eat approximately 6 ounces of meat group foods daily.

Milk and Milk Products These foods provide more calcium per serving than any other. Without milk or cheese, in fact, it is hard to

Figure 6.5 The food groups necessary for good nutrition: *(clockwise from top left)* milk and milk products, breads and cereals, fruits and vegetables, and the meat group.

meet the daily calcium requirement. Foods from this group also are good sources of protein, B vitamins, vitamin A, and vitamin D. If you're trying to control the number of calories or the amount of cholesterol in your diet, choose skim milk, dry skim milk powder, or low-fat milk. However, when using these products, check the labels to see that vitamins A and D have been added. These two vitamins will have been removed from whole milk along with the butterfat.

Fruits and Vegetables These foods supply all of the vitamin C requirement and 60 percent of vitamin A. They also provide other vitamins and minerals and much of the needed fiber. Four servings a day are suggested. One should be a food rich in vitamin C, such as citrus, tomato, or cantaloupe. Every other day, or more often, one of the dark green or deep yellow vegetables such as spinach or carrots should be added for vitamin A.

Breads and Cereals (Whole Grain or Enriched) The breads, rice, noodles, and similar products in this group provide carbohydrates, thiamine, riboflavin, niacin, and iron. Leaving out this group makes it difficult to get enough thiamine and iron (especially for women). While four daily servings from this food group are recommended, many people mistakenly eat less because they think these foods are fattening. In fact, a 1-ounce piece of bread contains fewer calories (65 to 70) than a 1-ounce piece of meat (75 to 90).

Talking Point
Organic and Natural Foods

Because of the various health hazards linked with chemicals used to grow or process our food, many Americans are making an attempt to eat foods that are free of such substances. So they are buying foods that are labeled "organic" or "natural." And they are paying far more than they would for similar foods without those labels.

But what do the terms *organic* and *natural* mean? Ideally, *organic* means that a food plant has been grown without pesticides or other synthetic chemicals, including fertilizers. And *natural* means that a food product has been prepared without artificial additives or preservatives.

In reality, people who buy such foods may be getting a lot more than they bargained for. They may be getting the very chemicals they are trying to avoid.

In the case of organic foods, tests show that plants grown without dangerous pesticides are still affected by them. In fact, organically grown produce may contain the same level of pesticide residue as plants grown the standard way. This contamination occurs in several ways. Most farmland now used to grow organic crops was once used to grow crops treated with pesticides. These chemicals remain in the soil for years, contaminating subsequent crops. Also, if nearby farmers are spraying their crops with pesticides, wind and rain can carry the chemicals to the fields of organic farmers. So that "organic" carrot that costs twice as much as a regular carrot may have the same amount of pesticide.

In the case of natural foods, the word seems to mean whatever the manufacturer wants it to mean. You can, of course, find many foods marked "natural" that fit the accepted definition. But far more common are foods labeled "natural" that aren't really natural at all.

In their efforts to get on the natural food bandwagon, companies have found a variety of ways to claim their product is natural. One way is to use the word *natural* to describe just one ingredient. So you may buy "natural banana" ice cream, only to find that it contains artificial ingredients along with the natural banana flavor.

Another technique manufacturers use to mislead customers is to suggest rather than state that a food product is natural. So they may use some form of the word *natural* in the trade name (*Nature's Finest,* for instance). Or they may put a back-to-nature drawing or photograph on the label—along with a higher price tag.

Until the government sets official standards for natural foods, then, the only way to be sure of what you are buying is to read the product label with care. As for foods that are supposed to be organic, chances are just as good that they're not—unless they've been certified by a laboratory. And the chances of that happening are pretty slim.

Sugar, Refined Fats, and Oils This fifth group contains foods that make up a large part of what Americans eat. These foods include butter, margarine, refined sugar, jelly, candy, soft drinks, pastries, cakes, and pies. Alcoholic beverages, which are high in sugar, are also included in this group. The foods in the fifth group are high in calories and low in nutrients, so there is no recommended daily intake. Nutritionists suggest that you limit your consumption of these foods.

Talking Point

Guide to Food Labels

Food labels provide a great deal of information that can help you learn what you're getting in the products you buy. Some of the information must be provided to satisfy requirements of the Food and Drug Administration (FDA). Other information may be included at the option of the manufacturer. This is a list of the information most often found on food labels:

- *The net contents or net weight* The net weight on canned food includes the liquid in which the product is packed, such as the water in a can of vegetables.
- *The name and place of business of the manufacturer, packer, or distributor*
- *The ingredients* The ingredient that represents the largest amount, by weight, must be listed first, followed by the other ingredients, in descending order of weight.
- *Additives* Any additives used in the product must be listed, but colors and flavors do not have to be listed by name.
- *The nutritional content* Under FDA regulations, any food that claims to provide nutrients, or that has a nutrient added to it, must have the nutritional content listed. The list tells you how many calories and how much protein, carbohydrate, and fat there is in a serving of the product. It also tells you what percentage of the U.S. Recommended Daily Allowances of protein and of seven vitamins and minerals the product provides.
- *A date* To help consumers obtain fresh and wholesome food, many manufacturers date their products.

Adapted from *A Consumer's Guide to Food Labels,* U.S. Department of Health and Human Services, HHS Publication No. (FDA) 82-2160, © 1982.

Vegetarianism

Vegetarianism, in general, is the practice of not eating meat. Some vegetarians avoid only red meat. Others do not eat fish, poultry, eggs, or any other food derived from animals.

People have different reasons for becoming vegetarians. Some believe that a meatless diet is more healthful than a diet with meat. Others believe that it is cruel to raise and slaughter animals for food. Some vegetarians point out that if the grain that is used to fatten animals was used to feed people, there would be less hunger in the world.

Vegetarianism may have health benefits. Meat is a major source of saturated fat and cholesterol. Because they do not eat meat, vegetarians get less saturated fat and cholesterol in their diets, and they avoid the chemical preservatives added to meat. Also, vegetarians who eat a variety of well-balanced vegetables, fruit, and grain products are less likely to be overweight than people who include a lot of meat in their diets.

Nevertheless, vegetarians do miss out on a major source of protein, especially if they do not eat poultry or eggs. Protein deficiency can have serious health consequences, and vegetar-

Figure 6.6 The processed foods you buy usually contain some preservatives and additives. Government dietary guidelines suggest that you choose fresh foods rather than those that are canned, frozen, or packaged.

ians must make sure that they achieve the proper combinations of amino acids to obtain complete protein. They also need to make sure they get enough calcium, iron, and vitamin B_{12}, which are found mostly in animal products.

Dietary Guidelines

To help Americans eat sensibly and maintain desirable weight, the federal government has published the dietary guidelines listed below. You should remember to follow these seven principles of nutrition when planning your meals. Make them a part of your life style.

1. Eat a variety of foods daily in adequate amounts, including fruits, vegetables, whole-grain and enriched breads, cereals, other grain products, yogurt, fish, and dried beans. Choose fresh foods over canned, frozen, or packaged foods.
2. Maintain a desirable weight by eating a variety of foods that are low in calories and high in nutrients and by increasing physical activity.
3. Avoid too much fat, saturated fat, and cholesterol. Do this by substituting fish and poultry for red meats and by replacing animal fats with vegetable oils. Broil, bake, and stir-fry foods rather than frying them.
4. Eat foods with adequate starch and fiber. Increase your complex carbohydrate consumption by eating more fruits, vegetables, and whole grains and by substituting complex carbohydrates for foods containing large amounts of fats and sugars.
5. Avoid too much sugar. Americans should reduce their sugar consumption by 40 percent by eating less sugar and fewer high-sugar foods.
6. Avoid too much sodium by using less table salt, eating less-salty foods, and substituting other spices for salt.
7. If you drink alcoholic beverages, do so in moderation. Alcoholic beverages are high in calories and low in nutrients. Heavy drinkers frequently develop nutritional deficiencies as well as more serious diseases.

CHECK YOUR UNDERSTANDING

1. List the five food groups. For each of the four recommended groups, list the nutrients that the foods supply.
2. What nutrients might be lacking in a vegetarian diet unless the vegetarian pays particular attention to them?
3. What do the government's dietary guidelines say about fats?
4. List the foods that are recommended for increasing the consumption of complex carbohydrates.

SECTION **3** **Weight Problems**

Many teenagers are not satisfied with their weight. Most think they are too fat or too thin. A large percentage of those who think they have weight problems are actually the correct weight for their height and frame. For some, however, their weight is, indeed, a problem.

Being overweight can have serious health effects. It can affect a person's life in other ways, too, especially during the teenage years. Because they feel self-conscious about how they look, and because they find it hard to move around, some overweight teenagers avoid sports and other physical activities that might help them reduce their weight. They might also avoid the kinds of social activities that would increase their enjoyment of life.

Being underweight carries similar burdens. People who are severely underweight may feel self-conscious about their appearance and may avoid social situations, such as beach parties or softball games, in which their bodies might be noticed.

Finally, there is the simple fact that carrying the right amount of weight for your body feels better. People who have gone from obesity to normal weight marvel at the difference in their energy level and in their movements. Even walking feels different. As one teenage girl explained, "I used to feel so awkward and heavy when I moved. Now that I've lost weight, walking down the street feels like dancing."

Are You the Right Weight?

Manuel and Gary are the same age and height, and they weigh the same amount. Manuel likes what he sees in the mirror, but Gary sees rolls of fat that tell him he needs to lose weight.

What makes the difference? Because Manuel has a large, broad-shouldered frame, his body can carry more weight than Gary's narrow, slender frame. Even though two people are the same height, then, they may need to weigh different amounts.

What is the right amount of weight for you? No one can give you a specific answer. What you can look at, however, are charts that give appropriate weight *ranges* for teenagers. These charts usually have three ranges for each height—one for small-framed people, one for those with medium frames, and a third for people with large frames. (You can determine the size of your own frame by comparing the size of your wrist with others of the same sex, age, and height.) Make sure that you look at a chart for your own age group, since charts for adults are not appropriate for younger people.

There are other ways to tell if you weigh more than you should. If a young man's stomach measurement is larger than his chest measurement, for instance, he probably needs to lose weight. You can also give yourself the *pinch test*. With your thumb and forefinger, grasp a fold of skin at your waistline. If the thickness of the skin fold is more than an inch, you are probably overweight. You must be careful, though, to grasp just skin, and not all the underlying tissue as well.

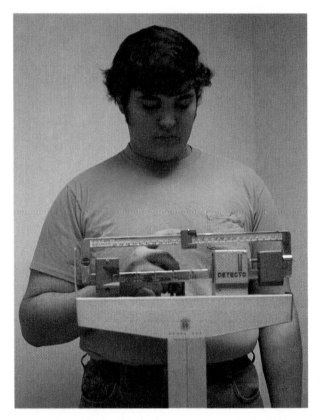

Figure 6.7 This young man is clearly overweight. He needs to combine exercise and diet to reach and maintain a weight appropriate for his age, height, and body type.

In general, your weight will not affect your health if it is not 10 percent more than the weight recommended for your height, body frame, and sex. A weight 10 to 20 percent above the table is generally considered overweight. Obesity usually begins at weights over 20 percent above the recommended level.

Body Composition

The amount that you'd like to weigh and the amount that you should weigh aren't necessarily the same. You can't tell if you're the right weight just by stepping on a scale. The right weight for you depends on your body composition: your height; your build; and the ratio of fat to lean tissue in your body.

Figure 6.8 About 25 percent of the average woman's body weight is fat, but athletic training may reduce this to as little as 14 percent.

Before adolescence, boys and girls have about the same ratio of fat to lean tissue. During adolescence, the ratio changes. At the end of his growth spurt, fat makes up about 14 percent of a young man's body weight; in a young woman, fat will make up about 25 percent of her body weight.

Because lean tissue weighs more than fat tissue, people can weigh more than the average without being obese. This is often true of football linemen and serious body builders. Because of their large muscles they may weigh 20 percent more than is recommended yet have no excess fat.

Two Types of Obesity

There are two distinct types of obesity. Some overweight people have a greater *number* of fat cells, sometimes two or three times the average. Other overweight people have the normal number of fat cells, but the cells are *larger* than normal.

People with an abnormal number of fat cells can lose weight. But they never lose the fat cells; the cells just shrink. The type of obesity associated with normal numbers of fat cells seems easier to overcome than obesity caused by excess cells.

Obesity from excess fat cells usually starts in childhood. Some evidence suggests that early overfeeding may be a cause of excess fat cells. Parents who make their children clean up their plates or who reward their children with food may be causing a lifelong problem. About 80 percent of overweight children become overweight adults.

Causes of Weight Problems

There's no mystery about the primary cause of overweight. If you eat more calories than your body can use, it stores the excess calories as fat. For every 3,500 calories stored, you gain 1 pound of fat. But why do some people eat more than they need? The underlying causes of overweight are not well understood. Research into a number of factors associated with overweight continues.

Scientists have been able to cause overweight in test animals in a number of ways. By inbreeding, they have been able to prove the existence of several "obesity genes" in rats and mice, which suggests that overweight may at times be hereditary. Scientists have also produced obesity in animals by injuring the brain mechanism that controls appetite. Other ways of producing obesity include changing hormone levels, overfeeding, and limiting physical activity. Researchers believe that in humans, too, there are probably different types and causes of obesity.

There are various theories about the causes of underweight, too. Like obesity, underweight tends to run in families: thin parents may have thin children. Some people are underweight because they skip meals, either because they are too busy or because they don't care about food; others can't afford to eat properly. A few people develop serious emotional disorders that cause them to lose weight (see the box on anorexia and bulimia, page 40).

Figure 6.9 Overweight tends to run in families.
This may be due to heredity, environmental
influences, or—most likely—a combination of both.

Psychological Reasons for Eating

Eating is not a purely physical reaction to hunger. People eat for psychological reasons as well. They may turn to food when they are lonely, depressed, anxious, bored, or under stress. Food gives them temporary comfort.

People also eat because something suggests the idea to them. They may, for example, have a dish of ice cream after watching an appealing commercial on TV. Some people associate eating with certain activities. They may, for example, have developed a habit of eating while reading or listening to music. Eating is also a way of socializing. Lavish meals are often prepared for family gatherings and parties.

Research suggests that overweight people are more likely to turn to food for psychological reasons than people of normal weight are.

strikingly less. Motion picture studies of children in playgrounds and adults in factories also showed that the obese exercised much less, in both amount and intensity. Without exercise, the body turns food into fat. With exercise, it converts food into energy.

Speed of Eating

Research suggests that speed of eating also may be linked to overeating. People who eat too fast may overeat regularly. A control mechanism in the brain, called the *hypothalamus*, regulates the appetite. However, by the time the hypothalamus signals fast eaters to stop eating, they may have already eaten too much. Over time, rapid eating may even cancel the control mechanism completely.

Junk Food

Junk food habits may contribute to overweight too. Many junk foods, such as potato chips and soft drinks, are high in calories but have little or no nutritive value and do not satisfy hunger. Junk foods tend to be habit-forming. Laboratory animals fed low-fiber, high-sugar foods later refused nourishing diets. Instead, they ate increasing amounts of the junk food. The easy availability of such foods in fast-food restaurants and vending machines may be an important cause of overweight.

In other words, they eat to fill needs other than hunger.

Lack of Exercise

Lack of exercise is also related to overweight. One study of obese and normal-weight girls showed that the obese girls actually ate less than the girls of normal weight—but exercised

CHECK YOUR UNDERSTANDING

1. Why might two people of the same age, sex, and height need to weigh different amounts? What are three ways to get an idea of what you should weigh?

2. How might overfeeding children affect their fat cells?

3. How many stored calories results in a pound of fat?

4. List three possible causes of obesity and three possible causes of underweight.

SECTION **4** **Methods of Weight Control**

The direct cause of overweight is eating more calories than the body is able to use up. The only way you can lose weight, then, is to change the calorie balance so that you consume fewer calories than you use. There are two ways you can do this. One is to eat fewer calories. The other is to increase the number of calories that you use by becoming more active.

The most successful weight-reducing programs combine both approaches. Long-term weight control requires *permanent changes in both eating and exercising habits*. Crash diets may enable a person to shed weight quickly, but they cannot help keep weight off over time. In the same way, people who want to gain weight must increase their food intake slowly and make a permanent change in their eating habits.

Planning a Weight-Control Program

Set clear, realistic goals when you begin planning a weight-loss or weight-gain program. Decide on the weight you want to be and the rate at which you want to gain or lose it. Then you can work out how you are going to achieve your goal.

Unless you are under a doctor's supervision, losing or gaining more than a pound or two a week is unwise. If you are 30 pounds overweight or underweight, you should give yourself a year to accomplish your weight goal.

The next step is to figure out how many calories you should eat daily to meet your goal. First, find the number of calories you need to hold your present weight. Use the Calorie Calculator and Activity Level Guide in Figure 6.11. Take as an example a 16-year-old boy who stands 5 feet 9 inches tall and weighs 180 pounds. As a student with a part-time clerical job, he would need about 3,150 calories daily to remain at 180 pounds.

His goal is to reduce his weight to 160 pounds by losing 20 pounds in 20 weeks. He does not intend to change his activity level, so he must reduce the number of calories he eats.

Since 1 pound of fat equals 3,500 calories, he must cut his weekly calorie intake by 3,500, or 500 calories a day. He must therefore reduce his present intake of 3,150 calories a day to 2,650 calories. If he weighed 140 pounds and wanted to increase his weight to 160 pounds by gaining 20 pounds in 20 weeks, he would add 500 calories a day for a total increase of 3,500 calories a week.

You must be patient when you work to change your weight. But it is worth it. Quick methods of weight gain or loss are only temporary, and they can be harmful.

The Need for Exercise

Exercise is an important element in weight control. If you were to walk only 1 mile extra each day (at a cost of about 116 calories), without raising your calorie intake, you would lose 12 pounds in a year.

If you are underweight, don't stop exercising. Exercise is important for everyone, and it will

Figure 6.10 Increasing the amount of exercise you get, without increasing your food intake, is an effective way to lose weight.

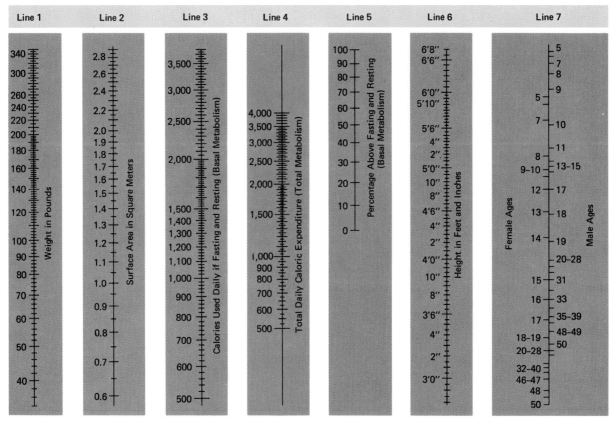

Figure 6.11 The calorie calculator and activity level guide. Your level of physical activity is the main indicator of your daily calorie needs. To determine the number of calories needed to maintain your present weight, follow these instructions:

1. Using a pin as a marker, locate your present weight on line 1.
2. Set the edge of a ruler against the pin. Swing the other end of the ruler to your height, located on line 6.
3. Remove the pin from line 1. Place it at the point where the ruler crosses line 2.
4. Keeping the edge of the ruler firmly against the pin on line 2, swing its right-hand edge to your sex and age on line 7. (Use the age of your nearest birthday.)
5. Remove the pin, and place it where the ruler crosses line 3. This will give you the calories you use daily (in 24 hours) if you are resting and fasting.
6. To the base number of calories thus determined, add the percentage above fasting and resting for your usual type of daily activity. Use the following guidelines:

Add 40 percent if you are a nonworking student whose physical activity is limited to walking to and from classes.
Add 50 percent if you are involved in physical activity (such as clerical or library work) that includes about two hours of walking or standing daily.
Add 60 percent if you participate in limited physical exercise (such as disco dancing) or light intramural sports.
Add 70 percent if your work involves heavy physical activity (such as construction work) or if you participate in a regular, daily exercise program (such as team sports).
Add 80 to 100 percent if you are engaged in strenuous physical work or participate in sports that have a high rate of calorie expenditure (i.e., basketball, track, and so on).

7. Leaving the pin in line 3, swing the edge of the ruler to the right to the proper percentage on line 5. Where the ruler crosses line 4, you will find the number of calories necessary to maintain you at your present weight if you maintain your present activity level.

TABLE 6.3 **Amount of Exercise Needed to Burn Off Calories**

| Food | Calories | Minutes of Activity | | | |
		Walking	Bicycling	Swimming	Running
Apple, large	101	19	12	9	5
Bacon, 2 strips	96	18	12	9	5
Banana, small	88	17	11	8	4
Carrot, raw	42	8	5	4	2
Cereal, ½ cup with milk, sugar	200	38	24	18	10
Cheese, cheddar, 1 oz.	111	21	14	10	6
Cheese, cottage, 1 tbs.	27	5	3	2	1
Chicken, fried, ½ breast	232	45	28	21	12
Cookie, chocolate chip	51	10	6	5	3
Egg, boiled	77	15	9	7	4
Egg, fried	110	21	13	10	6
Ham, 2 slices	167	32	20	15	9
Hamburger sandwich	350	67	43	31	18
Ice cream, 1/6 qt.	193	37	24	17	10
Mayonnaise, 1 tbs.	92	18	11	8	5
Milk, 1 glass	166	32	20	15	9
Milk, skim, 1 glass	81	16	10	7	4
Milk shake	421	81	51	38	22
Orange, medium	68	13	8	6	4
Orange juice, 1 glass	120	23	15	11	6
Pancake with syrup	124	24	15	11	6
Pizza, cheese, 1 slice	180	35	22	16	9
Pork chop	314	60	38	28	16
Potato chips, 1 serving	108	21	13	10	6
Spaghetti, 1 serving	396	76	48	35	20
Tuna salad sandwich	278	53	34	25	14

help you put on the extra pounds as muscle instead of fat. The early teen years are a time when a lot of calories are used for growing. As your growth rate slows down, you may start putting on weight.

Several points about exercise are well worth remembering:

1. How regularly you exercise is more important than the kinds of exercises you do.
2. Scheduling an exercise for a certain time of day is the best way to make it part of your routine.
3. You should choose an exercise that you enjoy and that fits your life style.
4. Steady, rhythmic exercise lasting at least 30 minutes burns the most calories without being exhausting. Swimming, bicycling, walking, and jogging are the best for weight control.

Changing Your Eating Habits

In order to change your weight and then keep the weight you want, you'll need to change your eating habits. To do this, you must become aware of your own eating patterns first. This requires some work because you took up these habits without thinking early in life. After you begin to study your eating habits, write them down. Include as much information as you can. Write down, for example:

- each meal and snack time (beginning and end)
- how hungry you were before eating
- what you ate and the number of calories it contained
- whether you were alone or with others
- your mood

- whether you were sitting, standing, or lying down when you ate
- which room you were in when you ate

You should also record your daily activities, including exercise periods.

Keeping a behavior record will enable you to spot eating patterns. Do you eat when you're alone? Idle? Watching television? When you discover these cues to your eating, you can find ways to change your habits. You can remove, avoid, or ignore the cues. Start with the most powerful ones. Take a walk instead of having an evening snack, for example. Some people make a point of not associating eating with any other activity they enjoy. That way, they do not change those activities into eating cues. Other people will not eat unless they sit down at a fully set table. This rule usually cuts out snacking.

Some other tips for a practical weight-control campaign are:

1. Eat a good breakfast, including a complete protein. It will keep you from eating the wrong foods late in the morning, and it will keep you mentally alert.
2. Do not skip meals and always eat at about the same time.
3. Keep portions small, with no seconds.
4. Keep especially small the servings of high-calorie, low-nutrient foods such as desserts.
5. Hold snacks down to three small portions a day of high-nutrient foods such as fruits, dry cereals, or raw vegetables.
6. Eat slowly, savoring each bite. Less food will satisfy you if you chew it well, eating a leisurely meal.
7. Select places at home, work, or school where you do nothing but eat.
8. Never eat because you are lonely, anxious, or depressed. Instead, call a friend, open a book, or take a walk.
9. Celebrate special occasions in some way that does not involve eating.
10. Pay attention to your own body signals. When you feel that you've eaten enough, stop eating.

If you are underweight, don't snack just before a meal. It tends to spoil your appetite. Eat your snacks at least two hours before your meal.

Try to put on some extra pounds by adding high-calorie snacks such as peanut butter and crackers, granola, milk and cookies, and nuts. Don't go into a frenzy of eating candy and cupcakes because you'll be getting empty calories.

Fad Diets

Fad diets are usually presented in books and promoted through advertisements and on television. Catchy titles abound—*Eat to Win, Carrots Are a Girl's Best Friend, Pasta Diet*. Many fad diets are wildly imbalanced, some are complete nonsense, and others can be deadly. Liquid protein diets, for instance, have led to a number of deaths from severe heartbeat irregularity caused by an imbalanced diet.

Many fad diets do work in the short run. But they cannot produce long-term weight loss. Most people can tolerate fad diets for a short time without harming themselves. Such diets are risky, however, for people with health problems.

Sweating

Sweating in steam baths, hot tubs, and plastic exercise suits is a popular way of losing weight. Water weight can be lost quickly. You can lose 5 or 10 pounds in a few hours. However, such rapid water loss can be dangerous. It can cause dehydration and kidney, liver, and heart problems. Even serious shock may occur. Sweating is not effective for losing weight. You gain the weight back again the next time you drink a glass of water.

Commercial Groups

For many people, a group approach to weight reduction is helpful. Among the commercial weight-reduction groups, *Weight Watchers* offers a sound diet and emphasizes the need to change eating habits. It offers understanding and encouragement from group sessions. It also has a special program to meet the needs of teenagers.

Some other commercial groups are *TOPS* (Take Off Pounds Sensibly) and *Overeaters Anonymous*. TOPS, founded over 30 years ago, is less expensive than Weight Watchers and involves less peer pressure. Overeaters Anonymous, as the name suggests, is organized like Alcoholics Anonymous. Clients pay on a voluntary basis and receive counseling and help from individuals and groups.

Many other small commercial programs are available locally. These programs can work well if they are run by experts and if they deal with the individual's entire behavior pattern. As with any weight-reduction program, you must change your way of living in order to change your weight.

CHECK YOUR UNDERSTANDING

1. In what two ways can people change their calorie balance?
2. Explain how exercise can bring about a weight loss. How does it help in weight gain?
3. Why is it helpful for people who want to change their weight to study their eating behavior? Why is it a good idea for people to set aside places where they do nothing but eat?
4. Describe the problems associated with trying to gain or lose weight by fad diets.

CHAPTER SUMMARY

- In order to function properly, we need protein, carbohydrates, fat, vitamins, minerals, water, and fiber.
- Protein is vital for the growth and repair of the body. Meat, eggs, and milk provide complete protein. Grains and vegetables can be combined with other foods to form complete protein.
- Carbohydrates include sugar and starches. They provide about 50 percent of the body's energy needs. They are also required for processing fat.
- Fats provide a source of energy, they insulate parts of the body, and they are vital to various chemical processes. Most Americans eat too much fat.
- Vitamins are necessary for triggering various chemical reactions in the body. Only tiny amounts are needed.
- Minerals help form body tissues and various chemical substances.
- Water has no nutritional value, but it is one of the most important food components. Fiber, too, is a nonnutrient, but it is a necessary aid to digestion.
- The simplest way to plan a balanced diet is to choose adequate amounts of food from each of the four basic food groups.
- The four basic food groups are the meat group,

milk and milk products, fruits and vegetables, and bread and cereals.

- There are two types of obesity. Some people have a larger number of fat cells than normal. Others have larger fat cells than normal.
- The direct cause of overweight is eating more calories than the body uses. The only way to lose weight is to consume fewer calories than you use. To gain weight, you must eat high-calorie, high-nutrient foods. The most successful weight-loss or weight-gain programs combine exercise with changes in eating patterns.
- In order to change your eating habits, you must first identify them. Keep a written record of your eating behavior. When you discover the cues to your eating, you can find ways to remove or avoid them.
- Fad diets don't work, and some are dangerous. They may provide a short-term loss or gain, but they usually don't produce long-term weight loss or gain. Some commercial groups have helped people gain or lose weight, but your motivation is the most important factor in your weight loss or gain. People with serious eating disorders need professional help.

DO YOU REMEMBER?

Give brief definitions of these terms:

amino acids   incomplete protein   carbohydrate   fiber
complete protein   glucose   cholesterol   calorie

THINK AND DISCUSS

1. What's wrong with the belief that athletes should consume excessive amounts of protein to give them strength?
2. What ways can you suggest for parents to teach their children healthy eating habits?
3. Why do you think that many teenagers tend to have poor eating habits?
4. What kinds of foods would you serve at a party where many of the guests are trying to lose weight?
5. Certain foods, such as diet soft drinks and potato chips, probably do more harm than good. Why do you think people buy such foods? Should such foods be banned? Why or why not?
6. Why do many people tend to gain weight during the winter and lose weight during the summer?
7. As time goes on, Americans are buying more processed foods and fewer fresh foods. Why do you think this is so? How do you think this affects us?

FOLLOW-UP

1. Obtain a copy of the diet recommended for teenagers by a commercial weight-loss group. Assess the diet according to the RDAs and the calorie content.
2. Clip out newspaper and magazine ads for weight-loss devices and diets. Display the advertisements in your class and discuss the promises they make.
3. Find out about the carbohydrate-loading system used by runners and other athletes for extra energy during a race or game. Write a report on this system.
4. Make a poster of the human body that illustrates the roles played by various vitamins and minerals.
5. Find out more about the hazards of obesity. Describe your findings to your class.
6. Monitor your television for one hour before dinner. Write down the kinds of food commercials that appear and the possible reasons that they are shown at that time.
7. Some people believe that large doses of vitamin C can prevent or cure the common cold. Find out more about this theory and write a report on your findings.
8. Make a poster that illustrates your favorite fast-food meal. Include a chart that lists the nutritional content of the foods. Display the poster in your classroom and discuss what should be added or subtracted to make the meal more nutritious.

CHAPTER 7

Caring for Your Body

After reading this chapter, you should be able to answer these questions:

1. How can you keep your teeth and gums healthy?
2. Can you protect your eyes from injury and eyestrain? How?
3. How do you choose the skin care products that are right for you?
4. Why should fair-skinned people avoid overexposure to the sun?
5. What should you know about buying shoes?

The way you look says a lot about you. It shows whether or not you care about yourself. Caring for your body begins with good nutrition and regular exercise. But in addition, certain parts need special attention. This chapter focuses on some parts of the body that require that special care: the teeth, eyes, skin, hair, and feet.

Some people take better care of their cars than they do of their own bodies. They know that if a car is neglected it will develop problems. So they have it serviced regularly, check tires, brakes, and other parts, and get it fixed when problems occur.

The human body, too, will develop problems if it is neglected. When basic health care routines are overlooked, teeth may be lost, skin permanently scarred, vision impaired, or feet damaged. Yet there are people who, while willing to spend the necessary time and money on their cars, don't bother to pay similar attention to themselves. And unlike a car, the human body cannot be traded in for a newer model.

Caring for your body is, then, a lifelong responsibility. The habits you develop now will affect the way you look and feel for years to come. If you understand your body, you can prevent many health problems. Brushing and flossing your teeth, bathing your body, and shampooing your hair should be parts of your regular routine. You already know a lot about basic hygiene, but now that you're a teenager, you must add to your knowledge about how to care for your body.

Another part of taking responsibility for your body is watching for signs of trouble. Toothaches, blurred vision, skin infections, and corns are signals that special help is needed.

But problems such as these can be avoided if you get regular checkups and if you make caring for your body a daily habit. Your main concern should be preventing health problems, not taking care of them after they occur. If preventive care becomes second nature to you, you will look and feel your best for years to come.

SECTION **1**　**Care of the Teeth**

Your teeth perform a variety of tasks. Their most important job is to prepare food for digestion. They tear food apart, cut off small pieces, and grind them into bits. Teeth are also needed for certain speech sounds. And teeth affect the way you look. Healthy teeth contribute to an attractive, youthful appearance.

Although dental disease can be prevented, almost all of the people in the United States have some cavities. By your own efforts you can prevent most tooth decay and gum disease. Routinely brushing and flossing your teeth are the most important things you can do. You can also eat right, watch for signs of dental problems, and visit your dentist regularly.

The importance of caring for your teeth cannot be overstressed. Neglecting dental care can mean unnecessary discomfort and expense—and eventually, it can cause the loss of your teeth. In America nearly half of all people over 20 wear a bridge or a denture of some sort to replace lost teeth. Yet, with proper care, tooth loss does not have to happen.

Tooth Decay

The outside of the tooth is covered by *enamel,* which provides a very strong, protective covering. In fact, the only substance occurring naturally that is harder than tooth enamel is a diamond. However, despite its hardness, tooth enamel can be destroyed. When this happens, *cavities* develop. As a cavity enlarges, it can destroy the hard, outer layers of the tooth and

reach the *pulp,* which is the soft, inner part. Because the pulp contains sensitive nerve endings, tooth decay can be painful.

Cavities are caused when the bacteria normally found in the mouth interact with sugar. The bacteria form a thin, colorless layer on teeth. This layer is known as *plaque.* The plaque turns sugar into acid that dissolves tooth enamel to start a cavity. This happens quickly. The worst damage to the teeth occurs during the first 20 minutes after sweet foods are eaten.

Your Diet and Tooth Decay

What you eat and when you eat it can determine whether or not you have tooth decay. Sugary snacks are especially harmful. Soft drinks and candy bars are not the only culprits. The kinds of sugar found in honey and raisins can also cause cavities. Sugar is also found in many processed foods that do not taste especially sweet. But sticky, sweet-tasting foods are the most damaging to your teeth because they are most likely to stick to tooth surfaces.

How often you eat is also important. Eating sweets between meals increases the number of times acid attacks your teeth each day. The amount of time teeth are exposed to acid is increased by sweets that stay in the mouth for a long time, such as cough drops and sugared gum. One solution is to stop eating between meals. Or you could choose snacks such as milk, yogurt, and fresh fruits and vegetables.

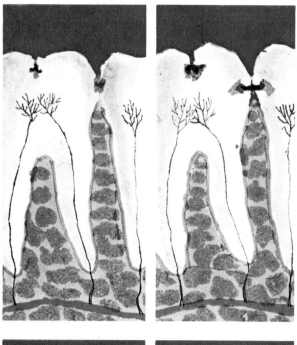

Figure 7.1 The progress of tooth decay. *Top left:* A cavity develops in the hard, outer layers of the tooth. *Top right:* The cavity enlarges. *Bottom left:* The pulp decays and nerve endings become diseased. *Bottom right:* The tooth is finally removed.

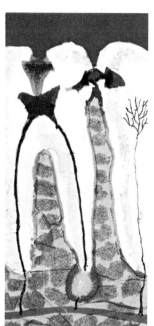
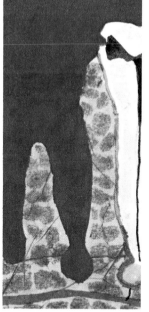

tant work of removing plaque is done by the toothbrush and dental floss.

Brushing your teeth removes some of the invisible plaque that sticks to your teeth. The American Dental Association recommends a brush with a straight handle and soft, rounded bristles that form a flat brushing surface. Be sure that the end of the brush is small enough to reach all the surfaces of your teeth. Replace the toothbrush when it looks worn. If the bristles have been worn down and spread out, they are no longer able to remove plaque effectively.

When brushing your teeth, use a gentle scrubbing motion, and be careful not to miss any of the surfaces of your teeth. Brush the outside and inside of your teeth, along with all

Figure 7.2 Sweets and snacks containing excessive sugar are a primary cause of tooth decay.

Cleaning Your Teeth

Tooth decay occurs when people do not keep their teeth clean. Luckily, toothbrushes and dental floss are all you really need to keep your teeth clean, and they are inexpensive and easy to use. Toothpaste is some help, but the impor-

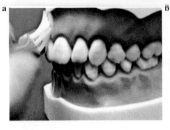
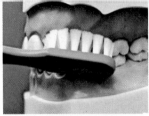
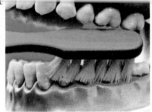

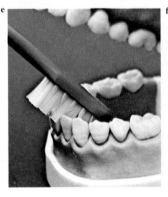
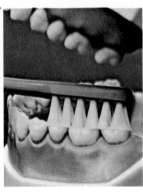

Figure 7.3 To clean the outside surfaces of all teeth and the inside surfaces of the back teeth, position the brush at the junction between the teeth and gums (a). Use short, back-and-forth strokes. Do the outer surfaces first (b, c). Then do the inner surfaces (d, e) in the same manner. To clean the inner surface of the upper front teeth, hold the brush vertically. Use several gentle, back-and-forth strokes over gums and teeth. Brush back and forth on biting surfaces (f). After brushing, rinse the mouth vigorously. Use dental floss to get into the crevices between teeth.

the chewing surfaces. Brush your tongue too. It will help to freshen your breath. But be gentle with your gums; hard brushing can actually make them recede.

Tooth decay often begins in areas that cannot be reached by toothbrushes. Dental floss can reach such places. This soft, waxed or unwaxed thread is gently pulled back and forth to clean between the teeth and under the gum line. Then the mouth is rinsed out with water to remove the loosened particles. Once you learn how, flossing takes only a few minutes. It should be done at least once a day.

Mouthwashes

Mouthwashes do not remove plaque, so they cannot prevent tooth decay. The best they can do is to temporarily freshen breath by scenting it. Extremely bad breath is a symptom that something is wrong, such as a throat infection or indigestion. Lack of cleanliness in the mouth can also cause breath odor, as can plaque, tooth decay, and gum disease. Since breath odor results from these problems, it makes sense to attack the causes of the bad breath rather than the bad breath itself.

The breath odor some people notice when they wake up is due to bacteria that acted on food particles in their mouths overnight. Brushing and flossing correct this situation, but a mouthwash does not. Even though a mouthwash may destroy some bacteria, the number of bacteria quickly returns to normal. Rinsing your mouth with water dislodges food particles as effectively as rinsing your mouth with mouthwash.

Fluoride

Fluoride, a substance that is found in drinking water and in many foods, helps the tooth surface to resist decay. It is especially helpful while children's teeth are forming. However, it cannot undo tooth damage that has already taken place.

When enough fluoride is not present naturally in drinking water, it can be added to a community's water supply. Fluoride can be applied directly to teeth by a dentist or dental hygienist. Fluoride tablets can also be used under a dentist's supervision. In addition, many types of toothpastes that contain fluoride are available.

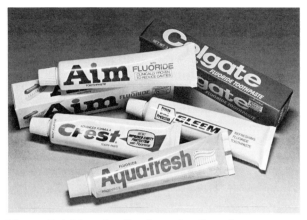

Figure 7.4 Most leading brands of toothpaste contain fluoride, a chemical that helps teeth resist decay.

Gum Disease

Periodontal disease, which affects the gums and the other structures that support the teeth, is the main cause of tooth loss in people over 35. Like tooth decay, periodontal disease is caused by plaque. In the first stage of gum disease, the plaque causes swollen, bleeding gums. Gradually, plaque builds up at the base of the teeth, forming a hard deposit known as *calculus,* or *tartar.* Then the inflamed gum pulls away from the teeth, and the plaque and calculus attack the newly exposed parts of the teeth. The bone that supports the teeth becomes infected, and the teeth loosen and eventually fall out.

If the teeth are out of position in the first place, the chance of periodontal disease increases. This is because the bad alignment of the teeth makes them hard to clean, encouraging the formation of plaque and calculus.

Good general health can help your gums to resist infection. Daily brushing and flossing and good eating habits are important too. You can also watch your gums for warning signs. In its first stages, periodontal disease causes no pain. But remember that bleeding gums are not normal. Even if your gums do not hurt, the bleeding is a sign that your gums are inflamed. You should see a dentist immediately.

At later stages, when gums are swollen and pus has formed between the teeth, treatment becomes more difficult. If teeth have loosened and bone has been lost by the time you take action, there may be little that can be done to save the affected teeth.

Some kinds of gum disease affect the bone very quickly. But regular dental checkups can help you to stop gum disease in time.

Poorly Aligned Teeth

A dentist can also help you to make sure that your teeth are lined up in their proper positions. When teeth are not located in their normal positions, people can have problems chewing their food. Also, irregularly placed teeth look less attractive than teeth that are properly aligned. They make it hard to keep the mouth clean, which can eventually lead to gum disease.

Some kinds of tooth-placement irregularities are caused by loss of teeth due to tooth decay. And sometimes the teeth in the upper and lower jaws do not meet correctly because of inherited irregularities. In both cases a dentist can correct the irregularities, usually with braces that slowly move the teeth into the proper position. Such work is done by an *orthodontist,* a dentist trained to treat problems with tooth location.

Visits to the Dentist

You should visit your dentist as often as he or she tells you to. Some people need checkups once a year, some every six months, and some more frequently.

Some dentists are better than others. A busy office does not necessarily indicate a good dentist. A dentist who always has patients waiting, and who spends little time with each one, may be trying to do too much. As a result, she or he may not give you the attention and treatment you need.

A good dentist will take the time to explain your treatment, showing you the x-rays and discussing the cost of your treatment. Your dentist should provide good care at reasonable cost and should remove teeth only as a last resort.

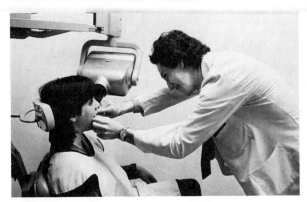

Figure 7.5 A dentist's job is twofold: to prevent dental problems and to repair damage when it occurs.

tal work is done. When a cavity is being filled, an anesthetic may be used to deaden the nerves around the tooth being worked on. After the filling is completed, the dentist will make sure that your upper and lower teeth bite together properly.

Your dentist can do much to improve the condition of your teeth. But he or she cannot provide the daily care that your teeth need. That's your responsibility. All it takes is a few minutes of careful brushing and flossing each day. Why risk getting cavities or losing teeth when dental care is so easy?

A good dentist is also interested in preventing dental problems rather than merely repairing damage after it has been done. The dentist or a hygienist should show you how to brush and floss your teeth and should carefully clean your teeth. The dentist, not the hygienist, should examine your teeth.

A good dentist does everything possible to make sure you are comfortable while your den-

CHECK YOUR UNDERSTANDING

1. What is plaque?
2. What kinds of foods are most likely to cause tooth decay? Why?
3. List the causes of bad breath.
4. Explain how gum disease develops.
5. What problems can be caused by poorly aligned teeth?

SECTION **2** **Care of the Eyes**

Your eyes provide you with most of the information you have about the world around you. They are constantly sending messages to your brain, enabling you to appreciate shapes, colors, distances—everything within your range of vision. You don't have to care for your eyes to the same extent that you care for your teeth. They have their own protective equipment and can keep themselves moist and clean. But you do need to protect them from injury. And you should get treatment for vision problems or eye infections.

Avoiding Eyestrain

Straining your eyes does not damage them, but it can cause discomfort. Along with red, watery eyes, headaches and dizziness can also result from eyestrain. You can avoid such discomforts by taking a few simple precautions.

Scheduling your homework so that you do not need to study for many hours at a stretch will keep you from feeling bleary-eyed. Reading in a well-lighted place is more comfortable than straining to read in dim light. When writing, you should have the light come from your left if you are right-handed and from your right if you are left-handed. That way, you will avoid working in your own shadow.

To avoid eyestrain while watching television, sit at least 2 meters (6 feet) from the set. Never watch television in a darkened room, and avoid long periods of viewing.

Too much glare can cause eyestrain. The eye responds automatically to bright light by narrowing the pupil. This is usually enough protection from sunlight. But if the sun is very bright, you can wear sunglasses to protect your eyes.

When you shop for sunglasses, look in a mirror to find out whether you can see your eyes through the lenses. If you can, the sunglasses are not dark enough. Sunglasses that go lighter or darker according to the amount of light are now available. To be effective, the lenses should be very dark when in bright sunlight.

Never wear sunglasses at night. Making a habit of doing so can damage your ability to see in dim light.

Avoiding Injury

Every year thousands of Americans suffer eye injuries that damage their vision. Sports and recreational activities alone account for more than 35,000 eye injuries a year that need hospital treatment. Yet the vast majority of these injuries could have been prevented if the victims had taken the proper precautions.

Rubbing your eye when you get a speck of dirt in it can injure it. You may scratch the *cornea,* which is the transparent layer of skin covering your eye. Instead of rubbing it, blink rapidly, and let the tear wash the object away. If something becomes embedded in the cornea, see a doctor rather than trying to remove it yourself.

Always point aerosol sprays away from your eyes. They may contain harmful chemicals. If a household chemical splashes into your eye, wash the eye in cool water immediately and call a doctor.

The sports activities that carry the greatest risk of eye injury are baseball and softball, followed by the racket sports—tennis, badminton, squash, and racketball. Players can be injured by a fast-moving ball or by a bat or racket. You should use safety eyewear when taking part in such activities. Lightweight, attractive safety glasses, eyeguards, and visors are available from most sports shops and some opticians.

Safety eyewear should also be worn when you are using power tools, trimming shrubs, spraying pesticides, paint, or other chemicals, or using a hammer and chisel.

Common sense can help you to avoid eye

Talking Point

Visual Display Terminals and Eyestrain

When desktop computers first became popular several years ago, some people worried that radiation from the visual display terminals (VDTs) might be harmful. There were suggestions that these machines might cause cataracts, miscarriages, and eyestrain. Research since then has found no conclusive evidence that VDTs cause cataracts or miscarriages. They do, however, contribute indirectly to eyestrain.

People who work at computer terminals for long periods of time sometimes suffer from headaches, blurred vision, and burning and itching eyes. The symptoms develop because VDT users stare constantly at a point 2 feet ahead of them. This strains the eyes muscles that are accustomed to more movement and to working at greater distances. Poor lighting and unsuitable furniture may also contribute to eyestrain and muscle fatigue.

To avoid eyestrain when using a VDT, you should reduce glare by positioning room lights so that they don't reflect in the screen. Also use shades or drapes to screen out light, and turn up the brightness of the VDT screen until it is about three times brighter than the room lighting.

Use an adjustable chair and terminal stand so that you can view the screen from a comfortable angle. The screen should be 14 to 20 inches from your eyes and slightly below eye level. If you plan to work at the computer for several hours, take a break and do something else for 15 minutes every 2 hours to give your eyes a rest. Be certain to see an eye doctor if you think you have a serious eye problem.

injury. Actions such as putting on eye make-up in a moving car are risky and foolish. Thinking about the possible consequences of what you do should help you to be more cautious.

Common Vision Problems

The human eye works much like a camera. An image enters an opening in the front of the eye and passes through a lens. The lens focuses the image on a "screen" (the *retina*) on the back wall of the eyeball.

But many people have eyeballs that are slightly longer or shorter than normal. When an eyeball is too short, the light rays focus behind the retina. This makes the person *farsighted*, which means that she or he sees things at a distance more easily than things that are nearby. A *nearsighted* person sees nearby objects better than those at a distance. Nearsightedness occurs when an eyeball is too long, causing the light rays to focus in front of the retina rather than directly on it.

Astigmatism affects vision at all distances. It is caused when the shape of the cornea or lens is irregular. Because of the distorted shape, light rays do not focus in one spot on the retina. As a result, vision is blurred.

Another common vision problem is *color blindness*. About 8 out of every 100 males, but fewer than 1 out of every 100 females, are color-blind. Most people who are color-blind have trouble telling red and green apart. There is no cure for color blindness, but it is not a serious handicap.

Eyeglasses and Contact Lenses

Glasses or contact lenses can correct many vision problems. They solve focusing problems by bending light rays to bring them into focus. A corrective lens that is curved in exactly the right way causes the light rays to focus directly on the retina.

Many people dislike wearing eyeglasses. They may feel unattractive in them or find them a nuisance. More and more people are turning to contact lenses as an alternative to glasses.

Contact lenses are round, plastic lenses held in place over the cornea by the natural tension of the tear layer on the surface of the eye. There are several types of lenses. *Hard lenses* are durable and easy to care for, but they may be uncomfortable at first. *Soft lenses* are more comfortable but require more care. Some soft

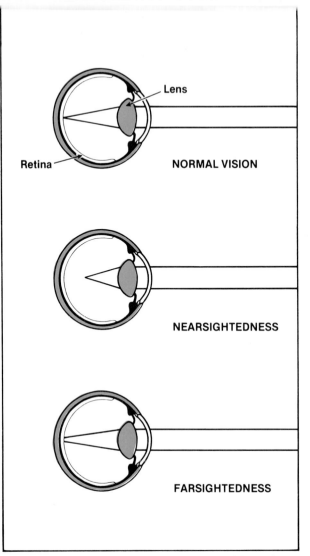

Figure 7.6 In order to produce normal vision, the eye's lens must focus light rays directly on the retina. If the light rays focus in front of the retina, the result is nearsightedness. The opposite problem, farsightedness, occurs when light rays focus beyond the retina.

contact lenses are known as *extended-wear lenses*. They can be left in the eye for more than a day. Some people, however, cannot wear contact lenses because they have allergies or because they live or work in a smoky or dusty environment.

Contact lenses do have certain advantages over eyeglasses. They improve the peripheral vision—the ability to see to each side—better

One of these drops of water is really a Bausch & Lomb soft lens. Can you find it?

Figure 7.7 Soft contact lenses, a relatively recent invention, contain a high proportion of water. They are easier to wear than hard contact lenses, but they must be sterilized frequently to prevent eye infection. (Note: The real lens is to the right of the letter *b*.)

than glasses do. They also make participation in certain sports easier.

However, they do have some drawbacks. Contact lenses are harder to keep clean than glasses. Hard lenses must be cleaned with a special solution every night, and soft lenses must be sterilized. Contact lenses can also cause eye injuries if they are left in too long. They reduce the amount of oxygen that reaches the eye, which, over time, can cause the eye to lose its natural fluid. When that happens, the cornea can be scratched by the lens or by dust particles.

Although advertisements claim that extended-wear lenses can be worn for up to 30 days, some doctors say that they shouldn't be left in for more than a week at a time. In fact, some doctors advise against extended-wear lenses altogether because of reports of eye damage. If you do decide to wear contact lenses, make sure they are prescribed and fitted by a specialist.

Eye Examinations

Even if you think your eyes are fine, you should have them checked periodically. Eye specialists not only test your vision, but they also look for eye diseases such as *glaucoma*.

Glaucoma is a disease in which pressure builds up in the fluid in the back part of the eye. In one form of the disease, pressure builds up so slowly that people do not realize that the delicate structures within the eye are being damaged. When treatment is begun too late, the pressure destroys the nerve that connects the eye to the brain, causing blindness. However, if treatment begins early, sight can be preserved for many years.

Sometimes poor vision is due to *cataracts*. A cataract is the clouding of the transparent lens behind the pupil. Usually this lens is clear, but it can gradually become cloudy, causing vision to worsen. Usually a cataract gets worse gradually until surgery becomes necessary. In most cases an operation will completely cure a cataract. Both cataracts and glaucoma occur most often in old people and are uncommon in teenagers.

Your eye specialist will tell you how often to have your eyes checked. Do not ignore this advice, since your eyes can change in a few months.

Eye Infections

If your eyes are sore or red, something is wrong. You may be suffering just from eyestrain, but if the soreness persists, you may have an infection.

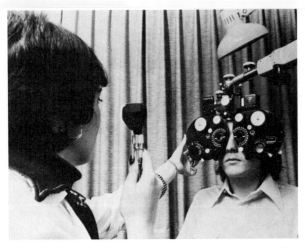

Figure 7.8 An eye specialist can detect changes in your vision and check for early signs of eye disease.

One fairly common eye infection is called a *sty*. A sty is an infection of the root of one of the eyelashes. Sties can be painful, but they are not usually serious. If you get a sty, do not touch it. It will open and then heal by itself. If you continue to get sties, or if a sty continues to be annoying, see a doctor.

You can minimize your chances of getting eye infections by following some common-sense rules. Never share towels or use someone else's make-up. Wash your hands carefully before you put on eye make-up. If your eyes do become infected, keep your hands away from them. If you must touch an infected eye, wash your hands thoroughly both before and after doing so.

CHECK YOUR UNDERSTANDING

1. Give five ways to avoid eyestrain.
2. When should safety eyewear be worn?
3. Explain the causes of nearsightedness, farsightedness, and astigmatism.
4. List three ways to minimize your chances of getting an eye infection.

SECTION **3** **Care of the Skin and Hair**

The skin is the largest organ in the body. With the glands, blood vessels, hairs, and nails that are found in it, one person's skin weighs about 4.5 kilograms (10 pounds). Like the other organs, such as the stomach and heart, skin is made up of several kinds of tissues that work together to perform the organ's functions.

One important function of the skin is to protect the body from injury and infection. The outer layer of the skin, the *epidermis*, provides a rugged, waterproof covering. The epidermis keeps out bacteria and other organisms that could cause disease, and it prevents internal organs and systems from drying out.

The epidermis also protects the body by producing skin coloring. *Melanin* is the substance that provides the coloring in the skin. Melanin protects the body from the harmful effects of the sun. A sun tan is caused by the darkening of the melanin that exists in the skin and the production of more melanin in order to provide extra protection. People born with darker skin have more built-in protection from the sun than lighter-skinned people do.

Most of the skin's work is done in the *dermis*, the layer below the epidermis. Structures located in this layer sense pressure, pain, heat, and cold and regulate the temperature of the body. Sweat glands, oil glands, and hair roots are located in the stretchable tissue of the dermis.

Caring for Your Skin

Your skin looks better when your general health is good. By eating a balanced diet, exercising regularly, and getting enough sleep, you will help your skin to look its best.

An important part of caring for your skin is knowing the best way to keep it clean. The best method for you will depend upon your skin

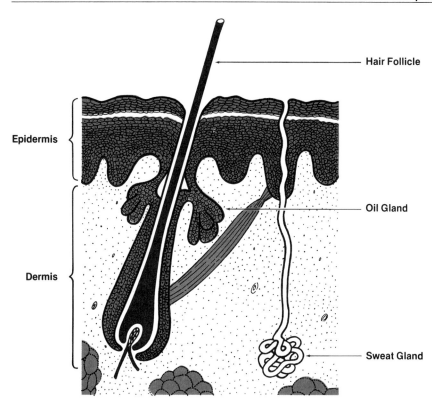

Hair Follicle

Epidermis

Oil Gland

Dermis

Figure 7.9 A cross section of the skin. While the epidermis provides protection, most of the skin's work is done in the dermis.

Sweat Gland

type, which is oily, dry, or a combination of the two. Your skin type can change with the seasons and as you grow.

The easiest and cheapest way to keep skin clean is to wash it with soap and water. If you have very dry skin, however, soap may cause further dryness. Some people with dry skin prefer to use cleansing lotions instead of soap. Others use soap, then a moisturizer, which adds oils to the skin. Some people with oily skin find that occasional use of a facial mask is an effective addition to soap and water for cleaning out the pores.

If you do use soap, be aware that any soap will keep you clean. Differences in the dyes, perfumes, and other substances added to soaps do not accomplish much. Usually, the deodorant ability claimed by a soap is just a perfume to cover up odors. Such a fragrance lasts only a few minutes. Oils and creams are also sometimes added to soap. However, since the soap is meant to remove oils from the skin, expecting a soap to add extra oils is contradictory. Anyway, the extra oils are washed away when you rinse the soap from your skin.

Some Common Skin Problems

Dry skin is often a problem during the winter months. The combination of cold winds, warm indoor temperatures, and low humidity can cause the outer layer of skin to lose moisture. The skin may also become dry and rough when too-frequent washing removes the skin's protective oil.

Because of the increased production of oil glands during puberty, teenagers are more likely to be troubled by oily skin than by dry skin. Gently washing the skin as often as necessary and avoiding creamy cosmetics can help.

Acne Increased production of body oil during puberty often leads to *acne*, which consists of eruptions on the skin, especially the face. A skin eruption is caused when a hair follicle, the cavity containing the root of a hair, is blocked. Layers of dead cells combine with body oil and bacteria to plug the hair follicle. When a plugged follicle is exposed to the air, it darkens because of the melanin in it. The result is a blackhead. A plugged follicle can also become

How to...

Treat Acne

Four out of five teenagers suffer from some form of acne at some time. In most cases, the condition is mild and can be treated at home. Here are some things you can do to treat occasional mild outbreaks:

- Wash your face gently several times a day. Don't scrub your face, and don't squeeze your pimples—this might cause a worse infection and could lead to scars.
- If you use make-up, be sure to remove every trace of it at the end of each day.
- Use a skin cleanser containing salicylic acid. Salicylic acid removes oil and helps dissolve pimples. You can find these cleansers at your drugstore. Ask the pharmacist to help you, or read the labels on the containers.
- If necessary, use a stronger cleanser that contains benzoyl peroxide. This antibacterial agent helps clear up pimples by drying them out. It should not be used too frequently, however, because it can cause excessive drying of the skin.

If over-the-counter remedies don't work, you might want to consult a dermatologist, who is a physician specializing in skin disorders. A dermatologist might prescribe an antibiotic or a stronger cleanser than those available over the counter.

inflamed, causing a pimple. Consult the box on page 124 for a description of acne treatments.

Boils are infections caused by bacteria. Because the bacteria can spread to other people, people with boils should not prepare or serve food. Boils generally occur where the skin is rubbed or irritated. The back of the neck and the armpits are common places for boils to appear. Small boils generally come to a head and break, after which the area should be covered until it has healed. Large, painful boils should be treated by a doctor.

Warts A *wart* is a small growth caused by a virus. The most common place for warts to appear is on the hands. If untreated, they can multiply and spread from one person to another. Most warts are not serious and they eventually go away without being treated. A wart that causes irritation or that continues to grow should be examined by a doctor.

Sun Damage You might think that a sun tan looks healthy, but too much exposure to the sun's rays has been linked to premature aging of the skin and to skin cancer.

Fair-skinned people run the greatest risk of developing skin cancer. Blacks, whose skin has more melanin, rarely get it. If you have fair-skin, you can take certain preventive measures. Limit the amount of time you spend exposed to the sun. Just slip a shirt on over your bathing suit, or move into a shady spot after you've been in the sun for a while. You can also help protect your skin by using a sunscreen containing the chemical PABA. Products that contain PABA are usually rated according to their sun-protection factor, or SPF number. For example, if you use a sunscreen rated SPF 15, it will take 15 times longer for your skin to show redness than it would without the sunscreen.

The Effect of Cosmetics

Some people use cosmetics to enhance their appearance; others like to protect their skin from the sun, pollution, and infections. Teenagers are generally advised to choose water-based skin products rather than oil-based ones because their skin tends to produce enough oil. They might find that heavy make-up bases, greasy sun tan lotions, and certain chemicals can cause skin problems.

If a particular cosmetic irritates your skin, it may be because you are sensitive to one of its ingredients. Try switching to another brand. Another way to avoid irritation, as well as infection, is to make a point of never borrowing someone else's make-up or lending anyone yours. You should also wash your hands before

Figure 7.10 While a sun tan may look healthy, sunbathing is not. Especially in fair-skinned people, overexposure to the sun can cause painful sunburn, premature aging, and skin cancer.

applying make-up and avoid using saliva, which contains harmful bacteria, to moisten cosmetics. Replace any make-up that is more than one year old.

Care of the Hair

No part of you grows faster than your hair. Brushing your hair stimulates your scalp and helps your hair grow. Brushing too vigorously, however, can damage your hair, especially if the bristles of your brush are made of synthetic fibers rather than natural ones.

Shampooing once or twice a week is usually enough to keep the scalp and hair clean. But air pollution or unusually oily hair may make more frequent shampooing necessary. Some teenagers need to wash their hair every day.

There are many different kinds of shampoos from which to choose. In general, an inexpensive shampoo can do as good a job as an expensive one. The main ingredients in shampoos are water, detergent, and fragrance. Although all shampoos are very similar, you may find that one brand does a better job of cleaning your type of hair and scalp than another. It's a good idea to experiment with different brands. Many people use conditioners after shampooing, to avoid dryness, dullness, or tangling. Conditioners work by coating the hair so it feels thicker and smoother, but too much conditioner can make the hair look greasy.

Some people also have problems with dandruff. *Dandruff* is formed when dead cells from the outer layer of the scalp combine with the natural oils. Regular shampooing usually removes both some of the oiliness and the dandruff itself.

Hair dyes, permanents, and straighteners contain harsh chemicals that can damage your hair. Some hair dyes have also been linked to cancer. Because there are many openings in your scalp for hair follicles and glands, chemicals from dyes can easily enter the bloodstream there. It is probably wiser, therefore, to avoid hair dyes until more is known about their effects. If you do decide to dye your hair or to have a permanent, go to a professional who is trained in the use of these chemicals.

Deodorants and Antiperspirants

During puberty, sweat and oil glands begin to produce more secretions. The extra sweat and oil make it necessary to wash more often. Also, some sweat glands, the *apocrine glands*, become active for the first time during puberty. They produce perspiration that contains small amounts of organic matter than can be broken

Figure 7.11 Gentle brushing keeps your hair looking attractive and helps remove loose dirt. But brushing too vigorously, especially with synthetic bristles, can damage your hair.

down by bacteria. The bacterial action causes an increase in perspiration odor.

Daily washing is the main way to control body odor and limit the growth of bacteria on the skin. Some people also use deodorants and antiperspirants. These preparations cannot be used as substitutes for bathing, but they can help to mask or control body odor and reduce perspiration flow. A *deodorant* contains chemicals that control the amount of odor that is produced or cover up the odor with fragrance. An *antiperspirant* does the same things a deodorant does, and it also somewhat reduces the amount of perspiration that is produced.

CHECK YOUR UNDERSTANDING

1. What is the function of melanin?
2. Explain the cause of the skin eruptions that occur in acne.
3. What are two hazards of overexposure to the sun?
4. Why does perspiration become more of a problem during the teenage years? What is the difference between antiperspirants and deodorants?

SECTION **4**   **Care of the Feet**

Your feet work hard for you, bearing your weight and accepting the bumps and jolts of all the movements you make. An average teenager takes 18,000 steps a day, a challenging job for the 26 bones and 13 muscles in each foot. The foot is a complicated structure. Many things can go wrong with it. In order for you to keep your feet healthy, you should be aware of the common foot problems and know what causes them.

To avoid foot troubles, you should give your feet some regular attention. You should keep them clean and dry and keep the nails trimmed. Buying shoes that fit properly and that are suitable for a particular activity is very important.

Basic Foot Care

Feet need regular washing because they pick up more dirt and dust than other parts of the body do and because they often perspire heavily. Like the underarms and the palms of the hands, feet contain sweat glands that are active at lower temperatures than those elsewhere in the body. These glands also produce more sweat in response to emotional stress. Enclosed shoes can increase perspiration and odor. Open shoes can help, as can absorbent socks or stockings. Some people also use foot powder to absorb perspiration.

Starting each day with clean, dry shoes is good for your feet. Try not to wear the same shoes two days in a row. Alternating pairs gives your shoes a chance to dry out, which helps them to last longer. If possible, vary the height of the heels you wear. It's good for the muscles in your feet and legs.

Choosing Shoes

When buying shoes, you should pay more attention to fit and comfort than to fashionable appearance. Even one pair of shoes that fits poorly can give you foot problems that last for years. Good fit is especially important if your feet are still growing.

If possible, buy shoes during the afternoon, since your feet tend to swell during the day. Wear the same kind of socks or stockings that you plan to wear with the shoes. Try to find shoes that are shaped the way your feet are. The widest part of the shoe and the widest part of your foot should be at the same place. There should be a small space between the end of your longest toe and the inside end of the shoe. The heel of the shoe should fit your heel snugly. It should not slip up and down when you bend your foot.

A new shoe should be comfortable. If a long, painful breaking-in period is necessary, you probably have bought the wrong shoes.

Choose shoes to match the activities in which you participate. Dressy shoes may be fine for special occasions but hard on your feet when you are doing a great deal of walking. Sturdy shoes and good fit are especially important for sports. Choose running shoes that cushion your foot and support the heel and arch. Look for ski boots and skates that fit well. Proper fit will improve your technique and help you to avoid injury.

Figure 7.12 Whether you are buying shoes, boots, or skates, fit and comfort should be more important to you than fashionable appearance.

Some Common Foot Problems

The majority of foot problems are caused by poorly fitting shoes. Women tend to have many more foot problems than men, mainly because women's shoe fashions are more extreme than men's are. Narrow toes, high heels, and platform shoes can all cause painful problems and, in some cases, permanent damage.

Blisters *Blisters* are uncomfortable reminders that skin has been injured or irritated. Shoes that rub are usually the cause. Usually, the best treatment for a blister is to leave it alone since the fluid in the blister provides an extra layer of protection for the injured area. If a blister does break, clean the area with an antiseptic and cover it with a sterile bandage.

Ingrown Toenails An *ingrown toenail* develops when the corner of a nail that was cut too short grows into the skin at the side of the nail. Shoes that are too narrow, and that crowd the toes together, increase the risk of ingrown toenails. The condition can be painful, and there is a risk of infection. If swelling or infection occurs, you should get medical help.

Corns and Calluses *Corns* and *calluses* result from the friction and pressure of poorly fitting shoes. Repeated rubbing causes extra layers of skin to build up. A corn is a round growth that feels painful when pressure is applied to it. A callus, which is larger than a corn, forms a hard, thickened area. Corns can develop when small areas, such as a toe, are repeatedly irritated. Calluses develop when the friction is over a larger area, such as the ball of the foot. You can remove simple corns and calluses by applying a medicated disk, covered by a cushioned pad. *Never* try to cut a corn or callus. You might cause infection. If the discomfort continues, see a doctor.

Bunions A *bunion* is a swelling in the joint at the base of the big toe. As it enlarges, it pushes the toes out of position, which can be very painful. Wearing shoes that fit is the best way to prevent bunions. If a bunion is allowed to develop, surgery may be necessary.

Athlete's Foot Tiny fungi are responsible for the condition known as *athlete's foot*. They cause red, itchy rashes and dry, scaly areas between the toes and on the sole of the foot. Athlete's foot is not limited to athletes. Anyone

How to...

Select Shoes for Sports

It used to be simpler—and cheaper—to buy a pair of sports shoes. You just went to a shoe store and picked out a pair of sneakers. Today, buying a pair of sports shoes is quite confusing. Before you can even try on a pair of shoes, you have to answer a whole series of questions: What sport are the shoes going to be used for? How many times a week do you plan to engage in it? If you're buying running shoes, how many miles a week do you expect to run? What kind of a surface will you run on? It's important to buy the right sports shoes to avoid discomfort and painful injuries such as knee injures and shin splints.

Today's sports shoes are designed specifically for certain sports. Running shoes have highly padded soles and specially designed heels. They are built for forward motion only, not for side-to-side movements. Court shoes, used for tennis and basketball, usually have less padding on the soles and are built low to the ground. They have a lot of lateral reinforcement to protect the feet because these sports involve a lot of sudden turning, pivoting, and side-to-side movements. Aerobics shoes are built to support both running and quick-turning movements.

Choosing a running shoe is more complicated than choosing a shoe for most other sports because more than 80 shoe manufacturers produce 300 to 400 models of running shoes, each of them with features you may or may not need. You don't need a pair of expensive racing flats, for example, if you don't run in marathons.

The most important feature of a running shoe—of any sports shoe, in fact—is its sole. The average runner lands on his or her feet 1,500 times a mile with a force three to six times his or her body weight. This is enough force to bruise bones and muscles and even crush blood vessels. Even if you are a very casual runner, you need a thick, soft-soled shoe to cushion that impact.

But do you need biokinetic soles, air wedges, poster cradles, diagonal roll bars, or thermoplastic heel counters, to name a few of the features that various manufacturers ballyhoo in their shoes? These high-sounding terms are simply the names shoe manufacturers give their own types of soles and heel stabilizers. You don't need to know these special names or be able to discuss them like a pro.

What you need to know is whether your ankles roll in (pronate) or roll out (supinate) or whether they roll at all. You can tell from looking at an old pair of running shoes or street shoes. If the heel or sole is worn down on either side, then you need shoes that can counter this tendency.

You should also follow these tips when choosing and wearing any type of sports shoes:

- Choose shoes with real leather or fabric uppers that let your feet breathe.
- Choose shoes that are flexible across the instep and have good arch supports.
- Wear thick, absorbent socks of wool or cotton or blends of these fabrics containing nylon or orlon.
- Be sure that you have a thumb's width of clearance between the end of your longest toe and the front of the shoe so your toes can move freely.

can get it if the conditions that encourage fungi are present. Fungi grow best in warm, moist places. Changing wet shoes and socks after exercising discourages fungus infections.

Washing the feet carefully and drying them thoroughly are also good precautions. Absorbent socks, such as those made entirely of cotton or wool, help to keep the feet dry.

Figure 7.13 Women tend to have more foot problems than men because women's shoe fashions have traditionally been more extreme. Narrow-toed, high-heeled shoes such as these can cause corns, calluses, bunions, and ingrown toenails.

Getting Treatment

Treating your own foot problems can make them worse. Never tear or cut away corns or calluses. And if any skin growth changes in size or appearance, see a doctor promptly to make sure that it is not a sign of cancer.

Be careful about diagnosing your own foot problems. A rash on your feet, for example, is not necessarily athlete's foot. Foot problems may be symptoms of serious diseases, such as diabetes or arthritis. If you have misjudged your foot problem, you could be using a drugstore remedy that can damage your foot. And you are delaying the professional treatment you need.

If you have any foot problems that need professional help, you should see a *podiatrist*. Podiatrists are concerned with the diagnosis, prevention, and treatment of foot disorders.

CHECK YOUR UNDERSTANDING

1. Why do feet perspire more heavily than most other parts of the body?
2. When is the best time of day to buy shoes? Why?
3. Explain the differences between corns and calluses. How should they be treated?
4. How can athlete's foot be prevented?

CHAPTER SUMMARY

- Although dental disease can be prevented, almost all Americans have some cavities.
- Cavities develop when plaque interacts with sugar to form an acid that dissolves tooth enamel. Sticky, sweet foods are the most damaging to teeth.
- Periodontal disease, which affects the gums and other structures that support the teeth, is the main cause of tooth loss in adults. Like tooth decay, periodontal disease is caused by plaque. Daily brushing and flossing prevent plaque from forming.
- Eyestrain can result in red, watery eyes, headaches, and dizziness. Reading in dim light, watching television in a darkened room, and prolonged spells in bright sunlight can lead to eyestrain.

- Sports and recreational activities account for more than 35,000 eye injuries requiring hospital treatment every year. Baseball, softball, and the racket sports carry the greatest risk of injury. Players should use safety eyewear.
- The most common vision problems are farsightedness, nearsightedness, astigmatism, and color blindness. Many vision problems can be corrected with glasses or contact lenses.
- To help your skin look its best, you should keep it clean, eat a balanced diet, exercise regularly, and get enough sleep.
- The increased production of body oil during puberty sometimes leads to acne. Blackheads and pimples should never be squeezed.
- Shampooing once or twice a week is usually enough to keep the scalp and hair clean. In gen-

eral, an inexpensive shampoo can do as good a job as an expensive one.

- Body odor and perspiration can be controlled by the use of deodorants and antiperspirants.
- Feet need regular washing because they pick up more dirt and dust than other parts of the body do and because they often perspire heavily.

- Shoes should be chosen with careful attention to fit and comfort. Just one pair of shoes that fits poorly can give you foot problems that last for years.
- Among the more common foot problems are blisters, ingrown toenails, corns, calluses, bunions, and athlete's foot.

DO YOU REMEMBER?

Give brief definitions of these terms:

enamel	cornea	cataract	aprocrine glands
plaque	retina	melanin	athlete's foot

THINK AND DISCUSS

1. Do you think mouthwashes are useful? Why or why not?
2. Why do you think some people avoid going to the dentist? What measures can you think of to persuade these people to go?
3. Do you think cosmetics enhance a woman's appearance? Why do you think women use cosmetics whereas men generally don't? Do you think men should use cosmetics?
4. Why do you think so many people who know the hazards of overexposure still spend many hours in the sun?
5. Now that you know that inexpensive shampoos work as well as expensive ones, do you plan to change your brand? Why or why not?
6. What current shoe styles do you think can cause foot problems? Why?

FOLLOW-UP

1. Find out about the controversy that exists over fluoride. Write a report that describes the two sides of the issue. Include your own opinion as well.
2. Learn about the new techniques orthodontists are using to straighten teeth. Make a poster that illustrates these techniques and display it in your classroom.
3. Obtain pamphlets on mouth care from your dentist and post them in your classroom. Discuss the new information in these pamphlets.
4. Find out more about the treatment of glaucoma or cataracts. Write a report on your findings.
5. Learn about the many dangerous cosmetics in use in the early part of the century. Write a report that describes these cosmetics and the actions that halted their manufacture.
6. Find out what to look for in shoes meant for different sports. Make a chart of the desirable characteristics for these shoes and post it in your classroom.

PART 3 The Life Cycle

Part 3 focuses on some key episodes in the human life cycle. It begins with the start of life. Chapter 8 describes the male and female reproductive systems. It explains how conception occurs and what happens during pregnancy. It also examines the role of heredity in determining individual characteristics.

Adolescence is the focus of Chapter 9. The chapter explores the many changes—physical, mental, and social—that take place during the teenage years.

Most Americans get married, and the majority of married couples become parents. Why do people marry? What makes a marriage work? What are the advantages and disadvantages of marriage? Questions such as these have become important topics of discussion, and they are addressed in Chapter 10. The chapter also discusses the complex and challenging task of parenthood.

Chapter 11 covers the final years of the life cycle. It examines the aging process and the challenges of the later years. It also discusses attitudes toward death, the needs of the dying, and the needs of the bereaved.

CHAPTER 8

Conception and Birth

After reading this chapter, you should be able to answer these questions:

1. How does the male reproductive system work?
2. How does the female reproductive system work?
3. What happens at the moment of conception?
4. What can parents do to ensure that they have a healthy baby?
5. What do you need to know about your genetic make-up?

No two people look alike. Consider your classmates. Some are short while others are tall, and there are equally large differences in weight and appearance. No two of you have the same nose, eyes, or hair. Yet you and your classmates—and everyone else on this earth—started out in exactly the same way, as two tiny cells too small to be seen with the naked eye. From these cells, as part of the remarkable process called reproduction, a whole and complex human being developed.

How does it all happen? Where do those two cells come from? How do they unite? What keeps them alive? How do they manage to develop into human beings, equipped with everything down to eyelashes and fingernails?

Like all other forms of life, human beings are biologically constructed to reproduce themselves. Every one of us is born with the special organs that will enable us, one day, to create a new human life. These organs begin to function at puberty. Once they do, boys and girls enter a new phase of life. They are capable of becoming parents, of bringing a new life into the world.

But with that capability comes the responsibility of protecting the health of this new life and of the mother who carries it. Knowledge of the reproductive process is, therefore, essential. Each year, for example, thousands of babies are born mentally defective because their mothers did not know how to eat properly during pregnancy. The knowledge these mothers could have gained from one pamphlet and one visit to a doctor could have prevented the problems of mental retardation in their children. Similarly, mothers who smoke, drink, or ignore the advice of their doctors during pregnancy are endangering the health, and possibly the lives, of their unborn babies.

This chapter explains the structure and function of the male and female reproductive systems. You will follow the growth and development of a baby from conception through birth. You will study the action of genes and chromosomes, those tiny particles that transmit physical and mental traits from parent to child.

The process of human reproduction is indeed a miracle, and this chapter will help you appreciate—and respect—that wonder.

SECTION 1   The Male Reproductive System

The system that enables a male to help create another human life becomes active at puberty. That's when a boy's body begins to produce *sperm*—tiny cells that are capable of fertilizing a female egg. Without these cells, an egg cannot develop into a baby.

A healthy adult male produces about 200 million sperm a day. Each sperm is shaped like a tadpole, with an oval head and a long, thin tail. The sperm are so small that 500 of them, placed end to end, would measure only 2.5 centimeters (1 inch). Any sperm that do not leave the body break down to be reabsorbed.

The sperm are produced by two small, oval-shaped glands called the *testes,* or *testicles.* These glands are suspended outside the body in a pouch called the *scrotum,* which hangs behind and slightly below the penis. The testes are made up of many slender tubes that serve two functions. They actually produce the sperm, and they provide a pathway through which the sperm can travel.

From each of the testes the sperm pass into a larger tube called the *vas deferens,* which carries them to the penis. Along the way, different glands send fluids into the tubes. These fluids mix with the sperm to form a thick, whitish fluid called *semen,* which carries the sperm and helps keep them alive.

The *penis* provides the final pathway for the sperm. Shaped like a cylinder, the penis is normally soft and hangs downward from the body. At birth, the tip of the penis is covered by a fold of skin called the *foreskin.* The foreskin is often removed a few days after birth in a minor operation called *circumcision.* Circumcision has long been a religious practice of Moslems and Jews, but it is now widespread as

Figure 8.1 Male reproductive organs.

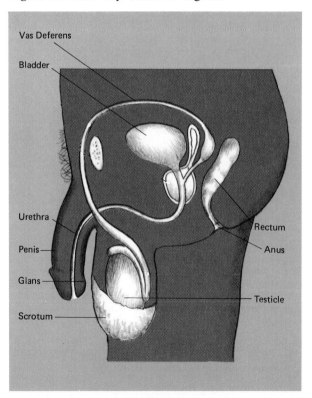

a hygienic measure. It is easier to keep the penis clean when the foreskin has been removed.

Role in Reproduction

In its soft state, the penis is used to pass urine. But for the purposes of reproduction, it becomes firm and erect. It also becomes larger—from 1½ to 2 times its normal size. These dramatic changes happen because extra blood flows into the vessels and spongy tissues of the penis. The erection makes it possible for the penis to enter the woman's body.

During erection, the *urethra,* the tube through which urine normally flows, serves as a route for the semen. First, though, strong muscles close off the bladder to prevent any urine from entering the penis.

Muscles also provide the force that ejects the semen from the penis. Rhythmic contractions spread through the reproductive system. When these contractions reach the penis, *ejaculation* occurs. In this final moment of the male's biological role in reproduction, a small amount of semen is discharged from the penis. This small amount contains from 300 to 400 million sperm. Such a large number is nature's insurance that enough sperm will reach the egg to fertilize it. Extra sperm are also needed to help break down the wall of the egg. Once this is done, a single sperm can unite with the egg to fertilize it.

Ejaculation can occur at night during sleep in what is called a *nocturnal emission,* or *wet dream.* Nocturnal emissions usually happen during adolescence, when production of sperm has just begun. They are considered a normal way for the body to relieve itself of sexual tensions.

CHECK YOUR UNDERSTANDING

1. Describe the appearance and function of sperm.
2. What are the two functions of the testes?
3. Why is it necessary for the penis to become erect? What causes the changes that occur to the penis during erection?
4. Describe what happens during ejaculation.

SECTION **2** # The Female Reproductive System

The female reproductive system serves three purposes. First, it supplies the egg that will grow into a new human life. Then it nourishes and protects this new life as it grows from a single cell to a fully formed baby.

The Uterus

The fertilized egg grows in the *uterus,* which is a sac made of the strongest and most elastic muscles in the body. Normally, the uterus, or womb as it is sometimes called, is the shape and size of a small pear. During the nine months of pregnancy, though, it expands greatly, growing as the baby grows.

The uterus rests within the pelvis on its narrow end, which is a ring-shaped opening called the *cervix.* This opening is normally smaller than one of the *o*'s on this page, but it expands during birth to allow the baby to pass through.

Once a female reaches puberty, her uterus goes through a monthly cycle that prepares it to receive a fertilized egg. During these times, the soft tissue of the lining becomes thicker and rich with blood. It is this lining that would nourish the fertilized egg if pregnancy should occur.

If pregnancy does not occur, the network of arteries beneath the lining constrict, cutting off the flow of blood. Now without nourishment, the lining breaks down and passes from the

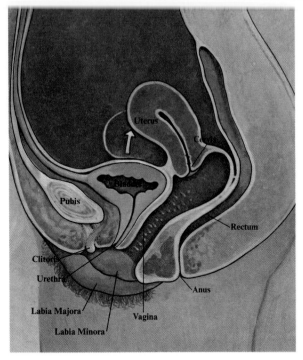

Figure 8.2 Female reproductive organs.

Cramps and backache are also common. Some women experience emotional changes such as depression and anxiety as well. A few women suffer such severe symptoms that their condition is considered to be a medical disorder. This condition is known as *premenstrual syndrome*, or PMS.

Many myths exist about exercising or swimming during menstruation. In reality, a healthy woman can take part in any activity that feels comfortable. Some doctors say that women who exercise regularly tend to have less trouble with cramps and other symptoms.

In most females, the menstrual cycle occurs regularly for 30 to 40 years after onset. Then, when a woman is about the age of 50, her ovaries gradually stop producing the hormones that control the cycle. Eventually, the cycle ceases completely, and the woman stops menstruating. She is no longer capable of becoming pregnant. The ceasing of menstruation is called *menopause*. Some people also refer to menopause as the "change of life," perhaps because it signals the end of a woman's childbearing years.

body, carrying the unfertilized egg with it. This flow generally lasts from three to six days and is called *menstruation*. The name comes from the Latin word *mensis*, meaning "month." Menstruation is the only instance in nature where loss of blood does not signify injury but is instead a sign of good health.

The menstrual cycle—the time from the beginning of one menstrual period to the start of the next—does generally take about a month, averaging from 27 to 30 days. But there are considerable variations. Some women have a 20-day cycle, others a 42-day cycle. The cycle may also vary within the same person from time to time. Illness, nutrition, and a woman's emotional state can all affect the frequency of her menstrual periods.

Most girls begin menstruating between the ages of 10 and 16. The age of onset is influenced by many factors, including heredity, health, and nutrition. Some temporary physical changes can accompany menstruation. Fluid can build up in body tissues, creating a feeling of discomfort, especially in the breasts.

The Ovaries

Every female is born with about a million immature egg cells inside her body. About 400 of these cells will reach maturity during her reproductive years. These large numbers are nature's way of ensuring that reproduction will occur.

Mature eggs are produced by the *ovaries*, two small glands about the size and shape of almonds. Besides producing eggs, the ovaries also produce the body chemicals, or *hormones*, that help control the whole reproductive cycle.

The ovaries usually take turns producing mature eggs, at the rate of about one a month. In another form of natural insurance, either ovary is capable of taking over the full load of egg and hormone production if the other one stops functioning.

Each egg is housed inside a capsule of cells. As the egg ripens, the capsule grows larger. When it reaches the size of a pea, it breaks open and the mature egg pops free. Some women can actually feel *ovulation*, as the pro-

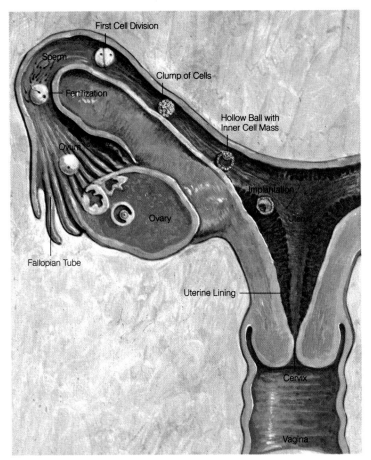

Figure 8.3 The path of an egg from the ovary to the uterus.

duction of a mature egg is called. They may feel pain or heaviness in their pelvic area. They may even feel soreness on the side with the ovary that is producing the egg that month.

The Fallopian Tubes

Each ovary lies close to the end of a *Fallopian tube,* or *oviduct.* These tiny, muscular tubes serve as passageways between the ovaries and the uterus. They also provide a meeting ground for the egg and the sperm. The small end of each Fallopian tube is attached to the uterus. The end that is near the ovaries has a funnel-shaped mouth, with many waving fingers that form a fringe around the opening.

When ovulation is about to occur, the fringed end moves closer to the ripening egg. The waving fingers then draw the released egg into the mouth of the Fallopian tube. Once there, the egg is moved along by tiny, hairlike structures and by muscular contractions in the walls of the tube.

If the egg is to unite with a sperm, the union will take place in the Fallopian tube. The fertilized egg will then move along the tube and drop into the uterus. If the egg is not fertilized, it soon dies.

The Vagina

The opening that allows sperm to enter the female's body is called the *vagina.* Ordinarily the size and shape of a flattened tube of toothpaste, it expands to receive the penis during sexual intercourse. During birth, it expands even further to become the exit for the baby. As such, it is called the *birth canal.*

The opening to the vagina is covered by two pairs of *labia,* flaps of skin shaped like lips. The outer labia, the *labia majora,* are broad and thick. When a female reaches adolescence, these labia become covered with pubic hair.

The outer labia cover the much smaller inner labia, or *labia minora,* which cover the vaginal opening directly. They join together in an arch above the opening. A small, sensitive organ called the *clitoris* lies at the point where they connect. About the size of a pea, the clitoris enlarges and becomes erect during intercourse. About midway between the clitoris and the vaginal opening lies the urethra, the canal through which urine passes from the body.

SECTION **3**   # Conception and Prenatal Development

Conception—the union of egg and sperm—depends on several "ifs." If ovulation has occurred, and if sperm have been deposited in the vagina, and if these sperm have moved into the right Fallopian tube at the right time, then conception may occur.

Once sperm have been deposited in the female's vagina, they swim up through the tiny cervical opening and into the uterus. From there they enter the Fallopian tubes, one of which may contain a ripe egg.

The protective coating of the egg is difficult to penetrate, but sperm cells contain a special chemical that can dissolve this coating. One sperm cell, however, cannot do it alone; it takes the combined action of a number of sperm to make an opening in the coating. One sperm cell can then enter and unite with the egg.

Once fertilized, the egg travels down the rest of the Fallopian tube into the uterus, a trip that takes about three days. During the journey the fertilized egg starts dividing rapidly into many cells. When it reaches the uterus, the cluster of cells floats free for three or four days. It then burrows down into the lining of the uterus. At that time there are about 200 cells in the developing cluster, which is now called an *embryo.* Still, it is only about the size of the dot over this *i.*

This tiny embryo has two layers of cells. The inner layer will develop into a baby, while the outer layer will develop into the baby's life support system—the *placenta.* This vital structure begins to form two or three days after implantation. It is a blood-rich tissue that absorbs nutrients and oxygen from the mother and carries them to the baby through the *umbilical cord.* The umbilical cord is attached to the baby at the navel.

Another important structure, the *amniotic sac,* also forms at this time. This transparent tissue surrounds the embryo and is filled with a warm liquid called amniotic fluid. The developing baby floats in this fluid, which protects it from being bumped or jarred. The amniotic fluid changes about once an hour, so it is always fresh.

Prenatal Development

During its first weeks of existence, the embryo looks something like a small, curved fish. Development is rapid; just a few days can bring remarkable differences. At the beginning of the fourth week, for example, a primitive heart forms and begins beating. The nervous system and internal organs also start to form. By the end of the same week, the brain and spinal cord and the eyes, ears, and nose are taking shape, as are the kidneys and lungs.

The first month marks the most rapid period of growth in a human being's development. The embryo that started out the size of a dot has grown to a length of about 3 millimeters (0.12 inch) and has increased its weight 500 times.

In the second month, the heart and limbs start to form. After the eighth week, the developing baby is called a *fetus*. At the three-month stage, the fetus is about 7 centimeters (2.75 inches) long and weighs 28 grams (1 ounce). It has arms and legs with fingers and toes. It can kick its legs, close its fingers, turn its head, and open and close its mouth.

Around the end of the fourth month, the fetus begins to stretch its arms and legs. From this time on, the mother will be able to feel it sleep and wake. It may even hiccup! The seventh month marks the start of the final period of development. With specialized medical care, the fetus could now survive outside the uterus. During the eighth and ninth months, fat forms over the fetus's body and the final touches are put on its internal and external organs.

By the ninth month the average fetus weighs from 2.25 to 5.5 kilograms (5 to 12 pounds) and is from 43 to 56 centimeters (17 to 22 inches) long. If you recall that nine months before, this fully formed human being was just a cluster of cells the size of a dot, you will appreciate the extraordinary process just described.

Multiple Births

Human beings generally give birth to one baby at a time. However, in about one out of every 88 births, twins occur.

Twins can form in two different ways. Sometimes a fertilized egg splits in half, and each part develops into an embryo. Because they develop from the same egg and sperm, such twins are *identical*. They are of the same sex and look almost exactly alike.

Sometimes the ovaries release two eggs at the same time, which are then fertilized by two

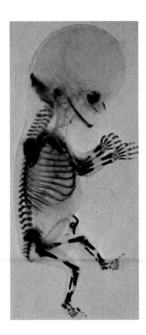
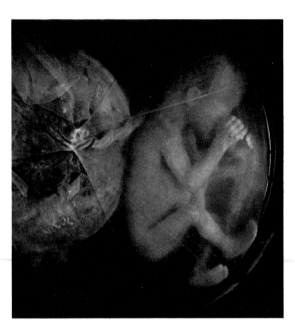

Figure 8.4 The developing fetus. *Left:* An x-ray, taken at 8 weeks, shows a well-developed skeleton. *Right:* By 12 weeks, the fetus looks unmistakably human. The transparent membrane surrounding the fetus is the amniotic sac; the pink spongy organ behind it is the placenta.

ternal. They do not resemble each other any more than two children born of the same parents at different times, and they may be of opposite sexes.

In very rare cases, triplets, quadruplets, and quintuplets are born. There have also been instances of six, seven, and eight babies born at a time. The survival rate in such multiple births is extremely low, though, and only one set of sextuplets (six babies) is known to have survived.

CHECK YOUR UNDERSTANDING

1. Where does conception take place?
2. What happens to a fertilized egg as it travels to the uterus?
3. Describe the functions of the placenta and the amniotic sac.
4. When does an embryo become a fetus?
5. Explain the differences between identical twins and fraternal twins.

SECTION 4 Pregnancy

As soon as a woman becomes pregnant, her body starts to undergo many changes. The early changes are subtle and internal, so most women do not suspect that they are pregnant until they miss a menstrual period. A missed period does not always signal pregnancy, however. It is not unusual for periods to be delayed by two or three weeks, especially in women whose periods are irregular. Stress, such as that caused by the anticipation or fear of pregnancy, can also lead to a delayed period.

If a woman is pregnant, she may notice changes in the way her body looks and feels within the first three or four weeks. Her breasts may become swollen and tender, and her pelvis may feel heavy. She may also experience nausea, especially at mealtimes.

Because a pregnant woman must care for herself in special ways to ensure her own health and that of her baby, the sooner a pregnancy is confirmed, the better. Urine tests and blood tests can diagnose pregnancy as early as the first missed period. By that time, the special hormone that a pregnant woman's body produces can be detected in the urine and blood. The blood test is far more accurate in very early pregnancy than the urine test, which frequently reports that a woman is not pregnant when in fact she is. Most of the do-it-yourself pregnancy testing kits now on the market are for testing urine. A blood-testing service is available in most cities at low cost. It usually requires no more than a brief visit to a clinic to leave a blood sample and a follow-up phone call for the results.

By about the seventh week of pregnancy, a doctor can usually tell, by examining a woman, whether or not she is pregnant. The pelvic tissue is slightly softened, the vaginal opening is slightly purplish, and the uterus has begun to enlarge. Still, without actually testing for the pregnancy hormone, a doctor cannot be certain that a pregnancy exists.

Visits to the Doctor

The ideal time for the first prenatal visit to the doctor is *before* pregnancy. Ideally, too, both partners should be examined and should provide the doctor with a thorough medical history. That way the doctor can determine whether there is any likelihood of the couple passing on a genetic disease to their offspring. If the likelihood exists, the couple may be advised to seek genetic counseling (see Section 6). A woman should also be tested to see whether she should be immunized against German measles.

If the examination has not been done before pregnancy, it should be done during the early weeks. The doctor, usually an obstetrician, will examine the woman carefully to determine her specific needs. The examination will also reveal any special problems that might affect pregnancy or birth.

The doctor will discuss special diets, vitamins, and exercises with the mother-to-be. She will be advised to return at least once a month up until the seventh month, when visits should become more frequent. During each prenatal visit, the doctor will check the woman's urine, blood pressure, weight change, and general condition. From the fifth month on, the doctor will also monitor the fetus's heartbeat.

Blood Tests

Early in a woman's pregnancy, an important series of blood tests will be performed. Her red blood cells will be examined for anemia, a condition caused by lack of iron. Anemia is fairly common in pregnancy because the baby absorbs iron from the mother's body to make its own red blood cells. If the mother's need for iron is not met by special supplements, she will feel tired and weak during her pregnancy.

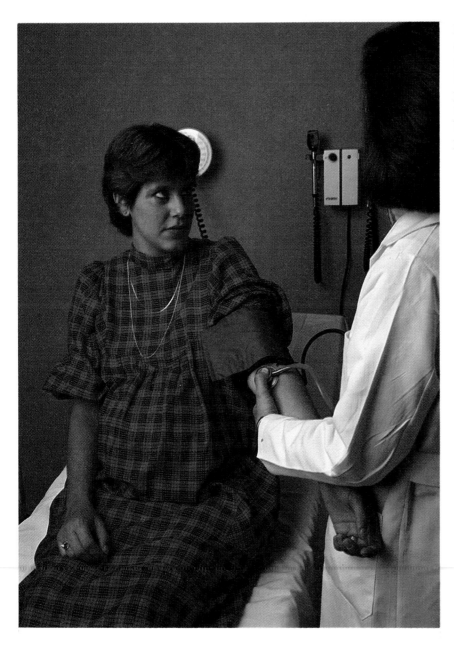

Figure 8.5 Regular prenatal care enables the doctor to watch for abnormal changes in a woman's blood pressure, blood, urine, and weight. Such changes may be warnings of potential problems.

The mother's white blood cell count will also be taken. An elevated count would warn that the mother has some infection or disorder that could affect her baby. In addition, the mother's blood is tested for German measles and for syphilis. Both these diseases can cause serious birth defects.

Another important blood test determines the risk of *Rh disease*. About 15 out of every 100 people lack a substance in their blood called the Rh factor. These people are called Rh negative (Rh−), while those who have the Rh factor are Rh positive (Rh+). An Rh− woman may conceive an Rh+ baby, a strong possibility if the father is Rh+. When this happens, the baby may be in great danger. If the baby is a first child, the risk is slight. But if the mother has already had an Rh+ baby, that baby's Rh factor may have stimulated her blood to produce anti-Rh substances. These anti-Rh substances can then destroy the red blood cells of the next Rh+ baby that the mother carries. The anemia this destruction causes makes it necessary to replace the baby's blood at birth through a transfusion. In severe cases, the baby may require a blood transfusion before birth.

Rh disease can be prevented by immunizing any Rh− mother who is carrying an Rh+ baby. The serum that is used prevents the mother's blood from forming anti-Rh substances.

Discomforts of Pregnancy

Pregnancy makes many demands on a woman's body. As her body changes and reacts to the new life that is growing inside her, various kinds of discomfort may occur.

One of the most common discomforts of early pregnancy is "morning sickness." Many pregnant women experience this unexplained nausea when they wake in the morning, but it can also occur around lunch and dinnertime, or any other time the stomach is empty. Small, frequent meals usually bring relief. For some unknown reason, morning sickness generally disappears around the third month of pregnancy.

The growing baby places many strains on the major organs of the mother's body. By the seventh month, for example, more than 15 percent of the mother's blood is in her placenta and uterus. Her heart must therefore work much harder than normal to keep her blood circulating. The growing baby also exerts pressure against her lungs, diaphragm, and bladder. As a result, the woman may have difficulty breathing. She may also have to urinate more often than normal.

Some women suffer during pregnancy from swollen, twisted veins, called *varicose veins,* in various parts of their body. Varicose veins in the rectum, a condition known as *hemorrhoids,* are most likely to occur in the later months, when the baby's head presses down into the pelvis. Varicose veins may also appear in the legs. Many women find that wearing elastic stockings helps relieve the discomfort. Elevating the legs on pillows will also help. This practice can also relieve pains in the ligaments that support the uterus. Varicose veins usually return to normal once the baby is born.

Spontaneous Abortion

The development of a new human being is a complex process, and, as in any complex process, something can go wrong. The fertilized egg may not implant itself correctly in the uterus, or something may have been wrong with the egg or sperm to begin with. In either case, nature prevents further growth of something that has no ability to survive by forcing the uterus to expel it. This process is called *spontaneous abortion,* or *miscarriage.* Ten to 20 percent of all pregnancies end this way.

In a miscarriage, the woman experiences cramps and bleeding. Medical attention is necessary, but the woman's ability to bear children in the future is not affected. Sometimes a miscarriage occurs so early in the pregnancy that the woman, unaware that she was pregnant, thinks it is her menstrual period.

Contrary to popular belief, miscarriages are not caused by falls or emotional shocks. There are, however, some women with disorders that prevent them from completing any pregnancy. These women suffer one miscarriage after another. They may be helped by special medical treatment.

Nutrition

A pregnant woman must pay special attention to nutrition. Her diet must provide the nutrients the baby needs to develop properly. Otherwise, both her own health and that of her baby can be affected.

A pregnant woman needs to eat a varied and balanced diet. Foods high in calcium, iron, phosphorus, magnesium, vitamin D, and folic acid are very important. These vitamins and minerals are needed for the baby to form healthy cells. A pregnant woman must get enough nutrients for both herself and the baby. If she doesn't, she may feel weak as the vitamins and minerals stored in her body are absorbed by the fetus.

Protein foods such as meat, fish, and eggs are equally necessary. Protein supplies the building blocks for all the baby's body tissues, so lack of protein can affect development of the baby's whole body. But it is the baby's brain that can be most affected. A baby's brain grows most rapidly just before and after birth. If the mother's diet does not supply enough protein, normal brain development does not take place. In fact, it will never take place, even if the baby later gets more protein. Throughout life, then, the baby will be mentally retarded, a victim of its mother's poor diet.

Alcohol, Smoking, and Drugs

Almost everything that enters a pregnant woman's body also enters the body of her baby. This fact is particularly significant in the case of alcohol, tobacco, and other drugs.

A woman who drinks alcohol during pregnancy could cause her baby severe harm. The alcohol that she drinks reaches her baby in concentrations as high as those in her own body. The baby's liver, however, is not mature and cannot get rid of the alcohol easily. As a result, the level of alcohol in the baby's brain and liver can be 10 times higher than that in the mother.

A serious condition associated with alcohol use during pregnancy is *fetal alcohol syndrome*, or FAS. Babies born with this condition are mentally retarded and have malformed heads and faces. Fetal alcohol syndrome is now thought to be one of the leading causes of mental retardation and birth defects.

Babies born to mothers who are alcoholics may also have to go through a painful withdrawal period. These babies have actually become dependent on alcohol. Withdrawal, which is difficult enough for an adult to go through, may cause death in a newborn baby.

You are probably aware of the hazards smoking poses to the health of the smoker. But smoking can affect a smoker's unborn baby as well.

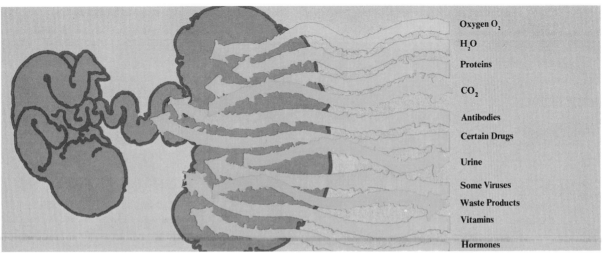

Oxygen O_2

H_2O

Proteins

CO_2

Antibodies

Certain Drugs

Urine

Some Viruses

Waste Products

Vitamins

Hormones

Figure 8.6 The blood of a fetus is kept apart from the blood of its mother by a porous membrane in the placenta. Many substances can, however, pass through this membrane. Some of these are necessary for the baby's development; others, such as drugs, can be harmful.

Pregnant women who smoke have twice as many miscarriages as nonsmokers and are twice as likely to suffer a *stillbirth*, which is the birth of a dead baby. They are also two to three times more likely to give birth prematurely. Furthermore, babies born to smokers run a 30 percent greater risk of dying shortly after birth than do babies born to nonsmokers. They are also likely to be smaller.

Many other drugs can affect an unborn baby. Cocaine, heroin, and other illegal substances can cause severe birth defects. Even such common substances as coffee and aspirin contain chemicals that may harm a developing fetus. You might be surprised to learn that a substance used to treat acne, called Accutane, has caused defects in babies born to women who used it during early pregnancy.

Most doctors today recommend that a woman take no drugs at all during pregnancy, unless they are medically prescribed. Equally important, they recommend that women who plan to become pregnant stop smoking, using alcohol, and taking drugs during the months before conception. That way, they won't risk harming the developing embryo before they realize they are pregnant. In addition, they won't have to deal with changes in habits at the same time that they are dealing with early pregnancy.

Figure 8.7 Pregnant teenagers are often afraid and worried. They do not want to face the truth or to tell their parents and friends.

Teenage Pregnancy

Every year more than 600,000 teenage girls in the United States have babies. Although teenagers are capable of having healthy babies—and many do—there are particular risks associated with teenage pregnancy. The biggest single problem is low birth weight.

The greatest hazard to the health of the teenage mother and her baby is poor diet. Because her own body is still growing, the pregnant teenager has greater nutritional needs than pregnant women over the age of 20. Yet, as a group, pregnant teenagers are far more likely to eat the wrong foods or not enough food. An inadequate diet greatly increases the probability of giving birth to an underweight or a stillborn baby.

Low birth weight has been identified as the greatest single threat to the life of a newborn baby. Many mothers who give birth to underweight babies do so because they do not receive adequate prenatal care. In fact, expectant mothers who receive no prenatal care are three times more likely to bear a low birth-weight infant than those who receive medical care.

Unfortunately, pregnant teenagers often fail to get the early medical attention they need. Studies show that 70 percent of all pregnant teenagers under the age of 15 receive no prenatal care during the first months of pregnancy. A substantial number of those over the age of 15 do not seek medical attention soon enough, if at all. This is usually because pregnant teenagers are afraid and worried. They do not want to face the truth or to tell their parents or friends. But a delay in seeking medical care can have serious consequences. One out of every four babies born to teenagers under 15 is premature and therefore underweight. Furthermore, babies born to teenage mothers are at least twice as likely to die during their first year of life as babies born to women in their twenties.

Lack of prenatal care threatens the life of the teenage mother as well as that of her baby. The lower the age of the mother, the greater is the risk that she will die from complications during pregnancy or birth.

Many of the physical problems of teenage pregnancy would be avoided if mothers got the right medical care. The teenager who visits a doctor regularly, eats properly, and takes care of her health has a good chance of delivering a healthy baby—and of maintaining her own well-being.

But there are other problems that cannot be avoided. Many pregnant teenagers drop out of school. Those who want to continue their education during pregnancy often find it difficult, for social or emotional reasons, to stay in school. There are still school districts that encourage expectant teenagers to drop out, without providing any sort of continuing education program for them. Thousands of teenagers, then, find themselves facing the difficult situation of having no diploma, no job, and a baby to take care of. While a number depend on their families, many find welfare their only means of support.

Prepared Childbirth

The more we know about a subject or experience, the more we tend to enjoy and appreciate it. The same holds true for childbirth.

Classes now exist to teach expectant mothers and fathers about the birth process. Prospective parents learn about all the stages of pregnancy, from conception through labor and delivery. They learn about hospital procedures and various ways to control pain. They

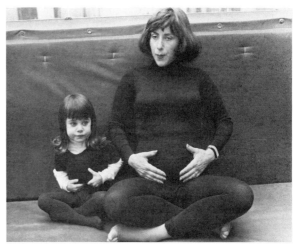

Figure 8.8 Prepared childbirth. *Right:* An expectant mother practices special Lamaze breathing exercises. *Below:* Wives and husbands get together for a practice session.

also learn about proper care of the new mother and baby.

Prepared childbirth is not the same as unmedicated, or "natural," childbirth. Unmedicated childbirth takes place without any sort of pain-killing drug. The mother reduces the pain of labor through special breathing and relaxation exercises. This technique of childbirth is often called the *Lamaze method.*

The goal of prepared childbirth is not an unmedicated delivery. Its aim is to allow parents to make informed choices about where and how their baby is to be born. There are other benefits as well. Women who have prepared for childbirth require less medication for pain. They know what to expect and what to do during labor. This knowledge can do away with many of the fears a woman may have about labor and birth.

Prepared childbirth helps make the experience of giving birth as rewarding as possible. Involving the father in both the preparation and delivery—a practice that has come about only recently—enriches the experience even further.

CHECK YOUR UNDERSTANDING

1. What physical changes might a pregnant woman first notice?
2. How can a woman find out if she is pregnant?
3. Why should a woman have her first prenatal visit *before* pregnancy?
4. Why do pregnant women sometimes become anemic? What condition can cause an unborn baby to become anemic?
5. What is the reason for most spontaneous abortions?
6. Why does a pregnant woman need to eat a varied and balanced diet?
7. List three substances that a woman should avoid during pregnancy.
8. What is the greatest danger to the health of a teenage mother and her baby? How can this affect the baby?
9. What are three benefits of prepared childbirth?

SECTION **5**   **Labor and Birth**

You may remember that the uterus is made up of the strongest muscles in a woman's body. They need to be powerful because their special task is to force the baby from the mother's body during labor. In fact, the uterus contracts gently all through pregnancy to keep the muscles exercised and ready for the birth process.

At the beginning of labor, contractions usually occur every 15 to 20 minutes and last for less than 30 seconds. Gradually, they become more frequent and longer lasting. By the time a woman is in heavy labor, the contractions are a few minutes apart, and each one lasts at least a minute.

The first signs of labor differ from woman to woman. Many women first experience the kind of contractions just described. The amniotic sac, or "bag of waters," may also break at this time, and the amniotic fluid flows from the woman's body. In other women, the onset of labor is signaled by a discharge of blood called "showing." This indicates that the cervix has begun to dilate, or enlarge, to let the baby through. The discharge is made up of blood from vessels that break as the cervix stretches.

The Three Stages of Labor

The stretching, or dilation, of the cervix is the first and longest stage of the birth process. In a 10-hour labor, for instance, almost 9 hours are taken up by dilation. You can understand this stage better if you recall the make-up and function of the cervix. For nine months this powerful muscle has remained tightly constricted to

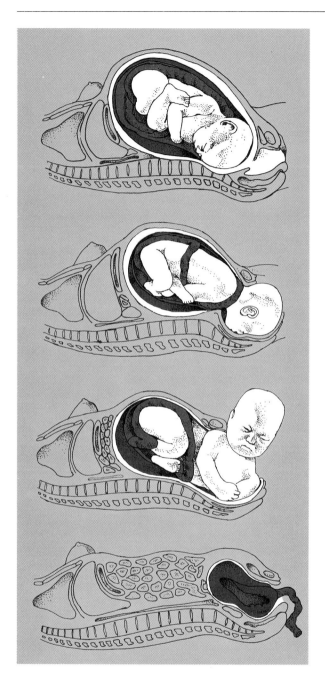

Figure 8.9 The stages of childbirth. When the cervix is fully dilated, the baby's head passes through the birth canal. The shoulders shift position, and the rest of the body squeezes through. Finally, the umbilical cord and the placenta are expelled.

When the cervix is finally dilated enough for the baby's head to pass through, birth can occur. The baby leaves the mother's body during this second stage, called expulsion. All the power of the uterine muscles are now concentrated on forcing the baby through the birth canal. Other powerful muscles in the woman's body also act now to help the baby enter the world. Her abdominal muscles contract, and she feels a compulsion to bear down.

At this point the baby begins to emerge. The top of the head appears first. Once the head is out, the shoulders rotate in the birth canal and the rest of the baby's body slips out. The baby is still attached to the mother by the umbilical cord, which will now be tied and cut.

The mother's labor is not over, however. Her body must still expel the placenta, which is sometimes called the *afterbirth*. This third and final stage of delivery, called the placental stage, usually occurs within minutes of the baby's birth. The uterus contracts again, pulling the placenta away from the lining and forcing it into the birth canal, from which it is carefully removed.

The Doctor's Role

Although birth is a natural process, most deliveries today take place in a hospital to ensure the health and safety of both mother and child. All during labor, a medical team works to make the mother comfortable and to assist the baby in its passage to the outside world. It is common practice, for example, for the doctor to enlarge the mother's vaginal opening by making an incision. This procedure, called an *episiotomy,* prevents the tissues from tearing as the baby's head emerges. After delivery, the incision is repaired with a few stitches, or sutures. At this time the doctor also checks to

keep the baby inside the uterus. Now it must be stretched to a diameter of at least 10 centimeters (4 inches) to allow the baby's head to pass through.

The contractions of the uterus stretch the cervix in two ways. As the muscles shorten, they pull the cervix open. Since the whole uterus gets smaller during a contraction, the baby's head is pressed against the cervix.

make sure all of the placenta has been delivered.

The doctor is also prepared to make labor less painful through the use of medication. Some women have general anesthesia, which makes them sleep lightly during the delivery. Many women, however, want to stay awake during the birth of their baby. Some have a regional anesthetic, which blocks pain in the lower part of the body. Others are given local anesthesia or a pain-relieving tablet.

Great care must be taken when medicating the mother, since any substance that enters her bloodstream passes through the placenta to the baby. Certain painkillers can affect the baby's breathing, and general anesthesia can make the baby, as well as the mother, sleepy.

The decision about whether to use drugs, and, if so, which drugs to use, depends in part on the mother's wishes. It also depends on what happens during labor and delivery. One reason a skilled doctor attends the birth of a baby is that a complication can arise. The baby may be in a poor position. The mother's pelvic opening may be so small that the baby's head cannot fit through. In cases when normal delivery is either impossible or dangerous, the doctor usually performs a *Caesarean section*. During this procedure, the baby is removed through an incision made in the abdomen and uterus. The Caesarean section gets it name from legends that say the Roman emperor Julius Caesar was delivered that way 2,000 years ago.

There can be other complications that require the presence of a doctor in the delivery room. A baby's heartbeat may drop to a dangerously low level right before it is born, or it may fail to breathe on its own after birth. Doctors then use their skills and the sophisticated equipment of the delivery room to help the baby. They must work with great speed, since lack of oxygen can cause infant brain damage in just minutes.

The doctor assists all newborns in their first attempts to breathe by clearing blood and other fluids from the baby's nose and mouth with a suction bulb or tube. The infant is then carefully examined. Heart rate, breathing, reflexes, muscle tone, color—all are checked to see if the newborn needs further medical help.

Midwifery and Home Delivery

In recent years there has been a small but growing movement in this country toward delivery of babies by a *nurse-midwife*. Although not doctors, nurse-midwives are well-educated professionals. They have been trained to manage normal pregnancies and deliveries. Just as important, they have learned to recognize complications in time to call a doctor. Nurse-midwives always work closely with a doctor to begin with, and most of their deliveries take place in a hospital.

Some women have recently been choosing to have their babies at home with the assistance of unlicensed "lay-midwives." This can be an extremely dangerous practice. At least half of the complications that arise during delivery are unexpected. No one can predict, for example, whether a newborn will have trouble breathing. In many cases, skilled medical attention is needed *within minutes* to prevent death or permanent damage.

One reason women give for choosing home deliveries is that they feel that hospitals are cold, uncaring places. Recognizing this, a number of hospitals have created a homelike setting within the hospital to make the mother feel as comfortable as possible.

Breast Feeding

The birth process stimulates the mother's breasts to produce milk. This milk is the natural food for infants; modern science has not yet been able to duplicate its composition for bottle feeding.

Human milk provides an infant with a number of benefits that bottle formula does not. It transfers disease-fighting substances from the mother's body, providing the baby with a greater resistance to infections. Breast-fed infants are also less likely to be overweight, constipated, or have diaper rash. Breast feeding is also thought to reduce the occurrence of allergies, and it is, of course, less expensive than bottle feeding.

Breast feeding has benefits for the mother as well. It causes the uterus to contract back to its normal size more quickly. Also, since produc-

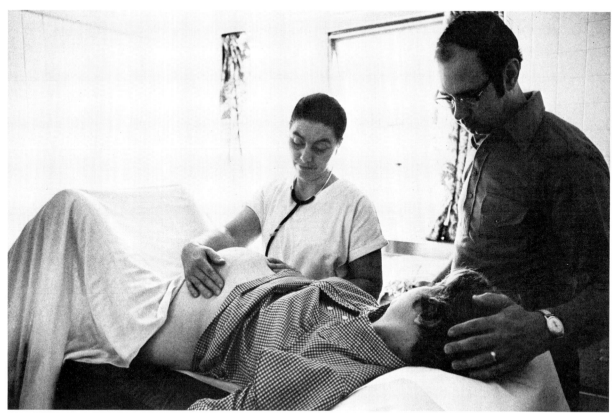

Figure 8.10 A growing number of women are choosing to have their babies delivered by nurse-midwives.

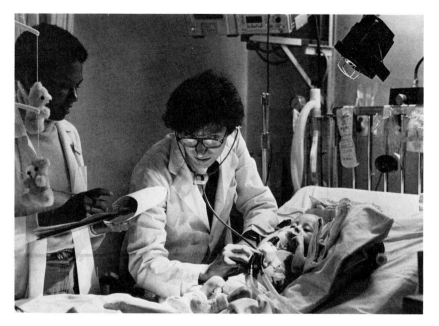

Figure 8.11 Equipment in the delivery room of a hospital may be needed for a baby who cannot breathe on its own after birth.

tion of breast milk uses up many calories, women who breast-feed readily lose the extra weight they gained during pregnancy. In addition, the intimacy involved in breast feeding may strengthen the emotional bond between mother and child. A breast-feeding mother can extract some milk from her breasts and store it. That way, the baby can be fed in her absence.

Almost all mothers are capable of breast-feeding their infants. To produce an adequate supply of milk, though, they must include in their diet an extra 500 to 1,000 calories a day. They must also drink an extra liter (quart) or more of liquid.

Despite the many benefits of breast feeding, some mothers choose to bottle-feed their babies. Others are unable to breast-feed, or they need to supplement their own supply of milk. Formula-fed babies do thrive and develop well. Bottle feeding does have an advantage over breast feeding. It enables the mother to be away from her baby for long periods of time—to go to work, for example. Another advantage of bottle feeding is that the father can be more involved in feeding the baby.

In a number of countries where breast feeding is encouraged, working mothers are allowed time during the workday to nurse their infants. Generally, this has not been the case in the United States. The American Academy of Pediatricians endorses breast-feeding a baby for the first six months. It also recommends that employers provide extended leave, part-time employment, or regular nursing breaks. Most American companies do not currently make these arrangements.

CHECK YOUR UNDERSTANDING

1. What are three possible first signs of labor?
2. What are the three stages of labor? Which stage takes the longest? Why?
3. What can a doctor do to make the mother more comfortable during labor and birth?
4. Why can home delivery be dangerous?
5. What advantages does breast feeding have over bottle feeding? What are the disadvantages?

SECTION **6** # From Generation to Generation

By the time a baby is born, much of what he or she will become has already been established. At the moment of conception, nine months before, a sequence of events started that would determine the child's appearance, influence health and intelligence, and establish many other physical and mental traits.

The fact that all children in one family often look like each other and like their parents has long made people realize that the mother and father pass on their traits to their children. But nobody knew how and why this happened until this century, when it was discovered that the egg and sperm carry complex hereditary material.

Traits such as eye color and hair color are passed on from generation to generation by means of *genes*. The science that studies the way genes are passed on and the way they are expressed is called *genetics*.

What Are Genes?

Genes, the basic units of heredity passed on by the egg and sperm, are composed of *deoxyribonucleic acid*. Called DNA, this chemical is made up of large, complex molecules shaped into double-stranded coils. DNA molecules contain the detailed set of instructions, often called the "code of life," for making and operating a new human being. This code is the blueprint for manufacturing *proteins*. Proteins are the vital substances that give shape to our bodies and regulate our life processes. They also produce more DNA as our cells grow and divide.

Each cell in the body contains identical molecules of DNA. Each molecule, in turn, contains the complete set of DNA instructions. But even though they start out the same, different cells "read" different portions of the in-

Figure 8.12 Through the hereditary process, traits such as hair color and eye color are passed from parents to children.

structions to develop into distinct body parts. Some cells develop into hair cells, others into fingernail cells, others into parts of eyes, and so on. Each body part is a complicated structure that requires many genes to develop properly and function correctly. Your eye, with its many parts, for example, develops because of the action of at least 150 genes.

What Are Chromosomes?

The genes in each cell are arranged in pairs making up structures called *chromosomes*. Human beings have 46 chromosomes arranged into 23 pairs. One-half of each chromosome pair is derived from the father, and one-half from the mother.

One of these chromosome pairs, the sex chromosome, determines whether a person is

male or female. This determination is made at the moment of conception, depending on which sperm fertilizes the egg. Females have two sex chromosomes shaped like the letter *X* and called the X chromosomes. Males have one X chromosome and one Y chromosome—so called because it looks like a *Y*. Egg cells and sperm cells contain only half the number of chromosomes that other cells contain. All female eggs, then, can contain only one X chromosome. Sperm cells, on the other hand, can contain either an X chromosome or a Y chromosome. If a sperm containing an X chromosome fertilizes the egg, the baby will be XX—a girl. If the sperm contains a Y chromosome, the baby will be XY—a boy. It is the father, then, who determines the sex of a baby.

The interaction of each gene pair, and of groups of similar genes, determines a person's characteristics. Genes for a particular trait, such as eye color, are either *dominant* or *recessive*. Dominant genes dominate, or overpower, recessive genes. The gene for brown eyes, for example, is dominant over the gene for blue eyes. That means a person can have blue eyes only if she or he inherits two genes for blue eye color. If a person inherits one blue and one brown gene, then the dominant brown gene will express itself, and the person will have brown eyes. That person can still, however, pass on a blue eye-color gene to the next generation.

Defective Genes

Of the many thousands of genes each of us carries, some five to eight are defective. Defective genes can occur if a cell does not divide properly. A gene may even get lost entirely. Radiation and chemicals can damage genes.

Genes direct the production of proteins with specific functions in the body. If the gene is defective, it may not make the protein properly, or it may not make the protein at all. In either case, a vital bodily function may be disturbed, with tragic results.

Some 2,000 different genetic diseases have been identified so far. Most are rare. Still, some 90,000 to 150,000 babies are born every year in the United States with a genetic disease. This number is not higher because most defective genes are recessive and show up only when both partners have the same defective gene. This is more likely to happen when the parents are closely related or belong to an ethnic group that has a genetic abnormality. For this reason, marriage between close relatives is prohibited by law.

Sickle Cell Anemia

One genetic disease is *sickle cell anemia.* In sickle cell anemia, a person's red blood cells have a sickle, or crescent, shape. These cells clog up the capillaries, the smallest blood vessels of the circulatory system, thus reducing the oxygen supply to the muscles and other body tissues. The result is tissue damage, along with pain in the muscles and joints. The illness can range from mild to severe.

Anemia occurs because the spleen, an organ that filters unwanted material from the blood, destroys the abnormal sickle cells faster than the body can replace them. The person feels weak and tired and may develop pneumonia or kidney failure.

Sickle cell anemia is most commonly found in blacks, although some whites are also affected. About 1 in 12 blacks in the United States carries one sickle-cell gene. This person may never be ill, but the individual can pass the gene on to his or her children. Sickle cell anemia is not a contagious disease. It can be transmitted only through genes.

To get sickle cell anemia, a person has to

Figure 8.13 The red blood cells of people with sickle cell anemia have a sickle, or crescent, shape.

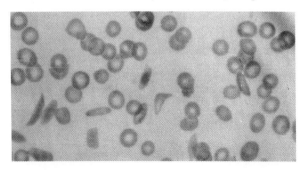

inherit two sickle-cell genes—one from each parent. About 1 in every 165 blacks is born with two genes for sickle cell anemia.

Scientists think that the sickle-cell gene developed thousands of years ago in Africa and in countries around the Mediterranean Sea. The sickle-cell trait does appear to have a beneficial side. It seems to protect its carriers from malaria, a disease that is common in the area where the sickle-cell trait originated.

Other Genetic Diseases

Many genetic diseases affect *enzymes,* proteins that cause specific chemical reactions in the body. Enzymes are responsible for turning the food you eat into body tissue. If a particular enzyme is not produced or is produced abnormally, certain substances in food can build up in the body to levels that can cause massive tissue damage.

In a genetic disease called *phenylketonuria,* or PKU, the victim's body lacks an enzyme that breaks down amino acids, which are the building blocks of proteins. Amino acids accumulate, resulting in severe mental retardation, epileptic seizures, and skin disorders. Because the missing enzyme is partly responsible for pigmentation, there is also a decrease in the normal coloring of hair, eyes, and skin.

PKU occurs about once in every 20,000 births. If it is detected at birth, or shortly thereafter, its effects can be controlled. Early detection is essential if severe damage is to be avoided. Many states now routinely test newborn babies for PKU disease.

Another group of genetic disorders, the *lipid storage diseases,* affects the body's ability to break down and use certain fatty substances. As with other enzyme disorders, the resulting build-up of substances in the body has tragic results. In *Tay-Sachs disease,* for example, affected children suffer blindness, convulsions, paralysis, and mental retardation. These children waste away and die by the age of five.

Like sickle cell anemia, Tay-Sachs disease is limited almost entirely to a specific ethnic group: Jews whose ancestors come from one small area on the Russian-Polish border. More than 90 percent of American Jews have this ancestry, and 100 to 200 children suffering from Tay-Sachs disease are born every year.

A special blood test can now detect carriers of the Tay-Sachs gene. This test is recommended for all people of Jewish ancestry who plan to have children.

Sex-Linked Genetic Diseases

Another group of genetic diseases is carried by the female sex chromosome (X). While the male sex chromosome (Y) seems to contain only genes that determine maleness, the X chromosome contains genes that determine many characteristics besides sex. Females have two X chromosomes, which means that a defective X chromosome, which is usually recessive, will be dominated by the healthy X chromosome. The female will not, therefore, be affected by the defective gene, but she can pass it on to her offspring.

Males, on the other hand, are XY. Because they only have one X chromosome, it is always free to express itself. There is no matching X chromosome to block it. They pass the defective X-linked gene on to all their daughters, but not to their sons. Of the genetic diseases transmitted by the X chromosomes, *hemophilia,* the "bleeder's" disease, is one of the best known. In hemophilia, the body is deficient in the substance that causes effective and rapid clotting of the blood. Because of this deficiency, even the smallest cut or bruise can result in excessive bleeding.

Red-green *color blindness* is another disorder that operates with the same pattern of inheritance. Females who receive the defective, recessive gene will not be affected, but they will transmit it to their offspring. Males who receive the gene will be color-blind and will also transmit the gene to their daughters.

Chromosomal Abnormalities

Genetic mistakes that involve whole chromosomes or large pieces of chromosomes can also occur. Such mistakes involve large numbers of genes and can interfere with the development and function of many body systems. Some pregnancies involving chromosome errors result in miscarriage. Others result in the birth of babies with abnormalities.

One common chromosomal abnormality causes *Down's syndrome.* About one out of every 1,000 babies is born with this condition, the result of an extra chromosome. The action of this chromosome affects almost every part of the body. Children with Down's syndrome have characteristically flat features, a dwarfed body, and are mentally retarded. Down's syndrome is, in fact, the most common cause of mental retardation.

Women over the age of 35 are much more likely to produce defective eggs that cause Down's syndrome than are younger mothers. More than half of all babies with this condition are born to women aged 35 or more.

Congenital Defects

The genetic and chromosomal abnormalities just described are also called *congenital defects*—that is, they are defects present at the time of birth. Congenital defects, more commonly called birth defects, can result from other causes as well.

A developing fetus can be harmed by a number of external factors. Almost everything that enters the mother's bloodstream enters that of the baby as well. If the mother smokes, drinks alcohol, is x-rayed, or takes even relatively harmless drugs, her developing baby can be killed, stunted, or deformed. Some defects can result from bungled attempts at abortion or from injury during delivery. Spastic cerebral palsy, for example, can be caused by almost any injury to the brain before or at birth.

Whether an abnormality will appear—and what it will be—is determined in large part by timing. Each part of the body develops according to its own timetable. If something disturbs that schedule, a body part may never be able to develop fully. The inner ear, for instance, forms between the seventh and tenth weeks of pregnancy. Any interruption in the fetus's development at this time may result in a baby who is born deaf.

Figure 8.14 One out of every 1,000 children is born with the extra chromosome that causes Down's syndrome.

German measles, or rubella, is another example of the relationship between timing and birth defects. The disease is relatively harmless in adults and children, who experience fever and a rash for a few days. But an unborn baby may suffer permanent damage if its mother gets German measles during the first three months of pregnancy. These babies may be born blind, deaf, mentally retarded, and with deformed limbs. An even larger number become the victims of spontaneous abortions or stillbirths.

Syphilis is another disease that can cause abortion, stillbirth, or physical defects such as blindness or deafness. Blindness can also result from gonorrhea or herpes simplex Type 2. All three of these diseases are sexually transmitted and are on the increase (see Chapter 16).

Genetic Counseling

Some genetic diseases can be treated. A special diet can reduce the damage of PKU, and injections of the missing clotting factor can help control the bleeding of hemophilia. But for most genetic diseases there is no treatment. Prevention, through *genetic counseling* and *prenatal diagnosis,* is the best that can be done. As mentioned earlier, the best time to get genetic counseling is *before* pregnancy occurs. In cases where the risk of passing on a serious genetic disease is high, a couple may be advised not to have children.

A developing fetus can now be tested directly for about 100 genetic disorders. Through a procedure called *amniocentesis*, a doctor withdraws some of the amniotic fluid that surrounds a fetus in the womb. The fluid contains cells shed by the baby, which are then tested. The sex of the baby is determined—important in sex-linked disorders—and the chromosomes are examined for abnormalities. The cells are also tested for the absence of vital enzymes that characterize other genetic disorders.

Another procedure for checking the condition of the fetus uses high-frequency sound waves. In *ultrasound*, a machine produces sound waves that are bounced off the fetus to create an image on a screen. The image shows the size, shape, and position of the fetus. No surgery is needed for this procedure.

Another technique for detecting fetal defects is *chorionic villus biopsy*. Chorionic villi are small pieces of tissue that surround the developing fetus. Doctors can remove pieces of this tissue after inserting a tube in the mother's vagina. The tissue can then be analyzed to provide genetic information.

If prenatal diagnosis reveals a genetic disorder, genetic counselors will discuss the disease with the prospective parents. Counselors help couples learn about the disease and put them in touch with service agencies and support groups.

The area of genetic disorders, however, is one in which "new" diseases, as well as new treatments, are constantly being discovered. Diseases that today are incurable may some day, through a new scientific development, respond to treatment.

Figure 8.15 If a woman contracts rubella during the first three months of pregnancy, the development of her baby may be affected.

CHECK YOUR UNDERSTANDING

1. What is the "code of life"?
2. Which parent determines the sex of a baby? What sex chromosomes does a girl have? A boy?
3. How can defective genes disturb a vital bodily function? Why do most defective genes show up only if both parents have the gene?
4. How does sickle cell anemia cause tissue damage?
5. What can happen to the body when a genetic disease affects enzymes?
6. Why do most sex-linked genetic diseases show up only in males?
7. What is the age groups of mothers most likely to have a baby with Down's syndrome?
8. What can happen if the development of the baby is disturbed between the seventh and tenth weeks?
9. Describe three methods for detecting genetic defects.

CHAPTER SUMMARY

- Human sperm are tiny, tadpolelike cells that are produced in the testes. Several hundred million sperm are released in a single ejaculation.
- Menstruation is the monthly flow of blood from the uterus. Most girls begin menstruating between the ages of 10 and 16.
- Human eggs are produced in the ovaries. Each month a ripened egg is released into a Fallopian tube. Conception occurs when sperm and egg unite in the Fallopian tube.
- After fertilization, the egg implants itself in the lining of the uterus. The placenta, which will nourish the developing fetus for the next nine months, begins to form.
- The sooner a pregnancy is confirmed, the better. A pregnant woman should get regular medical checkups. She should pay special attention to diet, and she should avoid unnecessary drugs, including alcohol and nicotine.
- Pregnant teenagers often fail to get the early medical attention that they need. They also tend to eat inadequate diets. One out of every four babies born to teenagers is premature.
- Childbirth begins with contractions of the uterus. Powerful muscles push the baby through the birth canal. The baby emerges head first, and the umbilical cord is cut.
- Breast feeding is beneficial for both mother and baby. It helps mothers regain their figures. It provides babies with greater resistance to infection.
- Certain physical and mental traits are passed from parents to their children by means of genes.
- Defective genes cause a variety of genetic diseases. Among the most common genetic diseases are sickle cell anemia, PKU, Tay-Sachs disease, hemophilia, and Down's syndrome.

DO YOU REMEMBER?

Give brief definitions of these terms:

semen	conception	genes	recessive gene
circumcision	Lamaze method	chromosomes	enzyme
ovulation	Caesarean section	dominant gene	Down's syndrome

THINK AND DISCUSS

1. What could be done to help persuade pregnant teenagers to seek medical attention?
2. Why do you think the survival rate is low for multiple births?
3. What policy do you think your school district should have regarding the education of pregnant teenagers? Why?
4. What do you think of the current practice of allowing the father to assist in the delivery of the baby? Why?
5. What could be the benefits of exercise during pregnancy?
6. Do you think employers should be obliged to allow women time off from work to breast-feed their babies? Why or why not?
7. Many women receive a temporary leave of absence from work, called maternity leave, when their babies are born. Some fathers are now requesting paternity leave as well. What do you think of this idea?

8. Do you think all couples intending to have a child should be required by law to undergo genetic testing and counseling? Why or why not?

FOLLOW-UP

1. Many couples have a fertility problem that makes it difficult or impossible for them to conceive a baby. Using recent magazines and books, report on one of the medical techniques used to help such people.

2. From a local clinic or doctor, obtain a typical recommended diet for a pregnant woman. Compare that diet with a standard recommended diet and report on the differences.

3. Obtain information on the Lamaze method of childbirth from your local YWCA, health department, or other local agency, and describe the special breathing technique to your class.

4. Find out more about one of the genetic diseases mentioned in this chapter and write a report on your findings.

5. Contact the La Leche League for more information on breast feeding. Share the information with your class.

9

Adolescence

After reading this chapter, you should be able to answer these questions:

1. What physical changes occur during adolescence?
2. What mental skills do you have now that you did not have as a child?
3. Why are teenage friendships particularly significant?
4. In what ways have roles of men and women changed in the past few years?

Many primitive tribes have special rites to mark the passage of boys and girls into adulthood. Some of the rites, such as tattooing, are quite painful. But the tribes believe that the ability to withstand pain is itself part of the proof that the child is ready to become an adult. Once the rites are over, the children frequently move away from their families, as a sign of independence. As new adults, they must start to act very differently from the way they acted as children. They are now ready to marry and start their own families.

In such societies, people know what is expected of them at all ages. In most cases, the skills they need to be independent are ones they learned during childhood by working with their parents. So when the time comes for young people to assume adult roles, they are ready.

In highly industrialized societies such as ours, the story is quite different. There is no clear-cut passage from childhood to adulthood. Instead, young people in America go through an in-between period called *adolescence*, which has no definite beginning and no definite end. Generally, boys and girls become men and women physically long before they are considered adults by society.

One reason for this transition period is the many years of schooling that an advanced society requires. Most jobs are complex and cannot be learned in childhood from one's parents. And the nature of being a student extends the years that young people are dependent, economically and perhaps emotionally, on their parents.

For many young Americans, the period of adolescence is a time of conflict and confusion. There is uncertainty about the physical and emotional changes that occur at this time and about the roles that adolescents are expected to take as adults.

One of the problems is that there is so much choice. There are, for instance, literally thousands of occupations from which to choose. Another problem is that there is so much change. It may be hard to decide on values in a society that is always in transition.

This chapter explores the physical and mental changes that take place during adolescence. It also discusses the new kinds of social relationships that develop during the teenage years. The final section examines the influence of relationships, as well as various social factors, in helping adolescents establish their own identities.

SECTION **1**   **Physical Changes**

Physically, adolescence is perhaps the most remarkable period in a person's life. Within a relatively short period of time, a number of complex and important biological changes take place. These changes affect not only a person's size and appearance but also his or her physical maturity.

The Growth Spurt

One of the most obvious events in adolescence is the *growth spurt*. Actually, the growth spurt is a series of spurts, in which different parts of the body reach full growth at different times and in a specific order. The head, hands, and feet are the first body parts to reach adult size. Because feet tend to have a growth spurt before the rest of the body, teenagers who are going through adolescence may feel for a time that they are "wearing someone else's feet."

In general, young women start their growth spurt at about age 10—two years before the average young man. Once a young man's height spurt begins, he grows an average of more than 6 inches in just two years. The average young woman grows about 3 inches in the same amount of time.

Body proportions change during this time, too, to create the body types that are characteristic of males and females. A female's hips start to broaden faster than her shoulders, while the opposite occurs with males. A young man's

Figure 9.1 Adolescents of the same age can show remarkable variations in height.

Figure 9.2 Portraits of the same person, taken six years apart. As the head enlarges during adolescence, the nose and lower jaw grow at a faster rate than the rest of the face.

legs also grow longer in proportion to his upper body, and his forearms grow longer in relation to his height.

For both males and females, however, the sequence of growth is the same. Their leg bones lengthen first. Then their hips and chests broaden, followed by their shoulders. Next their trunks lengthen, and then their bodies fill out.

The shape of the face changes during adolescence too. The head grows in length and width, with the nose and lower jaw growing at a faster rate than the rest of the face. These changes combine to make the adolescent's face look less like a child's and more like an adult's.

At about the same time that teenagers grow taller, they also grow heavier. Young women develop a thicker layer of fat under their skin than young men do, giving women a more rounded appearance. Young men show a greater increase in muscle mass.

The time it takes for growth to be completed varies greatly. Although the average age at which young men stop growing is 21, some continue to grow until they are 25. Young women, in general, reach full growth by about 17, but some keep growing until 21.

One of the major changes that occurs during adolescence is that the reproductive organs begin to mature. The *pituitary gland,* the same gland that regulates overall physical growth, controls the physical aspects of sexual maturation as well. The time during which this development takes place is called *puberty.*

Puberty in Girls

The sex characteristics of young women begin to develop at about the same time as their height spurt begins. These changes occur when the pituitary gland begins to release a hormone that stimulates the ovaries, which in turn produce other hormones, including *estrogen.* Estrogen causes the female's reproductive organs to develop. It also stimulates the outward and visible changes of puberty, such as pubic hair and breast growth. Frequently, one breast develops at a faster pace than the other. The difference in size lessens as the breasts reach their adult state.

While these visible changes are taking place, internal changes are occurring as the reproductive organs develop. The ovaries begin to produce mature eggs, and the uterus prepares to receive and nourish a developing embryo. The sign that these changes have occurred is *menarche*—the onset of *menstruation*. Menstruation can begin as early as age 9 and as late as age 18. (For a full description of menstruation, see Chapter 8.)

Puberty in Boys

The pattern of puberty is similar for boys, although, of course, the details vary. At the onset of puberty, the pituitary gland releases a hormone that stimulates the testes, which in turn produce a number of other hormones, including *testosterone*. Testosterone is the main hormone responsible for stimulating male sex characteristics. In about a year, the testes become capable of producing mature sperm. Usually, the sign that this has occurred is a *nocturnal emission*, an ejaculation of semen that occurs during sleep.

During early adolescence, the voice begins to deepen as well, and boys also begin to develop facial hair. In fact, the word *puberty* comes from the Latin word meaning "hairy."

Other Changes

Adolescence characteristically brings changes to the skin of both boys and girls. Their pores become larger and their skin texture coarsens. Hormones also stimulate the sebaceous glands, small oil-producing glands in the skin. This makes the surface of the skin oilier and contributes to a variety of skin problems. According to one survey, more than half of American 15-year-olds have acne, pimples, or blackheads. Boys tend to have acne more frequently than girls do, and it is generally more severe.

The oil glands in the scalp also become more active, making the teenager's hair oilier than it was before puberty. Stronger body odors also occur, caused by hormones that stimulate perspiration and odor-emitting glands.

When Does It Happen?

A glance at a picture of the freshman class in any high school will show boys and girls in all stages of adolescence. There will also be some students who have not yet begun to mature, as well as a few who are physically adults.

The age at which puberty begins varies markedly from boy to boy and girl to girl. No one knows exactly what triggers its onset, although the timing does seem to have a hereditary basis. Identical twin girls, for example, tend to begin menstruation within three months of each other.

Puberty is also affected by environment. The average age of menarche, for instance, varies worldwide from just over 12 to almost 19. Countries in which girls mature at an early age tend to have a higher standard of living than those in which girls mature later. In the United States the average girl now begins puberty at about age 10 and begins to menstruate during her twelfth year.

Still, the individual range for maturation is great. In a typical classroom of 11-year-olds, there will be about 1 girl in every 10 who has reached physical maturity. About 3 more will

Figure 9.3 Friends who are the same age may be at different stages of physical maturity.

be in the early stages. A year later, 3 out of every 10 will have matured. About 4 more will be on the brink, while 2 or 3 will not have started to mature yet. But by the end of their sixteenth year, almost all girls will have reached physical maturity.

Boys tend to begin puberty about two years later than girls do. For them, the average age at which their bodies start to change is 12. The ability to produce sperm and to ejaculate follows in a year or two. No one knows why the biological clock of males ticks at a rate different from that of females.

SECTION **2**   **Mental Changes**

When Sandi finally hung up the phone, her ear hurt. She and Steve had just spent two hours discussing a plan they had come up with to help the homeless in their city. They figured out how an old school could be converted into a low-rent apartment building. They even devised a system for finding jobs for the unemployed. Sandi and Steve didn't realize it yet, but their plans were made possible by a new development in their thought processes.

Formal Reasoning

The thinking patterns of people change significantly during adolescence. Instead of simply describing things, as they did in childhood, teenagers try to explain them.

When you were 11 or 12, you became capable of *formal reasoning*, an ability you use regularly in your daily life. For example, suppose your radio isn't working. When you were ten years younger, you wouldn't have known how to go about looking for the problem. Now you can examine the possible causes systematically, asking questions such as: Is the radio plugged in? Is the battery dead? Is a wire loose? You can use this approach because you have grasped the principle of varying some factors while holding others constant.

Figure 9.4 The ability to think through a problem systematically continues to improve throughout adolescence.

Abstract Thinking

Along with the ability to think logically comes the ability to think hypothetically—to develop theories and work from them. Adolescents can think in abstract ways that children cannot. It is much harder for a 9-year-old to describe a common object that is not visible than for a 14-year-old to do the same. The object can exist almost as clearly in the adolescent's mind as it does in reality.

This new skill becomes an important part of adolescent life. Children feel deep emotion only for living creatures. But teenagers feel great emotion for ideas as well. You find you can love an abstraction such as justice. You can also hate one such as tyranny.

Many teenagers spend hours at a time practicing this new ability to theorize. You probably have long "What if . . .?" conversations with your friends, and many of these conversations probably revolve around your ideas for reforming society. This kind of idealistic thinking is usually accompanied by a great deal of energy and enthusiasm, which can enable you to be a positive force in society right now.

Teenagers often work fervently for good causes. If you are active in an organization working to save endangered animals, for example, or do volunteer hospital work, you are probably motivated by strong ideals.

Thinking About Thinking

About 350 years ago, the French philosopher René Descartes wrote, "I think, therefore I am." Many teenagers can identify with this sentiment. As your thinking processes mature, you probably find yourself quite fascinated with the act of thinking itself. Thinking becomes a way of defining your own identity.

As you become more aware of your own thoughts, you also become more conscious of what other people think. You may, as many teenagers do, tend to assume that other people think the same way you do. This may lead you to believe that everyone wants to reform society the same way you do. When you find out that some people don't care about something that interests you passionately, you probably feel quite upset and angry.

The belief that others share your thoughts can also cause you to feel painfully self-conscious at times. Since your self-awareness is growing, you may think that everyone is thinking about you. For example, on a day when you dress quickly and put on socks that don't match or wear a shirt with a hole in it, you may think that everyone notices.

Many adolescents spend hours in front of the mirror trying to figure out how they look to others. And when they are together in groups, they tend to be more concerned with what others are thinking of them than with what they are thinking of others. This explains in part the show-off behavior that often takes place when a group of teenagers get together. For example, if you believe that everyone is watching you, you may feel that you have to show off to make yourself more interesting. This showing off may take the form of singing at the top of your voice or making faces behind someone's back.

Once they become aware of their own thoughts, teenagers tend to believe that their feelings are more intense than those of anyone else. Some construct what psychologists call a *personal fable*. They believe that what happens to others cannot happen to them. Thus many teenagers believe they cannot die, no matter how fast they drive. Some young women believe they cannot get pregnant, no matter how many chances they take.

Learning that your own thoughts don't always mirror reality takes time, as does realizing that other people's ideas aren't necessarily the same as yours. Some of these experiences can be painful, but they can help you become more realistic in your ideas about the world. You may also lose some of your self-consciousness as you see that you are not the center of attention in social situations. Learning more about the thoughts of others can let you see that other people have the same anxieties you have, which can lessen your own sense of isolation.

Sense of Right and Wrong

Children tend to see events only in terms of black and white. They judge an action strictly by its outcome. They would say, for example, that a person who runs over a dog is bad and should be punished, even if the action is an accident. But as people's thought processes mature during adolescence, their sense of right and wrong changes. The ability to think systematically leads them to consider an act within its context. They can now consider means and reasons as well as ends. So they would not want to punish the driver for the death of the

Figure 9.5 Taking action to right a wrong—such as demanding satisfaction when a product fails to work properly—is one outgrowth of an adolescent's developing sense of justice.

dog because they can see that it was an unavoidable accident.

Because you can think abstractly, you probably look at rules differently now from the way you viewed them when you were a child. Then, you saw rules as laws handed down by some person in authority. You knew that you had to obey the rules or else be punished. That was probably why, for example, you did the household chores that were assigned to you. Now that you are older, you can see such chores in a broader context. You can see the reasons for having rules in a household and understand that each person has an obligation to the family as a whole to share household chores.

This new understanding of the nature of rules often affects your attitude toward authority. When you reached adolescence, you became conscious of the concept of law itself. You realized that laws were more than just a set of rules to follow; they were necessary for people to be able to live together in a society.

Your evolving understanding of the reasons for rules affects the way you make decisions about your own behavior. For example, when you were a child, you may have decided not to cheat on a test because the rules said not to— and because you were afraid of getting caught and being punished. Now you may decide not to cheat for another reason—because it goes against your sense of right and wrong.

The changes in behavior described above, though, are neither universal nor consistent. A person's sense of right and wrong is shaped by many factors—not only by mental development, but also by the influence of family, friends, and culture. And the same person may make a mature decision on one day and a childish one the next. Also, many people, particularly early adolescents, have a tendency to conform to the standards of a group. In certain situations, the right action is seen as the one that pleases others, even if it goes against an individual's own beliefs. Few people can always match their actions to their beliefs.

CHECK YOUR UNDERSTANDING

1. How does an adolescent's reasoning ability differ from that of a child?
2. How does the ability to think abstractly affect an adolescent's emotions?
3. What assumption do adolescents tend to make about the thoughts of others? Describe two problems that can result from this assumption.
4. Briefly explain the way in which an adolescent's sense of right and wrong tends to differ from that of a child.

SECTION **3** **Social Changes**

Diana and Kirstin are both 15. They have been friends since childhood. These days they spend a lot of time together discussing almost every thought each of them has.

When they were children, Diana and Kirstin spent just as much time together as they do now. However, their friendship then was *situation-oriented*. That is, although they played together, they were more interested in the activity itself than in each other. As teenagers, however, their friendship has become *person-oriented*. Doing things together is often less important to them than expressing their thoughts and feelings to each other.

Relationships with Friends

As a teenager you begin to develop loyalties to friends in addition to the loyalties you have to members of your family. Teenage friendships are often models for the relationships you will form as an adult, both with members of your own sex and with the opposite sex. At a time when so much about you is changing, you gain emotional security from a friendship with someone who is going through the same kinds of changes that you are going through.

Figure 9.6 Talking with friends about the changes in their lives can help give adolescents a feeling of emotional security.

Besides being best friends, Diana and Kirstin are also members of an informal, but tightly knit, circle of friends generally known as a *clique*. At school, you are probably aware of a number of cliques—groups of friends that hang out together regularly. You may be a member of one yourself.

The members of a teenage clique generally come from the same social class and have similar interests and values. They often dress alike, have similar hairstyles, and like the same music. They might also use certain favorite expressions that mark them as members of their particular group. The members of a clique often also dislike the same things. They tend to categorize people and activities as being either "in" or "out." Cliques of young teenagers are generally composed of members of the same sex. By the mid-teens, however, the cliques begin to interact with one another, and cliques made up of members of both sexes form.

Many teenagers get great satisfaction from being members of a clique. The clique gives them a ready-made identity that they can use while they are trying to figure out who they are. Cliques can also be restrictive, however. They can prevent people from exploring other options, and they can cause some individuals to go against their own value systems.

Some teenagers also like to spend time with a larger crowd at a ball game or at the beach, for example. Being with a larger crowd gives them an opportunity to meet other people, and to enjoy activities that may not appeal to the members of their family or clique. In both cliques and crowds, teenagers are learning about appropriate social behavior.

Dating

For many teenagers, appropriate social behavior involves dating. Dating practices have changed over the years. A generation ago, dating was rather more formal than it is now. The young man usually did the asking and paid for the date.

Figure 9.7 Confused about their own identities, many teenagers turn to the ready-made group identity that comes from belonging to a clique.

Today, dating tends to be more casual. Teenagers are now far more likely to go out together in groups, with each member paying her or his own way. As they get to know each other better, a particular young man and young woman may spend more time as a couple. One recent change in dating practice is that the male is no longer necessarily responsible for planning the date. Also, it is no longer uncommon or considered improper for a woman to ask a man out.

Nevertheless, although you may find it easy to get along well with someone of the opposite sex, both you and your date may feel anxious about the other's expectations. This uncertainty is part of the process of learning the new roles that will be part of your adult life.

Sexual Involvement

In some parts of the country, standards for sexual involvement seem to be changing. Twenty or 30 years ago most people believed that sexual intercourse should be reserved for marriage. Today, though, more people are beginning sexual involvements before marriage.

Because standards are changing, many teenagers feel confused about sex. On the one hand, their parents or their religion may hold the belief that sex outside of marriage is unacceptable. Yet on the other hand, they see movies, books, and magazines that seem to promote the idea of sexual involvement. Teenagers who have sexually active friends may also feel pressured by those friends into sexual involvement before they are ready for it.

Clearheaded, responsible decisions can be especially difficult because of the new intensity of sexual feelings. Unfamiliar sexual feelings may be harder to control than adolescents expect at first. They also may not realize that surveys show that the majority of young people go through high school without any sexual experiences. Adolescents who want to go along with the crowd may be misjudging the amount of sexual experience their friends have had.

There are also those who pretend to have more sexual experience than they actually have had.

As time goes on, adolescents come to realize that they must take responsibility for their own decisions. They also learn that people have the right to say no to sexual involvement. A number of adolescents may be in love without feeling ready for sexual intercourse. They can explain that not being ready for sex is not a rejection of the other person—just of a particular activity.

Adolescents who have made the decision to avoid sex find it wise to avoid situations that invite sex. The privacy of a parked car is one such situation. They learn not to put themselves in a spot that they know will be hard to handle.

Relationships with Parents

As adolescents start trying out the independence that will be part of their adult lives, their relationships with their parents change. On both sides, there tend to be many uncertainties. The transition period between childhood and adulthood is confusing for both parent and child. Parents may be fearful of letting their children try their wings at being adults. At the same time, though, parents want their children to learn to make their own decisions, develop their own values, and take responsibility for their own actions.

Adolescents themselves feel pulled in two directions. They are eager to be independent, but they are also fearful of being on their own. Sometimes one feeling prevails, and sometimes the other. This frequently translates into unpredictable behavior. Adolescents may ask a parent for advice, but then resent receiving it. This can lead to a conflict which may last several years.

In many cases, though, adolescents do take their parents' advice. Studies show that there is much less of a ''generation gap'' than the media might have us believe. Teenagers may argue with their parents over immediate issues such as what to wear and when to come home.

Figure 9.8 Most adolescents find that their angry feelings toward their parents change, over time, to feelings of closeness.

But they tend to share the larger political and religious values of their parents.

When it comes to making decisions in specific situations, teenagers will listen to the advice of both their parents and their friends. They seem to be influenced by other teenagers on day-to-day issues such as appropriate clothing. But they tend to take the advice of their parents on larger issues such as career choices.

In many families, the major source of conflict between parents and adolescents is not about what to do, but when to do it. A 13-year-old may think she's ready to go hiking for a weekend with her friends. Her parents may feel that she's still too young to handle a situation that may involve an emergency. In another few years, they will be happy to let her go.

Many people have trouble in early adolescence dealing with the rude shock that comes when they realize for the first time that their parents are not perfect. Teenagers who see weaknesses in their parents may feel angry with them for a while. Later on in adolescence, though, the recognition that parents are "only human" may bring feelings of closeness instead of anger. In a number of studies, parents and older adolescents have reported pleasure at the friendship these changes in outlook have produced.

CHECK YOUR UNDERSTANDING

1. Describe some of the benefits of adolescent friendships.
2. What changes do cliques tend to undergo as adolescents get older? What can adolescents learn from being members of cliques and crowds?
3. Why do many teenagers feel confused about sex? What do surveys suggest about the sexual experience of high school students?
4. What are some of the causes of conflict between parents and their adolescent children?
5. In what kinds of situations do teenagers tend to take the advice of their friends? Their parents?

SECTION **4** **Seeking an Identity**

One reason that adolescents tend to fight with their parents and cling to their friends is that they are seeking to establish their own identities. The question "Who am I?" becomes primary as teenagers adapt to the changes in their lives and make decisions about their future. They must come to terms with the idea of evolving from one stage of life to the next. This involves learning that they can change in many ways yet remain the same person at the core.

Self-Image

An individual's self-image begins to develop during infancy, and the process continues throughout childhood. There is evidence that a person's relationship with her or his parents does the most to determine the way that person sees herself or himself. Someone who grows up feeling loved and trusted is likely to have a very different self-image from that of someone who feels unloved and mistrusted.

As children become adolescents, the way others in their own age group respond to them takes on great importance. Teenagers look to their friends to help them define themselves. At this time, being part of a group can provide a ready-made identity. This is one reason that the members of adolescent cliques tend to dress alike, act alike, and talk alike.

Adolescents often feel that they are walking a tightrope. They are under enormous pressure to conform to the standards of the group. Yet this desire to conform conflicts with the need to establish an individual identity. Many adoles-

Figure 9.9 The members of adolescent cliques tend to dress alike, act alike, and talk alike.

cents have had to make the difficult decision between going along with the crowd in an activity that feels uncomfortable or going their own way and risking banishment. For example, should an individual make fun of a new student who is "different" because the rest of the group does? Or should he or she answer an inner urge to be kind to that person?

With their closest friends, adolescents usually feel free to act the way they really want. They also feel free to experiment with different roles, often trying them out together. These new roles can range from changing their hair to the same new style through taking jobs together as hospital volunteers.

Close friends will also try out different roles on each other. In their attempts to find out if others see them the way they see themselves, such friends act as a mirror for each other. They depend on each other's honesty in these situations, and may spend hours analyzing each other's appearance and personality.

Gender Roles

There is yet another aspect to developing an identity—clarifying *gender roles*. At no other time are people as aware of being male or female as during adolescence. With this awareness comes the question of what is appropriate behavior for a man or a woman in our society.

Today the answers to that question are far less rigid than they were in the past.

Certainly, children are aware early in life that they are boys or girls. Traditionally, baby girls have been wrapped in a pink blanket at the hospital, baby boys in a blue one. Once home, they have been treated in different ways to develop character traits seen as male or female. Studies have shown, for instance, that mothers have tended to talk more to baby girls than to baby boys. And fathers have tended to be far more gentle with their daughters than with their sons. The toys boys and girls have been given have also been different. While girls have traditionally received dolls and toy sewing machines, boys have been given trucks and sports gear. These small differences have added up to an overall difference in the ways boys and girls have learned to act.

The way adolescents come to perceive their gender roles will affect all aspects of their future lives. It will color their personal relationships and their opinions. It will help determine the work they choose—and the way they do it. An adolescent girl who believes women should be passive will have trouble in the future asking for the promotion she deserves. And an adolescent boy who believes it is unmanly to show emotions may have trouble forming satisfying friendships as an adult.

The range of acceptable behavior for males and females of all ages has widened greatly in the past few decades. In one study, 50 percent of the college students polled described themselves as having character traits formerly used to describe only members of the opposite sex. Many male students, for instance, described themselves as gentle. And many female students saw themselves as ambitious and career-oriented.

Developing Values and Goals

Developing a personal set of values and goals is crucial to a teenager's search for an identity. As they mature, adolescents begin to look for something beyond their families to which they can attach themselves. They begin to develop loyalties to a school, club, or religious group. And they begin to feel a strong need to make a contribution to whatever it is they believe in.

For many adolescents, determining their values can be a difficult process. They ask themselves such profound questions as "What is important?" and "What do I believe in?" Finding the answers can involve conflict and confusion. Adolescents may find that influences such as television exhibit values far different from those they learned in their own homes. And in their quest for independence, teenagers may throw off their parents' values without studying them, only to adopt the equally unexamined values of their crowd.

Teachers and other adults may also present values that conflict with those teenagers have learned at home. In many cases, the influence these adults exert can be positive. They can show adolescents there are many goals they can aim at, many roles they can take on. There are many instances in which a dedicated teacher has helped an adolescent develop special talents and abilities.

In deciding what is important, adolescents also decide on their goals—what they want to achieve in life. Studies show that most adolescents seek satisfaction from setting and meeting their own goals. They need a sense of achievement. Thus they become more and more willing to take on responsibilities—especially outside the home, where they feel they are more likely to be judged by adult stan-

dards. It means much more for a teenager to receive praise for completing a salaried after-school job than for finishing a household chore.

Still, what goes on in the home can be crucial to the level of achievement an adolescent strives for. Parents who make realistic yet challenging demands on their children, reward success, expect achievement, and permit children to work on their own create a climate that teaches children they can accomplish a great deal.

Talking Point

Changing Gender Roles

Only a few years ago, it was unusual for a man to stay home and take care of the children while his wife worked. Now it is becoming more common as the roles of men and women change and merge. Today, the doctors, airplane pilots, police officers, and firefighters you encounter aren't always men; neither are the nurses, secretaries, and flight attendants always women.

The feminist movement opened many doors for women in the 1970s and 1980s. Women won admittance to formerly all-male military academies and universities. They became astronauts, building contractors, and corporate executives. By 1985, 68 percent of all married women in America worked at jobs outside the home. More women were elected to Congress and to state legislatures, and in 1984 a woman ran for the office of Vice President of the United States.

It is not only women who have changed. Men have learned that it is all right to show their emotions, and they now take on nurturing roles that were once uncommon for them. Some stay home and care for the house and children while their wives go out to work. Men participate in the birth of their children, and more and more men seek custody of their children in divorce cases. Men have also begun to gravitate to some traditionally female careers such as nursing and clerical work.

For most teenagers, the task of choosing a job for the future becomes a major concern. People have many different reasons for choosing the work they do. Abilities and talents are just two factors that influence career choices.

Matching themselves to an appropriate job is not easy for many teenagers. They may be attracted to a job because they think it is glamorous, without considering the actual work involved. Surveys show, for instance, that younger adolescents have a tendency to make career choices that do not match either their interests or their abilities. Ideally, adolescents should have the opportunity to ''try on'' different occupations, through part-time and summer jobs. In reality, few get that kind of hands-on experience. Most must make their choices through realistic assessment of both themselves and the jobs they are considering.

All in all, the adolescent's search for an identity is made difficult in our society. Because of the wide range of possibilities of what to be and how to be it, there are few clear guideposts on the road to adulthood. In the end, each person must travel that road as an individual.

CHECK YOUR UNDERSTANDING

1. How do close friends assist each other in forming their identities? What kind of conflict often disturbs teenagers who belong to a clique?
2. Describe some of the factors that influence the way a person perceives his or her gender role.
3. What makes some teenagers discard their parents' values without examining them? What creates their growing desire to take on responsibilities?
4. What aspect of a job do younger adolescents tend to focus on when choosing a career?

CHAPTER SUMMARY

- The growth spurt is a series of spurts during which different parts of the body reach full growth at different times.
- In general, girls start their growth spurt at about age 10, and boys at about age 12.
- The time during which the reproductive organs mature is called puberty. In girls the ovaries begin to produce eggs. In boys the testes begin to produce sperm.
- Thinking patterns change during adolescence. Teenagers become capable of formal reasoning and of abstract thinking.
- Many adolescents tend to believe that the thoughts of others mirror their own. This is one reason for the self-consciousness that teenagers often feel.
- The ability to think systematically enables teenagers to develop a sense of right and wrong. They become capable of understanding the need for rules and laws.
- Adolescent friendships are usually closer and more intense than childhood friendships. Adoles-

cents tend to form cliques—tightly knit circles of friends who share similar interests and values.
- Many people start dating during adolescence. Because standards are changing, many teenagers feel confused about sexual involvement in dating. Each person has to make her or his own decision about such involvement.
- Relationships between children and their parents change when the children reach adolescence. Some conflict is to be expected, although there seems to be much less of a ''generation gap'' than we are led to believe.
- Self-image is particularly important to adolescents. Teenagers often look to their friends to help them define themselves.
- The way teenagers perceive their gender roles will affect many aspects of their future lives. The range of acceptable behavior for males and females has widened greatly.
- Adolescents spend a great deal of time trying to decide on their values and goals. The task of choosing a career is a major concern.

DO YOU REMEMBER?

Give brief definitions of these terms:

growth spurt   menarche   personal fable
puberty   formal reasoning   gender role

THINK AND DISCUSS

1. What might be the advantages of maturing early? The disadvantages?
2. What does the term *generation gap* mean to you? Do you think one exists? Why or why not?
3. In what kinds of situations do you think a parent's advice would be more valuable than a friend's?
4. What issues do you think cause the most controversy between adolescents and their parents?
5. What kinds of decisions do you think adolescents should be allowed to make for themselves? Why?
6. What advice would you give to a teenager on how to be a member of a clique and still retain his or her own individuality?
7. What do you think is the biggest advantage of being an adolescent? The biggest disadvantage?

FOLLOW-UP

1. Find out more about the puberty rites that adolescents in certain societies must go through. Write a report on your findings.
2. Interview a member of your grandparents' generation about the differences between a teenager's life then and now. Describe these differences to your class.
3. Watch a popular television show that spotlights adolescents as the main characters. Write a description of the program, concentrating on whether or not the manner in which teenagers are depicted is realistic.
4. Examine two magazines aimed at teenagers and write a report on the kinds of issues and concerns dealt with. State in your report whether you think the magazines truly reflect teenagers' interests. What additional topics would you like to see covered?
5. Find out which services in your community deal with the problems of adolescents. Make a list of these services and post it in your classroom.

CHAPTER 10

Marriage and Parenthood

After reading this chapter, you should be able to answer these questions:

1. How is marriage today different from the way it was 50 years ago?
2. Why do many Americans choose to stay single?
3. What makes a marriage work?
4. How do people decide whether or not they want children?
5. In what ways to parents influence their children?

Marriage today is a greater challenge than ever before. Because of the liberation of both men and women from their traditional sex roles, marriage has become more of an equal partnership. Many husbands no longer expect to be the sole wage earner and major decision maker. Many wives no longer expect to devote themselves entirely to home and children. The challenge is to achieve a satisfying partnership that allows each person to pursue his or her individual goals.

Unfortunately, many people go into marriage expecting it to meet their every need. They are often disappointed. And many people marry before they are ready for it. Teenagers who marry are rarely mature enough to take on such a commitment. Three out of four teenage marriages end in divorce. And the divorce rate for the nation as a whole is now one out of three marriages. We shall explain some of the reasons for this situation in this chapter.

Despite the high failure rate and the problems of adapting to change, most Americans do marry. Statistics indicate that 9 out of 10 Americans marry at least once. And five out of six who divorce or lose their spouses marry again.

Marriage, then, remains one of the basic institutions of American society. And the majority of married couples become parents. Parenthood, like marriage, is changing in a number of significant ways. We shall explore the rewards and challenges of parenthood and the ways in which it is changing.

The first step toward a successful marriage is choosing the right partner. How can you be sure that you're making the right decision? Being in love is important, of course, but you also need to know many things about yourself and your partner. This chapter points to some of the right and wrong motives for marrying. It also examines some of the basic issues that couples need to resolve if they are to live happily together.

A successful marriage is not just a matter of luck. It requires communication, understanding, and flexibility. Marriages that work grow into families that work. The decision to marry is one of the most important decisions you'll ever make. It deserves to be treated seriously.

SECTION 1   Marriage Today

Over the past 50 years or so, the nature of marriage in America has changed significantly. Two or three generations ago, the roles of husband and wife were more clearly defined. In general, the husband was the wage earner, and the wife took care of the home and children. Life was harder. People tended to have larger families, and they had little time or money for travel or leisure. Men and women had only limited knowledge of other life styles, and their expectations were narrower.

Today, Americans are wealthier. They have more time for leisure. They travel more and have wider choices available to them. They have greater control over the size of their families. An increasing number of women are taking jobs outside the home. Men are participating in the housework. Marriage is a different kind of partnership, placing different kinds of demands on both husband and wife.

Marital Expectations

Most newlyweds realize quickly that married life requires cooperation and openness. They are now sharing a household and the responsibilities that go along with it. They have to learn to share the decisions and tasks.

Being able to compromise and communicate is becoming increasingly important in marriage. Today's changing roles and expectations make special demands on a couple. In the past, it was generally accepted that a man's responsibility was to earn enough money to support his family. In return, a woman was expected to take care of the household and raise the children. The demands of marriage on men and women was great, but their roles were fairly clear-cut.

Today, more than 50 percent of American wives have jobs outside the home, and the man's role of breadwinner is changing. Some men feel threatened when their wives pursue their own careers. They feel that their role as provider is being challenged, and they resent the fact that they are expected to help with those household chores that they consider to be "women's work." Other men are more able to accept the changing nature of marriage. They are willing to take on domestic responsibilities that include housework and child rearing. Some men have chosen to stay home after marriage while their wives pursue careers. It is estimated that about 70,000 men are doing this in America today.

This is not to suggest that traditional roles in marriage are gone. Thousands of married couples still choose the traditional type of marriage in which the wife stays at home to raise the children. Many of these women receive great satisfaction from maintaining a household, spending time with their children, and being able to pursue their hobbies and interests.

For other wives, the decision to stay at home brings problems. One problem is isolation. A young married woman often moves from the atmosphere of school or a job to the isolation

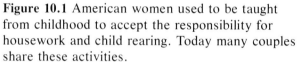

Figure 10.1 American women used to be taught from childhood to accept the responsibility for housework and child rearing. Today many couples share these activities.

of her home. She then begins to wonder why she is becoming dissatisfied. Having expected that marriage would bring more personal growth and fulfillment, she finds instead that the opposite is true. She has a home, a husband, often a child, and yet she is not happy.

In the past, the wife was not isolated. It was not unusual for a woman to share her home with other relatives and many children. There were plenty of people around to share her concerns and benefit from her abilities. Because families had to produce so much of what they needed, a woman knew that the work she did in the home was as necessary to maintain the family as the work the man did outside the home. For practical reasons, husband and wife were dependent on each other.

As families grew smaller and housework became less demanding and less time-consuming,

it seemed logical for women to move to work outside the home. Before World War II, only 15 percent of married women worked outside the home. By 1950 almost 25 percent did so. Today, more than half of all married women, 53 percent, hold jobs outside the home.

This figure shows several trends. Unlike in the past, when women automatically stopped working when they got married, most women now continue working. Like men, they consider their occupations a vital part of their lives. Those who did stop are returning to the labor force in increasing numbers. They do so for a variety of reasons. Some, of course, need the income. Some want to improve their standard of living. Some want to develop and use their skills. Others seek social and professional contact with other adults. Many feel a need to escape from the home environment. House-

Figure 10.2 In many marriages, the wife still bears the major responsibility for taking care of the home and family—even when she also holds a full-time job outside the home.

work, which involves many repetitive tasks for which there is no direct pay, does not satisfy them.

But this move out of the home and into the labor force has brought strains and conflicts into many marriages and families. Many working wives still bear the major responsibility for taking care of their homes and families. Research has shown that they have less than two-thirds the amount of free time enjoyed by husbands. The United Nations International Labor Organization has noted that many working wives are overworked to the point of constant exhaustion. It has urged men to help more with housework and child care.

Cohabitation

More and more people are examining their ideas about marriage. Some people are choosing to live together, or cohabit, instead. *Cohabitation* is highly controversial, and many Americans find the practice unacceptable.

People who live together sometimes say that they want to find out if they are ready for marriage. Does living with another person interfere with their personal and professional development? Can they adapt to the personality of their partner?

Many couples who live together find that they are suited and they get married. Many others break up. When that occurs, the absence of formal marriage does not relieve the partners of all legal responsibilities. Some courts have decided recently, for instance, that laws regarding property do apply to unmarried couples who live together. In any event, the breakup of such a partnership can be as emotionally painful as a divorce.

The Single Life

Not too long ago, many Americans believed that if you weren't married by the time you reached your late twenties, you would remain a bachelor or a spinster. Today, an increasing number of men and women are choosing to remain single or are delaying marriage.

Many who choose the single life value their freedom and independence. They may want time to concentrate on their careers before mar-

Figure 10.3 An increasing number of people are choosing to remain single or are at least delaying marriage.

rying. Others do not feel pressured to marry simply because they have reached a certain age.

There are, however, disadvantages to remaining single. People who live alone cannot always meet their needs for intimacy and security. They may feel lonely at times, and they carry the full economic responsibility for running their own homes.

Because attitudes toward marriage have changed, many single people today feel that they have more freedom to choose when to marry. Many feel that marrying later gives them time to prepare emotionally and financially for a lifelong commitment. They often feel that the wait is worthwhile.

CHECK YOUR UNDERSTANDING

1. In what ways have the roles of husband and wife changed in the past 50 years?
2. What advantages do the traditional marriage roles have?
3. Describe a major problem of women who stay at home after marriage.
4. List some of the reasons that married women work outside the home.
5. Describe some of the advantages and disadvantages of the single life.

SECTION 2 Choosing a Partner

Most Americans marry—or say they marry—for love. Love is a strong and exciting emotion. But does being in love guarantee a happy marriage? Obviously not. Many people have fallen in love and gotten married, and then their marriages have failed.

It is important to be realistic about choosing a partner for marriage. Being in love is important, but it is not all you need. It is quite possible, for instance, for two people to love each other but to be unsuited as marriage partners. You need to know many things about your partner—for example, her or his habits, interests, beliefs, and expectations. Equally important, you need to know yourself.

Self-Awareness

Right now you're going through a period of change. You have physical and emotional changes to cope with. You have many decisions to make. You are developing a sense of your own identity. This process may continue for several years.

Young people in their teens and early twenties often spend much time trying to figure out who they are and what they want to do with

Figure 10.4 Dormitory life often helps students become relaxed and comfortable with members of the opposite sex. This opportunity for open communication can help create a successful marriage.

Figure 10.5 Selecting a marriage partner. When couples feel "right" about each other, it is usually because they come from similar backgrounds and have similar values.

their lives. They spend many hours discussing their goals, relationships, and personal feelings with friends.

Some young people rush into marriage before they have gone through this process. Of those, some remain dependent and immature. Others develop their personalities later. In either case, these marriages may suffer. People who marry before they know themselves often choose partners who are similarly immature. Although the possibility of drifting apart in time exists in all marriages, there is a greater danger of that happening in marriages where neither partner is mature. Even teenagers who are relatively mature can stunt their personal growth through marriage.

Other young people concentrate on their own development. They find out who they are and discover the sort of work they want to do. They begin to develop career skills. They move from a state of dependency on their parents to one of independence. When these tasks are done, they may feel ready to move forward to the selection of a marriage partner.

Motives for Marrying

Anybody who is thinking of getting married should examine his or her motives carefully. People generally say they want to get married because they are in love. But deep down there may be other motives. Only by a process of self-examination can a person discover these motives.

There are plenty of "wrong" reasons for marrying. Some people get married before they are ready for it because parents and relatives pressure them into it. Some marry because all their friends are getting married and they don't want to be left out. Another motive may be to escape from an unhappy home life. Yet another may be to avoid loneliness. Then there are those who marry "on the rebound" to get even with a former girlfriend or boyfriend. Many couples, especially young ones, feel forced into marriage when the woman becomes pregnant.

Anyone who feels uncertain about her or his readiness for marriage probably should not get married. Nor should anyone who feels unsure that she or he has found the right partner. Some uncertainty about marriage is, of course, natural. In general, though, people with successful marriages speak about having had a strong feeling of rightness about their intended mate.

Couples feel right about each other for a variety of reasons. Very often it's because they come from similar backgrounds, have similar values, and want the same things out of life. In general, the more a couple have in common, the better their chance of being happy together. This is not always the case, however. There have been many successful marriages between people from different backgrounds and cultures.

Although no one can say with certainty whether two people are "meant" for each other, matches that succeed seem to share a number of characteristics. The partners consider themselves best friends and good companions. Each one trusts and confides in the other and feels totally accepted for what he or she is. Such people do not marry thinking they will change their partner or themselves. They like—as well as love—each other.

CHECK YOUR UNDERSTANDING

1. What kinds of things should people know about each other before they get married?
2. What are some of the problems encountered by people who marry before they reach emotional maturity?
3. List five "wrong" reasons for getting married.
4. Describe some of the characteristics common to marriages that succeed.

SECTION **3** # Making Marriage Work

There is no one recipe for a successful marriage. Every marriage, like every individual, is different. And in every marriage, two different individuals must find a way of creating a life together that satisfies them. Usually this requires compromise. For any marriage to work, a couple has to reach agreement on certain basic issues. These issues include personality differences, money, sex, and children. We shall look at each in turn.

Personality Differences

It is important that partners create a life style that pleases both of them. To do this, they must recognize each other's differences in personality and ability. They must adjust to such differences and allow each individual to fulfill her or his needs.

One young couple did this successfully by going against traditional sex-role expectations. The wife is outgoing and enjoys working with people. The husband, on the other hand, is shy and reserved. He enjoys spending hours on his own making furniture and working in his garden. They found a way of meeting their needs. She has a career outside the home, and he spends his time at home, doing the things he enjoys. Both are satisfied with their life together.

In one study of personality and marriage, researchers examined a group of college women. They noticed that the more independent women chose men who allowed them to develop their own talents and interests. For example, one woman writer married another writer. Together they shared a single teaching position. They both had strong interests in being parents. And, by sharing a job, both had time to enjoy their children and to write. Their arrangement allowed both of them to satisfy their needs for independence, creativity, and parenting.

The college women in the study who were less independent wanted a traditional marriage. They wanted to play a supportive role and did not want to cope with the complexities of the world outside the home. The only role that interested them was that of wife and mother.

In both groups, the women whose parents had gotten along well moved into marriage relatively easily. Those who came from homes where parents were in conflict often chose partners who tended to continue the process of conflict.

Figure 10.6 The way a couple handles decisions about finances reveals much about the relationship between the two partners.

may not think that money is important, but studies show that finances are a major cause of marital problems.

The way a couple handle decisions about finances reveals much about their relationship. Do they budget and decide priorities together? Do they take responsibility according to traditional sex roles? Or does the partner who has the better accounting skills take control? Is money used to create a position of power? Or is it used to enrich a mutual relationship?

Handling money in a fair way to achieve short- and long-term objectives is a challenging task. All financial decisions have meaning. The way couples handle their finances shows something about their ability to cooperate and act responsibly. Some couples agree to reserve some money for each person to spend however he or she wishes. By so doing, they show respect for each partner's individuality.

Money

A couple would be wise to consider their finances *before* they get married. Young people

Sex

In Victorian times, husbands and wives were not encouraged to enjoy their sexual relations. Wives were often pregnant every year or so.

Fear of pregnancy was common. Women were taught to view sex as one of the duties of marriage rather than as one of its pleasures. The sexual needs of men were frequently frustrated.

Attitudes today are different. There is a new emphasis on the enjoyment of sex, and couples who so choose can use birth control to avoid pregnancy. But this emphasis on sex can put its own strains on a marriage. Husbands and wives may feel pressured to attach more importance to sex than they would really wish. Greater expectations of sexual enjoyment can lead to conflict.

In stable marriages, individuals have an opportunity to adapt to their sexual needs and the needs of their partner. They can discuss their desires and problems and adapt to changes as they arise.

Children

The decision to have children is one of the most important choices a couple ever makes because children bring many changes to a marriage. For many years all of a couple's activities will be affected by the needs of their children. Although parents will no longer be free to come and go as they please, they will enjoy the many rewards that raising children brings.

Before they are married, couples should discuss whether or not they want to have children. Many marriages run into difficulties when the partners discover, too late, that they have conflicting opinions about children. Couples also need to discuss timing: do they want to have children early in their marriage, or do they want to wait until their careers are established or until they have bought a home and saved some money?

Couples who do decide to have children should be aware of what child rearing involves. Small children need attention and love. Some couples may resent the time and effort required to give a child a good start in life. Those who recognize and accept the responsibilities, however, often find that raising children is a truly rewarding experience. They enjoy paticipating in the development of a new human being.

Satisfying Needs

For a marriage to work, people have to be able to satisfy their own emotional needs and those of their partners. Recognizing and accepting those needs is the first step toward finding satisfaction.

One of the basic needs is the need for intimacy. This need can be satisfied if a couple can express their feelings freely. They should be able to feel unself-conscious about their sexuality. They should also be able to trust their partner with their deepest feelings. A person who lacks intimacy will feel lonely.

Another need is the need to share everyday experiences. Often husbands and wives live in different worlds much of the day. Experts suggest that they should make a point of spending a minimum of half an hour a day together, talking things over. This time allows the partners to keep in touch with what is going on in each other's lives. It also makes it easier to resolve problems as they arise.

A third type of emotional need is the need for nurturance—that is, the need to care for some-

Figure 10.7 For many couples, building a home and a successful marriage can, in itself, be a happy and fulfilling experience. Such couples are likely to delay having children, or they may choose not to have children.

Figure 10.8 Experts suggest that husbands and wives make a point of spending some time alone together each day.

body and to be taken care of. Many people feel that their lives have little purpose if they have no one to care for. A good marriage, in which partners can show their appreciation of each other, can satisfy this need.

Another need is that of security. People need to know that there is somebody to whom they can turn for help. A person who has no one to turn to in times of sickness or misfortune can experience great stress.

Marriage, then, can satisfy many of an individual's emotional needs. However, it cannot fill all needs. It is possible to overload a marriage by expecting too much from it. Many emotional needs can be met by friends, relatives, and co-workers. Individuals who expect their husband or wife to satisfy their every need are destined for disappointment.

Adapting to Change

People do not stop changing once they reach adulthood and get married. As time goes on, people frequently develop new interests, at-

titudes, and values. It is not uncommon, for example, for a person to decide that she or he wants to start a new career.

Married people need to be able to adapt to such changes in their partners. They need to be able to discuss what is happening openly and honestly.

Change in a marriage is inevitable. A successful couple learn in time to handle the conflicts that result. They see their lives with each other as a challenge. And they recognize that change can add to their relationship.

Teenage Marriages

Teenage marriages can succeed, but very often they do not. Teenagers who marry are two to three times more likely to get divorced than couples who marry when in their twenties or older. In fact, three out of four teenage marriages fail. Why?

The main problem is that most teenagers are not mature enough to cope with the responsibilities of marriage. They have not had time to decide what they want out of life. They have not learned to fend for themselves. And they tend to have unrealistic ideas about marriage.

Many teenagers marry because the girl is pregnant. When a child is born soon after the wedding, both parents are under a great strain. One of them will have to get a job. Both will find it difficult to continue school. They will have all the responsibilities of parenthood and their social life will be restricted. And because unskilled teenagers can rarely find well-paying jobs, the young couple will probably have financial problems.

Teenagers who marry—whether or not the girl is pregnant—are taking a great risk. They are committing themselves to each other at a time when both are still maturing, emotionally if not physically. The chances that each will change in ways that will pull them in different directions are great.

At the same time, they are limiting their opportunities to develop as individuals. Teenagers tied down by marriage have fewer opportunities to try new things, especially if they have a child. They miss out on many social activities, including dating a variety of people. Dating often helps people to develop their own values and to understand themselves better.

Despite all these problems, some teenage marriages do succeed. When they do, it is generally because the couple is unusually mature. Most teenagers are not ready for such a commitment. A teenage marriage that succeeds is the exception rather than the rule.

Divorce

Today almost one out of every three marriages ends in divorce. The failure rate for teenage marriages, as we have just seen, is three out of four. The divorce rate has increased more than four times since the beginning of this century.

In some cases, divorce is probably the wisest course of action. People sometimes choose unsuitable partners. Some marry for the wrong reasons. Some cannot accept or adapt to growth and change in partners. Others have unrealistic expectations of what marriage should be like.

Another reason for the higher number of divorces is that we live longer today. Eighty years ago, when people married in their early twenties, marriage was likely to end in death by the time the last child was leaving home. Today,

Talking Point

Delaying Marriage

Young people in the 1980s are getting married about two years later, on the average, than people did in 1960. It is no longer unusual for people to wait until they are in their mid- to late twenties before they marry.

Today's high cost of living is one reason that couples are delaying marriage. An increasing number of young people are choosing to continue living with their parents for several years after they finish school. That gives them an opportunity to begin a career and save money before they get married.

Census experts predict that the trend toward postponing marriage will have some far-reaching effects. People who marry later will have fewer children, and there will be more childless marriages. Thus, school enrollments will drop, and this, in turn, will affect employment prospects for teachers.

Because single people have different housing needs than couples with children, the housing industry will also be affected by later marriages. Singles affect the restaurant business, too, because they tend to eat out more frequently than do married couples. They also make greater use of health clubs, vacation resorts, and other facilities that cater to the special needs of single people.

The trend toward later marriage and smaller family size may also have an effect on the national economy. In the years to come, a relatively small work force will have to provide financial support for a growing population of older, retired people. National planners, along with business executives and community leaders, are exploring the many implications that late marriages may have for the decades ahead.

however, although people marry later, they also live longer. By the time they finish raising their children, they still have half their adult lives ahead of them. Boredom may set in.

Half of all divorces occur after 8 years of marriage, and a quarter happen after 15 years. The later divorces are usually not the result of bad initial choices, but of a growing apart of the individuals.

Divorced people are not usually seeking to escape from marriage for the rest of their lives. Most want to exchange unhappy marriages for satisfying ones. The vast majority do remarry. Many times their second marriages last the rest of their lives. Even when the second marriage fails, they often marry again. Divorcing people are actually marrying people.

Of course, divorce can have very upsetting effects on children. For this reason, couples would be wise to postpone having children until they feel confident about their marriages. Each year the parents of about a million children under 18 become divorced. Each one of those children has to cope with the emotional and practical problems of having divorced parents.

Some divorces probably could be prevented by marriage counseling. Marriage counselors work with troubled couples and can often help them to resolve conflicts. Unfortunately, many couples do not seek help until it is too late. Some counselors believe that many more marriages could be saved if couples would ask for advice as soon as a problem arises.

CHECK YOUR UNDERSTANDING

1. In what ways does the handling of family finances reflect the relationship between a husband and wife?
2. Why should couples discuss their feelings about having children before they marry?
3. Describe four of the emotional needs that can be fulfilled by a good marriage.
4. How many teenage marriages fail? What seems to be the main reason for this rate?
5. What is the failure rate for marriages in all age groups? What might be one way to reduce that rate?

SECTION 4 Parenthood

In the past, society expected all married couples capable of having children to have them. Today social expectations are changing. Society is recognizing the rights of each couple to decide whether or not they want children. The majority of married couples do become parents. But the percentage of those who choose to remain childless is rising.

In 1985 over one-third of all Americans under 30 who had ever been married remained childless. This compares with one-fourth in 1970 and one-fifth in 1960. In addition, many couples who do decide to become parents are having only one child.

There are several reasons for this shift in attitude toward parenthood. One is the awareness of world population problems and of limited natural resources. Another is the fact that couples can now state openly that they do not

want children without being considered "abnormal." The increased independence of women is also slowing the birth rate. Now that better jobs are available to women, many are choosing to remain childless rather than interrupt their careers. Finally, the wide availability of birth control methods makes it possible for couples to limit the size of their families if they wish to do so.

To Have or to Have Not

In the past, it was to people's economic advantage to have children. Sons could become farm hands or apprentices in a trade. Daughters could help with the household chores and marry men who could provide additional help and income to the family.

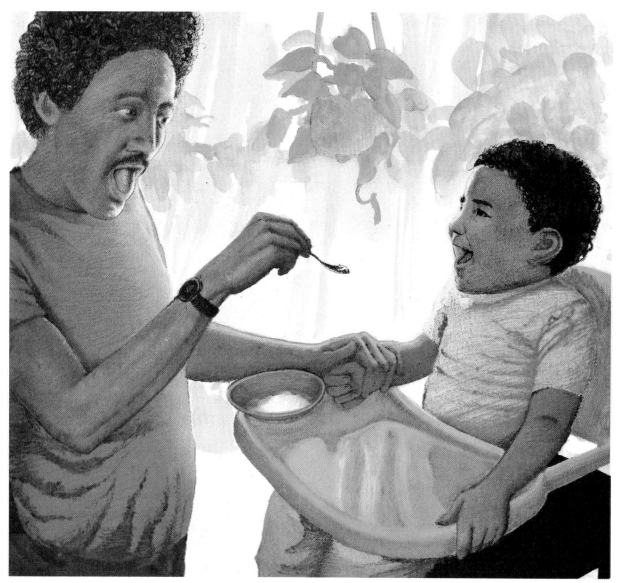

Figure 10.9 The best parents tend to be people who feel good about themselves and want to share these good feelings with their children.

Today people have children for different reasons. Studies on why people have children have revealed many motives. The reason least mentioned by parents is a love for children. There are many *wrong* reasons for couples to decide to have children. A few of them are—

- to try to bring stability to a shaky marriage;
- to provide objects for exercising parental authority;

- to give the parents immortality;
- to provide a love object for parents who do not love each other;
- to maintain family traditions;
- to equalize the number of children of each sex in the family or to provide playmates for an only child;
- to keep the wife at home;
- to give a bored wife something to do;

- to provide the couple's parents with grandchildren;
- to provide for security in old age.

What are some of the right reasons for having children? Consider the following:

- The couple enjoy and respect children.
- The couple have developed a strong, secure relationship. They would like to extend it and enrich it with a child.
- The couple feel good about themselves. They feel confident that they will make good and loving parents.
- The couple understand the change that having children brings.They are eager to accept the challenge.
- The couple are interested in learning how to be good parents.
- The couple are happy to have the opportunity to participate in the creation and development of another human being.

Coping with Change

Children cannot help but bring changes to a marriage. If both parents work, one parent must give up his or her job or else make arrangements for child care. The husband and wife are no longer as free as they were. Even a simple outing to the movies requires baby-sitting arrangements.

In a traditional marriage, the husband and wife come to live in two different worlds. He goes off to his job, and she becomes involved in the details of child care. Many husbands complain that their wives become duller and less fun once they become housewife-mothers. Wives complain that their husbands do not take enough interest in their activities and in the children.

Some tensions are inevitable as couples learn to cope with the changes that children bring. Those who have strong marriages and who can discuss their problems are most likely to resolve these tensions. Parents must learn to adapt to their new way of life. They must try to keep up with the activities that interest them, both as a couple and as individuals. The couple that can share in the care of home and children are more likely to have a happier marriage than couples who can't share. They are also more likely to raise happier, healthier children.

The Parents' Role

A parent is the most important teacher a child will ever have. It is important, therefore, that parents consider their various roles in the child's life. They are responsible for their

Figure 10.10 Love and attention are two of the most important things a parent can give a child.

Talking Point
Child Abuse

Karen isn't sick, but she's staying home from school again today. Her parents don't want anyone to see the burns they made when they scalded her with hot water to "teach her a lesson." The lesson? Not to cry when she trips and falls. Karen is six years old.

Karen is one of an estimated 1 million American children who are abused by their parents or guardians each year. They are beaten, burned, or otherwise battered. Some are starved. Many are sexually assaulted. So far, Karen is lucky; she has not become one of the 2,000 children who die from such treatment each year.

What kinds of people treat children this way? They come from all walks of life, all economic levels, and all races. They do share certain characteristics though. They themselves were usually abused or neglected as children. As adults, they have the same strict, disciplinarian attitude toward child rearing that their own parents displayed. No matter what the demand, instant obedience is expected. A child who does not obey deserves punishment.

As for abused children, they tend to be quiet and withdrawn. Understandably, they are terrified of authority. Rather than seeking help for their problem, they try desperately to hide or deny it. For one thing, they usually love the abusing parent. For another, they have been warned that they will be severely punished if they tell.

But help does exist—for both parent and child. Many communities have crisis intervention hotlines, where parents who realize they are losing control can get help at once. There is also a national organization, Parents Anonymous, that operates on the same principle as Alcoholics Anonymous. During meetings, parents help each other overcome their tendencies toward violence. Each parent has a buddy to call when a problem arises.

To protect the child involved, all states now have laws that require doctors and other health professionals to report suspected cases of child abuse. But anyone who knows of a child abuse situation is urged to call child welfare authorities. In too many cases, after the death of an abused child, it has turned out that neighbors suspected something was terribly wrong. But they did nothing, and tragedy resulted.

child's emotional, social, and intellectual development. It is a tremendous challenge and responsibility to provide a child with the right care and attention. The process requires a deep commitment of time and thought.

Emotional Development   The first five years are the most important for emotional development. The way parents deal with their child's emotional needs during this period is, therefore, crucial. Most important of all is the need for love. A child who is not loved will be emotionally handicapped.

All children want to be special. They want their parents to treat them differently from their brothers and sisters. Yet at the same time, they want to be like other children and to have what other children have. Parents can either help or hinder these natural tendencies.

Parents can hinder a child's development by being either too domineering or too permissive. They can make too many demands on the child in order to satisfy their own parental pride. Parents can also interfere with the child's development by imposing their own standards without giving an explanation. Just saying "We know best" will not help the child. On the other hand, children who have no limits tend to feel frightened and unloved. They may also have social problems.

Parents can help their child by leading and explaining. They can provide healthy models for dealing with emotions.

Social Development Children learn much of their social behavior by copying what adults do. Because parents are usually the most important adults in a child's world, they will be the ones whom the child imitates.

But parents are also important because they have the power to reward and punish. They can show or withhold love in response to a child's actions. Sometimes they train a child to behave in certain ways without even realizing it. For example, parents tend to show an interest in their child when he or she does or says something of which the parents approve. In contrast, they tend to be uninterested, or even hostile, when the child expresses an opinion that the parents don't share.

Parents also have a strong influence on a child's perception of the sex roles. Before children are even aware that there are two sexes, they learn from their parents the behaviors, attitudes, and feelings that fit each role. Because children imitate their parents, the model provided for them is extremely important. So is the quality of the relationship between the parents. The husband-wife relationship is the first model that a child perceives. It can have a strong influence on the child's response to sex roles.

Intellectual Development As with emotional development, the first five years are the most important for a child's intellectual development. Young children love to learn. They are naturally curious and will learn for the pleasure of learning. They need no other reward. It is only when they are forced to do it that learning becomes a chore.

Parents can assist their child's intellectual development in a number of ways. They should take time to explain their actions and let the child make decisions. They should also try to answer questions and encourage the child to try again when she or he makes a mistake. Parents can also introduce the child to interesting things and make everyday happenings into a learning experience.

Parenting for Health

Parents have a strong and lasting influence on their child's health. Many of our health ideas, attitudes, and practices are based on our family backgrounds.

Parents decide what and how much their children eat. If they allow children to overeat and get fat, the children may have a lifelong weight problem. If parents are physically active, children are also likely to enjoy physical activity. If parents smoke, their children are more likely to become smokers. And if parents misuse alcohol or other drugs, children are more likely to misuse them too.

Parent-Child Relations

The goal of parents should be to help children become responsible, mature individuals. However, parents should not neglect their own needs and interests in the process. They cannot spend all their time following a child around, nor would that be desirable.

Parents must, therefore, develop rules to govern their relationships with their children. Such rules generally fall under the heading of discipline. They should help the child's development, while keeping parent-child conflict to a minimum.

Among the methods of discipline that one child psychologist recommends are the following:

1. Parents should control the child's surroundings to avoid unnecessary problems. For example, a mother who allows her toddler to crawl around in a room full of things that should not be touched is inviting needless problems. Far better to remove the objects or to confine the child to a "safer" area.

Figure 10.11 The reflection-of-feelings technique. Parents should let children know that they understand the child's fears and problems.

2. Parents should give children freedom to explore their environment and to assume responsibility when they are able. As soon as children can feed or dress themselves, they should be allowed to do so. It may take longer, but it is better for children to do such tasks themselves.

3. Parents should make a distinction between feelings and actions. Children can learn to control their actions long before they can learn to control feelings. They can, for example, learn not to hit or kick people when they are angry. Instead, they should be taught to express such feelings in ways that are not harmful.

4. Parents should make sure that children know what they are permitted and not permitted to do. Such limits should be reasonable and consistent.

Parents should be able to explain why they set such limits.

5. Parents should try to understand their children's feelings. When children are afraid, helpless, angry, or hurt, they want their parents to understand. Parents can show they understand by putting the child's feelings into their own words and reflecting them back to the child (see Figure 10.12).

6. Children should be praised for their efforts. Parents often encourage bad behavior without realizing it. They ignore their children when they are good and punish them when they are bad. When that happens, the child knows that the best way to get attention is to misbehave. In such cases, punishment becomes a reward.

What Makes a Good Parent?

In addition to providing for the child's physical and emotional needs, good parents respect their child. They are honest with the child and admit mistakes. They provide the child with sympathy, understanding, and security. They make it clear, for example, that an episode of bad behavior does not mean they think the child is bad and unworthy of love.

Perhaps even more critical is that a couple should—before they even have children—know what they hope to achieve by becoming parents. Each partner should decide whether parenthood is what he or she really wants for a full and satisfying life. Once a person decides on parenthood, he or she must accept the responsibilities that go with it.

Parenthood may seem to be an awesome responsibility. In many ways it is. But it can also be a rewarding experience. It provides an opportunity to be fulfilled and to contribute constructively to the world. Parents can gain immense satisfaction from seeing their children develop and grow up.

Being a good parent involves relaxed living and family relationships. Even the best parents make mistakes. But children are quite tough. No child is ruined by occasional parental mistakes. Rather, the quality of the parent-child relationship is what, in the long run, makes for successful child rearing.

CHECK YOUR UNDERSTANDING

1. List five of the wrong reasons for having children. What are five of the right reasons?
2. Describe some of the ways a parent can hinder a child's emotional development.
3. How can parents foster a child's intellectual growth?
4. Explain five things a parent can do to help a child grow in responsibility and maturity.

CHAPTER SUMMARY

- The nature of marriage is changing. An increasing number of wives are taking jobs outside the home. Many husbands are participating more in housework and child rearing.
- Today's changing roles and expectations have placed new demands on married couples. Compromise and communication are becoming increasingly important.
- More than half of all married women have jobs outside the home. Many working wives still carry the major responsibility for taking care of their homes and families.
- An increasing number of men and women are choosing to remain single.
- There are many "wrong" reasons for marrying. Unfortunately, too many people do not examine their motives before marrying.
- For a marriage to work, a couple must reach agreement on certain basic issues. These issues include personality differences, money, sex, and children.

- Marriage should satisfy certain emotional needs. These include the need for intimacy, to share everyday experiences, for nurturance, and for security.
- Three out of four teenage marriages fail. The main problem is that most teenagers are not mature enough to cope with the responsibilities of marriage.
- The overall divorce rate in the United States is now nearly one out of every three marriages. The vast majority of the people who get divorced eventually remarry.
- The majority of married couples become parents, but the percentage of those who choose to remain childless is rising.
- Among the wrong reasons for having children are to bring stability to a shaky marriage and to give a bored housewife something to do. Among the right reasons are that the couple enjoy and respect children and that they feel confident that they will make good parents.

● Parents are responsible for their child's emotional, social, and intellectual development. They also have a strong and lasting influence on their child's health.

● Parents should develop rules of discipline to govern their relationship with their child. Such rules should help the child's development while keeping parent-child conflict to a minimum.

THINK AND DISCUSS

1. What is the purpose of an engagement period before marriage? How long should an engagement last?
2. Do you think a wedding should be a large social event or a small, private affair? Why?
3. Why might people who come from homes with parental conflict choose mates who continue that conflict?
4. Do you think remaining single for an extended period of time makes it easier or harder for a person to marry? Why?
5. What can a working couple do to make sure household chores are divided fairly?
6. Should finances be handled differently in a home where both partners work than in one where only one partner works? Why or why not?
7. Do you think more couples were happily married 50 years ago, when divorce rates were much lower? Why or why not?
8. Do you think the laws should make it easy or hard to get married and divorced? Why?
9. What ways can you think of for housewives to lessen feelings of isolation and boredom?
10. How can children benefit from fathers' taking an active role in child rearing?
11. What factors should working parents take into account when choosing a day-care center or baby-sitter for their child?
12. Do you think an unhappily married couple with young children should stay together "for the children's sake"? Why or why not?

FOLLOW-UP

1. Find out what was involved in running a typical home 100 years ago. Write a report on a housewife's daily routine.
2. Talk to a local clergy member about the kind of counseling she or he gives to couples planning marriage. Describe this advice to your class.
3. Contact your local Y or adult school to find out about courses in parenting. Post the information in your classroom.
4. Write an essay about someone you consider an outstanding parent. Describe the traits that make this person so successful at parenting.
5. Find out about the laws governing marriage and divorce in your state. Write a report on these laws, including any changes you would make.
6. Find out about the special programs in your area that help women reenter the job market after a long absence. Describe the program to your class.
7. Find out more about child abuse from your library or from the National Center on Child Abuse and Neglect. Write a report on an aspect of this problem you find especially interesting.

CHAPTER 11

Aging and Death

After reading this chapter, you should be able to answer these questions:

1. What happens to your body and mind as you grow old?
2. Can you stay younger longer?
3. What is the legal definition of death? Why is a legal definition needed?
4. What is a living will? Why do people write them?
5. Why is grief an important emotion?

Many people, when they think about aging, also think about death. They look upon both with fear. Because of this fear, they may avoid the company of old people. The sight of white hair and wrinkles makes them feel uneasy.

But old people are not all on the verge of death. Many lead active and enjoyable lives when in their seventies, eighties, even their nineties. How much they enjoy their later years depends largely on their attitudes toward aging. Those who look forward to their retirement and are able to adapt willingly to change are the ones most likely to value their later years. In addition, people who follow good health practices throughout their lives are more likely to enjoy a healthy, active old age.

At the same time, old people do have special needs. Their bodies are changing and they have less energy than younger people. The later years also bring many stresses and changes. Retirement, illness, and widowhood are three major events that many older people face. They need help to handle such events. They also have to come to terms with the idea of their own deaths.

Death is not always a sudden event. The big killers of today, cancer and cardiovascular diseases, often bring slow deaths. Many people know they are dying and have weeks or months in which to prepare for death.

Dying people have important needs. Friends and relatives should understand those needs and do all they can to help. And once a loved one has died, those who are left to grieve also need help and understanding.

This chapter explores the needs of the aged, dying, and bereaved. It explains what happens to people, both physically and emotionally, as they grow older and approach death. Being able to think and talk about death can be valuable at any age. It can help us to help others. And it can help us to face our own old age and death in a mature way.

SECTION **1**   # The Aging Process

As people grow old, their bodies are unable to perform as well as they once did. And when elderly people become ill, it usually takes longer for them to get better. The reasons for this are still a mystery. There are many theories about the aging process, but none of them fully explains how and why people age.

The "wear and tear" theory compares the body to a complex piece of machinery. As the years pass, the body simply wears out with use. The "waste product" theory maintains that damaging waste products build up in the body cells and eventually prevent the cells from functioning properly. Another theory holds that the body's immune system breaks down. Instead of fighting foreign substances, it begins to attack the body's own cells. According to another theory, highly active fragments of molecules cause aging by destroying essential body chemicals.

Some scientists believe that the body's chromosomes carry a genetic program that is scheduled to break down eventually. Others maintain that the aging process is linked to the formation of new body cells. As the cells divide and redivide, copying their DNA each time, errors occur in this genetic material. These errors build until the cells can no longer function normally. Yet another theory suggests that the brain contains pacemakers that control the aging process.

Gerontology, the study of aging and the aged, attempts to determine which of these theories is most valid. It may be that several of them are correct and that a combination of events leads to the aging process. Because the percentage of older people in our society is growing, gerontology will assume more importance in the years to come. Our understanding of aging should, therefore, increase.

Physical Changes

During later adulthood the hair turns white and tends to get thinner on top of the head. The skin loses its natural moisture and becomes more wrinkled. Many people lose their teeth. This loss causes the lower part of the face to become shortened. The nose tends to lengthen because the skin loses elasticity. Eyelids thicken and hollows develop beneath the eyes.

Many people become shorter with advancing age because the spine tends to curve. Shoulders become narrower and the pelvis broadens. Some older people's bones become porous and fragile—a condition known as *osteoporosis.* These people are very likely to suffer bone fractures if they fall. Osteoporosis is more common in women than in men.

Internal Changes

Other changes take place inside the body. The work capacity of the heart decreases. When an older person is exposed to stress, the heart does not react as fast or as well. And after stress, it takes longer for an older heart to return to its normal level of pumping.

The circulatory system no longer carries blood as well as it did. The artery walls thicken, causing circulation to slow down and blood pressure to rise.

The lungs, too, become less efficient. At age 85, one's lungs can hold only about three-fifths of the volume of oxygen that they held at 25. An older person thus has less energy.

The digestive and excretory systems also work less efficiently. Signals travel more slowly along the nervous system, so reactions become slower. And all the senses work less

Figure 11.1 Later adulthood brings many physical changes. Hair may turn white, skin becomes more wrinkled, the spine tends to curve, and movement becomes more difficult.

well. Vision, hearing, touch, taste, and smell tend to be less sensitive.

Health and Disease

Some older people sail through their later years active, vigorous, and the picture of good health. Others find themselves spending much of their time in doctors' offices and hospitals.

The course of illness in older people tends to be different from that in younger people. Young people generally get ill quickly, recover quickly, then seem to be as well as before. In older people illnesses tend to develop gradually and linger longer.

About 80 percent of older people have some sort of chronic health problem. Approximately one out of four people 65 or older is hospitalized each year. Older people also complain more about such discomforts as rheumatism, arthritis, and digestive problems. Yet despite all these illnesses, 81 percent of the elderly get around on their own, and only 5 percent live in institutions.

Old people are particularly likely to be affected by stress. They often have to face several of the most stressful life changes in a short period of time. Death of a spouse, retirement, personal illness or injury, and illness of a family member are just a few of the life changes most likely to affect older people. At any age, a major change in the pattern of a person's life is stressful and can lead to disease. But older people are physically less capable of tolerating stress. Such life changes can, therefore, lead to serious or even terminal illness. It is a vicious circle. Old age makes people more susceptible to disease; disease makes people age faster.

Mental Changes

Many people believe that old age invariably brings a decline in intelligence. This is not true. How well the mind works in old age depends on how much it has been challenged throughout life. People who believe they will go downhill after 65 will usually find that they do. But those who maintain an active mind will be able to find challenges in their old age.

How to...
Estimate How Long You Will Live

Of course, no one knows for certain how long she or he will live. However, various factors are known to lengthen or shorten a person's life. These include genetic and environmental influences and personal habits. Dr. Diana S. Woodruff of Temple University in Philadelphia has compiled a self-test that takes such factors into account. The results will not be scientifically accurate. But they may help you to increase your chances for a longer life.

The average life expectancy for people born between 1965 and 1975 is as follows:

Males   68 years, 8 months
Females   76 years, 6 months

To determine how your life expectancy is likely to compare with the average, study the following statements. Find out how many years you should add to or subtract from your life. Combine your total with the relevant life expectancy figure above. This is the age to which you can expect to live unless your life style changes.

1. Descendants of long-lived people tend to live longer themselves. Add one year for each grandparent who lived to be 80 or more.
2. First-born children tend to live longer. If you are the oldest or only child born to your parents, add one year.
3. Overweight is a health hazard and a killer. If you are overweight, subtract one year for each 10 pounds of overweight.
4. If you do not smoke, add two years.
5. If you do smoke, subtract 12 years for two or more packs a day, 7 years for one to two packs, and 2 years for less than one pack.
6. If you regularly go without breakfast and just have some snacks for lunch, subtract two years.
7. If you exercise at least two or three times a week, add three years. Exercise can include long walks, bike riding, swimming, jogging, or any athletics as well as calisthenics.
8. If you have lived most of your life in one of the following states, add one year: North or South Dakota, Nebraska, Kansas, Minnesota, Iowa, Missouri.
9. If you have lived mostly in New York, New Jersey, or Pennsylvania, subtract one year.
10. If you live (or intend to live) most of your life in a large city, subtract one year.
11. If you live (or intend to live) most of your life in a rural area, add one year.
12. If you intend to have regular annual medical examinations throughout your lifetime, add two years.
13. If you sleep more than nine hours a night (regularly), subtract four years.
14. If you plan to get married eventually, add three years.
15. If you don't use automobile seat belts or if you frequently drive or ride with someone beyond the speed limit, subtract one year.

People tend to improve some of their thinking skills in later years. Verbal skills—the use and understanding of words—are often better at 65 than they were at 40. Visual skills, such as finding a simple figure in a complex one, also tend to improve with age.

However, on tasks requiring eye-hand coordination, such as copying words, older people do not do so well. They also tend to do poorly on any task in which speed is important. Slowness is perhaps the greatest mental change in the elderly.

16. If you do use seat belts and observe speed limits, add one year.
17. If you intend to finish college, add one year.
18. If you are planning a professional career, such as law, medicine, or science, add two years.
19. If you intend to get a job that requires you to sit most of the day and not move around, subtract three years.
20. If you are planning a career that requires physical activity (for example, dancing or construction work), add three years.
21. If you sleep in a cool or cold room, add two years.
22. If you regularly read books or articles about good health or nutrition and try to live according to what you've learned, add five years.
23. If you're usually calm, reasonable, contented, and practical, you might be able to add up to five years.
24. If you're usually very competitive, intense, nervous, or unhappy, you might have to subtract several years—unless you seek professional help or do what you can to calm yourself and change your habits.
25. If you expect to become very rich, take a high-risk job (such as bomb removal or one involving much air travel), or remain single, you may have to subtract several years.

Adapted from Judith Bentley, "Will You Live to Be 100?," *Family Health*, January 1975. Reprinted by permission of the author.

Figure 11.2 Mental ability does not automatically decline with age. Visual and verbal skills actually improve in many people as they pass age 65.

thing. Older people, on the other hand, are unwilling to learn those things they consider unimportant.

Creative thought and ability also know no age barrier. Some writers, artists, and musicians have produced great work when in their seventies and eighties. Some people even become creative for the first time in their later years. The artist Grandma Moses, for example, did not begin painting until she was in her seventies.

Senility

The term *senile* is used to describe old people who suffer a severe loss of their mental abilities. They lose their memory, become very confused about time and place, and may be emotionally disturbed. About half of the elderly people who live in institutions are there because they have been diagnosed as senile.

Many of them may not be senile, however. Some older people who seem senile are simply depressed. Older people are particularly prone to severe depression because of the many losses in their lives. Other people who are thought to be senile are suffering from such conditions as anemia, malnutrition, gland disorders, and other physical ailments. Another major cause

It is not true that memory declines in later years. The ability to learn and remember is likely to be as good as ever, provided a person exercises that ability. The elderly may become more selective in their learning, however. Young people are willing to learn almost any-of mental confusion is the interaction of drugs. Older people are often given a variety of drugs. When taken together the drugs can have unexpected side effects.

It is estimated that as many as 20 percent of the people who have been diagnosed as senile have conditions that could respond to treatment.

Longevity

Children born today have a much longer life expectancy than did their parents or grandparents at their birth. An American born in 1900 had a life expectancy of only 49 years. The life expectancy of a baby born today is almost 75 years.

The length of time an individual will live depends on a number of factors. Where a person lives is one of them. People in advanced countries can expect to live longer than those in developing countries.

Another major factor is heredity. Longevity tends to run in families, so children of long-lived parents are likely to be long-lived themselves. Sex is also important. In countries where the risk of dying in childbirth is low, women generally live longer than men.

Other factors involved in longevity are environment, diet, activity level, social and economic status, marital status, cigarette smoking, use of alcohol, intelligence, happiness, and attitude toward aging.

Slowing Down the Clock

There are many things one can do to improve the chances of living a long and healthy life.

Talking Point

The Tragedy of Alzheimer's Disease

Every day, Arthur G. finds it more and more difficult to feed and dress himself. He can no longer remember his address or his wife's name, and he is convinced that his family is trying to kill him. Arthur is suffering from a progressive, incurable brain disease. He will continue to get worse and worse until, in a year or two, he will die. Arthur has Alzheimer's disease.

A few years ago, most people had never heard of Alzheimer's disease. Doctors used to think it was a rare brain disorder that affected only middle-aged and younger people, afflicting them with symptoms similar to senility in elderly people. Now researchers know that Alzheimer's is not rare at all and that it is, in fact, the cause of many cases of senility in the elderly. Alzheimer's afflicts an estimated 3 million Americans and takes more than 120,000 lives a year. Most people who have Alzheimer's are over age 65.

The first symptoms are forgetfulness and minor mental confusion. People forget where they left their car keys, or they can't recall familiar phone number. As the disease progresses, they fail to recognize their surroundings, and they can't remember the names of their spouses and children. Alzheimer's also often causes severe depression.

Alzheimer's is particularly hard on the victims' families, who must provide 24-hour-a-day care for them. Eventually, most people with Alzheimer's have to enter nursing homes where the cost of their care can use up all or most of the financial resources of their families.

Medical researchers don't know what causes Alzheimer's disease. It may be caused by a virus, or it may be genetic. They do know that it is the fourth largest cause of death among adults after heart disease, cancer, and stroke. This fact has generated millions of dollars in research grants, and many studies are now underway to try to determine the cause of Alzheimer's disease and to find a cure for it.

Figure 11.3 People who have stable family relationships are likely to live longer than those who do not.

Two of the greatest threats to longevity are cigarette smoking and excessive drinking. Poor nutrition, including overeating, also increases the risk of illness. And failure to keep physically fit may well affect longevity. Thus, people can increase the odds of living a long and healthy life by not smoking, drinking alcohol lightly or not at all, eating properly, and exercising regularly.

People are also likely to live longer if they are happily married and have stable family relationships. Learning to relax and avoid tension also helps. Other factors associated with a long life include avoiding high-risk occupations and activities and avoiding exposure to environmental pollution. It is also important to get early treatment for conditions such as diabetes and hypertension.

As people age, their mental and physical abilities generally follow the rule "Use it or lose it." Skills that are not used regularly tend to disappear. Unused muscles weaken; unused minds deteriorate. People who make full use of their capabilities seem to experience more meaning in their lives. They usually live longer than do those who withdraw and become passive.

Meanwhile, scientists are looking for other ways of slowing down the clock. One way might be to develop drugs and hormones to replace substances that wear out during the aging process. Another might be to inject an older person with his or her own *lymphocytes*. These disease-fighting white blood cells could be collected decades earlier and kept in cold storage. They could then be used when the body's immune system shows signs of weakening. Some scientists are looking into the possibility of altering the DNA in human cells in order to prolong life.

The aim of this research is not merely to prolong old age. Rather, it is to extend people's vigorous youths and productive middle years. Some scientists are even predicting that someday people may live 200 years or more.

CHECK YOUR UNDERSTANDING

1. Describe five theories about the aging process.
2. What happens to the heart and lungs when a person grows old?
3. List four stressful situations old people often have to face. How can such stress affect them physically?
4. Which mental skills improve with age? Which decline? Which remain constant?
5. List eight factors that influence longevity.

SECTION **2** **Dealing with Aging**

Childhood, adolescence, and young adulthood are years for gaining experience. This experience is put to productive use during middle adulthood. Then in the later years, people must adjust to a different way of life. They use their lifetime of experience to cope with the personal changes and losses that old age brings. The adjustment is easier for some than for others.

Attitude

Successful adjustment to old age depends largely on attitude. People who look forward to retirement adjust to it more easily and enjoy it more than those who dread it. Those who look forward to growing older also tend to grow old more gracefully than those who feel afraid of old age.

People who are willing and able to change and adapt also adjust more easily to older age. Those more likely to do so are those who challenged themselves to change and adapt earlier in life. People who always resisted change will continue to do so.

Adapting well to old age also means being willing to depend on others for help when necessary. In addition, a hopeful rather than a helpless attitude is essential. Those who continue to hope and to have control over their lives are more likely to handle the events of the later years successfully. They are also likely to live longer.

Marital Life

The great majority of older couples say that they are "happy" or "very happy" with their marriages. The divorce rate among the elderly is extremely low. This is partly because unhappy couples are likely to have divorced or separated years before.

Once a couple adjusts to having children move out and to retirement, the marriage relationship is often better than ever. For some, it may be the first time that they have been able to spend a lot of time together. They can enjoy each other's companionship and go at their own pace.

Figure 11.4 People's enjoyment of their later years depends largely on their attitudes toward aging.

Figure 11.5 Some elderly people report that grandparenthood is more enjoyable than parenthood. Grandparents can experience the joy of spending time with children without having the responsibility that parents have.

Figure 11.6 Happily married people tend to live longer, and elderly people tend to have unusually happy marriages.

Figure 11.7 Older people who have experienced the loss of a spouse may feel that they are no longer a part of the society around them.

Older couples who have happy marriages tend to have a more positive outlook. They are usually more active than those who are single or unhappily married.

Death of a Spouse

Many older people experience the grief of losing a spouse. More women face this experience than men because women live longer. Thus, among people over 65, there are many more widows than widowers.

The loss of a spouse is one of life's most stressful events. The surviving spouse goes through a period of intense grieving and readjustment. Many older people cannot deal with the loss. It is not uncommon for widows and widowers to die soon afterward. And suicides and mental disorders are more common among them than among married people.

Widows and widowers must develop a new way of living. They must often learn to live alone, perhaps for the first time. Many feel they are no longer a part of the society around them. Friends and relatives may avoid them for a while because they do not know what to say.

Once the grieving is over, however, most widows and widowers learn to deal with their new status. There may even be a new sense of freedom for some.

Remarriage

Many more older widowers remarry than do older widows. An older man generally finds many women of his own age to choose from. Widows, on the other hand, have less choice because there are fewer men of their own age around. Widowers rarely wait more than two years before remarrying; widows who remarry usually do not do so for about seven years.

Older people tend to marry those with similar economic, social, and religious backgrounds. The groom is usually a little older than the bride. Over half of the older people who remarry have known their new spouses for many years. Some couples had dated when they were young; others are friends or neighbors.

By remarrying, people can avoid living alone. They can also avoid living with friends or moving in with their children. Most couples who marry late in life have highly successful marriages.

Relationships with Children

The majority of elderly people stay in close contact with their children and see them frequently. Studies show that more than 80 percent of the elderly live an hour or less away from at least one of their children. Some 30 percent are 10 minutes or less away.

In most families, the two generations continue to exchange advice, services, gifts, and financial assistance. Most elderly people, however, become increasingly dependent on their families as they get older. About two-thirds of the elderly say that they receive money or gifts from their families. Nearly one-third depend on relatives to help with housework, meals, or shopping, and some of the elderly, of course, live with their children.

Family relationships are very important. Statistics show that older people who have no relatives living near them are the ones who face the greatest difficulties. Many of them have financial problems and have to turn to social agencies for help.

Changes in Living Patterns

Retirement brings with it a complete change in living patterns. It provides more time for leisure activities, but deprives a person of her or his daily contacts with co-workers. It makes some people feel useless. This is more likely to happen to people whose work was the main focus of their lives.

Only about 30 percent of older people, however, say that they have difficulty adjusting to retirement. Those who look forward to retirement and who have many other interests apart from their work adjust most easily.

How older people use their leisure time depends on their interests and activities in their middle years. Those who developed active and creative ways of using free time when they were younger continue to use that free time in interesting ways.

The elderly continue to participate in politics. They are generally well informed and like to discuss political issues. People over 60 vote more often than younger people. Some older people have joined a movement called the Gray Panthers. This organization is active in protecting the interests of senior citizens.

Living arrangements often change in old age. An older couple may sell a house that has become too large for them and move into a smaller house or an apartment. Some move to retirement communities. Those who do must learn to live in a new area, among new people, perhaps in a new climate. Some people thrive in retirement communities. They like being with people their own age and taking part in planned activities. Others miss the contact with younger people.

Many older people have serious financial problems. Retirement usually cuts a couple's income in half. At the same time inflation drastically reduces the value of savings and fixed-income pensions. These factors, combined with the high medical bills that some old people run up, cause many to run short of money.

Friendship

Older people adjust more easily to the stresses of the later years if they have someone in whom they can confide. Most older men name their wives as their best friends. Women, on the other hand, are more likely to name a child or a close friend. A woman rarely names her husband as her closest friend. This tendency may make it easier for women to adjust to the loss of a spouse than for men.

Having a close friend to talk with becomes particularly important when people must face death. Being able to confide in another person helps a dying person come to terms with his or her life, and with the end of it. It is not easy for most of us to talk about death, especially to

Figure 11.8 Having close friends in whom they can confide helps many older people cope with the stress of their later years.

someone who is dying. But those who understand the needs of an older person will be better able to provide comfort and support.

CHECK YOUR UNDERSTANDING

1. List the characteristics of people who adjust well to old age.
2. What are some of the reasons that most older couples are happy with their marriages? Describe what frequently happens to a person after the death of a spouse.
3. In what ways are elderly people helped by their children?
4. Give some reasons for the financial problems many older people face.

SECTION **3** **Attitudes Toward Death**

Most people do not like to think or talk about death. They often avoid referring to it directly by using other terms. Thus they may say that someone has ''passed away,'' ''departed,'' or ''gone away.''

But even though people are reluctant to discuss death, the subject is finding its way into conversations more and more. In recent years Americans have been exposed to a great deal of information about death. A new definition of death has been devised. The subject is being discussed more openly in magazines and on television. And colleges are now offering courses in *thanatology,* which is the study of death.

Why are people showing more interest in death? For one thing, Americans have more time to think about it. A baby born in 1900 could expect to live only 49 years. Today, the average life span is 75 years. For another, many infectious diseases are no longer a major threat to life because modern medicine makes it possible to prolong life. As a result, Americans are now more likely to die slowly.

New Definition of Death

Until very recently, people were considered to be dead when they stopped breathing and when their heart stopped beating. Today, however, special medical equipment is available. It can keep the heart and respiration working in people who would otherwise be dead.

The development of such equipment meant that a new definition of death was required. The Harvard Medical School suggested that the new definition be based on brain death, and it developed a set of criteria for defining brain death. Under the new definition, people are considered dead if they have no reflexes, cannot breathe, do not respond to pain, and if electronic measuring devices indicate no brain activity.

This definition has been widely accepted in the medical world. By the mid-1980s, 38 states had written it into their state laws. A legal definition of death is particularly important to doctors who want to use organs from accident victims in transplant operations.

Young Attitudes Toward Death

People's attitudes toward death are related to their ages. The majority of young people rarely talk or think about it. In a survey of 30,000 young adults, only about one-third said they had talked of death openly. Most first became aware of death between the ages of 5 and 10. For many, the death of a grandparent was their first personal experience with death.

Death is a difficult idea for a child under 10. Most young children know that it happens to everyone, but they don't always realize that it is final. They may expect dead pets to come alive again. Or they may expect a dead relative to come back someday. Some children see death as a punishment. It is something that happens to a person who has done wrong.

Figure 11.9 Until they reach the age of 9 or 10, most children have little experience with or understanding of death.

In both childhood and adolescence, death may be puzzling. Experience with death is rare. It rarely touches a young person's life in a deep and lasting way. Young people who do think about it usually see it as something that will happen in the far distant future. Young people usually feel safely removed from death.

Older Attitudes Toward Death

The middle years bring a greater awareness of death. Middle-aged people have usually experienced the death of one or both parents and perhaps of friends or people with whom they have worked. As they see others die, they begin to think more about their own deaths. A survey of 1,500 adults found that middle-aged adults were the most fearful of death. They often said that death comes too soon.

The same survey found that older people were least likely to think this way. The elderly were also the most likely to have made plans for their deaths.

Death is generally less frightening to the elderly. They think and talk about it often. Because they have finished many of their life projects, they may place less value on life. Ill health and financial problems may also affect their ideas about death. And as older people experience the deaths of friends and relatives, they may become more used to the idea of their own deaths.

Death also has special meanings for older people. The fact that they know they are close to death alters the way they use their time. They tend not to plan as far ahead as younger people do. In one survey people were asked what they would do if they had only six months left to live. The older people in the survey often said that they would not change the way they lived. Younger people were more likely to make major changes. Most of the elderly said they would spend their time in quiet contemplation.

The Influence of Education

People's attitudes toward death are also likely to be influenced by their amount of education.

People with little education are likely to think often of death and to have negative views of it. They are likely to believe that death comes too soon and that dying is a form of suffering. They are also the least likely to have made any plans for their deaths.

Educated people are more likely to have talked to others about death. They are also more likely to have made wills and to have discussed funeral arrangements.

Religion also affects people's views of death. Dealing with death and dying is likely to be easier for those who are religious and who regularly attend religious services.

SECTION **4** # The Process of Dying

Death can come in many ways. Some people die quickly from heart attacks or in automobile accidents. For others, such as cancer patients, death comes more slowly. Sometimes the process of dying is a long, slow, downhill process. Atherosclerosis and emphysema, for example, cause patients to get weaker and weaker as time passes. At other times, it is a series of ups and downs. A person with multiple sclerosis, for example, may have periods of improvement during the course of the illness.

The Circumstances of Dying

Given a choice, most young people would prefer to die a sudden but not violent death. Some say they want a quiet, dignified death. Most adults want a painless death. Older people are more likely than younger ones to consider unexpected deaths to be just as tragic as slow deaths. Most older people believe dying in one's sleep is the best way to die.

Few people suffer a painful, lingering death. Most patients with a terminal illness spend only a few days or weeks requiring special care. As they near death, people are likely to be unaware of what is going on around them. The disease and drugs may cause drowsiness.

Figure 11.10 As people approach death, they tend to distance themselves from the world around them.

Dying patients also tend to distance themselves from their surroundings. Only about 6 percent of dying patients are conscious shortly before death.

The moment of death is rarely distressful. There is even evidence that the brain releases a special chemical as death approaches. The chemical makes the moment of death pleasant instead of painful. For most, then, death does come as desired—painlessly and peacefully.

The Experience of Dying

People who have narrowly escaped death say the experience is not painful. Some say it is even peaceful and blissful. In one study of 35,000 dying patients, doctors found that fear was not common among those who were conscious just before death. Many patients reported seeing visions of heaven, beautiful pastures, or lush vegetation.

In another study, more than 50 people who had come close to death were interviewed. Some had been revived after being pronounced dead. Others had narrowly escaped death by accident. The experiences they reported included overhearing a doctor pronounce them dead, pleasant sensations, and noises. Some felt they were being pulled through a dark space. Others reported meeting with friends or relatives who had died. Some felt they were watching their own bodies from a point outside them. Others had visions of a radiant being surrounded by light. Reports of reviewing part or all of one's life were also common, as was the feeling of approaching a border or limit.

A sense of timelessness, peace, and tranquility was common among those interviewed. Many said that they had at first felt sad and had attempted to return to life. But when the pleasant feelings began, they felt unwilling to return. Most reported that after these brushes with death their attitudes toward life and death had changed. They were no longer afraid of death. At the same time they valued and enjoyed life more.

The Needs of the Dying

One of the first people to study the needs of the dying was the psychiatrist Elizabeth Kübler-Ross. She worked with more than 200 dying people of varying ages and backgrounds. Then she reported her findings in her book *On Death and Dying*.

One of the things she discovered was that terminally ill patients usually want to discuss their situation. They are anxious to talk frankly to people who can listen to them without feeling uncomfortable.

Kübler-Ross also discovered that dying people generally want to know the truth about their condition. Very often doctors do not want to tell patients about terminal illness. They are afraid that to do so will cause emotional outbursts, anger, or denial. Yet most patients can sense that they are dying, even if they are not told it.

Problems occur when the patient, the patient's family, and the doctor all know that a person is dying but are unwilling to discuss it. Patients find it easier to face death when they can discuss it openly. Friends and relatives also find it easier to cope with the patient's condition when they can talk about it. Dying people do not want to talk about their deaths all the time of course. But when they do, it is important that someone who cares is willing to listen.

Figure 11.11 When death can be talked about openly, the experience is easier for both patient and family.

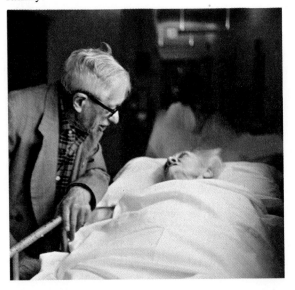

The Hospice Approach

Dying people and their families have special needs that a hospital cannot always satisfy. It was in recognition of those needs that the *hospice* movement started.

Hospices specialize in caring for people who are dying. Hospice workers, specially trained to deal with the dying, visit patients in their homes to provide medical care and counseling. An important part of their job is to help the patient's family deal with the approaching death. In order to give family members a rest, some hospices arrange for patients to spend short stays in the hospice, after which they return home. When patients become too sick to stay at home, they may be admitted to the hospice, where they will stay until they die.

One of the main differences between hospices and conventional hospitals is that hospices do not take any extraordinary measures to prolong the lives of their patients. They do not have the expensive, sophisticated lifesaving equipment found in hospitals. Their job is to make the patients' last days or weeks as comfortable as possible. They concentrate on emotional support and the relief of pain. In fact, patients may receive pain-killing drugs around the clock if they wish. Because the patients are dying and no measures are being taken to prolong their lives, the hospice doctors reason that there is little concern about patients becoming addicted to drugs.

Hospices also tend to be more homelike than hospitals. Patients are permitted to bring personal belongings, and rooms are furnished for comfort. If the patient wishes, death is openly discussed, and patients are given opportunities to make last requests and to take care of other legal matters.

The hospice movement started in England in the 1960s, and the idea quickly took root in the United States. Today, there are more than 1,200 hospices in this country. The vast majority of hospice patients—95 percent—have cancer. This is partly because cancer is one of the biggest killers today and partly because once cancer is diagnosed, the progression of the disease is fairly predictable.

It seems likely that the hospice movement will continue to grow because hospice treatment is less expensive than hospital treatment and because many people think it satisfies the needs of the dying.

In the mid-1980s the United States government recognized officially the important role of hospices in health care when it agreed to pay for hospice care for terminally ill patients receiving Medicare. Today, many private health insurance companies have extended their coverage to include hospice care.

Euthanasia

Modern medicine has created a problem. People can now be kept alive on respirators and other advanced machinery almost indefinitely. As a result, many people are concerned about the practice of *euthanasia*, or mercy killing. Should patients whose brains are dead be kept alive on respirators? If so, for how long? Weeks? Months? Or should somebody "pull the plug"? If someone does, is it murder? Or is it simply stopping useless treatment on a person who is, in fact, already dead? And who should decide whether to pull the plug? A family member? The doctor? Or a court of law?

Euthanasia can be either active or passive. In *active euthanasia*, death is brought on by the use of drugs or some other procedure. In *passive euthanasia*, no extraordinary life-prolonging measures are taken. The patient's life is not extended by the use of machines, drugs, or transfusions.

Most Americans admit to believing in passive euthanasia. Some doctors do practice it. They rarely admit it, however, because of legal complications.

It is impossible to determine how many people have practiced active euthanasia. Usually, it is done without anyone else knowing. Some doctors have privately admitted to ending the life of a patient who was in great pain and who had no hope of surviving. Some have given fatal drugs or allowed the patient or the family to use such drugs.

An increasing number of people are saying that they want to be involved in the decision making about their own deaths. Some say they would rather die than suffer pain or lose their mental capacities. Legally, people can refuse medical treatment. The major difficulty arises when patients are in a coma and cannot express their desires. Many people have begun to write "living wills." These are statements that set forth their wishes should they become unable to make life or death decisions. A living will explains the circumstances under which the writer would choose death over life. These wills are not legally binding, but they give doctors and family members a clear idea of the writer's wishes.

CHECK YOUR UNDERSTANDING

1. How does death come to most people? What kinds of feelings and experiences are reported by people who have come close to death?
2. According to Elizabeth Kübler-Ross, what is one great need of dying people?
3. What is the purpose of a hospice?
4. Explain the difference between passive and active euthanasia.
5. What is a living will?

SECTION **5**   # Coping with Death

How do people who know they are dying react to the situation? According to the psychiatrist Elizabeth Kübler-Ross, they go through five stages of emotion.

1. *Denial* At first patients refuse to accept the news that they are dying. Later in this stage, they drop their denial occasionally and talk about their illness. At other times they talk about their lives as though the illness does not exist.

2. *Anger* When patients can no longer deny the fact of their illness, they feel angry. They resent what is happening to them. Very often they direct their anger at doctors and relatives. Very little can be done to help patients at this stage.

3. *Bargaining* During this stage patients may offer their talents or services in exchange for a bit more time. A typical bargain is an offer to spend one's remaining days working for the church.

4. *Depression* As patients become more ill and less able to function, they enter the fourth stage—depression.

5. *Acceptance* Those who have enough time to work their way through the other four stages eventually reach the stage of acceptance. They seem neither depressed nor angry. This is not a happy stage. Rather it is a period without feelings. Patients tend to be calm and reflective. Often they prefer to be alone.

Not all psychiatrists agree that these five stages exist. Some say that only depression is common in all dying people.

The Nature of Grief

The dying person is not the only one, of course, who has to cope with her or his death. Friends and family, too, have to come to terms with it. And just as a dying person has special needs, so, too, do those who are left to grieve.

It is normal for people to grieve when they lose someone. The degree of sorrow is usually related to the importance of the loss and the circumstances under which it occurred. The more a loss affects the daily lives of the survivors, the greater its impact is likely to be.

A loved one's death brings a variety of emotions to the survivors. Shock, disorganization, hopelessness, frustration, anger, guilt, loneliness, terror, and relief may all be experienced.

Many people go through four phases of grief. First, there is a period of numbness. Close survivors have a difficulty in feeling anything but emptiness. Second, there is a time of yearning. Survivors long for the lost one to come back. Then there is despair, when the reality of the loss sets in. And finally, there is a period of reorganization. Survivors adjust their way of life in order to continue without the loved one.

Physical ailments often accompany grief. People may complain of headaches, backaches, insomnia, loss of appetite, dizziness, nausea, or diarrhea. Death rates among widows are higher during the first year of widowhood than among married people in the same age group. In extreme cases, grief can cause people to have hallucinations or suicidal impulses. Such cases sometimes occur among survivors of accidents in which a loved one has died. The survivors' loss is made worse by a feeling of guilt that they were spared.

Normally, physical and emotional problems tend to disappear as the grief becomes less intense. No time limit can be put on the period of recovery. It is different for each person. Most people suffer periods of grief, which gradually lessen in length and intensity. Many people have short bouts of grief long after the main period of grieving is over.

Figure 11.12 The death of a loved one brings a variety of painful emotions to the survivors. Openly sharing these feelings can reduce the more crippling effects of grief.

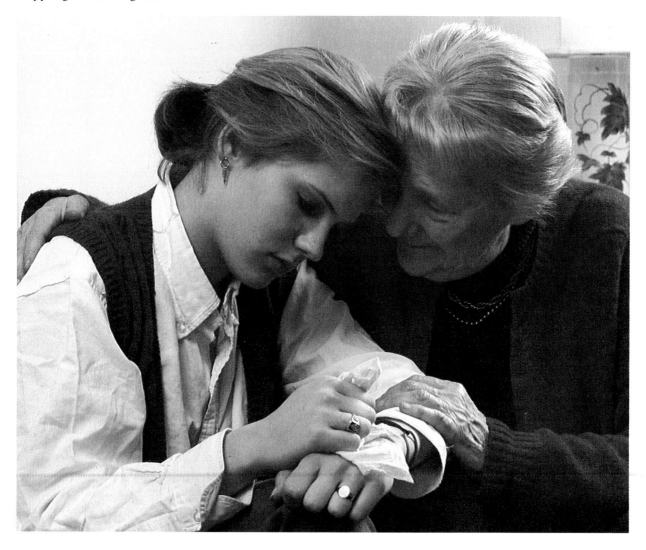

Anticipatory Grief

When people discover that someone close to them is dying, they go through *anticipatory grief*. That is, they deal with their feelings about death before the person actually dies. Thus, during a long terminal illness, survivors may do much of their mourning before the death occurs. When this happens, the mourning period afterward may be shorter and easier.

When family members hear of the approaching death of a loved one, they go through various emotional stages. Their first response is denial. They refuse to accept the idea that the loved one will die. They may even seek out another doctor in the hope that he or she will offer a different diagnosis. The second reaction is anger. Family members may get angry with the doctor, hospital staff, or even the dying person.

Guilt is another common feeling among families of dying people. They want to make up for past mistakes. Then, as they accept the idea of death, they become sad and depressed. For many families, the most difficult time is when the dying person is becoming detached from the world. This detachment is a normal way of dealing with one's own death. It can make the family feel rejected, however.

The Needs of the Bereaved

The *bereaved*—those who have lost loved ones—need understanding and comfort in dealing with their loss. Their needs vary, depending on whether the loss has been sudden or has followed a long illness. In cases of lingering death, their needs are greatest during the time that the person is dying. After the death they need support as they begin a new life.

In the event of a sudden death, the grieving period is often much longer. The real impact of the grief may surface months after the event. By then there is a danger that friends have stopped visiting or have grown too impatient to listen.

Animals, especially dogs and cats, often play an important role in the lives of grieving people. They provide companionship and give the bereaved person something to care for.

Figure 11.13 Pets can play an important role in the lives of grieving people. They provide companionship and give the bereaved person something to care for.

Grief Therapy

Some people can make grieving a way of life. Others find they are unable to mourn. Those who refuse to admit their loss may grieve for years. They may refuse, for example, to alter the personal belongings of the deceased.

For such people, professional therapy may be helpful. Both excessive grief and lack of grief are now looked upon as illnesses that can be treated. Grief therapy, like other forms of therapy, usually consists of talking out the patient's problems.

Research shows that the people most in need of grief therapy tend to be those who have suffered a sudden loss. People who have watched a loved one go through a long illness can prepare for their grief. But those who lose a loved one as a result of an accident or suicide cannot prepare in the same way. The unexpected shock makes it harder to accept and adjust to the death. In cases of suicide, the family and friends may also suffer deep feelings of guilt or shame.

Funerals

Death is almost always followed by some sort of parting ceremony. This ritual occurs in every human society. Like other rituals, funeral services satisfy some basic human needs. They enable survivors to share their feelings with one another.

Most Americans say they prefer burial to other forms of disposal, such as cremation. Usually, the dead person is placed in a casket, then praised during a brief service. The body is then carried to a cemetery, given religious blessings, and buried. Traditionally, funerals are conducted with dignity and ceremony.

The traditional funeral is expensive. Americans spend more money on funerals than on any other ceremony, except weddings. Yet despite the costs, surveys indicate that most Americans would not wish to change the funeral tradition.

There is evidence that funerals may be of psychological value to the survivors. The tradition of viewing the body or casket in a funeral home seems to be an important way of "giving up" the deceased. Research suggests that people who follow this tradition adjust to the death more easily than people who do not take part in a funeral ceremony.

CHECK YOUR UNDERSTANDING

1. What are the fives stages of emotion a dying person goes through?
2. Describe the four phases of grief.
3. What is anticipatory grief? List the emotional stages involved.
4. What two situations might call for grief therapy?
5. What purposes do funerals serve?

CHAPTER SUMMARY

- Among the theories about the causes of aging are that the body simply wears out, that waste products build up, that the immune system breaks down, that DNA errors build up, and that pacemakers control the aging process.
- Some of the physical changes that occur with aging are whitening of the hair, wrinkled skin, loss of teeth, shorter stature, and more fragile bones. Internally, the heart, circulatory system, and lungs work less efficiently.
- About 80 percent of older people have some sort of chronic health problems. About one out of four is hospitalized each year. Older people are particularly likely to be affected by stress.
- Aging does not diminish intelligence or memory. Older people do slow down mentally, however.
- Among the factors associated with longevity are heredity, sex, environment, diet, activity level, social and economic status, marital status, use of tobacco and alcohol, intelligence, and attitude toward aging.
- People's attitudes toward death are related to their ages. Young people rarely think or talk about it. Middle-aged people are the most fearful of it. Older people are less frightened and think and talk about it often.
- Death usually comes painlessly and peacefully. Few people are conscious just before death.
- Dying people generally want to know the truth about their condition and want to talk about it to people who can listen without feeling uncomfortable.
- The practice of euthanasia is highly controversial and raises many questions. Some people have begun to write living wills expressing their wishes about being kept alive.
- Some psychiatrists say that dying people go through five stages: denial, anger, bargaining, depression, and acceptance.
- Grief is a normal human response to the death of a loved one. It is often accompanied by physical ailments such as headaches, backaches, and insomnia.
- The grieving period is generally longer after a sudden, unexpected death than after a death following a long illness.

DO YOU REMEMBER?

Give brief definitions of these terms:

gerontology   senility   euthanasia

osteoporosis   hospice   bereaved

THINK AND DISCUSS

1. Why do you think more husbands consider their wives their best friend than vice versa?
2. Do you think young children should attend funerals? Why or why not?
3. Do you think retirement communities, where no one under a certain age may live, are a good idea? Why or why not?
4. Why do you think older people are more selective in their learning than younger people are?
5. Do you think people whose brains are dead should be kept alive by machines? Why or why not?
6. In what grade do you think students should start learning about death? Why?
7. If you had only six months to live, would you want to be told? Why or why not? If you were told, how would you spend your time?
8. What measures can you think of to ease the transition to retirement for people who are having difficulties?

FOLLOW-UP

1. Learn more about the work of the Gray Panthers. Write a report on their activities.
2. Find out the kinds of services your community offers old people. Make a list that describes these services and post it in your classroom.
3. Find out more about the hospice movement in this country. Write a report on your findings.
4. Read one of Elizabeth Kübler-Ross's books about death and dying. Discuss what you have read with your class.
5. Learn about funeral customs in other countries. Write a report that describes some of these customs.
6. Contact a nearby retirement community for information on the activities and services it offers its members. Post the information in your class.
7. Investigate one of the recent court cases on euthanasia. Write a report on the case, including your own opinion of its outcome.

PART 4 The Role of Drugs

At no time in history has drug use been as widespread as it is today. Vast numbers of over-the-counter and prescription drugs are used to treat physical ailments. We also have access to an incredible range of psychoactive, or mind-altering, drugs.

Part 4 is concerned with the role of drugs in American society. Abuse of the psychoactive drugs has become a critical health problem. Many people are so dependent on their drug taking that they can no longer lead normal lives.

Chapter 12 provides an overview of the drug problem. It outlines the stages of drug dependence and describes the effects and hazards of some of the more commonly used psychoactive drugs.

Chapter 13 focuses on this country's most widely abused drug—alcohol. And Chapter 14 is a study of cigarette smoking—a drug habit that can have disastrous long-term effects on overall health.

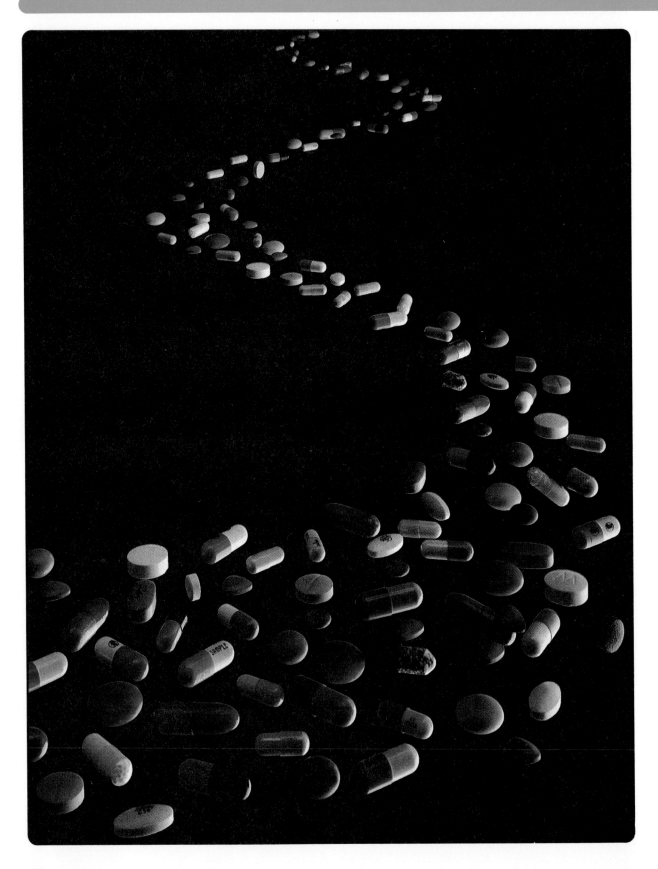

12

Drug Use and Abuse

After reading this chapter, you should be able to answer these questions:

1. How do drugs work? What determines how a particular drug will affect someone?
2. What reasons do people give for using drugs?
3. How do people become dependent on drugs?
4. What can you do to keep drugs out of your life?
5. What determines whether a drug is legal or illegal?

America today has been called the most drug-oriented society in the world. A huge number of chemical substances are available to us. Drugs are a part of almost every medical treatment, and they are used frequently at social occasions. They are commonly looked on as a way to relieve emotional as well as physical problems, and even as a way to give meaning to life.

Advertisements help persuade us to use drugs. Every day we hear and read about different brands of alcohol and tobacco, aspirin and cold remedies, eye drops and sleep aids. Not only do these ads sell products, but they also sell the idea that drugs can provide an immediate solution to our problems.

To some extent this is true. Many drugs do provide what people need, or think they need. Drugs do save lives and cure diseases. Alcohol does bring about relaxation. Tranquilizers do reduce anxiety. Barbiturates do bring sedation and sleep. Drugs are easy to take, and their effects are often immediate. So it is perhaps not surprising that so many people believe that ''relief is just a swallow away,'' nor that drugs are so popular as a means of escaping or coping.

But every drug that can help you can also harm you. Many people abuse drugs. They become so dependent on their drug taking that they can no longer lead normal lives. One reason for this is lack of knowledge. People often start taking drugs without knowing what the possible side effects are or how high the risk of dependence is. If Americans were better educated about drugs, they would be better able to decide if the hazards of a particular drug outweigh the benefits.

This chapter supplies some of this vital information. It starts with the basic questions—what drugs are and how they work—and then moves on to explore the complex issues of why people use and abuse drugs. It also provides information on some of the major psychoactive drugs. Finally, it deals with the important question of drugs and the law.

SECTION **1**

Drugs: What They Are and How They Work

Ask 10 people to give an example of a drug, and you're likely to hear the names of the illegal substances that so often appear in the newspaper. Probably no one will mention cola drinks or cigarettes or beer.

But these substances, and thousands more, contain ingredients that fit into the definition of a drug. A drug is *any chemical substance that changes living cells in any way.* Every organ and system in the human body is made up of living cells. Drugs act on those cells and affect the way a person feels and acts. The caffeine in just one glass of cola, for example, can make you feel nervous and irritable. It can also make your face flush and your heart beat fast.

Caffeine is one of the many drugs that act directly on brain and nerve cells. Drugs speed up, slow down, or even completely halt the transmission of impulses from nerve cell to nerve cell. Some drugs can reduce or do away with a person's perception of pain, for example. Others can change the way a person perceives the world or can alter or intensify a mood.

Drugs that affect thought, perceptions, or mood are called *psychoactive drugs.* They are also called consciousness-changing or mind-altering drugs. Because they are so frequently used—and abused—the psychoactive drugs will be the focus of this chapter. Bear in mind, though, that many of the use patterns and problems associated with the psychoactive drugs are also true of alcohol and cigarettes, as well as a number of over-the-counter (OTC) drugs. Specific information about individual psychoactive drugs is provided later in this chapter. Alcohol and tobacco are discussed in depth in the following two chapters.

What Determines a Drug's Effects

It is clear that drugs affect the workings of the human body, but how they do what they do is often shrouded in mystery. Different people vary enormously in the way they react to the same drug. The cold pill that works for one person, for example, may leave another sneezing and sniffling. One person may also react differently to the same drug at different times. Scientists are still trying to find out why there are such differences. They wonder if the same drug actually causes different biological changes in different people or in the same person at different times.

Although *pharmacologists*—the scientists who study drugs and their effects—have difficulty in predicting the exact effects a drug will have, they have identified a number of variables that affect a person's response.

Dosage

One of the most important variables is *dosage,* the amount in which a drug is taken. Different people need different dosages to achieve the same effect. The size of a person's body, the speed of the body's chemical processes, and inborn sensitivities are all important factors. In

The way a drug is administered, or given, also affects the dosage. Drugs that are injected into the bloodstream or inhaled produce greater and faster results than the same drugs taken by mouth or injected into a muscle.

Potency

The *potency,* or strength, of a drug is another factor that determines a drug's effects. Potency varies tremendously from drug to drug. It may take 1,000 times as much of one drug than another to produce the same level of response. It takes 200 milligrams of mescaline, for example, to produce the same effects as just 0.2 milligram of LSD.

Solubility

Another factor that affects the way a drug works is *solubility*. Some drugs dissolve only in fat, others only in water. Water-soluble drugs cannot reach the central nervous system because they cannot dissolve into cell walls, which are mostly fat. (Alcohol is a major exception. Its individual molecules are so small that they can pass through the spaces between the fat molecules of the cell walls.) Most psychoactive drugs are fat-soluble. This means they stay in the body longer. They must be broken down into water-soluble substances before they can be passed from the body. The breakdown process often takes several days.

Site

The *site*, or body part, where a drug acts is also relevant to its effects. For instance, the effects of a drug that changes the way the bladder works will certainly be very different from those of a drug that changes the rate of heartbeat.

But the functioning of body parts varies naturally to begin with. Fatigue or stress, for example, can greatly affect the way various organs in your body work. That, in turn, affects the way a drug works.

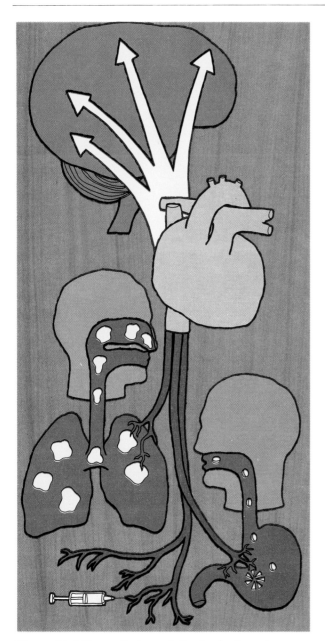

Figure 12.1 Drugs that reach the brain do so by way of the circulatory system. Some are injected directly into the bloodstream with a hypodermic needle. Others are inhaled and pass into the bloodstream from the lungs. Drugs taken by mouth are absorbed by the blood as they move through the digestive tract.

general, the larger the person, the higher the dose needed to produce a given effect. At least one cold remedy on the market recommends higher dosages for heavier people.

Set and Setting

The last two variables, *set* and *setting,* involve psychological factors. Set refers to a person's expectations about what a drug will do. For some reason that scientists have yet to figure out, a person's attitude influences a drug's effects. It may be that moods affect the body's chemistry. Anxiety, for example, may cause different chemical reactions from those caused by eagerness.

A person's social setting greatly influences his or her response to a drug too. This may be because people often respond to the expectations of others. An individual is likely to react quite differently to three drinks at a sedate dinner party than to the same three drinks at a sporting event with friends.

Drug Interactions

The number of drugs a person takes also influences the body's reactions. People who take more than one drug at a time, or in close succession, can be in for an unpleasant experience. When drugs are taken in that manner, they can interact *synergistically.* That is, the sum of their combined action can be far more than the sum of their separate actions. A classic example of drug *synergism* is the combination of alcohol and barbiturates. A less-than-lethal amount of alcohol and a less-than-lethal dose of barbiturates can, when combined, add up to a lethal dose.

One drug can also reduce the effectiveness of another with equally serious results. People who take certain antidiabetic drugs, for instance, are warned against drinking alcohol. The alcohol can cancel out the effects of the helpful drug, causing a dangerous diabetic crisis.

CHECK YOUR UNDERSTANDING

1. What is the definition of a drug? What common substances fit into this category?
2. Name six factors that determine the effects of a drug.
3. List four variables that affect the dosage of a drug.
4. Explain the workings of fat-soluble drugs. Why do they stay in the body longer than water-soluble drugs?
5. What can happen if a person takes two or more drugs at a time?

SECTION **2**   **Why People Use Drugs**

Americans use drugs at an astonishing rate. They smoke hundreds of billions of cigarettes every year. They consume vast quantities of alcohol. And they use an enormous amount and variety of prescription and over-the-counter drugs. One out of every 10 American adults, for example, will take the tranquilizer Valium this year. In addition, millions of Americans are regular users of illegal substances such as marijuana and cocaine.

Social Reasons

The reasons that drugs are used so frequently and in such great amounts are woven into the fabric of American society. There are, of course, genuine medical reasons for some drug use. But most drug use does not have a clear-cut medical purpose.

The truth is, we live in a culture that believes that no physical or mental discomfort, no mat-

Figure 12.2 We live in a culture that believes there is a drug to cure every ailment.

ter how mild or short-lived, should be tolerated. The advertisements we see and hear every day, while presenting cures, are part of the problem: "Tired? Take _____." "Got a headache? Take _____." "Tense and nervous? Take _____."

Both physicians and their patients share the responsibility for the large number of unnecessary prescriptions that are written. On the one hand, physicians themselves are bombarded with drug advertisements every time they read a medical journal or open their mail. On the other hand, they are faced with patients who do not want to be told that time is the best cure for their particular problem. Patients want instant relief, so many doctors prescribe a chemical for getting it.

Patients want fast relief from both their physical and emotional problems. The tranquilizer Valium, mentioned above, is one of the most frequently prescribed drugs in the United States today. Although it carries a risk of physical and psychological dependence, millions of American adults use it regularly to relieve anxiety instead of dealing with the reasons for that anxiety.

Adults set the examples that children follow. In this way, values are transmitted from one generation to the next. The child who sees adults drinking, smoking, and using other drugs comes to accept such behavior as normal and natural. There are other subtle persuaders, such as candy cigarettes, that tell children that drug use is acceptable in our society.

People are also subject to pressure from their own peer groups—their friends, classmates, or co-workers. The need to do what everybody else is doing can be very strong. It can tempt a person to try whatever drug the group uses, whether it be alcohol, cigarettes, or a psychoactive drug.

Politics and economics are also sociological factors that shape thinking about drug use.

Figure 12.3 Young people who use or abuse drugs may simply be following the example set by the adults in their lives.

They play a role in determining how available drugs may or may not be. For example, cigarettes are plentiful even though they are health hazards. One reason for this is the size of the tobacco industry. Tobacco growers are important voters. Through a strong tobacco lobby, they persuade their representatives in Congress to keep the cigarette business going.

Psychological Factors

The make-up of our society is not the only factor that influences drug use. People's personalities also determine their likelihood of using drugs. Many drug experts believe that, while social forces can determine drug use, psychological factors are the major forces in drug abuse. (The abuse of drugs is discussed in the next section.)

Drug experts know, for example, that different people will respond differently to the same amount of the same drug and that they will make different decisions about continuing to use that drug. Even people who respond similarly will "read" the response differently. One person may enjoy a drug-induced dizziness, for example, while another will find it very unpleasant.

Trying to untangle the various motivations that lead to drug abuse is a complex task. Scientists have come up with various theories which, while not completely satisfactory, do provide some explanations.

Some researchers think that people who consistently abuse drugs have not learned to cope with and accept the frustrations and disappointments of life. These people tend to feel like failures and may be angry at the world that caused their failure. So they turn to drugs to find an escape, a meaning in life, or an identity. They may also be rebelling against authority, which they believe has set up a social structure that is unfair.

Scientists have tried to define specific "pre-dependent" personalities, the people who are most likely to end up abusing drugs. So far they have not been successful. They believe that some abusers have serious psychological disturbances. But whether these disturbances led to or were caused by drug dependence has not yet been determined. The possibility does exist, though, that compulsive, long-term drug use can greatly worsen any existing disorder. There is also a possibility that heredity plays a part in how a person will be affected by drugs.

Not all people who have psychological problems end up with a drug problem, of course. Most find other ways to deal with the anxiety, depression, or anger that is affecting their lives. It is clear, though, that drug use is determined in part by people's inner landscape and in part by the world around them.

CHECK YOUR UNDERSTANDING

1. What is our general cultural attitude toward physical or mental discomfort?
2. Describe two ways in which doctors are pressured to prescribe drugs for their patients.
3. According to drug experts, what forces determine drug use? Drug abuse?
4. Describe some personality characteristics that some researchers think can lead to drug abuse.

SECTION **3**   # From Use to Abuse

There is no question that there is a great deal of drug abuse in America. Every year, for example, about 3,000 people die from barbiturate overdoses. Many thousands more die from the effects of alcohol.

But what exactly is drug abuse? And when does drug use cross the line and become abuse? The answers to these questions can be approached from several different angles. There are, of course, legal issues involved in the use

Talking Point

Changing the Social Scene

"You can get anything you want, anytime you want it, and it's cool to use." That is what some young people say about using drugs and alcohol. They seem to believe that partying can't be fun without them. This is not true of everyone.

Many young people want to go to a party and not be expected to get drunk or high. They are changing the social scene, showing that parties and social events can be free of drugs and alcohol. In several communities, teenagers are working with parents and other adults to establish guidelines for social events. They are making the point that it's okay to say no to drugs and to alcohol.

Billy Coletti, a high school junior in St. Petersburg, Florida, is one of the many young people who are finding ways to change the social scene. Billy is the founder and leader of a statewide organization called Florida Informed Teens, whose purpose is to prevent alcohol and drug use among teenagers.

The members of Florida Informed Teens go through training so that they'll be well informed about drugs and their effects. Then they visit schools in their area, where they make presentations about the hazards of drug use and the importance of a drug-free life style. The group also organizes drug-free parties and other activities. "We've developed a kind of club for middle-school students," Billy explains. "We have dances and parties for the younger kids every couple of weeks."

Billy and his friends are so enthusiastic about their work that they have started the National Federation of Drug-Free Youth. The purpose of this organization is to develop networks similar to Florida Informed Teens in other states throughout the country.

Adapted from *Teens in Action*, Tom Adams and Hank Resnik. National Institute on Drug Abuse, U.S. Department of Health and Human Services, DHHS Publication No. (ADM) 85-1376. Printed 1985.

of certain drugs. Some people consider the illegal use of drugs to be drug abuse. There are also religious and moral issues; at least two religious groups in this country, for example, consider the use of caffeine unacceptable.

None of these issues, though, is concerned with the effects of a drug on a person's body and mind. If drug taking causes harm to either, it can be considered drug abuse. Thus, drug abuse can be defined as *drug use that causes a person to become physically ill, mentally impaired, or incapable of carrying out the normal activities of daily life.* There can be short-term drug abuse, as when a person gets drunk at a party. Her or his body's reaction that night—and the next morning—says that it feels abused by alcohol. There can also be long-term drug

abuse, with equally long-term effects. Smoking, for example, can bring on an early death from a variety of diseases.

Patterns of Drug Use and Abuse

In an attempt to find out more about drug taking in America, the National Commission on Marijuana and Drug Abuse made a study in the 1970s of drug-taking behavior. The study revealed five different patterns of use: (1) experimental use, (2) social use, (3) situational use, (4) intensified use, and (5) compulsive use. These patterns go in steps; each one generally involves heavier drug use than the one before it. The five patterns are described below.

Experimental Use

By far the largest number of people who have ever used drugs are experimental users. Believing they are in no danger, they are curious about the effects a certain drug may have. In the case of psychoactive drugs, their friends may have told them the drug will give them new feelings or sensations.

Drug experimentation usually takes place at a party or other social gathering. Many people report that their first use of cigarettes, alcohol, or marijuana took place in such surroundings. Because fear of the unknown is usually mixed with curiosity, experimental drug doses tend to be low. Low dosage reduces the risk factor, but does not do away with it entirely.

Unfortunately, even experimental, "just this one time" use of a drug can have tragic results. Smoking one cigarette may do no more than make the smoker sick. But a novice drinker may get very drunk very quickly and then attempt to drive. Illegal psychoactive drugs pose special dangers. Because they are outside the law, no one regulates their purity, and they often contain a grab bag of ingredients—one of which may be fatal. And no one can predict the kind of mood or sensation a given psychoactive drug will produce at a given time.

Social Use

The next largest group, social users, also use drugs in a social setting. They wish to share the experience with their friends and are far less likely to use the drug when they are alone. Most people who drink wine at a dinner party,

Figure 12.4 Drug use falls into five different categories: *(from top)* experimental use (first-time use, usually in a social situation); social use (occasional use in a social setting); situational use (regular use to deal with a specific problem); intensified use (long-term use, often in combination with other drugs); and compulsive use (inability to function without the drug). Some users progress from stage to stage; others maintain a consistent level of use or move from heavier to lighter use.

for instance, would not think of doing the same thing if they were eating by themselves. Most drinkers, in fact, fit into this category.

Compared with experimental use, social use is more patterned and planned. Such users usually do not step up their use, and they are not dependent on the drug. The risks of social use are usually low, as are those of experimental use. But because social use is more frequent, the risk of sliding into dependence is that much greater.

Situational Use

Situational users are the people who turn to drugs for help. They may be trying to complete a task or cope with a situation. Such use tends to be regular, but limited to a specific circumstance. The student who takes caffeine to stay awake is a situational user. So is the athlete who takes a painkiller before competing or the sales executive who drinks a martini before facing a client.

This kind of drug use involves greater risks than does experimental or social use. The situational user perceives an actual need for the drug's effects and may come to rely on drugs more and more often. For example, the student who uses caffeine to stay awake may find that the body's need for sleep eventually becomes stronger than the drug. He or she may then seek a more powerful—and more dangerous—drug.

Situational use also poses a psychological risk. Reliance on a drug time and time again can undermine the user's self-confidence and prevent her or him from learning how to cope with problems. The student who consistently leaves studying to the last minute is in need of different work habits, not of drugs for staying awake.

Intensified Use

Intensified use may grow out of situational use. Here the drug taker uses drugs repeatedly and over a long period of time. The doses are high and may involve a combination of drugs. In general, intensified users are seeking help in facing emotional or physical problems. Often, like the homemaker who takes tranquilizers to relieve a constant feeling of boredom or anxiety, they believe they cannot function without the drugs. Still, they do function; intensified users can form personal relationships and hold down responsible jobs. However, they are teetering on the brink of a full-scale dependence.

Compulsive Use

Individuals who have lost control of their drug use are compulsive users. They are dependent, emotionally and/or physically, on heavy drug use, and all other activities frequently take a back seat to their habit. An example of the compulsive user is the man who regularly stops at a bar on his way home from work. He plans to have just one drink, knowing that his family is waiting for him. But after two hours and several drinks, he is still at the bar.

Compulsive users of drugs such as alcohol and heroin will often abandon family and friends who get in the way of their drug use. The physically addictive nature of those drugs exerts a stronger pull, caused in part by fear of the pain of withdrawal. Compulsive users are also often incapable of holding jobs. Since the frequency and amount of their drug use, especially with illegal drugs such as heroin, can add up to a large daily expense, they may also turn to crime to get the money they need to support their drug habit. They end up harming others as well as themselves, as statistics about drug-related crime indicate.

Stages of Drug Dependence

Somewhere in several of the five patterns described above comes the point when a person is dependent in some way on a drug. What happens to a person's body and/or mind to create the dependence that leads to a pattern of heavy drug use? Actually, there are three levels of drug dependence. The first involves the mind, while the other two involve the body. But all are alike in that the user has come to rely on the drug.

Psychological Dependence

Psychological dependence is the first level of drug dependence. Most of us feel dependent on a number of things, and we feel uncomfortable when these things are absent. For example, people who are used to starting every morning with a glass of orange juice may feel upset if there is none left one morning. If you are used to eating lunch with a certain friend each day, you may feel a sense of loss on the days your friend is out sick. To some extent, you are psychologically dependent on your habit. You count on it to fill a certain place in your life.

Drug users, too, may come to feel a sense of loss when they are deprived of the effects the drug creates. They may also become restless, irritable, or anxious.

Tolerance

Tolerance, the second stage of drug dependence, involves the body. As use of certain drugs continues, a person's body adapts to the drug. Larger and larger doses are needed to give the same effect that smaller doses once achieved. The person who at first takes one barbiturate pill to fall asleep may soon find it takes three or four to produce the same drowsiness.

Tolerance also means that a user can take larger doses without suffering overdose effects. A heroin user who has taken the drug for some time, for example, can tolerate dosages that would kill nonusers. But tolerance does not remain constant; if drug use stops, tolerance decreases again. If a person who stops taking heroin for a while suddenly returns to the old dosage, he or she may be in for a very bad time. Coma or even death could result.

Tolerance poses another problem too. As larger dosages are needed, the user spends more and more money on drugs. This can be disastrously expensive, particularly with illegal drugs that command high prices on the black market.

Physical Dependence

This is the final and most severe stage of drug dependence. *Physical dependence* means that actual changes have taken place in the body. The body has developed more than a tolerance for a drug. It now needs the drug to function. For the person who has developed this kind of dependence, drug taking often becomes the most important part of her or his life.

When the physically dependent user stops taking the drug, or does not receive a large enough dosage, the body reacts. Terrible symptoms can occur, including severe stomach pain, vomiting, and convulsions. The victim may also experience terrifying *hallucinations*, such as the feeling that bugs are crawling over his or her body. These reactions, known as the *withdrawal syndrome*, may even cause death. In most cases, though, the body could recover and lose its dependence.

Abuse of Over-the-Counter Drugs

Drug abuse is not limited to illegal or prescription-only substances. It can involve any number of the familiar items that can be bought in drugstores and supermarkets without a prescription.

Billions of dollars' worth of over-the-counter (OTC) drugs are purchased each year. How many of these drugs are effective? How many are safe? The Food and Drug Administration has been studying these questions for several years. It reports that some OTC drugs, such as daytime sedatives, are seldom truly needed. Advertising or popular beliefs may create an artificial need for them. Other effective drugs are frequently misused. For instance, many diet-conscious Americans mistakenly think that laxatives can help them lose weight or keep from gaining weight. They can't, but they can create a physical dependence that prevents normal functioning.

Aspirin is another OTC drug that is often abused. Because aspirin is so effective at reducing pain and inflammation, some people rely on it too much. Abuse of aspirin can cause abdominal bleeding. It can cover up the real

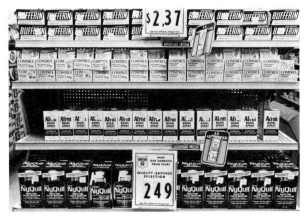

Figure 12.5 Billions of dollars' worth of over-the-counter drugs are purchased each year. Many of these drugs are not really needed, and many are abused.

problem and delay an important trip to the doctor, a delay that can pose a threat to health and even life. Self-medication without sufficient knowledge, then, carries its own forms of danger.

Multisubstance Abuse

There is yet another type of drug abuse, which can also involve all categories of drugs—*multisubstance abuse*. In this pattern, the user starts counteracting the effects of one drug with another. The person who feels groggy the morning after taking a sleeping pill may then take a stimulant to wake up. But at night the stimulant can prevent sleep, and the user takes a sleeping pill once again, creating a vicious cycle.

As you have already seen, drugs can interact in harmful ways. The person who takes a number of drugs on a long-term basis can be risking death. The late Elvis Presley is a tragic example of this syndrome. By the end of his life, he was consuming dozens of drugs each day—drugs to sleep, drugs to wake up, drugs to lose weight, and drugs for any number of other reasons. Eventually, this multisubstance abuse proved too much for his body, and he died at the age of 42.

CHECK YOUR UNDERSTANDING

1. How can drug abuse be defined?
2. Name and briefly describe five patterns of drug use.
3. Briefly explain the three stages of drug dependence.
4. What happens when a physically dependent drug user stops taking the drug?
5. Describe the cycle involved in multisubstance abuse.

SECTION **4** # The Psychoactive Drugs

The numbers of Americans who use, and abuse, psychoactive drugs are alarming. There are almost half a million heroin abusers. Between 1 and 2 million people use sedatives. At least 30,000 of these people have developed a physical dependence. About 4 million people regularly use cocaine, and 20 million currently use marijuana. Many of these drug users are young people. Roughly two-thirds of all American teenagers try a psychoactive drug before they finish high school. Of these, 40 percent use drugs other than marijuana. According to a recent survey conducted by psychologists at the University of Michigan, at least one in every eighteen high school seniors smokes marijuana daily. The survey also showed that 17 percent had used cocaine at least once and that 6 percent used it at least once a month during the previous year.

The tragic results of drug abuse—emergency room visits, mental hospital admissions, and deaths—point to at least one conclusion. Many people are just not aware of the nature of the psychoactive drugs they are using. Of those now abusing barbiturates, for example, many did not know that they could become physically dependent on such drugs when their physicians prescribed them.

It is also likely that few of the millions now using marijuana are aware of recent, disquieting evidence indicating that use of this drug can cause actual physical damage to the heart, lungs, and reproductive system. Scientists who once considered marijuana "safe" are now realizing that, as with cigarette smoking, it has taken years for the true effects of the drug to surface.

The purpose of this section, then, is to present the facts about some of the psychoactive drugs now in use. Only those who know the facts can make intelligent decisions about using them.

Depressants

A *depressant* is a drug that slows down or reduces the activity of the central nervous system, especially the brain. In small doses, depressants produce relaxation or sleep. In larger doses, they can produce coma and death. The most widely used of all depressants is alcohol, which is discussed in detail in the next chapter. The other depressants are divided into two broad groups—the *sedative-hypnotics* and the *opiates*.

Sedative-Hypnotics Among the most commonly used sedative-hypnotics are *barbiturates* and *minor tranquilizers* such as Librium and Valium. Their effects on people's moods and behavior are quite similar to those of alcohol. They reduce anxiety. They may also cause slurred speech and loss of coordination. In medicine, sedative-hypnotics are used to treat tension, anxiety, and insomnia. Abuse of sedative-hypnotics is widespread.

There are different patterns of sedative-hypnotic abuse. Some people go on occasional drug binges. They take large amounts of a substance in a short space of time in order to produce a feeling of intoxication. For other people, abuse takes the form of a dependence

developed over time. It may begin with a prescription for a sedative-hypnotic to relieve insomnia. The patient comes to rely on the drug more and more, and a psychological dependence develops.

When sedative-hypnotic drugs above a certain dosage are taken daily, the user develops a tolerance and begins taking larger amounts. The person might also begin to use the drug more often. Regular use of larger amounts of barbiturates usually results in physical dependence. If the drug is removed, withdrawal symptoms occur.

The withdrawal symptoms of people dependent on barbiturates are severe. They begin with nervousness, trembling, and weakness. If untreated, they can progress to terrifying hallucinations, unconsciousness, and epileptic-like seizures that can cause death. These symptoms can last as long as four days.

Barbiturates and other sedative-hypnotics are implicated in nearly 20 percent of all drug-related deaths. Many of these deaths are accidental, resulting from the combined use of alcohol and barbiturates. Barbiturates carry the highest risk of death among the sedative-hypnotics, but the others carry hazards as well. Abuse of Valium, for example, leads to more than 50,000 visits to hospital emergency rooms each year.

Opiates Most of the drugs in this group come from the dried juice of the opium poppy. *Opium* is the juice in its pure form. Three other drugs—*codeine, morphine,* and *heroin*—are derived from opium. The opiates are sometimes called *narcotics* because they can narcotize, or put to sleep, those who use them.

Morphine is the active ingredient in opium, and it is widely used for medical purposes. Any other use is illegal. Heroin, which is made from morphine, is used medically in England and some other countries. But in the United States the use of heroin is illegal for any purpose. Codeine, the mildest of the opiates, is a common ingredient in strong cough syrups. Medications containing codeine are available only by prescription.

The use of opiates is so tightly controlled because of their remarkably high potential for tolerance and physical dependence. A person who starts taking heroin can develop a need for a daily dose of the drug within a few months—a habit that can cost several hundred dollars a day. Despite the cost and dangers, heroin is the most common of the illegally used opiates.

In addition to the danger of dependence, other hazards are associated with the use of heroin. Its illegal status means that it is illegally manufactured. There are no controls over its purity. As a result, users constantly run the risk of illness or death from the chemicals that are mixed with the heroin. And because these street drugs vary in their strength, death from an accidental overdose is a constant risk. Finally, users place themselves at high risk of contracting fatal infections, such as heptatitis B and AIDS, when they become so anxious for their

Figure 12.6 Opiates were active ingredients in many medicines sold around the turn of the century.

next dose, or "fix," that they inject themselves with dirty needles.

An opiate abuser must receive both physical and mental treatment if she or he is to return to a normal life. Programs to help abusers offer medical help and long-term psychological counseling. Some of the most successful programs take a self-help approach similar to that offered by Alcoholics Anonymous.

Inhalants

Certain household products contain chemicals that give off psychoactive vapors. These substances include some cleaning fluids, paint thinners, and glues. When people inhale the vapors from these substances, they experience sensations similar to those produced by other types of psychoactive drugs. Low doses of *inhalants* cause users to feel stimulated, uninhibited, then drowsy. High doses can produce heart failure and immediate death. Repeated exposure can damage the liver, kidneys, blood, and bone marrow.

Stimulants

Stimulants are drugs that promote the activity of the central nervous system. They increase alertness, reduce fatigue, and prevent sleep. Their actions and effects are, therefore, opposite to those of the depressants.

Caffeine, amphetamines, cocaine, and nicotine are the most commonly used stimulants. Nicotine, an ingredient in tobacco, will be discussed separately in Chapter 14.

Caffeine   As the active ingredient in coffee, tea, cola drinks, and cocoa, *caffeine* is the psychoactive drug most widely used by Americans of all ages. It is also found in a number of over-the-counter drugs meant to overcome fatigue or suppress hunger.

Although caffeine is a strong stimulant, the low doses normally consumed produce only mild effects. Caffeine can, however, produce tolerance and habituation. People who consume six or more servings of coffee or cola drinks a day can suffer harmful effects. These people can experience trembling, heart palpitations, headaches, irritability, and insomnia. Caffeine abuse can also aggravate peptic ulcers and high blood pressure.

Amphetamines The *amphetamines* are a group of synthetic drugs that includes Benzedrine ("bennies"), Methedrine ("speed"), and Dexedrine ("dexies"). Amphetamines are also known as "uppers."

In low to moderate doses, amphetamines make users feel alert and energetic. The users' mood may be elevated, but they may also become anxious and irritable. Amphetamines also decrease appetite, so they have been used as diet pills.

Caffeine plays a larger role in American life than amphetamines do. However, amphetamine abuse is a much larger problem than abuse of caffeine. People who take amphetamines to lose weight or to combat fatigue may take average doses over a period of time. But then tolerance develops, and the user must take larger doses to achieve the same effect.

People who increase their amphetamine use suffer from a number of unpleasant side effects, which are also produced by long-term use of smaller dosages. Depression, exhaustion, insomnia, headaches, dizziness, and confusion are common. A small percentage of people become paranoid as a result of amphetamine abuse.

Amphetamine users often feel the need for a depressant to help them down from their drug-induced "highs." These people may experiment with heroin or barbiturates for this purpose. It is not uncommon for them to become heroin abusers as a result.

Cocaine The stimulant *cocaine* ("coke," "snow") is a natural drug extracted from the leaves of the South American coca bush. Cocaine's effects and abuses are similar to those of the amphetamines, but its great cost and scarcity make it far less common.

In medicine, cocaine is used as a local anesthetic. It numbs tissues and makes blood vessels constrict. It is used mainly in nose and throat surgery. When used nonmedically for its psychoactive properties, cocaine, in a powdery

Figure 12.7 Despite the severity of most states' drug laws, cocaine use continues to increase among young people.

form, is sniffed, or "snorted," through the nose. Repeated sniffing of the drug irritates the membranes lining the nose, leading to nasal congestion and a constantly runny nose. Long-term use can cause the septum, the wall between the nostrils, to break down.

Cocaine creates a very strong psychological dependence, or habituation. Chronic users may feel restless, anxious, and irritable. Some people develop a special kind of psychosis that often includes the sensation that insects are crawling on their skin. In rare cases, cocaine can cause death from seizures, respiratory failure, and coma.

Cocaine use is on the rise among young people. Users should be aware, however, that most states treat the illegal sale or possession of cocaine as severely as that of heroin. The legal risks of cocaine use are, therefore, particularly serious.

Psychedelic-Hallucinogens

A variety of drugs are known as *psychedelic-hallucinogens*. Among them are *LSD* and *PCP*. There is no sharp line separating these drugs from other classes of psychoactive drugs. At high dosages, or in certain circumstances, other drugs can produce equally powerful changes in mood and behavior, including delusions and hallucinations. The psychedelic-hallucinogens, however, are much more likely to produce these effects. And when they do, the effects are more intense and longer lasting.

LSD The scientific name for LSD is *lysergic acid diethylamide*. It is often known as "acid." Extremely small amounts of this synthetic chemical—as little as 0.1 milligram—will produce a wide variety of effects.

After taking LSD, the user experiences startling changes in perception. The word "tripping" has been used to describe the experience. Besides changes in perception, LSD brings about psychological changes. Thoughts pour into the user's mind in random combinations, and rapid mood changes occur. The user may go from euphoria and contentment to anxiety and fear in a matter of moments. The user may also feel that his or her body is distorted. Unlike the effects of some drugs, which are short-lived, the effects of a moderate dosage of LSD may last for several hours.

Some long-term negative effects can result from LSD use. For one thing, LSD can cause both occasional and chronic users to experience "flashbacks." Flashbacks are brief, sudden distortions of perception and thought—similar to an LSD trip. These uncontrollable episodes can occur months, even years, after the last dose of LSD. In some people, LSD can also lead to serious depression, feelings of persecution, or detachment from reality. Fatal accidents and suicides have also occurred following the use of LSD.

PCP This drug, which is often known as "angel dust," is an extremely dangerous and mysterious drug. Originally developed for medical use, PCP was discarded because of its unpredictable and negative side effects. It has become increasingly available as an illegal drug in recent years. Its availability is due to the fact that it can be made from common chemicals in makeshift laboratories.

In small doses, PCP produces a floating feeling and an overall numbness. Inhibitions may also be slightly reduced. Moderate doses tend to impair thought and speech and make the user feel as though her or his body is distorted. The user may become restless and unsure of place and time.

Large doses of PCP produce serious effects. The user may appear to be mentally ill, completely losing touch with reality. There are also people who become violent and self-destructive. In some cases, only physical restraint can prevent them from harming themselves or others. Hundreds of people who have become mentally disturbed after using PCP are in hospitals and institutions around the country. Some victims have experienced such severe loss of memory that they have even lost the ability to count.

Marijuana

Marijuana ("pot") and *hashish* ("hash") are natural drugs derived from the hemp plant, cannabis. Marijuana consists of the dried leaves of the plant, while hashish is a concentrated resin made from those leaves. Marijuana does not fit neatly into any of the major drug categories. In average doses, it acts somewhat like a sedative-hypnotic, somewhat like alcohol, and somewhat like a stimulant. It also has some unique effects of its own.

The effects of moderate doses of marijuana vary from user to user. The expectations of the individual, the setting in which the drug is used, and the user's previous experience with the drug all influence reactions.

Most drugs produce effects that build, peak, and begin to fade. Marijuana does not follow this pattern. Effects can begin to wear off, then

Talking Point

Look-alike and Designer Drugs

Sixteen-year-old John B. purchased two yellow and black capsules for $2 apiece from a friend who said they were a kind of amphetamine popularly called "yellow jackets." That night John took the two capsules and soon fell into a coma. Within a few hours he was dead of a cerebral hemorrhage. It was not amphetamines that killed John but a so-called look-alike drug. This powerful combination of legally available stimulants had raised his blood pressure so high it caused an artery to burst.

Most teenagers already know the dangers of such illegal drugs as marijuana, heroin, cocaine, and PCP. Now they also need to be aware of the hazards of two other classes of dangerous drugs—look-alike and designer drugs.

Look-alike drugs are pills and capsules that are made to look like popular illegal drugs. They do not contain the same substances as the drugs they imitate, however. Usually, they contain high concentrations of legally available stimulants. People who buy look-alike drugs may believe that they are buying the real thing—not the look-alike. What they might be buying, though, is a lethal dose of concentrated stimulants. Look-alikes have caused numerous deaths from heart failure and respiratory failure.

Designer drugs are different from look-alikes, and even more dangerous. They are usually produced in makeshift laboratories by people who use cheap chemicals to alter the composition of an existing drug to produce a potent new drug. One designer drug called China White, made from a surgical anesthetic, mimics the effects of heroin, but it can be as much as 3,000 times more potent. More than 100 people are known to have died from overdoses of this drug and its variations. The death rate may be much higher, however, because the drug is difficult to detect in the bloodstream after death.

Another kind of designer drug is MDMA, popularly known as Ecstasy. This drug helps relax inhibitions and break down barriers to communication in some people. Because of these characteristics, some psychiatric therapists have used it to treat their patients. However, because Ecstasy is chemically related to amphetamines, it may be toxic to people with circulatory problems or heart disease, and it can cause psychosis and, possibly, brain damage. In any event, drug treatment clinics have begun seeing numerous cases of overdoses, and law enforcement officials regard MDMA as having the potential for serious abuse.

grow strong again. The initial effects of moderate dosages of marijuana include a feeling of laziness. Sounds and colors may seem particularly vivid or may seem to flow in random patterns. Users often feel hungry because marijuana stimulates the appetite. Later, because of the drug's sedative-hypnotic properties, the user feels drowsy. In addition, the user's heart rate may increase by as much as 50 percent. Blood vessels become enlarged too, a reaction that gives marijuana users bloodshot eyes.

In larger dosages, the effects of marijuana are much stronger. Instead of mild alterations in sight, sound, and touch, the user may experience vast distortions of perception. Mental confusion is also common. The user's mood changes from one of relaxation to a state of anxiety and panic.

Exactly how marijuana affects the brain has still not been determined. However, early studies that suggested that marijuana was harmless have been shown to be poorly designed and unscientific. Recent studies are more likely to be accurate because they are based on data gathered over a significant period of time.

These studies suggest that long-term use of marijuana can affect the heart and lungs. One study, for example, found that smoking five "joints" a week caused more lung damage than smoking six packs of cigarettes. Marijuana smoke contains many of the same chemicals as cigarette smoke. Today, its cancer-causing qualities are assumed to be equal to, or greater than, those of tobacco.

It is also believed that marijuana can harm both male and female reproductive systems. Lowered levels of sex hormones have been detected in users. In males, abnormal sperm formation has been linked to marijuana use, and in females the menstrual cycle may be disrupted.

Refusal Skills

Peer pressure is recognized as a leading cause of drug involvement among young people. Friends often try to "turn a person on" to a drug by presenting it as a way to have fun, relax, or gain insight into life. Peer pressure can also sway someone who wants to turn down the drug but who does not want to feel "left out."

You are already aware of peer pressure, of course. It is natural that you should want to do the same things as your peers. You probably wear clothes similar to those of your friends and have a similar haircut. Such examples of peer pressure are harmless. Pressure to try drugs is quite different, however. It can have long-term effects on your health.

Learning to say no to things that go against your values is not always easy, especially at a time when your friends are so important to you. But, just as you can develop reasoning and listening skills, you can also develop refusal skills. Successful programs that help people say no to drugs suggest these guidelines:

- Learn the facts about drugs and alcohol, and let others know what you have learned.

- Know the dangers of combining alcohol with other drugs.

- Be objective about all the products that are advertised through the media; remember that advertising is done to promote products and to make money.

- Talk about drugs and alcohol with your parents.

- List the things that make you happy. If using drugs and alcohol is on that list, think it over. Try to find ways to get them off your list.

- Join with other teenagers who live a drug- and alcohol-free way of life, and promote it in your social activities.

- Get involved in prevention programs in your school, community, and neighborhood.

Figure 12.8 If you're tempted to try drugs, think about the possible consequences. Talk it over with a friend. Drug use can have serious effects on your health.

- If you cannot find a prevention program, consider starting one.

- Make a commitment to be healthy and in control of your own destiny.

- Develop the skills you need to handle pressure from friends who want you to do something you don't want to do. For example, think about how you would refuse to ride with someone who has been drinking.

- Confront friends who use drugs and encourage others to do the same.

- Identify sources of stress in your life and recognize how stress affects you (see Chapter 4). Do the ways you cope with stress cause other problems? Can you think of coping strategies that might be better?

- Seek professional help if alcohol or drugs are a problem for you or a member of your family

CHECK YOUR UNDERSTANDING

1. How do depressants affect the body? What are the medical reasons for using sedative-hypnotics?
2. Why is the use of opiates so tightly controlled? What are some of the other hazards associated with the use of heroin?
3. What effects do stimulants have on the body? What can happen to people who drink too much coffee or too many cola drinks?
4. What are some of the side effects of amphetamine use?
5. What are the effects of long-term use of cocaine?
6. What physical effects can result from the long-term use of marijuana?

SECTION **5**   **Drugs and the Law**

It is very important that anybody considering using a drug should take into account its legal status. The use of some drugs, of which heroin is the most notorious, is illegal under any circumstances. But many drugs have a dual status: their use can be either legal or illegal.

Very often, the legality of the drug depends on how it is obtained. There are many drugs that are legal when prescribed by a physician. But those same drugs are illegal when obtained from private individuals or from drug manufacturers who operate without government authorization. Age, too, determines the legality of two drugs—alcohol and tobacco—which may be sold legally only to people above a certain age.

The federal government first became involved in regulating drug use at the turn of the century. At that time, a household remedy called laudanum was as common as aspirin is today. It was considered very effective, and no wonder. Laudanum was made of two powerful psychoactive drugs, opium and alcohol. Laudanum was recommended for every member of the family, including children.

As use of this family remedy became widespread, the negative effects became apparent. Millions of people were sliding into physical dependence, and physicians began writing about the problem. The government soon took action, and in 1906 the Pure Food and Drug Act was passed. It obliged manufacturers to label all drugs that contained opium. Later, even stronger laws were passed, and opium-based drugs became illegal.

A similar situation occurred during the 1960s. Amphetamines were then manufactured and prescribed at the rate of more than a billion doses a year. Many people took them to suppress their appetites in order to lose weight, while others used them to fight depression and fatigue. But amphetamines can have serious side effects and can lead to physical dependence. Widespread abuse occurred. So in 1970 Congress passed the Controlled Substances

Act, which cut the legal production of amphetamines by 80 percent. Recently, the government acted again, declaring amphetamines both ineffective and dangerous as a weight-control measure.

Prohibition

Some drugs are so much a part of our culture that they are almost impossible to regulate. During the 1920s people who recognized alcohol as a harmful substance urged Congress to make it illegal. Eventually, prohibition laws were passed, forbidding anyone to make or sell alcoholic drinks.

The results of those laws were totally unexpected. It turned out that alcohol was so much a part of our society that the flow could not be halted. Millions of normally law-abiding citizens bought and drank "bootleg" liquor that was made and sold by notorious crime syndicates. After a few years, Prohibition was repealed, and the laws that regulate the use of alcohol are now more limited.

Some of these laws, such as the ones that set the legal drinking age, are determined by individual states instead of by the federal government. This age, therefore, varies from state to state and ranges from 18 to 21. Some states have two age limits: people can buy certain beverages with a low alcoholic content at the age of 18 or 19, but they must be 21 before they can buy stronger liquors.

The Marijuana Controversy

Marijuana is another psychoactive drug that is controlled by state laws as well as by federal law. Over the past few years, some states have relaxed their laws while others have strengthened them. Some states now allow marijuana to be used for medical purposes. Penalties for the illegal use of marijuana range from small fines to long prison sentences. The penalties are determined by a number of factors—for example, the amount of marijuana involved, and whether the person was caught selling, buying, or possessing it.

Figure 12.9 Young people who break the law by using marijuana may have to bear the consequences for the rest of their lives.

Like alcohol in the past, marijuana is the subject of controversy today. Some people argue that it should be legalized on the grounds that it is no more harmful than tobacco or alcohol. But no one can claim that tobacco and alcohol are not harmful. Unfortunately, until very recently there has not been much careful research on marijuana. Many statements made in the past about either the dangers or harmlessness of the drug were not supported by sound evidence. As a result of these past exaggerations, many people today scoff at any new information about marijuana. They assume the new information is also unfounded. But evidence mounts that marijuana can in fact do serious harm to the mind and body.

In the meantime, the fact remains that marijuana *is* illegal. Young people who use marijuana and break state or federal laws can affect their futures. They may have problems getting a job. Many employers, given a choice between two equally qualified candidates, would choose the one without a police record. Furthermore, a number of careers are closed to people with police records. They cannot be teachers or lawyers or hold government positions. And those who spend time in prison are often affected psychologically as well. Jail can be a harrowing experience.

Controlling Illegal Drugs

With a drug such as heroin, there is no controversy. It is illegal to buy it, sell it, or possess it, and all states have harsh penalties for offenders. In addition to its high potential for dependence, heroin poses another form of danger. The people who sell heroin (often known as "pushers") are frequently part of a drug ring or crime syndicate and have a record of violent crimes. These people often battle for control of various drug "territories." Some of them will stop at nothing and will harm innocent people who get in their way.

An international effort to stop illegal drug traffic has been underway for a number of years. Aimed at catching big-time pushers, it is also tough on small-time users who get caught. Luggage searches at ports and airports are one of the techniques used in this effort. In some cases, specially trained dogs who can sniff out drugs are used. Several hundred Americans are now in prisons around the world because they were caught trying to take illegal drugs into or out of foreign countries.

There is yet another controversy about the laws controlling drugs. Are all drug abusers criminals? If not, where should the line be drawn? And what of those people who commit crimes such as stealing, but whose actions are caused by their desperate need to support their drug dependence? Should they be punished, rehabilitated, or both? Finally, how effective are drug regulations in general? Do they actually control drug use or only cause a boom in illegal trade?

CHECK YOUR UNDERSTANDING

1. Name two factors that can make the difference between the legal and illegal use of a drug.
2. When did the federal government first start controlling drugs? Why?
3. What are some of the factors that determine the penalties for using marijuana illegally?
4. What kinds of careers are closed to people with police records?

CHAPTER SUMMARY

- A drug is any chemical substance that changes living cells in any way. Drugs that affect thought, perceptions, or mood are called psychoactive drugs.
- Several factors influence the effects of a given drug on an individual. These include the drug's dosage, its potency, its solubility, the site in the body where it acts, the setting in which it is taken, and the individual's own set, or expectations.
- Many drug experts believe that social factors determine whether or not a person will use drugs, while psychological factors are the major forces in determining whether or not that person will abuse drugs.
- Drug abuse is drug use that causes a person to become physically ill, mentally impaired, or incapable of carrying out the normal activities of daily life.

- The five patterns of drug use are experimental, social, situational, intensified, and compulsive.
- The three stages of drug dependence are psychological dependence, tolerance, and physical dependence. Once physical dependence is reached, a person may suffer withdrawal symptoms if he or she does not receive the drug.
- Depressants slow down the activity of the central nervous system. The most widely used depressants are the sedative-hypnotics, which include barbiturates and minor tranquilizers.
- The group of depressants known as the opiates includes opium, codeine, morphine, and heroin. They have a very high potential for physical dependence.
- Stimulants promote the activity of the central nervous system. The most widely used stimulants are caffeine, amphetamines, cocaine, and nicotine.

- The psychedelic-hallucinogens include LSD and PCP (''angel dust''). They can produce intense changes in mood, perception, and behavior. PCP is particularly dangerous because of its unpredictability.
- Marijuana acts somewhat like a sedative-hypnotic, somewhat like alcohol, and somewhat like a stimulant. Studies suggest that long-term use of marijuana can affect the heart, lungs, and reproductive organs.
- The use of some drugs is illegal under any circumstances. The use of other drugs can be legal or illegal, depending on how the drug is obtained, on the age of the user, and on individual state laws.

DO YOU REMEMBER?

Give brief definitions of these terms:

psychoactive	psychological dependence	depressant	narcotic
dosage	tolerance	stimulant	inhalant
synergism	physical dependence	withdrawal syndrome	hallucination

THINK AND DISCUSS

1. It has been suggested that some over-the-counter drugs be reclassified as prescription drugs. What would be the implications of such a measure?
2. Do you think there should be greater regulation of advertisements for over-the-counter drugs? Why or why not?
3. What aspects of modern life seem to lead to drug abuse?
4. Why do you think most drug experimentation takes place at parties?
5. What do you think are the effects of the various antidrug campaigns aimed at teenagers?
6. Why is selling illegal drugs usually considered a more serious offense than buying them?

FOLLOW-UP

1. Contact the National Clearinghouse on Drug Abuse Information for a packet of materials on marijuana and other drugs that are problems in your community. Set up the materials in a classroom information center.
2. Find out about the laws concerning drug use in your own state and community. Make a chart of the information and post it in your classroom.
3. Read a book about the harrowing experiences of young Americans who have been imprisoned in foreign countries on drug offenses. Tell the story to your class.
4. Visit or contact a local drug rehabilitation center to find out the kinds of assistance offered to people with drug problems. Describe these services to your class.
5. Find out more about the problems Elvis Presley had with drugs. Write a report of your findings.

CHAPTER 13

Alcohol Use and Abuse

After reading this chapter, you should be able to answer these questions:

1. How does alcohol "work"?
2. Why does alcohol affect different people in different ways?
3. In what ways is our society's attitude toward drunkenness contradictory?
4. What percentage of traffic deaths result from drinking and driving?
5. What are the signs of alcoholism? What treatment is available for alcoholics?

Vanessa often went to her friends' homes after school. But she never invited them to hers. For a long time, none of the girls in her group said anything about it. But then the pressure started. "It's your turn, Vanessa," her friends told her.

Vanessa made one excuse after another. Her mother was sick. A relative who hated noise was visiting. Her father was working at home that day. Eventually, she ran out of excuses, and the truth came out.

Her mother *was* sick. <u>She</u> was an alcoholic and had been for several years. Vanessa didn't invite anyone home because she never knew what she would find. If her mother was sober that day, it would be all right. But if she was drunk, there would be yelling and crying. Either way, the house would be dirty and messy.

Vanessa's mother is one of millions of alcoholics—people who have become dependent on alcohol. Millions more, while not alcoholics, abuse alcohol.

Abuse of alcohol is one of the biggest health and social problems in America today. More than half the fatal automobile accidents involve people who have had too much to drink. Alcohol is associated with crime and poverty, and it causes physical and mental illness.

Alcohol is a mind-altering drug. A moderate amount of it can relieve tension and help the drinker relax. It is readily available and widely advertised. Unfortunately, though, few societies have been able to enjoy the benefits of alcohol without suffering its harmful effects too.

Many people begin experimenting with alcohol during their teenage years. Today teenage drinking is a major problem. Over 3 million teenagers—and their families and friends—are having to cope with the problems of alcohol abuse. Users of this drug should be aware of the risks they are taking.

What are the effects of alcohol on the human body? How does it affect the drinker's mind and behavior? Why do people start drinking? What causes alcoholism? How can it be treated? These are some of the questions that will be answered in this chapter.

SECTION **1** # Alcohol: What It Is and What It Does

When people drink grape juice, they find that their thirst is quenched. But if they drink wine, another beverage made from grapes, they find that a lot more happens. They may start feeling relaxed or light-headed, angry or tearful. They may have trouble walking and talking. And they may feel even thirstier than before.

How can two liquids made from the same fruit have such different effects? Because one—wine—contains more than grapes. It also contains the mind-altering drug alcohol.

The alcohol in wine and other beverages such as beer and whiskey is a colorless liquid called *ethyl alcohol*. In small amounts, it causes intoxication. In large amounts, it is a poison.

Alcoholic Beverages

Alcoholic beverages result from the action of yeast, molds, or bacteria on grains and fruits. Through this action, the sugar in the plants turns into alcohol.

Different beverages contain greatly differing amounts of alcohol. Most wines, for instance, contain from 9 to 12 percent alcohol. But some wines, called fortified wines, have extra alcohol added to them. Examples of fortified wines are sherry and port. They contain from 18 to 22 percent alcohol. The different varieties of beer contain from 3 to 6 percent alcohol. That makes beer the least alcoholic beverage. Hard liquors such as gin, whiskey, and rum, on the other hand, contain the highest concentrations of alcohol—from 30 to 55 percent.

There is another kind of alcohol that is *not* a beverage. This alcohol is made from wood. It is called either *wood alcohol* or *methyl alcohol*, and it is poisonous in any amount. Even the fumes from wood alcohol are dangerous. Yet each year a number of people die from drinking wood alcohol, thinking it is the same alcohol used in beverages.

How Alcohol Works in the Body

Alcohol is absorbed directly into the bloodstream, first through the tongue, then through the stomach, and then through the small intestine. Once in the bloodstream, it travels to all the body tissues and organs. Alcohol dissolves in water, so it readily enters the water in the body tissues. There a chemical reaction burns up the alcohol and produces heat. It takes about an hour for the average adult to burn up the alcohol in one bottle of beer, one glass of wine, or one shot of whiskey.

How Alcohol Affects the Body

Alcohol changes the activity of all the body's tissues. The blood, for instance, must work to cool the tissues that are burning up the alcohol. To do this, it carries the heat to the surface of the body. The extra blood makes the skin flush.

After a few drinks, most people end up with a red face. They also feel warmer than they really are because of the extra heat on the surface of their bodies.

Alcohol also decreases the appetite. Over a period of time, people who drink may actually be starving themselves. The alcohol they consume cannot take the place of food. Although alcohol provides calories, it has no protein, no minerals, and very few vitamins.

People who drink also find that they have to urinate more frequently. That's because alcohol causes the kidneys to work overtime. This upsets the body's water balance, and the drinker develops a strong feeling of thirst.

Alcohol can have serious effects on the body's organs. It can increase heartbeat, which can lead to higher blood pressure. Alcohol also causes the stomach to secrete large amounts of gastric juices, which can inflame the stomach lining. Ulcers may eventually form.

The liver, too, does not function properly when large amounts of alcohol are consumed.

Figure 13.1 *Left:* A normal liver. *Top right:* A liver affected by cirrhosis. *Bottom right:* A close-up of the diseased liver, showing scar tissue.

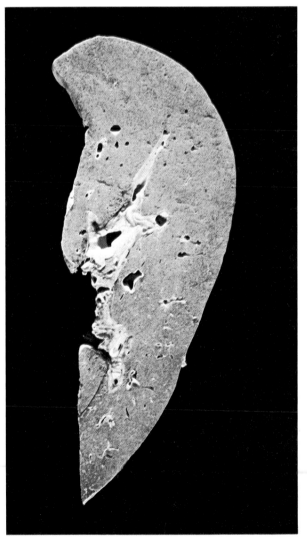

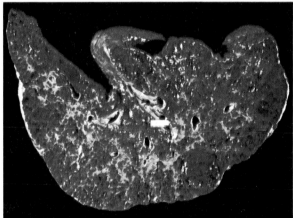

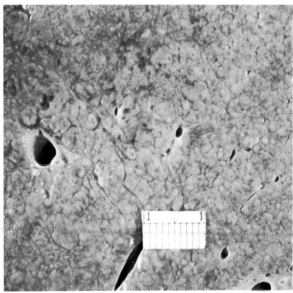

Instead of burning fat, it burns alcohol. The fat remains in the liver and can cause it to become enlarged if excessive drinking continues over a period of time. Even one episode of severe intoxication can cause the liver to enlarge and grow tender. Long-term drinking will eventually result in permanent liver damage. The liver develops scar tissue, a condition called *cirrhosis of the liver*. This disease is a leading cause of death among alcoholics.

Other chronic diseases can result from alcohol use. Heavy drinkers have a higher than normal incidence of cancers of the mouth, pharynx, larynx, and esophagus. If they smoke as well, these rates are even higher. Daily use of alcohol also can produce tolerance and physical dependence. More of the drug is needed to produce its effects, and the body needs the drug to function.

Hangover

One of the most noted effects of alcohol is the *hangover*—the terrible feeling that often hits people after a night of heavy drinking. People suffering from a hangover experience severe headache, vomiting, weakness, and rapid heartbeat. They may be nervous and unable to think clearly.

A hangover is actually a state of mild withdrawal from a powerful drug. There is no cure. Coffee, vitamins, more alcohol—none of these does any good. But solid food, liquids, aspirin, and rest can help ease the symptoms, which usually end within 36 hours.

People who have become physically dependent on alcohol experience far more serious withdrawal symptoms if they stop drinking. These can include severe seizures and hallucinations called *delirium tremens* or the DTs. Death from heart failure may result.

How Alcohol Affects Behavior

Besides affecting the body, alcohol also causes great changes in people's behavior. A person may suddenly start laughing or crying, for instance, or may become violent. Alcohol is a strong, mind-altering drug that affects the central nervous system, including the brain.

Some people think that alcohol stimulates them and makes them better conversationalists. What it really does, though, is paralyze those areas of the brain that exercise judgment and self-control. After a drink or two, people may indeed feel freer to talk—but may say things they will regret later. And their emotions also have free rein, again causing situations that may embarrass them when the effects of the alcohol wear off.

If the person continues to drink, the functioning of more and more areas of the brain will be affected. The next area to be deadened is the one that controls muscle movements. When this happens, it takes longer to react to, say, an oncoming car, because it takes longer for muscles to tense for action. The muscles of the tongue become affected, too, and the drinker begins to have difficulty forming words.

Next to go are the brain areas that keep the sense organs functioning precisely. Seeing is affected, resulting in blurred or double vision. Hearing, too, is dimmed. And the drinker's sense of balance is disturbed. Instead of walking normally, he or she will weave and stagger.

You may have read of situations in which a drinking "contest" resulted in the death of one

Figure 13.2 People suffering from a hangover can experience severe headache, weakness, vomiting, and rapid heartbeat.

Figure 13.3 After a drink or two, people generally feel freer to talk—but may say things they will regret later.

of the contestants. This person had consumed enough alcohol to reach the highest level of intoxication. At that point the brain centers that control the vital functions—breathing, heartbeat, and temperature—become paralyzed. Only immediate medical attention can save the life of someone in a state of such total paralysis. Any time, in fact, a person passes out from alcohol, careful attention is required. If the unconscious person is left alone to "sleep it off," she or he may vomit and then breathe the liquid into the lungs. Death from suffocation can result.

How Alcohol Affects Mental Processes

Because alcohol has such a powerful effect on the brain, the drinker's mental processes are affected. But as with the other mind-altering drugs, these effects can vary from person to person and from time to time.

Research shows that people under the influence of alcohol have trouble learning, performing, and remembering new tasks. They also have trouble solving problems. In short, the drinker cannot think clearly.

But at the same time, the alcohol affects the emotions, creating an illusion of well-being. Drunk drivers, for instance, believe that they are functioning better than normal. Yet they cannot see or react well. Their false sense of well-being can mislead them into thinking they can perform dangerous tasks with ease. So the drunk driver—already a menace—may decide to increase the speed of the car to match his or her "superior" driving ability.

The problem is made even worse by the effects alcohol has on the other emotions. Irrational fear, anxiety, or anger may surface. The speeding drunk driver may decide another car has cut him or her off and may try to go after the car to punish the driver. So the drunk driver speeds even more. He or she may indeed "punish" the other driver—with death by fatal collision. Thousands of accidents each year occur in this way.

CHECK YOUR UNDERSTANDING

1. Compare ethyl alcohol with methyl alcohol.
2. List the average alcohol content of the different kinds of alcoholic beverages.
3. Explain how alcohol affects different body organs.
4. Describe the order in which alcohol affects the various brain centers.

SECTION 2 What Determines the Effects of Alcohol

Two people drinking the same alcoholic beverage often do not react in the same way. One may feel relaxed and somewhat sleepy, while the other may get extremely drunk. Another time, the same drinkers may react in just the opposite ways to the same drink.

Figure 13.4 Blood alcohol levels and their effects on a drinker's behavioral state.

The effects of alcohol are not totally predictable. A number of factors interact to determine the way the body and the mind respond to alcohol. These factors vary from person to person and from time to time.

Blood Alcohol Level

Alcohol begins to be absorbed into the bloodstream as soon as a drink is taken. A small quantity is absorbed by the tongue and throat. A larger amount is absorbed once the alcohol reaches the stomach. About 20 percent of the total amount of alcohol consumed passes through the stomach wall into the bloodstream. The rest travels into the small intestine and is absorbed from there.

Once the alcohol has been absorbed, it is carried to the liver. There, through a process called *oxidation*, the alcohol turns into carbon dioxide and water. However, the liver can oxidize only a small amount of alcohol at a time. The rest is carried in the blood throughout the body. The amount of alcohol in the bloodstream is called the *blood alcohol level*. Alcohol remains in the bloodstream until all of it has been oxidized.

The liver oxidizes alcohol at the rate of about half an ounce an hour. Thus it may take several hours to get rid of the alcohol in a few drinks. Variations depend largely on the size of the liver. Liver size is closely related to body size, so a heavier person can generally break down alcohol faster than a smaller person can.

In general, most people will not experience any noticeable effects until the blood alcohol level reaches 0.03 to 0.05 percent. That means there are 3 to 5 parts of alcohol per 10,000 parts of blood. A 90-kilogram (200-pound) person who has two beers will probably fall into that category. His or her judgment will be impaired, and there will be a feeling of light-headedness. But a 45-kilogram (100-pound) person consuming the same amount of beer will have a blood alcohol level of 0.075. At that level, vision, hearing, and muscle control are affected. Driving would be dangerous.

Other Factors

A person who typically consumes one or two after-work or predinner drinks may sometimes find that, instead of feeling mildly relaxed, she or he feels drunk. What happened?

Something either increased the drinker's blood alcohol level above its usual percentage or changed the way the drinker's body reacted to the alcohol. You have already seen that the drinker's weight affects the blood alcohol level. A number of other factors also help determine an individual's blood alcohol level at any one

Figure 13.5 A small person and a large person will be affected differently by equal amounts of alcohol. Because liver size is closely related to body size, the smaller person will break down the alcohol more slowly—thus ending up much drunker much sooner.

time, as well as the way the drinker reacts to the alcohol.

Rate of Absorption Perhaps the drinker skipped lunch that day. An empty stomach greatly increases the rate at which the alcohol is absorbed into the blood. Absorption can take place so rapidly that even a small amount can affect the drinker. On the other hand, alcohol that is consumed with food or after a large meal will be absorbed much more slowly.

Rate of Consumption The drinker may also have gulped down the same drink that she or he normally sips slowly. For alcohol to reach the brain and cause intoxication, it must be absorbed more rapidly than the liver can break it down. How quickly it is absorbed depends partly on how quickly it is consumed. Two shots of whiskey can be downed in a moment. It takes much longer to drink two cans of beer. Even though there is the same amount of alcohol in each, the whiskey will have the greater effect because it can be consumed much more quickly.

Type of Beverage The drinker may also have changed the usual drink. Let's say the person normally drinks vodka and orange juice. But this time the orange juice ran out before the glass was full. This made the concentration of vodka greater. Or the drinker may have substituted a different beverage altogether, one with a higher alcohol content.

You have already seen that beverages vary greatly in the amount of alcohol they contain. A bottle of whiskey, for instance, has many times the alcohol content of the same size bottle of wine. The alcohol content of each drink or beverage, then, is very important in determining the effect it will have.

Physical Factors A person's physical condition can also affect his or her reaction to alcohol. If the after-work drinker was very tired that day or coming down with a cold, even the usual amount of alcohol would have a greater effect. People whose health is generally below par will also be extra sensitive. They will not be able to drink the way they usually do without experiencing uncomfortable effects.

Figure 13.6 Alcohol's effect on the drinker depends largely on psychological factors, such as experience, motivation, and mood.

Motivation   *Why* a person drinks is also important. Maybe the after-work drinker wanted to get drunk that day. People who really want to feel the effects of alcohol will behave very differently from those who resist the effects. They will drink faster and may choose stronger beverages.

Experience   Finally, the effects of alcohol are influenced by the drinker's past experience with the drug. First-time drinkers may act out the reactions they feel are expected of them. They may appear to be far more intoxicated than they really are.

Inexperienced drinkers will also become intoxicated more quickly than experienced drinkers. That's because experienced drinkers build up a tolerance to alcohol. Their bodies adapt to the drug and larger quantities are needed to produce the effects that smaller doses once achieved. Experienced drinkers also learn to minimize the effects of alcohol. They can appear to be less intoxicated than they really are. This is especially true of heavy drinkers who do not want to draw attention to their problem.

Alcohol and Other Drugs

When alcohol is taken with other drugs, there can be strong and unpredictable results. Drugs that would not be poisonous by themselves can combine to become toxic.

Alcohol figures in many such reactions. Each year hundreds of people die from consuming barbiturates along with alcohol. Tranquilizers and antianxiety drugs also pose a hazard when they are taken with alcohol. Over-the-counter drugs should not be forgotten either. Anyone taking cold capsules, sleeping aids, antihistamines, or other nonprescription remedies should not use these substances with alcohol.

High-Risk Groups

For some people, alcohol poses greater than normal risks. Even small amounts of alcohol can do serious damage to people with certain diseases. People with diabetes or epilepsy, for instance, run a special risk. So do people with certain heart diseases. There are also people who are so sensitive to alcohol that they seem to be allergic to it.

Researchers have also discovered that pregnant women who drink are risking the health and lives of their unborn babies. The action of alcohol can produce a variety of deformities, ranging from facial abnormalities to missing fingers and toes. The child may also be mentally retarded. Women who have more than six drinks a day run a 75 percent risk of bearing a defective baby. Even those who have just one or two drinks a day run a 14 percent risk of having a deformed baby. For this reason, pregnant women are advised not to drink alcohol at all.

CHECK YOUR UNDERSTANDING

1. How does body weight relate to blood alcohol levels? Why?
2. List six other factors that help determine the effect alcohol has on a specific person at a specific time.
3. What can happen if alcohol is taken with other drugs?
4. Why is it dangerous for pregnant women to consume alcohol?

SECTION **3** # The Development of Drinking Habits

The American people are constantly being invited to use alcoholic beverages. Television commercials and magazine ads make drinking look very appealing. One liqueur is advertised as "after-dinner magic." Another drink is referred to as "simply sublime." The public is told that alcoholic beverages taste "superb," "seductive," or just plain "smooth." These ads suggest that no one should serve dinner without wine, or after-dinner coffee without brandy.

Over the years, Americans have steadily increased their use of alcohol. Even when alcohol was illegal during Prohibition, from 1920 to 1933, people did not stop drinking. Beer, wine, and liquor were manufactured and sold on the black market. Drinking is now accepted in many social and business situations.

Drinking and the Family

Most people's first ideas about drinking come from their families. Children hear their parents express opinions about drinking and drinkers. More important, they see how the adults in their families use the drug. Children are naturally curious. Sooner or later, they want to know what their parents are drinking. Most children ask for, and some are given, a taste.

What children learn about drinking from their families can affect their future drinking habits. Children whose parents don't drink probably will not drink when they grow up. The children of moderate and heavy drinkers usually develop similar drinking habits.

Of course, there are exceptions. When an unhappy home life is caused by a parent who

Figure 13.7 The family is the earliest influence on a young person's attitude toward drinking.

drinks heavily, a child may become strongly opposed to alcohol. On the other hand, if alcohol is taboo in the home, children may come to view it as a "forbidden fruit." Alcohol use may then become a symbol of freedom and adulthood.

Other Influences

Children also learn about alcohol from friends, teachers, movies—the general social attitude around them. The influence of friends is particularly strong during adolescence. Many teenagers want to do what their friends do. If everyone is drinking at a party, they want to do the same. Also, some teenagers feel that they can forget their anxieties, frustrations, and conflicts by drinking. What they may be doing instead, however, is creating new problems for themselves.

Drinking and Teenagers

Some parents worry about drugs such as marijuana and cocaine, which they see as a major threat to their children's well-being. They aren't concerned about alcohol. But alcohol is, in fact, a much more serious problem than marijuana or any other drug.

More young Americans use alcohol than any other drug—including marijuana, cocaine, sedatives, and even nicotine. About 65 percent of all Americans between 12 and 17 years old have tried alcohol. In the 18- to 25-year-old group, 95 percent have tried the drug, while 68 percent are current users. These rates are actually higher than the rates for older adults.

Traditionally, people under 21 could not legally buy, sell, or use alcoholic beverages. However, during the middle 1970s many states lowered the legal drinking age to 18, 19, or 20. This was soon after the voting age was lowered

Figure 13.8 The legal drinking age is 21 in most states.

Figure 13.9 Three million American teenagers have drinking problems. Some of these people are actually alcoholics.

to 18. Many people, especially young people, reasoned that if 18-year-olds were old enough to fight for their country and to vote, they were old enough to drink legally.

But when drinking ages went down, the number of automobile accidents went up. In Iowa, for instance, fatal accidents involving drinking drivers aged 18 to 21 increased by 75 percent during the five years when the drinking age was lowered. The alarming rise of alcohol-related traffic deaths and injuries among young people caused lawmakers to review their decision. All of the 19 states that lowered the drinking age have passed laws to raise it again.

But no matter what the legal drinking age is, teenagers who want to drink will find a way to get alcohol. The statistics illustrate this only too clearly. There are about 15 million people in America between the ages of 14 and 17. Three million of those teenagers have drinking problems, and some are actually alcoholics.

Perhaps you have a friend or acquaintance who drinks too much. And perhaps you'd like to help but don't know how. First of all, you should show that you care. But don't lie or cover up for the person. You'll do more harm than good if you agree that she or he has no problem. You should try to convince the person to get professional help. Some schools and colleges provide counseling and medical help for those with drinking problems. There are also clinics in your community that can help. As with the treatment of any other drug problem, recovery requires recognition of the problem, treatment, and ongoing support and rehabilitation.

CHECK YOUR UNDERSTANDING

1. How do the drinking habits of parents tend to affect their children? What are some exceptions?
2. List three other influences on an adolescent's drinking habits.
3. What happened to the automobile accident rate when drinking ages were lowered in a number of states?
4. List three things you should do to help a friend who has a drinking problem.

SECTION **4**   **Intoxication and Society**

The attitude of our society toward drunkenness is at best confusing. At worst it is hypocritical. Drunkenness is sometimes tolerated and at other times condemned. If a person gets drunk at a party, friends may think it's funny. Yet if these same people were approached on the street by a drunken man or woman, they would be disgusted or angry. Even people who become drunk themselves at one time or another will, when sober, condemn drunkenness as sloppy, disgusting, and immoral behavior. And many people who think that all drunks should be put in jail would be upset if their next-door neighbor was jailed for being drunk in a bar or restaurant.

What Is the Answer?

For decades, society's answer to the problem of public drunkenness has been to put the offender in jail. For a number of reasons, jail does not seem to be the answer.

Dealing with intoxication places a great burden on law enforcement agencies, which are usually overtaxed to begin with. Over half of the time of all local police, jail, and courtroom personnel, in fact, is directed toward curbing public intoxication and disorderliness. And many of the people the police are arresting for drunkenness are repeaters. Each time they are released they start drinking again and end up in jail again. These people do not need "punishment." They need counseling and help. People who are arrested for major crimes committed under the influence of alcohol also need help. Releasing them from prison with an unsolved drinking problem will only cause the cycle of crime, arrest, punishment, and release to go on and on.

Putting an intoxicated person in a jail cell to "sleep it off" is also dangerous. Most people who die of intoxication die when they are alone and semiconscious. They vomit and then suffocate when the liquid is inhaled into the lungs.

Society has begun to look for other ways to deal with public intoxication. We have come a long way toward realizing that jail alone is not the answer. Many communities now "sentence" offenders to terms in rehabilitation centers. In many cases, hospitalization has proved more effective than jail.

Everyone Is Involved

The person who is obviously and repeatedly drunk in public is certainly of concern to society. However, many people who drink excessively can "hold their liquor." As a result, they do not seem drunk. These people are an even greater danger to themselves and society than the obvious drunk. They seem sober but their coordination, thinking, reaction time, and judgment are affected. They can cause serious injury or death to themselves and others.

Anyone who drinks too much—from the chronic drunk to the person who occasionally has "one too many"—can cause an accident. Motor vehicle accidents, private plane crashes, and machinery accidents frequently have

Figure 13.10 For decades, society's answer to the problem of public drunkenness has been to put the offender in jail.

drinking as their cause. And it may not always be the driver who is at fault. Some accidents are caused by cars or other machines that are poorly assembled by intoxicated workers. More subtle, but still dangerous, are errors made in business and government by people who have been drinking. Imagine a major military decision made by someone under the influence of alcohol!

Drinking and Driving

Drinking and driving is a lethal combination. About half of all traffic deaths are a result of that combination. Some 25,000 Americans die on the highways every year in alcohol-related accidents. Hundreds of thousands more are seriously injured. Young people between the ages of 15 and 24 are the most seriously affected—about 60 percent of the people who die in alcohol-related accidents are in this age group.

Drinking drivers are a threat to themselves and to others. Speeding, running red lights, improper passing, and other reckless behavior are common to the drinking driver. Pedestrians who are under the influence of alcohol also become involved in fatal and crippling roadway accidents.

Figure 13.11 About half of all traffic deaths are the result of drunken driving.

Attempts to teach the public a more sensible attitude toward drinking and driving have not been successful. Have you seen television ads urging people not to let their intoxicated friends get behind the wheel of a car? These commercials make sense, and everyone agrees with them. Yet when the situation actually happens, things often turn out differently. People are reluctant to take away their friends' car keys. They are afraid to strain the friendship. Matters are not helped by the fact that the intoxicated driver often insists that he or she can drive safely. If you are ever in such a situation, wouldn't it be better to risk ruining a friendship than to lose a friend in a car crash?

CHECK YOUR UNDERSTANDING

1. Why does jailing people for drunkenness seem to be a poor way of dealing with public intoxication?
2. Describe three ways in which intoxicated people can affect the well-being of other people.
3. How many of the 25,000 Americans who die of alcohol-related accidents each year are between the ages of 15 and 24?
4. What should you do if you think a friend is too intoxicated to drive?

SECTION **5**   **Alcoholism**

Good friends try to help each other. If you have a friend with an alcohol problem, you may already have tried to get her or him to stop drinking. You have probably failed, and you feel angry, frustrated, and sad. But some people simply cannot stop drinking by themselves. These people need professional help. It will also help if you know something about alcoholism.

What Is Alcoholism?

Alcoholics cannot stop drinking because they have become psychologically and physically dependent on alcohol. This does not happen overnight. From repeated use of alcohol, people build up a dependence on the drug. First they become psychologically dependent. They become nervous and upset when they can't have a drink. Continued use leads to the state of physical dependence that characterizes alcoholism. At this stage severe withdrawal symptoms—even death—can occur if the person is deprived of alcohol.

The earlier in life a person starts to drink, the shorter the time it takes to become an alcoholic. In adults, alcoholism can develop after 2 to 10 years of steady, heavy drinking.

However, among teenagers, the process is speeded up dramatically. It is possible for a teenager to become an alcoholic after only three or four months of heavy drinking. No one knows the reason for this.

Alcoholics cannot stop drinking once they have started. Or they cannot resist taking a drink at times when they know they shouldn't. Alcohol becomes the most important thing in their lives. They drink frequently, and they drink alone. Their physical and emotional health suffers, and so do their relationships with friends and family. Because these people are frequently intoxicated, they may lose their jobs.

The following are signs that might indicate that a person is heading toward alcoholism:

1. getting drunk four or more times in a year
2. needing a drink to go to work or school or to a social event
3. driving while drunk
4. becoming injured or hurting someone else because of an alcohol-related accident
5. getting into trouble with school officials or employers as a result of drinking
6. getting into trouble with the law as a result of drinking

Figure 13.12 Alcoholics are psychologically and physically dependent on alcohol. They drink frequently, and they drink alone.

7. doing things when intoxicated that one wouldn't do when sober
8. becoming angry when advice about drinking is given
9. experiencing blackouts

Not every alcoholic shows the same signs. You may think that to be an alcoholic, a person has to be drunk constantly. This is not always so. Some people are sober for long periods of time, then go on drinking binges. Others follow different patterns. They drink every night or only on the weekends. Often alcoholics deny that they have a problem because they *only* drink after 5 P.M. or some other specific time. A person's drinking pattern does not determine whether he or she is an alcoholic. What does determine alcoholism is the person's complete dependence on the drug.

What Causes Alcoholism?

Millions of Americans use alcohol without becoming problem drinkers. Why, then, do some people become alcoholics? What factors contribute to alcohol abuse? Some researchers believe that a person can simply learn to rely on alcohol. For example, when a tense person takes a drink, the alcohol in the drink has a calming and soothing effect. The next time the person is tense, she or he will again take a drink. The "learning" process has begun. If the behavior is repeated often enough, the person will become emotionally dependent on alcohol. Continued use will in turn lead to physical dependence.

Other possible factors leading to abuse include hormone imbalance, vitamin deficiencies, and personality problems. Researchers continue to look for a cause. But it does not seem likely that any one factor causes alcoholism. Instead, it is the result of a combination of physical, psychological, and sociological factors, all of which vary from person to person.

Physical Factors

Alcoholism definitely runs in families. This could be because children inherit the psychological traits associated with alcoholism. Or it could be that they learn to drink by imitating their parents. Or it could be a combination of the two factors. One Danish study shows that heredity may be a factor affecting at least some alcoholics. Researchers followed the lives of sons of alcoholic parents. One son in each family was raised at home. The other son was raised by nonalcoholic adoptive parents. The rate of alcoholism was the same for both groups of sons. A nonalcoholic environment, then, did not in itself prevent alcoholism.

Psychological Factors

A number of psychological traits have been found in people who drink too much. Alcoholics are unusually sensitive to stress and emotional discomfort. They may also feel inadequate about themselves and may suffer frequent bouts of depression and anxiety. Alcohol provides temporary relief and a false sense of well-being. Of course, the long-term effects of the drug only compound the problems. Alcoholics exchange long-term confidence and happiness for short-term relief and escape.

Sociological Factors

Alcoholics come from all parts of society. They are rich and poor, black and white, Christian and Jewish—and from all other economic, ethnic, and religious groups. They work in all occupations. They are executives and factory workers, waitresses and high-fashion models. They are homemakers, architects, students, and doctors.

According to statistics, there are many more male alcoholics than female ones. But alcoholism rates for women have risen quickly over the past few years. This may be due to the new place of women in society. As women pursue careers outside the home, they are exposed to the pressures and situations that contribute to alcoholism. Another possibility for this change in statistics is that when women stayed home, they could hide their problem more easily.

The impact of social change can also be seen in alcoholism rates among different ethnic

Talking Point

Alcohol and Crime

Danny and his friends were leaving the sports arena after watching a hockey game. As they tried to squeeze through the exit, a scuffle started and quickly got out of hand. Danny pulled out a knife and fatally stabbed another fan. When the police took Danny down to the station, they measured his blood alcohol level at 0.34, more than three times the legal level for intoxication. As it turned out, all of the fans involved in the fatal fight had been drinking.

Danny's case is not uncommon. According to the National Council on Alcoholism (NCA), 86 percent of all murders and 40 to 60 percent of all murder victims are drinking or drunk when the murders take place. Alcohol abuse is prevalent not only in murders but in most other violent crimes as well. The NCA estimates that half of all rapes and 72 percent of all robberies and assaults are committed by people under the influence of alcohol. In nearly 80 percent of all muggings, the victim is also under the influence.

People who abuse alcohol are not only violent to strangers and acquaintances; they also do harm to themselves and to members of their families. The NCA estimates that 10,000 people commit suicide each year while under the influence of alcohol and that two-thirds of all suicide attempts are made by people who have been drinking. In addition, alcohol abuse is involved in 52 percent of all wife battering cases and 38 percent of child abuse and molestation cases, according to the NCA.

It costs state and local governments billions of dollars each year to find, prosecute, and imprison alcoholic criminals. These costs are little, however, compared with the toll in human suffering and misery that alcohol-related crime costs its victims and their families each year.

groups. At one time, people of Italian, Jewish, and Chinese heritage were less likely to become alcoholics than other Americans. Their culture and religion endorsed moderation and opposed intoxication. But as these groups have been absorbed into the mainstream of American life, their alcoholism rates have risen. Today, ethnic heritage does not play much of a role in determining who becomes an alcoholic and who does not.

Treatment

Alcoholics are often secretive about their difficulties. They may deny their problem to themselves and others. Members of their families and friends may help to conceal the problem. They shield the alcoholic to help him or her keep job and respectability. Hiding or ignoring the problem helps no one. Alcoholism is an illness. It requires medical, psychological, and social treatment. The family, teacher, employer, and anyone else important in the alcoholic's life should be involved in the treatment. However, unless an alcoholic is willing to get help, little can be done. Anger, threats, and accusations will not help. The alcoholic is incapable of controlling her or his drinking—even if it means losing contact with friends and loved ones.

Once an alcoholic asks for help, though, there are many people and programs available. Very often medical attention is required to take care of physical problems, such as malnutrition or liver damage. Some doctors prescribe a drug called *Antabuse* to help alcoholics stop drinking while they are being treated. This medica-tion causes the person to become ill when he or she takes a drink. It is used along with emotional and psychological counseling.

Alcoholics Anonymous (AA) is the most well known of the many groups to help people recover emotionally and psychologically from alcoholism. AA members are recovered alcoholics who provide mutual support and guidance for alcoholics. Through the buddy system, members help each other get through one day at a time. Another organization, Al-Anon, is designed to help the spouses of alcoholics. Alateen is especially for the children of alcoholic parents. AA, Al-Anon, and Alateen meetings are held throughout the United States. Many community mental health centers also offer treatment programs for alcoholics.

Alcoholism is a disease, and alcoholics need support and understanding to recover. Group help and individual counseling can teach an alcoholic to change aspects of personality and life style that may have contributed to the problem. Some alcoholics need practical assistance in shaping their new lives. Recovery from alcoholism is a long-term process.

CHECK YOUR UNDERSTANDING

1. How long does it usually take for an adult to become an alcoholic? For a teenager?
2. List the signs that show a person is heading toward alcoholism.
3. Describe the kinds of treatment an alcoholic needs.
4. Describe the psychological traits that many alcoholics exhibit.

CHAPTER SUMMARY

- Alcohol is a mind-altering drug, resulting from the action of yeast, molds, or bacteria on grains and fruits. Beer, wine, and hard liquors contain different concentrations of alcohol.

- Among the diseases associated with heavy use of alcohol are high blood pressure, stomach ulcers, cirrhosis of the liver, and cancers of the mouth, pharynx, larynx, and esophagus.

- Alcohol affects behavior by paralyzing the parts of the brain that control judgment, muscle movement, sight, hearing, and balance. It slows mental processes and affects emotional responses.
- The effect of alcohol on a person's behavior is determined in part by the blood alcohol level. A heavy person will usually have a lower blood alcohol level than a light person after both have consumed the same amount of alcohol.
- Other factors that affect a person's reaction to alcohol include rate of absorption, rate of consumption, type of beverage, and the drinker's physical condition, motivation, and experience.
- When alcohol is taken with other drugs, such as barbiturates and tranquilizers, there can be unpredictable and sometimes fatal results.
- Alcohol use is linked to social influences, such as advertising, family drinking habits, and the influence of friends.
- Alcohol use by teenagers is a major problem in America today. Some 3 million teenagers have drinking problems. Alcohol use is well ahead of marijuana use.
- For a number of reasons, jail does not seem to be the answer to dealing with drunkenness. Rehabilitation and hospitalization are often more effective.
- Drinking and driving is a lethal combination. Some 25,000 Americans die in alcohol-related traffic accidents every year. About 60 percent of them are young people under age 24.
- Alcoholics are drinkers who have developed a physical and psychological dependence on alcohol. Alcoholism results from a combination of physical, psychological, and cultural factors.
- Alcoholism requires medical, psychological, and social treatment. Many alcoholics have been helped by the treatment program of Alcoholics Anonymous.

DO YOU REMEMBER?

Give brief definitions of these terms:

ethyl alcohol	cirrhosis of the liver	delirium tremens	oxidation
methyl alcohol	hangover	blood alcohol level	Antabuse

THINK AND DISCUSS

1. Do you think there should be greater controls over the advertising of alcoholic beverages? If so, what should these controls be?
2. What would you do if you realized that one of your friends had an alcohol problem?
3. What do you think should be the penalties for drunk driving? Why?
4. What aspects of our society do you think make drinking look attractive to young people?
5. Why do you think people who drink at parties sometimes try to force other guests to drink too? What would you do if you were a guest in such a situation?
6. Where would you draw the line between responsible and irresponsible drinking?
7. What could be the dangers of the false feeling of body warmth that alcohol produces?

FOLLOW-UP

1. Find out how your state controls the sale of alcohol and how it deals with drunk drivers. Write a report on your findings, including your own opinion of the laws involved.

2. Find out what services your community provides for alcoholics and their families. Make a chart that describes these services and post it in your classroom.

3. Learn more about Prohibition and why it failed. Write a report on the subject. Include your opinion of what would happen if a similar law were passed today.

4. Find out more about the methods now used to rehabilitate alcoholics. Describe these methods to your class.

5. Make a poster that illustrates how various body organs are affected by alcohol. Display the poster in your classroom.

6. Find out more about Alcoholics Anonymous or Alateen, the branch of AA that helps teenagers who have alcoholic parents. Write a report on the work of the group you choose.

CHAPTER 14

Smoking and Health

After reading this chapter, you should be able to answer these questions:

1. What warnings appear on cigarette packs?
2. What diseases are linked to cigarette smoking? What diseases are linked to smokeless tobacco?
3. Why do people smoke?
4. Why do people find it difficult to stop smoking?
5. How many Americans have quit smoking? How did they do it?
6. Does cigarette smoke affect nonsmokers?

According to a 1981 Federal Trade Commission staff report, cigarettes are the most heavily advertised product in the United States. "The dominant themes of cigarette advertising," the report states, "are that smoking is associated with youthful vigor, good health, good looks, and personal, social, and professional acceptance and success . . . conspicuously absent [is] mention of the numerous and specific adverse health consequences of using the advertised product."

The report also mentions that medical knowledge about the very serious health consequences of smoking is growing. On the other hand, although most Americans are aware of some of the health risks in smoking, more than 40 percent don't know that smoking causes most lung cancer, and 20 percent don't know it can cause cancer at all. More than 30 percent are unaware that smoking doubles a person's risk of heart attack, and 50 percent of women do not know that smoking during pregnancy increases the risk of stillbirth and miscarriage.

Among the commission's recommendations for ways to inform the public about these health risks are warnings that must appear on every package of cigarettes and on every cigarette advertisement:

Surgeon General's Warning: Smoking Causes Lung Cancer, Heart Disease, Emphysema, and May Complicate Pregnancy.

Surgeon General's Warning: Quitting Smoking Now Greatly Reduces Serious Risks to Your Health.

Surgeon General's Warning: Cigarette Smoke Contains Carbon Monoxide.

Surgeon General's Warning: Smoking by Pregnant Women May Result in Fetal Injury, Premature Birth, and Low Birth Weight.

As a result of the 1981 report, government and private agencies have launched educational programs to help smokers understand how dangerous smoking is and how specific smoking-related health risks apply to them personally. Yet, in spite of the warnings and programs, more than 53 million Americans smoke: 30 percent of adults and 16 percent of teenagers. Many of these people would like to stop, but they say that they cannot. Some have stopped for periods of time, only to go back to it.

What exactly is tobacco? In what ways is smoking harmful? Why do people smoke? Why is it so hard to stop smoking? How does cigarette smoke affect nearby nonsmokers? This chapter will discuss the answers to these and other questions.

SECTION 1   **What Is a Cigarette?**

How would you describe a cigarette? You'd probably focus on its size and shape, and you'd use the words *tobacco* and *paper* in your description. You probably wouldn't use the word *chemical*. Yet the fact is that scientists have identified more than 4,000 different toxic, or poisonous, chemicals in cigarette smoke. A cigarette may seem simple to describe, but it's actually a highly complex, and potentially lethal, chemical factory.

Few people smoked cigarettes until about 100 years ago. People had been using tobacco for over 3,000 years, but they usually smoked it in pipes or chewed it. Then in 1881 a cigarette-making machine was invented. A new industry sprang up that by 1900 was producing 4 billion cigarettes a year. In a single generation, that figure skyrocketed. By the 1920s, 80 billion cigarettes were being produced annually. Today Americans are puffing away their lives and polluting the air with the help of some 600 billion cigarettes every year. And they are spending more than $15 billion a year doing this. What exactly are they buying?

Components of Cigarette Smoke

When it burns, the average cigarette produces about half a gram of smoke. About 92 percent of that smoke is in the form of gases, some of which are known to be toxic. *Carbon monoxide,* for example, is a poisonous gas that is present in cigarette smoke. The other 8 percent consists of solid particles. These solids are high in tar and other harmful substances. Along with the gases, they make their way into the smoker's lungs.

Scientists have determined that the solids contain a high proportion of *carcinogens*. Carcinogens are substances that cause cancer. *Benzopyrene,* one of the deadliest carcinogens known, is found in smoke solids. Other chemicals found in the tarry solids do not actually cause cancer, but they can cause an inactive cancer cell to grow and spread.

Nicotine is the active drug in tobacco. It is found in smoke solids. Nicotine does not cause cancer, but it has been linked to other diseases. Nicotine works on the central nervous system. It speeds up the heartbeat and constricts certain blood vessels in the extremities. Researchers have taken special "heat pictures" of

Figure 14.1 A heavily carbon-pigmented lung, typical of smokers and coal miners, is compared to a normal lung.

smokers' hands and feet. These show that the temperature in the fingers and toes goes down after a cigarette is smoked.

Scientists are currently examining the effects of nicotine on certain lung muscles. They believe that nicotine may impair the functioning of these muscles and contribute to respiratory ailments.

Like many other psychoactive drugs, nicotine can cause psychological dependence. Regular use can also lead to tolerance, causing the smoker to increase his or her consumption of cigarettes.

What About "Safe" Cigarettes?

Perhaps you have heard certain brands referred to as "safe" cigarettes. When cigarettes first began to be linked to lung cancer, manufacturers did attempt to take some of the hazards out of smoking. They added filters to cigarettes to prevent some of the harmful gases from being inhaled. Cigarettes with less tar and less nicotine were developed.

Some smokers did not find these weaker cigarettes as satisfying as the stronger ones. The switchover was not an immediate success. But over the years, more and more smokers switched to low-nicotine, low-tar, filtered cigarettes.

Statistics show that, by smoking filtered cigarettes, people can lower their risk of lung cancer. However, the risk is still much greater than it is for a nonsmoker. And filters and lower levels of tar and nicotine do not solve another very serious problem. Carbon monoxide, one of the toxic gases in cigarette smoke, is not reduced by filters nor by lowering the tar and nicotine levels. Carbon monoxide has been linked to various types of heart disease.

Cigarette manufacturers have succeeded in producing "safer" cigarettes for their customers. They have not, however, managed to produce a cigarette that is safe.

CHECK YOUR UNDERSTANDING

1. How many toxic chemicals are known to exist in cigarette smoke?
2. What percentage of cigarette smoke is made of gases? Of solids?
3. Describe the effects nicotine has on the human body.
4. Explain what filters can and cannot do.

SECTION **2** **Smoking and Disease**

According to a report presented by the Surgeon General in 1982, cigarettes contribute to the deaths of some 350,000 Americans every year. That's enough people to fill a city the size of Miami, Florida, or Austin, Texas. Also, millions of smokers are chronically disabled by smoking-related diseases.

Most of the deaths are due to lung cancer, heart disease, and respiratory diseases such as bronchitis and emphysema. How likely a smoker is to get any of these diseases depends on a number of factors. The length of time people smoke and how much they smoke are important. Mortality rates are higher for people who start smoking at an early age. People who inhale as they smoke take more of the harmful chemicals into their lungs, and so run a higher risk of disease. The health history of the individual smoker is also important. Some people may have special problems, such as high blood pressure or asthma, that make cigarette use even more hazardous.

Have you heard a smoker argue that city air is so polluted it doesn't matter whether you smoke or not? True, polluted air isn't good for anyone. But nonsmokers in urban environments still have low rates of lung cancer while heavy smokers in clean environments suffer high rates of the disease. Smoke from an unfiltered cigarette contains 50,000 times as many harmful particles as does an equal amount of polluted city air. Environmental pollution can't compete with the "self-pollution" of cigarette smoking.

In all the bad news about cigarette smoking, there is some good news. Smokers can improve their odds by giving up cigarettes. The longer a person goes without smoking, the less chance she or he has of developing a smoking-related disease. The Surgeon General reports that, after 15 years without cigarettes, former smokers have mortality rates that are almost the same as those for people who have never smoked.

Figure 14.2 Pipe smokers are as likely as cigarette smokers to develop cancer of the lip, mouth, larynx, or esophagus.

Cancer

This year, over 110,000 Americans will die from lung cancer. The majority of them will be cigarette smokers. For every nonsmoker who contracts lung cancer, 11 smokers get this disease.

Lung cancer has been linked to the tarry particles in cigarette smoke. When the smoke is inhaled, these particles cling to the delicate lung tissues. An accumulation of these particles turns the normally pink lung tissue black. The particles cause cells in the lungs to become irritated and to form in abnormally thick layers.

Smoking can also destroy the top layer of cells in the lining of the lungs. Then these cells, which have hairlike projections to filter out dust and other harmful particles, can no longer do their job. The remaining cells become enlarged and flattened. When cancer develops, the abnormal cells spread rapidly through the lungs, destroying normal tissue. If the cancer is not checked in time, the cells can spread to other parts of the body. How soon the disease is detected, the extent of the disease, and its responsiveness to treatment determine the patient's chances for survival.

Other types of cancer are also affected by smoking. People who smoke a pack of cigarettes a day are twice as likely to die of bladder cancer as nonsmokers are. The toxic materials in cigarettes are eliminated in the urine. Their effects on the bladder are believed to promote cancer. Researchers also suspect cigarettes of contributing to higher than normal levels of cancers of the kidney and pancreas.

Fatal cancers of the lip, mouth, larynx, and esophagus are more common among smokers than among nonsmokers. In these cases, pipe and cigar smokers, who otherwise have almost normal mortality rates, are included in the high-risk group. Their risk is increased because of the heat and chemicals that are taken into the mouth and throat.

Heart Disease

A pack-a-day smoker is twice as likely to suffer a heart attack as a nonsmoker is. People who smoke more than a pack of cigarettes a day are three times more likely to die of a heart attack than nonsmokers. Diseases of the coronary blood vessels are also much more common in smokers than nonsmokers. Heart disease rates rise according to the number of cigarettes the person smokes and the length of time he or she has smoked. In the same way, rates begin to go down when the smoker gives up cigarettes.

Two parts of cigarette smoke—nicotine and carbon monoxide—have been blamed for the higher rates of heart disease suffered by smokers. Nicotine interferes with nerve messages and causes the heart to beat at an uneven rate. It constricts the coronary blood vessels, reducing the heart's supply of oxygen. Nicotine may cause clots to form in the blood. A blood clot in a coronary blood vessel is a serious problem and can be fatal. Nicotine is also believed to contribute to high blood pressure.

Carbon monoxide is the same toxic gas as is found in automobile exhausts. When it is inhaled, it reduces the amount of oxygen carried in the blood. Oxygen is the "food" that nourishes the body's tissues and organs. Carbon monoxide leaves important organs, such as the heart, starved for nourishment.

Bronchitis and Emphysema

People who smoke heavily often develop a nagging cough. A persistent, hacking cough and shortness of breath are symptoms of two serious pulmonary (lung) diseases, bronchitis and emphysema. Both conditions are characterized by damaged cells in the lungs. The chemicals in cigarette smoke are thought to cause such damage.

In bronchitis, the special cells that filter dust and harmful particles from the lungs are affected. When these cells are damaged, tiny particles get into the air passageways of the lungs. The passageways become clogged and irritated, and excess mucus is produced. The extra mucus and foreign particles cause coughing and lead to infections.

Emphysema is a disease that affects the millions of tiny balloonlike air sacs in the lungs. Normally, the air sacs serve two main functions. They fill with fresh air as a breath is taken. The oxygen in the fresh air passes to the bloodstream and is carried to all parts of the body. The air sacs also push out the stale air, or carbon dioxide, when it returns from the bloodstream. With emphysema, some of the air sacs stretch and break down. They become less elastic and cannot push out all of the stale air. This causes breathlessness. Damaged air sacs also affect the exchange of oxygen and carbon dioxide in the bloodstream.

The death rate from pulmonary diseases is six times higher for smokers than for nonsmokers. Although an improvement is noted when the person quits smoking, there is no such thing as complete recovery. Some of the damage

Talking Point

Tobacco—Unsafe in Any Form

How many times have you seen a clean-cut athlete chomping away on a huge plug of chewing tobacco or advertising a particular brand of snuff? Such images have led thousands of teenagers to believe that smokeless tobacco—chewing tobacco and snuff—is a safe alternative to cigarette smoking. It isn't.

According to the National Cancer Institute, there is a high correlation between the use of smokeless tobacco and cancers of the throat and mouth. About 9,000 Americans die of oral cancer each year, and others are disabled or horribly disfigured from the surgery and chemotherapy needed to halt the disease. Furthermore, the nicotine in smokeless tobacco has the same harmful effects on the cardiovascular system as the nicotine in cigarette smoke.

Another supposedly "safe" alternative to the regular cigarette is the clove cigarette, or "kretek," from Indonesia. Clove cigarettes, which have become very popular with young people, have been linked to serious lung disease. They are suspected of having caused several deaths among young smokers. Despite the advertising claims for various tobacco products, there simply are no safe forms of tobacco. The only truly safe course is to avoid them all.

done by bronchitis and emphysema is permanent. This is especially true of emphysema. The burst air sacs inside the lungs do not heal. Giving up cigarettes will, however, halt the progress of the disease.

Smoking and Pregnancy

Studies show that women who smoke during pregnancy double their chances of having a miscarriage or stillbirth. Mortality rates are also much higher for infants born to smoking

Figure 14.3 A pregnant woman who smokes increases her risk of having a premature and underweight baby.

mothers than for those born to nonsmokers. Pregnant women who smoke are more likely than nonsmokers to have premature and underweight babies, conditions that can affect the lifelong health of the newborn. In fact, there is evidence that children of smoking mothers are adversely affected in terms of physical growth, intellectual development, and emotional development.

Reduced levels of oxygen are believed to be the cause of much of the damage. A developing fetus gets its oxygen from the mother's body. If the mother smokes, she is reducing both her own oxygen supply and that of the fetus. The Public Health Service advises all pregnant women to stop smoking.

Other Health Problems

Three to four times more smokers die from *peptic ulcers* (ulcers in the digestive system) than do nonsmokers. Smoking increases the pain of the ulcer and decreases the effectiveness of drugs used to soothe the pain. Smoking probably does not actually cause ulcers, but it makes them worse because it stimulates the production of stomach acids. The activities that sometimes accompany smoking, such as drinking coffee or alcohol, may also contribute to the problem. These beverages irritate the stomach, particularly when there is no food present to absorb them.

Sinusitis is the mildest of the cigarette-related diseases. The gases and particles in cigarette smoke irritate the sinus cavities, causing pain and headaches. The condition quickly clears up when the smoker gives up cigarettes.

CHECK YOUR UNDERSTANDING

1. How many Americans die each year as a direct result of smoking cigarettes? Name four factors that affect a person's chances of developing a smoking-related disease.
2. Briefly describe the way smoking makes the lungs susceptible to cancer. What other kinds of cancer are linked to smoking?
3. How do nicotine and carbon monoxide affect the heart and blood?
4. Describe what happens in emphysema.
5. In what ways can smoking affect a woman's pregnancy?

SECTION **3** # Why People Smoke

When cigarettes first became big business at the beginning of this century, the typical smoker was a middle-class workingman. Perhaps he thought smoking made him seem more rugged and masculine. From this idea was built the advertising image of the tough, tan, and handsome smoker—an individual who stood for freedom and romance, strength and daring. At first, cigarettes were strictly for men only. Women who smoked in public were considered loose and decadent.

By the 1920s cigarette use had spread. Men of all economic levels took up cigarette smoking. The 1920s marked a new era for women as well. They had won the right to vote and they were demanding, and winning, new freedoms. For many women of this time, short hair, short skirts, and cigarettes were the ultimate marks of sophistication.

In the late 1930s and the 1940s smokers were portrayed in ads as heroes and heroines in all walks of life. Screen idols and leading ladies puffed their way through film after film. And all across America, the public lighted up with them. In the prosperous 1950s advertisers

Figure 14.4 In the early 1930s, smoking was considered a mark of sophistication. Today, slick advertising still lures many people to cigarettes.

promoted cigarettes as an important part of ''the good life.''

Cigarette advertising mushroomed in newspapers and magazines, on billboards, and on radio and TV. Smokers were portrayed as attractive, vigorous people, anxious to get the most out of life. Such ads were aimed at young people. As a result, college students and teenagers began to smoke in record numbers.

In January 1964, 50 years of uninterrupted growth in cigarette consumption came to an end, and a slow, but steady, decline in smoking began. The decline was caused in part by a report issued by the Surgeon General entitled *Smoking and Health*. This report linked cigarette smoking with cardiovascular and other diseases and identified smoking as a cause of lung and laryngeal cancers and chronic bronchitis.

Even though the decline in cigarette consumption is continuing today, millions of Americans continue to smoke, and young people continue to start smoking. Why?

Factors That Influence Smoking

People smoke for many reasons. Some do it to relax or to relieve boredom. Others smoke because of the comfort and physical gratification cigarettes give them. They enjoy the feel of the cigarette in their hands and in their mouths. Others say that they find the taste and smell of tobacco enjoyable.

Since cigarettes dull the taste buds, many people feel smoking helps them remain slim. They are afraid that, if they stop smoking, they will go on an eating binge and gain weight. This is a myth. The average weight gain for ex-smokers is slight, and most people are able to take the excess pounds off without trouble. But even if the pounds never came off, doctors agree that a pack-a-day habit poses a much more serious health hazard than a few pounds of excess weight.

People use cigarettes to see them through social encounters. Some say that smoking gives them something to do with their hands. Others say that it makes them feel mature and sophisticated. Of course, all that many people around the smoker notice are the choking smoke, the dirty ashes, and the offensive breath of the smoker. This certainly destroys

Figure 14.6 Cigarette packs reflect a harsher reality about cigarettes.

Figure 14.5 Cigarette manufacturers like to show active outdoor images in their advertisements to encourage people to associate cigarette smoking with successful living and good health.

any air of sophistication that the smoker may be trying to achieve.

Cigarettes have a special function for some young people. Like alcohol, they symbolize the forbidden and supposedly sophisticated pleasures of the adult world. Smoking provides a way of at once rebelling against adult authority and imitating adult behavior.

The home life of young smokers is also an important factor. Studies have shown that teenagers and young adults who smoke very often have parents who are current or former smokers. Understandably, teenagers are unwilling to accept warnings about the hazards of cigarette use from parents who smoke. Some parents don't even try to warn their children.

One study reported that one-third of smoking parents did not object to their children's doing the same.

We are all influenced by the standards and expectations of our peer groups. This is especially true of younger people, who often need the approval of a specific social group. Most young people who smoke have smoking friends.

Forming a Habit

Smoking a cigarette gives the smoker an immediate lift. This mildly stimulating effect soon wears off, giving way to mild depression. To relieve the depression, the smoker often reaches for another cigarette. This chain-smoking cycle can go on for hours. For some people, it occupies all of their waking moments.

The drug that produces these effects is nicotine. Can nicotine cause physical dependence? Experts disagree about this. Many smokers who have attempted to give up cigarettes claim to have experienced all of the discomforts of withdrawal syndrome. Many researchers, however, say that withdrawal is purely psychological. But whether nicotine dependence is physiological or psychological, it is difficult to overcome. About 40 percent of current smokers have made three or more attempts to quit.

Current Trends

Since 1964 the overall percentage of cigarette smokers has dropped. Today, 30 percent of the adult population smokes, compared with 42 percent in 1964. However, the decline has been mostly among men, down from 53 percent in 1964 to about 35 percent today. The percentage of women who smoke has dropped only slightly to 29 percent. Women also tend to smoke more heavily than they used to. As a result, lung cancer recently passed breast cancer as the leading cause of cancer deaths in women.

The most serious news is that, since the Surgeon General's first report, the number of smokers between the ages of 12 and 18 has actually gone up. Almost all of this increase is due to the larger number of teenage girls who smoke. The rates for boys have remained relatively stable. But, in the first decade after the Surgeon General's report, the rates for girls almost *doubled*.

Today, there are some 6 million teenage smokers. There are also some 100,000 smokers aged 12 or under. In one large West Coast area, one out of five children is smoking by the age of 12. This trend is very discouraging. Death rates from smoking-related diseases are higher for people who start smoking at younger ages than for those who start later in life.

CHECK YOUR UNDERSTANDING

1. List six reasons people give for smoking.
2. What special reasons might teenagers have for smoking?
3. What is the immediate effect of nicotine on the smoker? What happens after this effect wears off?
4. Describe the current smoking trends among men, women, and teenagers.

SECTION **4**   # Kicking the Habit

Nearly all smokers are aware of the Surgeon General's findings, and they agree that cigarettes *do* shorten life and promote disease. Most smokers would like to give up cigarettes. In fact, only 10 percent say they have no interest in quitting.

Why is it so difficult to kick the cigarette habit? Nicotine dependence, whether it is psychological or physical, is a powerful factor. The emotional comforts and physical pleasures of smoking may also be strong incentives. Cigarettes are convenient and, until recently, smokers were free to light up anytime and almost anywhere.

But times are changing. Smoking is no longer permitted in many public places. And nonsmokers are increasingly voicing their objections. It is estimated that there are more than 35 million ex-smokers in the United States today. Millions more could join them.

Ways to Quit

For the smoker who sincerely wants to give up cigarettes, there are many methods available. There are almost as many ways to stop smoking as there are brands of cigarettes. Each individual has to find the method that is best for her or him. What is easy for one person may not be easy for another.

There is evidence that quitting all at once brings the most successful results. The withdrawal symptoms fade more quickly than when a person just reduces the number of cigarettes gradually. The "part-time" smoker is in a constant state of withdrawal. He or she maintains a desire for nicotine and may quickly return to heavier smoking habits.

For many smokers, though, quitting "cold turkey" is too difficult. These people prefer to reduce their consumption of cigarettes gradually. Switching to a filtered cigarette or one of the low-tar, low-nicotine brands may be the first step toward quitting. Other gradual methods include not smoking to the end of a cigarette, taking fewer puffs on each cigarette, not inhaling as often, and reducing the number of cigarettes smoked each day.

Products and Programs

There are a variety of products on the market to help smokers stop. These include special filters that reduce the intake of tar and nicotine step by step, as well as a large number of books, records, and cassette recordings that outline quitting programs. There are also tablets and nicotine chewing gum designed to reduce the smoker's nicotine craving.

Some quitting programs involve *hypnosis*. The practitioner puts the smoker into a mild trance and then coaches him or her about stopping. Other programs use *aversion techniques*. They may have the person smoke continuously or breathe stale cigarette smoke. The aim is to make the smoker associate smoking with an unpleasant experience.

A wide variety of group programs and clinics have been developed to help smokers quit. Some are provided free of charge by voluntary organizations such as the American Cancer Society or the American Heart Association. Others are businesses and can be expensive. However, such programs are much less costly, both in terms of dollars and health, than a heavy smoking habit. A two-pack-a-day smoker can easily spend several hundred dollars a year on cigarettes.

Group programs provide education and moral support. Through lectures, films, discussions, or printed materials, smokers are made aware of the hazards of smoking and are given practical tips on how to stop. At the same time, smokers who are fighting for the same goal offer each other mutual encouragement. These programs can be brief and intensive or they can last for several weeks. Some hospitals even offer 24-hour-a-day, live-in programs.

It is difficult to measure the success rates of the various quitting programs. Many are designed for individual, at-home use, and experts find it hard to determine their effectiveness. Also, many people find it easier to give up cigarettes than to stay off them. They may go back to smoking after a few weeks or months. Good stop-smoking programs find that 30 to 40 percent of their participants are still not smoking after one year.

It is estimated that 95 percent of the 35 million Americans who have quit smoking stopped on their own without the aid of formal programs. These people talk of the benefits they gained by so doing. They say that they feel healthier and can get more enjoyment out of physical activities. They also appreciate food and fragrances more, and they feel that they look better.

How to...

Quit Smoking

If you are a teenage smoker, chances are you have been smoking for only a few months or years. If your habit is not yet deeply ingrained, you stand a good chance of kicking it.

Some schools and community groups have special programs to help teenagers quit. If these programs are not available in your community, you can enroll in an adult program or you can quit on your own.

The American Cancer Society offers a seven-day plan that calls for cutting down for the first five days, then quitting "cold turkey" on the sixth day. Here is how that plan works:

1. The day before you start, smoke an excess of cigarettes, three or four packs, to spoil their taste.
2. For the first five days, keep a record on a piece of paper wrapped around your cigarette pack. Write down the time and what you are doing (changing classes, waiting for a bus, etc.) each time you smoke. Grade each cigarette on a scale of 1 to 3 according to whether you "can't do without it"; "want it, but not desperately"; or "could do without it."
3. Change to a lower-nicotine brand of cigarette and buy only one pack at a time.
4. On days two through four, try to cut out all cigarettes you graded "3," then those you graded "2," until you are down to only those cigarettes you can't do without.
5. Write down your reasons for wanting to quit smoking. Reread your list often, and add to it whenever you can.
6. Try lighting up the first cigarette of the day an hour later each day. Smoke only during even- or odd-numbered hours.
7. On the sixth day, quit smoking altogether. Take up a new sport or engage daily in some moderate physical activitity, such as jogging or walking.
8. Substitute gum, celery, carrot sticks, or a cinnamon stick for a cigarette.
9. Whenever you feel a strong urge to smoke, sit down, relax, take several deep breaths, or drink a glass of water.
10. Until you are very sure of yourself, avoid situations in which you previously smoked.
11. On the seventh day, open a savings account and deposit in it weekly the amount of money you would have spent on cigarettes. After six months or a year without smoking, spend it on yourself as a well-deserved reward.

The Rights of Nonsmokers

At one time smokers would defend their habit by saying that it harmed no one but themselves. That argument is no longer acceptable. For the nonsmoker, cigarette smoke is much more than an annoyance. It is a proved health hazard.

As a cigarette burns, smoke pours into the air. This smoke, called *sidestream smoke*, ends up in the lungs of nearby nonsmokers. Sidestream smoke contains dozens of toxic gases and solids. Especially harmful are the large amounts of carbon monoxide. According to clean air standards set by the Environmental Protection Agency (EPA), there should be no more than 100 parts of carbon monoxide in every million parts of air. There is 420 times that much carbon monoxide in sidestream smoke.

Figure 14.7 Organized action by nonsmokers has led to the regulation of smoking in many public places.

Not all of this smoke is breathed in by people around the smoker. Some of it drifts away or is carried away by fans or air-conditioning systems. But enough can remain in a smoke-filled room to harm the health of everyone there. The Public Health Service reports that people with heart problems and those with heart and lung diseases run particular risks from exposure to heavy concentrations of smoke.

Another high-risk group of nonsmokers are those who are *allergic* to cigarette smoke. About 10 to 15 percent of all Americans suffer from eye irritations, breathing problems, and even severe asthma attacks after inhaling cigarette smoke. This problem is not commonly recognized because the allergic reaction usually takes place sometime after the smoke is inhaled. Also, allergic people have learned to avoid smoky rooms.

Whether they are allergic to tobacco smoke or simply object to it, nonsmokers are speaking out in increasing numbers. The right to breathe clean air, they say, is greater than the right to pollute it. Many are asking smokers not to light up in public places. Some have established no-smoking rules in their cars and homes. Some restaurants have created separate dining areas for smokers and nonsmokers. One woman who was allergic to smoke even sued her employer for the right to work in a smoke-free area. She won her case. The state court ordered a ban on smoking in the office she shared with others.

Group Action Against Smoking

Nonsmokers in many communities have formed groups to fight for their rights. Organizations such as ASH (Action on Smoking and Health) and GASP (Group Against Smokers' Pollution) are working for laws that will guarantee the rights of nonsmokers. They believe that smoking should be prohibited in offices, schools, hospitals, stores, elevators, buses, and other places shared by all members of the community.

Many states have passed laws that regulate smoking in public places. Minnesota's Clean Indoor Air Act, passed in 1975, is one of the strongest. It bans smoking in all areas shared by the public. Smokers may light up only in specified areas, and fines for lawbreakers can go as high as $100.

Laws such as this are not automatically obeyed. But smokers who light up in no-smoking areas are less likely to be tolerated than they would have been a few years ago. Nonsmokers are voicing their complaints and asking smokers to put out their cigarettes. In the long run, this may have a greater impact than all the scientific, educational, and legal efforts combined.

CHECK YOUR UNDERSTANDING

1. Why might quitting smoking all at once work better than stopping gradually? What are some gradual methods of quitting?
2. Describe some of the products on the market to help smokers quit.
3. Why might a group program work better for some smokers than quitting on their own?
4. What kinds of benefits do people say they gain from quitting smoking?
5. Describe sidestream smoke and its effects on nonsmokers.

CHAPTER SUMMARY

- Cigarette smoke contains more than 4,000 toxic chemicals. One of them is benzopyrene, one of the deadliest known carcinogens.
- The active drug in tobacco is nicotine, which affects the central nervous system.
- Cigarettes contribute to the deaths of some 350,000 Americans every year. Most of the deaths are due to lung cancer, heart disease, bronchitis, and emphysema.
- After 15 years without cigarettes, former smokers have mortality rates that are almost the same as those for people who never smoked.
- Smokers are 11 times more likely to die from lung cancer than are nonsmokers. They also run a higher risk of dying from cancers of the bladder, lip, mouth, larynx, and esophagus.
- A pack-a-day smoker is twice as likely to suffer a heart attack as a nonsmoker is.
- Millions of heavy smokers suffer from a persistent, hacking cough and shortness of breath—symptoms of bronchitis and emphysema.
- A woman who smokes during pregnancy can harm her unborn child. Smoking mothers-to-be are more likely than nonsmokers to have miscarriages, stillbirths, and premature babies.
- In recent years the overall percentage of people who smoke has dropped. However, the percentage of women who smoke has not changed significantly, and there has been a dramatic increase in the number of teenage girls who smoke.
- Some of the methods for giving up smoking include quitting "cold turkey" and using filters, hypnosis, aversion techniques, and commercial group programs.
- Carbon monoxide levels in smoke-filled rooms can become high enough to harm the health of nonsmokers. About 10 to 15 percent of Americans are allergic to tobacco smoke.
- Nonsmokers are increasingly expressing their right to clean air. Some have formed groups to fight for their rights. Many states now ban smoking in public places.

DO YOU REMEMBER?

Give brief definitions of these terms:

carbon monoxide	nicotine	emphysema	aversion techniques
carcinogen	bronchitis	sinusitis	sidestream smoke

THINK AND DISCUSS

1. Why do you think the percentage of teenage girls who smoke has risen so dramatically during the past 10 years?
2. Should the tobacco industry be allowed to advertise? Why or why not?
3. Why is it so important for athletes not to smoke?
4. In what ways can smoking damage your home? What do you think of people who tell visitors that they do not allow smoking in their homes?
5. What do you think the smoking regulations should be in public places?
6. Do you think your school should have a special smoking area? Why or why not?
7. How should nonsmokers handle situations in which they are disturbed by tobacco smoke?
8. How can you explain the fact that some government agencies encourage the tobacco industry, while others try to keep people from smoking?

FOLLOW-UP

1. Put together a collage of cigarette advertisements. Display the collage in your classroom and discuss the different appeals used in the ads.
2. Write a report on how the tobacco industry affects the nation's economy. Discuss your findings with your class.
3. Compute the average yearly cost of smoking one, two, and three packs of cigarettes a day. Post the results in your classroom.
4. Draw a cartoon figure that illustrates the effects of smoking on a person's appearance.
5. Ask five nonsmokers their reasons for not smoking. Make a list of their replies and post it in your classroom.
6. Interview five smokers about their efforts to quit. Describe their efforts in a written report.
7. Find out about the kinds of smoking regulations that exist in your community. Discuss these regulations with your class.
8. Contact the National Clearinghouse for Smoking and Health for information on teenage smoking. Display the information in your classroom.
9. Obtain information from your dentist about the effects of smoking on your teeth and gums. Describe your findings to your class.
10. Make a chart that lists the amounts of tar and nicotine in the most popular brands of cigarettes. Post the chart in your classroom.

PART 5

Disease

Disease is a threat that human beings have always had to face. The types of diseases that threaten us have changed, however. Most of the illnesses that our ancestors dreaded have been conquered by advances in medical science. Today the diseases of life style—notably, cancer and the cardiovascular diseases—are our major health problems.

Part 5 examines the struggle against disease from the highest levels of research to the personal level—what *you* can do to guard against illness. It highlights the factors that contribute to disease and emphasizes personal responsibility in disease prevention.

Chapter 15 discusses the causes and changing patterns of disease. Chapter 16 focuses on the infectious diseases that are still at large. Today's leading killers—the cardiovascular diseases and cancer—are the subjects of Chapters 17 and 18 respectively.

The Struggle Against Disease

After reading this chapter, you should be able to answer these questions:

1. How do scientists study disease? What do they learn from their studies?
2. How can you build up your resistance to disease?
3. Why is the life expectancy rate in the United States lower than that of some other highly developed countries?
4. What is chemotherapy?
5. What can you do to help prevent the spread of disease?

Have you had a cold lately? Or the flu? If so, you probably considered your illness one of the minor inconveniences of life. You knew that in a few days it would be over and you'd be back in school.

Fifty years ago, you would have worried about dying. The antibiotics used routinely by physicians today did not exist, and doctors had to watch helplessly as people died from complications such as pneumonia.

Two hundred years before that, you would have worried about the doctor. In those days, practices such as bloodletting could have killed you rather than cured you. Relatively little was known about disease, and—except for a few enlightened researchers—medicine was far from the sophisticated science it is today.

Through the work of thousands of medical researchers, we now know an enormous amount about how and why disease affects the human body. One of the first great breakthroughs occurred in the nineteenth century with the discovery that many diseases are caused by infectious agents that actually invade the body. The next important advance did not occur until the early part of this century, when scientists first discovered drugs that could destroy disease-causing agents. Now there are thousands of such drugs, plus thousands more to relieve the symptoms of disease.

Another breakthrough is far more recent and extends the fight against disease to another front—prevention. Scientists now know that infectious agents are not the culprits in many diseases. Most of the chronic diseases have a variety of causes. At least one factor, heredity, cannot as yet be controlled, but many others can. Medical researchers have discovered that the difference between a healthy body and a diseased one frequently depends on the way people live. What you eat, how much you exercise, whether or not you smoke cigarettes—these are just three of the factors that scientists have shown can cause disease.

This means, of course, that the fight against disease is not just in the hands of science. Each individual has to play an active role in his or her own health care. If you control the factors you can control, you can reduce your chances of developing a disease. In other words, you are the most important factor in maintaining your health.

SECTION **1** **Study of Disease**

In ancient times, no one knew how or why disease affected the body. Medicine was usually connected with religion, and often with magic. This does not mean that it was totally ineffective. But it did have a different basis and a different outlook from our modern medicine.

For instance, the very specific dietary and hygiene laws of the ancient Hebrews constituted an early attempt at public health measures. The first set of sanitation and hygiene laws on record comes from the Code of Hammurabi, introduced in Babylonia as early as 1700 B.C. And one of the first great physicians of Western civilization was Hippocrates, who lived in Greece from about 460 B.C. to about 360 B.C. Hippocrates based his treatment of patients on the experiences he had gained from treating similar cases, thus setting the stage for what in modern times is known as the scientific method of investigation. Incidentally, Hippocrates wrote a code for doctors to follow which is still subscribed to by physicians today—the Hippocratic Oath. Interestingly, the initial command in that code is "First, do no harm."

Possibly the greatest contribution to health in ancient times was the development of great public sanitation and water works in Crete, in Greece, and later in Rome. Fresh water was brought to the cities by aqueducts, and underground sewerage pipes, hot baths, and flush toilets were all part of the public sanitation systems.

Unfortunately, this limited development of health knowledge was followed by centuries of little progress. From the fifth to the fifteenth centuries, the study of medicine was almost completely abandoned. For religious and cultural reasons, autopsies were forbidden. Sickness was looked upon as punishment for sin.

The long-term neglect of the study and cure of disease had catastrophic results. By the fourteenth century, filthy and overcrowded cities existed in many parts of Europe. Rats scurried through streets littered with garbage and sewage. The cities were breeding grounds for disease. Personal hygiene was also ignored. People rarely bathed or used soap. They used perfumes to cover up disagreeable body odors. Such unhealthy living conditions led to an event which has been described as "mankind's nearest approach to complete annihilation."

In the mid-1300s, Europe was struck by the bubonic plague, the so-called Black Death. In four years, millions of people—at least one-third of Europe's population—died of the disease. Plagues continued to destroy populations into the sixteenth and seventeenth centuries. The Great Plague of London, for instance, killed about 70,000 people in that city in 1665.

So that such plagues would not continue, it was necessary to find out what caused them and then to contain them. The process for doing this scientifically was not discovered until the nineteenth century.

Figure 15.1 In the mid-1300s, the Black Death wiped out at least a third of the population of Europe. This drawing by an anonymous medieval artist shows a crier calling upon the people of London to bring out their dead.

Epidemiology

The branch of medicine that studies the source and spread of disease among groups of people is called *epidemiology*. Researchers called epidemiologists trace the causes and effects of disease. With this information, it is often possible to prevent disease as well as to treat it.

It wasn't until 1854 that John Snow, an enterprising London physician, conducted the first modern epidemiological study. For a long time, Snow had suspected that impure drinking water was responsible for London's frequent outbreaks of cholera. When 500 people died of the disease in a 10-day period, Snow decided to test his theory.

He observed 300,000 people, almost one-tenth of the city's population. He also drew a map of the houses and neighborhood water pumps of the people in the test group. By charting the disease patterns, he saw that a high proportion of the victims lived near the Broad Street pump. Further detective work proved that this pump was supplied with water from the most polluted part of the Thames River. Snow insisted that the pump be taken out of service. After that, the number of new cholera cases quickly declined.

Because of the research initiated by Dr. Snow and other early epidemiologists, plague and cholera have now been almost completely stopped in modern industrialized countries. Some countries, however, still have outbreaks because of their poor sanitation methods. There is even an occasional incident in the United States. As recently as 1924, an outbreak

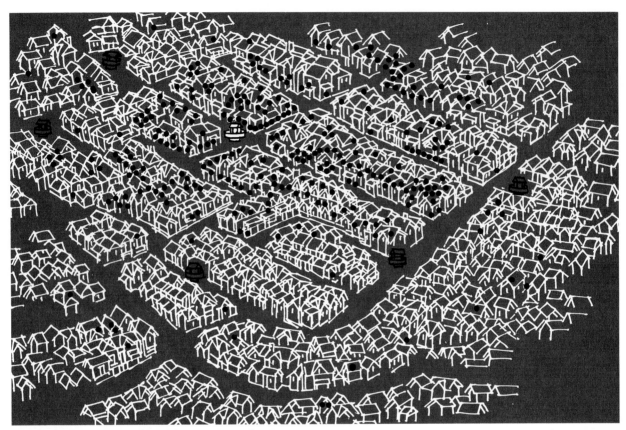

Figure 15.2 On a map like this one, Dr. John Snow indicated each house where a patient had died of cholera. Note the concentration of deaths around one of the water pumps.

of plague struck Los Angeles, killing 33 people. However, thanks to public health precautions, the disease was not allowed to spread.

Understanding Disease Patterns

Collecting data to find out what is causing a disease is a very complex process. It involves examining many variables, all of which affect the findings of a study. Just as Dr. Snow did, present-day epidemiologists look for patterns. They look for similarities and differences among the population they are studying. They try to sort out all the factors that influence who gets a certain disease and who doesn't. They look for a common denominator among all the victims, and they look for the absence of that factor among those who stayed well. In short, they look for a *disease pattern*.

Present-day health workers use a variety of statistics in their research. They look at the number of people who have died in a given population, the number of people who have a given disease, the number of years one may expect to live, the number of deaths among babies under the age of one, and the number of pregnancy-related deaths. From this information, the researchers hope to establish the who, the how, and the why of the disease.

Disease patterns are affected by many variables. Researchers must take these complex factors into account. They are divided into four basic groups:

1. *Host factors* include age, sex, genetic make-up, social and financial status, and life style. The host is the person who gets the disease.
2. *Environmental factors* include pollution, radiation, plant and animal life, climate, and work area.
3. *Time factors* (year, season, month, etc.) also influence disease patterns. For instance, sniffles, chills, and fever are much more common during the cool months than during the warm ones.
4. *Agent factors* include infectious bacteria or viruses, drugs, stress, and carcinogenic materials. Agents are those elements that cause the disease within the host.

Other variables also affect the outcome of a study. One factor in particular—age—can distort disease patterns. Statistics show that certain types of cancer are more common today than in 1920. However, the life expectancy in 1920 was only 54. Today it is above 70. Some of the increase in cancer is very likely due to the fact that people are living longer. It is the difficult task of the epidemiologist to determine how much of the increase is age-related.

Sometimes, it is not one factor but a combination of two or more factors that provides ideal conditions for a disease. Epidemiologists must discover the relationships among these interacting factors. This interplay of causes is discussed in the next section.

Disease Study Today

Epidemiologists of the past were mainly concerned with halting the spread of infectious diseases. Thanks to their efforts, those diseases are no longer a major health hazard in developed countries. However, they could become a major problem again through negligence or through a catastrophe. The major illnesses today are the chronic diseases, including cancer, heart disease, diabetes, and respiratory problems such as bronchitis and emphysema. It is to these that epidemiologists have turned their attention. Their work has already produced results.

Almost everything we know about the causes of cancer is a result of epidemiological studies. In addition to establishing a definite link between smoking and lung cancer, epidemiologists have discovered that fair-skinned people exposed to a great deal of sunlight have a higher rate of skin cancer than those not so exposed. They also know that children exposed to high-dose radiation have higher than normal rates of thyroid cancer as young adults.

Today, the principles of epidemiology are being applied to a broad range of health problems in addition to the chronic diseases. Studies are being made of degenerative diseases, mental disorders, and even social problems related to health, such as poverty, crime, drug abuse, and racism.

CHECK YOUR UNDERSTANDING

1. What is epidemiology? In what two ways can the results of an epidemiological study be useful?
2. List four types of factors that affect disease patterns.
3. Describe how age can distort a disease pattern.
4. How does the study of disease today differ from disease study in the past?

SECTION 2 Factors That Lead to Disease

Why do two-thirds of the students in a class become sick during a flu epidemic while the other one-third stay well? What makes some people more likely to have a heart attack than others? The process is not as random as it may seem. On the other hand, it is not always easy to sort out the reasons most responsible from among all the possibilities.

For instance, to get an *infectious disease,* a person must come into direct *contact* with the germ that causes the disease. She or he must also be *susceptible* to the disease. People who are susceptible to a disease have no resistance to it. They may not have received the vaccine against the disease, or they may have suffered another illness which left their body weakened. Or, and this is most important, they may have neglected to take proper care of themselves. Poor diet, lack of sleep, or prolonged stress can weaken the body's natural defenses against disease. One can become susceptible through negligence.

Chronic diseases are not caused by specific germs that invade the body, but by a wide variety of factors. These causes range from the kinds of food a person eats through the way he or she reacts to the stresses of daily life. The normal function or structure of the body becomes disturbed, and a chronic disease develops.

Generally, the main factors that determine a person's susceptibility to chronic disease are heredity, environment, infection, diet, drugs, stress, and degenerative processes. Sometimes it is the combination of two or more of these factors that causes a disease, as you will see below. Some of the factors are covered more fully elsewhere in this book, in which case you will be referred to the relevant chapters.

Heredity

Some diseases are passed on from parents to their children. Sickle cell anemia and hemophilia, to name just two, are diseases inherited by children through genes they receive from their parents (see Chapter 8). In some cases, gene-related diseases are noticed at birth. In other cases, though, the disease may not develop until the individual has grown up and had children of her or his own. Sometimes, the disease may skip a generation. Parents who do not suffer from a particular illness may still carry genes for that disease. For instance, hemophilia, a disease that prevents the blood from clotting, affects sons more often than daughters. Yet the daughters inherit the defec-

tive gene and pass the disease along to their own sons.

The role of heredity is not always so clear-cut. Heart conditions, for example, are not necessarily passed on from parent to child. Yet a child whose family has a history of heart trouble is more likely to have heart problems than a person who has no relatives with that condition. Certain types of cancer also seem to run in families although there is as yet no definite proof that these kinds of cancer are transmitted by genes.

Some scientists do not believe that the high rate of certain diseases within families is genetic. They believe, rather, that because the members of families live in the same environment, have the same eating habits, and follow the same life style, they run the same risks of developing a particular disease. In a certain family, for example, several members may have high blood pressure. That could be hereditary, but it could also be because of the family's habits. They may eat foods high in cholesterol and saturated fats; many of them may smoke cigarettes; they may argue a lot; and they may get little exercise. All of those factors are contributors to high blood pressure. Heredity may play no part in that family's disease. The culprit could be their environment.

Environment

As the example above shows, the environment in which people live can influence their chances of getting certain diseases and avoiding others. The influence of people's environment on their health is discussed in detail in Chapter 20. However, it is important to review a few key environmental factors to see how they influence a person's chances of contracting a disease.

Pollution Contamination of the air, water, and soil has serious effects on the public health. Polluted air is linked to lung diseases such as bronchitis, emphysema, and asthma. Noise, too, can be a pollutant. High levels of noise contribute to hearing loss and several stress-related diseases.

The very first epidemiological study traced an outbreak of cholera to polluted drinking water. Today, polluted water still poses a health hazard. The toxic chemicals found in many of our bodies of water can cause diseases among children and adults and can lead to birth defects.

Some researchers are discovering that "the good earth" may no longer deserve its name. Polluted soil can affect the foods grown in it. Such foods can be toxic or, at the least, low in vitamins and other important nutrients.

Socioeconomic Factors The economic and social standing of a family can affect the health of its members. Very poor families may not be able to afford a proper diet. Lack of information about hygiene, exercise, and sleep may foster bad habits that weaken the body's natural defenses against disease. Finally, lack of medical care may allow minor illnesses to become major ones through neglect.

While poverty has its obvious problems, affluence is no guarantee of good health either. The well-to-do may also eat a diet that is poor in nutrition. They may choose a diet that is too rich in fatty meats, cheese, or cream or one that contains too much sugar. They may not exercise enough.

Life Style A person's life style is to some extent determined by his or her socioeconomic status. Nevertheless, each of us makes individual decisions about how we live. How do you live from day to day? Do you swim, jog, or bicycle regularly? What role do cigarettes, alcohol, and drugs play in your life? Do you skip breakfast and for the rest of the day eat at irregular hours, gulping a quick sandwich and washing it down with soda? Your life style is an environmental factor that has a very important bearing on your health. As we have noted, many diseases and disabilities result from smoking, drug use, excessive drinking, poor nutrition, and lack of exercise.

In theory, you have a choice in determining your habits and activities. But studies reveal that most of us are conformists at heart. We tend to choose the options that are readily available. Social groups and even whole societies establish norms that influence the life style of the individual. Unhealthy habits, such as cigarette smoking, can become stylish fads within certain groups. But there are healthy fads too. The new concern with physical fitness and all-around good health has influenced many people to reexamine their ways of living.

Figure 15.3 The economic and social problems of the very poor often lead to living conditions that breed disease.

Infection

Infectious diseases (discussed in Chapter 16) are caused by an agent that reproduces within the host (person or animal with the disease). The agent could be a living cell, such as a bacterium, or a particle, such as a virus. Most infectious diseases are caused by bacteria or viruses, but other organisms can also cause infection. Fungi, for example, cause athlete's foot, and single-celled animals, known as protozoa, cause malaria.

In the United States, the fight against most infectious diseases has largely been won. But in certain segments of the population, the rates for some diseases are still very high. Tuberculosis is rarely a killer among white Americans, but for nonwhites the death rate is four times higher. Gonorrhea, a sexually transmitted disease that was almost eliminated at the close of World War II, has reached epidemic levels among American teenagers and young adults. Acquired immune deficiency syndrome (AIDS), a fatal infectious disease, presents a new challenge for epidemiologists and other health care workers.

Sometimes a new strain of bacterium comes to light. In the summer of 1976, an unknown disease killed 29 people attending an American Legion convention in Philadelphia. *Legionnaires' disease*, as it was called, has now been identified as the same illness that occurred in Washington, D.C., in 1965 and in Spain in 1973. Another outbreak occurred in 1978 when several workers in New York City's garment district came down with the disease. Researchers do not yet have all the facts about the bacterium. But they continue to study all these outbreaks to search for clues that will solve the mystery. They know that air-conditioning systems are one means of spreading the disease. They have also discovered that many more men than women have been affected and that heavy smoking increases a person's chances of getting the disease.

The Spread of Infection   Travel and migration, along with the importing and exporting of animals and food products, have been responsible for much of the worldwide spread of infectious diseases. For the most part, the spread of disease has been unintentional. There have been occasions, though, when people have deliberately tried to kill their enemies with disease. One particularly bizarre method of germ warfare was used during the Middle Ages. Warring groups shot the bodies of plague victims from cannons into enemy villages, thus wiping out entire communities with the disease organism.

The spread of disease has sometimes had tragic results. Early European immigrants to America brought some infectious diseases, to which the native American Indians had never been exposed. These "white man's diseases," which included measles and smallpox, wiped out entire tribes—far more than ever died from the white man's weapons.

Conquering Infection   Vaccination has been a major factor in preventing the spread of infectious diseases. People who receive vaccines become immune. That is, they are protected against the disease (see Chapter 16). In the late eighteenth century, the British physician Edward Jenner developed the first vaccine, which was against smallpox. The campaign to rid the world of this disease was often an uphill battle. People resisted the vaccine because of fear, superstition, or distrust. But by 1975 the World Health Organization (WHO) reported only 500 cases of the disease. The last new case was diagnosed in 1978, and in 1980 WHO reported that the disease had gone out of existence. Smallpox is the first disease in history to be completely wiped out.

Controlling other infectious diseases depends on maintaining immunization programs. For 25 years we have had the means to guarantee each person a polio-free life. But new cases of polio are reported each year. Rubella, or German measles, can also be prevented with vaccine. Since this disease in pregnant women causes birth defects, control is especially important. The United States government in 1978 instituted a massive immunization program for all schoolchildren. Even so, year after year, state and local medical authorities find it difficult to get all schoolchildren inoculated. But the success with smallpox is a great encouragement to keep up the pressure for the immunization program.

Diet

Millions of Americans do not eat properly. Some eat too much, while others don't eat enough or eat the wrong foods. Overeating—taking in more calories than the body uses—leads to overweight, or obesity. Doctors have linked overweight to infertility, heart disease, diabetes, and certain types of cancer. The poor in America are often undernourished. Some receive too few calories to function well. Others lack certain essential food substances, such as vitamins or proteins. Poor diet contributes to many diseases (see Chapter 6).

Figure 15.4 Edward Jenner developed the first vaccine in the eighteenth century. Vaccination has since played a major role in preventing the spread of infectious diseases.

Drugs

Medicines and other drugs that are used to treat disease have helped greatly to prevent, cure, or control many illnesses. Today, prescription and over-the-counter drugs are used to treat every ailment from heart disease to colds. But these substances can also be harmful if they are not used properly. People abuse medications in a number of ways. They take more than the recommended dose. They use old medicines or medicines that have been prescribed for someone else. And some take more than one drug at a time without asking their doctor's advice.

Some doctors also contribute to the problem by overprescribing drugs. Such has been the case with antibiotics. At one time, antibiotics were looked upon as "miracle drugs," and doctors prescribed them freely. But overuse of antibiotics has caused far-reaching problems. Some disease strains have built up a resistance to the drugs. Gonorrhea, once very responsive to antibiotics, has become more and more difficult to treat.

Drugs are also used for nonmedical reasons, and abuse leads to a wide variety of health problems. In addition, the use of some drugs in combination with alcohol is a lethal practice. This and other drug abuse problems are discussed at length in Chapter 12.

Stress

It is difficult to evaluate the role stress plays in the development of certain diseases. High blood pressure, heart disease, ulcers, and asthma are often named as stress-related ailments. Stress can lead to drug abuse, alcoholism, heavy smoking, and overeating—activities that are linked to serious chronic diseases. The role that stress plays in health is described at length in Chapter 4.

Degenerative Processes

Any disease in which a part of the body grows weaker over a period of time can be called *degenerative*. Arthritis, emphysema, and arteriosclerosis are examples of degenerative diseases. Such ailments are often associated with old age, but the degenerative processes may have been at work for many years. Degenerative hearing loss can begin as early as

How to...
Build Resistance to Disease

No one can avoid becoming ill occasionally. But there are ways to reduce the odds and to build resistance to disease in general. As you read through the following tips, take a look at your own life style. Perhaps you should make some changes.

1. Eat a well-balanced diet carefully selected from the four food groups (see Chapter 6). Good nutrition is of prime importance to good health and disease resistance.
2. Exercise regularly. If you are unused to strenuous exercise, start slowly and build up to a regular routine.
3. Get ample sleep and relaxation. Both are necessary for your well-being and for your ability to ward off infection.
4. If you are a cigarette smoker, think seriously about giving it up *now*. If you cannot give it up, at least cut down.

Cigarette smoking is the largest preventable cause of illness and death.

5. If you are allowed to drink alcohol, keep your consumption down to a moderate level, or don't drink at all.
6. Avoid habit-forming drugs of all sorts. Never take any kind of prescription drug unless you are under the care of a physician.
7. Give careful attention to personal hygiene. Keep yourself, your clothing, and your home clean. Always wash your hands before handling food.
8. Have regular medical and dental checkups. Seek immediate treatment for any illness or suspected disorder.
9. Take advantage of all immunization programs and screening tests.
10. Try to persuade your friends and family to follow these simple principles.

age 12. Arteriosclerosis, sometimes referred to as hardening of the arteries, may progress for decades before it is diagnosed.

Early diagnosis, changes in diet, and changes in life style can help prevent and delay some degenerative processes, or at least reduce their seriousness. High blood pressure can be helped by a diet low in salt. Atherosclerosis, which affects the arteries, may be prevented or lessened by a diet low in calories and fats. And osteoporosis, a disease that causes bones to become brittle, may be prevented or reduced by a diet that includes calcium and other minerals and vitamins and by exercise. As Chapter 5 points out, exercise can be a factor in the management of many degenerative processes that contribute to disease.

CHECK YOUR UNDERSTANDING

1. List the ways a person can become susceptible to an infectious disease.
2. Why is it difficult to determine the role of heredity in diseases such as high blood pressure?
3. Describe how socioeconomic standing and life style can affect a person's chances of contracting a disease.
4. List four diseases that doctors have linked to obesity.
5. What is a degenerative disease? What are some of the ways a person can delay or prevent such diseases?

SECTION **3** **Changing Patterns of Disease**

Disease patterns vary greatly throughout the world. Illnesses that are rare in one country may be quite common in another. Likewise, disease patterns change over time. A century ago, influenza, pneumonia, tuberculosis, and diphtheria were the leading causes of death in the United States. Today those diseases no longer take many lives, although many people still get influenza and pneumonia. These two diseases are perhaps the only serious acute infections that remain in the United States, except for certain sexually transmitted diseases.

Although tuberculosis has declined in the United States, there are some 15 to 20 million people in other countries who suffer from its effects. Similarly, leprosy, which has practically disappeared in the United States, is still common in parts of Asia and Africa. The development of vaccines and widespread immunization programs have brought other diseases under control. Polio, measles, smallpox, and rubella—once responsible for much death and disability—are no longer the serious threats they once were in the United States or other developed countries. To prevent these diseases from reappearing, the United States government has actively encouraged inoculation programs for schoolchildren. Over 85 percent of American schoolchildren between the ages of 5 and 14 are now inoculated.

Unfortunately, countries do not simply rid themselves of disease as their standards of living improve. Rather, they seem to replace one type of disease with another. In the United States, the chronic diseases—cancer, heart disease, and stroke—have become the new killers. These diseases are "new" in the sense that, just a few decades ago, many people didn't live long enough to develop them. Nor did most of them live in ways that made them susceptible to such illnesses.

The treatments given to combat chronic ail-

Figure 15.5 Death rates for selected countries (per 100,000 population).

	Austria Life Expectancy: Male 69 Female 77	Brazil Life Expectancy: Male 57 Female 61	Egypt Life Expectancy: Male 54 Female 56	Iceland Life Expectancy: Male 74 Female 79	Thailand Life Expectancy: Male 59 Female 63	United States Life Expectancy: Male 71 Female 78
Tuberculosis	3.8	6.4	4.5	2.2	11.8	0.7
Pneumonia	30.5	36.1	47.3	54.2	8.9	19.8
Heart Diseases	652.8	181.1	194.7	351.4	47.4	428.8
Malignant Cancers	255.2	57.1	19.2	158.1	24.7	179.6
Stroke	197.4	59.0	9.8	75.8	10.9	75.5
Cirrhosis of the Liver	29.3	9.2	9.4	1.7	6.9	13.2

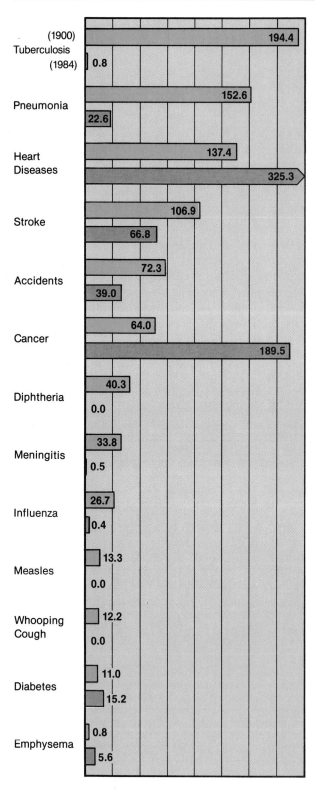

Figure 15.6 Leading causes of death in the United States, 1900 and 1984. (Rates per 100,000 people.)

ments also pose new problems. Frequently, these treatments tend to destroy an individual's natural defenses against infection. For instance, radiation treatments given for cancer weaken the patient's resistance to infection. Similarly, the drugs that kidney transplant patients must take to prevent rejection of the new kidney leave them open to infections. Some of these infections have never been seen by doctors before.

Life Expectancy

As we have seen, disease patterns in the United States have changed because people are living longer. Yet despite its high standard of living, the United States does not have the highest life expectancy rate in the world. We are among the highest, but Norway, the Netherlands, and some other countries are higher. This is mainly because there are people in the United States whose standard of living can be more closely equated with that of people in developing nations than with that of people in highly developed ones.

Some nonwhite Americans at low social and economic levels suffer many of the same diseases that are found in underdeveloped nations. On the average, nonwhite Americans can expect to live three or four years less than white Americans. The infant mortality rate among poor Americans is also comparatively high. This helps explain the shorter life expectancy rate in the United States compared with that in some other countries.

It is also interesting to note that average life expectancy figures hide an important fact: that women generally live longer than men. Today, a 15-year-old American male can expect to live to be about 72 years old. A 15-year-old female can expect to live to be about 79 years old. The differences have not always been so great. In the first part of this century, women lived only one or two years longer than men. The gap has been increasing slowly since then.

To some extent, this difference may be due to the different life styles of men and women. Men are more likely than women to drink and smoke heavily. They are often exposed to more stress factors, too, although this may be

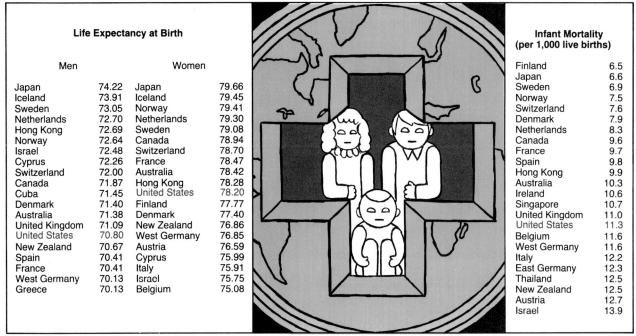

Life Expectancy at Birth				**Infant Mortality** (per 1,000 live births)	
Men		**Women**		Finland	6.5
				Japan	6.6
Japan	74.22	Japan	79.66	Sweden	6.9
Iceland	73.91	Iceland	79.45	Norway	7.5
Sweden	73.05	Norway	79.41	Switzerland	7.6
Netherlands	72.70	Netherlands	79.30	Denmark	7.9
Hong Kong	72.69	Sweden	79.08	Netherlands	8.3
Norway	72.64	Canada	78.94	Canada	9.6
Israel	72.48	Switzerland	78.70	France	9.7
Cyprus	72.26	France	78.47	Spain	9.8
Switzerland	72.00	Australia	78.42	Hong Kong	9.9
Canada	71.87	Hong Kong	78.28	Australia	10.3
Cuba	71.45	United States	78.20	Ireland	10.6
Denmark	71.40	Finland	77.77	Singapore	10.7
Australia	71.38	Denmark	77.40	United Kingdom	11.0
United Kingdom	71.09	New Zealand	76.86	United States	11.3
United States	70.80	West Germany	76.85	Belgium	11.6
New Zealand	70.67	Austria	76.59	West Germany	11.6
Spain	70.41	Cyprus	75.99	Italy	12.2
France	70.41	Italy	75.91	East Germany	12.3
West Germany	70.13	Israel	75.75	Thailand	12.5
Greece	70.13	Belgium	75.08	New Zealand	12.5
				Austria	12.7
				Israel	13.9

Figure 15.7 Highest life expectancy and lowest infant mortality rates worldwide. The position of the United States in terms of life expectancy has deteriorated in the past few years. At the same time, infant mortality rates in the United States have improved.

changing rapidly. But it is generally believed that the biological differences between the sexes in some way cause women to live longer than men.

World Population

Until recently, the populations of most Asian, African, and Latin American countries were growing at rates of more than 2 percent a year. At that rate populations double every 35 years. Such growth rates contribute to health problems, because disease is often linked to overcrowding and undernutrition.

Between 1970 and 1975, however, the "population explosion" in many of the underdeveloped countries began to slow down. Studies suggest that the lower rates are due to organized family planning. Some governments and private organizations have been encouraging people to use contraceptives and other methods of birth control to limit the size of their families. National family planning programs may play an important role in world health problems in the years to come. If countries limit the sizes of their populations, we can expect to see significant changes in worldwide health patterns.

CHECK YOUR UNDERSTANDING

1. What seems to happen to disease patterns of a country when the standard of living improves?
2. What problems can result from the treatments used for chronic ailments?
3. Explain why the United States has a lower life expectancy rate than some other highly developed nations.
4. Compare the life expectancy rates of American women and men. List some specific factors that contribute to this difference.

Control and Prevention of Disease

Since the earliest days of recorded history, people have been fighting the battle against disease. Over the years, this enemy has taken more lives than wars or natural disasters. Our attempts to eliminate disease have focused on two kinds of activities, *control* and *prevention*. Without the development of certain drugs, the death rate from many diseases would still be high. Without the introduction of new preventive measures, many infectious diseases would still be a problem. Prevention is also the keynote in the battle against chronic diseases.

Chemotherapy

You may have heard the word *chemotherapy* a great deal lately in the news and on radio and television. You may have heard it used in connection with the treatment of cancer. How-

Figure 15.8 Drugs used in chemotherapy may be given by injection or taken by mouth. Both methods get the medication into the bloodstream so that it can be distributed throughout the body.

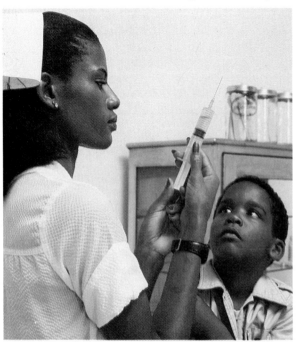

ever, chemotherapy is the use of any chemical substance to treat any disease. Even when you take an over-the-counter cold remedy, you are using chemotherapy.

Chemotherapy has been practiced for thousands of years throughout the world. The ancient Greeks, for example, extracted a pain reliever from plants that is similar to the one used in aspirin. A number of the drugs still used today have their roots in the folk medicines of centuries past.

Chemotherapy remained a primitive study until the late nineteenth century, when researchers such as Louis Pasteur and Robert Koch identified disease-causing bacteria for the first time. Their work enabled people to see, at last, how a disease developed. It also paved the way for people to understand how drugs worked.

It was not until 1932, however, that a drug effective against bacterial infections was discovered. *Prontosil*, the first of the landmark sulfa drugs, was originally developed as a fabric dye. One scientist, though, soon realized that the dye cured laboratory mice sick with bacterial infections. As soon as sulfa drugs were introduced to medicine, life expectancy rates rose as deaths from pneumonia and other bacterial diseases dropped sharply.

Death rates from infectious diseases dropped even further in the 1940s when *penicillin* was introduced. Penicillin was the first of the *antibiotics*. This group of drugs soon earned the well-deserved nickname of "wonder drugs." Produced naturally by molds and other microorganisms, antibiotics kill or prevent the growth of bacteria, viruses, or fungi. With their introduction, a broad range of diseases, including the major killer tuberculosis, came under control.

The search for new and more effective drugs continues all the time. The experimental substance called *interferon* was discovered in 1957. It is a protein that is naturally produced by diseased cells. It "interferes" with, or prevents, the disease from spreading to healthy cells. The first tests were done on cells affected with viruses. Experiments have also been conducted to test interferon's effectiveness on cancer cells. If interferon is successful, it might one day be used against a variety of diseases. It might even be used to combat the common cold.

Disease Prevention

The last, but by no means the least important, method for fighting disease is disease prevention. This is where you come in. No matter what medical wonders the future holds for us, prevention is still the most effective weapon in our battle against disease.

Government involvement is necessary in some areas of prevention. The government is concerned with water supply, sanitary facilities, environmental controls, vaccine programs, and disease screening.

Government programs can't work, though, without the cooperation of the public. Much can be done at the community level to prevent disease. Increasingly, communities are organizing themselves to foster programs that work to help people avoid needless illness and death.

For instance, government-funded programs on the community level provide nutrition education for pregnant women. Public schools feature health education and immunization programs for youngsters. Public and private programs have been developed to help people stop smoking or to overcome obesity. Similar programs for physical fitness and exercise regimens have also been developed. Many businesses, alarmed by illness among their employees and executives, foster workshops on stress control, physical fitness, and exercise.

On the individual level, each one of us can play a part in preventing disease. Most of us know that diet, exercise, and hygiene are important factors in good health. But if the human body required an operator's license, as automobiles do, many of us would be out of luck. "I can't help it if I love sweets," the overeater says, reaching for another cupcake. "I don't have time to exercise," the rushed executive says, puffing compulsively on a cigarette.

Figure 15.9 Government- and community-sponsored disease-prevention programs include efforts to control rats and other disease-carrying vermin.

"I'll wait until I'm *really* sick before I'll go to the doctor," you think, reaching in the medicine cabinet instead. Our willingness to follow the preventive measures we already know is crucial to maintaining good health.

CHECK YOUR UNDERSTANDING

1. What are the two main activities in attempts to eliminate a disease?
2. What is chemotherapy?
3. List five ways in which the United States government is involved in disease prevention.
4. What are some of the community programs that are aimed at preventing disease? What can an individual do to help in the prevention of disease?

CHAPTER SUMMARY

- Epidemiology is the study of the source and spread of disease among groups of people. The first epidemiological study was conducted by John Snow in 1854. It traced an outbreak of cholera to polluted water.
- Epidemiologists study patterns of disease and patterns of good health in order to reach the ultimate goal of disease prevention. The factors that influence disease patterns are divided into four groups: host factors, environmental factors, time factors, and agent factors.
- The emphasis of epidemiological studies has shifted from infectious diseases to chronic diseases.
- To get an infectious disease, a person must come into contact with the germ that causes the disease, and she or he must be susceptible to the disease. With chronic diseases, it is a person's exposure to various risk factors that leads to the onset of disease.
- The main factors that affect a person's susceptibility to disease are heredity, environment, infection, diet, drugs, and stress.
- Although the standard of living in the United States is very high, life expectancy rates are higher in some other countries. The infant mortality rate in the United States is comparatively high.
- Chemotherapy is the use of a chemical substance to treat disease. Chemotherapy has reduced the incidence of infectious diseases and it is now being used to treat chronic diseases.
- Disease prevention depends not only on government involvement, but also on community action and on individual awareness and cooperation.

DO YOU REMEMBER?

Give brief definitions of these terms:

epidemiology	agent	infectious disease	susceptibility
host	disease pattern	chronic disease	degenerative disease

THINK AND DISCUSS

1. Why do you think the Hippocratic Oath begins with the command "First, do no harm"?
2. What do you think could be done to improve life expectancy rates in the United States?
3. Why do you think people suffer more colds and flu in cold weather than in warm weather?
4. Which do you think is more difficult for epidemiologists to study—infectious diseases or chronic diseases? Why?
5. What do you think is going to happen to the difference between the life expectancy rates of American men and women in the future? Why?
6. Why do you think people become negligent about having themselves or their children immunized against diseases such as polio and measles? What could be done to encourage people to be immunized?

FOLLOW-UP

1. Find out more about the medical treatments used by Hippocrates. Write a report describing these treatments.

2. Learn more about the differences between infectious agents such as bacteria, viruses, fungi, and protozoa. Make a poster that illustrates these differences and post it in your classroom.

3. Make a graph that shows how the number of deaths from various childhood diseases has changed during this century. Display the graph in your classroom.

4. Explore the problems medical experts face in trying to develop vaccines against influenza viruses. Write a report on these problems.

5. Read an account of the discovery of penicillin. Describe the event and its significance to your class.

6. Using recent magazines, follow the case of Legionnaires' disease. Write a report that describes the detective work done to establish the cause and pattern of the disease.

7. Read more about the Black Plague and write a report that explains how lack of sanitation contributed to its spread during the Middle Ages.

16

Infectious Diseases

After reading this chapter, you should be able to answer these questions:

1. How do infectious diseases spread?

2. How does your body protect itself against disease?

3. Why should you keep a record of all your immunizations?

4. How can you avoid getting a cold? What's the best treatment if you do get one?

5. What can people do to avoid getting an STD?

Your body is teeming with billions upon billions of living organisms. On your skin, in your mouth, and in your intestines are some 15 million million minuscule plants and animals. Their presence was first discovered some 300 years ago by Anton van Leeuwenhoek, a Dutch scientist. He developed a powerful microscope and was the first person ever to see bacteria. In 1683 Leeuwenhoek wrote that there "are more animals living in the scum on the teeth in a man's mouth, than there are men in a whole kingdom."

Most of the organisms in your body are harmless. In fact, some contribute to your well-being by manufacturing essential vitamins and acids. There are times, though, when the balance between these normally harmless organisms and the part of the body they inhabit becomes upset. When this happens, disease can result. Disease also occurs when organisms that do not normally inhabit the body manage to get inside it.

Organisms that are capable of causing disease are called *pathogens*. When a pathogen attacks the body, *infection* occurs. Whether or not the infection becomes a disease depends on the number of pathogens invading the body or on how greatly their numbers increase once they are inside.

Your body has a number of defense systems to fight pathogens. But if the pathogens get past these defenses, infection spreads and causes an infectious disease. Most infectious diseases can be passed from individual to individual, either directly or indirectly. These are called *communicable* diseases.

In this chapter you'll find out what organisms cause infectious diseases and how an infection spreads. You'll also learn about the various defense mechanisms that your body has for fighting infection. In addition, you'll find out what measures you can take to avoid getting an infectious disease. Some common infectious diseases are discussed in detail, and special attention is given to the sexually transmitted diseases.

SECTION **1**   **Agents of Infection**

There are six main types of pathogens that cause infectious diseases. They are bacteria, viruses, rickettsiae, fungi, protozoa, and worms. These disease agents are responsible for a variety of illnesses, ranging from the common cold to life-threatening diphtheria.

Bacteria

Bacteria, a type of single-celled plant life, make up the largest group of microorganisms. They are found in the air, in soil, in water, and in the bodies of other organisms, including human bodies. Some bacteria are globe-shaped, some resemble rods, and some are twisted in thin, threadlike spirals.

Most bacteria are harmless, and many are vital to human existence. Some help to fertilize the earth by causing the decay of dead plants and animals. Those found within the human body perform a variety of important functions. Some play a role in digestion; others produce vitamins and destroy harmful pathogens.

Bacteria also cause disease, however. Some diseases occur when bacteria that are normally found in the body get out of hand. For instance, bacteria found on the skin may have a role in acne. And bacteria that live in the mouth can cause gum disease.

Other diseases are caused when harmful bacteria enter the body from an outside source. Gonorrhea, syphilis, meningitis, tuberculosis, tetanus, typhoid, strep throat, and diphtheria are examples of such diseases. Fortunately, antibiotics have proved effective against most of these bacteria, so the diseases they cause can largely be controlled.

Viruses

Scientists are not sure whether a *virus* is a living organism or complex inorganic matter. Viruses are parasites. They survive and multiply by invading living cells. Once a virus enters a cell, it "tells" the cell to produce hundreds of new viruses. When the cell is filled with new viruses, it breaks apart. Each virus then goes off in search of another cell to enter, starting the cycle again.

Among the many diseases that are caused by viruses are chicken pox, measles, German measles, mumps, polio, hepatitis, herpes, influenza, the common cold, and mononucleosis.

Figure 16.1 Diagram of a virus's invasion of a cell. The virus takes over the cell's machinery to make hundreds of new virus particles. When the cell breaks apart, these new viruses invade still more cells.

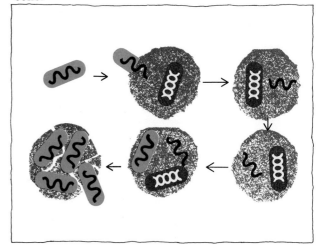

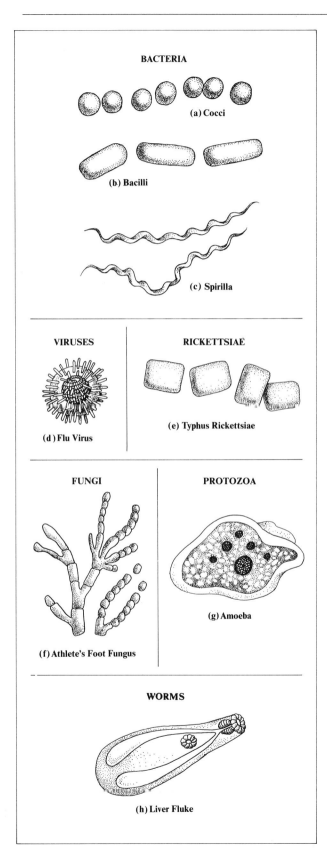

Many of the diseases that are caused by viruses can be prevented through immunization.

Rickettsiae

Rickettsiae are larger than viruses but smaller than bacteria. Like viruses, they cannot grow outside a living cell. Rickettsiae are most often found in the intestinal linings of lice, rat fleas, mites, and ticks. The insects spread these infectious agents to humans and also to some animals.

Rocky Mountain spotted fever is a disease that is transmitted by ticks infected with rickettsiae. Another disease caused by rickettsiae is typhus fever, which is transmitted by ticks, fleas, and lice. (Typhus fever should not be confused with typhoid, a disease that is caused by bacteria.)

Fungi

Fungi are plants that feed on organic materials. Plant and animal tissues provide the food they need. Certain kinds of fungi live off human tissues. Ringworm and athlete's foot are infections caused by fungi.

Protozoa

Protozoa are single-celled animals. Some kinds of protozoa are *parasites*. That is, they live in or on the body of another animal, known as the *host*. Disease can be transmitted when the parasite moves from one host to another.

One type of protozoan, found in the tsetse fly, can cause African sleeping sickness. The harmful protozoa are transmitted when humans are bitten by infected flies. Malaria is transmitted in much the same way, by the bite of a certain type of mosquito. Amoebic dysentery, another disease caused by protozoa, occurs when an amoeba, one type of protozoan, enters the human body in food or drink.

Figure 16.2 The six main types of pathogens, with examples of each.

Worms

Worms are another type of parasite. They are complex, many-celled animals, and usually they are large enough to be seen with the naked eye. Roundworms, pinworms, and tapeworms are parasites that can live in the human body. Dogs are major transmitters of roundworms, which deposit their eggs in dogs' feces. Humans can pick up the eggs if they touch something, such as a shoe, that has been contaminated by the feces.

CHECK YOUR UNDERSTANDING

1. What are bacteria? In what ways are they helpful?
2. Describe how viruses multiply. List some of the diseases caused by viruses.
3. What are the food sources for fungi?
4. Describe how protozoa-caused diseases such as malaria are spread.
5. How do dogs transmit roundworms?

SECTION **2**   **How Infection Spreads**

Most infectious diseases are communicable. That is, they can be passed from one person to another or from an animal or insect to an individual. Pathogens can enter the body through any of its natural openings, such as the mouth, nose, vagina, urethra, or anus, or through cuts in the skin. They can also be released through these same openings to be transmitted to other individuals.

Direct and Indirect Contact

Direct physical contact is the most common way for infectious diseases to pass from one person to another. Colds and flu are often transmitted in this way. The sexually transmitted diseases (STDs), including gonorrhea, NGU, and genital herpes, are most often spread by direct physical contact with an infected person.

Disease can also be spread by droplets in the air. These may be given off by sneezing, coughing, talking, or just breathing. When someone sneezes, as many as 20,000 droplets are released into the air. The droplets may contain thousands of virus particles, many of which may be capable of causing disease. The particles can be inhaled by people as far as 5 meters (16 feet) away.

Disease-causing organisms can also be passed by indirect means. Articles of clothing, eating utensils, and other objects that have been touched by an infected person can spread disease. Influenza, diphtheria, and meningitis are diseases that may be spread by such means.

Some types of pathogens can be transmitted through food and water. Typhoid, dysentery, and cholera are spread in this way.

Animal and Insect Carriers

Animals and insects can spread disease to humans. One example of a disease spread by animals is rabies. The bite of an infected dog, cat, bat, squirrel, or other animal passes the disease to humans. The immunization of dogs and cats helps keep this disease under control.

Insects carry disease in several ways. Flies and cockroaches, for instance, carry pathogens on their feet or other parts of their bodies. The pathogens are passed on to humans when an insect lands on a person's body, or on food, or on articles that the person handles. Insects can also infect humans by biting or otherwise piercing the skin. Typhus fever, Rocky Mountain spotted fever, malaria, and bubonic plague are all transmitted from insects to humans in this way.

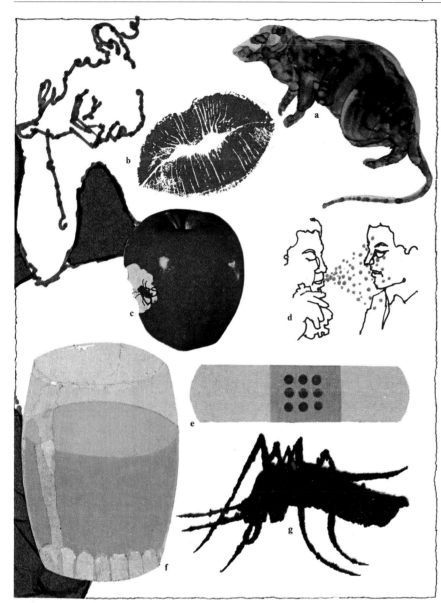

Figure 16.3 How infectious diseases are spread. (a) The bite of an infected animal can pass a disease to other animals and to humans. (b) Direct physical contact is the most common way for one individual to infect another. (c) Many insects carry pathogens on their feet or other body parts. (d) Sneezing, coughing, breathing, and talking can spray disease-carrying droplets into the air. (e) A cut or an open wound allows potentially harmful microorganisms to enter the body. (f) Pathogens can be passed by indirect means such as food, clothing, and other articles that have been handled by an infected person. (g) Some species of insects can infect humans by biting or otherwise piercing the skin.

The Course of an Infectious Disease

What happens when harmful pathogens enter the body? Most of them are destroyed by the body's natural defense system (see Section 3 of this chapter). Sometimes, though, disease does occur. When this happens, infectious diseases generally go through five stages.

1. The *incubation period* begins when the pathogens enter the body. During this phase the pathogens multiply and spread. The length of time this period lasts varies from disease to disease and from person to person for the same disease.

2. Incubation is followed by the *prodrome period*. This is a short interval during which the individual begins to experience discomfort. The general symptoms felt during the prodrome stage may include headache, fever, runny nose, loss of energy, and irritability. Diagnosis is often difficult at this time because the early symptoms are similar for most diseases. The disease is highly communicable at this stage.

3. *Clinical disease* is the full attack of the illness. General symptoms are replaced with ones that

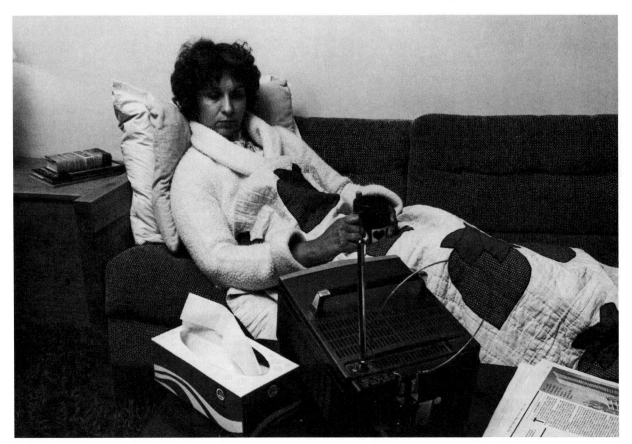

Figure 16.4 Even during the decline stage of an infectious disease, the patient must guard against overexertion and unnecessary contact with other people.

are specific to the disease. At this point a physician can usually diagnose the illness and treat it accordingly.

4. After the disease passes its peak, the *decline stage* sets in. The symptoms begin to go away, and the patient feels that he or she is on the road to recovery. At this point the patient should guard against overexertion. The body is in a weakened condition, and too much activity could cause a relapse. The disease is still communicable during the clinical stage and the decline stage.

5. *Convalescence* is the recovery stage of an illness. Even though the patient feels fine, the disease may still be communicable. Sometimes an individual can be completely recovered and continue to give off disease-causing pathogens. This person is a *carrier* and can unknowingly spread the disease to others.

CHECK YOUR UNDERSTANDING

1. What is a communicable disease?
2. List the ways in which communicable diseases are spread.
3. Describe two ways insects can transmit diseases.
4. List the five stages of an infectious disease.

SECTION **3** **Defense Against Infection**

The human body is exposed to a vast number and variety of organisms. To combat those that cause disease, the body has a system of natural defenses. Just how effective these defenses are depends upon a number of factors, not least of which is the state of health of the whole body. A person who keeps in good physical condition can usually resist a large number of infectious diseases.

The Role of the Skin

The first line of defense against disease is the skin. Just like the walls that protect a fortress, the skin surrounds and protects the organs of the body. To gain entrance, a pathogen must pass through the body's outer skin or through the "inner skin" that lines the body's natural openings.

It is not easy for an invading organism to penetrate the skin. Perspiration and skin oils contain chemicals that can kill bacteria. Bacteria-killing chemicals are also present in saliva, tears, mucus, and in secretions in the genital region. There are additional disease-stopping organisms inside body openings—in the respiratory, digestive, urinary, and genital tracts. For instance, fine, short hairs called *cilia* move back and forth in the respiratory passages. These hairs help to keep pathogens from settling in the lungs.

A cut in the skin is a weak spot in the defense system. This is one of the ways pathogens can get into the body. When this happens, a second line of defense goes to work to prevent the infection from spreading.

Blood and Tissues

Blood and tissues wage a counterattack against harmful organisms that have penetrated the skin. Chemicals in the blood go to work to kill bacteria and viruses. Blood also contains special white blood cells that surround and destroy

bacteria and other organisms by digesting them. These cells can move to the part of the body where they are needed most, clustering around the area of the infection. Tissues, too, contain cells that behave in a similar way. When a tissue is attacked, the cells work to keep the pathogens from taking over. Thus, many bacteria never gain a foothold in the body.

Inflammation

Suppose, however, that pathogens do become established and begin to multiply. When that happens, the body resorts to a third line of defense—*inflammation*. Inflammation occurs when the body detects the presence of an attacker. The attacker may be a disease-causing pathogen or a "foreign body," such as a splinter.

When inflammation occurs, the blood supply to tissues surrounding the infection is increased. Antitoxic and bacteria-fighting proteins are brought to the scene of the battle. The increased blood supply also brings reinforcements of white blood cells. While these disease fighters surround the infected area, the blood flow through the infected tissue is decreased. The body's strategy is to contain the invader and wage a local battle.

The outward signs of inflammation are usually redness, swelling, pain, and warmth in the area of the infection. These signs show that the invaders are being attacked. In the severest cases, this third line of defense fails, and the invaders begin to spread through the body. The infection then becomes widespread and highly dangerous.

In other cases, though, the local battle goes on and on. More and more healthy tissue around the infection is destroyed, creating a cavity, or *abscess*. The cavity fills with *pus*, a fluid that contains cells that have died fighting the infection. The fight goes on until the invading pathogens are killed or made inactive.

Fever

In severe cases, infection spreads from its original site to other parts of the body. At this point, the individual often runs a *fever*. This is caused in part by poisons that are released by the invading pathogens. The poisons interfere with the mechanism that controls the temperature of the body. A very high temperature is dangerous and can result in death.

A fever can also help the body fight off the disease. When the body's temperature rises, the production of white blood cells is speeded up. Also, most pathogens are very sensitive to heat. Since the body can tolerate temperatures a few degrees above normal and most pathogens cannot, this can be an effective way of killing off the invaders.

Interferon

In addition to these lines of defense, the body has another weapon in its battle against disease. The protein interferon, which you read about in Chapter 15, is produced by a cell that has been taken over by a virus. The interferon does not fight the virus particles directly; nor can it help cells that are already infected. Instead, it interacts with the membranes of healthy cells. Virus particles are unable to penetrate these healthy cells and the infection is kept from spreading.

Scientists are examining the possible use of interferon to prevent cancer from spreading in the body. They are also looking for ways to produce interferon synthetically. However, much research remains to be done.

Figure 16.5 An intrepid army of natural defenses awaits any disease-carrying organism that enters the body. These defenses include white blood cells, antibodies, and interferon.

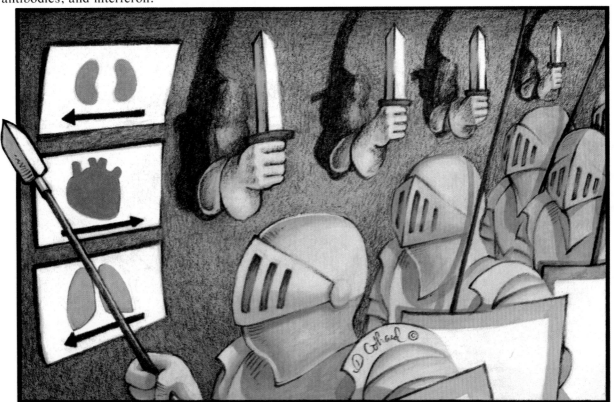

Immunity

Immunity is another form of defense against infection. It is the body's ability to resist infection or infectious disease. Immunity, or protection from a disease, depends on a certain type of white blood cell called a *lymphocyte*. When disease-causing organisms enter the body, they stimulate the lymphocytes to become plasma cells. These cells in turn produce *antibodies*. Antibodies are proteins that can make pathogens inactive. In the presence of antibodies, bacteria are much more easily destroyed by bacteria-killing agents that are in the blood and tissues. In addition, antibodies can combine with viruses and prevent them from invading healthy cells.

There are many different kinds of antibodies. But each type is effective against only one type of pathogen. For instance, if you had chicken pox when you were younger, your body went to work producing antibodies to deactivate the chicken pox virus. Your body continues to produce this type of antibody, so you will not get chicken pox again.

In the early 1980s, a mysterious new disease called *acquired immune deficiency syndrome,* or *AIDS*, was reported. Scientists have discovered that AIDS is caused by a previously unknown virus. When the virus enters the body, it attacks the cells that tell other cells to produce antibodies. As a result, the immune system becomes paralyzed, and the body loses its defense against infectious diseases. As yet, there is no treatment for this fatal disease.

The AIDS virus is transmitted by transfusions of infected blood, by infected hypodermic needles, and by sexual contact with an infected person.

Some vaccines introduce living pathogens into the body. These pathogens are weakened in the laboratory. They are not strong enough to cause the person to get the disease. But they are able to cause the production of antibodies. The Sabin oral vaccine for polio is an example of a vaccine that contains living pathogens.

Other vaccines that stimulate antibody production contain dead pathogens. These include the whooping cough and Salk polio vaccines. Still other vaccines are made from the poisons that cause certain diseases such as diphtheria and tetanus. The poisons, like the pathogens, have been weakened to the point where they cause the production of antibodies but don't cause illness.

Contracting a disease or being vaccinated for it produces *active immunity*. Active immunity is usually long-lasting. In some cases, the person is immune for life. *Passive immunity,* on the other hand, is short-term protection. It is used when a person is exposed to a disease for which there is no suitable vaccine. Temporary immunity can be created by injecting the individual with a special serum. The serum contains antibodies formed by another person or by an animal.

Today vaccines are available to protect people from a variety of life-threatening diseases. But they are only effective if they are used. Many people have become so used to living in a society free of diseases such as diphtheria, polio, and cholera that they don't bother to get protection against them. The immunization of children is especially important. Some diseases, such as tetanus, require boosters, or additional doses, at regular intervals throughout adulthood as well. You should keep a record of your immunizations and make sure you get booster shots when necessary.

Immunity Through Vaccination

Until quite recently, having a disease was the only way people could develop immunity to it. Today, immunity can be achieved artificially by the use of *vaccines*. A vaccine may be injected into the body or taken orally. It causes the body to produce antibodies against a specific disease.

Prevention and Treatment

The most effective weapon against infectious disease is prevention. Prevention centers on avoiding contact with harmful pathogens, or at least reducing the number to which you are exposed.

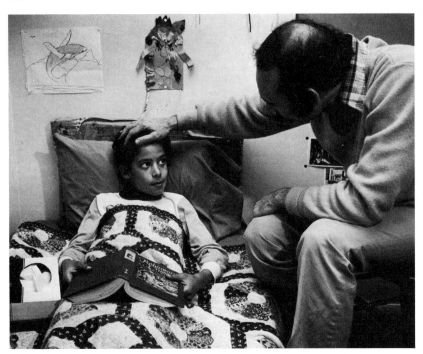

Figure 16.6 Because they have had no opportunity to develop active immunity, children are especially susceptible to infectious diseases. Most serious childhood diseases can now be prevented through vaccination.

You can prevent many diseases by taking a few simple precautions. Avoid any food or water that you suspect might be contaminated. Avoid contact with infected persons. When you have an infectious disease, keep away from other people. Always cover your mouth when you sneeze. Keep your body and your surroundings clean. And, as just mentioned, make sure you get the proper immunizations.

When infection does lead to disease, treatment is necessary. Some diseases, such as colds, may be relatively mild. The sufferer can identify the illness and is usually able to take the necessary steps without seeing a doctor. Other diseases are more severe. A doctor must analyze samples of blood, urine, or mucus in order to make the correct diagnosis. After the diagnosis is made, treatment can begin.

Although different diseases require different methods of treatment, there are some general procedures that you should know about. Rest of the entire body or of the affected part is important. Fluids are needed to nourish and cleanse the body. This is especially true if the infection is located in the urinary tract. It is also important to drain off pus, phlegm, or other infected matter. This can be done by coughing or, with a doctor's help, by opening

and cleaning an abscess. Elevating the inflamed area can also help draw these fluids away. Finally, heat may be applied to increase blood flow to the infected area.

For diseases caused by bacteria, such as gonorrhea and tuberculosis, doctors may prescribe an antibiotic. Penicillin and other antibiotics are effective against many bacterial infections. However, few drugs work against viruses. Over-the-counter cold and flu remedies, for example, may relieve symptoms, but they do little to control infection. They can have harmful side effects as well.

CHECK YOUR UNDERSTANDING

1. Explain the ways in which the skin fights off disease.
2. How does inflammation act as a disease fighter?
3. How does a fever fight disease?
4. Describe antibodies. How do they develop?
5. Describe the basic means for preventing disease. What are the general procedures for treating most diseases?

SECTION **4**   # Common Infectious Diseases

Although most infectious diseases have been brought under control, some continue to affect vast numbers of people. The common cold brings misery to practically everybody from time to time. Outbreaks of influenza occur regularly. In this section we shall discuss these two common infections, along with tuberculosis, pneumonia, hepatitis, and mononucleosis.

The Common Cold

The average person in this country gets between one and three colds a year. Sneezing, congestion, and a runny nose are the main symptoms of this illness. A tickling cough, sore throat, and mild headache can also contribute to the general discomfort of the sufferer.

It is very difficult to avoid contact with the viruses that cause colds. They are carried in the air from one person to another either in the spray of droplets from a sneeze or in the air exhaled by a cold sufferer. Cold viruses can also be transmitted by any form of direct contact, even a handshake. Once you have been exposed to a cold virus, it usually takes between 18 and 48 hours for the symptoms to appear.

There is little you can do to prevent colds, except to avoid people who have ''new colds'' (a cold is most communicable during the first 24 hours after symptoms appear). You can also help by staying away from others when you have a new cold. In addition, you can keep up your resistance to infection by eating properly, getting enough sleep, exercising, and controlling stress in your life. The value of such measures in preventing colds is disputed by some experts. However, taking such precautions can't hurt since they contribute to your overall health.

There is no cure for the common cold, but scientists are learning more about cold-causing viruses, and they have found that a nasal spray containing interferon can prevent some colds. However, much more research is needed.

Unfortunately, you don't develop an immunity to colds by having one. In this respect, cold viruses appear to be different from other viruses. This may be because cold viruses mutate, or change, rapidly. If this is so, then each cold you get could be caused by a different virus. The fact that there are many different cold viruses also explains why scientists have been unable to develop a vaccine for the common cold.

A cold does not usually last more than a week and sometimes is gone in just two or three days. You can help your body by taking special care of yourself while the disease runs

Figure 16.7 Covering your mouth when you sneeze will help prevent cold viruses from reaching other people.

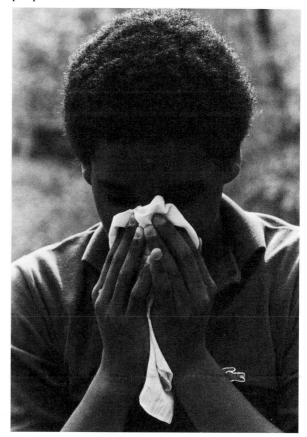

its course. This is necessary not only for your comfort but also to make sure a more serious illness does not develop. Rest and proper nourishment are important. A steam vaporizer can moisturize the air and help loosen nasal congestion. When you blow your nose, do it gently with your mouth open. In this way you will avoid forcing the infection back up the nasal passages to the ear.

Many cold sufferers turn to over-the-counter cold remedies. In fact, Americans spend almost $1 billion every year on nasal sprays, nose drops, cough medicines, and other cold remedies. Yet most of these products are useless, and some may even be harmful. For instance, products sold to relieve congestion may cause delicate mucous membranes in the lungs to dry out and crack. When this happens, the lungs fall prey to bacterial infections.

Aspirin has often been used to relieve cold symptoms. However, new research suggests that this may not be a good idea. While aspirin does ease discomfort and reduce fever, it may also interfere with the body's disease-fighting mechanism. Aspirin may allow the virus particles to multiply more easily, so that infection can spread more easily. The usefulness of massive doses of vitamin C, both as a prevention and as a form of treatment, is also disputed.

Influenza

Like the common cold, *influenza*, or flu, is a disease caused by several kinds of viruses. In its early stages, flu may resemble a cold. Symptoms include a runny nose, sneezing, and congestion. Flu also brings on fever, weakness, coughing, and aching pains in the back, arms, and legs. Flu sufferers often suffer mental and physical depression, which may continue after the infection is over.

The virus particles that cause flu are easily spread by coughing and sneezing. An infected person can infect others from the time just before the first symptoms appear until about a week later. The incubation period (the time between exposure to the virus and appearance of symptoms) is short, lasting from one to three days.

There are three major types of flu, which have been labeled types A, B, and C. Type A is much more serious than the other types. Each type contains many different strains, and new strains are being discovered all the time.

Flu viruses are constantly changing. For this reason, a single vaccine is not effective year after year. Each year a vaccine is developed to match the anticipated virus. Scientists are usually on target, and the vaccine prevents that year's flu in about 85 percent of those vaccinated. The Surgeon General's Advisory Committee on Influenza recommends that people over 65 and those with health problems that put them at high risk obtain the vaccine each year. Doctors also warn that children with the flu should not take aspirin. Aspirin has been linked to Reye's syndrome, a potentially fatal disease that strikes children.

Like the cold viruses, influenza viruses tend to mutate—to undergo small changes in their make-up. As a result, people may develop immunity to one type of flu virus, but they are not immune to it when it changes. A new flu virus can, therefore, affect large numbers of people. Several serious flu epidemics have occurred in the twentieth century, including one in 1918 that took 20 million lives worldwide.

Figure 16.8 An influenza virus.

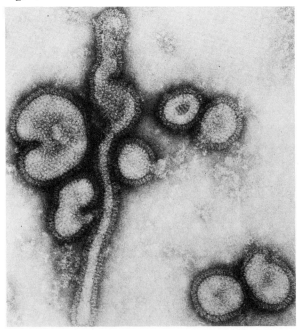

Tuberculosis

Half a century ago, about 80 percent of all Americans became infected by *tuberculosis* (TB) before they were 20 years old. Today the figure is less than 5 percent in most parts of the United States. This dramatic reduction in the number of infected persons does not mean that tuberculosis is under control, however. It is still a major problem among the poor and the elderly, both in the United States and in the developing nations.

Tuberculosis is caused by bacteria. These bacteria can travel through the air, and it is estimated that an infected person can exhale or cough out 2 to 4 billion of them in a 24-hour period. Once inside the body, the bacteria can cause inflammation of various tissues and organs, particularly the lungs.

The bacteria that cause tuberculosis were first identified in 1882. Since then, doctors have developed ways to diagnose and treat TB in its early stages. A simple skin test, called the Mantoux test, can indicate a tubercular condition. Chest x-rays, too, help doctors make a positive diagnosis. With careful treatment, a patient's prospects for recovery are good.

Following the ordinary rules of hygiene, avoiding contact with infected persons, and having regular physical checkups can greatly reduce your chances of contracting TB. Anyone who must be in contact with an infected person, such as a family member, should be checked regularly because TB is transmitted very easily from one person to another.

Pneumonia

Like TB, *pneumonia* used to be a major killer disease. Today, thanks to the use of antibiotics, its mortality rate is much lower. Nevertheless, it remains a leading cause of death in the United States, particularly among the very old and the very young.

Pneumonia is not caused by one specific kind of infectious agent. Viruses, bacteria, fungi, and other pathogens, and irritants such as dust or chemicals can cause pneumonia. Pneumonia can also occur as a complication of some other illness, attacking the body when it is in a weakened condition.

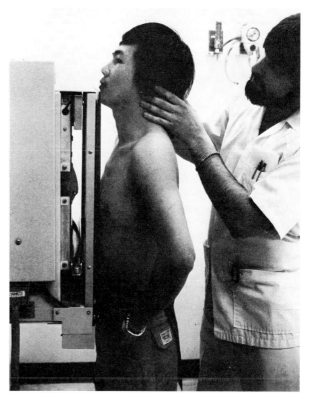

Figure 16.9 Doctors can use x-rays to diagnose pneumonia and other illnesses.

During a pneumonia infection, the lungs become inflamed. Chills, fever, coughing, and shortness of breath are among the common symptoms. Doctors use x-rays and laboratory tests to diagnose pneumonia. It is important to know what type of pneumonia the patient has in order to begin treatment. Antibiotics are very effective against the type of pneumonia caused by bacteria. Viral pneumonia will not respond to antibiotics, though, and other medicines must be used. A vaccine that prevents pneumonia is available at low cost. The vaccine is recommended for those at high risk for the disease. One inoculation is thought to be sufficient for at least five years.

Hepatitis

Hepatitis is one of the few infectious diseases that have increased significantly in recent years, especially among young people.

A hepatitis infection causes the liver to become inflamed. This produces an ache in the upper right abdomen. Fever, headaches, and nausea are also symptoms of the disease. Because the liver is affected, the patient often becomes jaundiced, with yellowish skin tone. The urine of a hepatitis patient is often a deep yellow color.

There are two distinct types of hepatitis. Both varieties are caused by viruses, and both have similar symptoms. *Hepatitis A* is sometimes called *infectious hepatitis*. It is the more common of the two types and the less serious. Hepatitis A is most often transmitted through food or water contaminated with fecal matter. Hepatitis A virus can also be conveyed by direct contact with an infected person. Persons exposed to this type of hepatitis can receive temporary passive immunity.

Hepatitis B is a much more serious form of the disease. It is referred to as *serum hepatitis* because it is transmitted through the blood. Contaminated needles shared by drug users or needles used for tattooing can pass the disease from infected persons to healthy ones. The hepatitis B virus can also be transmitted through a blood transfusion if an infected person donates blood. A vaccine for hepatitis B is available. It is quite expensive—about $110 for a three-shot administration. The three shots are needed over about six months. It is strongly recommended for those at high risk.

Mononucleosis

Probably every high school and college student has heard of "mono"—*infectious mononucleosis*. It occurs most frequently among 15- to 19-year-olds. Those 20 to 24 are next hardest hit. High schools, colleges, and military training camps are ideal settings for outbreaks of the disease because of the large numbers of young people there.

The symptoms can be severe although they usually don't last long. The main signs are fever, sore throat, nausea, chills, and general weakness. Infected persons may also get a rash, enlarged and tender lymph glands, jaundice, and an enlarged spleen. There are usually no permanent ill effects although jaundice and weakness may continue for a few weeks or months. Diagnosis can be made with a simple blood test.

Mononucleosis is caused by a virus. It has often been called the "kissing disease" because for a long time it was thought to be transmitted mainly by kissing. Actually, it is still not known exactly how the virus is spread. Kissing may be one of the ways it is transmitted, but it is certainly not the only way. Mononucleosis is not spread easily by ordinary contact. It is rare to have more than one case in a household.

One bout with mononucleosis usually makes the person immune to further attacks. However, in rare cases, the disease may linger for years.

CHECK YOUR UNDERSTANDING

1. Why have scientists been unable to develop a vaccine for the common cold? What problems can be caused by treating a cold with decongestants and aspirin?
2. List the causes of pneumonia.
3. Name an infectious disease that has become more common in recent years. What part of the body does it attack?
4. Describe the symptoms of mononucleosis. How is it spread?

SECTION **5** **Sexually Transmitted Diseases**

Sexually transmitted diseases (STDs) are infectious diseases that are almost always transmitted by sexual intercourse or other sexual activity. The most common diseases in this category are gonorrhea; nongonococcal urethritis (NGU), which includes chlamydia and ureaplasma; and herpes simplex Type 2. Other STDs, discussed later, include syphilis, trichomoniasis, and moniliasis. STDs are often referred to as *venereal disease,* or *VD.*

There was a dramatic increase in the number of STD cases in the 1960s and 1970s. These diseases still present a problem of epidemic proportions. In the past few years, however, the numbers have been decreasing. About 15 million people are affected by STDs each year. At least half of them are people under 24.

Anybody who contracts an STD should get treatment immediately. Most of the diseases can be cured if they are caught in their early stages. If not treated, they can cause very serious health problems. Infected people will also infect others.

STDs are by no means limited to people who have extremely active sex lives or who have many sexual partners. One experience with an infected person is all it takes to contract an STD.

Among the reasons for the high incidence of STDs are the following:

1. Changing life styles have permitted greater sexual activity.
2. People are beginning sexual activity at a younger age and may have several sexual partners.
3. Drug use often creates a false sense of security and causes people to be less cautious about the possibility of infection.
4. More cases are being revealed than previously because of improved methods of diagnosis and because people are more willing to seek help.
5. More people are using the pill and other methods of contraception that offer less protection against infection than the condom.
6. Some victims assume that STDs are easily and quickly treated with modern antibiotics so they do not bother to get immediate treatment.
7. Some victims are afraid or embarrassed to seek treatment.

Gonorrhea

Gonorrhea is one of the most widespread of all STDs. The average number of cases reported each year between 1980 and 1984 was 385,000.

In 1985, 330,000 cases were reported, and since then, epidemiologists have seen a downward trend of 10,000 fewer cases each month.

Gonorrhea is a bacterial disease. The bacteria that cause it can multiply in the urinary and genital tracts, in the rectum, and in the mouth. If left untreated, the disease can spread to the reproductive organs. Both men and women can become sterile as a result. In addition, the bacteria can enter the bloodstream and cause inflammation of the heart and joints.

Gonorrhea is almost always passed from one person to another through sexual intercourse. However, an infected person who touches an infected area of the body can also transmit the disease by hand. Personal hygiene is, therefore, very important in limiting the spread of this disease.

Figure 16.10 By increasing people's awareness of the danger of STDs, public health organizations hope to promote a more responsible attitude toward sexual activity.

It's a fact of life...
VD gets around

For more information, call toll-free
800-523-1885
N.Y.S. Health Department Public Health Education Unit

Talking Point

The Silent Venereal Disease

Laura and her husband Bill had been trying to have a child for nearly two years. Then Laura's doctor discovered that Laura had a form of NGU called chlamydia. The disease had scarred Laura's fallopian tubes so badly that she would never be able to conceive. Laura had never experienced a single symptom, however, and had no idea when or where she had contracted the disease.

Chlamydia is the most common sexually transmitted disease in the United States. It infects as many as 3 million people each year. Until recently, it received very little attention because its symptoms are often so mild that many people have it for years without knowing.

Even when symptoms are present, chlamydia is difficult to diagnose and is frequently confused with gonorrhea. In fact, many people who contract gonorrhea also get chlamydia. Symptoms can include painful urination and burning and itching of the genital area. Women may also experience abdominal pain, fever, vaginal discharge, and bleeding between menstrual periods.

With appropriate antibiotics, particularly tetracycline, chlamydia can be treated. It usually has no serious consequences for men. However, when it is left undiagnosed and untreated in women, it can develop into pelvic inflammatory disease (PID). PID, which can affect the cervix, the uterus, and the fallopian tubes, is a leading cause of infertility in women. It is also suspected of causing life-threatening complications in thousands of pregnancies annually.

Young women who take birth-control pills or who have more than one partner have the greatest risk of contracting chlamydia. Any woman who has experienced any of its symptoms or whose partner has experienced any symptoms should be tested for chlamydia.

The incubation period is from 3 to 14 days. After that period the disease is contagious. Because of differences in their anatomy, women and men are affected by gonorrhea in different ways.

Gonorrhea in Women Over 75 percent of the women who contract gonorrhea do not experience any symptoms of the disease in its early stages. Often a woman does not suspect that she has gonorrhea until a man reports that he caught the infection from her. Also, a woman whose sexual partner already has the disease and passes it on to her may be unaware of the infection unless the man tells her.

If symptoms do occur, the woman may feel a slight burning in the genital area. There may or may not be a discharge. As the disease progresses, it spreads from the vagina to the uterus and from the uterus to the Fallopian tubes and ovaries.

Gonorrhea can cause severe and painful inflammation of the Fallopian tubes. If it is not treated at this stage, noticeable symptoms may go away or lessen. However, the disease continues to cause serious problems. For example, pus can spread from the reproductive organs up into the abdominal cavity, and the whole pelvis can become inflamed. The infection can last for many years, causing extensive damage to the reproductive organs.

A woman should consult her doctor if she suspects that she has been exposed to gonorrhea or if she has a vaginal discharge.

Gonorrhea is sometimes difficult to diagnose. Many organisms other than gonorrhea bacteria can cause a discharge. Several laboratory tests may be needed to determine whether the person has gonorrhea. Because of the seriousness of the disease, some doctors treat patients for gonorrhea even before the diagnosis is confirmed.

Gonorrhea in Men Men are much more likely to show early signs of a gonorrhea infection than women are. Usually, the symptoms appear three to eight days after exposure to the disease. The man may experience a sharp, burning pain during urination. At the same time, pus begins to ooze from the penis. The pain and discomfort of these symptoms usually force even the most reluctant men to seek treatment.

If the infection is not treated promptly, it spreads to the prostate gland and testes. The resulting damage may cause sterility. The urethra can also become narrowed, making urination uncomfortable. If the infection is severe, men can also suffer arthritis and heart damage.

Treatment Gonorrhea is treated with antibiotics. Penicillin is usually the first choice for treatment. Other antibiotics can be used by people who are allergic to penicillin. These other drugs can also be used to treat a relatively new strain of gonorrhea that is resistant to penicillin.

The response to treatment is usually rapid if the disease is caught in its early stages. The antibiotics clear up the discharge from the vagina or penis almost immediately and kill the infecting bacteria. It is more difficult to treat more severe cases in which complications have appeared.

Nongonococcal Urethritis (NGU)

A little-known but very serious STD is called *nongonococcal urethritis (NGU)*, or *nonspecific urethritis (NSU)*. NGU refers to a wide range of bacterial infections, including chlamydia. Exact statistics are hard to get because many diseases go unreported. (Only

gonorrhea and syphilis are required, by law, to be reported to public health departments.) However, it is estimated that about 4 million cases of NGU occur each year.

NGU is an inflammation of the urinary tract. Symptoms usually start two to three weeks after exposure. They may include pain or tingling while urinating and a discharge. The symptoms are similar to those that signal gonorrhea. However, the drugs that cure gonorrhea do not work for NGU. Different antibiotics must be used. At times NGU may appear as an additional infection with gonorrhea, and each condition must be treated separately. The most effective treatments for the NGU infections, such as chlamydia, are the antibiotics tetracycline and ampicillin.

Serious complications can result from this infection. In women they include sterility and a very painful pelvic inflammatory disease. Men may get a painful condition in the testes. NGU may also cause stillbirths and infant deaths. In addition, pregnant women can pass it on to their unborn babies.

Herpes Simplex Type 2

Until a few years ago, the *herpes simplex Type 2* virus was a rare condition. Compared with gonorrhea and syphilis, it was considered a minor STD. Today this painful and highly infectious disease has reached epidemic levels with close to 500,000 cases reported each year. Worst of all, it is incurable.

Most people are familiar with the *herpes simplex Type 1* virus. It causes the painful cold sores or fever blisters that affect the lips and the sensitive lining of the mouth. In herpes simplex Type 2, the same type of painful sores appear in the genital region.

Herpes simplex Type 2, which is also known as *HSV-2* and as *genital herpes*, is caused by a virus. The infection spreads by sexual contact, and the first symptoms usually appear about six days after exposure. In addition to the sores, the infected person may experience difficult urination, swollen legs, watery eyes, weakness, and fatigue. Treatment can reduce the pain of these symptoms. Unfortunately, the disease itself cannot be cured.

Figure 16.11 Many communities have set up special information hotlines that can answer callers' questions about STDs. Callers do not have to reveal their identity.

Once a person contracts genital herpes, the disease can flare up at any time. Intercourse, fever, infections, fatigue, and exposure to the sun seem to trigger flare-ups of the disease. Sometimes, the herpes virus returns in such a mild form that the victim is not even aware of it. This is a problem because the disease can be transmitted whenever the symptoms occur, no matter how mild the attack is.

There is no blood test for HSV-2 and no vaccine against the disease. Aside from the discomfort of the infection, genital herpes also increases the risk of cancer. Men with HSV-2 show higher than normal rates of prostate cancer. Women with the disease are eight times more likely to develop cervical cancer than other women. Pregnant women with genital herpes also have more miscarriages than other women. Despite efforts to protect babies from the disease during the birth process, 25 percent of infants born to infected mothers develop the same incurable disease.

Syphilis

Syphilis is not as widespread as gonorrhea or NGU. There are about 150,000 new cases each year. But it is one of the most dangerous STDs. As with gonorrhea, the incidence of syphilis has been decreasing since 1984.

Syphilis is caused by bacteria that can thrive in the warm, moist areas of the body. The membranes of the genital tract, rectum, and mouth are ideal breeding places for the bacteria.

There are four major stages of the disease. Each stage has specific symptoms that appear and, after a time, go away. Between outbreaks of symptoms, the victim may feel completely well. For this reason, the infected person may believe she or he has recovered when the first symptoms disappear. When the secondary symptoms occur, weeks or even months later, the person may not connect them with the earlier problem.

Primary Syphilis The disease begins when syphilis bacteria enter the body and begin to multiply. The infected person may not be aware that anything is wrong for 10 to 28 days. Then he or she may notice a small, moist, painless, open sore in the infected area. In men, the shaft of the penis is a common site for the sore. In women, the vulva is often affected. The sore, which may be accompanied by swelling, is called a *chancre*. It is the first sign of the disease. At this point, a physician should be consulted. Diagnosis can easily be made, and treatment provides a complete cure.

Unfortunately, syphilis chancres are not always noticeable. They can occur inside the vagina, in the male urinary tract, or in the rectum. Thus, many people, especially women, are not even aware of the problem during the primary stage. But whether visible or hidden, the chancre is highly infectious and can readily transmit the disease from one person to another.

After several weeks, the chancre disappears—even if treatment is not received. This does *not* mean the disease has gone away. It only signals an end to the first stage of the disease.

Secondary Syphilis During the second stage of the disease, the syphilis bacteria are carried by the bloodstream to all parts of the body. Symptoms usually appear a few weeks to six months after the chancre. Sometimes, though, the secondary symptoms appear as much as a year later.

The infected person may experience general discomfort and uneasiness, low-grade fever, headaches, and swollen glands. Other signs can include small, flat sores on the moist areas of the skin, rashes on the skin, white patches in the mouth or throat, and temporary baldness or bald patches. Victims may have all of these symptoms or just a few of them. In some cases, the symptoms are so mild that they are not noticed.

This is the most contagious stage of the disease. That is, it is the time when it is most readily passed from one person to another. The sores are filled with bacteria. Any contact with one of these open sores—even without sexual intercourse—can transmit the disease. Secondary syphilis may last from three to six months. At this stage the disease can still be readily diagnosed and treated.

Latent Syphilis During this third stage all outward signs of the disease disappear. However, the disease is still causing much harm.

The bacteria are invading the body organs, including the heart and brain. This phase sometimes lasts only a few months, but it can also last for 20 years or until death.

During the latent stage, the disease is not usually contagious. One very important exception is that a pregnant woman can pass the disease to her unborn child at this time. All people in this third stage are potentially contagious though. This is because a relapse can occur and the person can go back to the highly contagious second stage. Despite the lack of symptoms, a blood test will reveal syphilis during the latent stage.

Late Syphilis This is the last and worst stage of the disease. The effects on the health of untreated persons can be devastating. Many people develop serious heart problems. In some cases the damage is severe enough to

Figure 16.12 Community clinics often provide confidential treatment for STDs free of charge or at a minimal cost

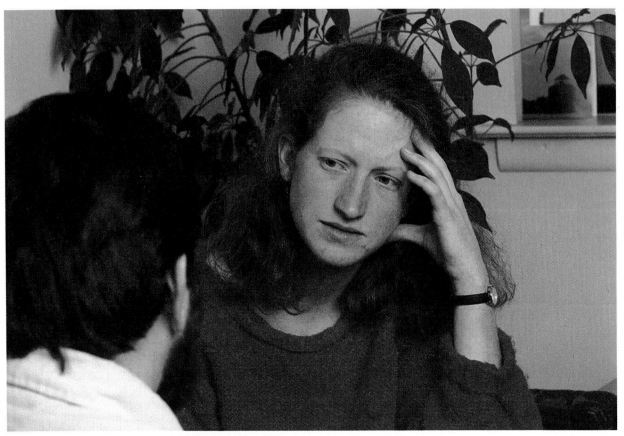

Figure 16.13 By immediately notifying all past and present sexual contacts, a person who has contracted an STD can stop the disease from spreading further. Individuals who learn that they might have an STD should seek immediate medical attention.

cause death. Other complications include damage to the brain or spinal cord, leading to blindness, insanity, or crippling. This stage may begin 10 or 20 years after the beginning of the latent stage.

Congenital Syphilis Syphilis can be passed from a pregnant woman to her unborn child. The child is born with the disease which, since it exists at birth, is known as congenital syphilis.

If the fetus is exposed to the disease in its fourth month of development, the infection may kill it. If the baby is born alive, it will have noticeable signs of disease, such as disfigurement. If the fetus is infected later in pregnancy, the disease may not be noticeable at birth. It may not show up for months or even years. At that time the infected child may become disabled, as in late syphilis.

If a pregnant woman who contracts syphilis gets treatment within the first four months, the disease will not spread to her unborn child.

Treatment Antibiotics can cure syphilis if the disease is diagnosed during its first three stages. Penicillin is the drug used most often. Some syphilis bacteria have shown a resistance to penicillin, but other antibiotics can be used. There are no vaccines for syphilis, and having the disease does not produce immunity. There is no limit to the number of times a person can become infected. Prompt diagnosis and treatment are essential.

Trichomoniasis

Trichomoniasis, often called "trich," is an infection caused by protozoa. The disease normally affects only women. The genital area becomes red, and there is a large amount of an odorous, white, bubbly discharge. Trichomoniasis can also bring on a bacterial infection, which causes a greenish yellow discharge. A doctor can diagnose trichomoniasis by identifying the protozoa in a sample of vaginal secretions.

Most men do not suffer from symptoms of this disease. Some may experience an irritation of the urinary canal, but this is not common. Men do serve as carriers though. Unless both partners are treated for the disease, a couple can pass the infection back and forth. Trichomoniasis is most often transmitted through sexual intercourse. But it can also be transmitted by underwear or washcloths used by the infected person.

Moniliasis

Moniliasis, which is also known as *thrush*, is another disease that usually affects women. Its symptoms include a white, lumpy discharge and an intense itching of the genital region. The disease is caused by a type of yeast fungus. It seems to occur when there is a change in the vaginal lining, such as during pregnancy or when a woman is taking antibiotics. Moniliasis can also occur on the skin, in the rectum or mouth, and in male genitals. It is important that both partners be treated for the disease.

Crab Lice

People who have *crab lice* (also known as *pubic lice*, or "crabs") do not have a disease. However, like the sexually transmitted diseases, the condition is spread by sexual contact, and it affects the genital region.

Crab lice are troublesome parasites, closely related to body lice. These tiny insects can be seen, but just barely, with the naked eye. As the name implies, crab lice resemble crabs in appearance. An infestation of crab lice causes persistent itching in the genital area. The parasites thrive in the pubic hair, and can wander off into the clothing of the infested person. Sexual contact can spread the parasites from one person to another. The lice can also be transmitted by contaminated clothing, sheets, towels, and toilet seats. Fortunately, the parasites can be destroyed by bathing with a special pharmaceutical preparation.

Prevention and Control of STDs

There are no vaccines to prevent STDs, and having one of these diseases does not produce immunity. So the only way of controlling them is by taking preventive measures that will reduce the number of infected persons. This is only possible if people realize the dangers of the diseases and become sufficiently concerned about their spread.

Clearly, the only way to minimize the risk of getting an STD is by avoiding sexual contact with an infected person or by avoiding sexual activity altogether. People who have many sexual partners are almost certain to become infected sooner or later.

Certain precautions can be taken, however. Men who use condoms reduce the risk of infection. Careful washing before and after sexual intercourse is another precaution. It is possible, though, for disease to be transmitted by kissing, by contact with broken skin, or by contact with items touched by an infected person.

Every state requires doctors to report all cases of syphilis and gonorrhea to the public health department. Public health workers try to reduce the spread of STDs by asking those seeking treatment to name all their sexual contacts. But even when patients are co-operative—and many are not—tracing contacts is time-consuming and costly. Obviously, not all who are infected are discovered.

Unlike most infectious diseases, STDs still carry a social stigma. This makes some people unwilling to seek treatment promptly. Embarrassment and ignorance also make some people reluctant to name their contacts or to avoid sexual contact themselves until they are cured.

To encourage reporting and treatment of STDs, many cities and states have set up special information hotlines. The person on the hotline will provide answers to the caller's questions about sexually transmitted diseases. The caller will not be asked for her or his name, and the call will be confidential.

Many communities have also set up special clinics. These clinics often provide treatment free of charge or at a minimal rate. Anyone who has been treated will be asked to return for a follow-up examination. The follow-up usually takes place two weeks after treatment and is extremely important. It is the only way for the doctor to make sure the disease has been completely cured. Patients who skip a follow-up visit run the risk of having the disease flare up again and of spreading it to others. Clinics treat their patients confidentially, and do not notify parents or other family members.

CHECK YOUR UNDERSTANDING

1. How is gonorrhea spread? How does it affect women and men?
2. What is nongonococcal urethritis? What complications can it cause?
3. Which STD can *not* be cured? What are its symptoms?
4. Describe the various stages of syphilis.
5. What are some ways to avoid contracting an STD? Why is it important for a person being treated for an STD to return for a follow-up visit?

CHAPTER SUMMARY

- The six main types of pathogens that cause infectious diseases are bacteria, viruses, rickettsiae, fungi, protozoa, and worms.
- Infections may be spread either by direct physical contact or indirectly by insects, animals, food, water, or articles touched by an infected person.
- Infectious diseases generally go through five stages: the incubation period, the prodrome period, clinical disease, the decline stage, and convalescence.
- The body has three main lines of defense against disease. The first defense is the skin. Second, there are chemicals in the blood and tissues that can kill bacteria and viruses. Third, inflammation and fever indicate that the body is resisting attack.
- A defense against viruses is interferon, a protein that protects healthy cells.
- The body produces antibodies that can provide immunity against specific diseases. Immunity can be achieved by having a disease or by the use of vaccines.
- Many infectious diseases can be prevented by simple precautions and proper vaccinations.

- The most common infectious diseases include the common cold, influenza, tuberculosis, pneumonia, hepatitis, mononucleosis, and some sexually transmitted diseases.
- Most Americans get between one and three colds a year. There is no cure for the common cold and most over-the-counter cold remedies are a waste of money.
- Sexually transmitted diseases have reached epidemic proportions. Some 15 million people are affected by STDs each year. At least half of them are young people under 24. The incidence of gonorrhea and syphilis has been decreasing since 1984, while the incidence of NGU has been increasing.
- Gonorrhea is almost always passed from one person to another through sexual intercourse. The early symptoms are more evident in men than in women. Penicillin is the usual treatment.
- The symptoms of NGU are similar to those that signal gonorrhea, but different antibiotics must be used.

- There is no cure for herpes simplex Type 2. Once a person contracts this disease, it may flare up at any time. Whenever the symptoms occur it may be passed on to other people.
- Syphilis develops in stages. During the primary, secondary, and latent stages, the disease can be treated. Left untreated, syphilis can cause blindness, crippling, insanity, and death.
- Since there is no immunity from STDs, the only way of controlling them is to take preventive measures that will reduce the number of infected persons.

DO YOU REMEMBER?

Give brief definitions of these terms:

pathogen	carrier	antibodies	passive immunity
parasite	inflammation	active immunity	chancre

THINK AND DISCUSS

1. What changes in the way people live do you think have helped bring about the decline of many infectious diseases?
2. What measures would you suggest to persuade people to receive immunizations and booster shots?
3. How might too frequent washing increase a person's risk of infection?
4. Why might it be a bad idea to try to reduce a slight fever during an infection?
5. What measures can you think of to make it easier for people to seek diagnosis and treatment of STDs?
6. What would you do if you found out that someone you knew had an STD but was doing nothing about it?

FOLLOW-UP

1. Find out about Typhoid Mary, who caused a major typhoid epidemic in the early part of the century. Write a report about her.
2. Contact your community health center for more information on infectious diseases. Post the information in your classroom.
3. Ask some adults what home remedies they have used for treating colds. Report your findings to your class.
4. Clip out magazine advertisements for cold remedies and make a collage to display in your classroom.
5. Study some of the conflicting theories on the causes and treatments of the common cold. Discuss these theories and treatments with your class.
6. Find out how STDs such as syphilis were treated in past centuries. Write a report on these treatments.
7. By using reference materials or by contacting a local health clinic, find out how victims of herpes simplex Type 2 can learn to deal with the disease. Write a report on your findings.

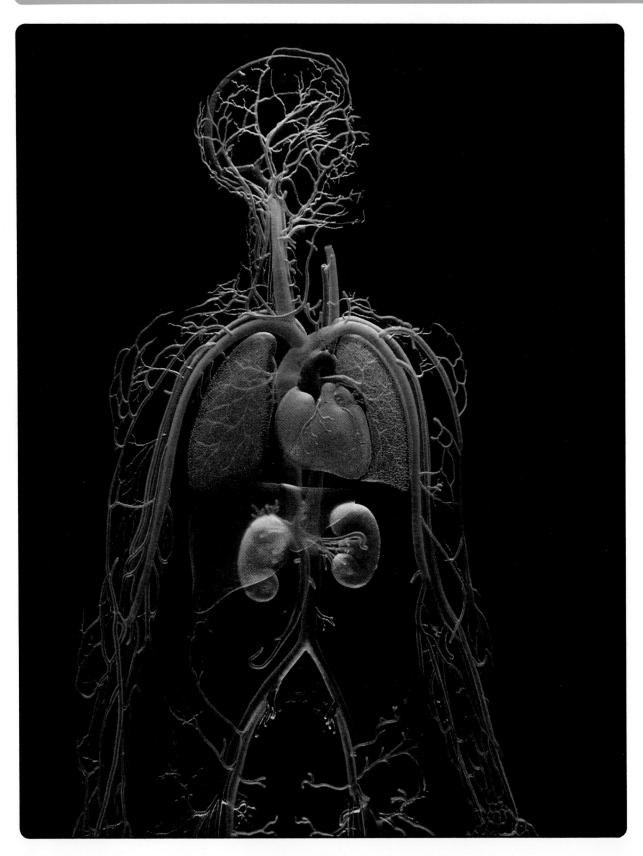

CHAPTER 17

Cardiovascular Diseases

After reading this chapter, you should be able to answer these questions:

1. What is high blood pressure? Can it be controlled?

2. Why do heart attack victims need immediate medical attention?

3. What is a stroke? What causes people to have strokes?

4. How can you reduce your risk of suffering cardiovascular disease?

In America today, we have little fear of dying from most of the diseases that plagued our ancestors. But we now face diseases that were rare among earlier generations of Americans. Among these are diseases of the cardiovascular system—the heart and blood vessels. High blood pressure, heart attack, and stroke all belong in this category.

So common are these diseases that they now cause more than half of all deaths in the United States. Why are we now experiencing an epidemic of diseases that hardly affected earlier generations? The main reason is that the American style of living has changed so drastically. Americans as a group now eat more, smoke more, and exercise less than their ancestors did. These three factors are strong contributors to cardiovascular problems.

Behind many cardiovascular problems lies the process of *atherosclerosis*—a gradual narrowing of the arteries caused by fatty deposits. This process can begin early in life—as early as the teenage years. So even though cardiovascular diseases themselves are not common among teenagers, many people lay the groundwork for later problems before they are 20.

Taking advantage of the knowledge provided by modern science, many Americans have already made changes in their habits to reduce the risk of getting one of the cardiovascular diseases. Their actions, combined with major advances in diagnosis and treatment, have led to a decline in the number of deaths from cardiovascular diseases.

Still, there are many Americans who are not doing what they can to help themselves. A blood pressure test, for example, is a quick and simple procedure. Yet millions of Americans have not been tested and are unaware that they have dangerously high blood pressure. Caught in time, high blood pressure can be kept under control. Ignored, it can lead to premature disability and death.

In this chapter you'll learn how cardiovascular diseases develop and how they are diagnosed and treated. You'll also learn how to reduce the risk of developing one of these disorders. Despite the dramatic advances that have been made in the treatment of these diseases, prevention is still the best weapon.

SECTION **1** # High Blood Pressure

Your heart beats constantly—about 100,000 times a day. Each contraction of the heart's powerful muscles pumps blood to all parts of your body through blood vessels called *arteries*. The surging blood pushes against the inner walls of the arteries. These walls are elastic; they stretch as the blood pushes against them. The pressure of the blood against the artery walls, or *blood pressure*, helps force blood into the most distant arteries, such as those in your fingers and toes.

Blood pressure is at its greatest during each contraction of the heart. After each contraction, the heart relaxes for a fraction of a second. When it does, the blood does not push so hard against the artery walls.

Blood pressure is measured with a simple device called a *blood pressure cuff*. The cuff is wrapped tightly around the upper arm and pumped up until the circulation is cut off. The air is then released from the cuff, and the force with which the blood surges through the arteries is measured. The device records both the high and low extremes of the blood pressure cycle.

One out of every six Americans has *high blood pressure*, or *hypertension*. With this condition, the blood constantly presses abnormally hard against the artery walls. Usually, this happens because the arteries have become narrowed. The heart, therefore, has to work harder than normal to force the blood through the smaller arteries.

The Dangers of High Blood Pressure

High blood pressure can lead to a number of serious disorders. As mentioned above, the heart has to work harder. The strain of this

Figure 17.1 Blood pressure is measured by means of an inflatable cuff wrapped around the upper arm.

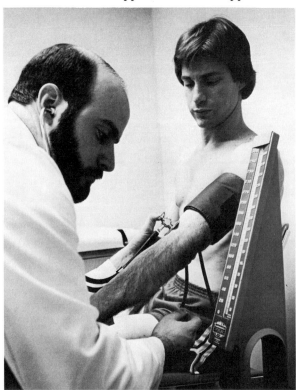

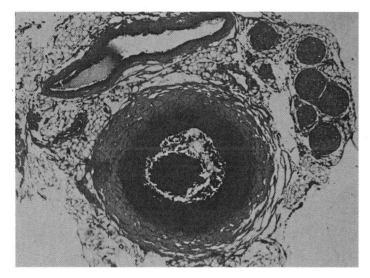

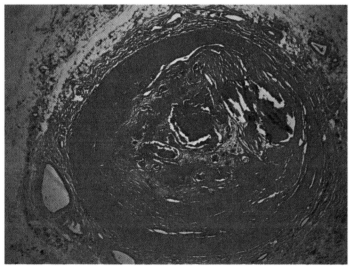

Figure 17.2 *Top:* Cross section of a normal artery. Note the clear passageway through the center. *Bottom:* An atherosclerotic artery. The passageway is almost totally blocked by fatty deposits.

overwork can cause the heart to enlarge and lose its strength. When this happens, the heart can no longer pump blood effectively.

High blood pressure can also speed the build-up of fatty deposits on the artery walls, a condition known as *atherosclerosis*. This condition makes it even harder for the blood to travel through the arteries. Atherosclerosis can also cause the walls of the arteries to harden and lose their elasticity. Hardening of the arteries, or *arteriosclerosis*, further reduces the ability of these vessels to carry blood. The blood supply to the legs and feet in particular may suffer. In extreme cases, body tissue may actually die from lack of nourishment.

The pressure of the blood against the walls of the arteries can be high enough to actually burst the walls. When this happens, blood pours into the surrounding tissues and forms clots. If this happens in the brain, a *stroke* can occur (see Section 3 of this chapter).

Another of the dangers of high blood pressure is the fact that so many victims are not being treated. According to the 1983 Surgeon General's report, about one-quarter of the 38 million Americans with high blood pressure are not even aware that they have it. Of those who are aware of the problem, only one-third are receiving adequate treatment. Thus, only about one out of every four people with high blood pressure is getting the right treatment for it. Some of the reasons for this problem are discussed below.

Causes of High Blood Pressure

Why is high blood pressure so common among Americans? A few people develop the disorder as a result of kidney disease or an imbalance of body chemicals. A large number develop it because they have atherosclerosis. But in many of the cases, no direct physical cause can be found. In these cases, small blood vessels all over the body tighten and remain tightened.

The real cause for many cases of high blood pressure seems to be the modern American life style. For many people, emotional stress and tension are built into their daily routines. The human body reacts strongly to stress and tension; the heart beats faster and small arteries throughout the body's system constrict, making blood pressure rise. When the stress is over, the body usually returns to normal. But some people feel tense constantly, which keeps their arteries constricted and their blood pressure high.

Overweight people are also prone to high blood pressure. Too much salt (sodium) can further increase high blood pressure, as can too much fat and cholesterol. One recent study suggests that calcium and potassium deficiencies might be contributing factors, but more research is needed.

There is a higher incidence of high blood pressure among blacks than whites, and the risk increases with age among all groups. Women, overall, have a lower rate of hypertension than men. However, black women have a higher rate than black men. A woman's risk increases if she is pregnant or taking oral contraceptives.

Symptoms of High Blood Pressure

In some people, high blood pressure causes headaches (especially at the back of the head), dizziness, flushing, fatigue, and insomnia. The great majority of people, though, experience no symptoms until high blood pressure is in an advanced stage. By then, the heart and blood vessels may be greatly damaged.

Because high blood pressure is so symptom-free, it is especially important to have your blood pressure checked at least once a year. Many communities set up screening booths or trailers in local shopping centers and other public gathering places. You can probably have your blood pressure checked during your next shopping trip. It takes just a few minutes, and it could save your life.

Why Me?

"Why should I have my blood pressure checked?" you ask. The figures give the answer. One out of every six adults in this country suffers from high blood pressure, including a significant number of young adults. In fact, cardiovascular diseases rank as one of the major causes of death among young adults aged 15 to 24. And in this age group, blacks are at least three times as likely as whites to suffer from high blood pressure.

Figure 17.3 For some people, nutritional changes, weight control, and salt reduction are effective enough to bring blood pressure back into normal range. For other people, medication is necessary to bring about the desired results.

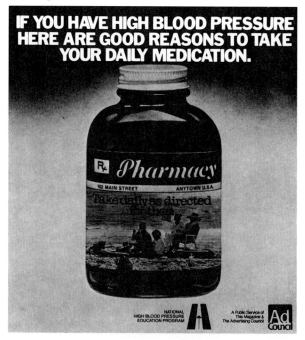

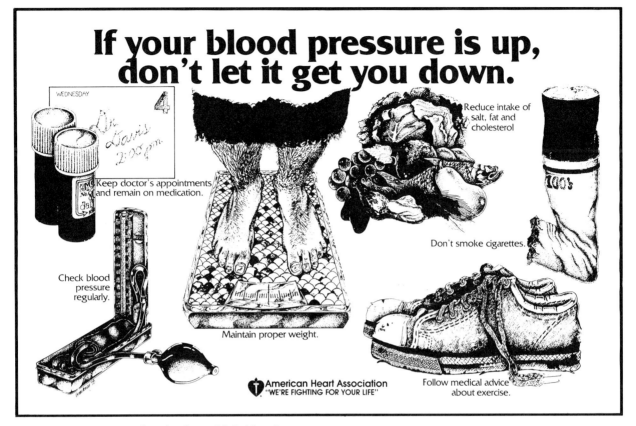

Figure 17.4 Most people who have high blood pressure can lead normal lives if they are willing to take a few simple precautions.

Treatment of High Blood Pressure

High blood pressure *can* be controlled. Modern drugs are extremely effective in bringing blood pressure into normal range. A low-salt or salt-free diet also helps to reduce blood pressure. In some cases, losing excess weight will bring blood pressure back to normal. Learning to cope more effectively with emotional stress is also an effective technique. Studies show that the proper treatment of hypertension can greatly reduce the risk of related diseases.

Many people, however, do not take their medications or adjust their diets because they do not feel sick. What they do not realize is that the damage caused by high blood pressure is not something they can feel. They cannot, for example, feel their hearts enlarge or their arteries harden. Just the same, these changes are taking place. High blood pressure, then, is a serious disease that deserves to be treated with serious concern.

CHECK YOUR UNDERSTANDING

1. When is blood pressure at its greatest? Its lowest?
2. Describe the ways in which high blood pressure can affect the heart and the arteries.
3. Describe what happens to the victim's small blood vessels in high blood pressure cases that have no physical cause. List the main causes of high blood pressure.
4. How can high blood pressure be treated?
5. Why are so many people unaware that they have high blood pressure? Why do many people who know of their condition neglect treatment?

SECTION **2** **Heart Attacks**

Jack's father was sure he was having an attack of indigestion. He felt nauseated and began to sweat. Soon he started to complain of a squeezing pain in the middle of his chest. He decided to get up from the table and go lie down until the heartburn passed. But when he tried to stand, a wave of dizziness passed over him and he had to sit down again. "Oh, it's nothing," he told his concerned son.

But Jack saw that it was far from nothing. He had taken a first-aid course, and he felt sure that his father was suffering something far more serious than heartburn—a heart attack. Jack called for an ambulance and made his father as comfortable as possible until help arrived.

What Is a Heart Attack?

A heart attack happens when the blood supply to an area of the heart is cut off. The heart attack itself is sudden. But it is the result of a disease that may have been present for many years. *Atherosclerosis*, mentioned earlier, is a condition in which fatty deposits build up on the inner walls of the arteries. When the arteries in the heart, called coronary arteries, are narrowed by atherosclerosis, the risk of heart attack is high. If a blood clot or spasm occurs in an already narrowed coronary artery, the flow of blood to the heart is blocked. The result is a heart attack.

During a heart attack, the part of the heart that is supplied by the blocked artery does not get oxygen and other nutrients. If denied nourishment for too long, it will die. The size of the dead area determines how severe the heart attack is. If it isn't too large, the heart can keep functioning. Other arteries develop to take on the work that was done by the blocked artery, and gradually scar tissue forms over the damaged area. Unlike normal tissue, scar tissue is not elastic. So it does not contract when the heart pumps. Therefore, the heart will never again function as well as it did before the attack.

Heart Attack Symptoms

People do not always realize they are having a heart attack. Sometimes the symptoms are mistaken for other conditions, such as indigestion. Usually, the symptoms consist of feelings of pressure, squeezing, or intense pain in the middle of the chest. The pain may extend to the arms, shoulders, neck, jaw, or back. Stiffness or numbness in these areas may be felt. The victim may also experience dizziness, nausea, fainting, shortness of breath, and profuse sweating. Vomiting may also occur.

The symptoms vary greatly from patient to patient. Some people suffer so intensely there is no question about what is taking place. Other people have heart attacks that are so mild that they are unaware of what has happened.

Regardless of the degree of pain or the number of symptoms, any suspected heart attack should receive prompt medical attention. More than half of all heart attack victims die outside the hospital, usually within two hours

Figure 17.5 When a blood clot occurs in an already narrowed coronary artery, the flow of blood to the heart is blocked. If this blockage continues too long, some of the heart's tissue may die.

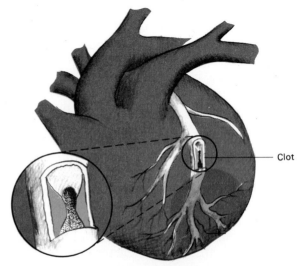

Clot

Talking Point

What Killed Jim Fixx?

Jim Fixx's father died of a heart attack at the age of 43. To avoid a similar fate, Fixx started running 10 to 15 miles a day when he was in his mid-thirties. He quit smoking, shed 60 pounds, and wrote two best-selling books on running.

In 1984 Jim Fixx died suddenly from a heart attack while he was running. He was 52. An autopsy disclosed that he had two completely blocked coronary arteries and a third artery that was partially blocked. Because the build-up of fatty material in the arteries is usually a slow process, medical experts agreed that his blocked arteries were the result of his heredity and his earlier bad habits. They also thought that Fixx's death was hastened by his refusal to get regular medical checkups, which would have shown the blockages.

Did running contribute to Fixx's death? The answer seems to be yes and no. Medical experts think that, over the long term, his running probably prolonged his life by improving his cardiovascular fitness. However, on the day he died, running placed too much stress on his clogged arteries.

About 20 percent of heart attack victims die without any previous warning. Fixx, however, appears to have had some warning signals. A few days before his death he complained to a fellow runner that he was exhausted. He told his family that he felt a tightness in his throat when he ran. These were probably signs of angina, a coronary disease.

According to doctors, there are lessons to be learned from the death of Jim Fixx. One is that warning signs are meant to be heeded. Fixx knew that his family history put him at high risk for heart disease, but he was negligent about seeing doctors. According to Dr. Kenneth Cooper, founder of the Aerobics Center in Dallas, Texas, Fixx refused to have his heart function evaluated with a treadmill stress test. According to doctors, people with coronary trouble often deny that they have a serious condition. For long-distance runners like Jim Fixx, the denial of any trouble can be fatal.

Running can be safe exercise, even for heart patients, but runners with heart conditions need to stick to strict limits and to train under close medical supervision. If Fixx had sought medical advice about his heart condition, he probably would have lived longer.

Another lesson to be learned from his death is that diet and exercise by themselves are not enough. You need to know what risk factors apply to you, and to keep those factors in mind when you make decisions about your life style.

of the first symptoms. It is essential, then, that the victim receives attention as soon as possible, preferably from a trained rescue squad or in a hospital emergency room.

It is not uncommon for a victim to deny that he or she is having a heart attack. If the symptoms are mild, the person doesn't believe that anything so serious can be happening. If you are ever with someone who is having the symptoms, and if they last more than two minutes, you should insist on getting emergency assistance.

Faltering Heartbeat

A heart attack not only damages the heart muscle; it may also drastically alter the rhythm of the heartbeat. The heart has a tiny piece of special tissue known as the *pacemaker*, which sends a current of electricity over the heart. This current makes the heart muscles contract. The pacemaker keeps the heart beating at an even, rhythmic rate. A heart attack may cause the pacemaker to go out of control. When this happens, the heart may beat hundreds of times a minute, a condition known as *fibrillation*. When the heart beats so rapidly, it is incapable of pumping blood. Unless fibrillation is stopped, the patient will die. This is one of the reasons why it is so important to get a heart attack victim to a hospital.

Sometimes a heart attack victim who seems to be recovering will experience a sudden slowing of the heartbeat. In this condition, known as *heart block*, the impulse that causes the heart to beat does not occur often enough. A physician can restore the normal rate with an electronic pacemaker. Usually, the heart can repair itself in a few days and return to its natural rhythm. If this does not happen, surgeons may insert an artificial pacemaker, a procedure that is described more fully below.

Cardiac Arrest and Emergency Treatment

Sometimes a heart attack makes the heart stop beating. Heart stoppage is also called *cardiac arrest*. Accidents such as drowning, strangulation, and electrocution can also stop the heart. When this happens, immediate action is essential. Once circulation stops, the brain can survive without damage for just four minutes.

In a hospital emergency room, a variety of techniques are used to start the heartbeat. External heart massage and mouth-to-mouth resuscitation are usually tried first. If these fail, an electrical shock may be given to the heart.

If immediate medical attention is not available, the patient can be saved by *cardiopulmonary resuscitation* (CPR). CPR involves massage of the chest area, which forces the blood

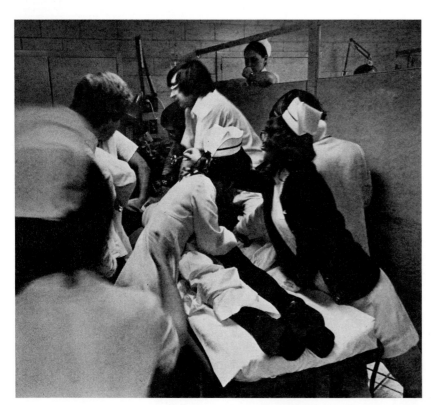

Figure 17.6 A medical team giving oxygen and heart massage to a man in cardiac arrest.

out of the heart and into the arteries. While the massage goes on, the victim also receives mouth-to-mouth breathing. In this way, the victim's lungs continue to supply oxygen to the body. Everybody should know how to perform CPR, but the procedure should *never* be attempted without proper training. Amateur attempts can do more harm than good. (See Chapter 19 for more information about CPR.)

Angina Pectoris

Many people whose coronary arteries have been narrowed by atherosclerosis do not have heart attacks. But whenever they exercise too much or get excited, they suffer symptoms similar to those of a heart attack. These people have a condition known as *angina pectoris*.

The symptoms of angina are pain, tightness, or pressure in the chest, sometimes extending to the neck, shoulders, arms, hands, or back. These symptoms occur whenever the heart is not getting enough oxygen. Coronary atherosclerosis reduces the flow of oxygen-carrying blood to the heart. Enough blood can pass through the narrowed arteries to meet the heart's ordinary needs. But when the heart must work harder, it does not receive enough blood. That is why people who suffer from angina usually feel the pain if they exert themselves or become excited. Eating a heavy meal can also cause this discomfort.

Angina pains may occur in people who have recovered from a heart attack or in those who have never had—and never will have—a heart attack. In some individuals the pains are so slight they are hardly noticed. In others they are quite severe. These people may have to limit their activity in order to avoid pain. With proper care, many angina sufferers are able to enjoy a normal life for many years. Medications exist to relieve the pain, and surgery may also help.

Treatment of Heart Problems

With proper management, many people survive heart attacks and live for many years af-

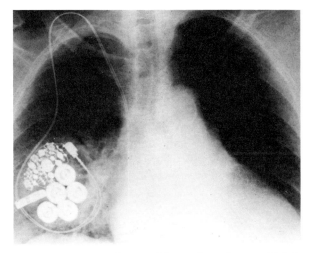

Figure 17.7 The wires and batteries of an artificial pacemaker are visible in the lower left-hand corner of this chest x-ray.

terward, as do those who develop angina. Proper care and treatment, though, is the key. Modern medicine can do wonders, but the patient must help as well.

After a heart attack, the patient must rest for a certain period of time. This reduces the work load on the heart to allow the wound to heal. After the healing period, most heart attack patients are started on an exercise program to strengthen the heart and increase the efficiency of the cardiovascular system. (A number of patients who have been on such a program say that they feel better than they had for years. Some even go on to become marathon runners!)

A change in diet may also be called for. Overweight patients are advised to lose weight to avoid straining the heart. In general, a moderate diet low in cholesterol and salt can help heart attack victims restore and maintain their health.

Other changes may also be called for. Cigarette smoking, which hampers circulation, must be ruled out. Stressful situations should be kept to a minimum; in some cases, doctors advise patients to change jobs to reduce stress. Heart patients frequently have to take medication. Those who have angina, for instance, often use nitroglycerin tablets to expand the coronary arteries and relieve discomfort. In all cases, frequent checkups are a must.

Heart problems may also be treated surgically. During the past few decades, dramatic advances in the treatment of cardiovascular disorders have taken place. Now surgery is commonly used to repair or replace damaged parts of the heart or blood vessels.

The development of the *artificial pacemaker* was a breakthrough in the control of certain heart disorders. This is a device that functions in much the same way as a natural pacemaker. It maintains a regular heartbeat for patients who suffer from weak or irregular heart rhythms.

The battery-operated pacemaker is implanted in the chest and wired to the heart. Additional surgery is needed regularly to replace the batteries. Each year about 200,000 Americans have pacemaker surgery.

When a heart can no longer function properly, surgeons may perform a *coronary bypass operation*. Some 170,000 of these operations are done each year. To perform this surgery, the doctor usually uses a section of a vein from another part of the patient's body. One end of the vein is stitched to a healthy part of the damaged artery; the other is attached to the heart. Because the vein bypasses the damaged section of artery, the operation improves the flow of blood and oxygen to the heart.

In 1984 the world's first artificial heart transplant was performed. In several such operations to date, the results have not proved satisfactory. Much more work is needed if the artificial heart is ever to become reliable.

As with any medical problem, the best way to deal with heart conditions will always be to try to prevent them. For those who do have heart trouble, understanding their own abilities and limitations and following a doctor's advice can help increase their chances of living long and full lives.

CHECK YOUR UNDERSTANDING

1. Describe briefly what happens during a heart attack.
2. List the symptoms of a heart attack.
3. Describe two ways in which a heart attack can affect the rhythm of the heartbeat.
4. What does CPR involve?
5. Why must heart attack victims rest for a period of time? What changes do they frequently have to make in their lives?

SECTION **3**

Strokes

When Joy went to visit her grandmother in the hospital, she didn't know what to expect. She knew her grandmother had suffered a stroke, but she wasn't sure what that was—or what its effects were. When she walked into her grandmother's hospital room, Joy saw that a great change had taken place. Her grandmother smiled in recognition, but she couldn't answer Joy's greeting. Nor could she move her right arm or leg. Later, the doctor explained to Joy what had happened.

What Is a Stroke?

A *stroke* is an injury to the brain. It occurs when the blood supply to the brain is interrupted. Strokes are the third leading cause of death in America today. Only heart disease and cancer claim more lives.

A stroke can occur in several ways. A diseased artery in the brain may burst. Or an artery may become blocked by a blood clot or a fragment of fatty material. Regardless of what triggers the stroke, some brain tissue dies because it is deprived of oxygen-carrying blood.

A stroke can announce itself in a number of ways. The victim may experience sudden dizziness, fainting, or severe headache. There may be numbness, tingling, or paralysis in one area of the body. It may also become difficult to swallow or speak. Impaired vision and an inability to think clearly are two more signs that a stroke is occurring. Any of these symptoms calls for immediate medical attention.

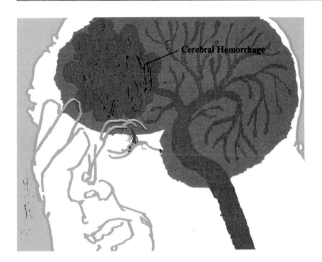

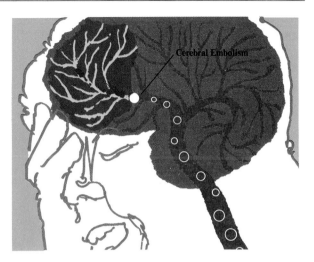

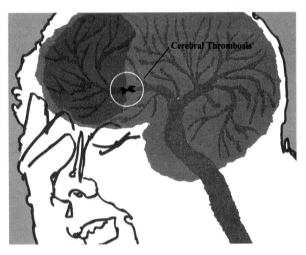

Figure 17.8 Three types of strokes: (*top left*) cerebral hemorrhage, in which a diseased brain artery bursts; (*top right*) cerebral embolism, in which a brain artery is blocked by a fragment of abnormal material; (*bottom left*) cerebral thrombosis, in which a blood clot forms within a brain artery.

A major stroke may be preceded by a "little stroke." This is a temporary attack with similar symptoms. It can last anywhere from a few minutes to a full day, and it can occur months before a major attack. A "little stroke" serves as a warning signal, since almost half of the victims later suffer a full-scale stroke. Prompt treatment, though, may prevent a future stroke.

Effects of a Stroke

When nerve cells in the brain die, the parts of the body controlled by these nerve centers can no longer function normally. As a result, stroke patients may become partly paralyzed or suffer a loss of coordination. Some may be unable to speak clearly. Others may have trouble understanding what is being said to them. Confusion and loss of memory are common following a stroke. For some reason, strokes are especially likely to affect short-term memory. Patients may be able to recall something that happened many years ago but not remember the events of the previous day.

It is also quite common for stroke victims to suffer emotional changes. Extremes of mood can occur, and the victim may have emotional reactions that don't fit the situation. For instance, the person may laugh during a sad occasion or cry when something funny happens.

In some cases, the effects of the stroke are temporary. They may disappear in a few days or weeks. Frequently, retraining, or therapy, helps another area of the brain take over for the damaged area. In other cases, the effects are long-term. Even with therapy, the patient may never make a complete recovery. Both the size and the location of the damaged area determine what the effects of the stroke are, how severe they are, and how long they are likely to last.

Causes of Strokes

Strokes are sudden occurrences. But the conditions that bring them about may have been developing for 30 or 40 years before a stroke actually occurs.

Atherosclerosis contributes to many strokes. A piece of fatty deposit can break off an artery wall and travel to the brain. The arteries of the brain itself can also develop this disease. About 40 percent of all Americans over 50 suffer from this form of atherosclerosis.

Hypertension, or high blood pressure, also greatly increases the chances of stroke. Smoking and diet also play a part. If an individual is exposed to two or more risk factors, the chances of having a stroke are greatly multiplied. (For a full discussion of risk factors, see Section 4 of this chapter.)

Treatment

Proper treatment is very important—not only to help the stroke patient recover but also to prevent her or him from having another stroke. A person who has suffered one stroke—even a mild one—is 10 times more likely to have a second stroke than he or she was to have the first one. Treatment following a stroke may include medicine, physical therapy, speech therapy, and control of risk factors. In some cases, surgery is useful.

If the stroke was brought on by a blood clot or a narrowed blood vessel, the patient may be given *anticoagulants*. These are drugs that reduce the clotting ability of the blood. Besides prescription medicines, simple aspirin has been found helpful in preventing second strokes. Even though aspirin can be bought without a prescription, it should never be used for preventing strokes without a doctor's advice. In any case, the use of aspirin is not likely to have any real value unless other risk factors (such as hypertension and cigarette smoking) are controlled.

It was once believed that stroke patients should have a long period of bed rest after the stroke. However, it is now believed that patients should get out of bed and start therapy as quickly as possible. Relearning basic skills such as walking and talking can be difficult, but the quicker the patient starts to do this the better.

In addition to physical therapy and speech therapy, many stroke patients need psychological help. They feel depressed and anxious about their inability to function. Doctors encourage the patient's family and friends to help create a feeling of independence by insisting that the patient do as much as she or he can. Whenever possible, the patient should not be treated as an invalid.

CHECK YOUR UNDERSTANDING

1. What is a stroke? What are two ways a stroke can happen?
2. List the symptoms of a stroke.
3. Describe some of the effects of a stroke. What determines these effects?
4. Give two reasons that proper treatment of a stroke is important. When are anticoagulants used?

SECTION 4   Risk Factors

As you have seen, most cardiovascular diseases develop over a period of many years. Someone who suffers a heart attack at 40 and a stroke at 50 may have started laying the groundwork for these conditions while still a teenager. The way you live right now, therefore, may determine the future state of your cardiovascular system.

There are a number of factors that increase a person's risk of cardiovascular diseases. Experts do not always agree on how significant some of the risk factors are. But on some there is general agreement. There is no doubt, for instance, that high blood pressure and cigarette smoking increase the likelihood of a heart attack. Recently, cholesterol has been found to be directly linked to heart disease. Other risk factors, such as stress, are being studied.

You have no control over some risk factors, such as your age, sex, race, or family medical history. All of these may affect your chances of getting a cardiovascular disease.

There are other factors, though, over which you do have control. Cigarette smoking is the

How to...

Maintain Your Cardiovascular Fitness

Heart disease takes decades to develop, but it can begin—or be prevented—with habits you are forming right now. Here are seven things you can do to reduce your risk of developing heart disease:

1. Reduce the proportion of saturated fats in your diet. Foods that are high in saturated fats should make up no more than 10 percent of your total dietary intake. These foods include meats, cream, cheese, whole milk, butter, and ice cream. By cutting down on saturated fats, you can significantly reduce the amount of cholesterol in your bloodstream.

2. Watch your blood pressure. People with blood pressure that measures 140 over 90 or more need to bring it down by losing weight, reducing use of table salt, exercising, or modifying their diet under advice of a doctor. Very high blood pressure is usually treated with medication.

3. Don't use tobacco products. All forms of tobacco are harmful to your cardiovascular health. Once nicotine is absorbed into the bloodstream, it can raise blood pressure,

increase heart rate, and cause vasoconstriction (narrowing of the blood vessels). When these effects are added to other risk factors, such as cholesterol build-up in the arteries, the smoker's risk of premature death increases sharply.

4. Exercise regularly. Studies have shown that the risk of death due to premature heart attack is lower for people who engage in moderate daily exercise than it is for sedentary people.

5. Watch your weight. If you are more than 20 percent heavier than the recommended weight for your height and age, you are putting an unnecessary strain on your heart.

6. Drink alcohol in moderation or not at all. Heavy use of alcohol increases the level of fats in the blood, which increases the risk of heart disease.

7. Control stress. Stress is an important facet of our daily lives. Without it we would be unmotivated and lazy, but too much stress can damage the cardiovascular system. When a stressful situation is not resolved and the stress continues, heart rate and blood pressure increase.

most obvious. Diet, exercise, and obesity are also within your control. Even high blood pressure is a reducible risk since it can be controlled if diagnosed early enough.

The presence of any risk factor puts you in danger of developing a cardiovascular disease. But when several factors exist, the chances are greatly multiplied. A person who has high blood pressure and who smokes a pack a day, for instance, is nine times more likely to suffer a heart attack than a nonsmoker with normal blood pressure. The fact that some factors are beyond your control makes it all the more necessary to control those over which you do have power. The elimination of just one factor can make a significant difference. The recommendations below do not guarantee protection against heart disease, but they can reduce the risks.

Cigarette Smoking

People who smoke a pack of cigarettes a day are twice as likely to have heart attacks as nonsmokers. The risk increases with the number of cigarettes smoked. Cigarette smoking also increases the likelihood of having a stroke.

Giving up cigarettes is one of the most effective ways to fight the odds. Within 2 years of

Figure 17.9 Giving up cigarettes is one of the most effective ways of reducing the risk of heart attack as well as of lung cancer and many other diseases.

quitting, the risk of heart attack drops greatly. And within 10 to 15 years, an ex-smoker's chance of death from heart attack is no greater than that of someone who never smoked.

Diet

Many experts believe that diet is the single most important factor in atherosclerosis. Scientists know that one of the substances that form the fatty deposits on the walls of the arteries is *cholesterol*. This build-up of cholesterol is directly related to the amount of cholesterol consumed in the diet.

The body obtains cholesterol from two sources: it is produced within the body, and it is obtained from the diet. Although we can do nothing about the cholesterol that our body makes, we can control our dietary intake. Studies done on animals have shown that when consumption of cholesterol is reduced, the development of atherosclerosis slows down. Researchers have also studied the diet patterns in different societies. They have found that people whose diets are low in cholesterol and fats have lower levels of cholesterol in their blood and fewer heart attacks.

In light of these and other findings, doctors suggest that people alter their diets by substituting carbohydrates and unsaturated fats for saturated fats. You can do this by cutting down on such foods as butter, cheese, mayonnaise, beef, pork, and lamb. Changing your diet in this way will reduce your risk of heart attack and improve your overall health.

Another risk factor related to diet is *obesity*. There is no proof that obesity itself is a cause of heart disease. But it is believed that when obesity is combined with hypertension and other factors, the risk of heart disease is greatly increased. A middle-aged, overweight person is two to three times more likely to have heart disease than a similar person of normal weight.

A link has been established between the consumption of large amounts of salt and high blood pressure. People who have high blood pressure are normally advised to reduce the amount of salt in their diets.

Figure 17.10 People who exercise regularly reduce their chances of developing cardiovascular disease. Exercise can help control weight and can help the heart work more efficiently by maximizing the use of oxygen.

The government's dietary guidelines suggest that all Americans should limit their salt intake. They advise people to cook with only small amounts of salt, to refrain from adding salt to their food at the table, and to avoid salty prepared foods. By reading labels, you can tell whether salt (which may be listed as sodium chloride) has been added to packaged foods.

There is no one diet that is right for everyone. But the key to good nutrition is a balanced, varied diet that includes all essential nutrients (see Chapter 6). Diet is one of the risk factors in heart disease over which you have some control. And since there is evidence that atherosclerosis begins at an early age, now is the time to take an interest in the food you eat.

Exercise

If you like to swim, run, cycle, or jump rope, stick with it. Studies show that people who exercise regularly improve their chances of escaping cardiovascular diseases (see Chapter 5). These people have fewer heart attacks than people who do not exercise and suffer less damage when heart attacks do occur.

Some forms of exercise are more helpful than others for improving cardiovascular fitness. Aerobic exercises such as walking and swimming are best. They strengthen the heart muscle and also increase the level of oxygen in the bloodstream.

Strenuous exercise also leads to the development of *collateral circulation*—that is, growth of additional coronary blood vessels. The value here is that if a coronary blood vessel becomes blocked, one of the new vessels can take over. People who develop collateral circulation rarely suffer death or disability from heart attack.

Stress

There is no proof that stress in itself helps to cause heart disease. How people cope with it is actually the more important factor.

Researchers have divided people into two categories. Type A people are competitive, aggressive, and impatient. They have fast-paced lives and are constantly under pressure—even if they have to create that pressure themselves. Type B people are the opposite—calm, patient, and relaxed. Most people are a combination of the two types, but generally one set of traits is dominant.

Extensive research indicates that the stressful Type A personalities are three times more likely than Type B people to develop heart disease. In fact, one study showed that 90 percent of all patients below the age of 60 who were treated for heart attack were Type A. Learning how to handle stress, then, may significantly reduce your own chances of having a heart attack. (For a detailed discussion of stress, see Chapter 4.)

CHECK YOUR UNDERSTANDING

1. List the cardiovascular disease risk factors that you can control and those that you cannot.
2. Describe the heart attack risk of one-pack-a-day smokers.
3. What can people do to reduce the amount of cholesterol in their diet?
4. What kind of exercise strengthens the heart? What is another benefit of such exercise?
5. Describe Type A and Type B personalities. What risk do Type A people run?

CHAPTER SUMMARY

- High blood pressure, or hypertension, is a condition in which the blood presses abnormally hard against the artery walls. One out of every six Americans has high blood pressure.
- High blood pressure can cause, or be caused by, atherosclerosis, a condition in which arteries are narrowed by the build-up of fatty deposits.
- One-quarter of the 38 million Americans who have high blood pressure are not aware of it. Only one out of every four people with high blood pressure is getting adequate treatment.
- Most people with high blood pressure experience no symptoms until the disease has reached an advanced state. Everyone should, therefore, have her or his blood pressure checked regularly.
- Heart attacks happen when a blood clot or spasm occurs in a coronary artery that has been narrowed by atherosclerosis. The flow of blood to a part of the heart is blocked.
- The symptoms of a heart attack include pain in the middle of the chest, dizziness, nausea, fainting, shortness of breath, and sweating.
- Any suspected heart attack should receive prompt medical attention.
- A person who regularly has pain, pressure, or tightness in the chest may have angina pectoris.

These symptoms occur whenever the heart is not getting enough oxygen.
- Treatment for heart attack patients usually begins with a period of rest, followed by an exercise program. A change in life style, to eliminate risk factors, may be necessary.
- The implantation of an artificial pacemaker and coronary bypass surgery are two surgical techniques used to remedy heart problems.
- A stroke is an injury to the brain. Strokes occur when the blood supply to the brain is interrupted by a burst or blocked artery.
- Among the symptoms of a stroke are dizziness, fainting, headache, numbness, partial paralysis, impaired vision, and mental confusion.
- Some stroke victims recover after a few days or weeks. Others suffer permanent effects.
- Treatment for stroke victims includes medication, physical therapy, speech therapy, control of risk factors, and psychological help.
- The risk factors associated with cardiovascular diseases include cigarette smoking, a high-cholesterol diet, obesity, lack of exercise, and stress. The existence of more than one risk factor greatly multiplies a person's chances of developing a cardiovascular disease.

DO YOU REMEMBER?

Give brief definitions of these terms:

hypertension	atherosclerosis	fibrillation	cardiac arrest
stroke	arteriosclerosis	heart block	angina pectoris

THINK AND DISCUSS

1. What reasons can you think of for the recent decline in the number of deaths from cardiovascular diseases?
2. What measures can you think of to persuade people to have their blood pressure checked regularly?
3. Why do you think high blood pressure is sometimes called "the silent killer"?
4. What aspects of our society do you think create the most tensions?
5. People with low blood pressure tend to live longer than the average life expectancy. Why do you think this is so?
6. What would you do if you were with someone who appeared to be having a heart attack but denied it and insisted on continuing with whatever he or she was doing?
7. What could be the dangers of self-treatment with aspirin to prevent stroke?
8. Should businesses schedule a daily round of exercise for their employees? Why or why not?

FOLLOW-UP

1. Contact the local chapter of the American Heart Association for more information on cardiovascular diseases, as well as for information on the services the association provides. Share the information with your class.
2. Keep a diary for one week that records the times you feel emotionally tense and the causes of your feelings. Write down the measures you could take to reduce the amount of stress in your life.
3. Find out more about the exercise programs doctors now recommend for heart patients.
(Your local Y may run such programs.) Write a report on your findings.
4. Do some research on the cholesterol controversy. In a written report, state which side you agree with and why.
5. Learn about the kinds of therapies used to help stroke victims regain their speech or the use of their limbs. Write a report on what you have learned.
6. Investigate the role salt plays in high blood pressure. Make a poster that illustrates your findings.

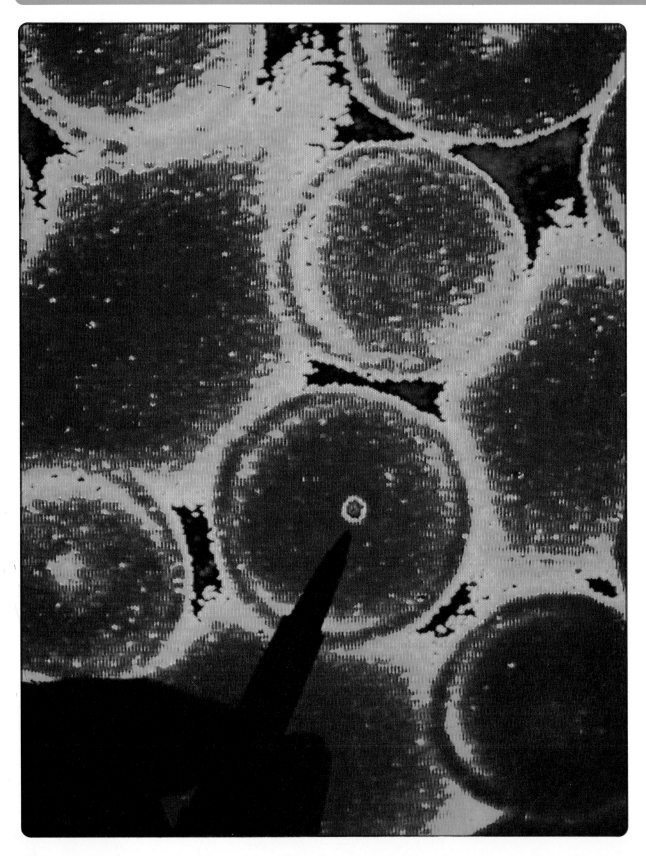

18

Cancer

After reading this chapter, you should be able to answer these questions:

1. What is the relationship between cancer and life style?
2. What are the main causes of cancer?
3. What can you do to reduce your risk of developing cancer?
4. What are the seven warning signals that may indicate cancer?
5. How is cancer treated?

Cancer is probably our most dreaded disease. In 1984 over 20 percent of all deaths in America were caused by cancer, compared with under 6 percent in 1900. As a cause of death, cancer is second only to heart disease, accounting for close to 400,000 deaths a year.

There are three reasons for the increase. First, new medical techniques can diagnose cancers that would not have been detected in the past. Second, the risk of cancer grows with age, and since Americans live longer today, the incidence of cancer has increased. And third, our modern life style brings more people into contact with cancer-causing factors such as cigarettes.

Although there is still much to be learned, our knowledge about cancer has grown steadily in recent years. Improved methods of diagnosis and treatment mean that cancer is no longer the death warrant it once was. Today, about 40 percent of all cancer patients live at least five years after the disease is diagnosed. In the 1950s only 30 percent of cancer patients survived that long.

Yet the cancer picture could be much better. The American Cancer Society estimates that about 50 percent of cancer patients could be saved with existing methods of treatment. The problem is to overcome the ignorance and fear that prevent people from seeking medical help early enough. The importance of early diagnosis and treatment cannot be overemphasized.

Even more important is the fact that some kinds of cancer are preventable. Most lung cancer, for example, is caused by cigarette smoking. And most skin cancer is caused by excessive exposure to the sun. When causes such as these have been established, it is only common sense to use the knowledge and avoid taking known risks.

This chapter explores the known, and suspected, risk factors associated with cancer. It also explains just what cancer is, how it spreads, and how it can be detected and treated. Many types of cancer *can* be cured. It is up to every individual to understand the disease and to join in the fight against it.

SECTION **1** **What Is Cancer?**

The word *cancer* refers to an uncontrolled growth of abnormal cells. Normal cells multiply in an orderly way. One cell becomes 2, 2 cells become 4, and so on. Cancer cells do not have this pattern. When they divide, 1 cell may become 3 or 4, and 4 cells may then become 9 or 10 cells. The cancer cells are also irregular in size and shape. And unlike normal cells, which form body tissues and organs, cancer cells serve no useful function.

The growth of cancer cells can start in any part of the body. Initially, just one or a few cells change. The changed—or *mutant*—cells then begin to multiply. Cancer cells multiply much more quickly than normal cells. If nothing is done to stop their growth, the patient will die.

Tumors

Sometimes a group of cells grows together to form a mass inside the body. This produces a lump or swelling called a *tumor*. A tumor will continue to grow, sometimes quite rapidly, until it is treated. As the tumor increases in size, it crowds nearby healthy cells and robs them of nourishment.

When a tumor is confined to a limited area and the cells do not spread to other areas, it is called a *benign* tumor. Benign tumors are *not* cancers. They generally grow slowly in a capsule that keeps the cells together in one solid clump.

The fact that a tumor is benign does not mean that it is harmless. It can place pressure

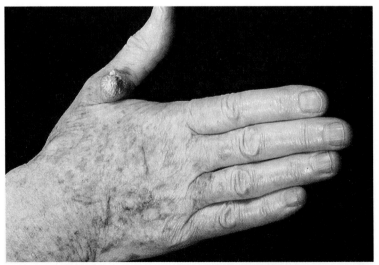

Figure 18.1 Each year about 400,000 Americans contract skin cancer. Of these, most have basal-cell or squamous-cell cancers, which are usually curable. These cancers are removed by freezing or surgery.

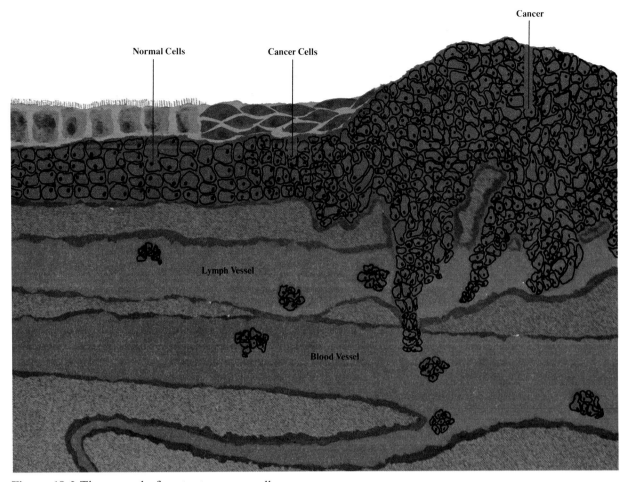

Figure 18.2 The spread of mutant cancer cells.

on surrounding parts of the body and can rob normal tissues of their blood supply. A benign tumor that occurs in a vital organ, such as the brain, can be particularly serious. Benign tumors can usually be removed by surgery, and only in rare cases do they grow back after removal.

Tumors that *are* cancerous are said to be *malignant*. Unlike benign tumors, malignant tumors do not grow within a capsule. Without the enclosing capsule, the tumor quickly branches out and invades and kills nearby healthy tissues. Diseased cells can break away and get into the bloodstream and lymph system. The cells are carried to other parts of the body where they settle and form new tumors. The process can occur over and over again. In this way, the entire body can become riddled with cancer.

The earlier the malignant growth is discovered, the easier and more successful treatment is likely to be. The physician's job is to seek out and destroy *every* harmful cell in the patient's body. If the tumor has not yet begun to spread, surgical removal is often simple and effective. But if the disease has invaded nearby tissues, complete removal is much harder. When the disease is so advanced that secondary tumors have begun to form in other parts of the body, the removal of all cancer from the body becomes exceedingly difficult.

During the first stages of growth, malignant tumors produce very few symptoms and rarely cause any pain. So unless the tumor is near the skin's surface, the patient is often unaware of what is happening. People who notice a lump or swelling sometimes believe it can't be too serious because it doesn't hurt. They postpone seeing their doctor, and this gives the disease a head start.

With many forms of cancer there is a certain period of time between the growth of the first tumor and the spread of the disease. If the tumor is discovered and diagnosed during this period, treatment *can* begin in time to cure the patient. However, it is necessary to do more than wait for symptoms to appear. Screening and regular medical checkups are important weapons in fighting this disease.

The different cure rates for certain forms of cancer show the importance of discovering the disease in its early stages. The cure rate for most forms of skin cancer, for example, is over 90 percent. That's because skin cancers are easily seen and are usually treated early. The cure rate for lung cancer, on the other hand, is less than 10 percent. This disease is *not* noticeable in its early stages. In fact, it often does not produce any symptoms that the patient would notice until it has caused widespread damage.

Types of Cancer

There are more than 100 different forms of cancer. Many of these forms are rare and ac-count for only a small percentage of the cases that occur each year. About 30 forms of the disease are fairly common, and these account for the majority of all cancer cases.

Each type of cancer has a specific medical name. This name tells something about the cancer and the part of the body that is affected. Look at the word *lymphoma*. The first part of the word tells where the disease occurs. Lymphoma is a form of cancer that affects the lymph system. Another form of cancer is called *myeloma*. The prefix *myelo-* refers to the bone marrow. Myeloma is a type of cancer that affects the marrow of the bones.

In medicine, *-oma* is placed at the end of a word to indicate a tumor. Since many cancers involve tumors, this word ending is fairly common. Not all types of cancer involve tumors though. *Leukemia* is a form of the disease that causes the overproduction of white blood cells (leukocytes). The last part of this word, *-emia*, shows that the disease affects the blood.

Unless you choose a career in medicine, you will probably never learn the technical names for most forms of cancer. For most of us, terms such as *lung cancer*, *breast cancer*, and *bone cancer* are accurate enough to be useful. It is important to remember, though, that these are only general terms. There are several forms of bone cancer, just as there are several forms of breast cancer and lung cancer.

Figure 18.3 The body sites where cancer occurs, in men and women. The figures indicate what percentage of all cancers each site represents.

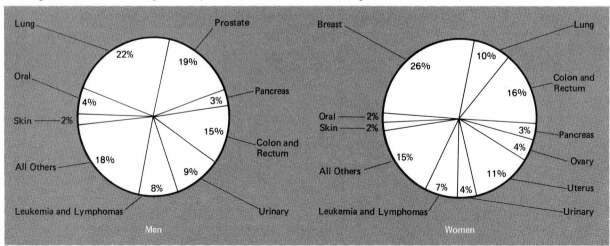

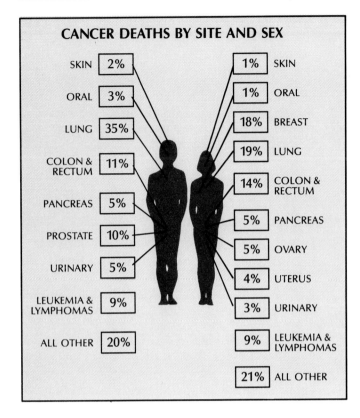

Figure 18.4 Cancer deaths by site in men and women.

Distribution of Cancer

Cancer rates vary from population to population, and forms of the disease that are common in America are not necessarily common elsewhere in the world. Even among Americans, rates vary according to age, gender, and other factors.

Some forms of cancer are obviously gender-related. Only women can get cancers of the ovaries, uterus, and cervix. Only men can get cancer of the prostate, a small gland located at the base of the bladder. Malignant tumors can form in the breast tissues of both men and women. In men such tumors are extremely rare. Women are susceptible to more forms of breast cancer and experience the disease much more frequently than men. Lung cancer is now the leading cause of death from cancer for both men and women.

Until the age of 50, more women than men get cancer. The cancer rates rise dramatically among men over the age of 60. The incidence of most cancers is greater among older people than young people. The young, however, are not immune to the disease. While accidents are the leading cause of death among young people, cancer kills more American children between the ages of 3 and 14 than any other disease. Leukemia and certain cancers of the bones, nerves, and kidneys are the most common forms of the disease among young people.

CHECK YOUR UNDERSTANDING

1. Describe three ways in which cancer cells differ from normal cells.
2. How does a tumor affect nearby healthy cells?
3. What is the main difference between a benign tumor and a malignant tumor?
4. Why do most forms of skin cancer have a very high cure rate? What does this suggest about cancers in general?
5. What are the two leading causes of death among American children aged 3 to 14?

SECTION **2**   **What Causes Cancer?**

Since cancer is actually a group of more than 100 diseases, it probably has no single cause. However, one cancer-causing factor can result in different forms of the disease. Cigarette smoking, for instance, does not only cause lung cancer. It can also lead to cancers of the bladder, larynx, mouth, and other sites.

An individual's environment and heredity are known to affect his or her chances of getting certain cancers. Skin cancer, for example, occurs most frequently among people with light skin who expose themselves to large doses of sunlight.

People of all colors, races, and environments have developed cancer of one form or another. There are some intriguing differences in the patterns of cancer in different populations. Stomach cancer, for instance, is more frequent in Scandinavia and Japan than in the United States. And cancers of the penis and cervix are more common in India.

Are such differences due to genetic factors or to environmental ones? Researchers are still looking for the answers. Their task is a difficult one. Hygienic, dietary, and social practices can be passed from one generation to another, making it almost impossible to tell where genetic factors stop and environmental ones begin.

Heredity

Some families seem to be genetically susceptible to certain forms of cancer. Heredity has been identified as a factor in cancers of the lung, stomach, large intestine, breast, and uterus. People whose immediate relatives have these cancers may be two to four times more likely to develop the same disease than are other people. In fact, one study found that relatives of patients who had suffered breast cancer before the age of 40 were *nine* times more likely to get the disease than people without such relatives.

What should you do if your family history includes a certain form of cancer? You cannot change your heritage. But you can learn what other risk factors are associated with that form of cancer and take steps to eliminate them. People who have a family history of cancer should also find out what tests are available and be sure they have regular checkups.

Diet

Why do cancer patterns vary throughout the world? Many researchers believe that one of the reasons is that eating patterns vary from country to country. The foods you eat, and the way those foods are prepared, may contribute to certain forms of cancer and help to prevent others.

Evidence to support this theory can be found in the cancer patterns of certain immigrant groups. For example, the Japanese tend to have higher rates of stomach cancer and lower rates of breast and colon cancer than the Americans. Yet among Japanese people who have migrated to the United States and who have adopted American eating habits, the cancer pattern is different. When the traditional Japanese diet is exchanged for a traditional

Figure 18.5 Eating a well-balanced diet, with sufficient fiber and low cholesterol, may reduce the risk of cancer.

American one, rates of stomach cancer decline, while cancers of the breast and colon increase.

Studies are being done to discover the relationship between diet and cancer. Early findings suggest that too much fat and cholesterol, and not enough fiber, may contribute to cancers of the colon, prostate, breast, and uterus. Foods rich in vitamin A and vitamin C, such as fruits and certain vegetables, may protect against cancers of the stomach, esophagus, lung, bladder, and larynx. One study estimates that the death rate from all cancers in the United States might be reduced by more than one-third if Americans made permanent changes in their diets. These changes include increasing consumption of fruits and vegetables and reducing consumption of red meat and salt-cured and smoked meats.

Sexual Activity and Childbirth

Some forms of cancer that affect women seem to be related to patterns of sexual activity. Cancer of the cervix is more common in women who have intercourse at an early age than in those who do not. It is also more common in women who have many sexual partners than in those who have few or none. Poor sexual hygiene also increases the likelihood of cervical cancer.

The sexually transmitted disease called herpes simplex Type 2 (genital herpes) is suspected of causing cancer in both men and women. Women with this disease run a higher than normal risk of developing cervical cancer, while men show increased rates of cancer of the prostate. Women who have their first child after age 30 increase their risk of developing breast cancer. The risk for these women—and for women who have never had children—is about three times greater than that for women who have a first child before the age of 18.

Tobacco

Many factors are still only "suspected" of causing cancer. This is not true of tobacco. Scientific studies have proved beyond any doubt that cigarette smoking causes lung cancer as well as a number of other diseases.

Both the tar and the smoke from tobacco contain *carcinogenic*, or cancer-causing, chemicals.

With each puff, the smoker draws the harmful chemicals into her or his lungs. Gradually, over a period of years, the chemicals accumulate inside the body. They collect on the fragile lung tissues and begin to cause significant changes.

Smoking destroys the special cells that keep dust and other harmful particles from entering the air passages of the lungs. Without these cells, the lungs are more susceptible to cancer-causing irritants. Smoking also causes lung cells to become enlarged and misshapen. These cells form thick, irregular layers, and this tissue can become the site of lung cancer.

The outlook for patients with lung cancer is not hopeful. The disease produces no symptoms until it is quite advanced, and diagnosis often comes much too late. Of all patients who develop lung cancer, only 15 to 20 percent are alive five years after the disease is diagnosed. Lung cancer now causes more deaths than any other form of cancer. Among women in the United States, it recently surpassed breast cancer as the leading cause of death from cancer.

Lung cancer is by no means the only form of cancer associated with tobacco use. Cancers of the mouth, larynx, and esophagus are more common among smokers than nonsmokers. Carcinogenic chemicals in cigarettes also contribute to bladder cancer. So-called smokeless tobacco—chewing tobacco—is not a safe substitute for smoking. On the contrary, research has proved conclusively that chewing tobacco is a major cause of oral cancers.

Drugs

Researchers believe that some drugs may contribute to certain forms of cancer. One such drug is *estrogen*. This is a female hormone that is often prescribed during menopause. Women who receive large amounts of estrogen over a long period of time have higher rates of cancer of the uterus than other women. At present, there is no evidence that moderate, short-term use of the drug contributes to any form of

How to...
Decrease Your Risk of Developing Cancer

Scientists believe that 80 percent of all cancers may be related to the environment and to things we eat, drink, and smoke, rather than to factors we can't control, such as our family background. If you change the things you *can* control, there is strong evidence that you can reduce your risk of getting cancer. Here are some of the things you can do:

1. Don't smoke or use tobacco in any form, including cigarettes, pipes, cigars, chewing tobacco, and snuff.
2. Vary your diet to include foods low in fat and low in calories. Include fresh fruits, vegetables, and whole grains in your daily diet.
3. Eat fewer meals that include heavily processed foods that contain suspected carcinogenic additives. Some of these foods are salted and smoked meats, such as hot dogs, bacon, ham, and luncheon meats.
4. If you drink alcohol, do so in moderation. Smokers who also drink increase greatly their risk of cancer.
5. Don't ask for an x-ray if your doctor or dentist does not recommend it. If you do need an x-ray, make sure that x-ray shields are used to protect other parts of your body.
6. Avoid too much sunlight, especially if you have fair skin. Use a good sunscreen and wear protective clothing, even on cloudy days. In particular, avoid exposure to sunlight between 11 A.M. and 2 P.M.
7. Regulatory agencies, industries, and unions have developed health and safety measures to control exposure to hazardous substances in the workplace Learn the health and safety rules of your workplace and follow them.
8. Avoid unnecessary drugs. If you take birth-control pills or hormone pills containing estrogen, a hormone that has been linked with cancer, discuss their use with your physician.

National Cancer Institute, National Institutes of Health Publications No. 85-2059 and No. 85-2711, 1985.

cancer. There is also no evidence that the contraceptive pill, which itself contains a synthetic form of estrogen, increases cancer risk.

Women who are pregnant should be especially cautious of taking drugs. Even prescribed drugs can be harmful to the fetus. During the 1950s and 1960s, doctors prescribed a drug called DES to certain women during pregnancy to prevent possible miscarriages. Many daughters of women who took DES during pregnancy have abnormal cells in the vagina and cervix. Initially, it was feared that the abnormality would develop into cancer. So far, however, the incidence of cancer in DES daughters has been average. Tests done to determine the increased risk of cancer—particularly testicular cancer—among sons of women who took DES have been inconclusive.

Certain drugs that are used during organ transplants have also been associated with cancer. The drugs are given to prevent the body's immune defense system from rejecting the new organ. The results of one study of 6,000 kidney transplant patients showed that they were 35 times more likely than other people to develop lymphatic cancer. The drugs themselves are not believed to contain any cancer-causing agents. Rather, the increased risk of cancer is believed to be associated with the reduction of the body's immunity to disease.

Chemicals

It is well known that a great many chemicals have cancer-causing properties. Certain pesticides and artificial sweeteners, preservatives, or other food additives have all been linked to cancer. What is not yet known, however, is what amounts of such chemicals have to be consumed in order for cancer to develop. Some chemicals may be unsafe in any amount; others may be safe only when they are used in limited quantities.

Much of the evidence that such chemicals cause cancer is based on experimentation done with laboratory animals. Scientists give large doses of a particular chemical to rats or mice. If the animals develop cancer, the scientists can suggest that the same chemical may cause cancer in humans.

Many people have criticized such tests. They point to the fact that it is almost impossible to make accurate comparisons between the human system and the system of a rat or a mouse. Moreover, they say, the quantities of chemicals given to animals are often far in excess of what humans would consume. This may be true. But scientists cannot experiment on human beings, and the animal tests do provide helpful warnings.

Pollution

The pollutants in the air have been linked with a number of diseases, and cancer is one of them. Two pollutants in particular are associated with cancer—benzene and asbestos. Benzene is given off by automobile exhausts. Exposure to high levels of benzene is known to be a cause of leukemia. Asbestos, long used as an insulating material, gives off tiny fibers that float in the air. Lung cancer and cancer of the intestines are associated with exposure to asbestos fibers.

The pollution caused by the dumping of chemical wastes is a matter of growing concern. After a number of years, these chemicals get into water supplies and even into food grown on polluted land. Some chemicals are known to be carcinogenic. Oil, for instance,

contains a group of substances known as PAH. PAH causes cancer in mice, even at low concentrations. Whether it can cause cancer in humans is not yet known.

Occupation

Workers in certain occupations are exposed to high doses of chemicals that are known to increase the risk of certain types of cancer. Carcinogenic chemicals are standard ingredients in many familiar products, including insulating materials, plastics, paints, rubber, and dyes. Generally, it takes a long period of exposure before the cancer develops. Today occupational cancers account for a sizable percentage of cancer deaths in the United States.

Extensive safety measures are being introduced to protect the health of workers in high-risk occupations. The importance of regular medical checkups and the elimination of other risk factors, such as smoking, are also being stressed. This is particularly the case for asbestos workers. Tests have shown that asbestos workers who smoke have significantly higher rates of lung cancer than nonsmokers in the same profession.

Radiation

X-rays can be helpful in all sorts of medical procedures. But they can also cause harm. Radiation from x-rays has been linked with increases in leukemia (cancer of the blood). Cancers of the thyroid, skin, and bone are also associated with excessive exposure to radiation. Besides x-rays, other sources of radiation include nuclear bomb tests, color TVs, and microwave ovens. Scientists disagree about safe levels of radiation. Some insist that even small levels can cause damage to the body.

Radiation comes from natural sources too. The sun gives off harmful ultraviolet rays. Excessive exposure to these rays can cause skin cancer. This is especially true for people with extremely fair skin. These people should wear protective clothing or use sunscreens to block the sun's powerful rays.

Viruses

Viruses have been found to cause several dozen types of cancer in animals. So far, there is no proof that the same is true of humans. But the evidence continues to mount in support of the idea that certain cancers are virus-related. Acute leukemia is just one of the cancers that have been linked with viruses. The association between the herpes simplex Type 2 virus and cancers of the cervix and prostate also supports the theory of virus-related cancer.

Figure 18.6 The typical "cancer personality" seems rigid, authoritarian, and in complete control. But on the inside, he or she suffers from doubt, self-pity, and repressed emotions.

The exact relationship between viruses and cancer is not known. Scientists are trying to discover how viruses transform normal cells into cancer cells. Once they know how this happens, they may be able to develop vaccines to guard against the disease.

Personality

Many scientists believe that a person's emotional make-up may determine whether he or she develops cancer. Just as there is a personality type that is prone to cardiovascular diseases, there seems to be a personality type that runs a higher than normal risk of developing cancer. Typically, the "cancer personality" is a victim of inner conflicts and problems. On the outside, the person may seem rigid, authoritarian, and in complete control. Inside, he or she suffers from doubt, self-pity, and repressed emotions. The cancer personality is unable to establish or maintain meaningful relationships. Depressed and lonely, this person is unable to get rid of tensions.

There are good reasons for suspecting that stress and depression could affect a person's chances of getting cancer. Many doctors believe that a person's mental state affects immunity. In people suffering from stress or depression, the brain may send signals to the immune system that cause it to function less efficiently than normal. Researchers are continuing to study this possibility.

Reducing the Risk of Cancer

Many factors suspected of causing cancer can be controlled, minimized, or even completely eliminated. Avoiding carcinogens whenever possible and following several commonsensible guidelines can reduce your chances of developing cancer. Cancer is not always preventable though, so you should also be prepared to spot early symptoms of the disease and get prompt treatment for them.

Many rules for cancer prevention are nothing more than the ordinary rules of good health. Keeping the mouth, skin, throat, scalp, and genitals clean and well cared for can lower the risk of several types of cancer. Your dentist can give you many reasons why broken teeth should be repaired. One of these reasons is that jagged teeth, scraping constantly against the tongue, can promote the development of tongue cancers.

While the relationship between diet and cancer is still unclear, a moderate and well-balanced diet is good for the health in general. You should not eat too much of any one particular food, and you should avoid excessive amounts of fats and cholesterol. You should also eat sufficient vegetable fiber, and your intake of calories should not exceed your daily needs. This type of nutritious eating is not only a factor in reducing cancer. It will also help you avoid obesity, diseases brought on by malnutrition, and a variety of cardiovascular problems.

In addition to developing good preventive habits, you should learn to avoid some dangers. If you have very fair skin, you should not expose yourself to excessive amounts of sunlight. When you do spend time in the sun, you should take care to use a special sun-blocking lotion. Workers should be aware of any carcinogenic materials found on the job and, where necessary, should follow recommended safety procedures. All individuals should avoid receiving excessive x-rays. If your doctor recommends an x-ray, ask her or him if it is essential. If possible, keep a record of all your x-rays.

The single most effective step you can take to safeguard yourself against lung cancer is to eliminate tobacco from your life. It is estimated that at least 80 percent of lung cancer could be prevented if people did not smoke. Cancers of the mouth, throat, larynx, esophagus, and bladder would also be significantly reduced.

Heavy drinking is also related to cancers of the mouth, throat, larynx, and esophagus. These cancers are sometimes brought on by the combined effects of an "alcoholic life style"—drinking, smoking, and poor nutrition. Cancer is only one of the life-threatening problems associated with alcohol (see Chapter 13). Excessive drinking should be avoided for a number of physical and psychological reasons.

Although we do not yet have the knowledge necessary to prevent all forms of cancer, the incidence of many varieties can be significantly reduced. Knowing what the risk factors are is only part of the story. To reduce cancer rates, we must be willing to act on this information.

CHECK YOUR UNDERSTANDING

1. List five types of cancer that can be inherited.
2. Describe an eating pattern that may lead to certain types of cancer.
3. Name two groups of women who have an increased chance of developing breast cancer.
4. Describe two ways in which smoking causes changes in lung cells that can lead to cancer. List five other forms of cancer associated with the use of tobacco.
5. Why do some people criticize the results of laboratory experiments that conclude that certain drugs and chemicals cause cancer?
6. List five sources of radiation.
7. How might stress contribute to cancer?
8. Describe six ways people can reduce the risk of cancer.

SECTION **3** **Detection and Diagnosis**

You have already studied several factors that help cause cancer. By minimizing or eliminating these factors, you can lower your chances of developing the disease. There is no way to guarantee prevention though. Anyone can get cancer. When the disease does occur, early diagnosis and treatment are essential. Many forms of cancer are curable today, but only if they are detected in time. A delay in treatment could allow the cancer to spread.

What You Can Do

No one knows your body as well as you do. You are aware of changes in your body that no one else, not even a doctor, would notice. Most of these changes are unimportant. However, sometimes a change that seems unimportant can indicate a larger problem.

The American Cancer Society has identified seven warning signals that may indicate cancer. These signals are the following:

1. unusual bleeding or discharge
2. a lump or thickening in the breast or elsewhere
3. a sore that does not heal
4. a change in bowel or bladder habits
5. persistent coughing or hoarseness
6. indigestion or difficulty in swallowing
7. a change in the size or color of a wart or mole

Every individual should know these warning signals and be alert to them. *None of these symptoms automatically means the existence of cancer. Most often they do not.* But they *are* warning signals. If you notice one of the symptoms, and if it does not go away within two weeks, you should see your doctor. Tragically, some people who notice a possible warning sign take no action thinking ''maybe it will go away.'' Such a reaction is foolish. The importance of early detection of cancer cannot be stressed enough.

Besides being aware of cancer's warning signals, you should make it a point to examine your body regularly. Use a mirror to check the inside of your mouth, your scalp, and your skin. Women should learn how to examine their breasts and should do this every month, preferably between menstrual periods (see Figure 18.7). Women usually detect breast cancer before a doctor does. Men should learn how to do a testicular self-examination.

Any irregularities should be reported to your doctor. Chances are good that he or she will tell you there is nothing to worry about. Any of the warning signals can appear for a number of reasons, and cancer is only one of several possibilities. This is not the time for you to play the odds, however. If a form of the disease is present, your prompt action may make the difference between life and death.

What Your Doctor Can Do

Physicians use many procedures to detect different forms of cancer. Some of these procedures should be conducted as part of a regular medical checkup. Other procedures are used only when the physician suspects that cancer is present. Persons who are in high-risk categories should have the appropriate tests conducted regularly.

Breast cancer, the most common form of cancer among women, can be detected in several ways. In a technique called *mammography*, an x-ray picture of the breast is taken. The x-ray can reveal tumors in the breast tissue. However, since this test involves exposing the breast to amounts of radiation, it is not routinely recommended for all women. A newer technique, called *xeroradiography*, requires less radiation and provides a more accurate picture of the breast. A third technique, *thermography*, does not use any radiation at all. This method shows different temperatures throughout the tissues of the breast. Since tumors give off more heat than normal tissues, the doctor can detect cancers in their early stages.

Another diagnostic method, called the *Pap smear*, helps detect cancer of the cervix in women. During a routine examination, the woman's doctor will take a sampling of cells from the cervix and vagina. These cells will be examined for abnormalities which may indicate an early stage of cancer. Over the past few years, this simple test has helped to decrease the number of deaths due to cervical cancer. The American Cancer Society suggests that women who have had a normal test two years in a row should have the test every third year after that. They should have their first Pap test at about age 20. High-risk women and women over 40 should have a Pap test every year.

Both men and women over the age of 45 should have a *proctoscopy* as part of their regular medical checkups. This simple rectal examination is an important aid in detecting cancers of the colon and rectum before they are too advanced to respond to treatment. Cancers of the colon and rectum are the second leading cancer killer in both men and women.

How to Examine Your Breasts

Before a mirror

Inspect your breasts with your arms at your sides. Then raise your arms overhead. Look for any changes in the contour of each breast, a swelling, dimpling of the skin, or changes in the nipples. Nipples should not be inverted unless they have always been so. The left and right breast will not exactly match. Few women's breasts do. Regular inspection will show what is normal for you.

Lying down

To examine the right breast, place a small pillow or folded towel under your right shoulder. Place your right hand behind your head. This distributes breast tissue more evenly on the chest. Keeping the fingers flat, press your left hand gently in small circular motions around the breast. Start at the outermost tip and move all the way around the breast until you reach the top again. A ridge of firm tissue in the lower curve of each breast is normal. Then move in an inch toward the nipple. Keep circling to examine every part of your breast. This requires at least three more circles. When you reach the nipple, squeeze it gently.

Now repeat the procedure on your left breast with a pillow under your left shoulder and your left hand behind your head.

You should make an appointment to see your doctor immediately if you find any lump or thickening in a breast. You should also notify your doctor of any discharge, clear or bloody, from either nipple.

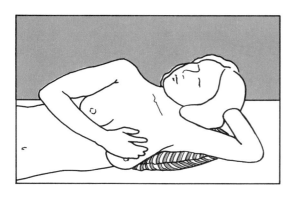

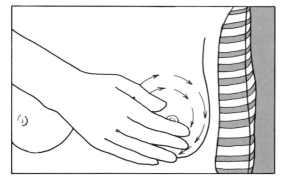

Figure 18.7 Breast self-examination. Women should examine their breasts every month, preferably between menstrual periods.

The normal methods for detecting lung cancer involve x-rays and examination of a specimen of lung tissue. Unfortunately, though, these procedures often detect the disease too late. Doctors of high-risk patients, such as cigarette smokers, may recommend *sputum cytology*. This is designed to pick up early signs of cancer. It calls for regular examinations of sputum coughed up from the patients' lungs.

Methods such as the Pap smear and the sputum cytology alert doctors to abnormal conditions that may be signs of cancer. If a cancer is suspected, a *biopsy* of the tumor will be performed. A small portion of tissue from the affected area is removed by surgery and examined under a microscope. Sometimes surgery is not needed to perform a biopsy. A new technique has been developed whereby cells can be taken from a tumor by means of a needle.

Surgery, one of the methods for curing cancer, can also be used as a preventive measure. Surgeons may remove tissue that is known to have a high potential for developing cancer. Such tissues include warts or moles and abnormalities in the mouth, vagina, and rectum.

CHECK YOUR UNDERSTANDING

1. What are the seven warning signs that may indicate cancer?
2. What parts of your body should you examine regularly?
3. Name some kinds of cancer a physician can test you for during an examination.
4. How often should women have a Pap smear?
5. Describe the procedure used by physicians to obtain tissue from a tumor for examination.
6. How is surgery used to prevent people from getting cancer?

SECTION 4 Types of Treatment

The goal of cancer treatment is to destroy or remove all cancer cells. Time is the key factor. The earlier treatment begins, the greater are the chances for survival. Any delay may allow cancer cells to spread to other parts of the body, making their removal more difficult. Many cancer patients, whether out of fear or ignorance, contribute to their own death. They do not take the steps that allow treatment to begin in time.

There are three forms of treatment for cancer: surgery, radiation, and chemotherapy. Often a combination of these methods is used.

Surgery

The removal of a tumor by surgery can be very successful if the cancer is found early enough. Surgeons try to remove the entire tumor, along with some of the surrounding normal cells. Sometimes they also remove the lymph nodes in the area of the tumor. Whether or not surgery is done depends upon the location and size of the tumor.

Radiation

In radiation treatment, x-rays are directed toward the tumors. The x-rays can penetrate deep into the body and destroy cancer cells. Cancer cells are more sensitive to x-rays than normal cells are.

The problem with radiation treatment has always been to avoid damaging normal cells. Scientists have come up with some solutions to this problem. New techniques have been developed that can locate tumors with great precision. Success has been reported in tests of a new radiation technique known as *pion beam therapy*. This technique enables physicians to focus high-energy particle beams on tumors without damaging surrounding health tissue.

Chemotherapy

Chemotherapy, the treatment of cancer by chemicals, has gained in importance in the past few years. The patient is given certain chemicals, usually by injection.

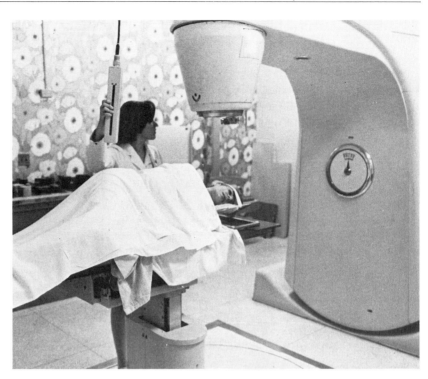

Figure 18.8 Radiation treatment using a linear accelerator. This machine can focus x-rays directly onto a tumor, with minimal damage to surrounding tissue.

There is no one drug that is used against all types of cancer. Rather, a number of different types of drugs are used. Hormones have been helpful in slowing the growth of cancers of the breast and prostate. Other drugs, specially developed to slow down the growth of malignant cells, have been useful against leukemia. A third type of drug has a highly toxic effect on cancer cells. Since this drug can also kill off healthy cells, it must be used with extreme caution.

New types of drugs are being developed and tested constantly. At present, there is no "miracle drug" that is completely effective, and chemotherapy often produces a number of unpleasant side effects. Nevertheless, many researchers feel extremely optimistic about the future role of chemotherapy in cancer treatment.

A cancer patient who survives five years after the disease is diagnosed and treated is usually regarded as "cured." Doctors are often reluctant to use this word, however, and stress that cancer may recur even after five years. All cancer patients should get regular checkups to make sure that the cancer has been completely destroyed or removed.

In some cases, it is not possible to destroy all the malignant cells in a patient's body. But medical treatment can prolong the patient's life. Chemotherapy and radiation can limit the spread of the disease. When cancer is kept from growing and spreading, the disease is said to be in remission. This phase of the disease can last for several years, allowing many patients to live near-normal lives.

Quackery

Although it is possible to cure or control many types of cancer, some victims do not go to physicians who could treat them. They go instead to quacks—frauds who promise miraculous cures. It is estimated that cancer sufferers spend $100 million every year on drugs, diets, devices, and all kinds of bizarre treatments.

One of the best-known quack cancer treatments is *laetrile*. The substance is derived from apricot pits and is often known as "vitamin B_{17}." There is no such vitamin as B_{17}, which ought to make people suspicious from the start. Laetrile costs about two cents per pill to produce, but it sells for $1.25 and more.

Laetrile was illegal in the United States until 1978. In that year the government gave permission for it to be used by cancer patients who were terminally ill. Studies at reputable cancer research institutes have found no evidence at all that laetrile will either cure or control cancer. Nevertheless, thousands of Americans use the drug.

It may seem puzzling that, in this age of modern medicine, people would even consider quack remedies. But people sometimes feel so desperate that they will try anything. Imagine, for example, a patient whose doctor has just told him that he has colon cancer. There is a possibility that some or all of the colon will have to be removed. If the patient hears about a "cure" that does not involve surgery, he may well be tempted to try it—probably with tragic results.

Cancer quacks make money because people are ignorant and afraid. People who fear that they have incurable cancer will grasp at any straw. The greatest tragedy is that victims who might be cured often delay trips to the doctor. They choose, instead, useless drugs and treatment. When the victim finally does seek proper treatment, it might be too late.

New Research

Research into the causes and cures of cancer continues all the time. Some of the most intriguing research concerns viruses and their relationship to human cancer. If cancer-causing viruses can be identified, preventive vaccines may be developed.

Other research focuses on the field of *immunotherapy*. Immunotherapy is concerned with making the body resistant to attack by diseased cells. Scientists hope eventually to find a way of making the body's own disease-fighting system effective against cancer invaders. One substance known as BCG has been successful in building up immunity to cancer in animals. It is now being tested on humans.

A branch of cancer research which has attracted much attention focuses on the use of *interferon*. This substance is produced naturally within the body. It acts as a sort of natural vaccine, enabling the body to resist certain diseases. Whether or not interferon can be used effectively against cancer remains to be seen. Research to date has not yielded especially positive results, but much testing must still be conducted.

Talking Point

Changing Attitudes About Cancer

When President Ronald Reagan underwent surgery for colon cancer in 1985, the nation's newspapers and magazines were filled with articles and drawings about the symptoms, treatment, and survival rates of colon cancer. Years ago, this kind of openness was unthinkable. People were so afraid of cancer that they didn't talk about it. A cancer-stricken President would have tried to keep it a secret to avoid alarming the public.

But in recent years, several well-known figures have spoken about their illnesses publicly, and their courage has helped change people's attitudes about cancer. President Reagan has done for colon cancer what former First Lady Betty Ford did for breast cancer in 1974. Actor John Wayne, who survived lung cancer for many years, did much to educate the public about the link between cigarette smoking and lung cancer.

These public figures have helped millions of Americans understand that they, too, can survive these diseases if they seek early diagnosis and treatment. People have become more aware of symptoms and less reluctant to ask for diagnostic tests. These changes are bound to save many lives.

Chemotherapy, mentioned earlier in this section, offers hope for those who already have cancer. *Chemoprevention* offers hope to those who do not yet have the disease. Chemoprevention is the prevention of disease by the use of drugs. Scientists believe that certain drugs could prevent people from getting some types of cancer. Although no such drugs are as yet available, several types are being tested in laboratories.

Other researchers are looking for improved screening methods. There has been some success in the development of a blood test to detect the presence of cancer in its earliest stages. Work is continuing to perfect such a test. Scientists hope to develop the test so that it can indicate exactly where the cancer is.

It is unlikely that a single permanent cure will ever be found for cancer. Instead, the victory may come in a much less dramatic way. Success in the separate areas of prevention, detection, and treatment may eventually combine to win the battle against this disease.

CHECK YOUR UNDERSTANDING

1. What is the most important factor in treating cancer?
2. What is the aim of cancer treatment? What three methods of treatment are used?
3. When removing a tumor, what else might physicians remove during surgery?
4. What is the biggest problem in treating cancer with radiation?
5. What two effects do the chemicals used in chemotherapy have on cancer?
6. How would the identification of cancer-causing viruses help doctors to treat the disease?

CHAPTER SUMMARY

- Cancer is a condition in which abnormal cells grow in an uncontrolled way.
- A tumor is a lump or swelling formed when a group of cells grows together. Benign tumors are confined to a limited area and are not cancerous. Malignant tumors contain cancerous cells that, if not removed in time, may spread to other parts of the body.
- There are more than 100 different forms of cancer. The incidence rate of different cancers varies from country to country. Rates also vary according to age and gender.
- An individual's heredity and environment affect her or his chances of developing cancer.
- Other factors that affect one's chances of developing cancer include diet, sexual activity, use of tobacco and other drugs, and exposure to chemicals, pollution, and radiation.
- An individual's emotional make-up may contribute to his or her chances of getting cancer. Many scientists believe there is a "cancer personality." That person suffers inner conflicts and repressed emotions. It is also believed that stress and depression can weaken the body's immune system.
- The risks of developing certain types of cancer can be reduced. At least 80 percent of lung cancers could be prevented if people did not smoke. Good hygiene and a well-balanced diet are important preventive measures. Avoiding excessive consumption of alcohol and unnecessary exposure to x-rays and sunshine will also be helpful.
- Every individual should know the warning signals of cancer and be prepared to act on them. The earlier cancer is detected, the greater are the chances of successful treatment.
- The three forms of treatment for cancer are surgery, radiation, and chemotherapy.
- Many cancer victims resort to useless and expensive quack cancer remedies, such as laetrile. By so doing, they delay getting medical care that could prolong, or save, their lives.
- Cancer research continues, and new methods of prevention, detection, and treatment are being tested.

DO YOU REMEMBER?

Give brief definitions of these terms:

mutant	malignant	mammography	biopsy
tumor	leukemia	thermography	chemotherapy
benign	carcinogenic	Pap smear	chemoprevention

THINK AND DISCUSS

1. Why do you think people put off seeing a doctor about a lump or swelling that does not disappear? What special characteristic of the early stage of many cancers makes this attitude especially tragic?
2. Why is it a good idea for a person to find out what caused the deaths of close relatives?
3. Why do you think the American Cancer Society seeks out famous people to appear in its public service advertisements?
4. What is the single most effective step people can take to reduce the risk of cancer? Why do you think so many do NOT take this step, and what might be done about the situation?

5. What measures would you suggest to make as many people as possible aware of the warning signs of cancer?
6. In recent years a number of famous people, including the President of the United States, have been treated for cancer. Many of these cases have received much publicity. Do you think this has had a good effect on the public's attitude toward cancer? What could be the drawbacks of so much media attention?
7. If interferon proves successful, but remains expensive and scarce, only a few of the many cancer victims could be treated with it. Who do you think should be given priority and why?

FOLLOW-UP

1. Call or write to the local chapter of the American Cancer Society to find out the kinds of services it offers to cancer patients and their families. Report your findings to the class.
2. Write a report on the measures used to protect workers in a high-risk industry such as asbestos or paint manufacturing. You can obtain information from newspaper and magazine articles or from someone who works in the industry.
3. Make up a personal profile that includes a description of your heredity and life style.

Then write a description of any changes you should make to reduce cancer risk factors.
4. Find out all you can about the laetrile controversy. Then make up a two-column chart. In one column, list all the arguments in favor of legalizing laetrile. In the other, list the arguments against it.
5. Many YWCAs offer free classes to women who have been operated on for breast cancer. Contact your local Y to find out what these classes offer, and report your findings to your class.

PART 6 Health and Society

Each one of us is responsible for our own health, but we do not function in isolation. We depend upon society to safeguard our health in many ways. Part 6 looks at those aspects of health for which society is largely responsible.

Chapter 19 is concerned with accidents—why they happen and what individuals, and society, can do to prevent them. The chapter also provides some basic information on first aid.

Environmental pollution is the subject of Chapter 20. The chapter discusses the scope of the problem and its effects on health.

Chapter 21 looks in detail at our health care system. We have the best equipment and facilities in the world, yet many Americans do not benefit from them. The chapter looks at various ways of improving the system.

The move toward self-care is the focus of Chapter 22. It explains the advantages and limitations of self-care and provides guidelines for making wise consumer decisions.

CHAPTER 19

Accidents and First Aid

After reading this chapter, you should be able to answer these questions:

1. What are the most common types of accidents?
2. What can you do to protect yourself from injury?
3. Why is drinking and driving a dangerous combination?
4. What is the first rule of first aid?
5. How can you prepare yourself to deal with some common emergencies?

Sharon was anxious to get home, so she accepted Keith's offer of a ride. She knew Keith had had a few beers, but she lived only a few miles away. Sharon never reached home. Keith failed to stop at a red light, and his car was hit from the side. Keith suffered a concussion; Sharon was killed.

Sharon is one of thousands of people who die or are injured on the roads every year as a result of drinking and driving. Keith is also one of tens of thousands to suffer disabling injuries because they don't use their safety belts.

Tough laws have been introduced to punish drunk drivers, and several states have made the use of safety belts compulsory. Laws can only do so much, however. Each one of us can do much more than laws can to prevent needless deaths and injuries.

The term *accident* is misleading. You've probably heard people say, "Accidents will happen" or "I couldn't help it; it was an accident." In fact, every accident is caused by someone or something. Moreover, almost every accident could have been prevented.

Nevertheless, hundreds of thousands of accidents occur every year. According to the National Safety Council, 10 people die from accidents in the United States every hour. An additional 990 people suffer disabling injuries every hour. About half of all accidental deaths occur on the nation's highways. About one-third of the injuries occur in people's homes.

This chapter explores different types of accidents and the reasons for them. You'll learn how you can prevent accidents and about the measures you can take to reduce your risk of serious injury if you are involved in an accident.

The final section of the chapter introduces you to some basic first-aid procedures. Knowing what to do if you are the first person to arrive at the scene of an accident could save a life or prevent unnecessary suffering.

SECTION 1   Accident Patterns

Although accidents may seem to be random events, statistics reveal certain patterns. They show, for example, that some sections of the population are more likely to have accidents than others. They also show how accident patterns change over the years. There are four main categories of accidents: motor vehicle, home, occupational, and public. We shall be looking at each type in turn.

Who Has Accidents?

Men have a much higher accident rate than women. In fact, more than twice as many men as women suffer injury or death from accidents. The difference is even greater among people aged 15 to 34. In that age group, four times as many men are killed in accidents as women.

One reason for this striking difference may be that American society expects men to take more risks than women. In addition, high-risk jobs, such as construction work and lumbering, are traditionally done by men.

In automobile crashes, three out of every four casualties are male. This may be because there are more male drivers and because men tend to drive greater distances than women. Male drivers are involved in five times more alcohol-related accidents than women are.

There is also a difference in accident rates between residents of towns and cities and residents of rural areas. People who live in rural areas have a 20 percent higher accident death rate than town and city dwellers. This may be

because rural residents tend to take part in more high-risk activities. They are also less likely to follow safety procedures or use protective devices.

Rural residents who have accidents are also less likely than city residents to get immediate medical attention. The nearest doctor or hos-

Figure 19.1 People who live in rural areas have a 20 percent higher accident death rate than town and city dwellers. This may be because rural residents take part in more high-risk activities.

pital may be many miles away. Moreover, rural hospitals cannot usually provide the specialized equipment and personnel that city hospitals can offer. Because of these differences, people injured in accidents in rural areas are almost four times as likely to die as those injured in urban areas.

Motor Vehicle Accidents

The automobile made its appearance nearly a century ago. Since then some 2 million people have died in motor vehicle accidents in the United States alone. Today, the motor vehicle is the number one cause of accidental death for all people under the age of 75. And for young people between the ages of 15 and 24, it is the leading cause of all deaths.

Among young people, fatalities are particularly high for overturning, running off the road, or colliding with fixed objects such as trees or telephone poles. In other words, young drivers have many accidents that do not involve a second vehicle. This is probably because they lack driving experience and tend to misjudge dangerous situations. Young drivers are also more likely to speed than older drivers are.

At least half of all fatal automobile crashes involve drivers who have been drinking alcohol. In an effort to reduce the number of alcohol-related accidents, many states have raised the legal drinking age to 21.

The most common injuries sustained in automobile crashes are injuries to the head and spine. Almost all cars are equipped with safety belts that are designed to protect passengers against such injuries in the event of a crash. It is estimated, however, that only about 20 percent of Americans regularly use their safety belts.

Home Accidents

If people do start driving less, they probably will start staying home more. And if they're home and off the road, they're safe, right? Wrong. Home is not always the refuge from harm it is thought to be. Take the case of John Glenn, the first American to orbit the earth.

Figure 19.2 Accidents in and around the home are the cause of one out of every five accidental deaths.

Glenn circled the planet and returned to earth without a mishap. Yet several years later he slipped and fell in his own home and suffered a serious head injury.

One of every five accidental deaths results from accidents in and around the home. The majority of the victims die from falls and fires. Others die from drowning, suffocation, poisoning, firearms, and electrical hazards. Altogether, some 20,000 people die in home accidents every year.

Children under 5 and adults over 65 are those most likely to die in home accidents. The very young die mainly of burns or suffocation. For older people, the main problem is falls.

In addition to the deaths, there are many injuries. In fact, home accidents cause more disabling injuries than any of the other types of accidents. Each year more than 2 million people are disabled by injuries suffered in the home.

Occupational Accidents

In this category, at least, the news is encouraging. Over the past 70 years, the number of deaths that occur in the workplace has gone down significantly. In 1912 about 20,000 workers lost their lives. In 1984, with more than twice as many people at work, there were 11,500 deaths. Most deaths are a result of automobile crashes, falls, burns, or accidents involving machinery. Occupational deaths account for about 12.5 percent of all accidental deaths.

Public Accidents

This last category includes accidents that happen in public places or on public transportation. Most accidents that occur in sports and recreation activities are public accidents, as are bicycle accidents.

Figure 19.3 Accidental deaths in the United States, 1984.

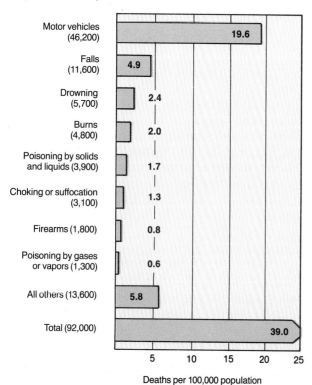

Cause of accident
(Number of deaths)

Cause (deaths)	Deaths per 100,000
Motor vehicles (46,200)	19.6
Falls (11,600)	4.9
Drowning (5,700)	2.4
Burns (4,800)	2.0
Poisoning by solids and liquids (3,900)	1.7
Choking or suffocation (3,100)	1.3
Firearms (1,800)	0.8
Poisoning by gases or vapors (1,300)	0.6
All others (13,600)	5.8
Total (92,000)	39.0

5   10   15   20   25

Deaths per 100,000 population

Figure 19.4 Accidents involving sports or recreational activities usually occur in public places. These and other public accidents account for 3 million injuries each year.

Each year some 20,000 people die in public accidents, and almost 3 million are injured. Almost half of the deaths in public accidents are from falls and drownings. Other major causes of death are fires and firearms.

CHECK YOUR UNDERSTANDING

1. Why is the accident rate for men higher than that for women?
2. What is the leading cause of death for young people? What types of automobile accidents are particularly prevalent among young people?
3. Which two groups of people are most likely to die in home accidents? What are the main causes of death for each group?
4. In what category of accidents has the death rate declined?
5. Name four major causes of death in public accidents.

SECTION **2**   # Why Do Accidents Happen?

Accidents rarely have one single cause. They usually result from hazards in the environment or unsafe behavior or a combination of the two. Consider this mishap:

A car driven by Jim Clarke zipped around a corner on a rainy evening. Jim was driving a bit faster than the speed limit. And his wipers were leaving greasy streaks on the windshield, so his visibility was reduced. As he rounded the corner, Jim didn't notice Mrs. Trumbull backing her car out of the driveway until it was too late. Mrs. Trumbull saw Jim but didn't react fast enough. Jim braked but lost control, and his car skidded on the slippery road. The two vehicles collided.

This accident had a number of causes. Both people contributed to the accident through unsafe behavior—Jim was driving too fast, and Mrs. Trumbull reacted too slowly. The rain-soaked road was a contributing factor. So was the oily windshield. Thus, a number of factors combined to cause the accident. We shall now consider some accident-causing factors in detail.

Unsafe Behavior

People cause accidents by *unsafe thinking* and *unsafe action*. Unsafe thinking involves misjudging hazards and underestimating risks. Sometimes people also think they are better able to cope than they really are.

Unsafe action includes using the wrong tools for a particular job. It also includes ignoring safety devices such as seat belts or helmets. In addition, people act in an unsafe way when they operate equipment or take part in an activity without the proper knowledge or experience.

As mentioned earlier, certain groups of people are more likely to have accidents than others. The factors that make some people more accident prone may be physiological, psychological, cultural, or a combination of these.

Physiological Factors

A person's general physical state plays an important role in accident causation. Someone who is very tired, for example, will be less alert than normal, and his or her reaction times will be slower.

It is not true, however, that people with physical handicaps or poor coordination have more accidents than those who are in good physical shape. In fact, the reverse may be

Figure 19.5 Accidents occur when people misjudge hazards and underestimate risks. Young people, especially, tend to think they are better able to cope than they really are.

true. People with known physical handicaps are aware of their limitations. They tend, therefore, to be more careful than those who have no physical problems.

Drugs can have a marked effect on a person's abilities to perform certain tasks. Even common cold remedies and antihistamines can be extremely dangerous. They can make people feel drowsy and therefore more likely to have accidents when operating machinery or driving. Other psychoactive drugs such as opiates, tranquilizers, and amphetamines also increase the risk of accidents.

By far the most dangerous of drugs, in terms of accident statistics, is alcohol. People under the influence of alcohol are a danger to themselves and to other people. Alcohol contributes to at least half of all automobile deaths and to a high percentage of on-the-job accidents.

Psychological Factors

Researchers have found that an individual's personality contributes to her or his likelihood of having accidents. They have identified a number of psychological traits that are shared by accident repeaters.

One of these traits is bad judgment. Accident repeaters do not get enough information before taking part in a risky activity. Their expectations may be faulty, and they tend to make decisions on impulse.

Another psychological trait found in accident repeaters is overconfidence. They tend to be less alert than other people because they are confident that they can cope. They also tend to overlook safety precautions.

Experts say that these character traits are common among people under 24. This may be why under-24-year-olds figure so highly in accident statistics.

Cultural Factors

Cultural factors include a person's home background and the habits and customs of the people with whom he or she mixes. These factors play a role in accident causation, partly because of their influence on personality. For example, many accident repeaters come from homes where there is a great deal of stress.

Certain cultural trends also play an important role. Ingroup fads bring about new activities which may be hazardous. The hero image of the "hot rodder" is one such example. Another example is the emphasis on drugs and alcohol in American society today.

Dangerous Objects

Most accidents involve the use by one or more individuals of a potentially dangerous object. The object may be an automobile, sports gear, or one of hundreds of other items. Any tool or material that people use can be dangerous if used in the wrong way. Among the objects that contribute to many accidents are the following.

Motor Vehicles All engine-powered vehicles, including minibikes, motocycles, and automobiles, represent possible hazards. When they are not taken care of properly and have bald tires, poorly adjusted lights, or worn brakes, motor vehicles become even more hazardous. In fact, the automobile is the biggest single source of death and injury in the United States.

The automobile itself does not cause accidents, of course. Most accidents are caused by either improper driving or improper vehicle maintenance. The automobile is dangerous only because drivers and owners make it that way.

Automobiles become particularly dangerous when handled by drivers who have been drinking alcohol. The main cause of highway crashes resulting in deaths is drivers who have been drinking. A drunk driver is 15 to 25 times more likely to be involved in a crash than a nondrinking driver. Alcohol affects a driver's judgment and overall sense of responsibility. It also increases the driver's willingness to take risks.

National data on motor vehicle crashes show that teenagers—especially males—run a high risk of being involved in fatal automobile crashes and also that many teenage drivers in fatal crashes have been drinking. Teenage drivers are more likely to have accidents than older drivers because of their combined inexperience with both drinking and driving.

Figure 19.6 People who use power tools often increase their risk of injury by neglecting to follow recommended safety procedures.

Household Objects Objects in and around the home offer many possibilities for accidents. Routine pieces of equipment such as knives, toasters, fans, and food blenders are all dangerous if used incorrectly. Lawn mowers, hedge trimmers, snow blowers, and other machinery are other sources of danger. If such equipment is left lying around, children may be tempted to operate it. And many adults fail to follow recommended safety procedures.

Falls, the main type of home accident, often result from slippery floors, slippery baths and showers, and poor lighting. Thus, an item as simple as floor polish can cause an accident.

Another household item that is potentially hazardous is the plastic bag. A young child could put it over her or his head and suffocate. Flammable liquids, such as some cleaning fluids, are also present in many homes. And many homes contain poisonous products. Even a bottle of aspirin, in the hands of a child, can be a killer. In addition, many pesticides and gardening products are highly toxic.

Workplace Hazards Any tool or piece of machinery used in the workplace can be an accident-causing agent. Hammers, saws, and drills can all injure or kill if used incorrectly. Most companies have strict safety standards for anyone using potentially hazardous equipment. Accidents usually happen when safety precautions are neglected.

Other hazards in the workplace are less obvious. Heat and noise, for instance, can lead to accidents. They can produce stress that, in turn, can cause people to be less alert.

CHECK YOUR UNDERSTANDING

1. Describe three ways in which unsafe action contributes to accidents.
2. Explain how drugs contribute to accidents.
3. Name three personality traits that are often found in accident repeaters.
4. Give three examples of automobile defects that cause accidents. What is the main cause of highway accidents?
5. List 10 objects found in or around the home that are potentially hazardous.

SECTION **3**   **Preventing Accidents**

By now it should be clear that accidents are not just random events over which people have no control. A great many accidents can be prevented. And even when they cannot be stopped, the results can be made less harmful by the use of safety devices such as seat belts or life jackets.

Accident prevention can be achieved in a number of ways. First, people need to be better educated about safety. They need to understand the risks involved in a particular activity and to know how to minimize those risks. Second, greater use of safety devices needs to be encouraged. And third, the design of certain accident-causing objects can be improved.

Let's look at the four main types of accidents again, and consider how accidents in each area can be prevented.

Reducing Auto Accidents

If you look at the causes of accidents, many of the ways to prevent them become clear instantly. For instance, half of all auto fatalities involve drivers who have been drinking. So it is obvious that there would be far fewer accidents if people did not drive when they had been drinking. The importance of the message "If you drink, don't drive" cannot be overemphasized. Far too many people ignore that warning.

Safety belts, too, have been widely ignored. Even though statistics have proved, beyond a doubt, that safety belts save lives and prevent injury, only about 20 percent of Americans use them regularly. It is expected that the use of safety belts will increase as more and more states make them mandatory. Still, only about 50 percent of drivers in New York State, the first state to introduce a safety belt law, actually obey the law.

Greater use of safety seats for children would also save lives and prevent injury. More than 3,000 infants and children die in automobile crashes every year, and more than 125,000 are injured. The number of such deaths and injuries could be reduced by well over half if children were secured in the correct kind of safety seat for their age.

Improvements in vehicle design have already helped prevent many crashes, as well as reducing injuries when crashes happen. Headrests and padded surfaces, for instance, protect passengers in a crash. Further improvements, including the installation of air bags, can be expected. Air bags would prevent occupants from hitting the dashboard in a head-on collision.

Preventing Home Accidents

The number of home accidents would be greatly reduced if every family took a few simple precautions.

Falls are the number one cause of home accidents, so a home safety program might begin with ways to minimize falls. Stairways should be kept free of clutter at all times. They should

Figure 19.7 Causes of residential fires, by percent.

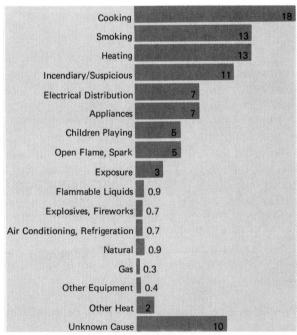

Cooking	18
Smoking	13
Heating	13
Incendiary/Suspicious	11
Electrical Distribution	7
Appliances	7
Children Playing	5
Open Flame, Spark	5
Exposure	3
Flammable Liquids	0.9
Explosives, Fireworks	0.7
Air Conditioning, Refrigeration	0.7
Natural	0.9
Gas	0.3
Other Equipment	0.4
Other Heat	2
Unknown Cause	10

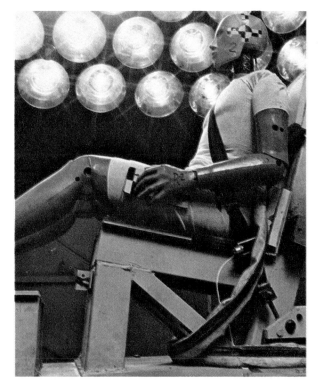

Figure 19.8 Automobile manufacturers, in response to public demand, have been working to improve the safety of their vehicles. Here, specially constructed dummies are being exposed to the conditions of typical automobile accidents. Analyzing the "injuries" that the dummies sustain will help manufacturers make lifesaving changes in future car designs.

also be equipped with adequate lighting and firm handrails. Nonskid throw rugs and nonskid floor wax also offer protection against falls.

Another major cause of home accidents is fire. Homes should be checked for fire hazards such as faulty wiring or piles of oily rags. Gasoline, kerosene, and other flammable products should be stored properly.

About 13 percent of household fires are a result of cigarettes. People who smoke should make sure they extinguish cigarettes completely. And they should never smoke in bed. Many people have died because they fell asleep while smoking and set fire to their own beds.

The installation of smoke detectors and fire alarm systems will help people escape once a fire has started. Fire extinguishers for home use can also be installed. In addition to minimizing fire hazards, every family should practice a fire safety plan. One such plan, known as EDITH (Exit Drills in the Home), is shown on page 364.

EDITH

Don't wait for smoke and fire to surprise you. Plan your home fire escape now. If you live in an apartment, ask the management to schedule drills. Practice during Fire Prevention Week and once or twice more during the year. If you move, make a new plan right away!

Discuss and Plan Ahead

- Sit down with your family today and make step-by-step plans for emergency fire escape.
- Diagram two routes to the outside from all rooms, but especially from bedrooms. Locate the enclosed exit stairs in an apartment building.
- Put the fire department number on your phone.
- Choose a place outdoors for everyone to meet for roll call, locate the call box or neighbor's telephone for calling the fire department.
- Discuss why you shouldn't go back inside once you're out. (People have died returning to a burning building.)

You May Need to Make a Purchase

- Buy a smoke detector for each level of your home. If the bedrooms are not all in the same area, you need a smoke detector outside each sleeping area, too.
- Each person should have a whistle (for warning others) to keep by the bed. Some family members may need a special escape ladder.

Practice

- Start now sleeping with the door closed, unless you have a good system of smoke detectors. The door holds back smoke and fire while you escape.

- Practice testing the door for fire. If it's warm, you'll have to use your alternative escape route. If not, brace your shoulder against the door and open it cautiously. Be ready to slam it if smoke or heat rushes in.
- Make sure children can operate the windows, descend a ladder, or lower themselves to the ground. (Slide out on the stomach, feet first. Hang on with both hands. Bend the knees while landing.) Lower children to the ground before you exit from the window. They may panic and not follow if you go first.
- Practice what to do if you become trapped. Since doors hold back smoke and fire fighters are adept at rescue, your chances of survival are excellent if you do the right thing. Put closed doors between you and smoke. Stuff the cracks and cover vents to keep smoke out. If there's a phone, call in your exact location to the fire department even if they are on the scene. Tell children not to hide. Wait at the window and signal with a sheet or flashlight.
- Practice crawling as if there were smoke.
- Have children practice saying the fire department number, the family name, street address, and town into the phone.

Figure 23.9 EDITH (Exit Drills in the Home) is a plan to save your life in case of fire.

In households with very young children, special precautions are needed. Adults should ask themselves, "What in this room could be harmful to a toddler?" An uncovered electrical outlet, for example, which is normally harmless, can be dangerous if a child sticks a finger or toy in it.

In the Kitchen The most dangerous item in most kitchens is the stove. Pots and pans should never be left on the stove with their handles sticking out. Someone could walk by and knock the pan off. Or a small child could reach up and grab the handle.

Cleaning supplies should also be kept out of the reach of young children, and electrical appliances should be unplugged when not in use. All members of the household should be taught the proper use of kitchen tools and appliances.

There should be a solidly built step stool in the kitchen for reaching high objects. Falls often occur because people perch on the edge of a chair or counter trying to get something from the top shelf.

In the Bathroom Shocks and falls are major problems in this room. Shocks occur when electrical appliances come into contact with water. Electric shavers and hairdryers should *never* be set on the edge of the sink or tub.

Falls are particularly dangerous because of the hard surface of sinks and bathtubs. Nonslip mats or strips should be used in bathtubs and showers. There should be a grab bar by the tub in any household with an older person.

All drugs and medicines should be kept out of reach of children or locked away. Old medicines should be thrown away.

In the Yard Here neatness counts. Many people have been injured by tripping over garden tools or toys left lying about. Power tools such as lawn mowers should be used according to the manufacturer's instructions. They should never be left unattended when children are present. Barbecues should be used with caution. Never, ever, pour lighter fluid on lighted charcoal.

Preventing Accidents at Work

Safety programs sponsored by employers and unions have helped reduce on-the-job accidents dramatically. Under the terms of the 1970 Occupational Safety and Health Act (OSHA), all employers must meet minimum safety and health standards. Employers who fail to meet these standards can be fined. They must keep records of all work-related injuries and deaths.

When an accident occurs, there is usually an investigation. Safety engineers can identify its causes and the machinery that was involved. They can then take steps to prevent a similar accident.

OSHA inspectors make inspections of factories, construction sites, and other workplaces. They make sure that employers and workers are following safety procedures.

Preventing Public Accidents

The prevention of public accidents requires a threefold approach. First, the public needs to be educated to understand and follow safety procedures. Second, public facilities should be made as safe as possible. And third, safety regulations must be strongly enforced.

A great many public accidents happen because people are unaware of, or ignore, safety rules. Water sports such as swimming, boating, canoeing, and water skiing, for instance, share some basic safety rules. Such rules include swimming only when a lifeguard is present or else employing the buddy system. Wearing a life jacket during boating is also a must.

Before you take part in any sporting or recreational activity, you should learn the safety rules. If you take up bicycling, for instance, you should learn the traffic laws, as well as how to minimize dangers specific to the sport. For example, there is a danger that drivers may not be able to see you at night. You can reduce the risk by having reflectors on your bicycle and by wearing light-colored clothing (the same applies to runners and joggers). Special reflector vests and sashes will make you even more visible.

Another way of preventing accidents is by using protective equipment. Sports stores now stock a wide range of protective gear, including helmets, padded gloves, kneepads, and, of course, life jackets. Such equipment is well worth its cost.

Inspecting and maintaining gymnasiums and play areas can also cut down on accidents.

Figure 19.10 Wearing a life jacket is an essential precaution for anyone who ventures out in a boat, raft, or canoe.

How to...
Avoid Drowning

This year about 6,000 people will drown. Half the victims will be from 15 to 24 years old. You can avoid becoming a statistic by learning the following skills and safety measures.

1. Learn how to swim with some degree of skill.
2. Never swim alone. If there isn't a lifeguard, take along a capable friend.
3. Don't swim or dive in unknown waters.
4. Don't try to swim underwater without coming up for air. You could lose consciousness.
5. Know your endurance, and stop swimming before you get too tired.
6. Don't swim on a full stomach or when you feel tired, cold, or overheated.
7. If you get a cramp while swimming, keep calm and keep kicking. Eventually, the cramp will ease.
8. If you get caught in a strong current, don't try to swim against it. Instead, swim in a diagonal line across the current.
9. Observe basic safety rules in backyard pools. Almost half of all pool drownings take place in home pools.
10. Don't swim out to save someone who is drowning unless you are a trained lifesaver. If you are not, throw the victim a rope or an object that will float.
11. Learn the proper procedures for handling a boat. Don't overcrowd it. Always wear a life jacket, and make sure everyone else wears one.
12. If a boat capsizes, cling to it until help arrives.
13. Don't ice-skate alone. Never build a fire on ice or skate on thin ice or on saltwater ice.
14. Never swim or go boating when under the influence of alcohol or drugs. Thousands drown each year while they are intoxicated or high on drugs.

Gymnasium floors, for example, can be specially treated to cut down the danger of slipping.

Most serious playground accidents involve falls from horizontal bars and jungle gyms. So the surface under such equipment is particularly important. Asphalt and concrete, the traditional surfaces, are too hard. A new type of rubber cushioning that decreases injuries is now being installed in some places.

Much more could be done to make play and recreational areas safer. But in the long run, the surest way of preventing accidents lies in public education. Safe behavior comes from learning to recognize potential danger, to judge the risks, and to make wise decisions.

CHECK YOUR UNDERSTANDING

1. Name three measures that would reduce automobile accidents.
2. What precautions should be taken to reduce the risk of fire in the home? What can people do to reduce the risk of injury or death if there is a fire in their home?
3. How can shocks and falls in the bathroom be prevented?
4. Describe the threefold approach to preventing public accidents.
5. How can gymnasiums and playgrounds be made safer?

SECTION **4** **First Aid—Some General Rules**

Every accident or emergency is different. However, there are some general rules for any situation in which first aid is needed before skilled medical personnel can treat a victim.

Keep Calm

The first rule is to stay calm. If the sight of blood or someone in pain makes you feel shaky, take a deep breath. Or sit down for a moment to collect yourself. Try to speak in a normal tone of voice. If the victim is conscious, talk to him or her quietly. Reassure the victim that everything necessary is being done.

Get Help

In any serious injury or accident, send or call for medical help immediately. First aid is not a replacement for skilled medical attention. It is a holding action until the victim can get that medical help.

The person who knows the most first aid should stay with the victim, while someone else goes or calls for medical assistance. If you are alone, however, don't leave the victim in order to find help unless it is absolutely necessary.

For medical help, call a hospital emergency room, rescue service, police department, ambulance service, or doctor. As a last resort, dial 0 and tell the operator the problem and your exact location.

If the victim is conscious and able to talk, ask what happened while you are waiting for medical help. Ask witnesses for details. Such information may be needed later by doctors who treat the injured person. If poison or drugs are involved, keep a sample for the doctor to analyze.

Do Not Move the Victim

In general, a badly injured person should not be moved until medical help arrives. The wrong movement can make fractures or other injuries worse. Make the victim as comfortable as possible, and keep her or him warm with a blanket or coat.

There are times, however, when you must move injured persons to get them out of a

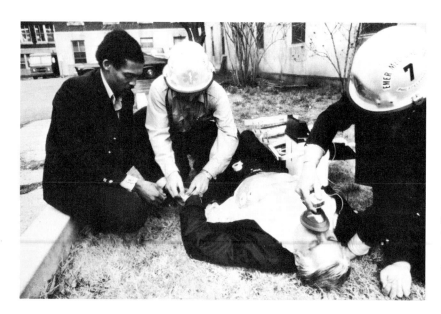

Figure 19.11 Calling for skilled medical help, such as an ambulance or rescue service, is the best way to ensure that a victim will get the treatment he or she needs.

dangerous place. Or you may have to move victims to get them to a hospital. General rules for moving injured people are the following:

- Keep the injured part of the body as still as possible. Before moving a person with broken bones, protect the broken place by making a splint.
- *Never* move anyone who might have a broken neck or back. Wait for an ambulance or trained rescue personnel.
- If you have to drive a badly injured or unconscious person to a hospital, try to use a vehicle in which the victim can ride lying down.

Give First Aid

If you are confused about what to do in an emergency, it is probably best to do nothing. Just send for help and keep the victim warm. The wrong action could cause great harm.

If you do know first aid, size up the situation and find out exactly what the problem is. When making your assessment, follow these two rules:

- If more than one person is injured, treat the person with the worst injuries first.
- When a person has several injuries, treat the most urgent or life-threatening problem first.

Instant action is needed if a victim—

- is not breathing;
- has no pulse;
- is bleeding heavily;
- has swallowed poison or an overdose of drugs;
- has been badly burned.

Check for Breathing and Pulse Find out immediately if the victim is breathing. If there is no breath, begin rescue breathing (described in Section 5 of this chapter) immediately. Speed is essential.

If the patient is not breathing, check to see if there is a pulse. The best place to check is on the neck, on either side of the windpipe. (Find the place right now on your own neck.) If there is no pulse, the heart has stopped. A technique called CPR (also described in Section 5) might save the person's life.

Look for Serious Bleeding Light bleeding is not dangerous, but the loss of large amounts of blood can cause death very quickly. Immediate first aid is called for.

Expect Shock and Act to Prevent It Expect any victim of an accident to go into shock. In shock, the person's blood circulation slows. Not enough oxygen reaches the brain. Have the victim lie down, and keep him or her warm. Do nothing that will alarm the victim.

Specific first-aid measures for bleeding, heart failure, shock, and other common emergencies are described in the next section of this chapter.

Be Prepared

Many accidents and emergencies occur at home and on the highways. Be prepared for such events by keeping a stock of first-aid supplies in your home and in the family car.

What should be kept in a home first-aid supply depends partly on the age and health of the people in the family. But in general, a basic list would include the following:

- sterile gauze pads and compresses
- sealed rolls of bandages
- adhesive-strip bandages in different sizes
- adhesive tape
- antiseptic
- syrup of ipecac (for poisoning)
- scissors
- large triangular bandages
- safety pins

People involved in car accidents often suffer large wounds. So a car kit might include larger sterile gauze pads, plus several large triangular bandages, rolls of bandages, as well as antiseptic ointment, scissors, safety pins, and adhesive tape.

Take a Course

The importance of getting training and practice in first aid cannot be overemphasized. The

American National Red Cross offers free first-aid courses in most communities. In these courses students learn the basics of first aid. They also practice applying bandages, making splints, giving mouth-to-mouth rescue breathing, and other first-aid skills.

First-aid classes are given in many high schools. They are also offered through Ys, churches, synagogues, and other community organizations. To learn where you can take a first-aid course, call the nearest chapter of the American National Red Cross or ask the school health office for information.

CHECK YOUR UNDERSTANDING

1. Name five sources of medical help that could be called in the event of an accident.
2. Why shouldn't a badly injured person be moved? If an accident victim must be moved, what precautions should be taken?
3. What five accident situations require instant first aid?
4. What preparations can people make for dealing with accidents?

SECTION **5**   **Some Common Emergencies**

Accidents and emergencies can happen any place, anytime. Would you know what to do if your hiking companion fell and broke a leg? Or if your little brother swallowed some poison? Or if you were first on the scene of an automobile accident? This section provides first-aid guidelines for some of the specific emergencies you are most likely to encounter. It should be seen as a guide only. Reading about first aid is no substitute for training and practice. You'll be far more effective in an emergency if you have taken a recognized course in first aid.

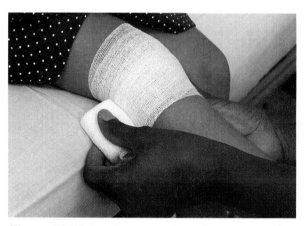

Figure 19.12 A minor wound, such as a scraped knee, should be cleaned and then covered with a sterile dressing.

Bleeding

Minor bleeding helps flush dirt out of a wound. It is not usually serious. The wound should be washed carefully, then covered with a clean dressing.

Heavy bleeding *is* serious. It is possible for a person who is bleeding heavily to die in a few minutes. Swift action is essential.

Apply Sterile Dressings To stop bleeding, press a sterile gauze pad over the wound. Use the palm of one or both hands to press down firmly. If blood soaks through one pad, add another on top of the first. Don't change the dressing. Just add another. If no sterile bandage is available, use the cleanest material available, for example, a ripped-up sheet or a handkerchief.

Press firmly with your palm until the bleeding stops. If the wound is on an unbroken arm or leg, use your other hand to raise the arm or leg. Elevating the limb slows the flow of blood. Direct pressure should not be applied if there is glass in the wound or if there is any possibility of a broken bone.

Pressure Points   If direct pressure and elevation don't stop the bleeding, or if you cannot use direct pressure, try to find the *pressure point* between the wound and the heart. The main pressure points on the human body are shown in Figure 19.13. At these places, arteries are close enough to the skin surface for hand pressure to slow the flow of blood. The four main pressure points are in the groin of each leg and on the upper inside arms between the shoulder and elbow.

Figure 19.13 The main pressure points on the human body.

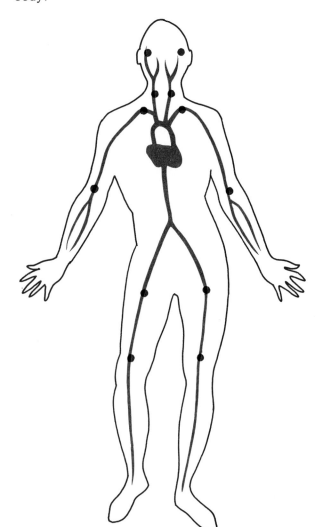

Tourniquets   A *tourniquet* is a band wrapped tightly around an arm or leg above the wound. The tight wrapping stops the flow of blood. A tourniquet should be used only as a last resort in very serious cases such as when an arm or foot has been severed. The use of a tourniquet raises the risk of *gangrene,* or tissue death.

To make a tourniquet, use a strip of cloth, a bandage, a necktie, or other material long enough to tie around the limb above the wound. Whenever a tourniquet is used, the victim must be rushed to a hospital because of the possibility of tissue damage.

Shock

After an accident or injury the body often goes into *shock.* In shock the body does not circulate blood properly, and not enough oxygen reaches the brain.

Shock is not the same as fainting. A person can be conscious, but in shock. A person in shock may feel weak, look pale, and have a forehead clammy with sweat. Other signs of shock are a rapid and irregular pulse, shallow breathing, and extreme thirst.

First Aid for Shock   Have the victim lie down, with the feet and legs propped up higher than the head. You can put a pillow or folded blanket under the knees to raise the feet. This position allows more blood to reach the brain.

Loosen tight clothing, particularly neckties, collars, and belts. Talk calmly to the person. Cover the victim with a blanket or coat to keep her or him warm. If the individual is conscious, offer a drink of water or other nonalcoholic liquid. Many people panic when they see their own injuries, so try to prevent the victim from seeing a wound.

Fractures or Broken Bones

A *fracture* is a break in a bone. There are two basic kinds of fractures, *closed fractures* and *open fractures.* In a closed fracture, the bone is broken but there is no visible wound in the skin. In an open fracture, the broken bone or bones may show through a flesh wound. Even if the bones do not show, there may be a wound at the site of the fracture.

Recognizing Fractures Signs of a broken bone include the following:

● The victim cannot move the injured part.
● The victim feels pain when trying to move the injured part.
● There is no feeling when the injured limb is touched.
● Swelling occurs or the skin looks blue around the injury.
● The affected part of the body looks misshaped.

If you are not sure whether an injury is a fracture, treat it as if it were one.

First Aid for Fractures If there is heavy bleeding, find the appropriate pressure point. Don't apply any antiseptics to the wound. Cover the wound with bandages, being careful not to jar the broken bone.

If the bone seems broken in several places or shattered, don't move the victim unless it is absolutely necessary. Keep the victim warm and treat him or her for shock.

Splints If the victim must be moved to get medical help, first make a *splint* to support the injured part. A splint will hold the injured arm, leg, hand, or foot firmly in place and prevent further injury from jarring.

Use any thick, sturdy material such as a piece of wood or cardboard or a thick magazine. It should be longer than the part of the body being placed in the splint. Wrap the splint with clean fabric or bandages to pad it. Tie the injured limb to the cushioned splint, using bandages, long strips of cloth, or a necktie. Do not try to straighten out the broken bones.

The splint should be tight enough to keep the injured limb from moving. But it should not be so tight that it shuts off the flow of blood to and from the wound. If swelling occurs, you may have to loosen the splint.

Sprains, Strains, and Dislocations

A *sprain* is the tearing or bruising of a ligament or muscle. Sprains are usually tender to the touch. There is rapid swelling around the area. Place ice bags or cold packs on the injury immediately to reduce swelling, and raise the injured part higher than the rest of the body.

A *strain* happens when a muscle or tendon is stretched or pulled too far. The victim feels a sharp pain at the time. Later the strained place feels stiff and painful when the victim moves it. Treatment consists of rest. The application of heat from a hot-water bottle or heating pad reduces pain.

A *dislocation* is the displacement of a bone from its normal position. A bump or sharp jolt, such as happens during a football tackle, can push a bone out of its joint. The joint swells and looks misshaped. Don't try to pull the bone back into place yourself. Let a doctor do it. First aid for dislocations includes the use of ice bags or cold packs to keep swelling down. Make a splint or a sling to hold a dislocation in place until a doctor can attend to it.

If you're in any doubt as to whether an injury is a fracture, a sprain, a strain, or a dislocation, treat it as if it were a fracture.

Burns

First aid for burns depends on how badly the victim has been burned. Burns are classified as first-, second-, or third-degree, depending on their severity. A *first-degree,* or minor, burn reddens the skin but does not blister it. A *second-degree* burn causes the skin to be red and blistered. A *third-degree* burn damages all layers of the skin and causes it to look charred or white.

Minor Burns Treat first-degree burns and small second-degree burns by pouring cold water over the affected area. You may then apply an antiseptic medication. Never apply grease or butter to a burn. Place a sterile gauze dressing over the burn.

Figure 19.14 Treat minor burns (such as those incurred while cooking) by running cold water over the affected area. Never apply grease or butter to a burn.

Major Burns Large second-degree burns and third-degree burns require urgent medical attention. Wrap the victim in a clean sheet and get medical help immediately. The sheet shuts off the flow of air and reduces the pain and possibility of infection.

If you cannot get the victim to a hospital, or if help cannot arrive quickly, you may offer some first aid. Treat the major burn like an open wound. Wash your hands with strong soap before you touch a burn victim. The danger of infection to burned skin is extremely high.

Very gently place sterile gauze bandages over the burned places. Don't use any salves or other substances. Don't press the gauze into place. If any charred cloth or other material sticks to the wound, leave it alone. You may cause further damage if you try to remove it. Now wrap the victim in a clean sheet and wait for medical help.

A burn victim generally goes into shock. Offer a drink of water and, if it is not too painful, have the person lie down.

Chemical Burns Strong acids and certain chemicals can cause serious burns to the skin. If a chemical splashes on someone, move fast. Don't take time to remove the clothing on which the chemical has spilled. Drench the victim with lukewarm water. If possible, rush the person into a shower, clothes and all. After the clothes are drenched, and with the shower still running, remove the clothes. Then treat the injury like any other burn and get the person to a doctor.

Convulsions

Convulsions are strong movements of the muscles and body over which the individual has no control. They may be caused by a variety of injuries or illnesses such as head injuries, high fever, or epilepsy. During a convulsion, the person loses consciousness. Sometimes the body goes rigid. Sometimes it shakes violently. Muscles tense and move involuntarily. Sometimes the person froths at the mouth.

It is important to find the cause of the convulsion. If fever has caused the convulsions, as it often does in very young children, first aid consists of bringing down the body temperature. This is done by sponging the body with cool water or with a mixture of rubbing alcohol and water. Whenever a child convulses from high fever or any other cause, contact a doctor immediately.

Do not try to hold or restrain a person who is having convulsions. Protect her or him from injury by clearing away any sharp or dangerous objects from the area. There may be quiet spots between convulsions. At these times the victim may regain consciousness. Check during a quiet time to see that the person's breathing passage is clear.

Epileptic Seizures   Some 2 million Americans—or almost 1 out of every 100—suffer from epilepsy. The name *epilepsy* covers several disorders of the nervous system. The word comes from a Greek word that means "seizures." The seizures result from an occasional imbalance in the brain's electrical activity.

In a seizure, the body goes still, then falls in whatever direction the person was leaning. Muscles of the arms, legs, and neck begin to convulse. The attack can last from 1 to 5 minutes, though some are as long as 20 minutes.

Clear the area around the victim. If possible, turn the victim on his or her side to assure free breathing. Loosen neckties or tight clothing. If the victim goes from one seizure to another without regaining consciousness, call a doctor. Look in the victim's wallet for an identification card or information on how to respond to an attack. Some epileptics wear identifying tags or bracelets.

Poisoning

Many of the substances that are used daily, such as bleach and some cleaning liquids, are highly poisonous if swallowed. Small children may decide to sample these liquids if they are not locked away.

In the event of poisoning, find out immediately what the poison was. Once you have identified it, read the label on the container. There should be directions on the label for first aid if the substance is swallowed. Follow the directions exactly.

Many cities have Poison Control Centers. To find the nearest Poison Control Center, look in the telephone book. Describe the poison and the symptoms, and you will be told what to do. If you cannot find a number quickly for Poison Control, dial the emergency room of a hospital, the police, or a doctor's office. Speed is essential. Don't waste too much time hunting for a telephone number.

Make the Victim Vomit   In most poisonings, first aid consists of diluting the poison in the stomach and then making the victim vomit up as much of the poison as possible. This should be done *only* if the victim is conscious. Give the victim plenty of warm milk or water. Then press your finger or a spoon on the back of the person's tongue to cause vomiting.

If that doesn't work, give an *emetic*, a substance that causes vomiting. Syrup of ipecac is an emetic that is available in drugstores without a prescription. Or you can mix your own emetic solution. To one glass of warm water, add either two teaspoons of salt or one teaspoon of dry mustard. Have the victim drink three to five glasses of the solution.

Force vomiting anytime someone has swallowed an overdose of medicine or drugs, including aspirin and sleeping pills.

When Not to Force Vomiting   Some substances are so harmful to human tissue that a person who swallows them must not vomit. Never induce vomiting if someone has swallowed a *corrosive*, or burning, substance. Such substances include strong acids, lye, gasoline, kerosene, ammonia, bleach, and lighter fluid. These substances eat away at the stomach and throat lining. If you force vomiting, additional damage can be done to the esophagus, throat, and mouth.

Get medical help immediately for anyone who has swallowed one of these corrosive poisons. In the meantime, give the victim something that will help coat the stomach lining. Milk, raw eggs, mashed potatoes, cornstarch, or milk of magnesia may be used.

If the person loses consciousness, don't force anything down her or his throat. Get help. Keep the victim lying face down, with the head lower than the body. This position helps keep the air passages clear.

Electric Shocks

Be sure the current is off before touching the victim of an electric shock. Otherwise, you could receive a shock yourself. If you need to move a victim to break the contact, use extreme care. Never touch the victim directly. Stand on a dry piece of wood or dry newspapers. Use a long, dry stick or other nonmetal tool to push the person off the source of electric current. Don't touch the person until he or she is no longer in contact with live current.

If the victim is not breathing, begin rescue breathing immediately. Check for a pulse. Get medical help.

Choking

If you're with someone who starts to choke, try to calm the person, and encourage her or him to cough up the object. If possible, look in the person's throat. You may be able to see the object. Young children sometimes swallow remarkable things such as safety pins, erasers, or bottle caps. If you can see the object clearly, and are quite sure you can grasp it with your fingers, reach into the side of the mouth with two fingers. Move your fingers from one side of the mouth across the throat to the other as you grasp the object. Take great care not to push it down further.

To remove something from the throat of a baby or very young child, turn the whole body upside down by holding the baby by the ankles. Slap gently but firmly between the shoulders.

If the victim is an adult, have him or her kneel across a stool or lean over a chair, head down. Slap firmly on the back. The strong taps may dislodge the object.

If these actions fail to dislodge the object and the victim cannot breathe, begin mouth-to-mouth rescue breathing and send for help. You may be able to force enough air past the throat blockage to keep the person breathing until medical help arrives.

The Heimlich Maneuver The *Heimlich maneuver* is a technique for forcing objects out of the windpipe. It should be used only in very serious choking emergencies, when the victim cannot get air, and only after a hard blow to the back has failed to dislodge the object.

To begin the Heimlich maneuver, stand behind the victim. Make a fist with one hand. Place the fist, thumb against the victim's abdomen, between the naval and the breastbone. Grasp the fist firmly in your other hand. Now press the fist into the victim's abdomen with a quick, upward thrust. Repeat the maneuver

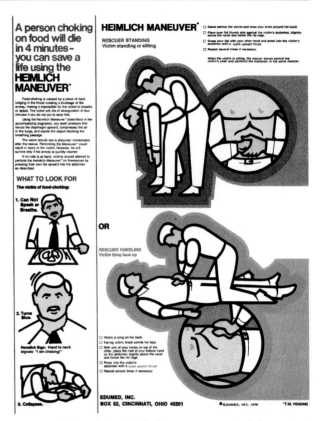

Figure 19.15 The Heimlich maneuver, which should be used only in very serious choking emergencies, is an effective technique for forcing objects out of the windpipe.

until the object is forced out or until the victim becomes unconscious.

If the person loses consciousness, begin rescue breathing. Also try rolling the person on the side and giving four quick blows to the upper back. Then continue the rescue breathing. You may be able to force enough air past the stuck object to keep the victim alive until medical help arrives. Do not attempt to practice the Heimlich maneuver on people, since it can cause broken bones.

Rescue Breathing

When someone stops breathing, every minute counts. Without a constant supply of oxygen, the brain can be permanently damaged within four minutes. Within six minutes the victim will almost certainly die. Rescue breathing can be used in many types of emergencies in which the lungs have stopped working. These include suffocation, choking, and drowning.

Even without special training, you can give mouth-to-mouth *rescue breathing*. The technique has several names, including *artificial respiration* and *mouth-to-mouth resuscitation*. You will not do any harm by attempting this procedure, and you may save a life.

Clear the Airway To begin rescue breathing, put one hand behind the victim's neck. Tip the head back as far as you can. This position allows the most air to flow through the air passage. Look inside the throat to see if anything is blocking the airway. If you see an obstruction, use two fingers to wipe out the mouth from one side to the other. Take care not to push anything further down the throat.

Start with Four Quick Breaths With one hand still under the victim's neck, place the palm of the other hand on the forehead. Use the finger and thumb of the second hand to pinch the victim's nostrils closed.

Take a deep breath. Open your mouth wide. Seal it over the victim's mouth and give four quick, full breaths. Do these four first breaths as quickly and strongly as you can. Pause between each breath just long enough to get another breath yourself. These four fast breaths should expand the victim's lungs fully.

Watch the victim's chest to make sure the lungs have expanded. If you do not see signs of lungs expanding, recheck the air passage. It may be clogged. Turn the victim on the side, and thump her or him on the back to dislodge the obstruction.

Maintain a Steady Breathing Pace After the first four quick breaths, keep up a steady pace of rescue breathing. For an adult, blow air into the lungs once every five seconds, or 12 to 15 breaths per minute. Even if the victim does not seem to respond, keep up the steady rescue breathing until medical help arrives.

Rescue Breathing for Babies A slightly different technique should be used if the victim is a baby. Instead of pinching the nostrils and

blowing into the mouth, the rescuer should place his or her mouth over the baby's mouth and nostrils and blow into both. The rate of breathing should be faster than for an adult, about 1 breath every three seconds, or 20 per minute. It should also be lighter, since forceful breathing could burst a baby's lungs.

CPR

CPR—cardiopulmonary resuscitation—is an emergency lifesaving procedure for use when both heart and lungs have stopped. CPR combines rescue breathing with chest compression,

Figure 19.16 Using a specially designed manikin, a young man is instructed in the technique of CPR. Although this procedure has saved many lives, it can cause injury if attempted by an untrained person.

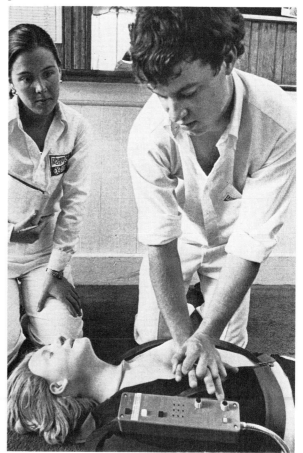

which forces the heart to pump blood. People trained in this technique have saved many lives.

Chest compression must be done *only* by someone who has received CPR training. An untrained person may crack ribs or injure kidneys or lungs. In a CPR course, students work with special manikins to learn chest compression. The Red Cross warns that chest compression must *not* be practiced on humans.

The American National Red Cross and the American Heart Association both offer CPR courses, which take from four to nine hours, in many communities. Contact these groups for more information about this valuable lifesaving technique.

CHECK YOUR UNDERSTANDING

1. Describe the procedure for stopping heavy bleeding. Why should a tourniquet be used only as a last resort?
2. List five conditions that may indicate a broken bone. Describe the procedure for making a splint.
3. What is the first-aid treatment for a victim of a major burn?
4. Under what circumstances should a poisoning victim *not* be made to vomit?
5. What is the Heimlich maneuver? Under what circumstances should it be used?

CHAPTER SUMMARY

- Men have a higher accident rate than women. People who live in rural areas are more likely to die in accidents than town and city dwellers.
- The four major categories of accidents are motor vehicle, home, occupational, and public.
- Accidents usually result from environmental hazards or unsafe behavior or a combination of the two.
- Individuals cause accidents by unsafe thinking and unsafe action. Certain groups of people are more likely to have accidents than others because of physiological, psychological, and cultural factors.
- Most accidents involve the use by one or more individuals of a potentially dangerous object, such as an automobile, a household appliance, or a piece of machinery. Almost any tool, equipment, or material can be dangerous if used in the wrong way.
- Half of all automobile accidents involve drivers who have been drinking. The importance of the message "If you drink, don't drive" cannot be overemphasized. Automobile accident fatalities and injuries would also be reduced by wider use of seat belts and proper education of beginning drivers.
- Safety precautions in the home should include keeping stairways free of clutter, using nonslip

mats and nonskid floor polish, checking for faulty wiring, and keeping dangerous objects out of the reach of children.
- The prevention of public accidents requires public education, safe facilities, and strong enforcement of safety regulations.
- The first two rules of first aid are to stay calm and get help.
- Instant action is needed if a victim is not breathing, has no pulse, is bleeding heavily, has swallowed poison, or has been badly burned.
- People should be prepared for accidents by keeping a stock of first-aid supplies in the home and car and by taking a recognized course in first aid.
- Among the common emergencies for which first aid is most likely to be needed are bleeding, shock, fractures, sprains, strains, dislocations, burns, convulsions, poisoning, electric shocks, and choking.
- Mouth-to-mouth rescue breathing should be used immediately if someone stops breathing. The technique can be applied without special training.
- CPR combines rescue breathing with chest compression. Chest compression must be done *only* by someone who has received CPR training.

DO YOU REMEMBER?

Give brief definitions of these terms:

pressure point	shock	sprain	convulsion
tourniquet	fracture	strain	epilepsy
gangrene	splint	dislocation	emetic

THINK AND DISCUSS

1. Why do you think that American society expects men to take more risks than women? In what ways is this attitude changing?
2. Should the wearing of seat belts be made compulsory? Why or why not? What could insurance companies do to encourage people to wear seat belts?
3. Do you think that people convicted of driving while drunk should lose their licenses permanently? Why or why not?
4. Do you think that licensed drivers should be required to take a driving test every few years? Why or why not?
5. What measures could be taken in your school to reduce the risk of accidents?
6. What features would you install in a standard bathroom to make it safer?
7. What ways can you think of to encourage people to follow the correct safety procedures for specific sports?

FOLLOW-UP

1. Find out about the different first-aid and lifesaving courses that are available in your community. Post the information in your classroom.
2. Visit a local sporting goods store and compile a list of the different kinds of protective equipment that are offered. Post the list in your classroom.
3. Clip all reports of accidents from your local newspaper for a week. Then make a chart showing how many accidents happened in each of the four major categories.
4. Contact your local first-aid squad and find out what types of accidents are most common in your community. Report your findings to your class.
5. Contact or visit a local factory or office building to find out what measures are taken to protect workers from accidents. Write a report on your findings.
6. Find out what new safety features have been introduced into automobile designs over the past 10 years. Make a poster that illustrates these features.
7. Check your home and garage for substances that are labeled poisonous. Make two lists, one showing the corrosive substances and the other the noncorrosive substances. Post the lists in your home and make sure all family members are aware of them.

20

Health in the Environment

After reading this chapter, you should be able to answer these questions:

1. What are the major causes of air pollution?
2. How can we keep our rivers and lakes clean?
3. Why does garbage disposal need to be controlled?
4. What can you do to protect yourself from excessive noise?
5. What can you do to help fight environmental pollution?

A number of years ago there was a popular song called "Don't Drink the Water, Don't Breathe the Air." It made people laugh.

They're not laughing anymore. There are places in the United States—in fact, throughout the world—where drinking the water and breathing the air have become hazardous to people's health.

Air and water, along with land, make up our environment. Without these natural resources, life would not be possible. Yet we are polluting the very things that keep us alive.

For years nobody gave much thought to pollution. We were concerned with progress. We invented machines to make our lives easier. We developed fertilizers and pesticides to help us produce more food. We built giant factories to make the goods we wanted. The automobile became part of the American way of life.

Certainly, our lives have been improved in many ways. But it is now becoming clear that all this progress has a cost. In our efforts to improve living conditions, we have created, or made worse, a variety of health problems. Environmental pollution is one of them.

What exactly is pollution? In simple terms, it is the presence of harmful substances in the environment. Some of these substances occur naturally. Volcanic dust, pollens, and animal wastes are examples of natural pollutants. Most pollution, however, is caused by people.

And the main culprits are automobiles and industry.

The effects of pollution are numerous. Besides harming plant and animal life, pollutants can enter our bodies and damage our health in a variety of ways. Even noise is now recognized as a pollutant. Exposure to too much noise can cause health problems.

Industrial nations such as ours have only recently awakened to the seriousness of the problem. The fight against pollution is still young; there is still much to be done. In this chapter we'll look at some of the main pollutants, their causes, and their effects on humans and nature. You'll see how you are involved in the problem and how you can be involved in the solution.

SECTION **1** **Air Pollution**

How can airplane passengers tell when they are approaching a city? Very often it's by the huge cloud of "smoke" that hangs over it. The movement of the air in our atmosphere cannot always disperse the tons of pollutants emitted by closely packed homes, factories, and cars. So pollutants hover around our cities causing great discomfort and threatening the health, and sometimes the lives, of the people who live in them.

What causes air pollution? Most of it comes from the burning of *fossil fuels*. Coal, petroleum, and natural gas are called fossil fuels because they are formed from the remains of plants and animals that lived millions of years ago. When fossil fuels are burned, certain substances are released into the atmosphere.

Every person in the United States uses over 10 tons of fossil fuel annually. We use fossil fuels to heat our homes, stores, and offices. Fossil fuels are used to make the steam needed to generate electricity and to power our cars, trucks, trains, and planes. Some fossil fuels end up as plastics and other petrochemical products and as tar and asphalt.

With only about 6 percent of the world's population, the United States uses about one-third of the world's production of fuels. Every bit of fuel that we burn adds to the pollution of our air, and not just in our cities. Harmful substances are also found in the air over the most rural areas of America.

No one knows yet what, or just how serious, the effects will be from continuous, long-term exposure to low levels of air pollutants. Events in the past have shown dramatically, though,

what happens when people are exposed to air that is unusually dense with pollutants. More than 4,000 people died as a result of London's "killer smog" in 1952. Fortunately, such acute air pollution episodes have occurred rarely.

Those who are most likely to be affected by air pollution are the very young, the very old, and those with chronic breathing problems. But all of us may be in danger. Experts fear

Figure 20.1 The United States uses one-third of the world's production of fossil fuels. Every bit of fuel that we use adds to the pollution of our air.

Figure 20.2 Volcanic dust—such as that given off by the eruption of Mount St. Helens in 1980—is an example of natural air pollution. Most pollution, however, is caused by people.

that anyone who constantly breathes polluted air may face serious health problems.

There are two major types of air pollutants—those that come mostly from stationary sources and those that come mostly from mobile sources. Power plants, which burn fuel to generate electricity, and manufacturing plants are the main stationary sources of air pollution. Cars and other vehicles that burn gasoline are the major mobile sources of air pollution. In fact, cars emit more than half of the pollutants that contaminate the air we breathe.

Pollutants from Stationary Sources

The most visible form of air pollution produced by stationary sources is *particulate matter*. These tiny particles of dust, ash, and other substances result from various types of burning and industrial processes. Particulates irritate the eyes, throat, and lungs, and they may contribute to disease.

Other pollutants are *sulfur oxides,* which are produced by the burning of coal and fuel oil in factories and power plants. These sharp-smelling, colorless gases are extremely irritating to the eyes, throat, and lungs. Sulfur oxides cause people who inhale them to cough and choke. They can also trigger attacks of bronchitis, emphysema, and asthma in chronic sufferers. Studies suggest that they may actually cause these diseases as well.

In recent years, a two-pronged attack has greatly reduced the levels of sulfur oxides in the air. Many places now forbid the burning of high-sulfur fuels. And many factories now use special chemicals to combat pollution. These chemicals remove the sulfur oxides from smoke before it is released into the air.

Most European cities banned the burning of soft coal some years ago. They wanted to put an end to smog, a deadly form of air pollution. Despite its name, smog is much more than a mixture of smoke and fog. It is a dangerous brew of pollutants that has taken many lives over the years.

The London variety of smog—*sulfur dioxide smog*—plagued European cities for centuries. These cities relied on soft coal, which gives off sulfur dioxide, for their heating. When the sulfur dioxide combines with foggy air and particulates, a dense smog can result.

When sulfur dioxide smog is breathed in, it can paralyze the hairlike structures that keep breathing passages clear. Smog particles can remain in the body, inflaming sensitive tissues. Breathing then becomes painful for everyone. But for people with chronic respiratory problems, breathing may become so difficult that they die. The strain of breathing smog can also make heart problems worse. Now that most cities have stopped using soft coal, London-type smogs happen only rarely.

Pollutants from Mobile Sources

Most Americans rely heavily on cars, buses, and trucks to satisfy their transportation needs. When gasoline is burned in internal combustion engines, *carbon monoxide,* which is a colorless, odorless, tasteless gas, is produced.

Carbon monoxide can affect breathing, hearing, vision, and thought. It acts by depriving the blood of oxygen. Lack of sufficient oxygen to the brain can lead to permanent brain dam-

age. If people are exposed to a very high level of carbon monoxide, they will lose consciousness and die.

High levels of carbon monoxide exist where there is heavy traffic, in both open and enclosed places. No one should spend more time than absolutely necessary at busy intersections or in garages and tunnels. Nor should people sit for long periods in a parked car with the engine running. When a car is not moving, there is a danger that carbon monoxide will seep into the passenger compartment. People who repair cars should never keep the engine running while the garage door is closed.

Automobile exhausts also contain *hydrocarbons*. Hydrocarbons are a large group of chemical compounds containing the elements carbon and hydrogen. Some hydrocarbons are linked with various types of cancer. The hydrocarbon benzene, for example, is known to be a cause of leukemia.

Besides resulting from the combustion of gasoline, benzene evaporates into the air every time a car is filled up at a gas pump. Some industrial processes also release benzene into the air, posing a special risk to workers in plants that use or produce this hydrocarbon. The government has now placed limits on the amount of benzene workers can be exposed to on the job. Some experts fear, though, that these levels are still too high.

Other air pollutants contained in automobile exhausts are *nitrogen oxides*. When these gases react with hydrocarbons in the presence of sunlight, *photochemical smog* is formed. This is the kind of smog for which Los Angeles is famous.

Los Angeles lies in a valley where the air circulation is poor and where the skies are sunny and the humidity low. Occasionally, a layer of cool, ocean air slips in under the normally warm air above the city, creating a *temperature inversion*. Motor vehicle emissions rise through the cool air, but cannot penetrate the warm layer, which acts like a lid on the Los Angeles basin. The action of sunlight on the trapped pollutants produces additional pollutants. One of them is *ozone*, which causes irritation of the eyes and nose. Ozone is also thought to cause pulmonary fibrosis, which forms scar tissue in the lungs.

Talking Point

The Bhopal Disaster

On the night of December 3, 1984, 25 tons of a highly toxic pesticide spewed out of a Union Carbide plant over the sleeping residents of Bhopal, India. The chemical killed more than 25,000 people and injured another 100,000.

Could such a nightmare happen again? Could it happen in the United States? Many people used to think that such an accident could not possibly happen here because most companies have elaborate safety regulations. Yet, despite safety controls, small-scale industrial accidents, such as explosions, derailments, and tanker truck spills, happen several times a week, all over the country.

The Bhopal disaster has been particularly worrying to Americans living near a Union Carbide plant in West Virginia. The plant produces the same pesticide as that produced in India. To ensure that a similar accident would not happen in West Virginia, Union Carbide spent more than $5 million on additional safety measures. Despite the company's precautions, there was a chemical leak from the West Virginia plant just nine months after the accident in Bhopal. Several people were injured.

The chemical industry as a whole responded to the Bhopal disaster by expanding its safety programs. It improved training procedures and introduced new hotlines to provide information on hazardous chemicals. It also organized a system to ensure that all chemical plants practice emergency procedures with local police and fire departments.

Pollution from Spray Cans

When it is near the ground, ozone is a harmful pollutant. Miles above the earth's surface, however, the ozone layer surrounding the planet screens out harmful ultraviolet rays from the sun and prevents them from reaching the earth. A reduction in the ozone layer could, therefore, lead to more cases of skin cancer, which is caused by overexposure to ultraviolet rays.

When scientists revealed that the *fluorocarbon* gases used to force the contents out of spray cans destroyed ozone, Americans reacted strongly. Within a year, sales of products in aerosol spray cans had dropped by 25 percent. The government now bans the use of fluorocarbon gases in spray cans.

Chemical Air Pollution

In addition to the pollutants already mentioned, a number of other chemical substances find their way into our atmosphere in a variety of ways. Among these are asbestos and lead.

Asbestos A naturally occurring mineral, asbestos is used to form fibers that are fireproof and practically indestructible. Products that contain asbestos fibers include cement pipes, shingles, floor tiles, and insulating materials. But working with asbestos is hazardous. People who inhale asbestos dust can get *asbestosis*, a sometimes fatal lung disease. Studies have also shown a higher than normal incidence of lung cancer and cancer of the intestines among asbestos workers, particularly those who smoke cigarettes.

Recently, some authorities have become concerned about the danger of relatively small amounts of asbestos fibers to the health of the general public. One London study found that one-third of patients who died of an asbestos-related cancer had no known history of direct exposure to asbestos dust. Asbestos fibers are commonly present in the lungs of people in cities, who breathe the fibers in with the air. Most of our homes and cars contain some asbestos in insulation, water pipes, and brake linings.

Figure 20.3 Acid ran has damaged these trees on Mount Mitchell in North Carolina.

Authorities and consumers are moving to reduce the use of asbestos. The spraying of asbestos fireproofing materials on new buildings has now been banned in many cities. The use of asbestos soundproofing materials in schools and other public buildings has also been prohibited. These and other such measures, combined with strict regulation of asbestos dust in the workplace, help to reduce the most obvious hazards.

Lead　Another naturally occurring material, lead has always been in the environment in low concentrations. Since the introduction of the automobile, however, the lead content of the air has greatly increased. That is because lead is used as an additive in most gasolines. It is also commonly used in paints, ceramics, glassware, pipes, and many other products, so it has many ways of finding its way into our atmosphere.

If too much lead enters the body, *lead poisoning* will occur. The effects of lead poisoning are weakness, loss of appetite, anemia, and damage to the nervous system.

The effects of long-term exposure to low concentrations of lead are not known, however. Studies indicate slight brain damage in city children who have been exposed to lead in the air. The increased use of unleaded gasoline should reduce the amount of lead in the atmosphere.

Acid Rain

Concern has been growing about another form of pollution known as *acid rain*. Scientists have discovered that sulfur and nitrogen oxides form acid particles as they travel through the air. When it rains, these particles are carried down to earth in the rain water. In some cases, rain water has been as acid as a weak solution of vinegar.

Acid rain could affect us in a number of ways. It could make lakes too acid to support fish life. This has already happened to hundreds of lakes in North America and Scandinavia. Acid rain could also lead to a reduction of crop yields. The acid would damage the crops themselves and would also affect the mineral content of the soil. Forests would be affected in a similar way. Finally, acid rain also damages buildings, monuments, and statues.

Cleaning Up the Air

In some cases we have improved the atmosphere by stopping or controlling the use of damaging substances. Fluorocarbons are no longer used in spray cans. The use of asbestos is now carefully controlled. The burning of soft coal is prohibited in most of our cities.

But we can't simply stop using all the substances that cause air pollution. Most of our energy comes from the burning of fossil fuels. Experts predict that, for the next 50 years at least, we will continue to use huge quantities of these fuels to keep our society going. There are techniques of cleaning up the pollution caused by burning fossil fuels, but they are very expensive.

Power plants can put devices on their smokestacks to remove particulate matter from the smoke. But when they do this, the cost of electricity goes up. Factories can install special equipment to remove most of the sulfur oxides from their exhaust gases. But the cost of doing this will be passed on to the consumer who will pay higher prices for the goods produced.

Automobile manufacturers now build *catalytic converters* into the exhaust systems of the cars they make. These devices convert harmful pollutants into harmless substances. Catalytic converters are an effective way of reducing pollution from automobile exhausts, but they are expensive. The consumer who buys a new car must pay the cost.

There are ways of cleaning up our air, but it will cost tens of billions of dollars to do it. It will take informed and concerned citizens to decide how much should be done and how to go about it in the most efficient way.

CHECK YOUR UNDERSTANDING

1. What are the two main stationary sources of air pollution? What is the main mobile source of air pollution?
2. Describe the effects of breathing sulfur oxides and sulfur dioxide smog.
3. How does carbon monoxide create its effects? Describe two dangerous practices that can lead to carbon monoxide poisoning.
4. What is a temperature inversion?
5. List some of the sources of asbestos and lead pollution. How do asbestos and lead affect the body?
6. Describe the cause and effects of acid rain.

SECTION **2** **Water Pollution**

Every day we Americans send billions of gallons of dirty water down the drain. This water contains food wastes, human wastes, detergents, and other substances. All the waste products that we send through our drains and pipes are classed together under the term *sewage*.

Throughout history, people have dumped sewage in rivers, lakes, and oceans. As a result, water has often been a major means of spreading diseases. Epidemics of typhoid and cholera, in particular, have often resulted from people drinking water contaminated by sewage. Today, modern sewage treatment plants remove many of the impurities from public drinking supplies. But there are still many communities in America that continue to dump untreated sewage into waterways.

Sources of Pollution

Water pollution comes not only from wastes discarded by individuals. Industries dump vast quantities of chemicals and other waste products directly into our waterways. Pesticides and herbicides eventually wash into rivers and streams. Even the salt that keeps cars from skidding on an icy highway may be carried to a nearby river.

One of the more dramatic forms of water pollution is that caused by oil spillages. You've probably seen pictures in newspapers of sea birds, unable to move because their bodies are coated with oil. Millions of tons of oil are spilled into our oceans every year. This happens when oil tankers collide, run aground, or spill oil as they are cleaning their tanks.

Mining, too, adds its contribution to water pollution. Strip mining for coal, which leaves the coal exposed, is particularly harmful. The sulfur in the coal reacts with water and oxygen to form sulfuric acid, which is then carried into waterways. This form of pollution is widespread in parts of Pennsylvania, West Virginia, and Kentucky.

Even heat can be a water pollutant. Power plants draw in large amounts of river or lake water for their cooling processes. They then return the water to its source, but at a higher temperature. This *thermal pollution* upsets the balance of life in the water. The warmer water kills off some kinds of fish and plants and causes others to flourish.

Effects on Water Life

Life in the water is delicately balanced. So it is easily upset. When tons of chemicals and other wastes enter a body of water, they can make life impossible for fish and other marine life in a variety of ways. Oil, as we have seen, kills birds by making them unable to fly. Some chemicals simply poison fish. And sometimes fish die for lack of oxygen.

Oxygen levels are reduced when chemicals cause large numbers of water plants to grow very quickly. Nitrates and phosphates from fertilizer and sewage have this effect. The plants grow quickly, then die and decay. The decaying process uses up oxygen in the water, causing fish to suffocate. This process of quick growth, death, and decay is known as *eutrophication*.

Figure 20.4 Once a common practice, dumping chemicals and waste products into waterways is now prohibited.

During the 1970s the United States and Canada started a program to save Lake Erie from being destroyed by eutrophication. Companies and townships near the lake were ordered to improve their waste treatment plants. Heavy fines were imposed on violators. The cleanup program has brought plant and animal life back to the lake. Its beaches are open once again.

Effects on Human Life

We need clean water for drinking, bathing, preparing foods, cleaning, manufacturing, and for many other purposes. When large bodies of water become polluted to the point where they are unfit for human use, the amount of water available to us is reduced. Water pollution could, then, lead in time to a serious shortage of water.

This, in itself, would be a health hazard. But water pollution threatens human health in other ways too. Water contaminated with sewage is a breeding ground for disease organisms. In countries where people take their drinking and bathing water from the same rivers that receive their wastes, outbreaks of typhus and cholera are common. Organisms that cause common diarrhea are also transmitted by polluted water.

People don't have to drink polluted water to suffer from its effects. Swimming in polluted waters may cause a rash. A cut or a scratch on the skin will also let pollutants enter the body, causing infections and other health problems. People can also take in pollutants by eating fish caught in contaminated waters.

Tragic instances of people being affected by eating contaminated fish have been reported around the world. A number of years ago, for example, many of the people who lived in a small Japanese fishing village on Minamata Bay began to suffer strange symptoms. Their arms and legs grew numb and weak, their sight and hearing grew dim, and some lost the ability to speak or think. A number of deformed babies were born. Fifty-two people died.

What these people had was acute mercury poisoning. Factories in the area had been dumping mercury wastes into Minamata Bay for over 40 years. Tiny organisms in the water changed the mercury into a form that was highly poisonous. This mercury was absorbed

Figure 20.5 This girl is only one of many Japanese villagers who were severely handicapped by Minamata disease.

by the fish and then by the people who ate the fish. As the years went by, the concentrations of mercury in people's bodies increased. Eventually, investigators discovered the link between mercury pollution and what was by then being called Minamata disease.

Mercury poisoning could be named after other places. Similar cases have shown up far away from Japan. Some Canadians have developed the same crippling symptoms. And people who have been eating fish from the Mediterranean Sea near the coasts of France and Italy recently received a fearful warning. They were told that the fish there contained high levels of mercury. Anyone who had been eating five pounds of this fish a week could expect to die within 20 years.

Once people realized what mercury pollution could do, many nations banned the dumping of mercury wastes in their waters. But other industrial and chemical wastes continue to be dumped. Many could turn out to be just as harmful as mercury.

Controlling Water Pollution

The control of water pollution operates on two levels. First, the dumping of pollutants in our waters must be reduced. Second, those waters that are already contaminated must be cleaned up.

The government has passed various laws banning the dumping of certain chemicals and other pollutants in our waters. Unfortunately, such laws are hard to enforce. Some companies

continue to pour harmful wastes into rivers, claiming that other disposal methods are too expensive. Meanwhile, many sewage treatment plants are being modernized and improved. These should greatly reduce threats to public drinking supplies.

Efforts to clean up polluted waters have met with mixed success. Some bodies of water have been made safe again, but others continue to be a health hazard, despite years of work.

The struggle to save Lake Michigan, for instance, has been going on for more than 20 years. The lake has suffered heavy contamination from the dumping of industrial wastes, sewage, and pesticides. The concentrations of some pollutants have been reduced, and some public beaches have been opened again. However, pollutants remain and some experts fear that the normal balance of life in the lake will never be restored. The history of Lake Michigan shows how persistent and complex a problem water pollution can be.

CHECK YOUR UNDERSTANDING

1. List seven sources of water pollution.
2. How does eutrophication occur?
3. Describe the three ways water pollutants can enter your body.
4. Explain Minamata disease and how it develops.
5. What are the two aspects of controlling water pollution?

SECTION **3**   **Land Pollution**

For years we have been polluting our land with garbage, industrial wastes, mining wastes, and chemicals. Ugly garbage dumps litter our landscape. Unsightly slag heaps surround our mining towns. Tons of industrial and chemical wastes lie on the ground and buried beneath it. Not only is this form of pollution ugly, but it can also be dangerous.

Garbage Disposal

Household garbage alone presents a formidable problem. Every week you and your family throw out about 50 pounds of trash. So do all the other families in America. What happens to it all?

We currently have three methods of disposing of garbage. All of them contaminate the environment and threaten our health. Open garbage dumps provide breeding grounds for rats and flies. Incinerators pollute the air. And dumping in lakes and rivers causes water pollution.

Discarding these materials is also wasteful. Many of the substances that make up trash and litter could be salvaged and *recycled*. For example, half the household trash in America is wastepaper. This paper could be reclaimed, processed, and made into useful paper again. The same is true of aluminum cans. Recycling would both reduce the amount of solid waste and lessen the drain on our limited natural resources.

Mining Wastes

The waste products from mining, in addition to being ugly, present two dangers. Slag heaps pose a constant threat of landslide to those who live beneath their shadow. Tragic instances of such slides have occurred around the world. One of the worst happened in Wales in the 1960s, when an avalanche of coal slag fell onto a school and killed dozens of children.

The other danger comes from the presence of toxic substances in the slag. If these are washed into the ground and into underground water channels, they can contaminate drinking water supplies.

Industrial and Chemical Wastes

Without knowing it, you may be living near a long-forgotten industrial dump. For years, factories were in the habit of dumping their wastes on the land or of burying them in landfills. The government estimates that there are more than 50,000 abandoned dumps around the country. Of these, many are dangerous because they contain toxic substances. A number of communities have already been affected. Their water supplies and land have been polluted by seepage from industrial dumps, sometimes with tragic results.

A number of years ago, for example, people who lived in the Love Canal area of Niagara Falls, New York, noticed something strange. Foul-smelling liquids were seeping into their yards and basements. At first most people dismissed the problem as a nuisance. But then the nuisance turned into a nightmare. The incidence of cancer and birth defects soared. Thirteen hundred people had to leave their homes, which were bulldozed over and sealed off. Today, most of the Love Canal area is deserted.

What had happened was this. In the late 1930s, a chemical company had dumped tons of highly poisonous chemical wastes into an abandoned canal. Years later a school and homes were built on land near the canal. Residents who moved into the area did not know about the chemicals. But gradually those chemicals made their way into the community's water supply. That's when people started getting sick. Efforts continue to clean up the area, but some of the chemicals are so poisonous that it may be years before they are made harmless.

Because of such incidents, the government has begun to regulate the dumping of potentially harmful wastes. But the dangers from abandoned dumps will be with us for many years.

Pesticides

In 1982 many of the residents of a town in Massachusetts became ill with what seemed like pneumonia. Investigators from the Environmental Protection Agency discovered that pesticides produced by a nearby chemical plant had leaked into the town's water wells. The plant was ordered closed, and the EPA began an emergency cleanup operation.

As with other toxic chemicals, pesticides that are dumped on the land pose a threat to our health if they seep into our water supplies. But they can affect us in other ways too. Not all of the pesticides that are sprayed onto fields reach the ground. Some are caught up by the wind and carried great distances. They stay in the air, adding to the problems of air pollution.

Pesticides have, in fact, proved to be far more dangerous than anyone ever anticipated. The story of DDT illustrates this. When DDT was first introduced as a pesticide in the 1940s, it seemed to be a great moment for humankind. DDT would kill off harmful insects that destroyed crops and brought disease to millions. DDT did do all this. All over the world crop yields increased, and deaths from malaria and yellow fever decreased dramatically.

But then the unexpected happened. DDT stopped working. Crops were once again being destroyed by insects, and deaths from malaria and yellow fever were on the rise.

What had happened? Nature had outsmarted science. The insects had become resistant to DDT. Something else happened too. DDT began to turn up in unexpected places—in the bodies of fish, birds, animals, and humans, where it could remain for years. DDT had polluted air, water, and land.

The effects of DDT on our bodies are not yet known. The evidence that exists is troubling though. Some studies link DDT to cancer. Others suggest it is related to birth defects. The United States has greatly limited the use of DDT and other dangerous pesticides, but they are still used in other countries. Since these pesticides can spread with ease throughout the

Talking Point

Dioxin: Today's DDT

Dioxin, an ingredient in some weed-killers, is the deadliest synthetic chemical known to exist. It is so deadly that the government considers the maximum "safe" concentration of dioxin to be one part per billion. Even in the smallest possible dosages, dioxin has been shown to cause cancer, miscarriages, birth defects, and death in laboratory animals. It is also suspected of having caused dozens of cancer deaths among pesticide industry workers.

Dioxin was an ingredient in Agent Orange, a defoliant used in the Vietnam War. Thousands of Vietnam veterans suffer medical problems that some people believe to be caused by exposure to dioxin. Dioxin was also one of the most alarming toxic substances found in Love Canal in 1978. When it was found at Times Beach, Missouri, in 1983, the federal government relocated virtually all of the 2,200 residents at a cost of $33 million.

Many uses of herbicides containing dioxin have been banned by the federal government; but in the mid-1980s, these chemicals could still be used for spraying around fences and parking lots, on industrial sites, on rangelands where cattle graze, and even on rice.

Each year, dioxin continues to accumulate in the environment, and it shows up in all levels of the food chain. No one knows how much of it is buried in toxic waste dumps. Even if dioxin were totally and immediately banned worldwide, it would remain a serious threat to humans for many years to come.

world, all countries must limit their use to have a lasting effect.

New pesticides have now been developed that, while still toxic, are less harmful than DDT. But the real answer to pests and pesticides may lie in biology instead of chemistry. Scientists are now trying to control pests with their own enemies. Ladybugs, for example, are now released into fields by the thousands to keep down the population of harmful insects. Pest-resistant plants are also being developed. In addition, scientists are trying to find ways to make harmful insects sterile so that they cannot reproduce.

Nobody knows what the long-term effects of such measures will be. The history of DDT illustrates how an apparent solution to a problem can turn out to be a problem in itself. Solutions are being sought to the new problem, as to all problems of land pollution. Meanwhile, though, we continue to produce billions of tons of garbage and other wastes every year for which no satisfactory means of disposal has yet been found.

CHECK YOUR UNDERSTANDING

1. How much garbage does the average American family toss out each week? What could be done with much of this material?
2. What are two dangers posed by the slag heaps that result from mining?
3. What are the problems with the two traditional methods used for the disposal of industrial and chemical wastes?
4. How do pesticides get into the air and water? What went wrong with DDT?
5. Give two ways in which pests could be controlled through biology instead of chemistry.

SECTION **4**   # Noise and Radiation

Pollution is generally defined as the presence of harmful substances in our environment. But there are two forms of pollution that do not quite fit this definition: noise and radiation. Both are invisible. Both are increasing. Exposure to large quantities of either one can damage a person's health.

Noise Levels

Stop what you're doing and listen for a moment. How many different sounds can you hear? You can probably hear people talking, maybe some traffic noise, perhaps an airplane, or footsteps, or a lawn mower, or chairs creaking. Some level of noise is always with us. But the amount of noise in our society grows every year.

The loudness, or strength, of a sound is measured in *decibels*. A noise measured at 130 decibels can cause pain. Prolonged exposure to sounds of 80 decibels or more may lead to hearing loss.

As with air pollution, noise pollution is worst in cities. There can be found some of the worst offenders: cars, trains, buses, construction equipment, and industrial machinery. A bus idles at 90 decibels, and a jackhammer creates 120 decibels of noise.

There's plenty of noise in and around the average home as well. A food blender, at 93 decibels, is louder than a bus, while a power mower, at 107 decibels, makes more noise than a subway train. Just eight hours of exposure to 90 decibels of noise can cause hearing damage. So if you mow lawns to earn money, you should consider wearing special earmuffs to protect your hearing.

Among the noisiest of all places are airport runways. A jet plane at takeoff creates a deafening 150 decibels. That's why people who work on runways wear earmuffs. But did you know that the average disco is almost as loud as an airport runway? Rock musicians and their fans run great risks of developing hearing problems.

Effects of Noise on Health

Prolonged exposure to loud noise may cause a person to suffer permanent hearing loss because cells in the inner ear will be destroyed.

Talking Point

A Deafening Noise

What do a jackhammer and a portable radio have in common? Both can damage your hearing. So can trombones, the ringing mechanism on some cordless telephones, and the use of headphones.

Medical researchers discovered long ago that people who worked for long periods of time at airports, on construction sites, and in noisy factories commonly experience varying degrees of hearing loss. In the past few years, researchers have also seen similar problems among rock and classical musicians and teenagers who listen to loud music through headphones or over portable radios.

A study of teenagers in Japan, for example, found that most of those who experienced unexplained hearing losses were in the habit of playing loud music through earphones for an average of four hours a day. The good news for those teenagers was that when they changed their listening habits, their hearing problems disappeared. Had they continued in their habit, permanent hearing loss may have resulted.

Loud noises of 80 decibels or higher can cause either temporary or permanent deafness. What counts is the length of exposure. In general, research has found that the ears can recover from short-term exposure to loud noises, but that long-term exposure eventually destroys the inner ear's ability to hear high-pitched sounds. The message is clear: Teenagers who want to go on listening to their favorite rock stars when they're 60 should turn down the volume on their radios and record players now.

But sound can affect the body in other ways too. Very loud noise actually causes physical changes. The heart beats faster, the blood vessels constrict, and the pupils of the eyes dilate. Such noise may even cause stomach pains.

Loud noise also tends to make people tense and irritable. So it may contribute to disorders related to stress, such as ulcers and high blood pressure. In tests done on animals, constant noise has resulted in heart, brain, and liver damage. Even fairly quiet sounds, such as distant traffic or a neighbor's stereo, can affect a person's health if they cause lack of sleep.

Controlling Noise Pollution

Some countries have managed to reduce noise levels by introducing special noise control laws. Britain, for example, has strict limits on the amount of noise a truck is allowed to make. And Japan has introduced noise limits for all types of machinery and vehicles. Signboards at busy intersections in Tokyo indicate noise levels, keeping the public aware of noise pollution.

In the United States, few communities have dealt with the problem successfully, although some are making an effort. In many cities it is illegal to sound a car horn, except in an emergency, or to play a radio in public. Some cities also demand that construction noise be kept below a specified level. The problem is that even when such laws exist, they are difficult to enforce.

Protection Measures

When noise levels cannot be reduced, people can be protected against their harmful effects. Some industries now provide workers in noisy occupations with special ear guards. Sound-proofing materials and sensible planning can help separate office workers from noisy machinery. Nevertheless, the problem is a long way from being solved. Insurance companies continue to pay out millions of dollars to workers who go deaf from exposure to excessive noise on the job.

Fortunately, there is plenty you can do to protect yourself and others from excessive noise. When at home, for instance, make sure you keep the volume of the TV and stereo down. Try not to use noisy appliances in places where other family members will be affected. If your family is planning to buy a new appliance,

Figure 20.6 This signboard in Tokyo indicates, among other things, the current level of noise pollution at the intersection. (At the time the photograph was taken, the level was 68 decibels.)

try to find out which brand is quietest. And if you go to a disco, keep away from the amplifiers.

Radiation Levels

Radiation is an invisible form of energy. Some level of radiation has always been present in our environment. It is given off by the sun's rays and by rays from outer space. Certain naturally occurring substances, notably uranium, also give off radiation. Such substances are said to be *radioactive*.

But human activity has begun to add more radiation to the environment. Sources of radiation include nuclear power plants, x-rays, microwave ovens, and color televisions. Nuclear bomb tests also release radioactive particles into the atmosphere.

Many people are concerned about the effects of this increased radiation on human health. Nobody knows how much radiation a human body can stand. But prolonged exposure to even small amounts could lead to health problems. This is suggested by the relatively high rates of cancer among people who work with radioactive materials.

Effects of Radiation on Health

Radiation alters or destroys individual cells. It has the most serious effects on those tissues in which cells normally reproduce rapidly, such as the lining of the digestive system and the tissues that form the blood. Sperm and egg cells are even more susceptible, as are developing fetuses. Significant doses of radiation, then, can cause infertility, miscarriages, and birth defects.

Prolonged exposure to high levels of radiation causes *radiation sickness*. Victims first experience nausea, diarrhea, and vomiting. Eventually, they lose their hair, suffer internal bleeding, and become highly susceptible to infections. In many cases, leukemia develops.

Various types of cancer also result from long-term exposure to lower levels of radiation, such as those experienced by workers in uranium mines and refining plants. In fact, recent studies indicate that there may be no safe level of radiation exposure, no dose of radiation so low that the risk of cancer is zero.

Nuclear Power

Public attention became riveted to the danger of radiation from nuclear power plants in 1979. In that year the Three Mile Island nuclear power plant near Harrisburg, Pennsylvania, was dangerously out of control for at least 48 hours. The people who were evacuated from the area soon returned to their homes, but their fears about the long-term effects of the radiation emitted during the accident continue.

Some people believe that all nuclear power plants should be shut down. They believe that the risks of an accident, resulting in the release of high levels of radiation, are too great. They also point to the fact that nuclear power plants produce tons of radioactive wastes. No safe method of storing or disposing of these wastes has yet been found.

Other people, however, see nuclear power as the answer to our nation's energy needs. They point out that it does not rely on fossil fuels, supplies of which are limited. It would also release the United States from its dependence on

Figure 20.7 The accident at Three Mile Island in 1979 turned public attention to the danger of radiation from nuclear power plants.

other nations for fuel. Furthermore, nuclear plants do not give off the air pollutants that conventional power plants do.

After the Harrisburg incident, the government halted the building of more nuclear plants. It also called for special inspections of existing plants and for strict safety precautions to be observed.

How large a role nuclear power will play in the future remains to be seen. Meanwhile, scientists all over the world are working to find safe ways of disposing of radioactive wastes. Until then, these wastes remain a hazard.

CHECK YOUR UNDERSTANDING

1. Describe the physical and the emotional changes that can result from noise pollution.
2. How long does it take for a sound of 90 decibels to affect your hearing? Name five sources of sound above 90 decibels.
3. How do significant doses of radiation affect the human body?
4. List some of the pros and cons of nuclear power plants.

SECTION **5**   **Solving Environmental Problems**

As we have seen, the problems of pollution in our environment are vast and complex. We have also seen that there are no quick and easy solutions. Nobody is going to invent some wonder machine that will vacuum all the pollutants out of the air or a tablet that will magically clear the waters in our polluted rivers and lakes.

Who Will Do It?

It's hard to get involved in such complex issues. It's also hard to deal with issues that do not touch us noticeably or directly. The consequences of most environmental problems are long-term. As long as we have air, water, and food—and feel healthy—we may not worry too much. Most of us find it easy to act only when we are directly affected. We're more likely to feel like doing something about air pollution, for example, after spending a week choking and coughing in a Los Angeles smog.

Some people do not get involved because they assume science will come up with the solutions. But as we have seen, technological solutions sometimes create new problems. Besides, experts do not always agree on the best way to tackle a problem. They may even disagree on whether there is a problem in the first place. Some scientists, for example, believe we are in no danger from exposure to low levels of pollutants that cause cancer in greater amounts. Other scientists say that any level of exposure is dangerous.

When the experts disagree, people become confused. Their uncertainty may make them withdraw from the issue instead of finding out more about it. When lack of concern leads to lack of knowledge, solutions become harder to find—harder to put into effect.

People also tend to assume the government will take care of environmental problems. Governments all over the world have, in fact, taken action. The government of this country, for example, has set strict controls on automobile emissions. It has also introduced rules to control the dumping of hazardous wastes. The British government's Clean Air Act brought a virtual end to London smogs. The Japanese government is also working hard to reduce all kinds of pollution.

Group Action

Governments cannot do it by themselves. The people must be willing to go along with government suggestions and rulings and to pay the cost of cleaning up the environment. The actions of citizens can also affect government policies. We can make officials aware of our concerns. Public opposition to the Concorde jet, for example, brought results. It caused the government to demand lowered noise levels before the Concorde was allowed to land or take off in this country. Groups of citizens have also banded together and forced the closing of factories that were polluting waterways.

Students acting in groups have also dealt with pollution problems. They have cleaned up beaches and birds after oil spills. They have cleaned up polluted ponds and streams and have cleared garbage from vacant lots. Such action reclaims natural resources. It may also

have an important ripple effect. When other people can see results, they may feel that they, too, can make a difference. When people feel they can make a difference, they can.

Individual Action

You too can make a difference. Think about the things you do that cause pollution. Then think of some of the changes you could make to reduce pollution. Almost certainly, you could use less electricity. Electric power plants are big polluters. You could probably walk more and drive less. You could use cloth napkins instead of paper ones. You could buy beverages in re-

Figure 20.8 One thing you can do to reduce pollution is to collect materials for recycling. If your community has no recycling center, you can organize a group to start one.

Talking Point

Superfund—Super Crisis

In 1978 a general-alarm fire broke out at a waste dump in the heart of a residential neighborhood in Chester, Pennsylvania. The dump included 50,000 barrels of unidentified industrial waste products that had been piled up and left there to rot. Clouds of dense black smoke forced the evacuation of nearby residents and the closing of a highway bridge spanning the Delaware River, which bordered the dump. Before the fire could be extinguished, 45 fire fighters were overcome by chemical fumes. Some fire fighters discovered that their rubber boots had partially melted from acids that puddled the ground around the ruptured barrels.

Throughout the 1970s, incidents involving toxic waste dumps were reported all too frequently. As a result, the federal government passed several laws regulating the dumping and transporting of waste products. It wasn't until 1980, however, that Congress enacted the first comprehensive cleanup measure—after Love Canal and after the Surgeon General of the United States labeled the toxic waste crisis an "environmental emergency."

The new law provided the federal Environmental Protection Agency (EPA) with $1.6 billion—which became known as Superfund—to begin the immediate cleanup of thousands of hazardous waste sites across the nation. The EPA was also given the power to collect as much of the cleanup costs as possible from the companies causing the pollution. It was to do this either through negotiation or by prosecuting the offenders in court.

At the end of Superfund's first five years, the EPA had completed the cleanup of only six sites. Moreover, its critics charged that three of those sites had been inadequately cleared. The cleanup work proved to be more complex and costly than anyone had anticipated. Superfund has, however, made a start on the nation's toxic waste problems by beginning cleanup and monitoring operations at hundreds of sites. Cleanup of the Chester dump, for example, was nearly complete by 1986. The operation, which cost more than $5 million in state and federal funds, involved the disposal of thousands of barrels of waste, the demolition of all buildings on the site, and the removal of several feet of contaminated topsoil.

In addition to its own direct efforts, the EPA works closely with state environmental protection agencies. It helps them speed up their cleanup and prosecution efforts, and negotiates or sues for the payment of millions of dollars in fines and cleanup costs from corporate polluters.

Until Superfund, few people realized the incredible magnitude of America's toxic waste problems. Superfund has identified up to 25,000 hazardous waste sites across the country. It has placed 786 of those sites on a priority cleanup list because they pose the most serious threat to public health and to the environment. The priority sites include landfills where hundreds of thousands of barrels filled with toxic substances were left rot. Also on the list are radioactive houses where doctors worked with cancer-causing radium in the 1920s and 1930s, as well as lagoons where various industries dumped liquid waste products such as paint solvents and corrosive acids. The toxic substances at the priority sites range from common poisons such as arsenic and mercury, to various chemicals such as dioxin, PCBs, and chlordane.

Many of the first sites to go on the Superfund list were put there because they threaten to pollute drinking water. Some dump sites and lagoons, located next to rivers and streams, overflow into these bodies of water during heavy rains or floods, polluting the water supply. The poisons in landfills leach out into the groundwater and contaminate nearby residental water wells and reservoirs.

Not surprisingly, the Superfund sites are concentrated in the older eastern industrial states. New Jersey has the most toxic waste sites on the priority list—a total of 95.

Some of the sites on the EPA's Superfund list have been polluting the environment for 40 or 50 years. Superfund administrators have discovered that the longer a toxic waste dump has been used, the more expensive it is to clean up. One Michigan firm agreed in 1982 to spend $38.5 million to clean up a 3.5-acre site where it had dumped and burned toxic chemicals for 40 years. The cleanup included removing the first 3 feet of soil on a nearby golf course—68,000 cubic feet—and pumping 1.25 million gallons of contaminated groundwater into a cement-lined well. Despite cases such as this where private industry pays most of the cost, federal experts estimate that it will cost American taxpayers millions of dollars to clean up some 10,000 toxic waste sites by the end of this century.

In land-rich America, the common method of disposing of toxic waste has been to bury it.

Even the EPA carts off wastes from one site for burial in another. Federally approved landfills, which are so-called state-of-the-art, are lined with clay and plastic; but even these landfills can leak toxic wastes into nearby groundwater. In some land-poor European nations, such as the Netherlands, ground disposal of toxic wastes has been banned. Instead, the wastes are detoxified at government plants or recycled for use by other industries. In some cases, industries are banned from producing toxic substances in the first place.

The United States is beginning to examine and adopt some of these alternatives. In 1984 Congress gave the EPA the authority to ban land disposal of some toxic substances, and some companies have discovered that recycling waste products can save money and improve the company's corporate image.

New technology is also being applied to the toxic waste problem with encouraging results. Gene splicing has created new bacteria that "eat" some kinds of toxic waste and break them down into harmless by-products. One company is experimenting with a chemical that can turn toxic PCBs into table salt, while others are using enzymes to separate toxic substances from liquid wastes.

In 1980 the EPA described the nation's toxic waste problems as a "ticking time bomb." Despite the technological advances and the governmental and private cleanup efforts since then, the situation has improved very little. Toxic waste will certainly remain a problem for the government and the public for many years to come.

turnable glass bottles instead of throwaway plastic ones.

There are other things you can do as well. You can collect materials such as bottles, cans, and newspapers for recycling. Many communities have set up recycling programs. If your community has no program, you can organize a group to start one. You can also make sure you use products, such as biodegradable detergents, that are easy on the environment. And you can avoid products that are "over-packaged," such as fast-food hamburgers that are wrapped in paper and placed in styrofoam containers, then put in a paper bag, only to be unwrapped and eaten minutes later. So much packaging is just not necessary.

Everything you do counts. It's up to all of us to join the fight against pollution and to help protect our environment.

CHECK YOUR UNDERSTANDING

1. What are some of the reasons that people do not get involved in the pollution problem?
2. Why can't the government deal with pollution problems on its own?
3. Describe two specific pollution problems that have been helped by group action.
4. List five ways individuals can aid in the battle against pollution.

CHAPTER SUMMARY

- Most air pollution comes from the burning of fossil fuels. Power plants and factories are the main stationary sources of air pollution. Pollutants from these sources include particulate matter and sulfur oxides.
- Cars emit more than half the pollutants in the air. Automobile exhausts give off carbon monoxide, hydrocarbons, and nitrogen oxides.
- The long-term effects of specific air pollutants are not known. Most pollutants affect the eyes, throat, and respiratory system. Those who are most likely to be affected by air pollution are the very young, the very old, and those with chronic breathing problems.
- Efforts to clean up the air include a ban on the use of fluorocarbon sprays, a reduction in the use of asbestos, and the introduction of catalytic converters into car exhaust systems.

- Sources of water pollution include human wastes, industrial wastes, chemicals, oil, pesticides, and herbicides.
- Drinking polluted water can cause disease. So can swimming in it or eating fish caught in it.
- Land pollution is caused by the dumping of garbage, industrial and mining wastes, and chemicals. Abandoned chemical dumps are particularly dangerous.
- Noise pollution may result in hearing problems, fatigue, and stress.
- The amount of radiation in the atmosphere is increasing. Significant doses of radiation can cause cancer, infertility, miscarriages, and birth defects.
- Cleaning up the environment requires action from governments, citizen groups, and individuals.

DO YOU REMEMBER?

Give brief definitions of these terms:

fossil fuels	photochemical smog	ozone layer	fluorocarbons	recycle
particulate matter	temperature inversion	hydrocarbons	thermal pollution	radioactive

THINK AND DISCUSS

1. If you had to make a choice between cleaning up existing pollution and finding ways to prevent future pollution, which would you choose? Why?
2. Because of existing laws, companies that pollute are fined, but they are allowed to continue in operation with a warning to change their ways. What are the pros and cons of forcing such companies to close down until they comply with the law?
3. Why is the death of plant and animal life that is found in water so serious?
4. Should the federal and state governments compensate people whose homes or neighborhoods have been made uninhabitable by pollution? Why or why not?
5. What changes could you make in your daily life to lessen the amount of pollution you create?
6. Why do you think discos and rock concerts are so loud? Do you think people really like them that way? How would you go about making them quieter?
7. What possibilities for group action against a specific pollution problem exist in your community? How would you institute such action?

FOLLOW-UP

1. Chart the number of car journeys—and the reasons for them—that your family makes each week. Rate each trip as necessary or unnecessary. How could the number of unnecessary trips be reduced?
2. Design a newspaper recycling project for your community. Consider where and when you would collect paper and what you would do with the paper you gather.
3. Contact your community's water treatment or sewage treatment plant to find out what techniques are used and what pollutants are removed. Also find out what improvements are planned for the future. Write a report of your findings.
4. The outdoor art treasures in famous European cities such as Venice are being ruined by acid rain. Find out about the extent of the problem and the measures being taken to save these treasures. Describe the situation to your class. If possible, use magazine photographs to illustrate your talk.
5. Find out more about the pollution problems of the Great Lakes. Choose one lake and write a report on the efforts being made to clean it up.
6. Gather more information about the nuclear power plant controversy. Make a chart that explains the pros and cons of the argument in detail. Which side are you on? Why?
7. Identify a Superfund site close to your area. Newspapers, government representatives, and the EPA are good sources of information. Write a report about the site that includes the scope and history of the problem, how it was discovered, what cleanup action has been taken, and how much it has cost.

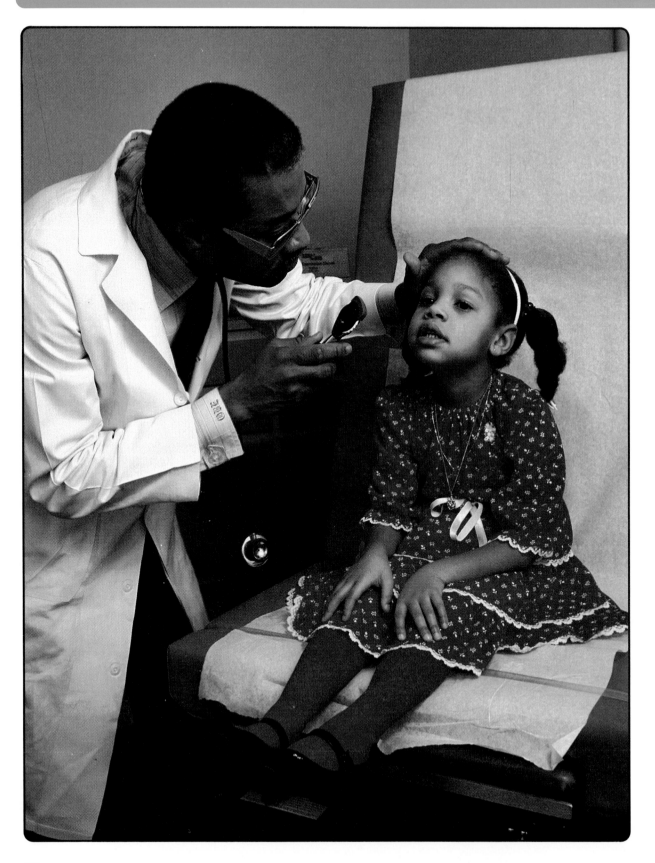

CHAPTER 21

Health Care in America

After reading this chapter, you should be able to answer these questions:

1. Who can you call when you're sick?
2. What does the World Health Organization do?
3. What special services can community clinics offer?
4. What career opportunities are there in health care?
5. What problems exist in our health care system?
6. What is being done to improve the system?

When Sam had an appendicitis attack, the nearest doctor was 100 miles away. He spent several hours in agony before help arrived.

Mrs. Jackson had major surgery for cancer. Her hospital bill came to over $10,000. She has no hospital insurance and will have to sell her house to pay the bill.

Unfortunate situations such as these happen all the time. They illustrate two of the inadequacies of our health care system: that it is not available to everyone and that it is expensive.

Despite such shortcomings, the United States has the most advanced health care in the world. Our hospitals have the most sophisticated equipment, and they are staffed by highly trained professionals. This chapter examines how the health care system works. We shall look at some of the organizations that work to promote good health and at the health practitioners themselves. You will learn about the training they undergo and the kind of care they can give.

We shall also point to some of the shortcomings of our health care system. You'll learn why medical care is so expensive and what is being done to try to bring costs down. You'll also find out why no medical care is available in some communities.

The majority of Americans have medical insurance to help reduce the financial burden of health care. But insurance, too, has its drawbacks. It is expensive, and it makes little or no provision for preventive care. This chapter examines the insurance industry and describes some alternatives to private health insurance.

One of those alternatives is the health maintenance organization, which emphasizes preventive medicine. Obviously, the more effort we make to prevent disease, the less time, effort, and money we need to spend on treating it. Disease prevention, then, should be encouraged. This chapter explores some of the ways we might accomplish this and other goals. If we strengthen the weaknesses of our health care system, it will truly be the finest in the world—in every way.

SECTION **1**   # Health Care Providers

The American health care system has undergone some major changes in the past few years. Once, the only choice people had was to go either to a general practitioner or, if they were seriously ill, to a hospital emergency room. Now they can receive medical treatment from a number of different types of providers.

Preventive care is also being given increased emphasis and consumers are recognizing the benefits of taking preventive action. Employers, too, are realizing that it is in their interest to spend money promoting employee health.

At the state, national, and international levels, various agencies and organizations work to promote health and prevent disease. Altogether, more than 6 million Americans work in health care. We will look at the different kinds of services they offer and at the choices available to those consumers in need of medical treatment.

The Consumer's Options

In the past, if someone was ill, the family doctor was summoned. He or she came to the patient's house and provided the necessary treatment. Today, house calls are almost unheard of. Individuals in need of health care must find a way to get to a doctor. Not only that, they must choose from a variety of facilities that offer health care.

The range of options available to an individual depends on a number of factors. City dwellers have access to many more types of medical services than people living in small communities. A person's income level, medical insurance coverage, and employer benefit package also influence his or her choice of medical provider. The individual's choice also depends on whether he or she is seeking emergency treatment, routine care, or preventive care. Listed below are the different kinds of professionals and organizations that provide medical services to consumers.

Private Physicians—Private physicians work out of their own offices and generally charge a fee for each service or treatment they provide. Many private physicians are members of group practices. Some group practices consist of three or four specialists in the same field, such as gynecology or sports medicine. Other group practices are made up of a number of different specialists. (The advantages and disadvantages of group practices are described later in this chapter.)

Health Maintenance Organizations—Health maintenance organizations, or HMOs, are group practices consisting of a number of different specialists and allied medical personnel. The main difference between an HMO and a private group practice is in the method of payment. Instead of paying a fee for services received, patients pay a fixed monthly sum. (A full description of HMOs appears later in this chapter.)

Hospitals—Most hospitals provide a full range of medical services for patients in need of emergency treatment or treatment that cannot be provided in a doctor's office. A few hospitals specialize in the treatment of one particular dis-

Talking Point

The Fight Against AIDS

It is ironic that just at the time when smallpox was finally conquered, a new disease began to appear. After years of painstaking work in many nations, the World Health Organization was able to announce, in the late 1970s, that smallpox no longer existed. At about the same time, the Centers for Disease Control in Atlanta began to receive reports of some unusual deaths among young males. Nobody knew what had caused these young men to get sick and die. As the reports continued to come in, epidemiologists studied medical records and looked for patterns that would give them information about the deaths.

By 1981 the cause of the deaths had been identified as AIDS—acquired immune deficiency syndrome. AIDS is a disease that destroys the body's natural immune system, leaving victims with no defense against disease. No one who has developed AIDS has recovered from it.

Once it became apparent that AIDS was fatal, that it was spreading, and that there was no known cure for it, a massive effort to deal with the disease began. The effort involved several approaches:

- to identify the cause of the disease
- to establish how it is passed from one person to another
- to develop a vaccine against the disease
- to develop a cure
- to prevent the spread of the disease
- to educate the public about the disease

Throughout the United States, federal, state, and local organizations rallied to combat AIDS:

- The Centers for Disease Control collected and analyzed data on deaths, searching for clues that might lead to a method of prevention, a cure, or a vaccine.

- The National Institutes of Health focused their massive research capabilities on identifying the virus that caused the disease and on experimenting with possible cures.
- Community networks throughout the country provided counseling and care facilities for people who had contracted AIDS and for the friends and families of victims.
- Private foundations and public health agencies conducted widespread health education campaigns to provide information on the facts of the disease, as they became known, and to explain prevention measures.

By the mid-1980s, thanks to all the research efforts, it had been established that AIDS is caused by a virus, identified as HTLV-III. The virus is present in the body fluids (blood, semen, vaginal discharge, tears, and saliva) of infected individuals. It is communicable and can be transmitted through sexual contact with an infected person, through the use of a hypodermic needle contaminated by the virus, or through transfusions of blood donated by an infected person. Pregnant women who have AIDS can pass the disease on to the baby. Work on developing a vaccine and a cure for AIDS continues.

ease. There are more than 7,000 hospitals in the United States, and each year more than 40 million patients are admitted to hospitals.

Freestanding Emergency Clinics—Introduced in the past few years, freestanding

emergency clinics, or FECs, offer emergency care and routine testing. Many FECs are open 24 hours a day, and many are conveniently located along major highways. Because they offer limited services, they generally charge lower fees than a hospital emergency room would.

For more information on FECs, see the box on page 415.

Public Clinics—Public clinics offer health care services for people who may be unable to afford the services of a private physician. The clinics receive their funding from federal, state, or local government resources. Patients may pay no fee at all, or they may be charged according to their ability to pay.

Nursing Homes—More than 1 million Americans are residents of nursing homes. Nursing homes offer long-term care for the elderly and for others who are unable to care for themselves. There are both private and public nursing homes.

Hospices—Hospices, described fully in Chapter 11, provide care for people who are dying. They specialize in the relief of pain and in the special counseling that dying patients and their families need.

Corporate Health Care

In the past few years, a number of corporations have introduced programs to promote the health of their employees. They have come to realize that the money they use to promote their employees' health is money well spent. Healthy employees work more efficiently, take less time off, and have fewer accidents.

Figure 21.1 Educating the public about the problems they are fighting is only one of the functions of volunteer health organizations. By soliciting contributions of time and money, these agencies are able to help the victims of various diseases and support research into possible cures for these diseases

Corporate health care programs generally focus on disease prevention and health promotion. Programs offered by some corporations include couses to help employees stop smoking, and courses in weight control, physical fitness, nutrition, and stress control. Some corporations have even installed exercise facilities on the premises and give employees time off to use them.

Companies provide for the health care of their employees in other ways too. Many organizations buy health insurance or pay HMO fees for their workers. Some large companies hire physicians and nurses to provide emergency services. They may also have physicians come in from time to time to conduct screening tests.

Volunteer Agencies and Private Foundations

Hundreds of organizations have been formed to deal with specific health problems at the local, regional, or national level. Most voluntary organizations focus on a given disease or health problem. The best known of these are probably the American Cancer Society, the American Heart Association, and the National Foundation–March of Dimes. Almost all of their money comes from private donations. Voluntary agencies have three main functions: (1) to educate the public about the disease they are

fighting; (2) to provide money for research to find out more about the disease; (3) to provide aid for victims of the disease.

You have probably seen television commercials produced by voluntary agencies. The American Cancer Society, for example, makes antismoking messages for television. Some voluntary agencies run telethons to raise money. Funds are also raised in drives by the United Fund, which collects for all agencies in a community.

Unlike volunteer agencies, private foundations are financed by wealthy individuals or families. The Rockefeller Foundation is one of the best known of the private foundations. The activities of private foundations range from providing education for health to donating money for medical research. Some run their own research laboratories. Others concentrate on solving health problems in particular communities.

International Organizations

International organizations deal with worldwide health problems. The best known of these organizations is the *World Health Organization (WHO)*. WHO is mainly concerned with providing basic primary care in the poor, underdeveloped countries of Asia, Africa, and South America. In these countries disease and malnutrition are widespread. WHO helps by sending doctors and other trained people, medicines,

Figure 21.2 Activities of the World Health Organization. *Left:* An African doctor performs a

minor operation by the light of an oil lamp. *Right:* A health center for mothers and children in Uganda.

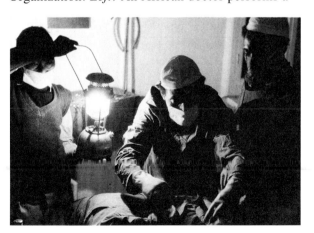
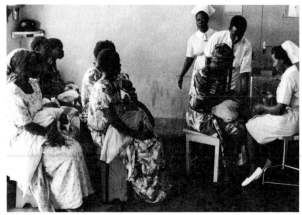

supplies, equipment, and money. When epidemics and other major disasters break out, WHO sends in special teams of doctors.

WHO is also concerned with preventing disease. For example, since the 1940s it has been fighting a war against malaria, in part by fighting the mosquitoes that carry the disease. It has been only partly successful, however. The number of people with malaria is much lower than it was 30 years ago, but there are still millions of people who suffer from the recurring chills and high fevers of this disease.

WHO has claimed victory over another disease, however—smallpox. For centuries, smallpox had been a dreaded disease, killing millions and leaving survivors disfigured for life. During the 1960s WHO launched a worldwide vaccination campaign. It was so successful that by 1980 the organization was able to announce that the disease had been completely eliminated.

CHECK YOUR UNDERSTANDING

1. List four factors that influence an individual's health care options. Name seven kinds of professionals and organizations that provide medical services.
2. Why do some corporations offer their employees programs that focus on disease prevention and health promotion?
3. What are three functions of voluntary health organizations?
4. What activities does the World Health Organization carry out to help prevent the spread of disease?

SECTION **2**   # The Role of Communities

Recently, community groups made up of concerned residents have become involved in health care. Although individual communities in general do not have the primary responsibility for the health care of their members, community action can sometimes result in swift and significant health reforms. Indeed, a new kind of health activism is growing in communities across the country.

The story of screening children for lead poisoning in New York City is a case in point. Parents in poor neighborhoods became aware that thousands of children were suffering from lead poisoning. The children had been eating old lead-based paints that had peeled off walls and window sills in run-down buildings. If lead poisoning is found early enough, it can be cured and the brain damage it causes can be prevented. The concerned parents pressured the city to screen the children in their neighborhoods for lead. The city agreed but was slow in setting up a program. A group of young people quickly took matters into their own hands. Through their efforts, vans containing mobile testing laboratories soon moved through the streets. The publicity this action aroused embarrassed the city to move more promptly.

Another example of community involvement in health care is the community clinic program. Community clinics have sprung up in most major cities, especially in poor areas. These clinics are largely run by members of the community, and in some cases doctors and nurses provide their services free of charge. Much of the nonmedical work, such as keeping records, cleaning, and maintenance, is done by local volunteers.

Community clinics are often better able to meet the needs of the community than large urban hospitals are. They are accessible. People don't have to travel great distances to get to them. They are inexpensive. Their charges are lower than hospital charges, and some offer free services to people who cannot afford to pay. And those in non-English-speaking communities are generally staffed by people who speak the language and know the customs of the people.

Community clinics also cut through much of the red tape that many people find so frustrating at hospital clinics. They are dealing with

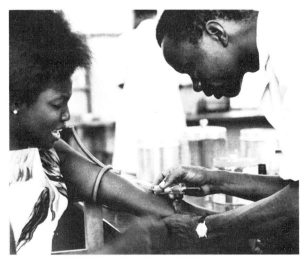

Figure 21.3 A woman who cannot afford private health care receives free treatment at a community clinic.

Figure 21.4 A mother at a free clinic for migrant workers describes her health problems with the aid of an interpreter.

smaller numbers of people and can offer a more personal service.

Community clinics could be part of the answer to providing health care in poor areas. But as things stand now, they often do not last very long. Some become the victims of poor management, but the usual problem is money. Many of these clinics get started with a grant from the government, a voluntary agency, or a private foundation. When that money runs out,

the clinic must close. Community clinics do show, however, that people have a new attitude toward taking direct action about their own health care needs.

Future Role of Communities

The efforts of community members to improve neighborhood health care are currently taking two directions. In the past, government agencies worked on their own to identify community health needs. They then decided how funds should be distributed to satisfy those needs. The trend now is for representatives from individual communities to take part in identifying local needs. The community representatives can point out problems that may not be apparent to agency representatives who do not live in the neighborhoods.

The work of consumer advocate Ralph Nader and his Public Interest Research Group (PIRG) is an example of the other way in which communities are becoming involved in health services—through community coordination. Communities throughout the nation often have groups and individuals who share the same health concern. PIRG helps these far-flung groups to organize around this concern and make a plan for action. Part of their work is to rally political support for the project. The recent and dramatic upgrading of care for patients in nursing homes around the country is a direct result of PIRG-sponsored community coordination.

CHECK YOUR UNDERSTANDING

1. Give four reasons that community clinics are often better able than large hospitals to meet the needs of local residents.
2. Why do some community clinics last for just a short time?
3. What do community clinics show about people's attitudes toward their own health care needs?
4. Describe the two directions in which community involvement in health care is moving.

SECTION **3** **Health Practitioners**

As you have seen, many groups work to support our health care system. But it is the millions of specially trained health practitioners who actually care for and treat individuals.

There are more than 60 health fields concerned with caring for the health of the human body and mind. Of these, many are involved in behind-the-scenes activities that support the work of doctors, or physicians. Many health practitioners are legally and professionally entitled to use the title *Doctor*, but only certain ones can dispense medicine and perform surgery. Others are trained to use different methods for treating disease. In this section we will discuss a few types of medical practitioners in detail.

Physicians

Physicians are the health professionals most people associate with the word *doctor*. Fewer than 10 percent of all health practitioners are physicians, but the vast majority of other health personnel either work directly for physicians or receive patients on a referral from physicians.

There are two kinds of physicians in the United States: the doctor of osteopathy (D.O.) and the doctor of medicine (M.D.). A D.O. is generally called an *osteopath* or *osteopathic physician*, while an M.D. is generally called a physician or doctor of medicine.

Years ago, osteopathy was quite different from the kind of treatment given by M.D.'s. Osteopaths then believed that most physical problems were caused by bones that were out of position. Treatment involved manipulation, or adjustment, of the bones and muscles. Drugs were avoided.

Many people think osteopaths still treat their patients only through manipulation. Today, though, osteopathy is much the same as medicine. There is very little difference in the way osteopaths and doctors of medicine take care of their patients. The requirements for entrance into osteopathic and medical colleges are almost the same, and the course of study in the colleges is similar.

Talking Point
Family Practice

Depending on their needs, an American family today might see several medical specialists, including a gynecologist, a pediatrician, and a doctor of internal medicine.

Many people, however, would prefer to receive comprehensive treatment from one physician instead of specialized treatment from several.

The medical community has responded to this preference by creating a new specialty: family practice. Family practitioners are different from general practitioners, or G.P.'s, who receive basic medical training, do a one-year internship, and then go into practice. Because G.P.'s do not undergo advanced specialized training, they must refer patients with complex medical problems to specialists. Family practitioners, on the other hand, must take a full three-year residency in addition to the one-year internship after basic training. They must also take a qualifying exam every seven years.

Family practitioners receive advanced training in a number of areas:

- health promotion and disease prevention
- gerontology, including preventive care and the physiology and psychology of aging
- psychiatry, including psychotherapy, drug therapy, and treatment of substance abuse
- internal medicine, including heart and lung diseases and infectious diseases
- obstetrics and gynecology, including marriage counseling and sexuality
- surgery, including surgical emergencies, referrals, and counseling

Family practitioners still refer patients to specialists. However, they are able to provide more comprehensive care than G.P.'s can. The idea of family practice appears to have caught on. Family practice residencies are now the third most popular choice for medical students.

Physicians must go through a lengthy period of schooling and training before they can apply for a license. First, there is premedical education at a college or university, which generally lasts four years. The student then spends four years in a medical school, followed by a year as an *intern* in a hospital. As an intern, the graduate physician gets direct experience working with patients and works in many different specialties. Should the intern choose to pursue a specialty, internship is followed by *residency*, which may last as long as five years. As a resident, the physician learns more about a particular specialty.

The American Medical Association has recently moved to shorten the training period for physicians. It has suggested that the internship become the first year of residency. That way, instead of first experiencing a number of different specialties, the physician would begin training immediately in one particular specialty.

In the United States today, about half of all physicians are in private practice. They see patients in their own offices and charge a fee for each service. There is a growing trend, however, for physicians to form groups or to become salaried employees of hospitals and clinics.

Most physicians today are specialists who work only in a specific area of medicine, such as dermatology or psychiatry. Fifty years ago, in contrast, most physicians were general practitioners (G.P.'s) who did a little bit of everything. But more new medical discoveries have been made in the past 50 years than in the previous 1,000. It is impossible for one physician to keep up with all the new discoveries. This fast growth of medical science is the main reason that so many physicians are becoming specialists.

Other Independent Medical Practitioners

This category is made up of practitioners who work independently of physicians. Like physicians, a number hold degrees that entitle them to be called doctor. Only certain ones, however, can prescribe medication and perform surgery.

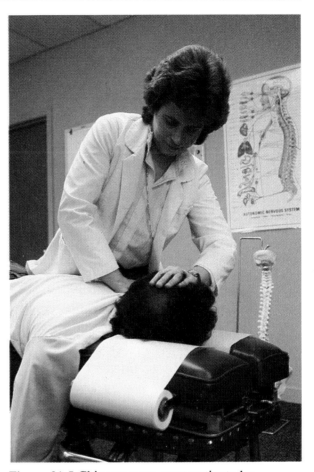

Figure 21.5 Chiropractors treat patients by manipulating parts of the body, particularly the spinal cord.

Chiropractors believe that many disorders can be traced to the central nervous system. However, the scientific basis for this belief is weak. Chiropractors treat patients by manipulating parts of the body, particularly the spinal cord. They cannot prescribe drugs or perform surgery. Chiropractors must complete a four-year training program in a chiropractic college. They then receive the degree of doctor of chiropractric (D.C.). All states require that chiropractors be licensed.

Podiatrists specialize in diseases of the feet. They perform surgery and prescribe and administer drugs. They also administer physical therapy and prescribe devices for correcting foot problems. Podiatrists must graduate from a college of podiatry and pass a state board examination before they can receive a license.

Optometrists examine the eyes and surrounding structures to detect vision problems. They are often confused with *ophthalmologists*. However, ophthalmologists are physicians; optometrists are not. They cannot prescribe drugs, perform surgery, or treat eye diseases. But they can prescribe lenses and other visual aids, and they are trained to recognize eye diseases, which they refer to physicians.

Optometrists receive their training in one of 16 colleges of optometry. They can enter an optometry college after two years in an undergraduate college. They then study for four more years. After receiving a doctor of optometry (O.D.) degree, they must pass a state licensing examination before they are allowed to practice.

Clinical psychologists diagnose and treat mental and emotional problems. They work in hospitals, clinics, and private offices. They also serve as consultants to community mental health programs and to schools. Many are engaged in research.

The training of clinical psychologists requires three to four years of graduate study, which include a year of internship. The Ph.D. (doctor of philosophy) degree they are awarded entitles them to be called doctor.

Dentists

Dentists specialize in the care and treatment of the teeth and gums. It takes almost as long to become a dentist as it does to become a physician. Although most dental schools require two or three years of predental education, most students earn a bachelor's degree before entering dental school, which takes four years to complete.

The first two years of dental school, which concentrate on basic sciences, are so similar to medical school that medical and dental students sometimes take these courses together. During the second two years, dental students treat patients and learn to work with assistants. Upon graduation, they receive the degree of D.D.S. (doctor of dental surgery) or D.M.D. (doctor of medical dentistry).

Allied Dental Personnel

Dental hygienists are the only dental aides who need a license to practice. Dental hygienists clean teeth, take x-rays, and give fluoride treatments. They also teach patients proper brushing and flossing techniques and advise them about good nutrition.

Most dental hygienists are graduates of two-year programs, but some go through a four-year bachelor's degree program that allows them to teach or work in public health.

Dental assistants prepare the patient for treatment and then work with the dentist during treatment by passing instruments and mixing filling materials. They also take x-rays, sterilize instruments, and keep office records and accounts.

Figure 21.6 Dental hygienists clean teeth, take x-rays, and advise patients about dental care. They are the only dental aides who need a license to practice.

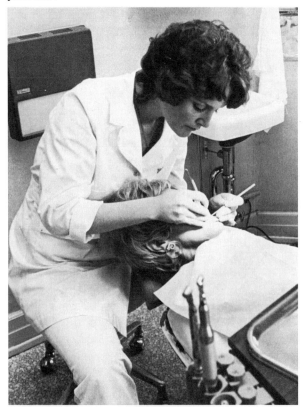

Talking Point

Careers in Health Care

Have you considered a career in health care? Perhaps you think you're not dedicated enough to be a doctor or patient enough to be a nurse, so you've dismissed the idea. Think again. America's health care systems offers hundreds of different kinds of jobs. There is almost certain to be a job in the health care system that suits your interests and skills.

Careers in health care range from those requiring only a few weeks of training to those that take many years of study. If you like the idea of working directly with patients, your options include the jobs of paramedic, physician assistant, nursing aide, physical therapist, nurse, and physician. If you prefer the idea of working behind the scenes, there's an equally wide range of possibilities. You could be involved in hospital or office management—working on budgets, ordering supplies, hiring and training staff, and overseeing maintenance. Another job possibility involves working with medical records, which must be organized,

transcribed, analyzed, coded, and stored. If you want to do laboratory research, you can choose a specialty such as genetics, microbiology, or pharmacology, among others. There is also a rapidly growing need for technicians to operate equipment and perform diagnostic tests.

The health care business is extensive, employing more than 6 percent of the total work force in the United States. It employed 6.2 million people in the mid-1980s. About half of all health care workers work in hospitals. The others are employed by clinics, laboratories, community and mental health centers, nursing homes, hospices, and the military. Businesses and schools also offer employment opportunities for health care professionals.

If you are interested in a health career, your guidance counselor and local librarian can help you explore the different opportunities available and determine the education and training you will need.

There is a new trend in the training of dental assistants. In the past, they were trained on the job by the dentists who hired them. Now, though, many receive formal training in one- and two-year programs offered by community colleges.

Nurses

Nurses form one of the largest groups of health practitioners. They assist physicians and care for patients by monitoring their conditions, administering medications, and making them comfortable. They also keep records and supervise the work of other health personnel.

Most nurses work in hospitals as *general duty nurses*. A small number become *operating room nurses*, assisting before, during, and after surgery. Thousands of others work as *office nurses* for physicians, performing office and laboratory work besides regular nursing duties.

There are also nurses who work in the community. *School nurses*, for example, promote good health among children, while *public health nurses* teach the public at large about good health practices. *Visiting nurses* provide health care to patients in their homes.

Recently, there has been a steady increase in the relatively new field of *nurse-midwife*. Nurse-midwives are specially trained to deliver babies and to recognize problems requiring the attention of a physician. They also help the new mother learn to care for herself and her infant.

All states require nurses to pass a state board examination after they graduate from an approved school of nursing. There are three different types of programs that lead to a nursing license. In the past, most nurses received their training in three-year programs provided by hospitals. These courses, which qualify students to be registered nurses, or R.N.'s, are still offered by some hospitals. They provide students with a combination of clinical knowledge and on-the-job training.

In addition, two different courses are offered by universities and colleges. Students who take a four-year course become bachelors of science in nursing, or B.S.N.'s. The bachelor's course focuses more heavily on clinical knowledge than does the course for R.N.'s, and it offers less practical training. Students who complete a two-year course earn an associate degree and become licensed practical nurses, or 'l.p.'n.'s. Licensed practical nurses generally work under the supervision of an R.N. or a B.S.N.

CHECK YOUR UNDERSTANDING

1. Describe the stages of training that physicians go through.
2. List and briefly describe the services offered by four other kinds of independent medical practitioners.
3. Explain the differences between dental hygienists and dental assistants.
4. What are six different jobs for nurses?

SECTION **4** **Problems with the System**

The United States has the finest health care facilities in the world. But this excellent medical care is not equally available to everyone. For a number of reasons, millions of Americans do not receive the kinds of health care they need.

Distribution of Physicians

If you live in a big city and have an appendicitis attack, you're in luck—medical care is probably just a few minutes away. But if you live in a small town in a place such as North Dakota, you may have to travel many miles to get to a hospital or even to a doctor. There are thousands of remote towns all over the country that do not have even one physician. They are too small to provide enough of an income to attract one.

About half of our nation's physicians are in private practice. As self-employed people, they can choose where they will work. As a result, the availability of physicians varies greatly from state to state and from one area to another within a given state. One area in Los Angeles, for example, has just 9 physicians for every 100,000 people, while Beverly Hills has 1,800 physicians for the same number of residents.

This unequal distribution cannot be blamed on the physicians themselves. Just as it costs a great deal of money to become a doctor, it can cost a great deal of money to work as one. Setting up an office today can cost more than $40,000, money that must come out of the physician's own pocket. Physicians in private practice must also pay the costs of office personnel and the rising costs of insurance against malpractice suits brought by dissatisfied patients. They must also have money left to support themselves and their families. It is understandable, then, that most choose to practice in places where there are patients who can pay their bills.

Physicians who are not in private practice are salaried employees of hospitals, HMO's, corporations, and government agencies. In recent years, an increasing number of physicians have been accepting salaried positions. It is projected that by 1990, 85 percent of our nation's physicians will be employed by hospitals, HMO's, corporations, and the government. This change may not relieve the problem of an undersupply of physicians in poor and rural areas, however. Large hospitals and corporations tend to be located in heavily populated areas.

Another factor contributing to the shortage of physicians in remote areas is that in recent years only a small percentage of all new physicians have been entering general practice. A small town that can support only one doctor needs a general practitioner. The new family practice specialty, discussed on page 408, might help relieve this problem.

Insurance Coverage

Although the majority of Americans have some kind of medical insurance, it is often very limited. Moreover, the number of people with no health insurance at all is growing. It is estimated that more than 23 million Americans

have no insurance protection, mainly because of unemployment or because they can't afford the cost of it.

The amount of insurance coverage people have is often determined by their income and by the kinds of worker benefits their employers offer. People with higher incomes are much more likely to be covered by insurance than are those with low incomes. And the higher the income, the better the insurance package. This means that lower-paid workers—those most in need of insurance coverage—often have the poorest insurance, or no insurance at all.

There are more than 1,500 insurance companies. They offer a confusing assortment of policies, written in difficult language. The result is that millions of people do not know just what kind of coverage they really have. Many think they have full protection when they do not, while more than 50 million have too much protection. This last group has what is called

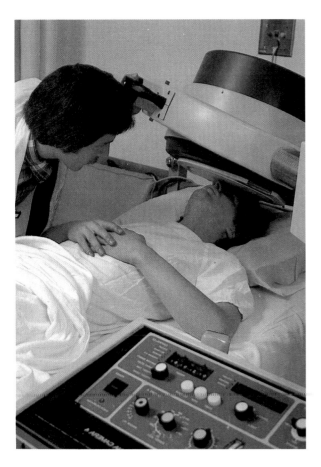

Figure 21.7 Among the reasons for the high cost of hospital care are the need to purchase complex equipment and the admission of patients who do not really need to be hospitalized. Expenses could be reduced if hospitals shared equipment and allowed people who need simple tests to be treated as outpatients.

double coverage—they are insured twice for the same protection. Yet most companies will not pay a medical bill if another company has already paid it. Double coverage, then, is usually a complete waste of money.

Much money is spent on health insurance. Yet, the insurance companies pay for only about 37 percent of hospital and doctor bills. The government pays for about 53 percent of hospital bills and 28 percent of doctor bills. About 8 percent of hospital bills and 28 percent of doctor bills come out of the pockets of the patients. Medical bills are one of the leading causes of bankruptcy in the United States.

The Cost of Medical Care

We have already mentioned the high cost of health care in the United States. In 1984 the nation was spending an average of about $1,300 per person on health care, an amount that continues to rise. To some extent, patients themselves are responsible for the high costs of health care. Many of our health problems are a direct result of the life styles that we choose. Smoking, drinking, poor nutrition, and lack of exercise are just four factors that contribute to disease. If people took better care of themselves and made a greater effort to prevent illness, health care costs would be significantly reduced.

There are many reasons for the high costs of health care. Let's look at two of the main components of health care and see why costs have reached such high levels.

Hospital Care

The largest portion of health expenses goes for hospital care, which can cost up to $500 a day. Some of the reasons for this high price are unavoidable. A hospital has many expenses it must always pay, no matter how many beds are occupied. The hospital staff must receive their salaries, the building must be maintained, and emergency and operating room equipment must be ready for use 24 hours a day. The high quality of American health care is also involved: the average patient is attended by three to five staff members.

But there are also factors that make hospital costs much higher than they need to be. Some hospitals have been built without first studying the need for them. As a result, there are now 100,000 unused hospital beds in this country. And the cost of maintaining these empty beds runs between 60 and 70 percent of the cost of maintaining the occupied ones.

As for the patients in the occupied beds, experts estimate that 3 out of every 10 do not even need to be there. Many of them are there because most insurance policies do not cover out-of-hospital expenses. So doctors try to save their patients money by admitting them to a hospital for simple tests that could be performed during an afternoon visit as an outpatient. But as outpatients, many of these people would not be able to afford the tests.

Finally, the amount of money hospitals and physicians spend on malpractice insurance has increased dramatically in recent years. The increases are due to the growing number of patients who are suing their doctors and to the sharp rise in the amounts of money awarded in malpractice suits. The average amount awarded jumped more than $300,000 in just one year. Approximately $4 billion was spent on malpractice insurance premiums in 1985. These costs are, of course, passed on to patients. Hospitals, physicians, and insurers are pressing for new legislation that will help alleviate the problem, but there is little agreement on how it should be handled.

Surgery

Surgery is another major area of health care. Some experts believe that thousands of unnecessary operations are performed in this country each year, encouraged by our present system of health care.

Most surgeons are paid by the operation. How much money they make depends on how many operations they perform. There is strong evidence that this system of payment results in extra operations. In some places where surgeons have been put on salary, the number of operations has dropped by half.

Insurance companies also contribute to the problem. They will pay for surgery done in a hospital. Most, however, pay little or nothing

Talking Point

Walk-in Clinics

Walk-in medical clinics have become popular with medical consumers in the 1980s. Known for their convenience and low rates, they have been called "McDoctors" and "Doc-in-a-Box" because of their similarities to fast-food chains. They prefer to be called freestanding emergency clinics, or FECs.

These small clinics are equipped to treat minor injuries and illnesses and to carry out routine tests. Because they have small staffs and much less equipment than hospitals, FECs are able to charge less for their services than hospital emergency rooms do.

Is an FEC a viable alternative to the hospital emergency room? The answer depends on the patient's needs. FECs can take care of minor medical problems. However, they do not have the equipment or the staff to handle serious injuries or illnesses.

Some people also see FECs as an alternative to the family physician. Consumers like the fact that they can go to an FEC without an appointment, whereas they might have to wait several days to see their own doctor. Critics point out, however, that FECs cannot provide the continuity of care that a family physician can. Most FECs employ a number of physicians; patients who make several visits may see a different doctor each time. Furthermore, FEC fees for routine examinations and treatments are often higher than those charged by a private physician.

FECs have had one good effect. Some hospitals have responded to this new form of competition by opening their own clinics. Known as surgicenters, these clinics offer minor surgery to patients who do not need to stay overnight. The cost of running a surgicenter is lower than that of running a conventional surgery unit. The surgicenter can, therefore, charge less for its services than the main hospital would charge.

---

for medical services done outside a hospital. Often a health problem can be solved without surgery. But the insurance company will not pay, so the patient ends up on the operating table.

Medicaid and Medicare patients are now advised to get a second opinion from another doctor before having *elective surgery*. Elective surgery is surgery by choice; the patient can choose whether or not to have the operation. Medicaid and Medicare will pay for the second opinion. Many insurance companies now follow the same practice. They have found it saves them money in the long run because patients who receive a second opinion choose surgery less often than those who do not.

CHECK YOUR UNDERSTANDING

1. What are some of the reasons for the unequal distribution of physicians in the United States?
2. How many Americans have no health insurance at all? What is double coverage and why do people have it?
3. List three expenses a hospital always has to pay.
4. Explain three factors that make hospital costs higher than they need to be.
5. Describe two aspects of our health care system that encourage unnecessary operations.

SECTION **5**   **Improving the System**

There is no doubt that our health care system is in need of improvement. Physicians should be available to care for people in all communities. Everybody should have adequate insurance coverage. The cost of medical care should be brought down. And, most importantly, the focus of our system should be on prevention rather than on treatment.

A number of reforms have been introduced in recent years, and others are being discussed.

Distribution of Physicians

Measures have been taken to persuade physicians to move to areas that need more doctors. Some medical schools are offering students reduced tuition fees if they agree to practice for a specified period of time in areas where doctors are needed. Other programs provide grants and low-interest loans to encourage doctors to set up practices in unpopular areas.

The popularity of the new family practice specialty may also help answer the need for doctors in more remote areas. These specialists are able to provide the primary care services that poor and rural areas need.

If some experts' predictions come true, the problem of physician distribution may, in fact, take care of itself. Medical schools are attracting record numbers of students. Not all of them will be able to find jobs in the cities that have traditionally attracted doctors. It can be anticipated, then, that more doctors will move to areas they would not have considered in the past.

Group Practices

Group practices are not new, but the number of physicians who belong to group practices has been growing rapidly. It is expected that this trend, which brings benefits to both physicians and their patients, will continue.

For physicians, group practices offer a number of cost-saving benefits. Members of a group can share expenses by using the same building, equipment, laboratory, technicians, and support staff. Income arrangements in group practices vary. In some groups, each member is paid on a fee-for-service basis. In other groups, members are paid a salary from the total group income.

For patients, group practices offer a number of benefits. Most services are available under one roof. There is always at least one physician on duty, so patients can be seen at any time. And if the patient's personal physician is away, another doctor can easily obtain his or her medical records and provide treatment.

Health Maintenance Organizations

Health maintenance organizations (HMO's) first became popular in the late 1970s. The main difference between an HMO and a regular group practice is in the method of payment. Instead of paying each time they see a doctor, the patients (or their employers) pay a monthly fee. In return for the fee, the patients receive medical care whenever they need it. HMOs generally hire physicians in a number of different specialties so that they can offer patients comprehensive health care. Physicians who work at HMOs are generally paid a fixed salary.

There are many advantages to HMOs. Patients do not have to fill out complicated forms every time treatment is needed, as they must do when making health insurance claims. They also know what their medical costs are going to be, since they pay a fixed monthly rate.

HMOs encourage preventive medicine. Patients are urged to have regular checkups instead of waiting until they are sick before seeing a doctor. Both doctor and patient benefit from this. The doctor may earn more by promoting good health, since less money will be taken

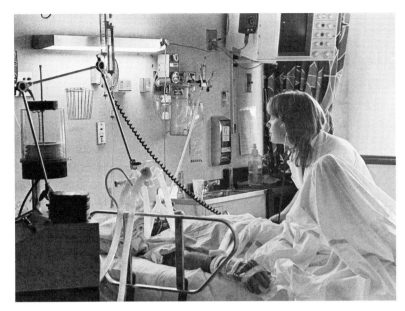

Figure 21.8 Physician assistants are trained professionals who work under the supervision of a physician. By taking care of routine medical procedures, they free the physician for more complex tasks of evaluation and treatment.

from the HMO's funds to pay for treatments or hospital stays. And the patient knows that any illness will be detected early. In the event that extensive and costly treatment is required, the patient does not have to worry about the expense.

Studies have shown that HMO patients go into hospitals less frequently than other people. They also spend shorter periods of time in hospitals and have less surgery.

Although HMOs offer advantages over conventional health insurance plans, they are not a magical solution to America's health care problems. Most people who join an HMO do so when their employers offer them a choice between insurance coverage and HMO fees. If they choose the HMO, they give up their conventional insurance. That won't affect them as long as they use physicians at the HMO. If they wish to consult a physician outside the HMO, however, they will have to pay the physician's fees.

By the mid-1980s there were more than 300 HMOs in the United States, and the number was increasing. In the early 1980s the federal government introduced a new law concerning HMOs. Under this law, companies that provide their employees with conventional health insurance must offer them the option of joining an HMO plan instead. The new law applies only to companies above a certain size and only to companies that are located near an HMO.

Hospital Reform

Disillusionment with hospital costs and inefficiencies finally started to bring about hospital reforms in the early 1980s. Much of the pressure for reform came from large corporations whose annual costs for employee health insurance had skyrocketed. The federal government, too, wanted to reduce the amount it was spending on Medicare and Medicaid payments.

In 1983 the federal government introduced a new payment system for Medicare and Medicaid patients. Under the old system, hospitals and doctors who treated Medicare and Medicaid patients sent their bills to the government and the government paid them. There was no control over the size of the bills. The new *prospective payment system* specifies how much the government is willing to pay for certain procedures. The government states, for example, the sum it will pay for a tonsillectomy or for a coronary bypass operation. The sums are based on calculations of how much the treatment should cost under normal circumstances.

If the hospital bill is higher than the government figure, the hospital must pay the difference.

By introducing the prospective payment system, the government hoped to force hospitals to become more efficient and cost-conscious. However, the system has not always had the desired results. Some hospitals have begun to turn away Medicare and Medicaid patients; or to cut back on their care in order to save costs.

Another aspect of hospital reform concerns the way hospitals are run. Hospitals run according to traditional methods provide support services for private physicians. These physicians are self-employed, working on a fee-for-service basis. Under this system, the hospitals provide the nursing staff, equipment, and facilities that support the work of the doctor. The patient is billed both by the hospital and by the doctor.

The traditional system may have been adequate when hospitals were smaller and when their operating costs were lower. Nowadays, however, hospitals are big businesses. They have to spend enormous sums on sophisticated equipment. Increasingly, therefore, they are being run like big businesses, which has led to a number of significant changes.

To help them control their costs, many hospitals are now employing their own physicians instead of providing support services to independent physicians. Some hospitals are also entering into contracts with large corporations. A contract might set reduced fees for employees of a particular corporation, and in exchange, the corporation will agree to send its employees to the hospital named in the contract.

Stiff competition among hospitals has had welcome side effects for consumers. Some hospitals have introduced disease prevention programs, such as clinics to help people stop smoking, and weight-control classes. They hope that people who attend the classes will also choose that hospital for treatment when they need it.

Because of the reforms mentioned above, it is expected that about 85 percent of the physicians in the United States will be salaried employees by the early 1990s. It is also expected that many smaller hospitals will be forced to close. They won't be able to compete with the large hospitals. Small hospitals have limited resources. They can't afford to keep buying new equipment at a time when medical technol-ogy is constantly changing. Nor can they afford to advertise or run the aggressive marketing campaigns that larger hospitals are conducting.

Many people are worried that hospitals will become *too* businesslike. There is concern that life-and-death decisions will be based primarily on financial considerations. There is also concern that cost-cutting procedures will lead to a reduction in the quality of care offered to patients. Further reforms can be expected.

Prevention Through Screening

Several of the improvements to our health care system are expected to promote the idea of disease prevention. The HMO system, with its monthly payment plan, encourages people to schedule regular checkups. Thus, doctors in an HMO system spend much of their time examining healthy people. Some HMO doctors find this frustrating; they would prefer to spend their time diagnosing and treating illnesses.

Two different programs have been introduced to help deal with this dilemma. *Triage* is a low-cost system for determining what medical care a patient needs. Specially trained people talk to patients and determine whether they need immediate care and treatment, health testing, or just general health information that can be given over the telephone.

Health testing takes the form of *multiphasic screening*. This combines a detailed computerized medical history and a series of tests on the heart, lungs, and other parts of the body. X-rays are taken and blood samples are examined. The information is then fed into a computer. The computer indicates whether further tests are needed or whether the patient should see a doctor immediately. Multiphasic screening can sometimes detect diseases that have no outward symptoms. It also provides doctors with a basic health profile for future reference.

Triage and multiphasic screening separate the well from the sick. They enable health personnel to make the best use of their time, and they free physicians to treat patients who are seriously ill.

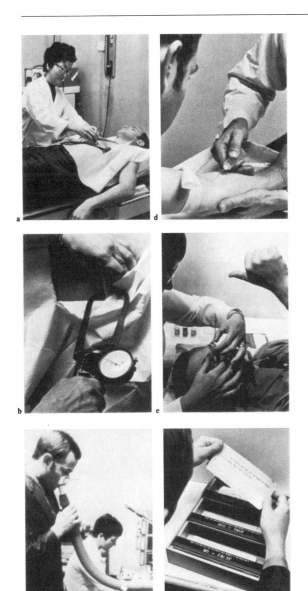

```
                    PERMANENTE MEDICAL GROUP - OAKLAND
          DUPLICATE REPORT - MULTIPHASIC HEALTH CHECKUP (MHC)  -  5/20

TEST,PATIENT                    RETIRED                      S.F. DR. SMITH
MR: 225859C J1    AGE 5C    FEMALE    WIDOWED                 LAST MHC  6/16

                            SUMMARY OF REPORT
          ***********************************************

          (TEST)                 (NORMAL)    (THIS EXAM)
     CIRCULATORY:
 **   B.P.SUPINE(GODART): 90-159/ 50- 89      164/100
     HEMATOLOGY:
 **   HEMOGLOBIN GM.:       12.0- 16.0          9.2
 **   MHC MCMCG:            26.0- 34.0         20.6
 **   MCHC %:               32.0- 38.0         25.6
 ~   BLOOD CHEMISTRY:
 **   GLUCOSE 1 HR MG%:     UNDER-  263         332
 **   GLUCOSE 2 HR MG%:     UNDER-  150         164
 **   VDRL:                     NEG             POS
 **   QUANTITATIVE VDRL:                       RKWWWN
     URINE:
 **   GLUCOSE:                   NEG            MED
 **   CLINITEST:                 NEG            3+
 **   ACETONE:                   NEG            POS

 ** BREAST X-RAY:  FIBROCYSTIC DIFFUSE CHANGES
 ** HEARING:       CLINICALLY IMPAIRED HEARING LEFT

    PATIENT RECEIVED FOLLOWING (ADVICE RULE) DIRECTIONS:
    700-REQUEST PT.RET. AMS LAB FOR 2-HR SERUM SUGAR
    801-NOTICE SENT TO PHYSICIAN: CONSIDER EARLY APPTMT.

 *    IN PAST YEAR SPELLS OF WEAKNESS OR PARALYSIS OF ARMS OR LEGS
 *    IN PAST YEAR BLURRING OF EYESIGHT LASTING OVER A FEW MINUTES
 *    IN PAST YEAR ANY LOSS OF HEARING WHICH IS STILL PRESENT
 *    IN PAST 6 MONTHS OFTEN HAD PAIN IN THE EAR
 *    IN PAST 6 MONTHS 2 OR MORE NOSE BLEEDS NOT FROM INJURY OR A COLD
 *    IN PAST YEAR COUGHED UP ANY BLOOD




TND = TEST NOT DONE   PRT = PAT. REFUSED TEST   TNI = TEST NOT INDICATED
BND = BLOOD NOT DRAWN  UNSAT = TEST UNSATISFACTORY  - = DATA NOT AVAILABLE
NSA = NO SIGNIFICANT ABNORMALITY
*  = PATIENT ANSWERED YES ON THIS MHC AND NO ON LAST MHC
** = CONSIDER POSSIBLE ABNORMAL        ~ = NOTE          242-11:57:21
```

Figure 21.9 *Left:* Several steps of a multiphasic screening: (a) an electrocardiogram is taken; (b) a skin-fold test measures body fat; (c) lung capacity is measured; (d) a blood sample is taken for analysis; (e) the eyes are checked for glaucoma; (f) the patient sorts a set of cards as part of a psychological test. *Right:* A computer print-out shows test results for a woman who underwent a similar screening.

Focus on Prevention

The greatest improvement to our health car system would be to place still more emphasis on disease prevention. We know so much about what causes disease. Now we have to find ways to persuade people to act upon that knowledge.

Each one of us can do more to our own health than any doctor, hospital, or drug. Yet millions of Americans spend more money to pay for medical treatment than to keep themselves well. Millions more spend their dollars on cigarettes, alcohol, and illegal drugs—substances that they know will harm their health.

The keys to prevention are education and motivation. We need to find ways of educating more people to practice disease prevention techniques. Schools, communities, employers, and individuals could all expand their health promotion efforts.

Certain incentives could be offered to help encourage people to take care of their own health. Health insurance policies could be written so that they offer discounts to people who get regular checkups and practice healthful habits. Similarly, employers could offer bonuses to workers who participate in corporate fitness courses.

If we placed more emphasis on disease prevention and health promotion, we could, indeed, have the finest health care system in the world. That would be far better than having the most expensive sickness care system, which leaves millions of Americans unable to receive adequate treatment.

Many health care professionals hope that America is on the verge of a new kind of health breakthrough. This breakthrough—involving greater public attention to health promotion—cannot happen in a laboratory or a hospital. Instead, it has to happen in our homes, our schools, and our workplaces. Most of all, it has to happen in our attitudes and in our health practices.

CHECK YOUR UNDERSTANDING

1. What are two ways to encourage physicians to move to poor and rural areas?
2. Describe the workings and benefits of a health maintenance organization.
3. Name three hospital reforms that have taken place since 1980. List some benefits and disadvantages of each.
4. What are the two keys to preventive health care?

CHAPTER SUMMARY

- The American health care system has expanded. Today, medical services are offered by private physicians, health maintenance organizations, hospitals, freestanding emergency clinics, nursing homes, and hospices.
- Community clinics can satisfy a number of health care needs. Community members can also play a significant role in identifying local needs and in organizing consumer action groups.
- Health practitioners include physicians, independent medical practitioners, dentists, allied dental personnel, and nurses.

- The main problems with the American health care system are the uneven distribution of physicians, inadequate insurance coverage, and high costs.
- Efforts to reform the health care system include improving the distribution of physicians, increasing the number of group practices and HMOs, introducing cost controls in hospitals, and promoting disease prevention.
- The keys to prevention are education and motivation. Although the motivation to stay healthy must come from within, certain incentives could be offered to help encourage people.

DO YOU REMEMBER?

Give brief definitions of these terms:

chiropractor	optometrist	dental hygienist	double coverage	triage
podiatrist	clinical psychologist	nurse-midwife	group practice	multiphasic screening

THINK AND DISCUSS

1. What reasons can you give for a company to provide an employee health care program that includes courses in weight control and fitness training?

2. What opportunities for health activism exist in your community?

3. If a community clinic is having financial problems, what measures might help?

4. What kinds of people do you think would best be able to point out local health needs to a government agency?

5. Do you think the training period for physicians should be shortened? Why or why not?

6. Why might it be better for dental assistants to be trained in a formal program instead of on the job?

7. In order to ensure an equal distribution of physicians, should the government tell physicians where to practice? Why or why not?

8. Many doctors now wear regular street clothes instead of dressing in white. Why do you think they do this?

9. What benefits do you think group practice offers the doctors in the group?

FOLLOW-UP

1. Find out more about how Ralph Nader and his Public Interest Research Group have helped community efforts to improve health care. Write a report on your findings.

2. Contact or visit your local health department to find out the kinds of services it offers the members of the community. Make a chart to illustrate these services and post it in your classroom.

3. Bring in a health insurance contract that belongs to a relative or friend. Compare the contract with those brought in by your classmates, and then discuss the kinds of health services the insurance covers, as well as the kinds it excludes.

4. Learn more about the National Health Service plan of Great Britain. Describe the good and bad points of the plan to your class.

5. Contact several large and small companies in your area to find out about the health care plans they offer to their employees. Write a report on your findings.

6. Obtain information from the local chapter of a volunteer agency such as the United Fund to find out how money is collected and distributed. Post the information in your classroom.

7. Find out more about the workings of health maintenance organizations. Make a chart that lists the advantages and disadvantages of HMOs.

CHAPTER 22

Self-Care and the Consumer

After reading this chapter, you should be able to answer these questions:

1. What should you do to protect your health?
2. What should you think about when you choose a doctor?
3. What signals should warn you that you might be dealing with a health care "quack"?
4. What is the government doing to protect health care consumers?

In colonial times families often lived in isolated homes. The nearest doctor was likely to be days away by horseback. So when people got sick, they had to know how to take care of themselves.

As the country grew and transportation improved, it became easier to get a doctor. At the same time, new drugs were developed that could cure and control many diseases. Gradually, the self-reliance of the pioneer days disappeared.

Now the pendulum is swinging back. People are taking a new and active interest in caring for themselves. They are reading about health and asking their doctors questions. People have come to see that they, individually, can do much to care for their own minor illnesses.

The idea behind self-care is that people can, by learning more about their bodies, treat many ailments themselves. Self-care stresses the ability to identify when you are ill and to choose a course of action to combat the problem.

The self-care movement came about for a number of reasons. One is the high cost of health care. It makes economic sense to avoid as much as possible expensive visits to the doctor. Another reason is the overall interest in consumer concerns. We are all consumers of health care products and services. Thanks to the consumer movement, we are now learning to evaluate those products and services, to choose the right ones for our needs, and to recognize useless cures and remedies.

This chapter looks at the advantages and the limitations of self-care. It tells you what skills and knowledge you need in order to practice self-care. It identifies what ailments you can treat yourself and when you should see a doctor. It also explains how you can get the most out of your visit to your doctor and tells you what you need to know about prescription and over-the-counter drugs. Finally, it shows you how to protect yourself against quacks.

SECTION **1**   # The Self-Care Movement

The trend toward self-care is closely linked to other changes in our society. The consumer movement, for example, has made people more aware of the effectiveness, or the inappropriateness, of health care products and services. The growing interest in physical fitness has led to a widespread concern about personal health. Community clinics have spread the idea that people can do much to protect and maintain their own health. There is also an increased awareness that many illnesses can be self-treated.

Goals of Self-Care

Self-care does *not* mean you should never see a doctor. Medicine is a very complicated and specialized area of learning. There are many things you cannot and should not do for yourself. The primary goal of self-care is to know the difference between the health problems you can treat yourself and those that require a doctor's help. With self-care *you* have the main responsibility for your health. Your doctor becomes an adviser—a consultant.

Limitations of Self-Care

There are several pitfalls in the self-care movement. The most serious is ignorance. *Don't treat yourself or your family without first gaining the knowledge you need to do it properly*. Otherwise, you are apt to do more harm than good. There are many books and courses that can help you. The courses should be taught by a qualified person—a health educator, doctor, nurse, or other health professional. Guidelines on choosing books are given below.

Another problem involves going to extremes. Some people refuse to seek any kind of medical help from doctors. In times of illness, they are liable to fall prey to unscrupulous quacks who take their money in return for worthless remedies.

Preparation for Self-Care

Self-care requires knowledge and skill in several areas. You should know how to administer first aid in emergencies (see Chapter 19). You should be familiar with over-the-counter drugs and basic home health care equipment. You should also understand how to take prescription drugs and why you are taking them. You should know how to recognize and treat common minor ailments. You can also learn to participate in the treatment of more serious chronic ailments.

To practice self-care, you will need to keep certain items in the house. They include current information on health care and first aid, orderly medical records, and basic equipment and medicines.

Sources of Information

An overwhelming amount of material has been written about health care. There are many books on health for the layperson. Many private companies, professional groups, and government and voluntary health agencies also publish pamphlets and brochures.

However, there is probably no one source that will contain all that you need to know about self-care. Some books cover the topic very generally. Others treat only one disease, or they address a particular group, such as children or women.

How can you tell which sources are accurate? Your librarian or health education teacher can help you select the right books. Also, here are some guidelines to help you choose a useful publication.

1. Look at the qualifications of the authors. Do they have appropriate credentials in the areas in which they write? Do they represent a special interest? Do they appear biased in any way?

2. Check that the book is current. A 5- or 10-year-old book may contain out-of-date information.

3. Do the authors back up any claims they make? This is especially important when they are talking about new products or treatments. If research has not been completed on a product or procedure, they should state that. Also, the research offered in the publication should be properly documented. Do the samples referred to seem adequate or does the case for the new treatment rest on only a few isolated examples?

4. Is the material clearly organized? Can you find the topic you want quickly, in case of an emergency? To test this, you may choose several topics and look them up as you would expect them to be listed.

5. Is the content clear and to the point?

6. Can you understand the terminology? If there are many medical terms that you don't understand, the book will not be useful to you.

Regardless of what books or pamphlets you choose, if the information there contradicts advice given to you by your doctor, follow the doctor's recommendation.

Medical Records

Near the telephone you should keep the names and the numbers of people you may need to call in an emergency: doctors, dentist, ambulance,

Figure 22.1 Every time you have a medical treatment of any sort, you should list it in your health notebook.

hospital, fire department, police, poison control center, suicide hotline, and a close relative or friend. In case you can't reach any help by telephone, make sure you know the quickest route to the nearest hospital emergency room.

You should also have a family health notebook. Every time a member of the family has medical treatment of any sort, it should be listed in this book. Important information includes (1) dates and types of immunizations; (2) doctor and dentist visits; (3) test results; (4) treatments given for any illnesses or accidents; (5) pregnancies and births; (6) hospitalizations (including surgery); and (7) a brief health history of relatives not living with you.

This information is valuable for a number of reasons. It can be helpful in identifying hereditary diseases or tendencies. It can also help a doctor diagnose any future illness you may get. You may think now that you will remember all your medical treatments. But be safe—write them down. If you know, for instance, that you have been immunized against a particular disease, it could save you from being immunized again unnecessarily. Also, if you had an allergic reaction to a certain medication, a note in the book could save you from getting that medicine again.

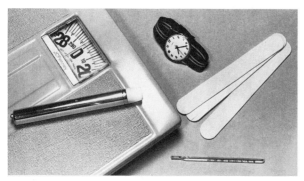

Figure 22.2 Basic tools for self-care. These should be kept neatly in one place, and every member of the family should know where to find them.

Self-Care Equipment

Simple tools that can help you examine yourself or your family are listed below. All these health care supplies should be kept neatly in one place. Every member of the family should know where to find them.

Thermometer You should have at least one good-quality oral thermometer for taking temperatures. If there is a baby or young child in the family, you should also have a rectal thermometer. Young children often cannot hold an oral thermometer in their mouths. They can also hurt themselves by biting the thermometer and breaking it.

Tongue Depressor and Small Flashlight These items are needed for examining the throat. Wooden tongue depressors are inexpensive, but they make some people gag. You can use a butter knife or spoon handle instead. The flashlight can also be used for examining eyes and ears.

Scale Most bathroom scales sold in department stores are not accurate. Accuracy, however, is not the most important feature. Just be sure that you always weigh yourself at the same time of day. Your weight does change somewhat during the course of the day. If you check your weight regularly, you will be able to spot sudden gains or losses that may be signs of illness.

Watch with a Second Hand You will need a watch to count your pulse (heartbeat) and respiration (breathing) rate.

Self-Care Examination

You should start to use this equipment when you and your family are well. If you know how your body acts normally, you will be able to notice changes that may indicate illness. When you do need professional help, you will be able to give the physician better information about your symptoms. The self-care equipment is used to check *vital signs*. These signs indicate the condition of your body. They include pulse, respiration, temperature, size of pupils, color and condition of skin and tongue, and reaction to verbal and physical stimuli. Changes in any of these signs can be a warning about a health problem.

Self-examinations should be triggered if you or anyone in your family notices any general signs that something is wrong. Your body and mind constantly monitor your well-being and often give off signals that a problem may be developing. Learn to identify the most common of these signals: excessive fatigue, nagging aches or pains, insomnia, unwarranted anxiety or irritability, tenseness, and sudden feelings of chill or of excessive warmth. Go through a self-examination as soon as you become aware of one or more of these signals.

Pulse (Heartbeat) The pulse should be taken when you or the "patient" is resting. Any exertion, even just standing up, will change the pulse rate.

With the patient's palm up, place one or two fingers on the thumb-side of the wrist. Press gently. (Do not use your thumb. It has a pulse of its own.) Using a watch with a second hand, count the number of pulse beats you feel for 15 seconds. Multiply your count by four. The result is the heart rate in beats per minute.

In healthy young children at rest, the normal heart rate is 90 to 120 beats a minute. In adults the rate is slower, 60 to 80 a minute. Athletes in top condition can have pulse rates as low as 40 to 60 a minute. Remember, these are just

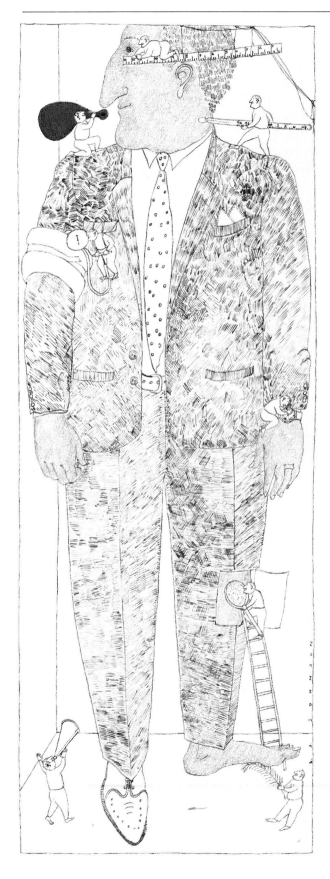

Figure 22.3 Your vital signs are good indicators of the overall condition of your body. These signs include pulse, respiration rate, temperature, size of pupils, color and condition of skin, and reaction to verbal and physical stimuli.

ranges. By taking a pulse regularly, you can find out what is normal for you and your family.

Respiration (Breathing Rate)   Watch the patient's chest as it rises and falls. Count each complete breath (a breath in and out) as one. Count for 15 seconds using a watch with a second hand. Multiply the count by four. Try to do this without the patient's knowledge. It could affect the person's breathing rate.

After age 15, a person's respiration rate should be about 20 breaths a minute. Older adults can have lower rates, for instance 14 to 16 a minute at age 70. The rates for younger children are higher, averaging about 25. Infants have an average rate of 35 to 40 breaths a minute.

Temperature   See Figure 22.4 to find out how to take a person's temperature. Clean the thermometer with rubbing alcohol after each use.

While normal mouth temperature is 98.6°F, it can vary by several degrees and still be normal. Eating, drinking, and smoking can change mouth temperature. If an individual has done any of these things, wait at least a half-hour before taking his or her temperature.

Temperatures above 100.4°F and below 96.8°F are usually indications that something is wrong. High fevers should not be ignored, especially in children, because a high temperature that lasts for more than a short time can cause brain damage.

Eyes   First look at the whites of the eyes. A yellowish or reddish color may indicate illness. Then gently draw down the lower lid. The inner lining should be moist and pink. A grayish or reddish color and swelling of this lining are also trouble signs. Crustiness around the eyelashes could also be a sign of illness.

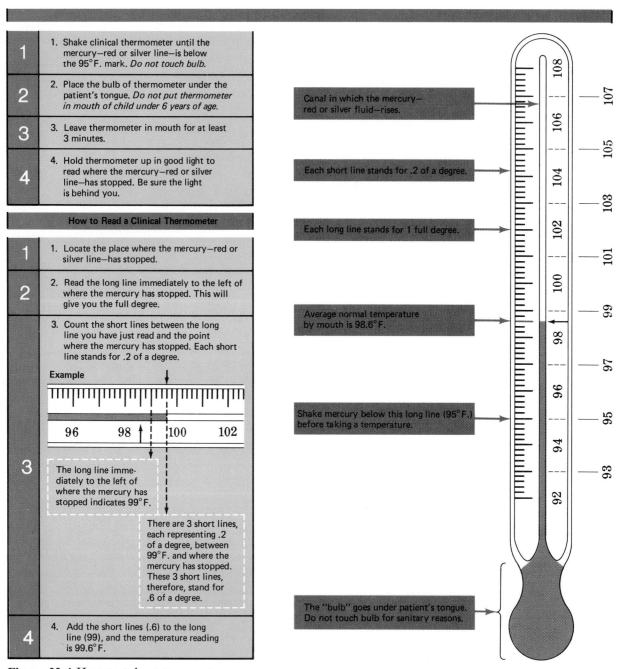

1. 1. Shake clinical thermometer until the mercury—red or silver line—is below the 95°F. mark. *Do not touch bulb.*

2. 2. Place the bulb of thermometer under the patient's tongue. *Do not put thermometer in mouth of child under 6 years of age.*

3. 3. Leave thermometer in mouth for at least 3 minutes.

4. 4. Hold thermometer up in good light to read where the mercury—red or silver line—has stopped. Be sure the light is behind you.

How to Read a Clinical Thermometer

1. 1. Locate the place where the mercury—red or silver line—has stopped.

2. 2. Read the long line immediately to the left of where the mercury has stopped. This will give you the full degree.

3. 3. Count the short lines between the long line you have just read and the point where the mercury has stopped. Each short line stands for .2 of a degree.

Example

96   98   100   102

The long line immediately to the left of where the mercury has stopped indicates 99°F.

There are 3 short lines, each representing .2 of a degree, between 99°F. and where the mercury has stopped. These 3 short lines, therefore, stand for .6 of a degree.

4. 4. Add the short lines (.6) to the long line (99), and the temperature reading is 99.6°F.

Canal in which the mercury—red or silver fluid—rises.

Each short line stands for .2 of a degree.

Each long line stands for 1 full degree.

Average normal temperature by mouth is 98.6°F.

Shake mercury below this long line (95°F.) before taking a temperature.

The "bulb" goes under patient's tongue. Do not touch bulb for sanitary reasons.

Figure 22.4 How to take a temperature.

To check the size of the pupil, first darken the room. This will cause the pupil to dilate (get larger). Hold a flashlight about one-third of a meter (about a foot) above the person's head. Bring it down and shine the light directly into the pupil. Repeat for the other eye. The pupil should get smaller when the light flashes into the eye. If it does not, it may be a sign of head injury. Another sign of head injury is that the pupil stays small after the light is removed.

Throat To examine a throat, have the patient tilt her or his head back, open the mouth wide, and say "Ahhh." With a tongue depressor or spoon handle, press down the tongue. At the same time, shine a light down the throat. You should look at healthy throats to become familiar with their appearance. If someone in your family complains of a sore throat, examine it carefully. If the throat is red and swollen or if there are whitish or yellowish patches, call the doctor and describe the way the throat looks.

Breasts Breast cancer is the second leading cause of cancer death among women in the United States. If it is detected and treated early, however, nearly 85 percent of its victims recover. The American Cancer Society recommends that women examine their own breasts every month. Although most women who get breast cancer are middle-aged or older, the Society also recommends that girls begin the habit of breast self-examination while in high school. (Instructions for self-examination are given on page 347.)

Over-the-Counter Drugs

Almost every family uses over-the-counter drugs from time to time. Exactly what you should keep in your home depends on your family's health situation. Whatever drugs you have should be kept out of the reach of children. Always read the labels carefully, and take note of the warnings and the recommended dosages. Some of the drugs you are most likely to keep in your medicine cabinet are listed below.

Pain Relievers *Aspirin* is probably the most widely used of all drugs. It is sold by itself and in combination with other drugs. Aspirin offers temporary relief from headaches, muscle pain, and toothaches. It also lowers fever and reduces the inflammation of joints.

Aspirin is safe for most people, but there are some dangers. Aspirin is a leading cause of poisoning deaths among children under five. Children's flavored aspirin can be particularly dangerous because it looks like candy. Aspirin can upset the stomach, cause ringing in the ears, or cause ulcers to flare up. It also makes the blood take longer to clot.

Acetaminophen is a nonaspirin pain reliever. It is sold under many trade names such as Tylenol and Datril. For most people it is as safe and effective as aspirin. But it can damage the liver and upset the kidneys. This can happen when large doses are taken over an extended period of time. Acetaminophen can also cause problems if the patient is already suffering from an existing liver condition or if it is used by someone with an alcohol problem.

Research has shown that *ibuprofen*, a new over-the-counter pain reliever, is as effective against pain as aspirin and acetaminophen. It is the most effective of the three in blocking *prostaglandins*, the main cause of menstrual cramps; and like aspirin, it is good for treating sprains and joint aches because it reduces inflammation as well as pain.

Antacids *Antacids* overcome the effects of too much acid in the stomach. These effects—indigestion, sour stomach, and heartburn—are usually caused by overeating or by not relaxing during or just after eating.

Antacids come in tablet and liquid form. The liquid is more effective. It coats more of the stomach wall. To do their job, antacid pills must be chewed thoroughly.

Figure 22.5 Most families keep a number of over-the-counter preparations on hand. Before using any of these medicines, read the label carefully.

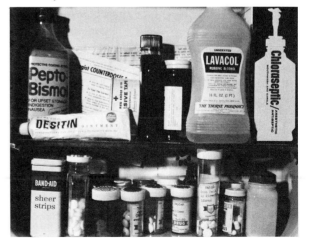

Some antacids contain sodium bicarbonate. This neutralizes acid quickly. However, the disadvantage of these antacids is that they are absorbed into the bloodstream. When this happens, the acid-base balance of the body can be disturbed. The result can be that the stomach will just produce more acid in a rebound effect.

Other antacids contain magnesium or aluminum. They are not absorbed into the bloodstream. However, they can cause diarrhea or constipation.

Antihistamines These drugs are used to relieve the symptoms of colds and allergies. *Antihistamines* can shrink swollen membranes and ease runny noses, watery eyes, and itching. They do not cure the cold or allergic reaction. They only reduce the discomfort.

Antihistamines have many side effects. They include drowsiness, dizziness, blurred vision, nervousness, nausea, and headaches. If used for long periods of time, these drugs can cause permanent damage to the membranes of the nose, throat, and sinuses. They can also lessen the body's defenses against infection.

Laxatives *Laxatives* are used to relieve constipation. They are among the most misused of all nonprescription drugs. Many people take laxatives because they think it is harmful not to have a bowel movement every day. This is not necessarily true. The normal range is anything from three a day to three a week.

When a person takes a laxative, the bowels are completely emptied. Several days can go by before the system returns to normal. This may lead the person to take more of the laxative. After a while the person may develop a laxative habit.

Unless it is ordered by a doctor, no laxative should be taken for more than a week. A proper diet, one that includes raw vegetables, fresh fruits, and whole-grain foods, will usually prevent constipation. Drinking enough water is also important, as is a proper amount of exercise.

Antidiarrhea Preparations These drugs should be used only if the diarrhea is very serious. You should try a clear liquid diet before you use any drug. Diarrhea usually goes away by itself. However, it can sometimes be a sign of a serious illness. If it lasts more than a few days, with or without medication, you should see a doctor. It should also be noted that diarrhea often follows an antibiotic treatment. Try drinking a few glasses of milk after you have stopped taking the antibiotic treatment to remedy this side effect.

Emetics An *emetic* is something that will make you vomit. In case of accidental poisoning there should be an emetic in your medicine cabinet. This is especially important if there are small children in the house. The most widely used emetic is syrup of ipecac. For information on how to treat a poisoning victim, see Chapter 19.

Care of Chronic Conditions

Chronic conditions, such as diabetes, arthritis, kidney disease, and ulcers, usually last a long time, and in some cases a lifetime. They generally require some type of continuing medication, exercise, diet, or other treatment. The patient or the patient's family may have to learn special skills. These may include giving injections, taking blood pressure readings, performing kidney dialysis, carrying out a physical therapy program, or maintaining a special diet. Good daily care can prevent setbacks and can help the patient feel better and live longer.

CHECK YOUR UNDERSTANDING

1. What is the primary goal of self-care? What are two pitfalls?
2. List six guidelines to help you select useful sources of self-care information.
3. What kinds of information should be listed in your family health notebook?
4. What are the five basic pieces of self-care equipment? When should you start using them? Why?
5. List the vital signs that indicate the condition of the body. Why shouldn't you take a pulse with your thumb?

SECTION **2**   **You and Your Doctor**

Practicing self-care can reduce the need for professional medical help. Sooner or later, though, most of us need to see a doctor. But how do you go about choosing a doctor? And how can you make sure that you get the most out of your visit? In this section you'll learn what you can do before and during a visit to the doctor in order to get full benefit from it.

How to Choose a Doctor

It is often difficult to choose a doctor, particularly if you have just moved into a new area. In some parts of the country there is a shortage of doctors. Physicians in those regions may not want to accept new patients. If you are planning to move, you may ask your present doctor to recommend a physician in the area of your new home. You may also ask friends, relatives, and schoolmates. Remember, though, that nonmedical people are not always the best judges of a doctor's qualifications.

Local medical societies will usually give out names of physicians who are willing to take new patients. However, they will not evaluate them for you. Another thing you may do is to choose a doctor who is associated with the nearest hospital. Or, if you live near a university medical center, you may want to go to a physician who is on staff there.

Most libraries have reference books that list physicians' education and experience. One such book, put out by the American Medical Association, is the *Directory of Medical Specialists*. It lists, by state, doctors who are certified by the professional board of their specialty.

When you have found a physician, it would be a good idea to set up an appointment to discuss your health care needs and expectations. Don't wait until you get sick. If you find that the doctor does not want to give you an appointment unless you're sick, try someone else. Of course, this visit will cost you money because you are taking the doctor's time, but it very likely will be worthwhile in the long run. If

Figure 22.6 A good doctor should be willing to take the time to discuss your health needs and expectations, even if you are not ill.

the doctor is familiar with you and your health history, he or she will be better able to help you when you are ill.

Physical Examinations

Physical examinations can range from extensive multiphasic screenings that involve many tests (see Chapter 21) to simple ones in which only the heart, weight, and blood pressure are checked. Most doctors agree that an extensive physical examination every year isn't necessary. However, the older a person gets, the more useful this type of examination is likely to be. It may help the doctor find illnesses that have no obvious symptoms in their early stages.

Most illnesses in children and young adults are discovered when symptoms appear. Therefore, a routine checkup may not be worth the money. Some doctors recommend a physical examination every five years for people between ages 30 and 40. For those between 40 and 50, every three years is recommended, and every two years for those between 50 and 60. These are only general recommendations for those people with no specific problems or special circumstances. In all age groups there are exceptions. For example, a woman of any age who is planning to have a baby should have a complete physical examination.

People who are exposed to dangerous chemicals or radiation at work should be examined frequently. Anyone who has a chronic condition, such as heart disease or diabetes, should also have frequent checkups. Also, people who have a family history of a serious disease should be checked regularly for signs of that condition.

There are some things that all people should have checked regularly. A complete physical exam is not necessary to have these items tested.

Blood Pressure   Everyone should have her or his blood pressure checked about once a year. High blood pressure can be very dangerous if not treated. It can lead to problems with the heart, arteries, brain, and kidneys. Frequent checking is necessary because a person may feel fine and have no symptoms even though her or his pressure is high.

Pap Test   In 1980 the American Cancer Society revised its recommendations about the Pap test. In the past an annual test was advised. The new guidelines, which are being challenged by some cancer specialists, are as follows. Women between 20 and 65, and younger women who are sexually active, should have this test at least once every three years. The test is done to check for cancer of the cervix. A few cells are taken from the cervix in a simple, painless procedure. The cells are then examined under a microscope. This type of cancer is completely curable if detected early. Women who have a family history of cervical cancer should have the test done more frequently.

For women aged 20 to 40, the doctor can also check for breast cancer during the same visit. Women over 40 should be checked for breast cancer every year.

Other Tests   Eyes, ears, and teeth should be checked regularly. Your doctor can decide whether your blood and urine should be checked or whether you need other tests.

When to See a Doctor

As mentioned earlier, one of the goals of self-care is to know when you can treat yourself and when you should consult a doctor. The following is a list of some situations that call for a doctor's help. It is by no means a complete list.

1. broken bones
2. heavy bleeding that does not stop
3. chest pain or any other heart attack symptoms (see Chapter 17)
4. severe pain in any part of the body
5. blood in the urine or feces or coughing up blood
6. cold sweats, especially when combined with light-headedness and chest or stomach pain
7. major burns
8. unconsciousness
9. disorientation (The person cannot tell who or where he or she is.)
10. fever that continues for more than a few days or fever above 104°F
11. suspected poisoning
12. sudden, unexplained weight loss or gain
13. lump in the breast or any of the other warning signs of cancer (see Chapter 18)
14. possible pregnancy

You will need to see a doctor for immunization injections. A visit to the doctor is also necessary if you need antibiotics or other prescription drugs.

Many people put off going to the doctor because they are afraid. They may fear that they have a serious or fatal disease or that they will not be able to pay their medical bills. Do not let any of these reasons stop you. Many conditions can be treated successfully if they are caught in time. And many times what you think is a sign of a serious condition is something minor. As far as cost is concerned, medical insurance often covers part of the bill. When patients have to pay large bills themselves, they may be able to make financial arrangements.

How to Talk with Your Doctor

Once you get to the doctor, make sure you know what you are going to say. Be as specific as possible in explaining your symptoms. "I feel terrible" is not enough. Information such as "I have a temperature of 102°F, and my throat has been sore for three days," is much more useful.

So that you won't forget any important points, it may be helpful to write down what you want to say or ask. You should also write down what the doctor tells you to do. Whether the doctor asks you or not, tell her or him the following information: (1) if you are seeing another doctor for another problem; (2) what medicines, prescription or over-the-counter,

you have been taking; and (3) what allergies you have, if any.

If the doctor uses words you don't understand, don't be afraid to ask for an explanation. If you have a long-lasting health problem, get to know the medical words associated with it. This knowledge will save time for both you and the doctor. You may find a medical dictionary useful.

Before you leave the doctor's office, make sure you understand what problem you have and what the treatment will be. Find out how soon you should come back for another visit. If you are given a prescription, you should ask additional questions (see below).

Figure 22.7 A check list of questions to ask yourself and your doctor.

Before the visit, ask yourself these questions:
1	Why am I going to the doctor? (the main reason or "chief complaint")
2	Is there anything else that worries me about my health? If so, please list.
3	What do I expect the doctor to do for me today? (in ten words or less)

During the visit, complete with help of your doctor:
1	What is the diagnosis?
2	What exactly does that mean? (If you already understand the diagnosis, omit this question.)
3	Why did I get it, and how can I prevent it next time?
4	Are there any helpful patient-education materials available for the condition? or special organizations I should look into (for example, the Diabetic Association, Muscular Dystrophy Association, and so on)?
5	Are there any medications for me to take? If so, are there any special instructions, concerns, or possible side effects I need to know about the medicine?
6	When am I to return for another visit, if any?
7	What should I do at home in the way of activity, treatments, or precautions?
8	Am I to phone in for lab reports? Will you notify me even if my lab tests are negative?
9	Should I report back to the doctor for any reason?

Prescription Drugs

When you take any drug, you should know something about its effects, both short-term and long-term. This is particularly important with prescription drugs, because they are often stronger than over-the-counter drugs. Over-the-counter drugs can only relieve symptoms. Some prescription drugs, on the other hand, can actually cure disease. But they can also cause serious side effects. Before leaving a doctor's office with a prescription, you should know the answers to the following questions.

What is the drug? How much will it cost? Ask for the name of the drug. The doctor should tell you the brand name and the *generic name*. The generic name indicates what the drug is made of. Ask the doctor if you can buy the drug by the generic name. Often that will save you money. Also prices can vary from pharmacy to pharmacy. Shop around if you can.

What is the drug supposed to do? Ask the doctor to tell you exactly what the drug will do. An answer such as "It will make you feel better" is not enough.

How should I take the drug? Drugs come in many forms—pills, capsules, liquids, and more. They can be swallowed, inhaled, injected, and so on. If you are taking a drug orally, ask if it should be taken with or without water or other liquids. In some cases, water is needed to help dissolve the pill and prevent stomach upset. Some liquids, on the other hand, can cause medicines not to work. Tetracycline, for instance, cannot be taken with milk or milk products.

When should I take the drug? An instruction to "take three times a day" can be confusing. Does it mean three times in a 24-hour day? Does it mean three times during the time you are awake? Ask the doctor. Also ask if the drug should be taken before, during, or after meals.

Do I have to change my diet or activities while I'm taking the drug? Some drugs cannot be taken with certain foods. Others cannot be combined with alcoholic beverages. Check with the doctor. Some drugs might make you sleepy. If that is the case, you should not drive, work with dangerous machinery, or do other hazardous activities while taking the drug.

How long should I take the drug? Some prescription drugs are one-time only medicines. Others are intended to be used for a long time. With some drugs, you must keep taking the prescription even after the symptoms go away. This is often true of antibiotics—if you stop taking them too soon, the infection may flare up again.

What happens if I miss a dose? Never take a dose sooner than you should and *never* take a double dose when you have missed a dose. If you are concerned about what to do if you forget to take your medicine, check with your doctor.

What side effects can I expect? All drugs can cause side effects. Some can be quite serious. Make sure you know what side effects you can look for. Also find out what to do if you experience these effects. Be prepared.

Is this the mildest drug that will help me? Because newer and often stronger drugs are continually coming on the market, physicians may prescribe a drug that will do the job but that is more powerful than necessary just because it is new. Make it clear to your doctor that you are not "pill happy." You want to get well, of course, but you want to do it with the simplest and least strong remedy possible. Taking stronger drugs than are necessary will not

Figure 22.8 The patient's bill of rights.

#	
1	The patient has the right to considerate and respectful care.
2	The patient has the right to obtain from his physician complete current information concerning his diagnosis, treatment, and prognosis in terms the patient can be reasonably expected to understand. When it is not medically advisable to give such information to the patient, the information should be made available to an appropriate person in his behalf. He has the right to know, by name, the physician responsible for coordinating his care.
3	The patient has the right to receive from his physician information necessary to give informed consent prior to the start of any procedure and treatment. Except in emergencies, such information for informed consent should include but not necessarily be limited to the specific procedure and/or treatment, the medically significant risks involved, and the probable duration of incapacitation. Where medically significant alternatives for care or treatment exist, or when the patient requests information concerning medical alternatives, the patient has the right to such information. The patient also has the right to know the name of the person responsible for the procedures and/or treatment.
4	The patient has the right to refuse treatment to the extent permitted by law and to be informed of the medical consequences of his action.
5	The patient has the right to every consideration of his privacy concerning his own medical care program. Case discussion, consultation, examination, and treatment are confidential and should be conducted discreetly. Those not directly involved in his care must have the permission of the patient to be present.
6	The patient has the right to expect that all communications and records pertaining to his care should be treated as confidential.
7	The patient has the right to expect that within its capacity a hospital must make reasonable response to the request of a patient for services. The hospital must provide evaluation, service, and/or referral as indicated by the urgency of the case. When medically permissible, a patient may be transferred to another facility only after he has received complete information and explanation concerning the needs for and alternatives to such a transfer. The institution to which the patient is to be transferred must first have accepted the patient for transfer.
8	The patient has the right to obtain information as to any relationship of his hospital to other health care and educational institutions insofar as his care is concerned. The patient has the right to obtain information as to the existence of any professional relationships among individuals, by name, who are treating him.
9	The patient has the right to be advised if the hospital proposes to engage in or perform human experimentation affecting his care or treatment. The patient has the right to refuse to participate in such research projects.
10	The patient has the right to expect reasonable continuity of care. He has the right to know in advance what appointment times and physicians are available and where. The patient has the right to expect that the hospital will provide a mechanism whereby he is informed by his physician or a delegate of the physician of the patient's continuing health care requirements following discharge.
11	The patient has the right to examine and receive an explanation of his bill regardless of source of payment.
12	The patient has the right to know what hospital rules and regulations apply to his conduct as a patient.

help you and may, in fact, cause you to undergo unnecessary side effects.

Are there any alternative treatments besides drugs? Particularly in cases involving tranquilizers, sedatives, and the like, you should question whether there is another way of coping with the problem. Americans today are much too accustomed to solving everything with a pill. Let your physician know you are not like that.

Your Rights as a Patient

The self-care movement has brought new attention to the rights of patients. Patients in hospitals and those being treated outside of hospitals do have certain legal rights. They also have certain ethical rights. Accordingly, a Patient's Bill of Rights was drawn up by the American Hospital Association (see Figure 22.8). While it is not a legal document, it does put forth guidelines for both patients and health professionals. Among other things, it emphasizes the patients' rights to be fully informed about their treatment and their rights to expect reasonable care.

As mentioned, this bill of rights is *not* a legal document. If you have any legal questions about health care, you should consult a lawyer or local legal aid society.

CHECK YOUR UNDERSTANDING

1. What are some ways to help you choose a doctor?
2. List the recommended physical examination schedule for people in different age groups. Who are some of the exceptions to this schedule?
3. List 10 situations that require a doctor's aid.
4. Describe the points to make when you talk to your doctor during an office visit.
5. What questions should you ask your doctor about prescription drugs?

SECTION **3** **Guarding Against Quackery**

Americans spend more than $10 billion a year on quackery—useless treatments and medicines that have no healing powers whatsoever. These unwise consumer decisions are partly a result of ignorance. People who have little knowledge about health and medicine are more likely than informed people to believe in quack remedies and health fads.

Many people also turn to quack remedies because they are afraid of pain, illness, or death. Often they delay seeing a doctor because they don't want their fears confirmed. Quacks take advantage of such fears. They promise that their so-called cures will be painless, and they guarantee success.

Sometimes the cures seem to work. That's because of the *placebo effect.* Placebos are substances, such as sugar pills, that have no medicinal value but which are given for their psychological effect. Patients who believe that they are taking a medicine, when in fact all they are taking is sugar, often claim that they feel better. Wishful thinking, hope, and the promises of a quack therapist, then, all have a placebo effect.

The placebo effect also illustrates the fact that many illnesses have a *psychosomatic* basis. The patient's mental state has led to, or made worse, a physical condition. Quack remedies seem to work in such cases because they relieve the anxiety that was causing the illness. It would be far better, though, if the patient were to deal with the cause of the anxiety instead of taking useless medicines.

Quack remedies seem to work at times because people with certain diseases do get better when they take them. But what they overlook is the fact that these illnesses only last for a limited time. How long does a cold last, for instance? A week if you treat it, a week if you

 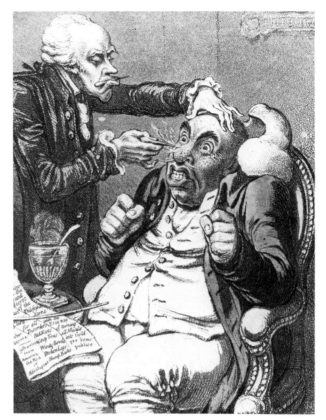

Figure 22.9 People throughout history have turned, out of ignorance or fear, to quack therapists who promised quick and easy cures for their ills. Even today, Americans spend more than $10 billion a year on quackery.

don't. A large number of useless remedies are bought to treat illnesses that would cure themselves in time.

Not all illnesses cure themselves, however. The tragedy of fake cures for such diseases is that sick people may be risking their lives, as well as wasting their money. Time spent taking useless cures is time taken from proper treatment.

How to Recognize Quackery

The best line of defense against quackery is to learn about health and about how quacks work. Quacks often follow certain patterns. If the answer to any of the following questions is yes, beware.

1. Does the seller of the product or service claim that the medical profession is trying to keep this "great discovery" from the public?
2. Does the seller say that doctor-prescribed medical treatments such as x-rays, surgery, and medication will do more harm than good?
3. Is the product or service sold door to door or advertised at public lectures?
4. Is the product or service advertised in sensational magazines, by a faith healer's group, or by a crusading organization?
5. Does the seller use statements by so-called satisfied customers to prove the product's worth?
6. Does the seller use scare tactics such as pictures of the "awful consequences" of not using the product?

7. Is the product or service promoted as a "secret remedy"?
8. Does the seller guarantee a quick cure?
9. Is the product or service claimed to cure many illnesses?
10. Is the address of the seller only a post office box number?

Quacks usually go after people who have chronic or incurable diseases. The victims of arthritis and cancer are particularly likely to fall prey to health quacks. For a discussion of specific forms of cancer quackery, see Chapter 18.

Close to $1 billion is spent on arthritis quackery each year. For every dollar spent on legitimate research, 25 are spent on false cures. One of the most common is the copper bracelet, which quacks claim cures arthritis magnetically. Other false cures include vibrating pillows and chairs and even visits to uranium mines. There is no medical cure for arthritis as yet, but proper treatment may be able to eliminate or reduce the symptoms. Quackery can do no good at all.

Buyer Beware

There are hundreds of thousands of health care products and services that we can buy without a prescription. How can we tell which ones are reliable and useful, and which are fraudulent? Unfortunately, we usually have to rely on the seller for most of the information about a product. That information is given on packaging and in advertisements. Often, though, sellers don't provide the information we need to make an intelligent decision. And sometimes, they deliberately try to obscure the facts.

Rather than providing facts, advertisers often make emotional appeals. Their aim is to create a desire for their products. Ads for a certain brand of toothpaste, for example, may suggest that you will be lonely and have no friends if you don't use the product. But they may never tell you how the product works. Thus, you have no way of judging how effective it is.

When you are about to buy any health care product, you should ask the same questions you would ask about prescription medicines: How does it work? Is it safe? What are the side effects? Are there other solutions to this health problem?

If you do have a bad experience with any over-the-counter remedy, you should report it to a government or private consumer agency.

CHECK YOUR UNDERSTANDING

1. Give two reasons that people turn to quack remedies.
2. Explain two reasons that quack remedies seem to work.
3. List five of the warning signs of quackery.
4. What kinds of people are usually the targets for quacks?
5. List four questions you should ask before you buy any health care product.

SECTION **4** **Who Helps the Consumer?**

There are relatively few agencies with direct responsibility for protecting consumers against unsafe or worthless health products. Moreover, their budgets are much smaller than the advertising and promotional budgets of the product manufacturers. Some consumer protection is provided by government agencies. There are also private organizations that provide consumers with information about products and services.

Federal Government Agencies

Food and Drug Administration (FDA) The FDA works to protect consumers against unsafe and worthless health products. It was established in 1931 to regulate food and drugs shipped across state lines. At that time, it enforced the rules of the Pure Food and Drug Act of 1906. Over the years Congress has given the FDA more powers. The present Food, Drug, and Cosmetic Act, which was passed in 1938, makes it a crime to put false or misleading information on drug labels. The act also requires that active ingredients be listed on labels. In addition, it demands that all manufactured foods, drugs, and cosmetics be proved safe before they can be sold.

In 1962 the FDA's powers were extended further. The Kefauver-Harris Drug Reform Act requires drug manufacturers to prove that their drugs are not only safe but also effective. It also requires that drug labels list side effects. And it authorizes the immediate recall of hazardous drugs. This law was broadened in 1972 to cover over-the-counter drugs as well as prescription drugs.

The FDA's responsibilities were also expanded by the passage of the Hazardous Substance and Labeling Act of 1969. The act requires that all household products that are poisonous, flammable, or dangerous in some other way carry a warning label. If the products are poisonous, antidotes must be listed. Since 1976 the FDA has also been responsible for checking medical devices such as x-ray equipment and artificial heart valves.

As part of its drug evaluation process, the FDA checks the research data of drug manufacturers. This includes closely regulating any drug testing that is done on humans. The FDA also does some research and testing in its own laboratories.

Federal Trade Commission (FTC) Since 1938 the FTC has protected consumers against harm that could result from false advertising. By law, a company is responsible for claims it makes about its products. It can also be held responsible if it omits important information from product labels.

Every year the FTC investigates hundreds of cases of false claims in advertising. It issues orders telling companies to stop making the claims. A company that does not obey may be fined as much as $10,000 a day. Many cases, however, are in the courts a long time. It took the FTC 16 years, for instance, to get Carter's Little Liver Pills (which do nothing for the liver) to drop the word *liver* from the product name. During all that time the company continued to use the word. Even today, many people still believe that Carter's pills are good for the liver.

Consumer Product Safety Commission Every year thousands of Americans are killed and some 2 million are injured while using household products. The Consumer Product Safety Commission was created in 1972 to reduce risk of injury from household products. It develops and enforces safety standards for about 10,000 products. These range from household appliances and power tools to toys and skateboards.

Just how much power the agency has, though, is still unclear. There are many cases being heard in courts. Manufacturing companies often claim that people get hurt only if they don't use the product correctly. The government tries to prove that the company could have designed the product to be safer. It also encourages companies to provide information on the safe use of their products.

United States Postal Service One of the functions of the Postal Service is to guard the public against the sale of fraudulent products by mail. Anyone convicted of mail fraud can get five years in jail and/or a $1,000 fine. The Postal Service can also refuse to deliver mail to fraudulent mail-order companies and thus put them out of business.

Private Consumer Agencies

Better Business Bureau (BBB) Most urban areas have a Better Business Bureau. This is a nonprofit organization that is supported by private firms. The BBB protects companies and individuals against unfair competition, misleading advertising, and other unfair practices. The BBB also handles any complaints people may have about dealings with business firms. Local chambers of commerce do similar work.

Consumers' Research and Consumers Union
These are private groups that test and rate consumer products. They get their funds from donations and from the sale of their publications. Consumers Union publishes the monthly *Consumer Reports*. This magazine compares the price, performance, and safety of many items, including drugs and health care products.

Local Radio, Television, and Newspapers
Consumer reporters and consumer complaint columns can use the power of publicity to solve consumer problems. They often get very quick results. One local television station, for example, ran a story about a chain of drugstores. It reported that the stores were charging more for prescriptions in the poorer parts of the city than in wealthier areas. The stores were doing this, said the TV station, because the poor people had no automobiles and *had* to buy from the store in the neighborhood. As a result of this bad publicity, the drugstore chain changed its policy on pricing.

CHECK YOUR UNDERSTANDING

1. Compare the work of the FDA with that of the FTC.
2. Describe the work of the Consumer Product Safety Commission.
3. How does the Postal Service protect consumers?
4. What kind of information can be found in the *Consumer Reports* magazine?

CHAPTER SUMMARY

- The primary goal of self-care is to know the difference between the health problems you can treat yourself and those that require a doctor's help.
- To practice self-care, you should obtain reference books, keep your own medical records, and stock diagnostic equipment and certain over-the-counter medications. You should learn how to use them *before* someone gets sick.
- Doctors disagree about the need to have an extensive physical examination every year. There is general agreement, though, that the older a person gets, the more useful this type of examination is likely to be.
- Among the situations for which you should seek prompt medical attention are broken bones, heavy bleeding, severe pain, unconsciousness, prolonged or very high fever, and disorientation.

- If your doctor gives you a prescription, find out all you can about the drug being prescribed. You should know its generic name, what it is supposed to do, how and when you should take it, and what side effects to expect.
- Americans spend more than $10 billion on quack remedies every year. Quack remedies sometimes seem to work because of their placebo effect. Many illnesses, if left untreated, would cure themselves in time.
- To protect yourself from quackery, you should learn how quacks operate and what patterns they follow.
- Among the organizations that regulate or provide information about consumer health products are the FDA, FTC, Consumer Product Safety Commission, Postal Service, and private consumer agencies.

DO YOU REMEMBER?

Give brief definitions of these terms:

pulse	antacid	emetic	quackery
respiration	antihistamine	Pap test	placebo
acetaminophen	laxative	generic name	ibuprofen

THINK AND DISCUSS

1. What are the benefits for the medical profession of people's becoming more involved in self-care?
2. What are your courses of action when you feel dissatisfied with the way your doctor is treating you?
3. Why would it be a good idea to check your family's medicine cabinet from time to time?
4. Besides savings in money, what other advantages does self-care have?
5. What changes or additions would you make to the Patient's Bill of Rights?
6. What do you consider the most important qualities a doctor can have?
7. Do you think doctors should be allowed to advertise? Why or why not?

FOLLOW-UP

1. Clip out newspaper and magazine advertisements for health care products you suspect promise far more than they can deliver. Bring them to class and explain the reasons for your suspicions.
2. In your local drugstore or supermarket, compare store brands and name brands for a variety of over-the-counter drugs (aspirin, antacids, etc.). Make a list showing the differences in price and in ingredients. Explain how you would decide which ones to buy.
3. Make a chart of your pulse rate at different times of day and after different activities. Compare your chart with those of your classmates to see the range that exists in your age group.
4. By talking to friends and relatives, make up a list of common household remedies (e.g., putting mud on a bee sting) and sayings about the treatment of disease (e.g., Feed a cold and starve a fever). Discuss the validity of these remedies and sayings with your class.
5. Contact your local Y or library to find out what courses in self-care are available in your area. Post the information in your classroom.
6. Find an account by an early American settler that describes the kinds of treatments used when someone was sick. Write a report on these treatments.

The
Body Systems

The human body is enormously complex and highly efficient. Day after day it performs a variety of functions, many of them beyond our conscious control. Well within our control, though, is the maintenance of this complex mechanism.

In order to promote or maintain health, we need some understanding of the workings of the human body. Most complex systems can be broken down into subsystems, and the human body is no exception. It is made up of groups of systems that work closely together and that depend upon each other for the overall functioning of the body.

This appendix provides an overview of the structure and function of the major body systems. One major system—the reproductive system—is not included here because it is covered in detail in Chapter 8.

The Skeletal System

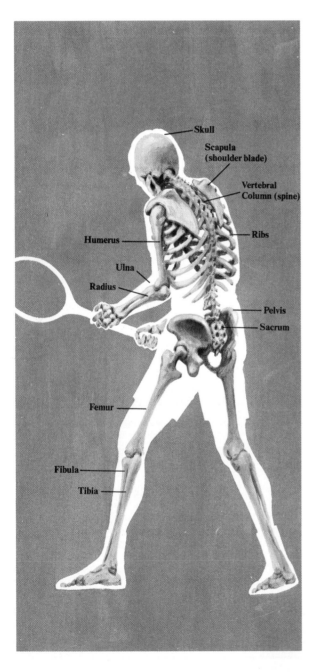

The skeleton is the framework of the human body. The 206 bones that make it up serve many functions. Some determine the types of movement that can be made. The shoulder joints, for example, are of the ball-and-socket type, which allows for circular movement. Hinge joints, such as the elbow, allow for open-and-shut motions.

The bones are connected at most joints by tough, fibrous cords called ligaments. The ligaments are elastic to allow the joints to move. Most joints are surrounded by a capsule containing a special fluid called synovial fluid, which allows the bones to slide over each other without wearing away.

Some parts of the skeleton serve to protect soft body organs. The breastbone, or sternum, looks and acts like a shield to protect the heart. The ribs curve around the heart and lungs like barrel staves. The skull surrounds the brain like a helmet. The pelvis cradles the reproductive and digestive organs. The bones of the spinal column fit together like a flexible pipe to provide protection to the delicate spinal cord that passes through it.

The other bones of the skeleton are also shaped according to their purpose. The bones of the hands and feet are many, small, and delicate to allow for an almost infinite variety of hand and foot movements. Thigh bones are long and heavy to provide levers for lifting the upper part of the body. Their round shape helps provide the strength they need. In contrast, the bones of the arms are light in weight to enable the arms and hands to move easily.

The materials that the bones are made of are vital to the functioning of other body systems. The same calcium that makes bones hard is also released into the bloodstream to enable blood to clot and muscles to contract. The red, spongy marrow that is at the core of certain bones manufactures most of the red and white blood cells in the body.

The Muscular System

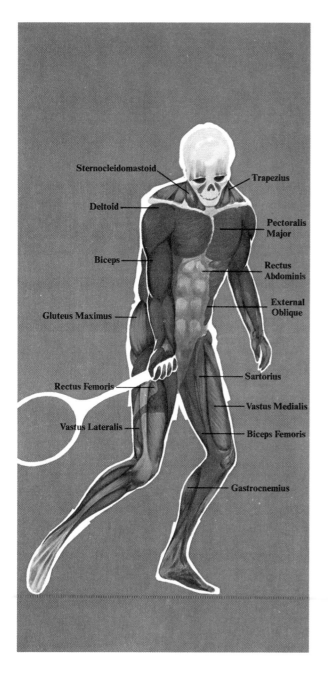

Sternocleidomastoid

Trapezius

Deltoid

Pectoralis Major

Biceps

Rectus Abdominis

External Oblique

Gluteus Maximus

Sartorius

Rectus Femoris

Vastus Medialis

Vastus Lateralis

Biceps Femoris

Gastrocnemius

The human body has over 600 muscles. Some muscles allow for movement, some play a role in digestion, and some control the circulation of the blood.

Many muscles are attached to the skeleton. Strong tissues called tendons hold them to the bones. The skeletal muscles are usually long, fibrous bundles. Each muscle bundle can contract, or shorten, like an accordion. When it contracts, the distance between its two ends is reduced.

The skeletal muscles usually work in pairs. One muscle contracts to cause a joint to bend, and the other contracts to straighten it. The biceps muscle on the upper arm, for instance, contracts to bend the arm at the elbow. Muscles on the back of the upper arm contract to straighten the arm.

The arrangement of the muscles determines what kinds of movements can occur. The muscles in the forearms extend partly around the bones, making rotation of the lower arm possible. Muscles in the tongue allow the many complex movements involved in eating and talking. All these movements are made possible by muscle contractions.

The muscles that move the skeleton are voluntary muscles. An individual can move them at will. The body also has many muscles that are not attached to bones and that are largely beyond individual control. These involuntary muscles control the actions of internal organs such as blood vessels and intestines.

The involuntary muscles can remain contracted for long periods of time as they push blood through the vessels and food through the intestines. They work by squeezing these tubular structures to force material through. Many of the body's organs consist of such tubes surrounded by muscles. There are also involuntary muscles around circular openings, such as those that surround the pupils of the eye. They act to change the size of the opening.

In general, muscles do mechanical work. They move bodily parts, or their contents, which means that they require energy—no work occurs without the expenditure of energy. Muscles, then, are energy converters. They convert the chemical energy provided by food into mechanical energy.

The Circulatory System

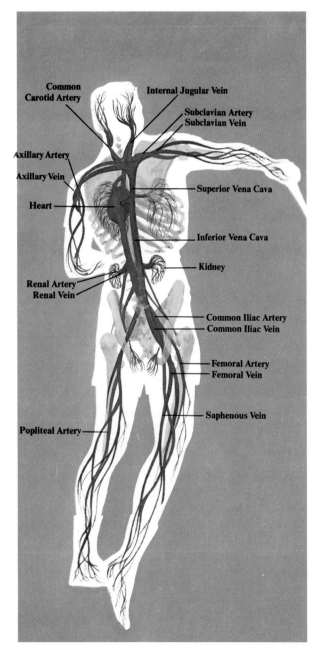

Common Carotid Artery

Internal Jugular Vein

Subclavian Artery
Subclavian Vein

Axillary Artery

Axillary Vein

Superior Vena Cava

Heart

Inferior Vena Cava

Kidney

Renal Artery
Renal Vein

Common Iliac Artery
Common Iliac Vein

Femoral Artery
Femoral Vein

Saphenous Vein

Popliteal Artery

The circulatory system services all the tissues of the body by bringing nutrients to them and carrying away waste products. It has three main components: blood, the liquid that carries the nutrients and wastes; vessels, the tubes through which the blood is transported; and the heart, a powerful muscle that pumps the blood through the vessels.

The body of the average adult contains about 5 litres (5 quarts) of blood. Blood consists of cells floating in a liquid. The liquid portion, plasma, contains minerals, proteins, and hormones. It can clot to seal broken or cut blood vessels.

The cells that float in the plasma are of three main types. Red cells carry oxygen to body cells and remove waste carbon dioxide. White cells act to surround and destroy any disease-causing organisms that enter the body. Platelets, the smallest blood cells, help repair damaged blood vessels. They also make clotting possible.

The vessels that transport the blood form a 100,000-mile network throughout the body tissues. Capillaries, the smallest vessels, service the cells directly. They are finer than a hair and have walls only one cell thick. The spaces between those cells allow nutrients and oxygen to pass from the blood into the body cells. Waste products from the body cells pass into the capillary blood to be transported to the lungs and kidneys.

The capillaries connect to two kinds of larger vessels. Arteries carry freshly oxygenated blood from the heart to the capillaries, while veins carry oxygen-depleted blood back to the heart. Both kinds of vessels depend on muscle contractions to help force the blood through them.

The heart contracts rhythmically to keep blood circulating constantly through the vessels. This powerful muscle consists of two pumps side by side, separated by a wall. Each pump has an upper and lower chamber. The right pump receives waste-laden blood from all the veins in the body. It forces this blood into the lungs, where the blood releases waste carbon dioxide and absorbs oxygen. The oxygen-rich blood then enters the left side of the heart, which pumps it through the arteries back to the capillaries.

The Respiratory System

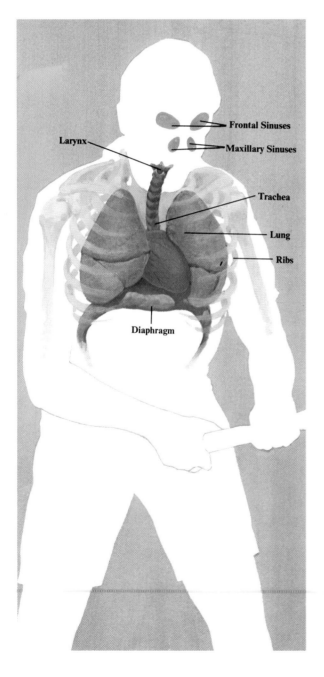

The respiratory system brings into the body the oxygen cells needed for converting nutrients into energy. It also disposes of the waste carbon dioxide given off in the process. These functions are accomplished by breathing.

The major organs of the respiratory system are the lungs. The lungs hang inside the chest cavity and are opened to the atmosphere by a series of breathing passages. Breathing results from an alternating increase and decrease in the size of the chest cavity. When the chest grows larger, the lungs expand to fill the space, and air is sucked into them. When the chest grows smaller, the lungs contract, and air is forced out of them.

Chest size is changed through the action of muscles. When the diaphragm, a large muscle beneath the lungs, contracts, it flattens downward to enlarge the chest cavity. At the same time, muscles in the chest contract to raise the ribs up and outward.

Air enters the body through the nose and mouth, travels through the voice box, or larynx, and down into the windpipe, or trachea. The trachea divides into two main branches, the bronchi. Each bronchus leads to one lung, where it divides into smaller and smaller tubes, the bronchioles.

The upper air passages are lined with mucous membranes to warm and moisten the incoming air. The mucous membranes are covered with many tiny hairs called cilia. Together, the mucus and the cilia purify the air by trapping dust and other particles. The cilia then wave the unwanted material upward and outward.

Inside the lung, the bronchioles release the air they carry into tiny air sacs called alveoli. Each air sac is surrounded by a network of capillaries. The thin walls of the alveoli allow gases to pass through. The exchange of oxygen and waste carbon dioxide occurs here, where the capillaries and alveoli touch each other. The oxygen that the blood in the capillaries picks up from the alveoli is distributed to the tissues. The carbon dioxide deposited in the alveoli is breathed out when the lungs squeeze inward.

This process takes place about 12 times a minute in a normal resting adult.

The Digestive System

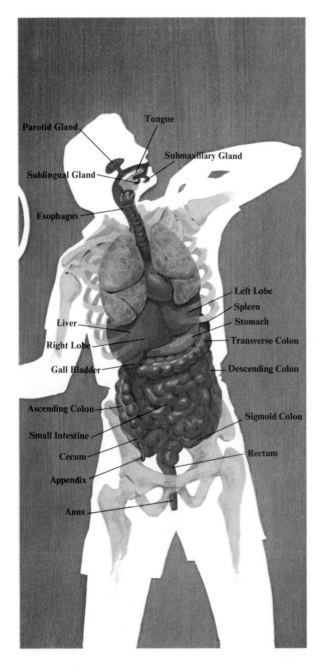

Parotid Gland
Tongue
Submaxillary Gland
Sublingual Gland
Esophagus
Liver
Right Lobe
Gall Bladder
Ascending Colon
Small Intestine
Cecum
Appendix
Anus
Left Lobe
Spleen
Stomach
Transverse Colon
Descending Colon
Sigmoid Colon
Rectum

The digestive system breaks down food so that nutrients can be absorbed by the blood. The aim of digestion is to split the food into molecules small enough to pass through membrane walls into the blood. This physical and chemical process takes place in a continuous tube, more than 9 meters (30 feet) long, that runs from the mouth to the anus.

The first section of the digestive tract, the mouth, breaks food down physically through chewing. It also starts chemical breakdown by pouring saliva over the food.

The food is next swallowed into the esophagus, which pushes it along into the stomach. There the stomach walls churn the food and bathe it in powerful gastric juices. A sphincter muscle then opens to allow the liquefied food to pour into the small intestine.

A major section of the digestive tract, the small intestine is 6 to 7 meters (20 to 24 feet) long. Here the breakdown of food is completed, and the nutrients are absorbed into the circulatory system through tiny projections called villi, which are located on the intestinal walls. Each one of the villi contains blood capillaries and a lymphatic vessel. Nutrients made up of small molecules pass through the capillary walls into the blood, which carries them to the liver for processing before they are distributed to the body. Larger molecules, particularly fats, enter the lymphatic vessels, which carry them to fat-storage depots.

Undigested material in the small intestine is carried to the large intestine. After further processing there, it moves into the rectum where it is stored until it is eliminated from the body.

When food is digested and turned into energy by the body, a number of by-products result. Many of these would be poisonous if left to build up. The excretory system rids the body of such substances.

The kidneys, two bean-shaped organs, are the major organs of the excretory system. One of their main jobs is to convert the ammonia that results from protein breakdown into urea. They also filter out water, salts, and other wastes. These substances combine with urea to make up urine. Urine is stored in the bladder until it leaves the body.

The Endocrine System

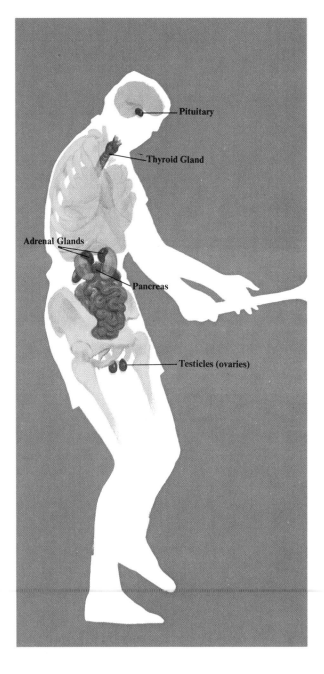

Pituitary

Thyroid Gland

Adrenal Glands

Pancreas

Testicles (ovaries)

The endocrine system produces hormones, which are chemical messengers that travel through the body to trigger the activities of other systems. Hormones also control the rate at which those activities occur. The glands that make up the endocrine system are located in the head, neck, and torso. They secrete their hormones directly into the bloodstream.

The pea-sized pituitary gland, located within the brain, is considered the master gland. It produces hormones that control the hormonal output of other endocrine glands. Some of the pituitary hormones regulate skeletal growth, controlling both the size of the body and the rate of growth. Others affect the rate at which the kidneys excrete urine. And others activate contractions of the uterus during childbirth.

The thyroid gland, situated in the neck, secretes a hormone that affects the rate of cell activity. Too little of this hormone, and cell activity slows down, resulting in sluggishness. Too much of this hormone, and the body becomes overactive.

The adrenal glands, which lie above the kidneys, trigger the increased body activity that makes up the fight-or-flight response. When a tense or dangerous situation occurs, the adrenal glands send a rush of adrenaline through the body. This hormone makes the heart and lungs work faster and stronger than normal. It decreases the blood flow to the digestive tract and increases the flow to the skeletal muscles. At the same time, it stimulates the liver to step up its output of sugar. These changes increase energy, at times to a remarkable degree.

The pancreas, which sits behind the kidneys, secretes insulin, the hormone that enables the body to use sugar properly. If the pancreas produces too little insulin, diabetes develops.

The sex glands in men are the testes and in women the ovaries. The testes produce sperm; the ovaries produce eggs. The sex glands also secrete sex hormones. These hormones cause sexual characteristics to develop during puberty.

The Nervous System

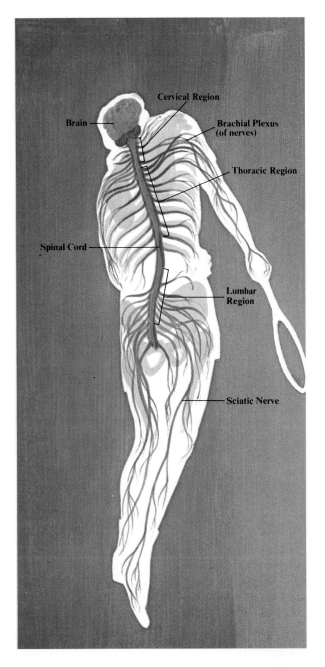

The nervous system is a network of nerve cells that reaches throughout the body to transmit information from one part to another. These nerve cells, which number in the billions, are controlled by the brain and spinal cord, which themselves are masses of nerve cells.

Each nerve cell sends out one or more branches called nerve fibers. It is through these fibers that the nerves communicate with one another. Some fibers receive messages, others send them. Through the release of special chemicals, signals can travel through the spaces between fibers.

Many of the longer nerve fibers bundle together to form nerves, which link portions of the nervous system with other body organs. The same kind of message leap that takes place between nerve fibers occurs across the space that separates nerves from a particular muscle or gland.

Most of the nerve cells are massed together in the central nervous system, which consists mainly of the brain and spinal cord. The peripheral nervous system branches out on both sides of the body from the central nervous system. This network spreads out through the limbs.

Each part of the nervous system acts like a two-lane highway. One lane, the sensory branch, gathers information from the outside world and all parts of the body and carries it to the nerve centers. The second lane, the motor branch, sends out the directions that control all body activities.

The motor branch consists of two systems, the voluntary nervous system and the autonomic nervous system. The voluntary nervous system controls the skeletal muscles by sending them orders to contract. Some of its actions, such as picking up a book, are the result of a conscious decision. Others, such as body posture, are the result of habit. The nerve impulses travel along their pathway without any voluntary effort on the part of the individual. The voluntary nervous system also controls the reflex actions that remove the body from danger.

The autonomic nervous system is not under a person's control. It directs the activities of such vital functions as breathing, heart action, and digestion.

Cervical Region

Brain

Brachial Plexus
(of nerves)

Thoracic Region

Spinal Cord

Lumbar Region

Sciatic Nerve

Glossary

A

abscess A pus-filled cavity formed by the destruction of tissue from a severe infection.

acetaminophen A pain reliever frequently used in place of aspirin.

acid rain Rainfall containing acids that result from the presence of sulfur and nitrogen oxides in the air.

active immunity The immunity acquired through the production of antibodies resulting from contact with live disease-causing organisms or with vaccines.

adrenaline The hormone that prepares the body to respond to danger by making it temporarily stronger; its effects include increased heart rate and deeper breathing.

aerobic exercise Any form of exercise that does not make the body's need for oxygen exceed its supply; usually an extended exercise that does not involve extreme physical exertion.

afterbirth See *placenta.*

agent Something that causes an effect, such as a virus that causes a disease.

AIDS (acquired immune deficiency syndrome) an incurable, fatal disease caused by a virus that destroys the body's natural immunity against diseases; transmitted by sexual contact with an infected person, by infected hypodermic needles, and by transfusions of infected blood.

alcoholism An illness in which a person becomes psychologically and physically dependent on alcohol; severe withdrawal symptoms occur if regular use of the drug stops.

allergy Extreme sensitivity to certain substances; exposure to those substances causes allergic reactions such as sneezing, coughing, itching, and swelling.

amino acids Tiny particles found in plant or animal protein; the body combines them in different ways to manufacture cells.

amniocentesis A diagnostic procedure in which a needle is inserted into the amniotic sac surrounding a fetus and fluid is withdrawn for examination; used to detect genetic diseases.

amniotic sac The fluid-filled sac that encloses the fetus during prenatal development.

amphetamines Stimulant drugs that increase alertness, reduce fatigue, and prevent sleep; also known as "uppers."

anaerobic exercise Any form of exercise that demands more oxygen than the body can supply; usually an extreme exertion over a short time.

anemia A disease characterized by a lack of red blood cells and/or hemoglobin, which carries oxygen to the body's cells; people who are anemic feel weak and tired.

angina pectoris A condition marked by chest pains resulting from an insufficient supply of blood to the heart muscle.

Antabuse A drug that causes a person to become violently ill when he or she consumes alcohol; used in the treatment of alcoholism.

antacid A substance that neutralizes acid in the digestive tract.

antibiotic A substance, produced by a living organism, that can kill or inhibit other organisms, especially bacteria.

antibody A protein substance manufactured by the body to destroy specific bacteria, viruses, or other disease agents that invade the body.

anticoagulant A substance that prevents or delays blood clotting.

antihistamine A medication used to relieve the symptoms of colds and allergies.

apocrine glands Sweat glands located only on the hair-covered areas of the body.

appraisal The second stage in forming an emotional reaction, during which a person judges whether a situation is harmful or not.

arteriosclerosis A circulatory disease characterized by thickening, hardening, and loss of elasticity of the walls of the arteries.

artery A blood vessel that carries blood from the heart to the body tissues.

artificial pacemaker A battery-operated device that is surgically implanted in the chest and that transmits electrical impulses to the heart in order to make it pump at a steady pace.

asbestosis A lung disease caused by inhalation of asbestos particles.

astigmatism An irregularity in the shape of the cornea or lens of the eye that results in blurred vision.

atherosclerosis A condition characterized by the buildup of fatty deposits on the inner walls of the arteries.

athlete's foot A fungus infection characterized by a red, itchy rash and scaliness between the toes and on the soles of the feet.

atrophy To waste away; used to describe muscles that have not been used.

autonomic nervous system A part of the nervous system that regulates involuntary body functions and prepares the body to respond to stress or danger.

aversion technique A method of making someone abandon an undesirable habit, such as smoking, by getting the person to associate the habit with something unpleasant.

B

bacteria Single-celled, plantlike organisms.

barbiturates Sedative-hypnotic drugs that depress the central nervous system and reduce anxiety; also known as "downers."

basic needs The primary human needs, including physical needs, such as the need for food, and emotional needs, such as the need for affection.

benign Not malignant; harmless.

bereaved Deprived of a loved one as a result of the loved one's death.

biopsy The examination by microscope of surgically removed tissue to aid in diagnosis.

birth canal The vagina during childbirth, when it expands to become the exit for the baby.

449

blood alcohol level The amount of alcohol in a person's bloodstream.

boil A severe tissue inflamation caused by bacterial infection.

bronchitis A lung disease in which the mucous membranes of the bronchial tubes become inflamed; characterized by chest soreness, congestion, and coughing.

bunion A swelling in the joint at the base of the big toe.

C

Caesarean section Delivery of a baby through an incision made in the abdomen and uterus.

caffeine A central-nervous-system stimulant that reduces fatigue; the active ingredient in coffee, tea, and cola drinks.

calcium A mineral that keeps bones and teeth hard and strong; found in dairy products, leafy vegetables, and apricots; depletion causes bones to become brittle and susceptible to fractures.

calculus A hard deposit on the teeth caused by a buildup of plaque; also known as tartar.

calisthenics A form of exercise that builds strength through repeated movements that use the body as a weight; examples are push-ups and pull-ups.

callus A hard, thickened area on the skin caused by friction.

calorie A measure of the energy produced by a given amount of food when it is eaten.

cancer A disease characterized by an uncontrolled growth of abnormal cells.

carbohydrates Nutrients made up of carbon, hydrogen, and oxygen that provide energy for the body; examples are sugars and starches.

carbon monoxide A poisonous gas present in cigarette smoke and motor vehicle exhaust fumes; acts to prevent red blood cells from attracting oxygen.

carcinogen Any substance that causes cancer.

carcinogenic Cancer-causing.

cardiac arrest Any complete stoppage of the heart.

cardiopulmonary resuscitation (CPR) An emergency technique for forcing a stopped heart to beat again by using a combination of cardiac massage and mouth-to-mouth breathing.

carrier A person who harbors and transmits disease-carrying organisms or genes, but who exhibits no symptoms; also an insect or animal that carries infectious organisms.

cataract A cloudy area on the lens of the eye that causes poor vision or blindness.

cervix The narrow, necklike opening of the uterus that leads into the vagina.

chancre A small, open sore; usually the first sign of syphilis.

chemoprevention The prevention of disease by the use of drugs.

chemotherapy The use of chemicals to treat disease.

chiropractor A medical practitioner who believes that many disorders can be traced to the central nervous system; treats patients through manipulation of the body, particularly the spine.

cholesterol A fatty substance necessary for proper body functioning that is found in animal tissue and manufactured by the body; implicated in atherosclerosis.

chorionic villus biopsy A diagnostic procedure for detecting defects in a fetus; involves analyzing small pieces of tissue surrounding the fetus, which are removed by inserting a tube in the mother's vagina.

chromosomes Structures composed of genes within the nucleus of each cell; they contain the program for the inheritable properties of the cell and enable the cell to reproduce itself.

chronic disease A disease that lasts a long time or that recurs frequently over a long time; often marked by slowly progressing seriousness.

cilia Hairlike structures projecting from the walls of the nasal passages and bronchi; they wave excess mucus and foreign particles upward and outward.

circumcision The surgical removal of the foreskin from the head of the penis.

cirrhosis of the liver A chronic disease characterized by severe scarring of the liver; frequently a result of alcohol abuse.

clinical psychologist A medical practitioner who diagnoses and treats mental and emotional disorders through therapy and counseling.

cocaine A stimulant extracted from the leaves of the South American coca bush; also known as ''coke.''

collateral circulation The growth of additional coronary blood vessels as a result of strenuous exercise over a period of time; reduces the likelihood of heart attacks.

color blindness A sex-linked genetic trait marked by the inability to perceive certain colors correctly.

communicable Capable of being passed from one person to another through direct or indirect contact.

complete protein Protein containing all eight of the essential amino acids; used to describe the make-up of certain foods.

complex carbohydrates Starches, found in such foods as pasta and beans; provide the body with more energy than simple carbohydrates do because

they usually contain additional nutrients.

conception The union of an egg and a sperm; also called fertilization.

concrete operational stage According to psychologist Jean Piaget, the third stage of development of a child's ability to think, during which the child learns to solve problems with physical objects.

conditioning A learning process based on the rewards or punishments that result from various actions.

congenital Present at birth.

convalescence The recovery period after an illness.

convulsion An attack of strong muscle contractions.

cornea The transparent outer coating of the eyeball that covers the iris and pupil.

coronary bypass A surgical technique in which a diseased portion of a coronary artery is replaced with a segment from a healthy blood vessel.

corrosive Able to burn; if swallowed, corrosive chemicals can destroy body tissues.

crab lice Insects that infest the genital area causing persistent itching.

D

decibel A unit of measure used to assess the loudness or intensity of a sound.

decline stage The period in an illness during which the symptoms subside.

defense mechanism An unconscious emotional reaction that helps a person cope with stress; examples are repression and rationalization.

degenerative disease A disease characterized by the deterioration or impairment of bodily organs and functions.

delirium tremens A mental disorder in which a person experiences anxiety and hallucinations, accompanied by tremors; associated with excessive and prolonged use of alcohol.

delusion A false belief; sometimes a symptom of schizophrenia.

dental assistant A dental aide who performs tasks such as passing instruments, preparing materials, sterilizing equipment, and keeping office records.

dental hygienist A dental aide who cleans teeth, takes x-rays, and informs patients of proper oral hygiene.

deoxyribonucleic acid (DNA) A highly complex protein molecule that contains the ''code of life,'' the genetic blueprint for a human being; the material of which genes are composed.

depressant A drug that slows down or reduces the activity of the central nervous system; examples are alcohol, the sedative-hypnotics, and the opiates.

depression A mental disorder marked by sadness, anxiety, fatigue, underactivity, sleeplessness, and reduced ability to function and relate to others.

dermis The middle layer of the skin, containing the sweat glands, oil glands, hair roots, and nerve endings.

disease pattern The characteristic distribution of a disease, the study of which can lead to an understanding of its causes.

dislocation The displacement of a bone from its normal position in its joint.

disorder Term used by psychologists to refer to any of the major categories of mental illnesses, e.g., anxiety disorders or thought disorders.

dominant gene A gene that will express itself whenever it is present. See also *recessive gene*.

dosage The amount in which a drug is taken.

double coverage A situation in which a person carries insurance from two companies to cover the same occurrences.

Down's syndrome A genetic disease caused by an extra chromosome and characterized by mental retardation and several physical defects.

drug Any chemical substance that changes body cells in any way and affects the functioning of the body.

drug abuse The use of a drug to the extent that it produces physical illness, mental impairment, or an inability to function in daily life.

E

elective surgery Surgery that is a matter of choice and not necessity either because the condition is not life-threatening or because other courses of treatment are available; the removal of a birthmark for cosmetic reasons is an example.

embryo A developing human organism during the first three months of pregnancy. See also *fetus*.

emetic A substance that induces vomiting.

emphysema A chronic disease in which the air sacs in the lungs become stretched or ruptured; characterized by extreme shortness of breath.

enamel The hard substance that forms the protective covering on the teeth.

endocrine system The group of ductless glands that secrete hormones, which are substances that set off and regulate the activities of other body systems.

endorphins Natural substances produced by the body during exercise that scientists feel relieve depression and stress.

enzyme A substance, produced by body tissue, that causes specific chemical reactions in the body; most enzymes are found in the digestive tract, where they assist in the breakdown of food.

epidemiology The study of the frequency, distribution, causes, and control of diseases within a population.

epidermis The thin, outer layer of the skin.

epilepsy A chronic disease of the central nervous system, characterized by convulsions.

episiotomy Surgical incision in the vagina during childbirth to prevent tearing in the vaginal walls.

estrogen A hormone, produced by the ovaries, that causes the female reproductive organs to develop and stimulates development of outward signs of puberty in girls; may be prescribed for women during menopause.

ethyl alcohol A colorless liquid that acts as a depressant and produces intoxication; the active ingredient in beer, wine, liquor, and liqueur.

euthanasia The act of ending the life of someone who is suffering from an incurable disease.

eutrophication The rapid and abundant growth, death, and decay of plant life in a body of water; refers especially to the rapid multiplication of algae in highly polluted waters, resulting in oxygen depletion of the water.

F

Fallopian tubes The two tubes that carry eggs from the ovaries into the uterus; also called oviducts.

farsightedness A vision disorder that results in a blurring of nearby objects; caused by an abnormally short eyeball.

fetal alcohol syndrome A medical condition suffered by babies born to women who used alcohol during pregnancy; characterized by mental retardation and malformation of head and face.

fetus A developing human organism during the last six months of pregnancy. See also *embryo*.

fever A raising of the body temperature above the normal range.

fiber The indigestible portion of certain foods that provides roughage to aid in digestion; examples are the skins of fruits and the bran of cereals.

fibrillation Rapid, ineffective, nonrhythmic contractions of the heart.

fight-or-flight mechanism The process that enables the body to adapt to a stressor.

fluoride A chemical substance that helps the tooth enamel resist decay.

fluorocarbons Chemical substances that were used in aerosol spray cans until evidence showed that they destroy the ozone layer surrounding the earth.

foreskin A fold of skin that covers the tip of the penis; frequently removed after birth. See also *circumcision*.

formal operational stage According to psychologist Jean Piaget, the fourth stage of development of a child's ability to think, during which the child learns to understand abstract concepts.

formal reasoning The mental ability to reason systematically.

fossil fuels Substances, such as coal and oil, formed from the remains of ancient plants and animals and burned as fuel.

fracture A break in a bone.

fungi Parasitic plants that lack chlorophyll.

G

gangrene The death and decay of body tissue resulting from lack of blood supply.

gender role The behavior society considers appropriate for each sex.

generic name The descriptive, nontrade name of a drug or pharmaceutical preparation.

genes Tiny particles, made of DNA, that transmit hereditary traits from parents to their offspring; the components of chromosomes.

genetic counseling A professional service to advise prospective parents on the possibilities of their conceiving a child with a genetic disease.

genetics The science that studies the transmission of hereditary traits and the ways in which they express themselves.

gerontology The study of aging and the aged.

glaucoma An eye disease in which the fluid within the eye builds up to an abnormal level, causing pressure that can damage the retina and optic nerve; a common cause of blindness.

glucose A simple sugar formed from carbohydrates during digestion and burned by the body for energy.

gonorrhea A sexually transmitted disease caused by bacteria and characterized by inflammation of the genital region, although at times the infection produces no noticeable symptoms.

group practice A group of physicians and other health professionals who work as a team.

growth needs A term for those needs not

essential to physical survival but important to psychological well-being; they include the needs for justice and beauty.

growth spurt A rapid increase in height and body size that takes place during adolescence.

H

hallucination A false perception that has no relation to reality and cannot be accounted for by any external stimulus.

hangover The aftereffects of drinking a large quantity of alcohol; symptoms may include headache, nausea, vomiting, and weakness.

hashish A psychoactive drug consisting of a concentrated resin made from the leaves of the hemp plant.

health maintenance organization (HMO) A group medical practice in which patients are charged a fixed monthly fee for health care.

heart block A cardiac condition in which the heartbeat slows down.

Heimlich maneuver An emergency rescue technique for choking victims in which the windpipe is cleared by a sharp, upward thrust to the abdomen.

hemophilia A genetic disease in which the blood lacks the substance necessary for rapid clotting, thus causing excessive bleeding when an injury occurs.

hemorrhoids Painfully swollen veins in the anal region.

hepatitis Inflammation of the liver, caused by viruses or toxic substances.

heroin An opiate drug derived from morphine.

herpes simplex Type 2 An incurable, sexually transmitted disease characterized by periodic outbreaks of sores in the genital area.

high blood pressure Abnormally high pressure of the blood against the artery walls, often associated with atherosclerosis.

hormones Body chemicals, produced by the endocrine glands, that stimulate the activity of various body systems.

hospice A home for people who have terminal illnesses.

host An organism on which or in which another organism lives for nourishment; a person who has an infectious disease is the host to the disease-causing pathogen.

hydrocarbons Pollutants that result from incomplete burning of fuel; produced mainly by automobile emissions.

hypertension Persistent high blood pressure.

hypnosis An induced, trancelike state of great suggestibility.

hypothalamus The part of the brain that controls the autonomic nervous system and affects a variety of body functions, such as the rate at which the body uses food.

I

ibuprofen An over-the-counter pain reliever that is as effective against pain as aspirin and acetaminophen; especially effective in relieving menstrual cramps.

immunity The ability to resist infection or the development of a disease. See also *active immunity; passive immunity*.

immunotherapy The use of the body's disease-fighting system against cancer or other diseases.

incomplete protein Protein that does not contain all eight of the essential amino acids; used to describe the make-up of certain foods.

incubation period The first phase of an infectious disease, during which the invading organisms multiply within the host.

infection The presence of disease-causing organisms within the body.

infectious disease A disease caused by an organism capable of reproducing within the body.

inflammation Redness, local warmth, swelling, and pain in body tissues resulting from the presence of a disease-causing organism or a foreign body.

influenza An infectious disease caused by a virus and characterized by fever, extreme weakness and fatigue, headache, muscle aches, congestion, and coughing; also called flu.

ingrown toenail A painful condition in which the corner of a toenail grows into the flesh at the side of the nail.

inhalants Household products, including glues and paint thinners, that give off vapors which, when breathed in, cause psychoactive effects in the user; effects include stimulation, lack of inhibition, then drowsiness.

interferon A protein, produced by the body, that fights viral infections and that may be effective in the treatment of cancer.

intern A medical school graduate who is receiving postgraduate training by working in a hospital, a requirement for becoming licensed to practice medicine.

iron An important nutrient that is necessary for hemoglobin production in

the red blood cells and that enables the cells to carry oxygen.

isometric exercise A form of exercise that involves pushing or pulling against a stationary object to develop strength; an example is pushing against a wall.

isotonic exercise A form of exercise that develops strength through repeated rhythmic movements; examples are calisthenics and weight lifting.

L

laetrile A substance extracted from apricot pits and sold as a quack cancer treatment; also known as "vitamin B_{17}" and "aprikern."

Lamaze method Natural, unmedicated childbirth using special methods of breathing and relaxation.

laxative A medication used to relieve constipation.

Legionnaires' disease A recently discovered bacterial infection that can be fatal.

leukemia Cancer of the white blood cells.

lipid storage disease A genetic disease that affects the body's ability to break down and utilize fats.

lymphocyte A type of white blood cell produced by lymph tissue.

lymphoma A cancerous tumor in the lymph nodes.

M

malignant Dangerous to health or life; cancerous.

mammography An x-ray technique used to detect breast cancer.

manic-depressive illness A mental disorder in which the sufferer alternates between extreme sadness and extreme joy.

melanin The pigment that gives color to the skin and the hair.

menarche The onset of menstruation.

menopause The end of menstruation; usually occurs in middle age.

menstruation A bloody discharge from the uterus that occurs at regular monthly intervals in women of childbearing age.

methyl alcohol A highly poisonous type of alcohol made from wood; also called wood alcohol.

minerals Substances, such as iron and potassium, needed daily by the body to help it form tissues and function properly.

minor tranquilizer A drug in the depressant group that calms or relaxes a person; examples are Valium and Librium.

miscarriage See *spontaneous abortion.*

modeling Learning to behave in certain ways by observing and imitating the actions of others.

moniliasis A genital infection caused by a yeast fungus and characterized by a white discharge and intense itching; most common in women.

mononucleosis A viral disease characterized by fever, enlarged lymph glands, and general weakness; also known as glandular fever.

morphine The active ingredient in opium; the drug from which heroin is made.

multiphasic screening A type of health testing that combines a computerized medical history with a series of diagnostic tests.

mutant Changed; a term used to describe cells that have become cancerous.

myeloma A tumor originating in the bone marrow.

N

narcotic See *opiate.*

nearsightedness A vision disorder characterized by a blurring of distant objects; caused by an abnormally long eyeball.

neuroses Mental disorders characterized by anxiety and partial impairment of functioning, although neurotic people can still function in most areas of their lives. See also *psychoses.*

nicotine The active drug in tobacco; it affects the central nervous system and produces habituation and tolerance.

nitrogen oxides Air pollutants that come from motor vehicle exhaust emissions and the burning of fossil fuels.

nocturnal emission An involuntary discharge of semen during sleep; also called wet dream.

nongonococcal urethritis (NGU) A sexually transmitted disease characterized by inflammation of the urinary tract.

nurse-midwife A health practitioner trained to manage normal pregnancies and deliveries and to recognize complications for which a physician is needed.

nutrients Substances, obtained from foods, that provide energy and building materials for the body.

nutrition The science that relates the health and well-being of people to the food they eat.

O

obesity Excessive weight; usually applied to people whose weight is more than 15

percent above the average for their age, sex, and body frame.

ophthalmologist A physician who specializes in diseases of the eye.

opiates Drugs derived from the opium poppy; also called narcotics.

opium An opiate whose active ingredient is morphine.

optometrist A health practitioner who examines eyes and prescribes corrective lenses.

osteopath A physician who attended a school of osteopathic medicine; also called an osteopathic physician.

osteoporosis A medical condition, caused by a depletion of calcium, in which bones become porous and fragile and are thus susceptible to fractures; usually occurs in older people, more often in women than in men.

ovaries Two endocrine glands in the female that produce eggs and sex hormones.

oviduct See *Fallopian tubes.*

ovulation The periodic discharge of a mature egg from an ovary.

oxidation The chemical process that turns alcohol into carbon dioxide and water.

ozone layer The layer of the atmosphere that contains a large amount of ozone, a form of oxygen; it absorbs ultraviolet rays and keeps the earth from losing heat.

P

Pap smear A diagnostic test to detect the presence of cancer cells in the cervix.

paranoia A mental disorder characterized by intense feelings of persecution and self-importance.

parasite An organism that lives in or on another organism known as the host.

parasympathetic system The division of the autonomic nervous system responsible for conserving energy; it acts to balance the sympathetic system.

particulate matter Tiny particles of dust, ash, and other substances that contribute to air pollution.

passive immunity An immunity acquired through means other than the production of antibodies, usually through transfer of antibodies from an actively immune person. See also *active immunity; immunity.*

pathogen A disease-producing organism.

perception The process of becoming aware of objects or of receiving sensory impressions.

personal fable A belief that one is unique and therefore not subject to the cause-and-effect relationships that govern the world.

pharmacology The study of drugs, their origin and characteristics, and their effects upon living organisms.

phenylketonuria (PKU) A genetic disease caused by the absence of an enzyme that helps break down milk; characterized by progressive mental retardation.

phobia A strong, irrational fear.

photochemical smog The type of smog resulting from the interaction of automobile emissions and a temperature inversion; also called Los Angeles–type smog.

physical dependence A drug-induced condition in which a person requires frequent administration of the drug in order to avoid withdrawal symptoms. See also *tolerance.*

pion beam therapy A radiation technique that focuses high-energy particle beams on tumors without damaging surrounding healthy tissue.

pituitary gland The endocrine gland located at the base of the brain; it secretes hormones that regulate many bodily functions, such as growth and reproduction.

placebo A substance with no medicinal value that is used by some physicians to satisfy patients who demand unnecessary medication.

placenta The organ that absorbs nutrients from the mother and distributes them to the developing fetus.

plaque A sticky substance that accumulates on the teeth; made up of food particles, bacteria, and debris.

pneumonia Inflammation of the lungs, often caused by bacterial or viral infections.

podiatrist A physician who specializes in disorders and diseases of the feet.

pollution The release of biological, physical, and chemical wastes into the environment.

potency The strength of a drug.

premenstrual syndrome (PMS) A medical disorder suffered by some women at the time of menstruation; symptoms, which are usually in severe form, include fluid build-up, cramps, backache, depression, and anxiety.

prenatal diagnosis The testing of a developing fetus for genetic diseases. See also *amniocentesis.*

preoperational stage According to psychologist Jean Piaget, the second stage of development of a child's ability to think, during which the child begins to imagine objects and learns to talk.

pressure point An area on the body where an artery is close to the surface and in front of a bone so that pressure applied there will control bleeding beyond that point.

preventive medicine The practice of

maintaining health by identifying risks to health and taking action to prevent those risks from leading to disease or disability.

proctoscopy A procedure for conducting a rectal examination.

prodrome period The second phase of an infectious disease; it is a short interval characterized by headache, fever, runny nose, and other common symptoms, making diagnosis difficult.

progressive relaxation A technique for relieving muscle tension.

prospective payment system A payment system set up by the federal government for Medicare and Medicaid patients; specifies how much the government will pay for certain medical procedures.

prostaglandins Substances, present in body tissues, that are the main cause of menstrual cramps.

protein A category of vital substances that make up the basic material of body cells; includes enzymes, hormones, and antibodies; also a critical food substance.

protozoa Single-celled animals.

psychedelic-hallucinogens Psychoactive drugs that produce excitement, agitation, hallucinations, depression, or other psychosislike changes.

psychoactive Referring to any drug that produces a change in a person's mood, thoughts, feelings, or behavior.

psychological dependence A drug-induced condition in which a person requires frequent administration of the drug in order to feel a sense of well-being; the first level of drug dependence.

psychoses Severe mental disorders, characterized by loss of contact with reality, that prevent an individual from functioning in everyday life. See also *neuroses*.

psychosomatic Referring to the development of physical symptoms as a result of psychological stress.

psychotherapy A method of treatment for emotional and behavioral problems.

puberty The period in life when a person's reproductive system begins to work.

pulse The rhythmic beating in the arteries caused by the alternating contraction and expansion of the arterial walls as a result of the heartbeat.

pus The yellowish white liquid produced in certain infections and consisting mainly of bacteria, white blood cells, and blood serum.

Q

quackery The fraudulent practice of health care by an unqualified person.

R

radiation sickness A serious illness caused by prolonged exposure to high levels of radiation; in its later stages it leads to hemorrhaging, hair loss, sterility, and cataracts.

radioactive A term used to describe certain elements and their products that give off particles or rays from the natural disintegration of their atomic nuclei.

recessive gene A gene that will express itself only when the other gene in the pair is not dominant. See also *dominant gene*.

recycle To use again; a term applied to used items that, through cleaning, repair, or conversion to raw materials, are returned to productive use.

reinforcement An occurrence that follows a person's action and that increases the probability that the person will repeat the action.

reproduction The process by which living creatures produce offspring.

rescue breathing An emergency rescue technique for restoring respiration in a person who has stopped breathing by rhythmically breathing into the person's mouth to inflate the lungs; also called artificial respiration and mouth-to-mouth resuscitation.

respiration The act of breathing; the taking in of oxygen and the giving off of carbon dioxide.

retina The inner coating of the back part of the eyeball that is sensitive to light and upon which images are formed.

Rh disease A condition in which the blood of an Rh-negative pregnant woman forms antibodies that destroy the red blood cells of the Rh-positive fetus she is carrying.

rickettsiae Bacterialike organisms responsible for typhus fever and other diseases.

risk factor Any element of a person's heredity or life style that presents a health hazard; some are preventable, such as smoking, improper diet, and lack of exercise; others are not preventable, such as age, sex, race, and family medical history.

S

schizophrenia A severe form of psychosis in which the person suffers from disturbed thinking, moods, and behavior; hallucinations, delusions, and

loss of contact with the surrounding environment are common.

scrotum The pouch that contains the testes.

sedative-hypnotics Drugs that cause relaxation and sleep by depressing the activity of the central nervous system.

self-esteem The regard people have for themselves.

semen The thick, whitish fluid produced by male sex glands; it contains sperm.

senility A mental disorder of the elderly characterized by loss of memory and a disoriented sense of time and place.

sensorimotor stage According to psychologist Jean Piaget, the first stage that a child goes through in developing the ability to think, during which the child learns that there are external objects and that actions have consequences.

set The expectations a person has about the effects of a certain drug.

setting The social environment in which a person takes a drug.

sexually transmitted disease (STD) A disease usually transmitted through sexual intercourse.

shock A state of collapse caused by failure of the peripheral circulation, often resulting from severe injury and characterized by weak and rapid pulse, extremely low blood pressure, and rapid but shallow breathing.

sickle cell anemia A genetic disease in which the red blood cells have an abnormal crescent shape; characterized by tissue damage resulting from lack of oxygen.

sidestream smoke The smoke that is released into the air as a cigarette burns.

simple carbohydrates Sugars, which provide the body with energy; include sugars that occur naturally in foods such as fruit and milk and the refined sugar that is added to many processed foods.

sinusitis An irritation of the sinus cavities.

site The body part upon which a drug acts.

solubility The capability of being dissolved.

sperm The male reproductive cells.

splint A firm object used to keep an injured body part, such as a broken arm, in one position.

spontaneous abortion The natural expulsion of an embryo or fetus from the uterus before it is capable of surviving; also called miscarriage.

sprain An injury in which a tendon or ligament is torn.

sputum cytology The examination of material coughed up from the lungs to detect disease.

stamina The ability to mobilize energy in order to maintain movement over an extended period of time.

stillbirth The birth of a dead baby.

stimulant A drug that increases the activity of the central nervous system.

strain A muscle injury caused by overuse or overstretching.

strength The basic muscular force required for movement.

stress A strain or tension that disturbs a person's normal physical, mental, or emotional balance. See also *stressor*.

stressor An event, such as the loss of a job or the death of a loved one, that produces stress. See also *stress*.

stroke A sudden brain injury usually caused by a blood clot or a rupture in a blood vessel.

sulfur dioxide smog The type of smog produced by the burning of fossil fuels; also called London smog.

suppleness The quality of muscles and joints that permits a full range of movement.

susceptibility Lack of resistance to a disease.

sympathetic system The branch of the autonomic nervous system that carries signals to activate such internal organs as the heart, lungs, and liver.

synergism The joint effect of a number of drugs that is greater than the total effect of each drug working on its own.

syphilis A sexually transmitted disease characterized in its initial stages by open sores in the genital region; if left untreated, it can cause blindness, insanity, and death.

T

tartar See *calculus*.

Tay-Sachs disease A genetic disease in which the body is unable to break down certain fats; characterized by mental deterioration, blindness, and death before the age of seven years.

temperature inversion A weather condition characterized by a layer of cold air sandwiched between the surface air and a top layer of warm air, which tends to trap pollutants.

testes The two male reproductive glands that produce sperm and the male sex hormone, testosterone; also called testicles.

testosterone A hormone, produced by the testes, that stimulates the development of male sex characteristics.

thanatology The study of death and dying.

thermal pollution Water pollution in the form of excessive heat.

thermography A technique for detecting breast cancer by measuring temperatures throughout the breast tissue.

tolerance The adaptation of the body to a particular drug whereby an increased dosage of that drug is needed to produce the same effect. See also *physical dependence*.

tourniquet A very tight band placed around a limb to control bleeding.

toxic Poisonous.

triage The classification of patients according to who needs treatment, testing, or information; it is done to ensure the efficient use of medical personnel and equipment.

trichomoniasis A sexually transmitted vaginal disease caused by protozoa and characterized by burning and a frothy, white discharge.

tuberculosis An infectious disease that usually affects the lungs but can affect other parts of the body; it is characterized by the formation of tubercles, or hard swellings.

tumor An abnormal mass of new tissue growing independently of its surrounding tissue structures.

U

ultrasound A nonsurgical diagnostic procedure used to check the condition of a fetus; high-frequency sound waves produce an image of the fetus that allows doctors to check the size, shape, and position of the fetus.

umbilical cord A ropelike tissue that attaches the fetus to the placenta and serves to transport nutrients and waste products between the mother and the fetus.

unconscious mind The part of the mind made up of thoughts, memories, and desires which influence a person's behavior and emotions without his or her realizing it.

urethra The canal that carries urine from the bladder to the outside of the body; in males it also transports semen.

V

vaccine A preparation containing dead or living viruses, bacteria, or rickettsiae; it is administered to provide immunity to a particular disease.

vagina The canal that leads from the uterus to the outside of the body.

values Those principles, qualities, or things that a person holds in esteem and considers worth striving for.

varicose veins Swollen, twisted veins.

vas deferens The tube that leads from a testicle and carries sperm.

venereal disease (VD) A sexually transmitted disease.

virus A microscopic particle that can cause disease and that can reproduce only in connection with living cells.

vital signs The bodily signs that indicate a person's physical condition; they include pulse, respiration, and temperature.

vitamins A group of substances essential in small amounts for normal functioning of the body.

W

wet dream See *nocturnal emission*.

withdrawal syndrome A set of physical and mental symptoms, such as nausea and hallucinations, that results from removal of a drug upon which a person is physically dependent.

worms Long, limbless animals such as tapeworms that live as parasites in the human body.

X

xeroradiography An x-ray procedure used to detect breast cancer.

Y

yoga A system of exercise involving special postures and movements, controlled breathing, and relaxation.

Credits

Chapter 1

2—Guy Gillette/Photo Researchers, Inc.; 5—(*left*) Melchior DiGiacomo/The Image Bank, Inc.; (*right*) Tom Dunham; 6—(*left*) Tom Dunham; (*right*) John Freeman; 8—Tom Dunham; 10—(*top*) Stock/Boston; (*bottom*) Les Armstrong; 11—Tom Dunham.

Chapter 2

14—Michael de Camp/The Image Bank, Inc.; 17—Barbara Loudis; 18—Tom Dunham; 19—Harry F. Harlow/The University of Wisconsin Primate Library; 20—Joel Gordon; 22—Irene Roman/Gwen Goldstein rep.; 23—Linda Ferrer Rogers/Woodfin Camp & Assoc.; 24—Peter Vilms/Jeroboam; 28—Jeffrey Foxx/Woodfin Camp & Assoc.; 29—Joel Gordon.

Chapter 3

32—Howard Sochurek; 35—Frances Kuehn; 37—Diane Tong; 39—Cliff Feulner; 42—Frank Ferri/Barbara Bell rep.; 45—Steve McCarroll; 46—David Strickler/Monkmeyer Press Photo; 48—Lonni Sue Johnson; 49—Michal Heron.

Chapter 4

52—Design Photographers, Inc.; 55—Sports Illustrated, Inc.; 56—Courtesy, Air France; 58—David W. Hamilton/The Image Bank, Inc.; 59—David Gothard; 60—David Gothard; 62—Doug Magee/EPA/Art Resource, Inc.; 65—Watriss-Baldwin/Woodfin Camp & Assoc.; 66—Janos Kalmar/Black Star.

Chapter 5

70—Douglas Kirkland/Contact Press; 72—Courtesy, General Motors Corporation; 73—Joel Gordon; 74—Guy Gillette/Photo Researchers, Inc.; 75—(*top left*) Peter Menzel/Stock, Boston; (*bottom*) John Freeman; 76—(*top left*) Michal Heron;

(*bottom left*) Sylvia Johnson/Woodfin Camp & Assoc.; (*right*) Leif Skoogfors/Woodfin Camp & Assoc.; 78—Pat Pereira; Information adapted from Leonore R. Zohlman, *Beyond Diet . . . Exercise Your Way to Fitness and Heart Health* (CPC International, Inc., Englewood Cliffs, NJ, 1974, pp. 20-21); 82—Sports Illustrated, Inc.; 84—Martin Rogers/Stock, Boston; 86—Barbara Pfeffer/Peter Arnold, Inc.

Chapter 6

88—Jerry Howard/Stock, Boston; 90—David Madison/Bruce Coleman, Inc.; 92—(*top left*) Steve Allen/Peter Arnold, Inc.; (*bottom right*) Tom Dunham; 95—Joe Rodriguez/Black Star; 98—Tom Dunham; 100—Helena Frost; 102—Tom Dunham; 103—J. Schweiker/Photo Researchers, Inc.; 104-105—Courtesy, The Ad Council; 106—Joel Gordon.

Chapter 7

112—Wolf/The Image Bank; 115—(*left*) Tom Lewis; (*right*) John Freeman; 116—Gerry Efinger; 117—Tom Dunham; 118—Peter Southwick/Stock, Boston; 120—Pat Pereira; 121—Courtesy, Bausch & Lomb Soft Lens Division; 122—American Optometric Association; 123—Pat Pereira; 125—(*top left*) Herb Snitzer/Stock, Boston; (*bottom right*) Karen Leeds; 127—John Freeman; 129—Tom Dunham.

Chapter 8

132—Erika Stone/Peter Arnold, Inc.; 139—From Rugh and Shettles, 1971; 141—John Troha/Black Star; 143—Tom Lewis; 144—Mimi Forsyth/Monkmeyer Press Photo; 145—(*top right*) Erika Stone/Photo Researchers, Inc.; (*bottom*) Ed Lettau/Photo Researchers, Inc.; 147—John Dawson; 149—(*top*) Robert Goldstein/Photo Researchers, Inc.; (*bottom*) Sepp Seitz/Woodfin Camp & Assoc.; 151—Frank Siteman/Stock, Boston; 152—Gabriele Wunderlich; 154—Richard Hutchings/Photo Researchers, Inc.; 155—The Metropolitan Life Insurance Company.

Chapter 9

158—Helen Marcus/Photo Researchers, Inc.; 160—Cary Wolinsky/Stock, Boston; 162—Jae Carter; 163—Les Armstrong; 165—Tom Dunham; 166—Tom Dunham; 167—Peter Vandermark/Stock, Boston; 168—Joel Gordon; 170—Jae Carter.

Chapter 10

174—Pakenham/International Stock Photo Agency; 177—(*left*) American Standard/The New York Public Library; (*right*) Michal Heron; 178—(*top left*) Helena Frost; (*bottom right*) Cary Wolinksy/Stock, Boston; 179—Rick Smolan; 180—Dagmar Frinta; 182—Tom Dunham; 183—Sybil Shelton/Peter Arnold, Inc.; 184—Harry Crosby; 187—David Biedrzycki/Gwen Goldstein, rep.; 188—Wasyl Skodzinsky/Photo Researchers, Inc.; 191—Howard Saunders.

Chapter 11

194—Burk Uzzle/Woodfin Camp & Assoc.; 197—Bruce Davidson/Magnum Photos, Inc.; 199—Costa Manos/Magnum Photos, Inc.; 201—Hella Hammid/Photo Researchers, Inc.; 202—(*left*) Lowell J. Georgia/Photo Researchers, Inc.; (*right*) Ed Lettau/Photo Researchers, Inc.; 203—(*left*) Cary Wolinsky/Stock, Boston; (*right*) Elliot Erwitt/Magnum Photos, Inc.; 205—Ginger Chih/Peter Arnold, Inc.; 206—Costa Manos;Magnum Photos, Inc.; 207—James Motlow/Magnum Photos, Inc.; 208—Leonard Freed/Magnum Photos, Inc.; 211—Tom Dunham; 212—Erika Stone/Peter Arnold, Inc.

Chapter 12

216—Sigrid Owen/International Stock Photo Agency; 219—Patty Peck; 221—(*top left*) Owen Franken/Stock, Boston; (*bottom right*) Ray Ellis/Photo Researchers, Inc.; 224—Pat Pereira; 227—Tom Dunham; 229—National Audiovisual Center; 230—Amy Meadow; 233—Lenore Weber/OPC; 235—Charles Gatewood/Magnum Photos, Inc.

Chapter 13

238—Cecile Brunswick/Peter Arnold, Inc.; 241—Dr. Max E. Elliot/University of California, San Diego; 242—Tom Dunham; 243—Tom Dunham; 244—Lonni Sue Johnson; 245—Isabelle Tokumaru; 246—Lonni Sue Johnson; 248—Larry Mulvehill/Photo Researchers, Inc.; 249—(*top*) Tom Dunham; (*bottom*) Jim Anderson/Woodfin Camp & Assoc.; 250—Charles Gatewood; 251—Michael Bonotto; 253—Tom Dunham.

Chapter 14

258—Louis Fernandez/Black Star; 260—Dr. Max E. Elliot/University of California, San Diego; 262—Tom Dunham; 264—The American Cancer Society; 265—Courtesy, American Tobacco Company; 266—(*left*) Keith Gunnar/Bruce Coleman, Inc.; (*right*) Laura Dwight/Peter Arnold, Inc.; 270—(*left*) Tom Dunham; (*right*) Bohdan Hrynewych/Stock, Boston.

Chapter 15

274—Stacy Pick/Stock, Boston; 277—Culver Pictures; 278—Tom Dunham; 281—Eric Kroll/Taurus Photos; 283—National Library of Medicine; 288—FPG International; 289—Tom McHugh/Photo Researchers, Inc.

Chapter 16

292—Raymond/Bruce Coleman, Inc.; 294—Tom Lewis; 295—Felicia Fry; 297—Tom Lewis; 298—Tom Dunham; 300—David Gothard; 302—Tom Dunham; 303—Tom Dunham; 304—Lester V. Bergman & Assoc.; 305—Elizabeth Wilcox/Photo Researchers, Inc.; 307—Courtesy, The Advertising Council; 310—Tom Dunham; 311—Tom Dunham; 312—Tom Dunham.

Chapter 17

316—Steve Allen/Peter Arnold, Inc.; 318—Ed Lettau/Photo Researchers, Inc.; 320—Courtesy, The Advertising Council; 321—The American Heart Association; 324—Dan Budnick/Woodfin Camp & Assoc.; 325 Renald von Muchow; 327—Tom Lewis; 330—John Freeman; 331—Ken Heyman.

Chapter 18

334—Chuck O'Rear/Woodfin Camp & Assoc.; 336—(*left*) Martin M. Rotker/Taurus Photos; (*right*) Patrick Thurston/Transworld Feature Syndicate, Inc.; 337—Tom Lewis; 338—The American Cancer Society; 339—The American Cancer Society; 340—Tom Dunham; 344—Isabelle Tokumaru; 347—Pat Pereira; 349—The American Cancer Society.

Chapter 19

354—Tom Tracy/The Image Bank; 356—Tom Dunham; 357—Tom Dunham; 358—(*top right*) John Freeman; (*bottom left*) Pat Pereira; 359—Joel Gordon; 361—Jack Beeler; 363—Courtesy, General Motors Corporation; 365—John Blaustein/Woodfin Camp & Assoc.; 367—John Freeman; 369—Ron Maratea/International Stock Photo Agency; 370—Isabelle Tokumaru; 372—Tom Dunham; 374—Edumed, Inc.; 375—Timothy Eagan/Woodfin Camp & Assoc.

Chapter 20

378—Stephen J. Krasemann/Peter Arnold, Inc.; 380—EPA-Documerica; 381—Larry Ikenberry/West Stock; 384—Katharine S. Thomas; 386—George Hall/Woodfin Camp & Assoc.; 387—W. Eugene Smith/Magnum Photos; 392—Sekai Bunka Photo; 393—Bill Pierce/Woodfin Camp & Assoc.; 395—John Freeman.

Chapter 21

400—Elliot Varner Smith/International Stock Photo Agency; 402—World Health Organization; 405—(*left*) The American Foundation for the Blind; (*right*) The American Cancer Society; 409—Tom Dunham; 410—Mort Slavin; 413—(*left*) Joel Gordon; (*right*) William Hubbell/Woodfin Camp & Assoc.; 417—Visiting Nurse Service of New York; 419—C. Koreneff, Project Director, "Systems Approach to Mental Health in an HMO Model," National Institute on Mental Health Grant MH24109.

Chapter 22

422—Tom Dunham; 425—Les Armstrong; 426—Tom Dunham; 427—Lonni Sue Johnson; 428—American National Red Cross, District of Columbia Chapter, Nursing Service; 429—John Freeman; 431—John Freeman; 433—Adapted from *How to Be Your Own Doctor–Sometimes* by Keith W. Sehnert, M.D. and Howard Eisenberg. All rights reserved. Used by permission of Grosset & Dunlap, Inc.; 434—© 1975, The American Hospital Association; 436—(*left*) Courtesy, American Medical Association; (*right*) James Gillray/Courtesy, National Library of Medicine.

Appendix

422-428—Millsap/Kinyon

Index

A

Abscess, 299
Abstract thinking, 163-164
Accidents, 355-366
  and alcohol use, 243, 250-252, 360, 362
  causes of, 359-361
  and drug use, 360
  motor vehicle, 243, 250-252, 355, 356, 357, 360, 362
  occupational, 358, 361, 365
  prevention of, 362-366
  in the home, 357, 361, 362-365
Accutane, 144
Acetaminophen, 429
Acid rain, 384
Acne, 123-124, 124 (box), 162, 294
Acquired immune deficiency syndrome (AIDS), 229, 282, 301, 403 (box)
Additives, 100 (box), 342 (box), 343
Adolescence, 159-173
  and behavioral changes, 164, 165, 168
  and choosing a career, 172
  and dating, 166-167
  definition of, 159
  developing goals and values in, 171-172
  and friendships, 166, 169-170
  and identity search, 169-172
  and mental changes, 163-165
  and physical changes, 160-163
  relationships with parents during, 168-169
  self-consciousness during, 164
  and sense of right and wrong, 164-165
  and sex, 167-168
  and social changes, 166-169
  see also Teenagers
Adrenaline, 59, 73
Advertising, cigarette, 259, 265, 266 (Fig. 14.5)
Aerobics, 79 (box), 81-83, 331
Afterbirth, 147
Agent Orange, 389 (box)
Agents of infection, 279, 281, 294-296
Aging, 195-214
  attitude toward, 202
  and death, 206
  and disease, 197
  effects of exercise on, 73, 76, 77, 82
  friendship and, 204-205
  and life changes, 127, 204
  and marriage, 202-204
  and mental changes, 197-199

  and physical changes, 196-197
  and relationships with children, 204
  and stress, 73, 197
  theories about, 196
AIDS (Acquired immune deficiency syndrome), 229, 282, 301, 403 (box)
Air pollution, 380-385
Al-Anon, 255
Alarm stage, 59
Alateen, 255
Alcohol, 239-257
  and accidents, 243, 250-252, 356, 357, 360, 362
  alcoholism, 252-255
  and cancer, 342 (box), 345
  and crime, 254 (box)
  definition of, 240
  developing drinking habits, 247-249
  and driving, 243, 250-252, 360, 362
  effects of, on behavior, 242-243
  effects of, on the body, 240-242
  effects of, on the mind, 243
  factors affecting reaction to, 243-247
  and heart disease, 329 (box)
  interaction with other drugs, 220, 246-247, 429
  and pregnancy, 143-144, 247
  and Prohibition, 235
  public drunkenness, 250
  and teenagers, 248-249, 252
  types of, 240
Alcoholics Anonymous (AA), 255
Alcoholism, 252-255
  causes of, 253-255
  signs of, 252-253
  treatment for, 255
Allergies, 270, 430
Alzheimer's Disease, 200 (box)
American Cancer Society, 269, 335, 346, 405, 429, 432
American Heart Association, 376, 405
American Hospital Association, 435
American Medical Association, 409, 431
Amino acids, 92, 152
Amniocentesis, 155
Amniotic fluid, 138
Amniotic sac, 138
Amphetamines, 230, 234-235
Ampicillin, 309
Anaerobic exercises, 83
Anal stage, 24
Anemia, 96, 141
Anemia, Sickle cell, 152

Angel dust, 231
Angina pectoris, 323 (box), 325
Anorexia, 40 (box)
Antabuse, 255
Antacids, 429-430
Antianxiety drugs, 46
Antibiotics, 283, 288, 302, 305, 308, 309, 312, 430, 434
Antibodies, 301
Anticipatory grief, 212
Anticoagulants, 328
Antidepressants, 46
Antidiarrhea drugs, 430
Antihistamines, 430
Antiperspirants, 125-126
Antipsychotic drugs, 46
Antisocial personality disorder, 42
Anxiety, 40
Apocrine glands, 125-126
Arteries, 318
Arteriosclerosis, 283, 284, 319
Arthritis, 283, 309, 430, 437
Artificial respiration, 375
Asbestos, 343, 383-384
Asbestosis, 383
ASH (Action on Smoking and Health), 271
Aspirin, 226-227, 304, 328, 429
Asthma, 261, 280, 283, 382
Astigmatism, 120
Atherosclerosis, 91, 284, 317, 319, 320, 322, 325, 328, 330
Athlete's foot, 127-128, 295
Atrophy, 73
Authority, attitude toward, 165
Autonomic nervous system, 17, 59
Autonomy vs. shame and doubt, 25
Aversion techniques, 268

B

Bachelor of science in nursing (B.S.N.), 412
Bacteria, 91, 282, 288, 294, 301, 302, 305, 307, 310
Barbiturates, 220, 222, 227, 228
Basic needs, 18, 19
BCG, 350
Behavior therapy, 44
Benign tumors, 336-337
Bennies, 230
Benzedrine, 230

T

U

V

W

X

Y